MW01703211

McGraw Hill create

Course	Entrepreneurship & Small Business Management & Growth Vol. 2
Course Number	**BES 218/219**
	Manchester Community College
	Business

The McGraw-Hill Companies

create

http://create.mcgraw-hill.com

ISBN-10: 0390461377 ISBN-13: 9780390461377

Contents

Credits

Cash, Accounting, and Finance in the Small Business

PART FOUR

4

Cash, Accounting, and Finance in the Small Business

CHAPTER

13

Small Business Accounting: Projecting and Evaluating Performance

● Tracy and Brad Butler of Acropolis Computers, pictured here, learned the power of careful accounting practices when their consultant uncovered thousands of dollars of lost income due to poor pricing strategies. Armed with these facts, Acropolis Computers began to grow steadily into a more solid business. In what ways did Tracy and Brad use accounting in determining their cost structures?

LO

LEARNING OBJECTIVES

When you complete this chapter, you will be able to:

LO1 Describe the basic concepts of accounting.

LO2 Specify the requirements for a small business accounting system.

LO3 Explain the content and format of common financial statements.

LO4 Use accounting information as a tool for managing your business effectively.

LO5 Develop a complete set of budgets for your business.

LO6 Use accounting information to make better business decisions.

Focus on Small Business: Tracy and Brad Butler and Acropolis Computers[1]

After three years of hard work, Tracy and Brad Butler still did not seem to be making very much money. The reason for this was not obvious to the brothers. Sales were growing. The business was regularly working on the computers of between 600 and 700 loyal customers. Customers were satisfied, and it showed in their high rate of referrals.

At a loss as to what they were doing incorrectly, the brothers engaged a consultant to analyze their business processes. What the consultant showed them changed the way they ran their business.

The brothers, engineers by education, were masters of the computer but novices at accounting. They simply did not understand the relationship among costs, revenues, and profits. For example, they charged customers only what Acropolis paid for the parts, without any markup to pay for the time Acropolis spent ordering, storing, and carrying the part in inventory. When they went to a client's home to do repairs, they did not charge a service fee for their travel time or for the wear and tear on their truck. Although they charged for labor by the hour, if the labor was only a few minutes, they gave it away for free. Those lost minutes alone accounted for a $40,000 shortfall in income annually.

"We were actually losing $200 a job," Tracy said.

The process of pricing out their real costs, and then mapping those costs to the work they did for clients, helped Acropolis Computers finally become profitable—even after paying off the consultant's eventual bill for $27,000!

But that was just the start.

"Only 4 percent of our revenue was coming from individuals, but they were a large number of people: 600 to 700," Tracy said.

Once they understood the nature of the costs of their business, the brothers trimmed it drastically, moving away from serving individuals and focusing instead on providing service to businesses with between 15 and 150 employees. As the nature of their business changed, they changed its name to Acropolis Technology Group, www.acropolistech.com, moving from the basement to commercial locations in Wood River, Illinois, and Creve Coeur, Missouri.

"The success we have enjoyed has come directly from understanding the relationships among Revenue, Gross Margin, Overhead, and Burdened Labor rates," Tracy Butler said.

Acropolis was ranked for three consecutive years by *Computer Resellers News (CRN)* in their yearly Fast Growth list. In 2004, they grossed over $3.1 million in sales.

Success came, but only after they got their numbers under control.

DISCUSSION QUESTIONS

1. What is the nature of the " . . . relationship between costs, revenues, and profits . . ." that Tracy and Brad Butler did not understand?
2. What do you infer about Acropolis' accounting system during the years leading up to this crisis?
3. Why was it important for Acropolis to begin marking up the price of computer parts over their cost?
4. How is it possible for a business to succeed by deliberately getting rid of loyal customers?

Why Accounting Matters to Small Business

LO1 Describe the basic concepts of accounting.

The way many people think of it, what makes a business businesslike is its focus on making money, and in the end, the only way an owner knows or can prove to others that money is being made is through keeping careful accounting records. Accountants themselves think of five reasons why accounting is important to a small business:

- It proves what your business did financially.
- It shows how much your business is worth.
- Banks, creditors, development agencies, and investors require it.
- It provides easy-to-understand plans for business operations.
- You can't know how your business is doing without it.

managerial accounting Accounting methods that are specifically intended to be used by managers for planning, directing, and controlling a business.

tax accounting An accounting approach based on specific accounting requirements set by governmental taxing agencies.

financial accounting A formal, rule-based set of accounting principles and procedures intended for use by outside owners, investors, banks, and regulators.

There are three types of accounting, **managerial accounting**, which is used by managers for planning and control, **tax accounting**, which is used for calculating and reporting taxes, and **financial accounting**, which is used by banks and outside investors.

Managerial accounting is forward-looking and attempts to predict the results of management decisions.

Tax accounting is used to produce tax returns and schedules. Tax accounting is important for avoiding penalties for noncompliance and for minimizing how much money you have to pay in taxes.

Financial accounting is a formal, rule-based system intended primarily for absentee owners, bankers, investors, and regulators.

Basic Accounting Concepts

If you, as do many folk, have an aversion to even thinking about accounting, let alone trying to *do* accounting, then you are about to gain a new perspective on the topic. As you read the next couple of pages you'll come to realize that accounting is actually a very simple process that is based on common sense.

The most basic concepts of accounting are:

1. The idea that a business has an existence that is separate from its owner, called "business entity concept."
2. The expectation that a successful business will stay in business, or the "going concern concept."
3. An extremely simple equation called the "accounting equation."
4. The premise of revenue and expense.
5. The principle that accounting information must be useful to the owners and managers of businesses.[2]

Business Entity Concept

Because of the **business entity concept**, it is possible to separate business transactions from your own personal transactions. Thus we can distinguish between money that your business borrows, and money that you borrow for personal needs. It is the business entity concept that underlies the legal forms of establishing businesses, such as corporations, limited partnerships, and limited liability companies. (These are explained in detail in Chapter 18.)

business entity concept
The concept that a business has an existence separate from that of its owners.

Going Concern Concept

The assumption that a successful business will stay in business enables long-range planning and strategy. Accounting assumes that this year's business results will affect next year's, and that the intent of business is to make money over a period of many years. The **going concern concept** also implies that, as a separate entity, the business may continue in business even if it is sold to other owners.

going concern concept
The accounting concept that a business is expected to continue in existence for the foreseeable future.

The Accounting Equation

Of all the concepts and ideas of accounting, the **accounting equation** is the simplest, but least understood. The entire system of accounting entries, reports, and financial statements is developed from this simple equation. The primary value that accounting produces for owners and managers is that of keeping records. The accounting equation is the method that is used to place these records into understandable categories that are useful for managing your business.

accounting equation
The statement that assets equal liabilities plus owners' equity (assets = liabilities + owners' equity).

This equation has its basis in keeping track of everything that the business owns, while at the same time keeping track of what the business owes to others and what it is worth to its owners. This is done as a simple two-part equivalence, which is best understood by presenting an example.

Suppose you decide to start a business making executive desks of fine hardwoods. You already have a hobby of woodworking, and have collected tools during the pursuit of your hobby. These tools, especially the power tools, are very valuable, and you want to transfer their ownership to your new business. You will also need some cash for working capital, and your local banker (who already has one of your desks) has agreed to loan money to your business. Let's take a look at how these transactions are recorded, using the accounting equation.

First, you give up ownership of your tools, transferring them to your new corporation:

What the Business Owns		=	Claims on the Business	
Woodworking tools	$50,000		Capital donated by owner	$50,000

Notice that the business now owns the tools worth $50,000, but you as the owner have a "claim" on the business equal to the value you gave up. Should you change your mind right now, and dissolve the business, you could take back the tools. Or, were you to sell the business to someone else, you would expect to receive no less than the value of the tools.

Next, the bank makes a $50,000 loan to the business:

What the Business Owns		=	Claims on the Business	
Cash	$ 50,000		Loan payable to bank	$ 50,000
Woodworking tools	50,000		Capital donated by owner	50,000
Total value	$ 100,000		Total claims	$ 100,000

Now the business owns money and equipment. The total value of what it owns is $100,000. At the same time, the business owes $50,000 to the bank, and once the bank debt is paid, there will still be $50,000 value left for the owner. It may be hard to believe, but this is the entire accounting equation. The value of everything that the business owns is exactly equal to the sum of what the business owes to others plus any claims the owner has. Of course, the accounting equation is stated a bit differently. Its formal expression is:

Assets = Liabilities + Owners' Equity

So, let's take a look at the equation in the example, rewritten to use accounting terms:

Assets		=	Liabilities + Owners' Equity	
Current Assets			***Current Liabilities***	
Cash	$ 50,000		Loan payable to bank	$ 50,000
Long-Term Assets			***Owners' Equity***	
Woodworking tools	50,000		Capital donated by owner	50,000
Total assets	$ 100,000		Total liabilities & equity	$ 100,000

liabilities
Legal obligations to give up things of value in the future.

owners' equity
The difference between assets and liabilities of a business.

Notice that, except for using different terms, this is exactly the same as the earlier example. The only part that might be confusing is understanding what the terms "assets," "liabilities," "equity," "current," and "long-term" mean. An *asset* is simply something the business owns that will have value in the future. A **liability** is a legal obligation to pay some amount (or to give up product or services) at a time in the future. **Owners' equity** is simply whatever value is left after all liabilities have been paid. "Current" means that the value of the item can be realized, or must be paid as cash within one year. "Long-term" simply means that the asset will still be valuable more than one year in the future, or that the business may take longer than one year to pay the amount owed. The format used here is called a *balance sheet* because assets *must* equal the sum of liabilities and owners' equity. Simple, huh?

Revenues, Expenses, and Costs

Now suppose you purchase $10,000 of hardwood and $5,000 of supplies. What does this do to the accounting equation?

Assets		=	Liabilities + Owners' Equity	
Current Assets			***Current Liabilities***	
Cash	$ 35,000		Loan payable to bank	$50,000
Inventory	10,000			
Supplies	5,000			
Long-Term Assets			***Owners' Equity***	
Woodworking tools	50,000		Capital donated by owner	50,000
Total assets	$100,000		Total liabilities & equity	$100,000

cost
The value given up to obtain something that you want.

As you can see, making these purchases of inventory and supplies does not change the value of the business. All that you did was trade an asset called "cash" for assets called "inventory" and "supplies." However, the inventory has a cost of $10,000 and the supplies have a cost of $5,000. You gave up $15,000 in cash to obtain them. So, a **cost** is the value of what you *give up* to gain something you need or want.

To explain revenues and expenses it is best to continue our example. Suppose that, having started the business and purchased inventory and supplies, you produce and sell one desk to a local attorney. In making the desk, you use $1,000 of your inventory. You pay your employee $400 in wages. You present the attorney with an invoice for $2,500, and he promises to pay you in 10 days. How do these transactions affect the accounting equation?

First, recognize that only $400 has changed hands. You used inventory that you'd already paid for, and you accepted the attorney's promise to pay in lieu of cash. It should be obvious to you that the value of inventory has gone down by $1,000. But what do we do with the $2,500 sales price? We recognize $2,500 of revenue, and we deduct $1,400 of expenses in this manner:

Assets		=	Liabilities + Owners' Equity	
Current Assets			***Current Liabilities***	
Cash	$ 34,600		Loan payable to bank	$ 50,000
Accounts receivable	2,500			
Inventory	9,000			
Supplies	5,000			
Long-Term Assets			***Owners' Equity***	
Woodworking tools	50,000		Capital donated by owner	50,000
			Revenues earned	2,500
			Expenses for inventory used	(1,000)
			Expense for wages paid	(400)
Total assets	$ 101,100		Total liabilities & equity	$ 101,100

Now we can see the differences among costs, revenues, and expenses. Costs are the value of whatever you give up to get what you need or want. Revenue is an increase in owners' equity that is the result of selling your product or service. **Expenses** are reductions in owners' equity that recognize the value of goods (inventory) and services (labor) used to produce your product or service. When you sold the desk, the business received the attorney's promise to pay, which is called "accounts receivable." The business gave up the value of the inventory used and the value of labor expended.

expense
A decrease in owners' equity caused by consuming your product or service.

Of course, if we continued to record transactions in this way, pretty soon the owners' equity part of the balance sheet would become unreadable. Just imagine a year's worth of sales and expenses being recorded as in the example, above. So, as a matter of practicality transactions are not actually entered directly into the balance sheet. Rather, we create an *account*. An account is simply a record of transactions that are similar in nature. Thus we have an account for sales revenue where we record each sale as it is made. Similarly, we have an account for wage expense in which we record wages as they are incurred. At the end of the accounting period, whether it is a day, a month, a quarter, or a year, we simply add up all revenues and all expenses. We then subtract expenses from revenues and the remainder is our profit (or our loss if it is a negative number).

A complete discussion of basic accounting is available as a set of interactive slides in the online learning Web site for this text: http://www.mhhe.com/katz3e.

Information Usefulness

There are only two reasons to do accounting: first, to produce information that is useful to you for managing your business, second, to meet legal or contractual requirements. To be useful, information must be accurate and relevant.[3] You can ensure that your accounting information is accurate by using a computerized accounting program, as discussed in the following section. Relevance of information must be evaluated for each decision as it is made. If having the information helps you make a smarter decision, a faster decision, or a decision you feel more comfortable about, then the information was relevant.

The skill module shown on the next page illustrates the issues discussed in this section.

Accounting Systems for Small Business

LO2 Specify the requirements for a small business accounting system.

The primary reason to acquire and use a computerized accounting system is to ensure the accuracy of your accounting information. Computerized systems also simplify the accounting process by providing automatic error checking, entry screens that look like the common business forms, and automatic production of financial statements and management reports.

The most commonly used small business systems are QuickBooks, Peachtree, SimplyAccounting, One-write, and Great Plains. All these systems automatically produce financial reports that meet legal requirements for content and format. Although, as with any computer program, you will have to invest some time in learning to use it effectively, each of these accounting programs is very user-friendly. Its use can be mastered in a very short time, a matter of a few hours. Most community

SKILL MODULE 13.1

Why Does Accounting Matter?

Suppose you are operating a buffalo wings restaurant, and you purchase a high capacity fryer as discussed in the text above. Suppose you have estimated the following costs of operating your restaurant for one month:

Variable costs:	
food (chicken, potatoes, etc.)	$ 15,000
beverage (soda, tea, beer)	4,500
supplies (napkins, cleaning materials, etc.)	2,000
labor	21,600
Total monthly variable costs	$ 43,100
Fixed costs (rent, insurance, depreciation, etc.)	$ 21,900

Now suppose that you are currently using a battery of three fryers that you originally bought used for $4,000. Because the purchase price was small, you recognized the entire $4,000 cost of the fryer as an expense in the year it was purchased.

The Vulcan representative is trying to sell you a new four-basket computer-controlled battery fryer. The purchase price is $25,000 and the costs of shipping, installation, and testing will be $5,500. The representative has shown you how the new fryer, because of its improved insulation, safety features, and cooking capacity will save you $1,000 per month in reduced electricity use and lowered insurance premiums. The fryer also has much greater capacity than the one you are currently using, so you will be able to cook more wings and serve more people.

You have spoken with your accountant, and she told you that for tax purposes the fryer will have to be depreciated in six years, using the "5-year **MACRS rate**" set by the IRS. The amount of **depreciation** expense you will recognize will be the following:

MACRS rate
An Internal Revenue Service acronym for the Modified Accelerated Cost Recovery System. The MACRS approach lets taxpayers depreciate more of the cost earlier in the life of a capital expense.

depreciation
Regular and systematic reduction in income that transfers asset value to expense over time.

Year	Depreciation
1	$ 6,100
2	9,760
3	5,856
4	3,513
5	3,513
6	1,758

1. What is the cost of buying the new fryer?
2. How will your expenses change if you buy the fryer?
3. How will your fixed costs per year change if you buy the fryer?
4. If you predict that sales will increase by 10 percent per year, should you buy the fryer?
5. Suppose that your accountant called you and said that the fryer could be depreciated for seven years, using straight line depreciation of $4,357 per year for the first six years and $4,358 in the last year. Would this change your decision of whether to buy the fryer?
6. Under what conditions is the amount of depreciation expense relevant to deciding whether to buy the fryer?

colleges offer night and weekend classes in QuickBooks and Peachtree, and you may have (or have even taken) similar courses at your school. There are also numerous online sites that offer tutorials. Each program itself includes a tutorial, help files, and a printed manual to help you master its use.

To ensure that your accounting information is accurate, reliable, and useful, the accounting system that you choose should easily and efficiently accomplish the following tasks:

- Provide a simple, easy-to-understand user interface.
- Have an exhaustive context-sensitive help function.
- Produce an income statement that clearly lists revenues and expenses by appropriate categories for your industry and type of business.
- Produce a classified balance sheet that clearly shows the financial position of your business.

- Facilitate the development of a cash budget.
- Facilitate the task of developing operating and investment budgets.
- Produce financial statements in approved formats to be furnished to outside investors, bankers, and regulators.
- Produce multiple-year comparison financial statements for management use.
- Provide a method for you to define and produce custom reports to meet your management needs.
- Be able to export financial data in a form that can be used by your accountant and can be imported into tax preparation and spreadsheet programs.
- Maintain an internal "audit trail" that records all entries and changes to the accounting system in order to facilitate the identification and correction of errors.
- Enforce security measures to reduce the opportunity for employee misuse or fraud.
- Have provisions that will either allow the program to grow with your business or to easily export its data into programs that can handle larger businesses.

Setting Up an Accounting System

Your specific accounting needs are largely determined by the industry you're in and by the size of your business. The smallest businesses often need little in the way of accounting records beyond an accurate check register. As businesses become larger, the difficulty of any one person being able to remember all its details increases exponentially. When a business is large enough to have one or more employees, formal record keeping is a must.

Regardless of your business's size, the one essential element of an accounting system is *cash accounting* that is accurate, easy to use, and tracks all checks written and all deposits made.

As your business grows the following accounting functions will become important to your success:

- *Accounts payable* records to track what you owe and to make timely payments in order to capture prompt pay discounts and to maintain a good credit rating for your business.
- *Payroll* records to ensure that payroll and employment taxes are kept current.
- *Fixed asset* accounting that automatically calculates and accumulates depreciation.
- *Inventory* accounting that facilitates maintaining the appropriate levels of inventory and aids in calculation of appropriate stocking and reorder levels.
- *Credit card sales* function to enable reconciling your sales records with the amount of discount and charge backs taken by your credit card provider.
- *Accounts receivable* records if you provide credit to your customers. Accurate and timely accounts receivable records are essential for making decisions concerning the extension of credit. Accurate records also help produce accurate billing of customers, and thus help to maintain good customer relations.
- *Insurance register* to ease the problems of keeping necessary insurance coverage current and in force.
- *Investments* records if your business keeps surplus cash invested in securities.
- *Leasehold* records if your business has made improvements to leased property or equipment.

The actual task of setting up a computerized accounting system for your business is quite easy. All the small business accounting systems listed above include all the functions that you are likely to need. Additionally, each program has a method to establish a set of records that is appropriate for your specific business. Should you have a business that is unique, setting up a set of records from scratch takes less than an hour. Quickbooks and Peachtree include an "interview" function that will guide you through the setup process by furnishing a series of questions and prompts.

Often in such situations, you can get help for free from your local Small Business Development Center (www.sba.gov/sbdc/sbdcnear.html) or SCORE (the Service Corps of Retired Executives; www.score.org). Alternatively, for a small fee (generally $200 to $1,000) many CPAs (certified public accountants) will set up any of these accounting programs for your specific needs. You can find CPAs in your phone book (hard copy or online) or even through Google searches for a CPA directory. As when you choose any other professional (like doctors or lawyers), it makes sense to check with others about a professional before making a major commitment.

Financial Reports

LO3 Explain the content and format of common financial statements.

financial statements
Formal summaries of the content of an accounting system's records of transactions.

The final output of a computer system is a set of **financial statements** and reports. Although there is certainly room for you to customize financial reports in many ways, the overall content and form of financial statements have been made standard by long usage. Bankers and investors are familiar and comfortable with standard financial statements. When you apply for a loan or seek equity investment, you will be expected to present financial information in the format and containing the information that is standard for your industry.

Figure 13.1 shows examples of the most common formats. When you are familiar with them, you will find that you can easily understand and adapt them to the differences unique to your industry.

There are five common financial statements:

- Income statement
- Statement of retained earnings
- Statement of owners' equity
- Balance sheet
- Cash flow statement[4]

FIGURE 13.1

Flow of Information in Financial Statements

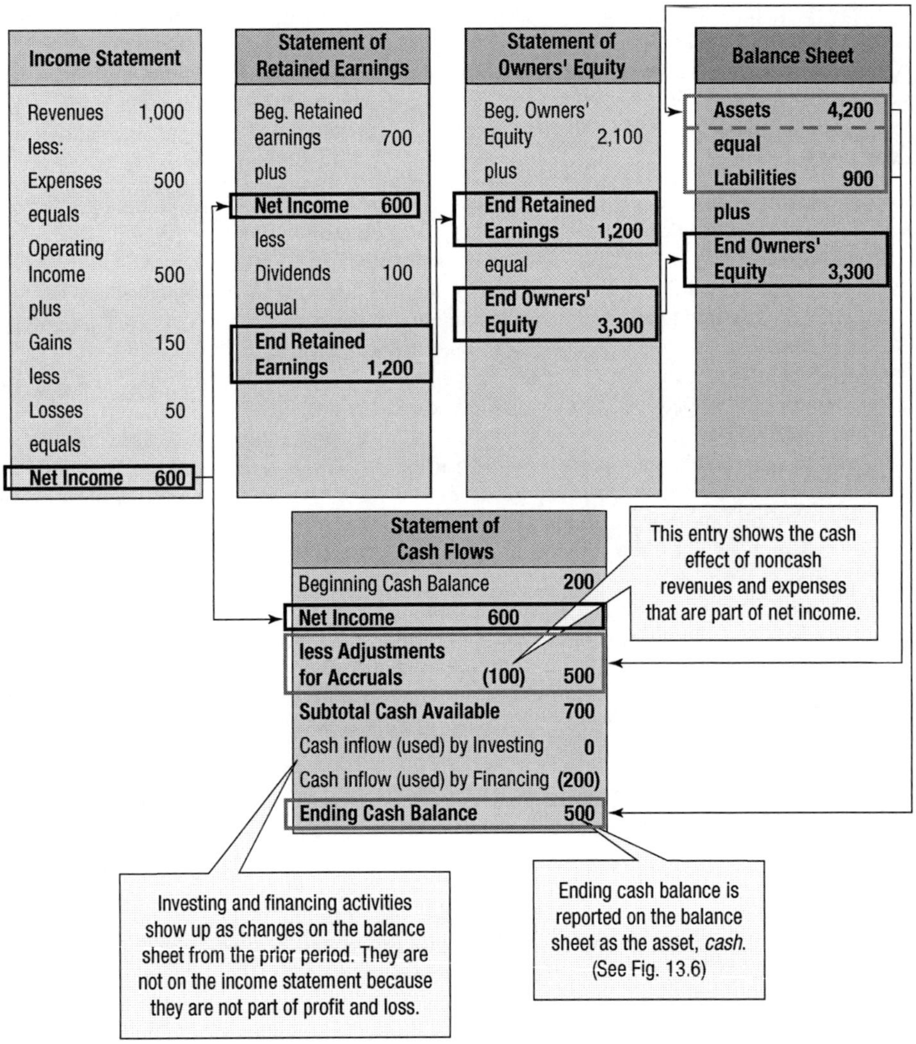

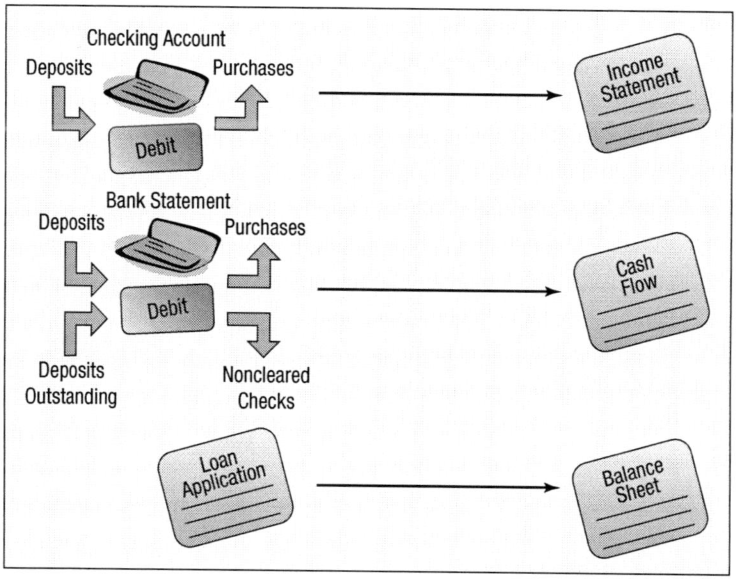

FIGURE 13.2

Everyday Financial Documents and Similar Financial Reports

To the uninitiated these financial statements can seem almost alien, but in reality each type is similar in concept and operation to financial records we use in everyday life (see Figure 13.2):

- Think of your checking account or the account tied to your debit card. You put money in and write checks or use your debit card to take money out. That is similar to the use of the income statement.
- The exact amount you have in the account at any moment depends on the deposits credited to your account (which can take anything from minutes to days, depending on how you made the deposit and the speed of your bank) and which checks have been handled by the bank. Figuring that exact amount (which some people do with their check registers or by keeping a running tally in their heads) is the idea behind the statement of cash flow.
- The monthly bank statement gives you the check and deposit information as well as any fees the bank charged you or interest it paid into your account. That parallels the statement of **retained earnings**.
- When you apply for a student loan or for a loan to purchase a car, you must fill out a loan application. This form asks you to list what you own and how much it is worth. It also asks you to list all debts you owe to others. This is very similar to the balance sheet on which financial accounting is based.

retained earnings
The sum of all profits and losses, less all dividends paid since the beginning of the business.

The important thing about these financial statements is that they **articulate**, that is, information flows from the income statement through the statement of retained earnings, the statement of owners' equity to the balance sheet. Information from the income statement and the balance sheet flows to the cash flow statement (see Figure 13.1).

articulate
The concept that information flows from the income statement through the statements of retained earnings and owners' equity to the balance sheet.

Income Statement

The **income statement** is the primary source of information about a business's profitability. The income statement shows the amount of revenues earned minus its expenses which equals net income:

income statement
A statement that lists revenues and expenses and shows the amount of profit a business makes for a specified period of time.

$$\text{Revenues} - \text{Expenses} = \text{Net Income}$$

All income statements follow the same simple general format. Reading from the top down, the income statement presents answers to the questions shown in Figure 13.3.

The usefulness of the income statement for managing a small business is related to the amount of detail available in the statement. There are two formats for income statements: (1) a *single-step*

FIGURE 13.3

Organization of the Income Statement

Question	Income Statement Content
How much revenue did the business produce?	Sales
	−
What did it cost to produce its product?	Cost of goods sold
	=
How much is available to pay expenses and provide profits?	Gross margin
	−
How much did the business use in its continuing operations?	Operating expenses
	=
How much income did the business produce?	Operating income
	−
What costs did the business have for financing?	Interest expense
	=
	Net income before tax
	−
How much tax must the business pay?	Income tax
	=
How much profit did the business make?	Net Income

format, illustrated in Figure 13.4A, which provides little detail—it simply lists all revenues and gains together, then lists all expenses and losses together, and (2) a *multiple-step* format, illustrated in Figure 13.4B, which lists revenues from operations separately from other income and gains.

Most owners and managers of small businesses prefer the multiple-step format because of its greater detail. Notice that in Figure 13.4B operating income of $105,800 is reported separately from the nonoperating gains and income from leasing. The two most commonly used computerized accounting systems for small businesses, QuickBooks and Peachtree, by default produce income statements in the multiple-step format.

FIGURE 13.4A

Typical Single-Step Format Income Statement

Real Wood Furniture Co.
Manufacturers of Fine Wooden Desks
Income Statement
for the Year Ended December 31, 2012

Revenue and gains		
Sales		$255,000
Income from leasing		4,000
Gain on sale of equipment		500
Total revenues and gains		259,500
Expenses and losses		
Cost of goods sold	$84,200	
Sales, marketing, and administrative	50,000	
Depreciation	15,000	
Interest expense	5,000	
Income tax expense	22,000	
Total expenses and losses		176,200
Net income		83,300

Income is the result of operations for a specified period of time (one year).

All revenues and gains are grouped together.

All expenses and losses are grouped together.

Only net income after tax is shown.

FIGURE 13.4B

Typical Multiple-Step Income Statement

Real Wood Furniture Co.
Manufacturers of Fine Wooden Desks
Income Statement
for the Year Ended December 31, 2012

Sales revenue		$255,000
Less cost of goods sold		84,200
Gross margin		170,800
Less operating expenses		
Marketing	$25,000	
Sales and administrative	25,000	
Depreciation	15,000	
Total operating expenses		65,000
Operating income		105,800
Income from leasing		4,000
Less interest expense		5,000
Gain on sale of equipment		500
Income before taxes		105,300
Income tax expense		22,000
Net income		$83,300

Income is the result of operations for a specified period of time (one year).

Marketing is separated from general expenses.

Gross margin is shown.

Operating income is shown as a line item.

Nonoperating revenues and gains are reported separately.

Shows both income ***before tax*** and income ***after tax***.

Difficulties in Understanding the Income Statement

There are two typical difficulties that arise in understanding and interpreting the income statements. First, there are disagreements about *what* exactly should be reported as revenue. The second problem arises from disputes over *when* to recognize revenues.[5]

Suppose your business is a water park that is open for only 120 days between June and September. In the late fall you run a promotion to sell season tickets as holiday gifts. Through this promotion, you sell for cash $200,000 worth of season tickets. Have you realized a revenue? No, to be recognized as revenue, you must have earned the money. This means that even though you have $200,000 in your bank account, it really isn't yours until the holders of season passes use them to visit the park. In fact, the amount of the season passes would be shown on your balance sheet as a liability—you owe the pass holders either access to the park or their money back.

Similar problems arise in determining the amounts and timing of gains, losses, and expenses. Suppose your business sells motor scooters. Customers who buy one will expect to receive a warranty. If they have a problem within the warranty period, they will expect that the scooter will be promptly repaired or replaced. So how much expense should you recognize for warranty? And when should you recognize it? When you sell the scooter, or when it comes back for repair? The amount of warranty cost and the timing of returns are not known at the time of sale.

Despite the difficulties and limitations of the income statement, it provides valuable information. Most small businesses do not have any difficulty deciding how much and when revenues and expenses occur. In many small businesses, all sales to customers are made either for cash or as credit card transactions that are essentially the same as cash. Subscriptions and warranties are not an issue. So in many cases, the income statement of a small business is a reliable report of just how well the business is doing in producing profits.

Use of the Income Statement

The income statement is used by you, by lenders, and by investors to analyze the effectiveness of business operations. *Operating income* is the most used item on the statement. It represents just how well management achieved sales and controlled costs to produce profits. Lenders use operating

FIGURE 13.5

Organization of the Balance Sheet

Question	Balance Sheet Content
What does the business own that can be turned into cash within one year?	Current assets
	+
What does the business own that will produce revenues for more than one year?	Fixed assets
	+
What other things does the business own, such as investments, patents, and copyrights?	Other assets
	=
What is the value of everything that the business owns?	Total assets
What debts does the business have that must be paid within one year?	Current liabilities
	+
What debts does the business have that will take longer than a year to pay?	Long-term liabilities
	+
How much is the business worth to its owners?	Owners' equity
	=
	Total liabilities and equity

income as a measure of how much debt a business can support. Interest is deductible for determining income tax, therefore net income before tax is available to make interest payments. Equity investors similarly look to operating income as an indication of future sales, so operating income becomes a favorite indicator of the value of their investment.

Balance Sheet

balance sheet
A statement of what a business owns (assets), what it owes to others (liabilities), and how much value the owners have invested in it (equity).

The **balance sheet**, also called the *Statement of Financial Position,* presents a "snapshot" of the financial holdings and liabilities at the close of business on a specified date. The balance sheet explicitly details the accounting equation for your business. The balance sheet provides answers to the questions shown in Figure 13.5.

The usefulness of the balance sheet is determined by the detail it includes. As shown in Figure 13.5, the minimum level of detail is to report both assets and liabilities in two categories: current, which will either produce or use cash within a year, and long term, which will convert to cash over a period of time greater than one year. However, your balance sheet may be made in greater detail if there is a need to do so. A common practice is to present multiyear balance sheets to facilitate analysis, as is shown in Figure 13.6.

Use of the Balance Sheet

The information in the balance sheet is used to determine the liquidity, financial flexibility, and financial strength of the business, which are detailed below. These measures of a business's financial position are used by owners, lenders, and equity investors in making financial and investment decisions.

liquidity
A measure of how quickly a company can raise money through internal sources by converting assets to cash.

Liquidity is a measure of the expected time before an asset can be converted into cash, and of the expected time before a liability must be paid. A completely liquid asset is one that can be converted instantly to cash, at its full value.[6] Cash is the most liquid of assets, as it does not have to be converted. An illiquid asset *cannot* be sold quickly without suffering a significant discount from its true value. Specialized machinery is not a liquid asset. Certainly, given enough time, specialized machinery that is not technologically obsolete can be sold. However, it is not likely to be sold quickly, and is quite likely that when sold, it will sell for only a portion of its true value as a productive asset. Think of a hot rod automobile. You might spend $20,000 or more building it. But if you must sell it,

FIGURE 13.6

Typical Balance Sheet

Real Wood Furniture Co.
Manufacturers of Fine Wooden Desks
Balance Sheet
for December 31, 2012 and 2011

	2012	2011
Assets		
Current assets		
Cash	35,000	18,800
Accounts receivable	15,500	3,500
Inventory	18,300	8,000
Total current assets	68,800	30,300
Fixed assets		
Property, plant and equipment	217,000	177,000
Accumulated depreciation	(50,000)	(35,000)
Net fixed assets	167,000	142,000
Total assets	235,800	172,300
Liabilities and owners' equity		
Current liabilities		
Accounts payable	6,000	9,500
Note payable to bank	1,500	1,700
Credit card payable	2,500	4,500
Deposits from customers	2,000	5,600
Total current liabilities	12,000	21,300
Long-term mortgage	120,000	126,000
Total liabilities	132,000	147,300
Owners' equity		
Common stock	10,000	10,000
Retained earnings	93,800	15,000
Total owners' equity	103,800	25,000
Total liabilities and equity	235,800	172,300

Current assets are things that are expected to be turned to cash within one year.

Fixed assets include machinery, buildings, land, and so on, that will be used for a long time.

Current liabilities are *debts* that will have to be paid within one year.

Owners' equity is what is left over after all debts are paid.

Retained earnings is the sum of all profits and losses, less any dividends paid from the start of the business to the date of the balance sheet.

A balance sheet may be shown for one year, or for multiple years.

Cash is the most *liquid* of all assets.

PP&E is always shown at its original cost—its *historical cost.*

Deposits from customers are liabilities because you owe your customers either the product they bought or their money back!

you are unlikely to get more than a tiny fraction of your cost. The same is true for any custom asset, and the more illiquid it is, the greater the discount.

Liquidity is a measure of the ability of a business to meet both short-term and long-term obligations. Lenders are concerned with liquidity because it indicates the level of risk that a loan will not be repaid as contracted. Equity investors are concerned with liquidity because it affects a business's ability to pay dividends.

The most common ratio used to estimate liquidity is the **current ratio**. The current ratio is calculated by dividing the value of current assets (those assets expected to be converted to cash within one year) by the value of current liabilities (those liabilities that must be paid within one year). The rule of thumb for evaluating current ratio is that the minimum acceptable ratio is 2.0, and higher is better. The calculation and use of financial ratios are discussed in detail in Chapter 15.

current ratio
The value of current assets divided by current liabilities.

Financial flexibility is an indicator of the business's ability to manage cash flows so that the company has the financial ability to respond appropriately if an unexpected opportunity or problem arises. There are no accepted financial ratios that are indicators of financial flexibility. Financial flexibility is a matter of judgment, usually based on experience. What owners, managers, bankers, and investors look for to help indicate levels of financial flexibility include (1) the ability to sell nonoperating assets, (2) the ability to obtain loans or to sell additional stock, and (3) the ability to increase efficiency and to lower costs of operation.[7] You can see that what is similar across the three indicators is the business's ability to rapidly and efficiently raise additional capital.

financial flexibility
A business's ability to manage cash flows in such a manner that the company can respond appropriately to unexpected opportunities and needs.

The **financial strength** of the business is also a matter of informed judgment. The balance sheet provides information about the nature of the assets and liabilities of the business. In evaluating financial strength, more cash and cash equivalents indicate higher strength. Current assets that comprise cash, short-term investments, and accounts receivable are more indicative of strength than are inventories

financial strength
The ability of a business to survive adverse financial events.

and prepaid expenses. In fact, excessive amounts of inventory in the current assets are indicative of management problems and financial weakness. For example, a large inventory may indicate lagging sales or products that have become obsolete or fallen out of favor with customers—all indicators of out-of-touch management. Long-term assets that are relatively new, low current liabilities, low long-term debt, and fully funded retirement plans for employees are all indicative of financial strength.

Problems in Interpreting Balance Sheet Information

For all its usefulness to the owners and managers of businesses, the balance sheet has several limitations. First, all values listed in a balance sheet are *historical* values—the cost of the asset when it was acquired. In the case of long-lived assets, such as land, buildings, and equipment, the value recorded in the accounting records can be widely different from the asset's current value. Given even a small level of inflation, the original cost of such assets is likely to be a much smaller number of dollars than its current value. On the other hand, cash is always current. This means that ratios such as return on assets (current income/net average asset value) have a current value as numerator and a denominator that, at best, is measured in older dollars of greater purchasing power. At the extreme, the true value of the asset may have changed because of changes in population density, demographics, highway access, and economic development.

Additionally, every balance sheet typically contains estimated amounts, such as estimated loss from uncollectible accounts receivable, estimated warranty cost, accumulated depreciation, depletion, amortization, and income taxes. Sometimes these estimates can be significantly wrong, such as when an unexpected product defect appears.

Finally, certain assets and liabilities are omitted from the balance sheet. Assets that are not listed include the value of licenses, established business with vendors, established customers, organizational knowledge and expertise, employee loyalty and morale, and research and development. When such assets represent a major strength of your company, the balance sheet will underreport your firm's financial strength.

SKILL MODULE 13.2 Applying for a Loan

You are going to apply for a loan for your business. Your banker told you that you will need to bring him a set of financial statements that show your business income, your business's financial position (balance sheet), and your cash flows for the year to date. To complete this task, you have collected the following information from your accounting records, which you keep manually in a three-ring binder.

Use the information to make a balance sheet in the format shown in Figure 13.6. (You can complete only the current year balance sheet.)

Account	Balance
Accounts payable	2,500
Accounts receivable	5,000
Building and equipment	112,000
Note to bank	27,500
Customer deposits	3,000
Cash	15,000
Accumulated depreciation	35,000
Capital portion of owners' equity	50,000
Retained earnings	14,000

1. What is the amount of current and long-term assets that you have?
2. Can you pledge the retained earnings of $14,000 as collateral for the new loan? Why or why not?
3. Calculate the current ratio. Using the rule of thumb given in the text, is this a good or bad ratio?
4. Why would the current ratio matter to your banker?

Cash Flow Statement

You compute the **cash flow statement** in order to see the sources and uses of cash by the business. Cash flow statements can be either direct statements or indirect statements. The direct statement is developed solely from the cash records of the business (only those things bought and sold) and does not make any reconciliation to the income statement. **GAAP** (Generally Accepted Accounting Principles) now specifies that the direct method should be used. The indirect statement of cash flows starts with net income and adjusts the accruals and deferrals to provide cash flow information that can be easily reconciled to the other financial statements. Most owners, lenders, and investors prefer the indirect method because it explicitly links net income and the balance sheet to cash flows.

There are six items that must be reported in the statement of cash flows (see Figure 13.7A):

1. Cash flows from operating activities.
2. Cash flows from investing activities.
3. Cash flows from financing activities.
4. Net effect of foreign exchange rates.
5. Net change in cash balance during the period.
6. Noncash investing and financing activities.

cash flow statement
A statement of the sources and uses of cash in a business for a specific period of time.

GAAP
Generally Accepted Accounting Principles are the standardized rules for accounting procedures set out by the Financial Account Standards Board and used in all audits and submissions of accounting reports to the government.

FIGURE 13.7A
Organization of the Cash Flow Statement

Question	Cash Flow Content
Cash flows from operating activities	
1. How much money did I receive from my customers?	Cash collected from customers
2. How much did I pay for merchandise?	(Cash paid for merchandise)
3. How much did I pay for leased equipment?	(Cash paid for equipment leases)
4. How much did I pay my employees?	(Cash paid for wages and salaries)
5. How much did I pay for other expenses?	(Cash paid for miscellaneous expenses)
6. How much cash did I receive from interest earned?	Interest received
7. How much did I pay in interest on borrowed funds?	(Interest paid)
8. How much cash was provided (used) by operations?	Net cash provided (used) by operating activities
Cash flows from investing activities	
9. How much cash did I receive (use) from disposing of obsolete or surplus equipment?	Cash proceeds (use) from disposal of equipment
10. How much did I use in paying credit deposits?	(Cash paid in security deposits)
11. How much cash did I receive from selling stock in another company?	Cash proceeds from security sales
12. How much cash did I pay to acquire equipment?	(Acquisition of equipment)
Cash flows from financing activities	
13. How much money did I invest in my own business?	Owner's contributions
14. How much did I borrow from banks?	Proceeds from bank loans.
15. How much did I pay back to banks on loans?	(Principal payments on bank loans)
16. How much money did I take out of the business for personal use?	(Owner's draws)
Net effect of foreign exchange rates	
17. How much money did I gain (lose) through foreign currency conversions?	Gain (loss) due to foreign currency exchanges
Net increase (decrease) in cash	
18. Do I have more or (less) cash now than at the beginning of the year?	Net increase (decrease) in cash
Noncash investing and financing activities	
19. What was the value of barter transactions that I made?	Schedule of noncash investing and financing activities

FIGURE 13.7B

Typical Cash Inflows and Outflows on the Cash Flow Statement

Inflows	Outflows
Cash Flows from Operating Activities	
1. Cash received from customers	1. Cash paid to purchase inventory
2. Interest received on accounts receivable	2. Salaries and wages
3. Dividends received on investments in other firms	3. Cash paid for rent, utilities, royalties, and license fees
4. Cash refunds from vendors	4. Income taxes, duties, and fines
5. All interest received from loans to other entities	5. All interest paid on liabilities
Cash Flows from Investing Activities	
1. Disposal of property, plant, and equipment	1. Acquisition of property, plant and equipment
2. Disposal of investment securities	2. Acquisition of investment securities
3. Receipt of the capital amount of loans made to customers and vendors	3. Loans made to other entities
	4. Acquisition of assets other than inventories
Cash Flows from Financing Activities	
1. Cash received from owners of the business	1. Cash paid to owners as dividends and draws
2. Cash received from borrowing	2. Cash paid to acquire the firm's own stock
	3. Repayment of the principal of borrowed funds

operating activities
Activities involved in producing and selling goods and services.

investing activities
The purchase and sale of land, buildings, equipment, and securities.

financing activities
Activities through which cash is obtained from and paid to lenders, owners, and investors.

Common *cash inflows* (receipts) and *outflows* (payments) are shown in Figure 13.7B.

Operating activities include all the functions that are performed to create your product or service. Thus the receipt of cash from customers is an operating activity. Funds received from obtaining a loan at a bank is not an operating activity; rather, it is a financing activity.

Investing activities include the acquisition and disposal of property, plant, equipment, and investment securities of other firms. The outflows are the cash investments made by the business to acquire noncash assets. Investing outflows arise from the sale or disposal of noncash assets acquired from prior investments.

Financing activities are those actions taken by management to finance the operations of the business. Thus cash inflows come only from investments by owners and from money borrowed through notes, mortgages, and bonds. Cash outflows from financing activities comprise capital repaid to owners and repayment of the principal amount of borrowings.

Net effect of foreign exchange rates is becoming ever more important to small businesses. The Internet has opened foreign trade to businesses of all sizes. Exchange rates often vary rapidly, affecting the value of contracts and sales made in currencies other than the currency of the home nation of the business.

Net change in cash balance simply reconciles the net increase or decrease with the beginning cash balance and the ending cash balance.

Noncash investing and financing comprise transactions in which an exchange of value other than cash takes place. An example of a noncash transaction is when a debt is settled by issuing stock to the creditor. These types of transactions are rarely made by small businesses. A more common transaction for small businesses is a barter transaction, which is discussed in detail in Chapter 14.

Uses of Financial Accounting

LO4 Use accounting information as a tool for managing your business effectively.

Although financial accounting is not specifically designed for management purposes, it can be a highly valuable aid in decision making. Financial and business managers are familiar with the format, content, and interpretation of financial statements. Obtaining loans, answering Internal Revenue Service inquiries, and satisfying the reporting requirements of regulatory agencies are all made easier when an appropriate set of financial statements is provided.

As the accounting scandals of recent years have made evident, the existence of financial accounting statements, even when audited by major accounting firms, does not guarantee that the representations of management are complete, accurate, or even true. In this respect, financial accounting is much like a lock on the door. A lock will keep honest people honest. Crooks will pick the lock, jimmy a window, or find another entry to commit burglary. Similarly, a business manager who is determined to commit fraud might be inconvenienced by accounting standards, but will find some way to do the crime.

Thinking about the lock idea, if you have locked something, doesn't it just make sense to double-check that the lock is in fact locked? Doing that just shows a healthy skepticism. Similarly for owners and managers of small businesses, all representations by owners, managers, employees, and providers of business outsourcing should be examined with an attitude of informed professional skepticism. It is just a healthy attitude to have.

Reporting to Outsiders

The greatest value of financial accounting for small business owners and managers is reporting the results of operations and the financial condition of the business to entities outside the business. Outsiders can include absentee owners,[8] creditors and lenders, unions, and taxing and regulatory agencies. Each of these groups has some interest in the conduct of the business. Each has either or both legal rights and political power to enforce honest disclosure of your business's finances. You are less likely to be accused of misrepresentation if your disclosures comply with accepted accounting principles.

Record Keeping

The primary criteria for a small business's record keeping system are: (1) simplicity of use, (2) accuracy of detail, (3) timeliness of reports, (4) understandability to the manager of the business, and (5) security of data. An appropriate accounting system keeps records of the details of financial transactions that facilitate the task of corroborating the conduct of the business. The most convincing evidence that can be provided to outsiders is a set of complete and accurate records that can be substantiated by third-party sources.

Taxation

Current Internal Revenue Service (IRS) regulations require that employers withhold federal income, social security (FICA), and Medicare taxes from the wages of each employee. Employers must also pay the federal unemployment tax (FUTA). The amount withheld, and the employer's share of taxes, must be paid to the IRS regularly, on a schedule determined by the amount of withholding. At the year's end, each employer is required to submit summaries of each employee's total earnings and withholdings for the year and to report the information to the IRS and to each employee on a Form W-2. This process can be automated by using one of the small business computerized accounting systems mentioned earlier.

Similarly, businesses need to pay taxes each year, and having the financial records makes the task dramatically easier. In fact many of the computerized accounting packages have tax modules or are designed to feed information to tax programs such as Intuit's TurboTax or H&R Block's TaxCut.

Control of Receivables

Accounts receivable—money owed your business by customers—is often the key to survival. An appropriate record-keeping system provides detailed reports of amounts due from customers including purchases, payments, and current contact information. The key in controlling receivables is to have them *aged,* by sorting them into groups of those that are 30, 60, 90, and over 90 days past due. If you don't receive payment when due, you should take immediate and appropriate action to collect it. Often businesses step up collection efforts when the receivables are more than 30 days overdue, with many businesses treating receivables more than 90 days old as delinquent. In such cases the owners may refer the account to a collection agency or even factor the account, selling it (at a substantial discount) to a company that will take aggressive actions to collect the entire amount owed and keep all the money it obtains.

Analysis of Business Operations

Your accounting records contain information that can be easily used for analysis of the results and state of your business. Experience in your business provides a benchmark to which all items may be compared. Those items that appear unrealistic—either too high or too low—should be carefully examined. The examination should attempt to answer the following:

- What are the appropriate levels of sales and expenses?
- Why do certain expenses appear too high or too low?
- Can any expenses be reduced or eliminated?
- Are profits appropriate for your investment, risk, time, and effort?

Uses of Managerial Accounting

Managerial accounting—the forward looking form of accounting—is one of the three types of accounting, along with tax and financial. Mastering certain managerial accounting techniques will make you a better small business manager.[9] The techniques of managerial accounting will help you become more accurate at forecasting profits, planning operations, and conserving scarce resources. Managerial accounting information and reports are used in the conduct of all managerial functions: planning, organizing, staffing, directing, and controlling.

Managerial accounting is based on understanding how costs change as a result of business changes. Some costs, such as the cost of food for a restaurant, change because of increases or decreases in gross sales. If you sell more steaks to customers, you must buy more steaks from your meat supplier. Other costs, such as rent on your building, do not change when you sell more or when you sell less. Rent is usually determined by a contract called a lease. For most stores outside of malls, leases have a specified term (for example, one year) during which rent will not change.

Many things both external to the business and internal can cause costs to change. External forces that cause cost changes can be anything from inflation, to changes in supply and demand, to economic shocks such as war. Internal forces are functions of how your business works. Consider a commuter airline. The amount of fuel used changes as a result of how long, how high, and how fast the airplane is flown. Flying a long trip at a low altitude and a high speed will use much more fuel than flying a short trip at high altitude and low speed. The cost of fuel, therefore, changes with (1) **external factors**, the cost per gallon that you have to pay, and (2) **internal factors**, how you decide to operate your planes. Other costs of your airline will change according to the operating decision you make. For example, costs of landing the airplane are caused by the cost of a landing fee at the airport, wear on the tires and brakes, and fees for parking and using airport facilities. Costs for ticket agents, baggage handlers, and onground fleet service are largely driven by the number of airports which the airline serves.

external (cost) factors
Aspects of the world outside the business which could cause the business's costs to change.

internal (cost) factors
Aspects of or choices within the business which could cause the business's costs to change.

Notice that none of the costs for this commuter airline are related to the revenues paid by passengers. Fuel burn is very nearly the same whether the airplane is empty or full. Landing costs are based on landing, no matter how many passengers are aboard. Costs for ground crew are determined by how many people are working, and how many hours they work, not how many passengers they help.

cost-volume-profit analysis
A managerial accounting technique which looks at the fixed and variable costs of a business to arrive at a number of unit sales (volume) to maximize profits.

Cost-Volume-Profit Analysis

The most common application of managerial accounting, called **cost-volume-profit analysis** (CVP) is based on sorting costs into only two categories: **variable costs** and **fixed costs**. The total cost is the sum of variable costs and fixed costs. To make this analysis, all costs that change with changes in output (which can be units made or sold, or sales revenue) are called variable costs. All costs that do not change because of changes in output are called fixed costs. In the example of the commuter airline, which uses a measure of the number of passengers for output,[10] every cost listed is considered to be fixed. None of them change as passenger loads change.

variable costs
Those costs that change with each unit produced, for example, raw materials.

fixed costs
Those costs that remain constant regardless of quantity of output, for example, rent.

Fixed costs are those costs that cannot be (or are extremely difficult to be) assigned to a specific item sold or manufactured. Imagine that *MyLibros.com,* whose business plan you saw at the end

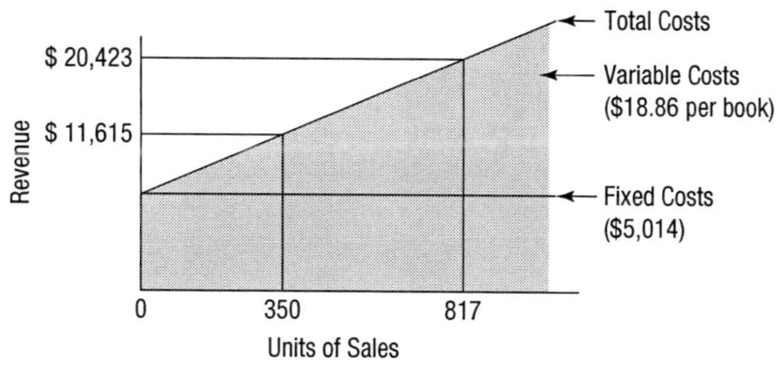

FIGURE 13.8
Total Costs

of Chapter 8, rents an office. The firm pays for utilities to heat or cool the building, for lighting and operating their computers. MyLibros has all the paperwork expenses of running a virtual business that relies on other entities for supply and distribution. It has legal fees and accounting fees. Eventually, MyLibros will have to hire additional workers, secretaries, office managers, Web programmers, purchase agents, and salespersons. MyLibros must pay for security, cleaning, or other services. None of these items is directly connected to the sale of any single book, but MyLibros cannot do business without them. The effect of variable costs and fixed costs is shown graphically in Figure 13.8.

It is important to understand that fixed costs are paid whether you sell or make one product, one million products, or no products. If MyLibros hires an office manager, he or she will want to get paid whether anything is sold or not. The electric company expects to be paid regardless of what MyLibros's sales are.

Most variable costs are the costs directly related to the production or sale of one item. For example, MyLibros must purchase every book that they sell. The more books sold, the greater the cost of books sold will be. The same is true for magazines and other media that the business sells. The books all have to be shipped to the customer. Again, the more books sold, the greater the cost of shipping will be. MyLibros is also paying Internet sites for "click through" advertising. Each time an Internet user clicks on the MyLibros link to buy a book, the company is charged 15 cents.

As does MyLibros, most retail businesses usually have primarily variable costs for the goods they sell. In contrast, many businesses have very few variable costs. An airline, for example, has minimal variable costs which include a small addition to fuel burn due to the added weight of carrying more passengers or cargo, the food and service item that a passenger consumes en route, and sometimes a per-person fee for using airport facilities.

Expendables are often variable costs. Expendables (also called indirect materials) are products used in the sales, manufacturing, or delivery that are not part of the finished product. MyLibros may need a $0.25 cardboard carton in which to ship the books, some bubble wrap for protection, tape to seal the container, etc. These items are necessary, but MyLibros's product is the book which these items contain.

Other variable costs are not directly related to an individual product but still change in proportion to changes in output. For example, there is usually some amount of waste or scrap in a production process. MyLibros may have to discard shipping boxes that are dirty, torn, or have become wet. Books may be dropped, wrinkling the cover, or tearing pages. Bonuses paid to salespersons as a percentage of sales, the cost of creating and fulfilling an order for product, and the cost of shipping product commonly vary with changes in output, and thus are variable costs. See Figure 13.8.

Generally, both fixed and variable costs are averaged over a year. For example, MyLibros might have a clogged drain that causes several shipping boxes to have to be discarded in a single day. The business will not charge a greater scrap rate for that event, but will expense the average scrap rate for the year over time. Legal fees might be paid only once a year, but part of this cost will be shown as a cost for each month of the year, not just for that particular month. There are some accounting exceptions to this, but using averages is both perfectly acceptable, and about the only reasonable way to handle the situation.

To understand how this works, consider what MyLibros's cost structure would be if they were selling only books, not books, magazines, and other media. (These numbers come from the MyLibros

FIGURE 13.9

Example of Fixed and Variable Costs Based on *MyLibros.com*

	Books 91% of gross sales	Magazines 9% of gross sales
Revenues:		
Price	$23.50	$17.02
Shipping fee	1.50	0
Gross price	$25.00	$17.02
Variable costs:		
Discount	2.35	0
Cost of goods sold	14.57	13.94
Selling	1.94	0.20
Monthly fixed costs:		
General	835.00	
Administrative/wages	1,750.00	
Rent	1,500.00	
Depreciation	429.00	
Other	500.00	
Total fixed costs per month	**5,014.00**	

Note: Selling costs are divided between books and magazines in proportion to gross sales.

financial planning Excel® workbook on the textbook Internet site.) The costs are placed into the variable and fixed categories in Figure 13.9.

Suppose MyLibros sold only one book in the month. What would the financial results be? MyLibros would lose $5,008: revenue of $25.00 minus variable cost of $18.86 minus fixed costs of $5,014. If MyLibros sells 350 books, as forecast, the loss decreases to $2,865 (revenue of (350 * $25) minus (350 * $18.86) minus $5,014). How many books must MyLibros sell in one month before the company starts earning a profit? This is easy to calculate, if you rephrase the question: How many books must MyLibros sell in a month so that gross revenue exactly equals total cost? Let *X* be the number of books that must be sold. The question now can be made into an equation (see Figure 13.10):

Key points

- Fixed costs plus variable costs equal your total cost.
- Fixed costs remain constant in total, but variable costs increase as output increases and decrease if output decreases.
- The more books MyLibros sells, the less its fixed costs *per item* become. In our example, at one book, the entire fixed cost of $5,014 needs to be applied to that book. At 350 books, fixed cost per book drops to $14.33, and at 817 books, it is a mere $6.14 per book. This truism is called **economy of scale**.

economy of scale
The idea that it is cheaper (per item) to make many of an item than few.

FIGURE 13.10

Figuring the Breakeven Point

$$\text{Revenue} = \text{Variable Cost} + \text{Fixed Cost}$$
$$\$25X = 18.86X + 5{,}014$$
$$25X - 18.86X = 5{,}014$$
$$6.14X = 5{,}014$$
$$X = 5{,}014 / 6.14$$
$$X = 816.6 \text{ books}$$

Of course, MyLibros cannot sell 6/10s of a book, so the answer must be 817 books.

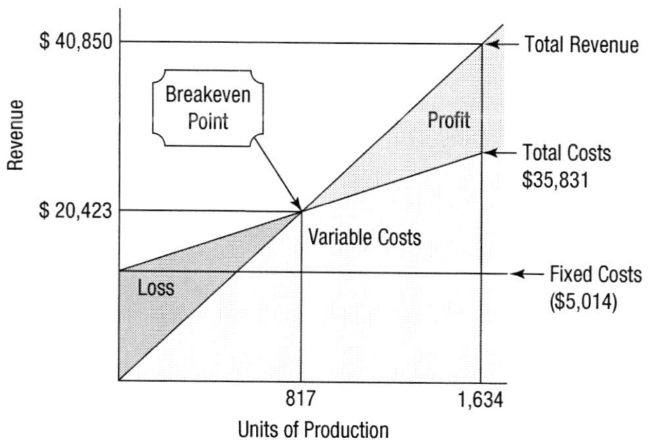

FIGURE 13.11
Breakeven Point

You have certainly encountered these concepts before. The point at which gross revenue exactly equals total costs is called the **breakeven point**. At breakeven you neither make any money nor lose any. In the example above, MyLibros must sell 817 books to break even. These relationships are shown graphically in Figure 13.11. Of course, no one goes into business to break even. For this reason, the concept has been expanded into cost-volume-profit analysis (CVP). MyLibros has determined that the best price for their books is $25.00. Suppose management would like to earn $100,000 per year. How many books must MyLibros sell to make a $100,000 profit? There must be enough sales to cover all MyLibros's costs, then to produce $100,000 in profit:

breakeven point
The point at which total costs equal gross revenue.

$$\text{Total Revenue} = \text{Total Variable Cost} + \text{Total Annual Fixed Cost} + \text{Desired Profit}$$
$$\$25X = 18.86X + (12 \times 5{,}014) + \$100{,}000$$

If you solve this equation as is done in Figure 13.10, above, you will find that MyLibros must sell 26,086 books to earn an annual profit of $100,000. These relationships are shown graphically in Figure 13.11.

This formula can easily be expanded to account for income taxes. If MyLibros's management wants to have $100,000 after tax, and the firm's tax rate is 25 percent, then the formula would become:

$$\$25X = 18.86\,X + (12 \times 5{,}014) + (\$\,100{,}000/(1 - .25))$$

The discussion above was simplified by assuming that MyLibros would sell only books. In fact, the firm currently sells magazines in addition to books. In practice, having more than one product greatly complicates the determination of breakeven. In a two-product situation like that of MyLibros, the business can break even with either product, alone. There is a near infinite number of combinations of the two products that will provide breakeven. To handle this problem, you must do one of two things: (1) assume fixed proportions of each product, as MyLibros does, or (2) use a percentage average of each, sales price and variable cost.

No one starts or buys a business for the purpose of losing money. Rather, you go into business for the express purpose of making profits and creating wealth. It is unfortunate that, as business failure statistics show, a significant number of small business owners do not achieve this basic goal. One of the underlying causes of financial failure of small businesses is the lack of a coherent plan to produce the profits necessary for continued existence and growth.[11]

Accounting data contain the information necessary to create detailed plans of how to make a desired level of profit. The problem is coaxing the information out of the data.

The process of profit planning comprises creating a *model* of the business which will allow you to test various situations, assumptions, and occurrences without risking financial loss. If the model "crashes," simply reset it and try again.[12] Models can be as simple as a schedule of expected profits at differing levels of sales, or as complex as a full, interactive computerized simulation of the business and the economy.

The Business Plan and the Budget Process

LO5 Develop a complete set of budgets for your business.

The most common model used for small businesses planning is the familiar business plan, like those described in Chapter 8. Looked at the managerial accounting way, a business plan specifies the amounts and types of inputs required to achieve a set of desired outcomes. It is based on assumptions concerning how costs will change in response to changes in the business operations, how risks can be controlled, and what opportunities can be taken. The financial projections in your business plan are a form of a budget which can easily be expanded to be useful for day-to-day management of your business. In fact, the budgeting techniques we show here use exactly the same estimates and calculations as you must make to create pro forma financial statements for a business plan. The budgets here, however, have the advantage of being comprised of a series of small, easy-to-understand schedules. When they are linked and printed as a single set of financial statements, they are identical to the familiar business plan **pro forma** statements.

pro forma
Latin for "in the form of" when used to describe financial statements, indicates estimated or hypothetical information.

Planning/Budgeting

Strategic planning, as discussed in Chapter 7, results in statements that are expressed in broad terms. For example, your strategic marketing position may be a price strategy, a luxury strategy, or a value strategy. However, if your broad strategic goals are to be achieved, you must take specific tactical steps. Budgeting is the process through which strategy is mapped into a series of tactical and operational actions.[13]

The process of achieving your strategic goals requires complex activities, cooperation among the people in your business, and the use of significant valuable resources. You will be better able to direct all this if you have a documented quantitative plan of action for your business. Such a plan is called a **budget**.

budget
A financial plan for the future, based on a single level of operations; a quantitative expression of the use of resources necessary to achieve a business's strategic goals.

Once a budget has been prepared, it becomes a standard against which performance can be measured.[14] Your budget establishes resource restraints within which your managers and employees must operate. Your budget becomes the basis for controlling activities and the use of resources. By constantly comparing actual performance to budgeted amounts, determining the causes of the inevitable differences, taking necessary corrective action, and providing feedback concerning performance, you may ensure that you attain your business goals.

Despite the many benefits to comprehensive budgeting, few small business owners consistently budget.[15] Those who do create budgets often set them aside in the rush of business activities.[16]

Let's face it, budgeting is seen by many entrepreneurs as a tedious and difficult job. We are going to try to convince you otherwise. In fact, business planning is a *simple* process of applying your knowledge of your business to make estimates of future operations and results. In many ways it is little more than an expanded application of the break-even analysis that was discussed earlier. However, business planning uses more detail than break-even analysis, and thus provides a basis for analyzing, directing, and controlling your day-to-day business operations at the level of detail that is most effective for you.

The first step in budgeting (as in any other method of business planning) is to make a forecast of your future sales. From the sales forecast, and from your knowledge of cost behaviors, collections, payments, and expenses, a complete business plan will be developed. Although this sounds daunting, in practice, you can adjust the level of detail you need to provide a comprehensive budget that is both compact and understandable (see Figure 13.12).

You may create as many or as few supplemental budgets and schedules as you need to model your business. The budgets and schedules that you will find most useful are listed in Table 13.1.

Completing a Master Budget

As you will have to do when you develop your own business plan, the founders of *MyLibros.com* had to make a set of assumptions about how their business would work. Some of the assumptions that they made were for the purpose of simplifying the task of planning. Other assumptions, however, are unique to doing business online with a minimum of physical assets and employees. Because of these facts, the MyLibros business plan cannot be simply copied and applied to "brick and mortar" businesses.

Therefore, to provide you with as useful an application as possible, one which can be easily modified to fit a wide variety of businesses, we will not develop budgets here exactly as is done in

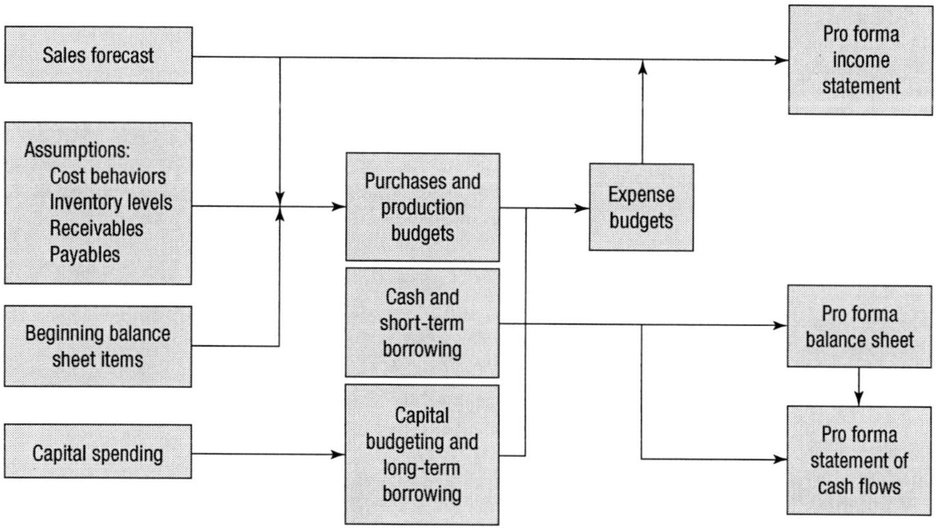

FIGURE 13.12

Budgeting Relationships

TABLE 13.1 Useful Budgets and Schedules

Budget for a Manufacturing Business	Budget for a Retail or Wholesale Business
1. Sales budget	1. Sales budget
2. Schedule of budgeted cash receipts	2. Schedule of budgeted cash receipts
3. Production budget	3. Purchases budget
4. Direct materials budget	4. Cost of goods sold budget
5. Direct labor budget	5. Labor budget
6. Manufacturing overhead budget	6. Overhead budget
7. Cost of goods manufactured and sold budget	7. Selling and administrative budget
8. Selling and administrative expense budget	8. Cash disbursements budget
9. Cash disbursements budget	9. Cash budget
10. Cash budget	10. Budgeted income statement
11. Budgeted income statement	11. Pro forma cash flow statement
12. Pro forma cash flow statement	12. Pro forma balance sheet
13. Pro forma balance sheet	

the *MyLibros.com* plan. Rather, we will use it as the basis for a teaching case which will include assumptions that are more generally applicable to the most common small businesses.

For the purpose of illustrating both how simple it is to create a **master budget**, and the specific techniques to do so, we will use the following assumptions which differ from those of the business plan for *MyLibros.com.*

master budget
A budget, also referred to as a *comprehensive budget,* consists of sets of budgets that detail all projected receipts and spending for the budgeted period.

1. Each month's sales will be a specific whole number of books and magazines.
2. The unit sales price of books will be $23.50 and of magazines will be $17.02.
3. Shipping fees will be $1.50 per book, which is collected from customers.
4. All customers will pay by use of credit cards.
5. Credit card processing fee will be 2.8 percent of gross sales.
6. All books will be sold at a 10 percent discount from the unit sales price.
7. The ending inventory of books will be equal to 60 percent of the next month's gross sales in units.

The master budget that is developed from these assumptions contains the budgets and schedules for a retail business, as is shown in Table 13.1. The specifics of producing these budgets are detailed below. To make the discussion more compact, we will use only the first three months of the second year of the original *MyLibros.com* financial projections as the basis for this discussion. The rest of the projections in the business plan are created in exactly the same way, in a reiterative process. A copy of the entire Excel® workbook, which contains both the original *MyLibros.com* financial projections and this teaching case, can be downloaded from the Web site for this textbook. In the workbook you can see all the details of the assumptions and calculations used.

Sales Budget

The first step in preparing a master budget is to prepare a sales budget. The sales budget shows the projected future level of sales in units multiplied by the sales price per unit. Chapter 12 discusses the many methods you may use to project future sales. *MyLibros.com* calculates sales from an estimate of Web traffic to their site. For teaching purposes, we assume a specific number of book purchases and magazine subscriptions for each month. This simplifies setting up the spreadsheet formulas, but it does cause minor differences from the original *MyLibros.com* business plan in Chapter 8.

SCHEDULE 13.1

MYLIBROS.COM

Sales Budget
For the Quarter Ending March 31, 2012

Note that April sales forecast is needed to determine the ending inventory for March.

Month/Quarter	Jan	Feb	Mar	Apr	Quarter 1 Total
Sales in units					
Books	608	621	634	648	1,863
Unit sales price	23.50	23.50	23.50		23.50
Revenue from books	14,288.00	14,593.50	14,899.00		43,780.50
Magazines	81	83	85		249
Unit sales price	$17.02	$17.02	$17.02		$17.02
Revenue from magazines	1,378.62	1,412.66	1,446.70		4,237.98
Shipping fees @ 1.50 per book	912.00	931.50	951.00		2,794.50
Misc. media	0.00	0.00	0.00		0.00
Gross sales	16,578.62	16,937.66	17,296.70		50,812.98
Less credit card processing fee	464.20	474.25	484.31		1,422.76
Less discounts on book sales	1,428.80	1,459.35	1,489.90		4,378.05
Net sales	14,685.62	15,004.06	15,322.49		45,012.17

Notice also that unit sales prices, gross sales, and net sales are all carried to a whole penny. While this level of detail is necessary for accuracy when using unit prices, it is not necessary and is somewhat misleading at the net sales level. Remember that all the numbers both in an initial business plan and in later budgets are based on lots of estimates. There simply is no way that you are ever going to estimate the exactly "correct" amount. For the purposes of planning, controlling, and directing, it is sufficient for any small business to carry calculations only to whole dollar amounts, or even to round to the nearest one hundred dollars.

Purchases Budget

Once sales have been projected, the next step is to plan for inventory purchases. The business plan for MyLibros was designed with the idea of buying 100 percent of inventory in the month before it will be sold, which is a reasonable simplifying assumption because of the nature of on-line businesses. However, there are almost as many patterns of buying and holding inventory as there are businesses that need inventory. Restaurants and bars usually purchase food and alcoholic beverages, especially meats and beer, two or three times per week. It is common for restaurant food suppliers to require payment in cash when the goods are delivered. The common practice for consumer electronics (stereos, DVD players, car radios, etc.) is for the retailer to place annual orders for product which will come in the form of only a few future deliveries. This annual ordering is usually done at the Winter Consumer Electronics Trade Show which is held in Chicago every January.

Most often a retail business will start each month with some amount of inventory already in hand (often around 60 percent of projected sales) and the rest is ordered for delivery in that month. If MyLibros operated this way, what would its Purchases Budget look like? Schedule 13.2 shows this more common approach, which can easily be modified to fit any pattern of ordering and holding inventory.

SCHEDULE 13.2

MYLIBROS.COM

Purchases Budget
For the Quarter Ending March 31, 2012

Month/Quarter	Jan	Feb	Mar	Quarter
Books:				
Sales in units	608	621	634	1,863
Desired ending inventory (60% of next month's sales rounded up to next higher whole number)	373	381	389	389
Inventory required	981	1,002	1,023	2,252
Less beginning inventory	365	373	381	365
Books to be purchased	616	629	642	1,887
Cost per book	$14.10	$14.10	$14.10	$14.10
Total cost of books purchased	$8,685.60	$8,868.90	$9,052.20	$26,606.70
Magazines				
Sales in units	81	83	85	249
Desired ending inventory	—	—	—	—
Inventory required	81	83	85	249
Less beginning inventory	—	—	—	—
Magazines to be purchased	81	83	85	249
Cost per magazine (rounded)	$13.94	$13.94	$13.94	$13.94
Total cost of magazines purchased	$1,129.14	$1,157.02	$1,184.90	$3,471.06
Total cost of inventory purchases	$9,814.74	$10,025.92	$10,237.10	$30,077.76

The purchases budget shows the number of units that are expected to be acquired during the budget period. The specific number of units that must be bought in each period is a function of how many units are on hand at the beginning of the period, how many are projected to be sold, and the desired number of units to be held in inventory at the end of the period. Examine the column for February. Sales are predicted to be 621 books. Management wishes to have approximately 60 percent of the next month's sales on hand at the end of the quarter: 381 books. Thus, 1,002 books are needed to meet the demands of sales and ending inventory. However, management plans to start the quarter with 373 books in stock. Thus, only 629 books must be purchased during February. This simple formula is used over and over to produce most of the schedules of a master budget: the amount needed = the amount to be used + desired ending amount – predicted beginning amount. Other inventory items to be purchased are estimated in exactly the same manner. Notice that in the purchases budget there is no beginning and ending inventory for magazine subscriptions. This is because a subscription is a contract which cannot be held in inventory. The formula for calculating budget items is often presented in the accounting format, as is shown in Figure 13.13.

FIGURE 13.13

Formula For Master Budget

Amount used
+ Ending balance
= Amount required
– Beginning balance
= Amount to be added

Cost of Goods Sold Budget

cost of goods sold budget
A schedule that shows the predicted cost of product actually sold during the accounting period.

The **cost of goods sold budget** shows the predicted cost of product actually sold during the accounting period. The calculation is simply the quantity of goods sold times the price that you expect to pay for each product.

At this point, the first quarter of the second year, *MyLibros.com* is expecting to sell only books and magazines. The firm expects to begin selling other media items beginning in July of the second year. Budgeting for other media items would be done in the same manner as is done for books and magazines. Because MyLibros never handles magazines, an acceptable alternative accounting method would be to simply show the expected commissions received from magazines. However, the management of MyLibros elected to show a cost of goods sold for magazines, and it is included here for that reason, and to illustrate the budgeting process.

SCHEDULE 13.3

MYLIBROS.COM

Cost of Goods Sold Budget
For the Quarter Ending March 31, 2012

	Jan	Feb	Mar	Quarter
Units sold				
Books	608	621	634	1,863
Cost per book	$14.10	$14.10	$14.10	$14.10
Cost of books sold	$8,572.80	$8,756.10	$8,939.40	$26,268.30
Magazines	81	83	85	249
Cost per magazine	$13.94	$13.94	$13.94	$13.94
Cost of magazines sold	$1,129.14	$1,157.02	$1,184.90	$3,471.06
Net cost of goods sold	$9,701.94	$9,913.12	$10,124.30	$29,739.36

Labor Budget

The labor budget shows both the amount and cost of labor needed to meet output goals. MyLibros, as it is currently being operated, has very little cost of labor, and management has chosen not to show labor as a separate amount. Rather, labor is included in the category Administrative and Wages. This treatment is not uncommon because for many small businesses, labor is not a major expense, and the cost of separate budgeting and accounting is greater than the value of these processes for the management of the firm. For other small businesses, such as plumbing companies, electricians, restaurants, etc., labor is the single largest cost and thus requires substantial management attention. The budget shown in Schedule 13.4 is an example of the most commonly used method to forecast labor cost.

SCHEDULE 13.4

MYLIBROS.COM

Labor Budget
For the Quarter Ending March 31, 2012

Month/Quarter	Jan	Feb	Mar	Quarter
Number of units shipped	608	621	634	1,863
Time per shipment (1/10 hours)	0.215	0.215	0.215	
Hours to be worked	130.72	133.55	136.31	400.545
Wage rate, including employment taxes	10.00	10.00	10.00	
Cost of employee benefits				
Total labor cost	1,307.20	1,335.15	1,363.10	4,005.45

Selling, General, and Administrative Expense (SG&A) Budget

The selling, general, and administrative (SG&A) budget illustrated here contains both costs that change with production and costs that do not. Selling costs, including freight, are a variable cost in respect to sales. General and administrative costs are fixed.

SCHEDULE 13.5

MYLIBROS.COM

Selling, General, and Administrative Budget
For the Quarter Ending March 31, 2012

Month/Quarter	Jan	Feb	Mar	Quarter
Selling	1,216.79	1,242.34	1,268.43	3,727.56
General	835.00	835.00	835.00	2,505.00
Administrative & wages	442.80	414.85	386.90	1,244.55
Total SG&A	2,494.59	2,492.19	2,490.33	7,477.11

Administrative & wages is the $1,750 monthly budget from the MyLibros business plan, less the amount allocated to labor in Schedule 13.4.

Overhead Budget

activity-based cost estimates
An accounting method which assigns costs based on the different types of work a business does in order to sell a particular product or service.

Traditionally, all overhead costs have been treated as fixed, not changing with changes in output as measured by either volume of production or gross sales. It is becoming more common for managers to use **activity-based cost estimates** for overhead. As was discussed above, many costs that do not vary in proportion to output levels do vary in response to changes in other business activities. If the cost behaviors are known, they can easily be included in the budget process. For simplicity, the example given here assumes that overhead costs are fixed with respect to sales.

SCHEDULE 13.6
MYLIBROS.COM
Overhead Budget
For the Quarter Ending March 31, 2012

Month/Quarter	Jan	Feb	Mar	Quarter
Rent	1,500.00	1,500.00	1,500.00	4,500.00
Maintenance	500.00	500.00	500.00	1,500.00
Depreciation	429.32	429.32	429.32	1,287.96
Total overhead	2,429.32	2,429.32	2,429.32	7,287.96

Budgeted Income Statement

The budgets that have been completed to this point can now be combined into a "pro forma" budgeted income statement. It is common to create the budgeted income statement in only a fiscal period format (one quarter or one year) as is done here. While the income statement could be produced in months or even in days, that level of detail, while possibly helpful for management, is not helpful to bankers, investors, or others outside management for which the income statement is intended. Thus the detailed planning that is included in the budget is condensed for the income statement. The entire budgeted income statement is based on the assumption that all budgeted items, sales, production, purchasing, labor, overhead, and SG&A will be incurred exactly as planned in the supporting budgets. During the year, comparisons of actual results are made to the budgeted items. If the budget is met, then the projected profit will be realized.

Completing a Comprehensive Budget

The final schedules to be completed to produce a master budget are (1) a cash receipts budget, (2) a cash disbursements budget, and (3) a cash budget. From these schedules, a pro forma cash flow statement and a pro forma projected balance sheet are prepared.

The management of cash is so important to small business that it deserves a chapter to itself. Therefore, the discussion of cash and cash budgeting is included in the next chapter.

Controlling

variance
The difference between an actual and budgeted revenue or cost.

Managerial accounting, primarily through the budget process, provides information that allows managers to determine how well the business is doing in attaining its goals. This is done by comparing actual results to budgeted results. The difference between actual and budget is called a **variance**. Management can determine where the business is not meeting goals through examining a report of variances.

SCHEDULE 13.7
MYLIBROS.COM
Budgeted Income Statement
For the Quarter Ending March 31, 2012

Sales revenue		50,812.98
Less discounts on book sales		4,378.05
Net revenues		46,434.93
Less cost of goods sold		29,739.36
Gross margin		16,695.57
Operating expenses:		
Labor	4,005.45	
Selling, general, & administrative	7,477.11	
Rent	4,500.00	
Other expenses:	1,500.00	17,482.56
Income before depreciation, interest, and income tax		(786.99)
Interest		0
Depreciation		1,287.96
Net income before provision for income tax		(2,074.95)

Variances should be evaluated to determine the significance of a particular variance. Small variances from budget are expected to occur, as the budget is a collection of estimates. No business manager, in fact, no person, no computer, is capable of making estimates that are exactly what future results will be. For this reason, it is customary for management to determine a range of acceptable variances. Individual variances that fall within the predetermined acceptable range are ignored. Variances that exceed the acceptable range are examined in detail, with the manager tracing the activities that drive the cost to determine the cause of the variance and appropriate methods to deal with it.

Variance analysis is a topic that is simple in concept but complex in execution. At the most basic level, variances occur because of one of two events: (1) Prices are different from what was estimated, or (2) Quantities are different from what was estimated. Thus variances can be reduced to determine the amount of variance caused by price changes and the amount of variance caused by changes in volume.[17] The specifics of variance analyses are detailed in the Thoughtful Entrepreneur box on the next page.

variance analysis
The process of determining the effect of price and quantity changes on revenues and expenses.

Preparing a Master Budget

SKILL MODULE 13.3

Go to the McGraw-Hill Web site for this textbook (**http://www.mhhe.com/katzesb**) and download the Excel budget template for *MyLibros.com*. Using the information in the downloaded spreadsheet, complete a monthly master budget for the remainder of the second year of operation, following the examples shown in this chapter.

THE THOUGHTFUL ENTREPRENEUR

PERFORMING VARIANCE ANALYSES

Suppose that you operate a business that produces aluminum window frames for the replacement window industry. You have used all your expertise to budget the next year's operation of your business. Based on prior years' results, the current state of the economy, and projections for the replacement window industry, you developed the following budget items:

Materials to produce one window frame	**Budget**
Aluminum extrusions 16 ft @ 1.20 per ft	$19.20
Sheet aluminum 25 sq in @ $ 0.08	2.00
Screws 22 @ .06 each	1.32

For the past month, you estimated total production to be 6,000 window units. You actually produced 5,800 window frames. You used 93,960 feet of extrusion that cost $109,933 in total. As a manager, how would you answer the questions, "How did the price of aluminum affect us?" and "Did we use the extrusions efficiently?"

Logically, the answer to the first question can be found by answering the question, "What would I have paid for the aluminum I actually used if the price had been what I expected?" The difference between that and what you actually paid is the difference caused by price changes.

The second question, "Did we use the material efficiently?" can be answered by asking, "How much material should I have used to make the number of window units that were actually completed?" The difference between what you should have used and actually did use multiplied by the price you expected to pay for aluminum is the difference resulting from efficiency.

These questions are answered by variance analysis, which uses the information mentioned above to produce quantitative results. The equations that make up variance analysis are given in Figure 13.14. Figure 13.15 shows how the calculations are made.

FIGURE 13.14

Fundamental Variance Analysis

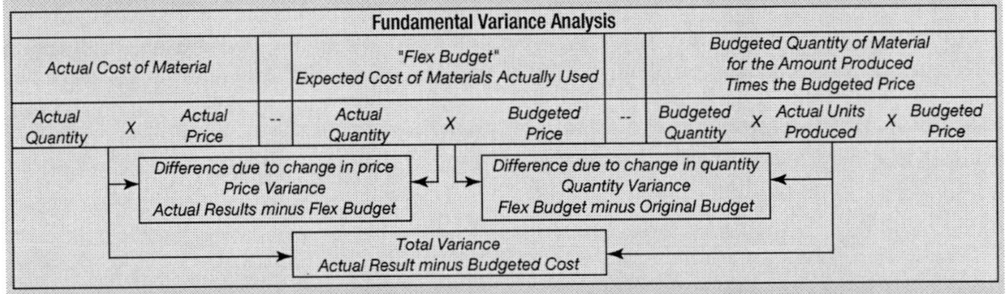

FIGURE 13.15

Variance Analysis Example

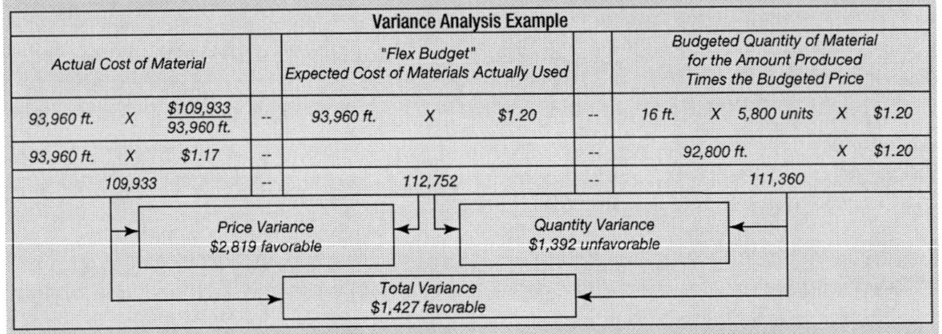

Thus we can see that the actual cost of material was $2,819 less than the expected cost for the amount actually used. This is called a **favorable price variance.** On the other hand, the cost of the amount of materials actually used is greater than the budgeted cost of materials to make 5,800 window frames. This is called an **unfavorable quantity variance.** The terms *favorable* and *unfavorable* are determined by the variance's effect on profits, all other things being as budgeted. Paying 3 cents a foot less for extrusions than was budgeted would cause a greater profit than budgeted, if all other budget items were exactly correct. Conversely, using more extrusions to make 5,800 window frames than was budgeted for that level of output would cause a decrease from budgeted profit.

Note that although the variances are labeled as favorable or unfavorable depending on the direction of the variance from budget, no value judgment can be made from the label. A favorable price variance could be a bad event for the company; if, for example, the reason for the lower price was lower quality of materials that would prevent the business from attaining its strategic goals. Additionally, managers must use judgment to determine if the variance is worth the effort to investigate. For example, the price of aluminum extrusions is set by the world price for aluminum. It is not likely that any amount of investigating would result in determining a way to get a lower price. On the other hand, using 0.2 feet more of material than was budgeted might indicate that cutting tools are out of adjustment or that worker efficiency is not as great as expected. Management could reasonably expect to find the cause and to devise a way to improve the use of this resource.

favorable/unfavorable variance
A label applied to variances to indicate their effect upon the income statement; favorable variances would result in profits being greater than budgeted, all other things being equal; unfavorable variances would result in profits being less than budgeted, all other things being equal.

Decision Making

LO6 Use accounting information to make better business decisions.

Managers have five primary functions in a business: planning, organizing, staffing, directing, and controlling the combined efforts of the firm. Each of these functions requires making decisions, both large and small. The primary purpose of managerial accounting is to support good decision making.

To use accounting information for decision making, you need to have some understanding of the processes by which people make decisions.

All current theories of decision making are based on the belief that people are rational, that is, people think, reason, and consider alternatives before they act. Although this assumption may be a bit optimistic, it applies (or *should* apply) to decision making in business situations. The assumption of rationality itself comes in several "flavors." At one extreme are theories that assume that the human mind has essentially unlimited reasoning powers. At the other extreme are theories that assume that people have limited abilities to obtain and process information.

The theories of unlimited reasoning powers have been largely discredited. Research shows that people use incomplete information and incomplete analyses of alternatives to make decisions. Today, it is generally assumed that people are inefficient processors of information. Theories based on the assumption of limited human abilities are called *bounded rationality models.*[18] One implication of the assumption that people are limited in their ability to use information is that the more information available to be included into the decision process, the less efficient that process will be.

Thus to make good decisions we need (1) good information, (2) efficient ways to condense information so it is understandable, and (3) methods to help compare alternatives.

Managerial accounting is both a source of information that is used in decision making and a methodology to reduce the complexity of the information used to make a decision. By definition, managerial accounting deals with only financial information. By limiting the information being considered to financial concerns, the complexity of the alternatives is reduced. Managerial accounting further reduces information complexity by evaluating information for relevance to the decision to be made. For financial purposes, any decision that was made in the past cannot be changed and is therefore irrelevant to any decision to be made today. Information that is the same for two or more alternatives cannot be used to choose between them. For these reasons, managerial accounting decision support is based solely upon the differences in expected financial outcomes among identified alternatives.

Examining some of the common management decisions that can be aided by the use of accounting information and procedures will illustrate these concepts.

Investments are a constant management problem. To reduce the difficulty of choosing from among investment alternatives, managerial accounting has developed two basic methodologies to reduce the magnitude and complexity of the information that must be considered in making an appropriate decision.

The first of these simplification methods is called *differential revenues and expenses.* This methodology comprises estimating the *changes* in revenues and expenses from current operating results that will occur if each alternative is taken. The decision rule that is applied is to accept the investment that produces the greatest profit.

The second simplification method is called *net present value analysis* (NPV). NPV analyses are based on the concept that a dollar to be received right now has more utility (value) than does a dollar to be received at some time in the future. To perform NPV analyses, only cash flows are considered. The decision rule is to accept the largest positive NPV. The theory and application of NPV is covered in detail in Chapter 17.

Outsourcing requires that a decision be made whether the business should make a component of its own product or purchase the component from another business. As is done in investment decisions, accounting information relevant to the decision is reduced to differential revenues and costs, or to cash flows. Depending upon the methodology chosen, either the differential profits (losses) or the net present value of each alternative is calculated. Once the information is developed, decision rules are applied.[19]

A simple example of an outsourcing decision is the provision of salad for a local restaurant. Suppose that the restaurant is a barbeque that serves cole slaw as its only salad. The restaurant may either make the slaw on premises at a cost of $2.87 per pound or purchase it from a wholesaler at $2.40 per pound. Should you make the slaw or purchase the slaw? A superficial examination of the problem would indicate that purchasing it is less expensive. Examining only the differential costs offers a very different conclusion (see Exhibit 13.1).

EXHIBIT 13.1

Using Differential Costs to Make an Outsourcing Decision: Make or Buy?

Current Costs to Make Slaw on Premises	
Pounds of slaw served per month	900
Materials per pound	$0.87
Direct labor per pound (2.4 hrs @ $10 per 30 lbs.)	0.80
Variable overhead per pound	0.20
Allocated fixed costs per pound	1.00
Total cost per pound	$2.87

Differential Costs between Alternatives

	Alternatives	
	Make	Buy
Materials	$0.87	–0–
Direct labor	0.80	–0–
Variable overhead	0.20	–0–
Purchase price	–0–	2.40
Total	$ 1.87	$2.40

The difference arises from the fact that fixed costs will not change if the decision is made to purchase the slaw. By definition, fixed costs are costs that do not change with changes in output (here output is slaw). As a result, the amount of fixed cost allocated to making slaw is irrelevant to the decision. If you have trouble understanding this, simply put a line for fixed cost into the decision criteria above. Put the allocated amount of $1.00 in the columns for making and buying the slaw. Add the columns and see if your decision would change.

Accounting is useful for managers of small businesses, for record keeping, for reporting to absentee owners and other stakeholders, for substantiating assertions made to regulators and taxing agencies, for support of the five functions of management, and for decision making. Accounting information is a financial model of the operations of the business and provides a wealth of useful reports, analyses, and measures that are valuable to the management of small businesses. Accounting is a rich source of information. It is not, however, the only source of information needed by managers.

CHAPTER SUMMARY

LO1 Describe the basic concepts of accounting.

- Accounting matters to small businesses because:
  - Accounting proves what your business did financially.
  - Accounting shows how much your business is worth.
  - Banks, creditors, development agencies, and investors require accounting statements.
  - Accounting provides easy-to-understand plans for business operations.
  - Accounting provides information about how your business is doing.
- There are three types of accounting:
  - Managerial accounting attempts to predict the results of management decisions.
  - Tax accounting is used to produce tax returns and schedules.
  - Financial accounting is a formal, rule-based system intended primarily for absentee owners, bankers, investors, and regulators.
- Accounting is based on a few basic concepts:
  - A business is believed to have an existence that is separate and different from the owner's (business entity concept).
  - Because a business exists, it is expected to continue to exist (going concern).
  - The accounting equation is simply an expression of the common sense statement that your net worth is whatever is left over after all your debts are paid.
- To use accounting effectively for management purposes, you must understand the difference between costs and expenses:
  - Costs are real changes in the value of what you own.
  - Expenses are simply entries made in your accounting system to record your use of goods and services in the conduct of your business.
- There are only two reasons to do accounting:
  - To produce information that is useful to you for managing your business.
  - To meet legal or contractual requirements.

LO2 Specify the requirements for a small business accounting system.

- The primary reason to acquire and use a computerized accounting system in your business is to ensure the accuracy of your accounting information.
- Your accounting system should easily and efficiently accomplish the following tasks:
  - Provide a simple, easy-to-understand user interface.
  - Have an exhaustive context-sensitive help function.
  - Produce financial statements in the format used by your industry and type of business.
  - Facilitate the development of a cash budget.
  - Facilitate the task of developing operating and investment budgets.

- Provide a method for you to define and produce custom reports to meet your management needs.
- Be able to export financial data in a form that can be used by your accountant and can be imported into tax preparation and spreadsheet programs.
- Maintain an internal "audit trail" that records all entries and changes to the accounting system in order to facilitate the identification and correction of errors.
- Have provisions that will either allow the program to grow with your business or to easily export its data into programs that can handle larger businesses.

- Your specific accounting needs are determined by the industry you are in and by the size of your business.
- When a business is large enough to have one or more employees, formal record keeping is a must.
- Essential elements of an accounting system are:
  - *Cash accounting* that is accurate, easy to use, and tracks all checks written and all deposits made.
  - *Accounts payable* records to track what you owe and to make timely payments in order to capture prompt pay discounts and to maintain a good credit rating for your business.
  - *Payroll* records to ensure that payroll and employment taxes are kept current.
  - *Fixed asset* accounting that automatically calculates and accumulates depreciation.
  - *Inventory* accounting to facilitate managing inventory.
  - *Credit card sales* function to enable reconciling your sales records to those of your credit card provider.
  - *Accounts receivable* records if you provide credit to your customers.
  - *Insurance register* to ease the problems of keeping necessary insurance coverage current and in force.
  - *Investments* records if your business keeps surplus cash invested in securities.
  - *Leasehold* records if your business has made improvements to leased property or equipment.

LO3 Explain the content and format of common financial statements.

- The final output of an accounting computer system is a set of five financial statements and reports.
  - Income statement.
  - Statement of retained earnings.
  - Statement of owners' equity.
  - Balance sheet.
  - Cash flow statement.
- It is common for these statements to be presented as only three separate documents by combining the statements of retained earnings and owners' equity into the equity section of the balance sheet.
- The income statement is the primary source of information about a business's profitability.
- The primary difficulties in understanding and interpreting the income statement arise from two causes:
  - Disagreements about what should be reported as revenue.
  - Disputes over when to recognize revenues.
- The income statement is used in the following ways:
  - The income statement is used to analyze the effectiveness of business operations.
  - Lenders use operating income as a measure of how much debt a business can support.
  - Equity investors similarly look to operating income as an indication of future sales and thus the value of their investment.
- The balance sheet presents a snap-shot of the financial holdings and liabilities at the close of business on a specified date.
- The balance sheet is used in the following ways:
  - The balance sheet is used to determine the liquidity, financial flexibility, and financial strength of the business.
  - These measures are used by owners, lenders, and equity investors in making financial and investment decisions.
- The following are problems in interpreting balance sheet information:
  - All values listed in a balance sheet are *historical* values—the cost of the asset when it was acquired.
  - A balance sheet contains several estimated amounts.
  - Certain assets and liabilities are omitted from the balance sheet.
- The purpose of the cash flow statement is to disclose the sources and uses of cash by the business.
- There are two primary formats of cash flow statement:
  - The direct statement is developed solely from the cash records of the business and does not make any reconciliation to the income statement.

- The indirect statement of cash flows starts with net income and adjusts the accruals and deferrals to provide cash flow information that can be easily reconciled to the other financial statements.

LO4 Use accounting information as a tool for managing your business effectively.

- Financial accounting is useful for decision making.
- Financial and business managers are familiar with the format, content, and interpretation of financial statements.
- Obtaining loans, answering Internal Revenue Service inquiries, and satisfying the reporting requirements of regulatory agencies are all made easier when an appropriate set of financial statements is provided.
- Financial accounting is used for reporting to outsiders.
- Managerial accounting is used internally for management purposes.
- By mastering managerial accounting techniques, you will become more accurate at forecasting profits, planning operations, and conserving scarce resources.
- Managerial accounting information and reports are used in the conduct of all the managerial functions of planning, organizing, staffing, directing, and controlling.
- The most used managerial accounting technique is cost-volume-profit analysis.
- Accounting data contain the information necessary to create detailed plans of how to achieve a desired level of profit.
- The process of profit planning comprises creating a model of the business which will allow you to test various situations, assumptions, and occurrences, without risking financial loss.
- The most common model used for small businesses planning is the familiar business plan.
- The financial projections in your business plan are a form of a budget which can easily be expanded to be useful for the day-to-day management of your business.

LO5 Develop a complete set of budgets for your business.

- Budgeting is the process through which strategy is mapped into a series of tactical and operational actions.
- Once a budget has been prepared, it becomes a standard against which performance can be measured.
- Business planning is a *simple* process of applying your knowledge of your business to make estimates of future operations and results.
- The most common budget schedules are:
  - The sales budget which shows the projected future level of sales in units multiplied by the sales price per unit.
  - The purchases budget shows the number of units expected to be acquired during the budget period.
  - The cost of goods sold budget shows the predicted cost of product actually sold.
  - The labor budget shows both the amount and cost of labor needed to meet required output.
  - The overhead budget details both fixed and variable overhead costs.
  - Selling, general, and administrative expense (SG&A) budget shows both costs that change with production and costs that don't.
- These budget schedules are combined into pro forma financial statements.
- The difference between actual results and budgeted amounts is called a variance.
- Variances occur because either actual prices or volume is different from what was budgeted.
- To understand the effect of price changes, you must answer the following questions:
  - What would I have paid for the amount I actually used, if the price had been what I expected?
  - How much material should I have used to make the number of units that were actually completed?

LO6 Use accounting information to make better business decisions.

- The five primary functions in a business—planning, organizing, staffing, directing, and controlling—are combined as input for decision making.
- To make good decisions we need:
  - Good information.
  - Efficient methods to condense information so it is understandable.
  - Methods to facilitate comparing alternatives.

- Managerial accounting is both a source of information that is used in decision making and a methodology to reduce the complexity of the information used to make a decision.
- Common management decisions that can be aided by the use of accounting information and procedures include investments and outsourcing.
- Managerial accounting uses two primary simplification methods to handle information: differential revenues and expenses and net present value analysis (NPV).

KEY TERMS

managerial accounting, 402
tax accounting, 402
financial accounting, 402
business entity concept, 403
going concern concept, 403
accounting equation, 403
liabilities, 404
owners' equity, 404
cost, 404
expense, 405
MACRS rate, 406
depreciation, 406
financial statements, 408
retained earnings, 409
articulate, 409
income statement, 409
balance sheet, 412
liquidity, 412
current ratio, 413
financial flexibility, 413
financial strength, 413
cash flow statement, 415
GAAP, 415
operating activities, 416
investing activities, 416
financing activities, 416
external (cost) factors, 418
internal (cost) factors, 418
cost-volume-profit analysis, 418
variable costs, 418
fixed costs, 418
economy of scale, 420
breakeven point, 421
pro forma, 422
budget, 422
master budget, 423
cost of goods sold budget, 426
activity-based cost estimates, 428
variance, 428
variance analysis, 429
favorable/unfavorable variance, 431

DISCUSSION QUESTIONS

1. Which of the three types of accounting is most important to small business? Which is the least? Why do you think so?
2. How does the accounting equation relate to the balance sheet?
3. How are costs and expenses different?
4. Why should you, as a business owner, care about the distinction between costs and expenses?
5. Defend the statement, "The function of accounting is to produce information that is useful for decision making."
6. What are the three most important characteristics of a small business computer accounting system? Why do you think these are the most important?
7. What are the three most important functions (think cash, accounts payable, owners' equity, etc.) that a computerized accounting system should have? Why are they the most important?
8. Which financial report is most important for managing a small business? Why?
9. You can sell your product (have revenues) without receiving any money. You can receive money (customer deposits) without having any revenue. Because revenue, expenses, and cash are so different, why should a small business owner care about the income statement?
10. Why would a small business ever need an accounting system more complicated than a simple checkbook register?

11. A budget is a collection of estimates—a big word that means the same thing as "guess." If you are guessing what future results will be, what value can a budget really have?
12. How are budgets related to business plans, as described in Chapter 8?
13. Is there any advantage to making a series of budget schedules, rather than just producing a pro forma income statement and balance sheet? What are the advantages, if any?

EXPERIENTIAL EXERCISES

1. Assume that you have decided to purchase a computerized small business accounting system. Visit the Web site of each of the accounting systems named in this chapter. From the information there determine:
   a. The price of the accounting system.
   b. The minimum computer requirements for the program.
   c. The availability and cost of training to learn to use the program.
   d. The availability of trained accountants and consultants in your geographic area who can be retained to assist you in setting up and using the program.
2. Choose an industry in which you would like to own a small business. Use the Internet, the university library, and the public library to find the names and addresses of industry trade associations. Examine the Web sites of the trade associations for availability of financial statistics of your industry. Examine governmental agency sites, such as those of the Department of Commerce, Department of the Treasury, Securities and Exchange Commission, and the Small Business Administration, for benchmark statistics.
3. Choose a public business that is in the same industry as the business you would like to own. Go to the company's Web site and find "investor relations." Download a copy of the business's most recent annual report. Examine the financial statements in the annual report. Make a list of the ways in which their content and format differ from the examples in this text.
4. Either by yourself or in a group of other students, select a business that you could reasonably expect to be able to start and run right now. (This could be as simple as a T-shirt company.) Using the techniques learned in exercises 2 and 3, above, develop a set of estimates of (a) sales, (b) variable cost of product or service and (c) the amount of other costs (rent, electricity, transportation, etc.) that you would expect to incur. Using these estimates, create a set of budget schedules through the schedule of cost of goods manufactured and sold.
5. Go to either the QuickBooks or the Peachtree Web site. Download and install a demonstration copy of its accounting program. Using either the budget schedules you developed in exercise 4, or the *MyLibros.com* example from the text, set up the program to do accounting as if this were a real business.
6. Do a Google search on the terms "accounting system" and "small business." Follow the Google returns to the Web sites of the companies (other than the ones named in the text) that you can find that sell computerized accounting systems. Examine the site to determine if its program would be suitable under the criteria specified in the text.

MINI-CASE

PHIONIA'S FINICKY FELINE GOURMET CAT DINNERS

Phionia Phelps has developed a gourmet cat food. Not only is this food eagerly eaten by the most finicky felines, but it is specially formulated to prevent the many health problems of aging cats. Phionia has been making the food on her kitchen range and selling it at $250 per case only to close acquaintances who are also cat lovers. One of her wealthy acquaintances has now offered to invest in her business if Phionia will begin selling the product through her Web site. However, the investor wants Phionia to produce a budget for the first six months of operation.

Based on her experience to date, Phionia predicts the following sales in cases:

Nov	Dec	Jan	Feb	Mar	Apr	May	Jun	Jul	Aug
4,300	4,600	5,000	5,500	6,100	6,800	7,000	7,200	7,400	7,500

Each case of Finicky Feline Gourmet Cat Dinner requires 5 pounds of prime lamb meat, 10 pounds of short grain Chinese rice, 2 pounds of wild caught Alaskan salmon, and 1 pound of secret vitamins and supplements. Phionia plans to maintain end-of-month inventories equal to 10 percent of the next month's projected sales, to meet expected sales growth. All the ingredients inventories are to be maintained at 5 percent of the production needs for the next month, but not to exceed 1,000 pounds of any one ingredient. January will begin with all inventories at the projected levels.

Phionia has the following price quotes good for the following year:

Item	$ per pound
Lamb	$15.00
Rice	1.20
Salmon	24.00
Vitamins	45.00

The production process requires direct labor at two skill levels: (1) ingredient preparation, $18 per hour, and (2) cooking and canning, $24 per hour. Two workers are willing to work part days if there is not enough demand for them to work full time. It takes one hour to process one batch. Because of preparation and cleanup time, only six batches can be produced per day. Each batch produces enough food to fill 100 cases. Manufacturing overhead is $6,000 fixed per month plus $15 per case.

CASE DISCUSSION QUESTIONS

1. Prepare the following budgets for the period, January through June:
   a. Sales budget in dollars.
   b. Production budget in units.
   c. Direct materials purchases budget in pounds.
   d. Direct materials purchases budget in dollars.
   e. Direct manufacturing labor budget in dollars.
2. Comment on the viability of this business and the advisability of the investor making a $50,000 investment to get it started.

SUGGESTED CASES AND ARTICLES

- Parker Mountain Products, Inc.

Available on PRIMIS:

- Lexington Valley Medical Associates
- Michaels Ballet Company
- Thermal Remediation, Inc.
- Majsperk
- Wilmont Chemical Corporation
- Ratios Tell a Story: 2003
- ENTERTAINMENTNOW.COM
- Belle Air Charter

SUGGESTED VIDEOS

eClips Videos:

- Brian Qualey States Importance of Outlining Breakeven Point In Business Plan
- Laurie Linn Discusses Need to Understand Accounting to Better Run the Business

SBTV Videos:

- Start-Up Costs
- Three Tips for Accounting

STVP Video:

- Keeping a Financial Focus

CHAPTER 14

Cash: Lifeblood of the Business

- Be Our Guest learned the hard way how much a crippled cash flow can hamper a business. Faced with several different options, they eventually expanded their credit line in order to handle the annual peaks and declines of the party supply business. Which route would you have chosen, and why?

LO

LEARNING OBJECTIVES

When you complete this chapter, you will be able to:

LO1 Explain the importance of managing your business's money.

LO2 Explain the concepts of money, cash, and cash equivalents.

LO3 Explain the basics of managing cash flow.

LO4 Reconcile bank and company book balances.

LO5 Develop a cash budget.

LO6 Develop strategies for preventing and coping with cash flow problems.

LO7 Implement strategies for coping with cash shortages.

Focus on Small Business: Stephen Lizio, Al Lovata, and Simone Williamson of Be Our Guest, Inc.

Stephen Lizio, Al Lovata, and Simone Williamson had run out of financing options. Their firm, Be Our Guest, Inc., of Boston, Massachusetts, had a long-term loan with a principal balance of $315,000 and at $140,000 had also maxed out their revolving credit line. This came about in a year that had seen sales increase by a remarkable 22 percent, but their sky-high debt made it clear that too many customers owed Be Our Guest too much. There were bills to pay, but no money with which to pay them.

Be Our Guest, Inc., rents party supplies. Its business is highly seasonal, with peaks in June, as many weddings occur, and in November–December during the holiday party season. During the rest of the year, especially in the first quarter, revenues are always less than expenses. The instant cash flow problem facing Be Our Guest came about because of a busy December, with high sales and therefore high receivables. Now, facing January bills themselves, many customers were not paying on time. Although the owners expected all the customers to pay eventually, right now Be Our Guest was scraping for cash for daily operations.

The owners had few alternatives available to fix the current problem. Having maxed out their bank credit, additional bank borrowing was not available. The firm could borrow against the receivables, but this was not an attractive option. Many of the receivables accounts were past due, so lenders would loan no more than 70 percent of the amount to be collected from customers. Also, the past due accounts would mean paying the lender more than the customary 5 percent fee, on top of a sky-high 20 percent annual interest rate. Another way would be for the owners to cut what they were paying to themselves, leaving more money to pay the creditors, but that was the last thing they wanted to do, since technically the business had enough money—their marketable assets far exceeded liabilities. It was just that Be Our Guest didn't have enough cash.

"What should we do now?" they asked themselves.

For a time, they did nothing. They continued to scrape by on the cash flow that could be generated, while cutting back on every expense and payout they could. By the midsummer party season, the problem had again resolved itself. Given some financial breathing room, the owners took several steps to find a permanent solution to the seasonal peaks of cash inflows. First, with their financials once again strong and a year of increased sales to show, they arranged for a $60,000 increase in the line of credit to a total of $200,000.[1] Then, in the following year, based on continuing improved results, the line of credit was refinanced, converting it into long-term debt. This reduced the interest rate, resulting in an immediate reduction in cash outflows.

The business (http://www.beourguestpartyrental.com) is successful and growing today. It still encounters peaks of business in June and December, but it has developed methods to ensure that cash will be available when needed.[2]

DISCUSSION QUESTIONS

1. Why did the current amount of debt limit how much the business could borrow to solve the current cash crunch?
2. Why does the fact that some customers are late paying in January make using the receivables for collateral so expensive?
3. Should the owners have reduced payments to themselves to be able to pay more to vendors and suppliers?
4. How is it that a business could "have enough money," but still not be able to pay its bills?

The Importance of Money Management

LO1 Explain the importance of managing your business's money.

Have you ever considered the question, "What is money?"

Certainly you have thought about money. It is a rare small business person who does not think about money—making money, investing money, spending money, having enough money. In fact, money can seem so important to business that sometimes people make the error of believing that money is all that business is about. Of course, as you have already learned in the earlier chapters, business is about many important things, of which money is only one.

But this still leaves the question, "What is this *'money,'* and why is it so important?"

Throughout this book, terms that refer to money are tossed about: money, cash, cash equivalents, profits, and banking, to name a few. Have you given any consideration to what these terms mean? How are they alike? How are they different? How are they related to each other? The differences are important because in the end money in its different forms represents the lifeblood of the business, and knowing which form to use, and when to use it, can make the difference between boom and bankruptcy.

In this chapter, the meaning of these terms and how they are important to managing small businesses is discussed. If you are like most people, this chapter will contain some surprises. Things that you think you know are going to turn out to be false. Things you might think are trivial will turn out to be of great importance. It is part of what makes cash and money fascinating.

Money In/Money Out—Just How Important Is It?

A recent poll conducted by the National Federation of Independent Business (NFIB Foundation) found that almost two-thirds of small businesses experience money problems (see Figure 14.1). Businesses either do not have enough money, or if they have money, they cannot get to it when it is needed. Nearly one-fifth of small business managers reported that cash flow—*how much* and *when* money will come into and go out of the business—is a continuing problem, one they face daily. The owners reported that the three primary causes of cash flow problems were (1) difficulty collecting money due from customers, (2) seasonal variation in sales, and (3) unexpected decreases in sales.[3] Approximately 55 percent of small businesses that fail do so because of cash flow problems with an immediate impact, not because of lack of profitability.[4]

Cash flow management is a problem for small businesses because of the difficulty of matching the *timing* of the *receipt of cash* to the *timing* of the need to *expend cash.* Figure 14.2 illustrates the flow of money into and out of your business as you buy what you need and sell your product or your service. This repeating flow of money is called the **cash-to-cash cycle** or the **operating cycle** of your business.

cash-to-cash cycle
The time that is required for a business to acquire resources, convert them into product, sell the product, and receive cash from the sale.

operating cycle
See cash-to-cash cycle.

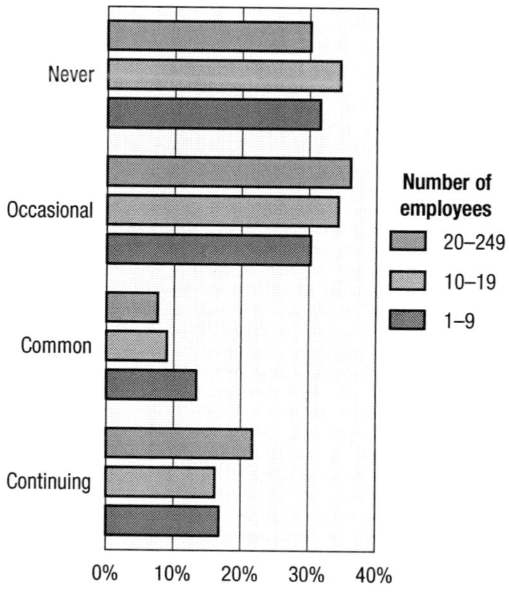

FIGURE 14.1

Percentage of Small Businesses that Experience Cash Shortages by Number of Employees

When you start a new business, you put in some money. You then buy all the things necessary to run the business, such as materials, supplies, rent, and labor. Some of these you purchase for cash. Other things you may buy on credit, creating **payables**, which you will have to pay next month. You then use labor to convert materials and supplies into your product or service, which you sell to your customers. Your customers then either pay you immediately, or agree to pay you soon. The promises of your customers to pay are **receivables**, which you will collect in the future. The money you collect will then be used to buy the things necessary to run your business, and thus the cycle repeats.

payables
Amounts owed to vendors for merchandise or services purchased on credit (see receivables).

receivables
Amounts that are owed to a business for merchandise that was sold on credit (see payables).

The time that it takes to complete this cycle can be as short as a few hours or as long as several years, dependent upon the type of business you are in. The ubiquitous pushcart vendors of hot dogs in New York City purchase inventory on credit every morning. They sell their product for cash during the day. Each evening they pay for the merchandise sold that day. The cash-to-cash cycle of a pushcart vendor is only a few hours. Construction projects, on the other hand, can easily take years to complete. A contractor will borrow money to begin construction. That money is paid out

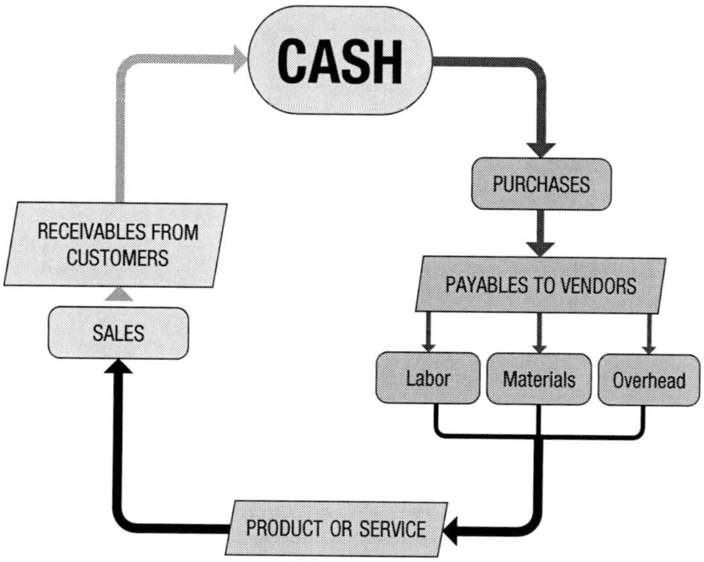

FIGURE 14.2

The Cash-to-Cash Cycle

• Pushcart vendors, such as the ones pictured here, enjoy a very short cash-to-cash cycle, due to the nature of their business. Each day, their receipt of cash from sales enables them to then expend cash back to their suppliers for exactly what has been sold. Though small in scope, the simplicity of their business set-up allows for the immediate assessment of their profitability. Does this kind of a set-up appeal to you?

across the time that it takes to complete the project. The contractor, however, receives from his customer either a single payment upon completion or a few payments as prespecified completion targets are met.

Many small businesses experience difficulty or even failure because of (1) the mismatch in time between receiving cash and spending cash and (2) the mismatch between the size of payments received and the size of payments that must be made. In some businesses, such as restaurants, cash comes into the business in a reasonably dependable pattern that is affected by the state of the economy, the season, the day of the week, and the weather. Expenses, on the other hand, tend to occur less frequently but in larger amounts, as suppliers are paid monthly, and employees are paid weekly. Other businesses, such as construction firms, plumbing contractors, ski resorts, and equipment manufacturers, have cash receipts that tend to occur irregularly but in large amounts. However, the cash payment needs of these businesses are relatively smaller amounts paid consistently from month to month. (See Figures 14.3 and 14.4.)

Although maximizing your wealth may not be your highest priority, managing your business's money is critical to succeeding and being able to attain goals that are more important to you.

FIGURE 14.3

Cash-to-Cash Cycle

Many vendors, few customers.

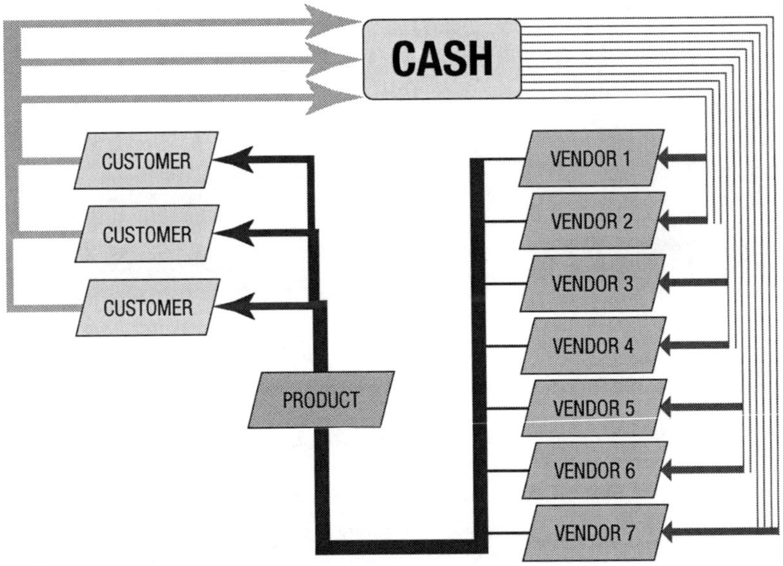

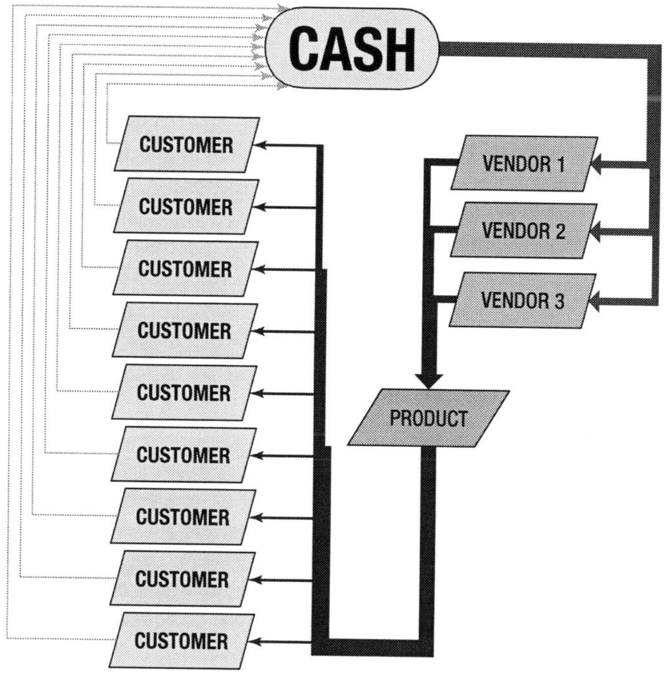

FIGURE 14.4

Cash-to-Cash Cycle

Few vendors, many customers.

John Mackey, founder of Whole Foods, Inc., said, "Business is the most transformative agency in the world. [Business leaders] can make money and do good. . . . I always wanted to make money. . . . To be sustainable, business has to be profitable."[5]

Money as the Key Idea

Ask people, "What is money?" and most likely they talk about currency—the bills and coins that you use to make purchases. That answer is right, but it tells only part of the story, because while all currency is money, all money is not currency.

LO2 Explain the concepts of money, cash, and cash equivalents.

Today we use many electronic and plastic forms of money: debit cards, online bill payments, electronic bank drafts, and wire transfers. These forms of money make an important point—money in the end is a form of *information.* Money is a very special type of information. The U.S. Dallas Federal Reserve Bank provides the following definition:

> Money is a medium of exchange accepted by the community, meaning it's what people buy things with and sell things for. Money provides a standard for measuring value, so that the worth of different goods and services can be compared. And lastly, money is a store of value that can be saved for later purchases.[6]

This definition gives us the two purposes of **money**: (1) to make exchanges and (2) to keep track of wealth or value. More importantly, it also defines the essence of money. In the Federal Reserve's qualifying phrase, "accepted by the community," what makes money "*money,*" is the *belief* users have about the information contained in the money. This information (and belief in it) reflects the two purposes above as well as a third purpose—wealth accumulation as in saving money. Money can even be used for quantifying the value of nonmonetary assets, such as when juries make awards for pain and suffering.

money
An accepted medium of exchange.

Knowing the meaning of money is important so that you can recognize where you have money in your business. For example, are profits money? You might think so at first, but consider the following example.

Suppose you own a business that details used automobiles to prepare them for sale. You complete work on a car, removing dings, rubbing out scratches, shampooing the carpets and upholstery, and giving the car a hand-buffed wax job. You promised your brother-in-law that for his help you would pay him $100 when you received payment for the work. When you delivered the car to the dealer, you presented an invoice for $500.

How much profit do you have? How much money do you have?

As is discussed in the previous chapter, profit is simply the difference between two accounting items, revenue and expense. You have revenue of $500, because the work is finished and you trust the customer to pay you in the ordinary practice of business. You also have an expense of $100, which is the cost of your brother-in-law's help. Your **profit** is the difference between the revenue and the expense, $500 − $100 = $400.

profit
The amount that revenues exceed expenses.

But you have no money, at all. Nada, zip, zero!

Suppose for a moment that you're in this situation. Your heating and air-conditioning company has profits, but no money. You owe your equipment wholesaler for last month's purchases. As a result, you cannot get the air conditioner unit needed to finish a job right now.

"Sorry," the credit manager said, "but we just can't extend any more credit until you bring your account up to date."

What are you going to do? If you don't pay what you owe, you cannot get equipment. If you cannot get equipment, you cannot stay in business. If you do not stay in business, you cannot pay what you owe. You are in a classic "catch-22!"[7]

You're in a bind, certainly, but now is not the point to give up. You have several options to help you deal with this problem. Think about your situation. You have profits that are not money, but they are information about money that shows the amount of revenue and expense your business generates.

Your problem is that information about money to come is not the same thing as the money itself. You cannot use your customer's promise of payment to purchase groceries at a supermarket, any more than your brother-in-law can spend your promise of payment to him at the local tavern. You will receive money if and when your customer pays you. You will give up money if and when you pay your brother-in-law.

The identical situation exists for your heating and air-conditioning company. You have promises to pay from customers, and you have made promises to pay your vendors. The promises of your customers, your receivables, can be quickly turned into money by using them as collateral to obtain a loan from your banker or a factor.

Remember: a profit on your accounting spreadsheet or in your account book is *not* money in your hand. Money is a medium of exchange, store of value, and measure of wealth. Until backed by the actual money, profits in your account books are none of these things.

Cash and Cash Equivalents

To this point we've been throwing around the terms *money* and *cash* as if everyone knows just what they are; just how they differ. Although we have carefully defined the meaning of money, we have not done so for cash.

Cash is money, but it's only one form of money, a subcategory of money that is immediately available to be spent. Not all money is "spendable." For example, think of certificates of deposit. Although you may well have a lot of money in CDs, you may have very little cash because your money is tied up in the CDs and would take time to convert into cash. Cash is composed of the three forms of money that can be immediately used to make payments: currency, demand deposits, and traveler's checks.

cash
Money that is immediately available to be spent.

Businesses, on the other hand, use a concept called **cash equivalents** to measure how much money is available to be spent. Cash equivalents are assets that may be turned into cash in a slightly longer time, from a few hours to a few days, such as marketable securities, commercial paper, and debt investments that mature in less than three months. Businesses use cash equivalents because they provide a better measure of the resources available to pay current bills than is provided by cash alone.

cash equivalents
Assets that may be quickly converted to cash.

Currency is the most familiar form of cash: bills and coins that represent money. In December 2003, the Federal Reserve Bank of St. Louis reported that the supply of currency in circulation was $663 billion, or approximately $2,300 of currency for each individual living in the United States.

currency
The bills and coins printed by governments to represent money.

Demand deposits make up most of the noncurrency cash. Demand deposits are accounts that let you withdraw (what bankers call demand) any amount of the balance immediately, without any advance notice to the institution: That is, owners may withdraw money on demand by using a check,

demand deposits
Money held in checking and savings accounts.

draft, currency, or electronic transfer. Checking accounts and savings accounts are the two most common forms of demand deposit accounts.

Marketable securities are made up of stocks and bonds for which there is an active auction market, such as the NASDAQ or the New York Stock Exchange. Marketable securities represent either ownership or debt of publicly held firms and government issued debt, in the form of bonds, notes, and bills.

Commercial paper and **short-term debt** are two forms of short-term financing (30 days to 1 year) whereby a company with good credit can issue a note for cash to another company. Commercial paper is issued to be paid to the **bearer** of the note, and thus is fully transferable. Short-term debt is expected to be collected in less than a year, but it can be sold to other investors at any time.

marketable securities
Stocks and bonds that are traded on an open market.

commercial paper
Notes issued by credit-worthy corporations.

short-term debt
Any debt that must be paid in less than one year from the date of the financial statement on which it is reported.

bearer
Any person or business entity who possesses a security.

Managing Cash Flow

LO3 Explain the basics of managing cash flow.

Suppliers, vendors, employees, and lenders all demand payment in cash. Because of this, a small business must have access to cash to be able to remain viable. Cash can come from only three sources: (1) Cash can be obtained by selling the products and services of the business and collecting cash from customers. This is called *cash flow from operations.* (2) Cash can be obtained from investments the business has made, such as stocks, bonds, land, buildings, or equipment. This is *cash flow from investing.* (3) Finally, a business may obtain cash through financing. Financing may be in the form of cash donated to the business in return for ownership or in the form of money borrowed from other entities.

Just as many businesses have failed by failing to manage cash, many businesses have credited their success to good cash management. Baby Einstein is a case in point. Because of the careful cash management of the founders, Julie and Bill Clark, Baby Einstein was able to grow to a $25 million company without once using outside investment.

The starting point in understanding cash management is understanding how banks, and especially your own bank account, work. This is because the vast majority of small businesses depend on banks to store cash, handle checks and credit cards, and finance their debt through credit.[8] You can see how much debt the banks support in Figure 14.5.

Company and Bank Cash Balances

Because most cash is held as bank deposits, understanding how banks actually work is essential. For example, money you have deposited today may not be immediately available to you. Money that you have spent by writing a check may well remain in your bank account for days after you have made payment. The first step in managing your cash flows is to understand how the bank's idea of your business's cash flow and your own view of the business's cash flow differ.

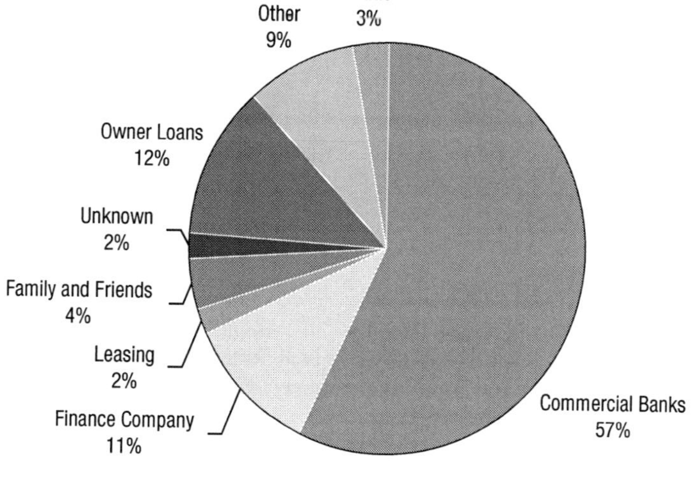

FIGURE 14.5

Sources of Credit and Debt for Small Businesses

Share of outstanding debt for all small firms, by supplier of credit, 1998. (Total value = $700 billion)

Source: U.S. Small Business Administration, Office of Advocacy from data provided by the Federal Reserve Board's 1998 SSBF, Table 1.5a. http://www.sba.gov/advo/stats/ssbf_98.pdf, page 14.

SMALL BUSINESS INSIGHT

THE BABY EINSTEIN COMPANY[9]

When Julie and Bill Clark started The Baby Einstein Company to produce videos for infants, they made a conscious decision to fund the business using only their own resources. They had been involved in an earlier business that produced educational software.

"I struggled through the experience of dealing with a venture capitalist. Julie lived through it with me and wanted to avoid a repeat experience at all costs," Bill said.

They started the business in their home with an initial capital of $10,000 from their savings. Their determination not to use bank debt, private placements, or venture capital meant that they had to have strict control of cash. They had to budget carefully and conduct constant oversight to prevent spending from exceeding cash receipts.

To conserve cash, marketing was initially conducted by word-of-mouth. As the company grew, the product line was gradually extended to include discovery cards and audio CDs.

How well did they succeed? By setting conservative revenue projections and carefully monitoring cash flows, Baby Einstein was able to grow rapidly, financed solely with internally generated cash. By the fourth year of the company's existence, annual sales were approximately $17 million.

In November 2001, the Clarks sold The Baby Einstein Company to Disney. Their one splurge has been to buy a share in a business jet. "We want the kids to see the world," Julie said.

Julie Clark of Baby Einstein knows what it means to strictly manage cash flow. By adhering to conservative revenue projections and rigorously monitoring their cash intake and outtake, she and husband Bill got to experience first-hand both the substantial growth of their company and the eventual personal payoff it granted them.

company book balance The sum of cash inflows and cash outflows recorded in the firm's accounting records.

Let us start with the company. The **company book balance** is the name given to the sum of the company's internal accounting record of all transactions that affect cash. This account (usually called the *cash account*) includes records of all inflows of cash, such as cash from sales, receipts on receivables, checks received from customers, and deposits made directly to the bank through electronic transfers. The cash account also includes records of all outflows of cash, such as checks written to pay for wages, salaries, inventory, services, taxes, and so on. The difference

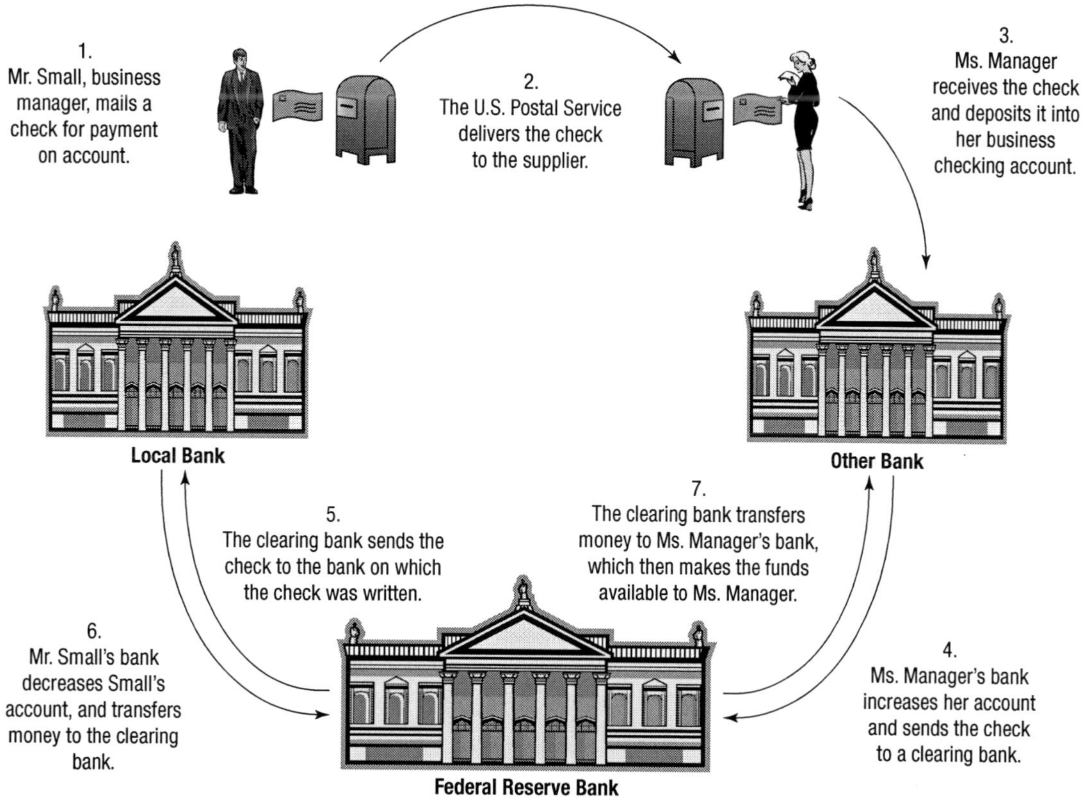

FIGURE 14.6

How Checks Get Cleared

between inflows of cash and outflows of cash is called either *company book balance*, or simply *book balance*. Book balance usually does not reflect the actual amount of cash that is available to the firm at any specific time, because the actual cash amount depends on which checks have cleared or been cashed.

Now let us consider the bank's side. The **bank ledger balance** is the name given to the bank's accounting system for all recognized transactions that affect the account, including deposits, electronic transfers, service fees, and checks presented to the bank for payment. However, just as a company book balance may differ significantly from the actual value of cash of the firm, a bank ledger balance may vary significantly from the actual value of cash that the bank is holding for the depositor because of delays in collecting deposits and delays in making cash transfers.

bank ledger balance
The sum of deposits and withdrawals recorded in a bank's accounting records.

The key measure is called the **bank available balance**, which is the actual cash value of the account and can vary significantly from the ledger balance. The bank available balance is the amount of money that has been received from or on behalf of the customer less all amounts of money that have actually been paid out of the depositor's account by the bank. Bank policies, such as how long checks are held, or when new deposits are added to your account, determine a great deal of the difference between the two balances.

bank available balance
The sum of money that has actually been received and paid out of a depositor's account.

Deposits of cash, electronic transfers, and cash withdrawals result in immediate changes in the available balance because money has been received or disbursed by the bank. Checks, drafts, and automated **clearinghouse** payments result in receipts or disbursements of money only after some delay. The delay can range from as little as a single day up to several days in the event of a check paid across national boundaries. (See Figure 14.6.)

clearinghouse
An entity that processes checks and electronic fund transfers for banks and other financial organizations.

Banks differ in how the ledger balance and available balance are used. Some banks will allow established customers to **overdraft** their accounts by paying a check when the available balance is not sufficient to cover the check amount, but the ledger balance is.

overdraft
A negative balance in a depositor's bank account.

Float is the term used to describe the delay in movement of money among depositors and banks. There are two primary causes of float: (1) delays in transferring money among banks due to internal

float
Delays in the movement of money among depositors and banks.

procedures, called *availability float,* and (2) delays in delivering checks from the writer of the check to the recipient's bank, called *processing float. Processing float* is the time required to move checks among payers, payees, and banks. Processing float is what individuals refer to when they say, "The check is in the mail."

Reconciling Bank Balances with Company Book Balances

LO4 Reconcile bank and company book balances.

reconciling
An accounting process that identifies the causes of all differences between book and bank balances.

The key to managing your daily cash flow is knowing how much cash is available to you in your bank account at that moment. Some banks report available balances only once a day, so that amount can be misleading. To get a more realistic number, you need to **reconcile** the differences between bank and book balances caused by float to know how much cash is currently available and how much will soon be available for your business needs. Most small business managers concentrate their attention on maintaining a positive book balance and assume that this means there will be an adequate available balance. However, when this assumption is not correct, it often leads to cash flow crises.

If you want to be able to manage your cash flow in real time, it is important to choose a bank that gives you online access to account information that is continuously updated. Check to make sure how quickly transactions get posted and are reflected in your online account statement. If you feel you can afford a more leisurely approach to cash flow management, remember that day-old information is much more timely than the month-old information furnished by a traditional bank statement. A manager can, with a bit of effort, use yesterday's bank transactions and the current business book information to estimate cash availability and demands with reasonable accuracy.

The process of reconciling bank balance and book balances is quite simple. There are only two reasons why the balances differ:

1. The bank knows information about your account that you cannot know until the bank tells you.
2. You know information about your account that the bank cannot know, because relevant transactions have not yet reached the bank.

nonsufficient funds
A situation that occurs when a check is returned to a depositor because the writer of the check did not have a bank available balance equal to or greater than the amount of the check.

Information that the bank knows about your account that you do not know includes (1) the amount of service charges taken from your account, (2) the amount of any direct payments made to your account by your customers, (3) the amount of any interest received or charged, (4) and the amount of any checks that were returned because of **nonsufficient funds** (NSF).

Information that you know about your account that the bank does not know includes (1) the number and value of checks that you have written and mailed but that have not been received by the bank, and (2) deposits that you have mailed or made after bank closing.

The process of reconciling the bank and book balances is, therefore, a two-step process:

1. Add (subtract) to the bank balance those things that you know about your account that the bank does not know.
2. Add (subtract) to your book balance those things that the bank knows about your account that you do not know until you receive the bank statement.

When this is done the *corrected* bank balance and the *corrected* book balance will be identical. The appendix to this chapter presents a complete example of performing a bank reconciliation.

Accepting payments by credit card causes significant differences between the bank and book balances for three reasons:

- Your business will record the gross amount of each credit card sale, while the credit card service provider will deposit to your account the sale amount less the credit card service fee.
- Your business will show the amount of the sale deposited on the date of the sale, while the service provider will take up to three working days to actually make the deposit to your account.
- Credit card clearing services also will reduce the amount deposited, or will **charge back** the amount, removing it from the business's account in the event of fraud or customer challenge.

charge back
A reduction in the bank account of a merchant by a credit card company.

Similar patterns of the timing and the amounts of various deposits, fees, and transfers exist for other electronic transactions. A bank may accept payment, charge a handling fee, and deposit only the net amount, or it may deposit the gross amount and show a separate charge for handling fees. Regardless, the use of electronic payment systems, of all types, creates significant differences between bank and book balances.

Why go to all this trouble? Because reconciling differences in the bank and book balances serves four purposes:

- Reconciliation gives you a way to estimate the bank's available balance for the purpose of managing your cash flows.
- Regular reconciliation of bank and book balances identifies any mistakes that were made by either the bank or by your own bookkeeper—and those mistakes happen.
- Performing a reconciliation checks the accuracy of both the bank and business records, providing an accurate statement of the value of cash held by the business.
- A reconciliation lets you know about items on the bank statement that would not otherwise be included in the business's accounting records.

Planning Cash Needs

For small businesses, the key to cash planning is the **cash budget**. Simply put, the cash budget identifies when, how, and why cash is expected to come into the business, and when, how, and why it is expected to leave. The quality of those expectations is important. Making more realistic or accurate estimates about expected incomes and expenses means that the budget becomes a more useful tool for understanding and managing your cash flow and financial situation.

LO5 Develop a cash budget.

cash budget
A cash budget identifies when, how, and why cash is expected to come into the business, and when, how, and why it is expected to leave.

All business budgeting begins with a forecast of sales. As is discussed in Chapters 12 and 13, there are several methods that are used to make sales forecasts. We will illustrate the process of creating a cash flow budget for the first quarter of the second year of business using the predicted sales of MyLibros.com. The sales forecast is shown in Schedule 14.1.

SCHEDULE 14.1
MYLIBROS.COM
Sales Budget
For the Quarter Ending March 31, 2012

Month/Quarter	Jan	Feb	Mar	Quarter 1 Total
Sales in units				
Books	608	621	634	1,863
Unit sales price	23.50	23.50	23.50	23.50
Revenue from books	14,288.00	14,593.50	14,899.00	43,780.50
Magazines	81	83	85	249
Unit sales price	$17.02	$17.02	$17.02	$17.02
Revenue from magazines	1,378.62	1,412.66	1,446.70	4,237.98
Shipping fees @ 1.50 per book	912.00	931.50	951.00	2,794.50
Misc. media	0.00	0.00	0.00	0.00
Gross sales	16,578.62	16,937.66	17,296.70	50,812.98
Less credit card processing fee	464.20	474.25	484.31	1,422.76
Less discounts on book sales	1,428.80	1,459.35	1,489.90	4,378.05
Net sales	14,685.62	15,004.06	15,322.49	45,012.17

THE THOUGHTFUL ENTREPRENEUR

THE BUSINESS COSTS OF USING CREDIT CARDS

Credit card use fees quickly add up to material amounts. Consider a successful restaurant that grosses approximately $80,000 per month, with an average per-customer ticket of $20. If 90 percent of customers pay with a credit card, 3,600 credit card charges will be made in a month ($80,000/$20 × 0.9). Assume that the credit card company charges 20 cents per transaction plus 2 percent of the amount charged. The credit card fee for the month will equal $2,160 (3,600 transactions × 0.20) + (80,000 × .9 × .02). The restaurant will also pay the 2 percent fee on any tips that are added to the bill. If the average tip added is 15 percent, then the added fee on tips charged per month will be another $216. Thus the restaurant will average paying an amount greater than $28,000 in credit card fees per year.

So why, you may ask, do small businesses use credit cards? First, accepting credit cards creates increased sales. Second, the credit card issuer assumes the cost and risk of determining credit worthiness.

Sales Budget: Forecasting Sales Receipts

For many small businesses, the sales forecast *is* the cash receipts forecast. Businesses such as barbershops, muffler repair shops, restaurants, and all kinds of retail merchandisers do not provide credit to customers. All sales are made either in cash or by credit card. Despite this, this type of business *can* have cash flow problems created when sales are insufficient to cover required payments. Each type of business has a different pattern of sales and cash receipts. Some businesses, whose customers make heavy use of credit cards, can face serious cash drains as a result (see Thoughtful Entrepreneur: The Business Costs of Using Credit Cards).

Many businesses have either relatively few large sales events or highly seasonal sales that complicate forecasting cash inflows. Examples include:

- Retailing
- House builders
- Custom electric sign shops
- Machine shops
- Providers of custom software
- Real estate brokers
- Consultants
- Ski resorts
- Water parks
- All businesses that depend upon tourism

Cash Receipts Budget

As we discussed earlier in this chapter, how much and when money will come into your business is of critical importance. Later, we will discuss specific techniques that you can use to help control both how much and when you will receive money. However, the basis to being able to control your business's money is to understand and be able to predict the patterns of cash flows. Understanding and predicting begin when you prepare a **cash receipts budget**.

cash receipts budget
A schedule of the amounts and timings of the receipt of cash into a business.

Many small businesses operate on pretty much a cash basis, as does *MyLibros.com:* customers purchase and pay at the same time. If, on the other hand, you do provide credit to your customers, sales and cash receipts can be very different. If you provide credit, you will always wait some period of time for some of your money—that's what providing credit means, after all. You also, sooner or later, will have some customer who never pays. These two facts about selling on credit create significant differences between the amount of sales and the amount of cash received in any month.

The pattern of collections greatly affects the timing of cash flows. For example, assume that, on average, 10 percent of your sales are made for cash, collected immediately. The remaining 90 percent of sales are made on credit. You collect 60 percent in the month following the sale and the remaining 40 percent in the second month following the sale. To forecast cash receipts, simply combine the expected collections by months. To illustrate this, assume for a moment that MyLibros, instead of using credit cards, sells its product on credit as described above. The cash receipts budget for the last quarter of the first year and the first quarter of the second year would then look like this:

SCHEDULE 14.2A

MYLIBROS.COM

Cash Receipts Budget for Credit Sales
For the Quarter Ending March 31, 2012

		Last quarter previous year			First quarter current year			
Month of sale	Forecast sales amount (no credit card fee subtracted)	Cash collected in October from sales made in August, September, and October	Cash collected in November from sales made in September, October, and November	Cash collected in December from sales made in October, November, and December	Cash collected in January from sales made in November, December, and January	Cash collected in February from sales made in December, January, and February	Cash collected in March from sales made in January, February, and March	Total cash collected
August	11,785.84	4,242.90						4,242.90
September	12,289.90	6,636.55	4,424.36					11,060.91
October	13,654.66	1,365.47	7,373.52	4,915.68				13,654.66
November	15,948.07		1,594.81	8,611.96	5,741.31			15,948.07
December	15,749.98			1,575.00	8,504.99	5,669.99		15,749.98
January	15,149.82				1,514.98	8,180.90	5,453.94	15,149.82
February	15,478.31					1,547.83	8,358.29	9,906.12
March	15,806.80						1,580.68	1,580.68
Totals	91,787.64	12,244.91	13,392.69	15,102.63	15,761.28	15,398.73	15,392.90	87,293.14

10% of January sales are cash

40% of 90% of November sales

60% of 90% of December sales

Total cash collected in January

Of course, as noted above, this is *not* how *MyLibros.com* is actually making sales. The *MyLibros.com* business plan explicitly states in the "Financial Plan Assumptions, Expenses" section:

> We anticipate 100 percent of sales to be purchased by customers using credit cards. The cost of selling through credit cards will be about 2.8 percent of net sales on the Web site.

Although the assumption is that processing credit cards will cost 2.8 percent, its effect is not in the business plan. The business plan also assumes that all revenue will be collected in the month of the sale. This assumption is reasonable, to simplify the business plan projections. However, it is not exactly correct. It takes approximately three to five working days for credit card charges made online to be transferred into the merchant's bank account. Thus, sales made in the last few days of the month will be collected in the following month. For this reason, the cash budget in MyLibros's business plan at the end of Chapter 8 is slightly inaccurate. The inaccuracy is *not* material to the business plan. But, for purposes of illustrating how this cost could be explicitly included in your planning, consider what the cash receipts budget for their actual operation would be if these two effects were included in the cash receipts budget. To make the changes explicit, we put the credit card fees on the cash receipts budget. We also assume that the credit card processor takes the full five days to transfer cash into MyLibros's account.

SCHEDULE 14.2B

MYLIBROS.COM

Cash Receipts Budget for Online Credit Card Sales
For the Quarter Ending March 31, 2012

				First quarter current year			
Month of sale	Forecast sales	Credit card fee: 2.8% discount	Net sales	Cash collected in January from sales made in the last 5 days of December and the first 26 days of January	Cash collected in February from sales made in the last 5 days of January and the first 23 days of February	Cash collected in March from sales made in the last 5 days of February and the first 26 days of March	Total cash collected
December	$15,749.98	$441.00	$15,308.98	$2,469.19			$2,469.19
January	15,149.82	424.19	14,725.63	12,350.52	2,375.10		14,725.63
February	15,478.31	433.39	15,044.92		12,358.32	2,686.59	15,044.92
March	15,806.80	442.59	15,364.21			12,886.11	12,886.11
Totals				$14,819.71	$14,733.43	$15,572.70	$45,125.84

$15,308.98 / 31 x 5

$14,725.63 / 31 x 26

You can compare the numbers above with the numbers in the *MyLibros.com* business plan at the end of Chapter 8. You will see that the effect of not including the credit card charge results in MyLibros slightly overstating cash receipts. Because MyLibros is forecasting even daily sales, the delay in receiving payment for the last few days of the month has no material effect. Over time, MyLibros will collect for all sales.

Businesses for which the delay in receiving cash from credit card sales is important are those which make most of each week's sales on Friday and Saturday evenings, such as theaters, restaurants, bars, and lounges. Purchases made over the weekend usually will not be transferred to the business's bank account before the next Wednesday.

You can never know exactly when you will collect cash. However, your experience in business, the experience of other businesses in the industry, and careful monitoring of your credit process lets you make very good estimates. While resort owners may on occasion get advance bookings a year or more in advance, on average, deposits are received about one month in advance. Thus a reasonable estimate of their amount and timing can be made.

Forecasting Cash Disbursements

A similar approach is used for the forecasting of cash disbursements. The estimates of expenses that you develop in your budget, and your knowledge of your business's payment patterns are combined to predict how much and when cash must be paid out. (See Schedule 14.3.)

MyLibros.com states in the business plan, "Inventory is paid for and delivered in the month prior to sale." In other words, the management of MyLibros intends to prepay for all inventory. This is a reasonable assumption for many small businesses including online retailers, restaurateurs, liquor stores, and bars. If we follow this assumption, but use the more common inventory purchases practice developed in Chapter 13 (Schedule 13.2), then *MyLibros.com*'s **cash disbursements budget** would be:

cash disbursements budget
A schedule of the amounts and timings of payments of cash out of a business.

SCHEDULE 14.3
MYLIBROS.COM
Cash Disbursements Budget
For the Quarter Ending March 31, 2012

	First quarter current year			
	January	February	March	Total cash disbursed
Purchases for next month's inventory	9,814.74	10,025.92	10,237.10	30,077.76
Selling expenses	1,216.79	1,242.34	1,268.43	3,727.56
Rent	1,500.00	1,500.00	1,500.00	4,500.00
Maintenance	500.00	500.00	500.00	1,500.00
General	835.00	835.00	835.00	2,505.00
Administrative/wages	442.80	414.85	386.90	1,244.55
Labor	1,307.20	1,335.15	1,363.10	4,005.45
Totals	15,616.53	15,853.26	16,090.53	47,560.32

With the cash receipts and cash disbursements budgets complete, we need to know only how much money we expect to have on the first day of the year to put together a cash budget for the first quarter. The amount of cash we will have at the beginning of the year is simply the amount of cash we had at the end of the prior year. We can get this number from either of two sources: (1) the balance of our cash account after the year end reconciliation is complete, or (2) the amount of cash shown on our year-end balance sheet. You will find the beginning cash balance for the first month of year two in MyLibros's business plan on the balance sheet for the end of year one: $40,472. However, to illustrate more general budgeting techniques, we assumed earlier that MyLibros would extend credit to customers. If indeed, MyLibros were to offer credit, then there would be $19,916 from November and December sales that had not yet been collected. Because of this, the beginning cash balance for the first quarter of the second year would be $20,556 and accounts receivable would be $19,916.

Also, to illustrate how projected cash shortages may be handled, assume that MyLibros desires to have a minimum ending cash balance of $35,000 each month. If the projected cash balance is less than this, money will be borrowed from a line of credit. If the projected balance exceeds the desired minimum, then the surplus may be used to pay back some or all of the outstanding line of credit. Because most business lenders will not make loans for "odd" amounts, we assume here that any money borrowed will be the amount of the shortage, rounded up to the next higher $100.

SCHEDULE 14.4
MYLIBROS.COM
Cash Budget
For the Quarter Ending March 31, 2012

	First quarter current year			
	January	February	March	Quarter 1 Total
Beginning cash balance	20,556	35,000	35,046	20,556
Cash receipts	15,761	15,399	15,393	46,553
Total cash available	36,317	50,399	50,439	67,109
Cash disbursements	15,617	15,853	16,091	47,560
Forecast balance	20,700	34,546	34,348	19,548
Desired minimum balance	35,000	35,000	35,000	35,000
Excess (shortage)	(14,300)	(454)	(652)	(15,406)
Borrowings	14,300	500	700	15,500
Repayments	-0-	-0-	-0-	-0-
Ending balance	35,000	35,046	35,048	35,048

SKILL MODULE 14.1

Planning Cash Needs

1. How would sales for custom electric sign shops, machine shops, providers of custom software, real estate brokers, and consultants vary with (a) changes in the economy and (b) season of the year?
2. Use the spreadsheet, ComprehensiveBudget.xls, from the text Web site, **http://www.mhhe.com/katzesb**, to complete the following tasks:
   a. Complete the cash collection forecast for MyLibros for the current year.
   b. Complete the cash disbursement forecast for MyLibros for the current year.
   c. Complete the cash budget for MyLibros for the current year.
   d. Complete annual (i) income statement, (ii) statement of retained earnings, (iii) balance sheet, including statement of owners' equity.

(Note: All needed data and step-by-step instructions are included in the spreadsheet.)

The Comprehensive Budget—the Pro Forma Cash Flow Statement

It is a fact that no matter how daunting, you will budget, one way or another. The budgeting process presented here is specifically designed to feed directly into your business plan. The final step in this part of business planning is to put everything together to create a complete set of pro forma financial statements that you can use for raising money, for evaluating your operations, and for managing your business. All the budgets from Chapter 13 *and* the cash budget developed here are combined at this point to make the **comprehensive budget**. (Comprehensive budgets are also often referred to as "*master budgets.*")

comprehensive budget
Comprehensive budgets are often referred to as *master budgets.*

The cash flow statement is essentially a restatement of the cash budget, but with the cash coming into your business and the cash going out of your business placed into the categories of cash from operations, cash from investing, and cash from financing. The format illustrated here is the direct method, which is the format now required by GAAP. Many owners of small businesses prefer the indirect method, which explicitly links net income to cash flows. An example and explanation of the indirect method of cash flow statements is available on the Web site for this text: http://www.mhhe.com/katzesb. Notice also that although we did the budgeting process to the nearest dollar, when pro forma statements are prepared, they are usually stated with an accuracy no greater than whole dollar amounts. In fact, for businesses that gross in excess of $10 million per year, pro forma amounts are usually rounded to the nearest one thousand dollars.

SCHEDULE 14.5

MYLIBROS.COM

Statement of Cash Flows
For the Quarter Ending March 31, 2012
(Direct Method)

Cash flows from operating activities		
Cash received from customers		46,553
Cash paid to vendors		
Inventory providers	30,078	
Labor	4,005	
Rent	4,500	
Maintenance	1,500	
Selling	3,728	
General	2,505	
Administrative & wages	1,245	47,560
Net cash provided (used) by operations		(1,007)
Cash flows from financing activities		
Borrowings against line of credit		15,500
Cash flows from investing activities		0
Net cash inflows (outflows)		14,493
Beginning cash balance		20,556
Ending cash balance		35,048

From the Cash Budget: Cash Receipts, Schedule 14.4

From the Purchases Budget, Schedule 13.2

Total Cash Disbursements from Cash Budget, Schedule 14.4

Investing activities include owner contributions, purchases and sales of property, plant and equipment, and investments in other businesses

The Comprehensive Budget—Pro Forma Balance Sheet

The final step in preparing a master budget, and also in preparing the pro forma financial statements for a business plan, is to prepare a balance sheet for each accounting period. As discussed in Chapter 13, the balance sheet provides a "snapshot" of the financial position of your business as of the date it is prepared. The sample balance sheet below illustrates how the various schedules of the master budget are collected and reported.

SCHEDULE 14.6
MYLIBROS.COM
Balance Sheet
For the Quarter Ending March 31, 2012

Assets:			
Cash and cash equivalents			35,048
Accounts receivable (based on hypothetical credit sales)			19,798
Inventory			5,485
Fixed assets at cost		22,750	
Less accumulated depreciation		6,440	16,310
Total assets			76,641
Liabilities and owners' equity			
Short-term liabilities		15,500	
Long-term liabilities			
Total liabilities			15,500
Equity			
LLC membership shares		100,000	
Beginning retained earnings	(36,783)		
Net income (loss)	(2,075)		
Ending retained earnings		(38,859)	
Total owners' equity			61,141
Total of liabilities & owners' equity			76,641

Ending cash balance from Cash Budget

Uncollected amounts from Feb & Mar on the Cash Receipts Budget (Schedule 14.2A)

Ending inventory of 389 units at $14.10 each on the Purchases Budget (Schedule 13.2)

Borrowings to meet desired minimum ending cash

Sum of all profits and losses since the business began

From Schedule 13.7

The spreadsheets used to prepare the budget examples are available on the Web site for this textbook, www.mhhe.com/katzesb. They may be used as models to develop other planning spreadsheets appropriate for businesses other than retail.

SKILL MODULE 14.2 A Comprehensive Budget

Choose a business that you are interested in owning.

1. Prepare a complete list of the costs of operating this business. To determine the costs of your selected business, examine sources such as *Entrepreneur* magazine's start-up manuals (**http://www.smallbizbooks.com/cgi-bin/SmallBizBooks/index.html**) or perform a Google search on the term "business startup guide" for other books, manuals, and Web sites. You may also obtain cost information from the Internal Revenue Service, audit guides, franchisors, and industry organizations.
2. Place each cost that you identify into one of the following categories: fixed cost, variable cost, or mixed cost. (Remember: variable costs are costs that vary with changes in sales or production.)

3. From industry sources, determine what the customary payment terms are from vendors and what terms, if any, your business will be expected to provide to customers.
4. Use this cost information to produce a comprehensive budget, based on the ComprehensiveBudget.xls from the McGraw-Hill Web site, **www.mhhe.com/katzesb**.
5. From the cash budget that you have prepared, identify any cash flow shortages. Prepare a plan to deal with the expected shortages.

Preventing Cash Flow Problems

LO6 Develop strategies for preventing and coping with cash flow problems.

Benjamin Franklin's adage, "An ounce of prevention is worth a pound of cure," truly describes the best way to manage cash flows in a business. It is much, much easier to prevent such problems than to solve them once they begin.

Several techniques can help prevent getting into a cash flow problem in the first place. The best prevention is attending to and understanding your business's operations—its patterns of generating cash inflows and outflows—which should help you maintain an accurate forecast of cash needs. However, planning alone usually is not sufficient to ensure that cash flow needs are met. The assumptions made may be incorrect. The economy may suffer an unforeseen shock, such as a natural disaster, war, or energy shortages. Fashions and preferences change, often in unexpected and unpredictable ways. As airline pilots often point out, "Careful planning is no substitute for full fuel tanks."

Protecting Cash from Being Stolen

Cash is the most desired asset and easiest asset to steal from your business. While there is some chance that theft will be committed by criminals coming into your business carrying a gun, the vast majority of business theft is committed by employees. This is so for two reasons. First, employees have access to cash in the course of doing their jobs. Second, employees are often in a position to be able to hide the theft.

According to the U.S. Chamber of Commerce,[10] the most common means by which employees steal cash from their employers are through misappropriations of cash accomplished using one of three categories of theft: (1) Larceny and embezzlement, which are methods employees use to steal cash after it has been received and recorded in your books. (2) Skimming, which is the practice of "pocketing" money from customers and hiding the theft by not recording the sale. (3) Phony disbursements, which are most commonly accomplished by making fake invoices that are subsequently paid by your ordinary cash disbursement procedure. There are many, many variations on these broad categories, including such practices as creating "phantom employees," whose paychecks go to the accounts of the thieves, tampering with legitimately processed checks, and conducting billing scams.

Of these three broad categories, skimming is the most prevalent. Embezzlement, however, is the means by which the greatest dollar loss occurs. Partly, this is because of the nature of the transactions used in each fraud. Skimming is usually done at the point of sale: a bartender who "forgets" to enter a sale into the register or a sales clerk who scans the code for a $20 jacket while checking out a $500 leather coat for a confederate. Embezzlement, on the other hand, usually happens in your accounting office. Any single skimming incident is limited to the sales amount. A crooked accountant can steal the entire value of your business.

To protect your business from having its cash drained by employees, you need to take specific steps, the first and most important of which is to hire honest and ethical people into your business. Do really good preemployment background checks, including criminal records, previous employer, credit history, official transcripts from colleges, and references.

Other steps you should take are:

- Run credit checks periodically on all employees who have material access to your finances.
- Identify opportunities employees have to steal from you. Examine every aspect of how money flows into and out of your business, and evaluate the inherent risks.
- Divide financial duties among two or more people. The person who prepares the payroll should not be allowed to hand out checks or to authorize direct transfers. The person who authorizes payment of a bill must not also be able to write the check for payment.

- Investigate budget variances carefully.
- Have a formal audit conducted, including your internal and external control procedures.
- Implement a formal statement of ethics policies.
- Provide coaching, counseling, and training to employees to ensure they understand the ethical standards set for your business.
- Terminate the employment of those who fail to achieve standards within a reasonable time.
- Provide education about the economics of your business to employees. Be sure each understands that the theft of a single dollar means that you will have to increase sales by $10, just to recover the value of the theft.

Techniques to Increase Cash Inflows

There are several simple methods that can be used to increase the amount of cash flows while simultaneously reducing the effects of irregular or seasonal patterns of receipts. Five proven techniques are:

- Taking deposits and progress payments.
- Offering discounts for prompt payment.
- Asking for your money.
- Taking on noncorc paying projects.
- Factoring receivables.

deposits and progress payments
Cash payments received before product is completed or delivered.

Deposits and progress payments can greatly smooth the receipt of cash in businesses which otherwise have highly variable levels of cash flows. For example, many businesses that involve summer activities, such as water parks, are open as few as 100 days per year. However, many costs, such as rent, taxes, maintenance, security, and utilities, continue year-round. These types of businesses often choose to obtain cash flow during the closed season by selling season tickets or other forms of advance purchase.[11] Progress payments are payments that are received from your customer as you achieve predetermined goals in a lengthy project. Progress payments are very common in the construction industry where individual projects may take years to complete.

Requiring deposits is advisable in many kinds of businesses in which the process to fulfill a contract with a customer requires significant amounts of time or additional capital. Examples of this type of business are building contractors, consultants, and manufacturers of custom machinery.

discounts for prompt payment
A reduction in sales price provided to credit customers for paying outstanding amounts in a timely manner.

Discounts for prompt payment will often motivate your customers to make payments in a timely manner. It is common for wholesale suppliers to offer their customers terms of a 2 percent discount for payment within 5 to 10 working days. You must carefully balance the cost of providing the discount with the cost of obtaining needed cash from other sources.[12] The cost of a discount for prompt payment is deceiving. Consider that you are operating a wholesale distributorship of plumbing supplies, with an average margin on sales of 22 percent, and you provide a 2 percent discount for prompt payment. A customer purchases $100 of supplies on account. What is the effect on your profitability? Your profit margin will decline from $22 to $20, a decline in gross margin of 9.1 percent. (See Table 14.1.)

Asking for your money is at once the most simple and the most effective way to obtain payment from customers.[13] Surprisingly, many owners and managers of small businesses are loath to call

TABLE 14.1 Effect of Prompt Payment Discounts on Gross Margin

Gross sales amount	$100.00
Less cost of goods sold	78.00
Gross margin	22.00
Less prompt pay discount of 2 percent	2.00
Net margin	$20.00
Percentage reduction in margin ($2/$22)	9.1%

customers and request that they pay what they owe. However, you will find that few, if any, businesspeople will be offended by a polite phone call requesting payment. This is especially true of the owners and managers of small businesses who have encountered cash flow difficulties themselves. Very often, a request for prompt payment will be honored, if possible. Of course, there is an implied obligation that, if at some time in the future the customers encounter cash flow problems, you will also be understanding and cooperative, helping them through their own rough spot.

Taking on **noncore projects** can often provide desperately needed cash during slow business periods. Possibilities are limited only by your imagination. Many sign installers, during slow times in early spring, often will send a crane truck and operator to hoist air-conditioning and other equipment onto the roofs of buildings. Bill Millers' Barbecue of San Antonio, Texas, for a fee, deep-fries whole turkeys for customers during the slow restaurant periods immediately preceding Thanksgiving and Christmas. Rowan Oak House B&B in Salisbury, North Carolina, as do many bed and breakfasts, during its slow seasons, sells "murder mystery weekends" that include lodging, breakfast, dinner, and a role-playing mystery game, complete with costumes and props.

noncore projects
Revenue-producing tasks and activities related to, but not part of, the primary strategy of a business.

Factoring receivables should be considered only if other, less expensive methods to increase cash flows have not been sufficient.[14] Factoring is a method of borrowing against receivables. The factor will usually lend between 75 percent and 80 percent of the amount of uncollected receivables. As the receivables are collected, the factor deducts a proportional principal amount and remits the remainder, less its fee, typically 5 percent of the gross receivables, to the business.[15]

factoring receivables
Borrowing money secured by a firm's accounts receivable.

To factor your receivables, your customers must have good credit ratings. Your credit rating is irrelevant because it is the customers who pay the factor, not you. To provide for losses on uncollectible accounts, some factors either hold back some of the remittances or charge back any uncollected amounts at the end of a specified contract period.

Techniques to Decrease Cash Outflows

Decreasing cash outflows is as important as increasing cash inflows. Regardless of how much money you're making, conserving cash is essential. All companies have certain costs that cannot be avoided and cannot be financed. Examples of unavoidable cash payments include payroll, rent, utilities, and withholding taxes. If you do not have enough cash to pay your employees, keep the door open, the lights burning, and the tax collector at bay, the business will fail, no matter its potential or

THE THOUGHTFUL ENTREPRENEUR

DANGERS OF TAKING ON NONCORE BUSINESS PROJECTS

There are several caveats to be considered in taking on noncore projects:

- First, any noncore project should be such that it can be completed in a reasonable time.
- Second, the project should be clearly specified, with clearly defined outcomes or stopping points.
- Third, no noncore project should be taken solely for the purpose of "churning dollars."

Noncore projects can sometimes provide desperately needed cash. However, the time for such projects is taken from time that otherwise would be used for your core business. When the environment for the core business improves, noncore projects can become very costly distractions.

Specifying outcomes and stopping points prevents making noncore projects into permanent business, which then competes for limited resources with the core business.

It is always tempting, when faced with a need for cash, to offer deep discounts to gain cash inflows. This is counterproductive, however, for two reasons: (1) discounting in either your core or in an associated business devalues your product or service, which will limit the price that can be charged when conditions improve, and (2) accepting business that does not provide an adequate margin reduces profitability for the entire year, which can negatively affect your ability to arrange financing and investment when business conditions improve and additional funding is needed for growth.

THE THOUGHTFUL ENTREPRENEUR

EFFECT OF BORROWING AGAINST YOUR RECEIVABLES

Although it is tempting to use your receivables to obtain immediate cash, doing so is quite expensive. Suppose, for example, your business has $100,000 in accounts receivable. If you factor these receivables, you will obtain an immediate $75,000. Now suppose a customer who owes $10,000 pays the full amount. The factor will deduct 75 percent in repayment plus 5 percent of the gross payment amount. You will receive the remaining $2,000:

Customer payment	$10,000
Repayment to factor	(7,500)
5% factor fee	(500)
Balance received	2,000

If your factored receivables are all collected within 90 days, you will have paid $5,000 to receive $75,000 immediately plus $20,000 over three months, a total of $95,000. On an annual basis, this is essentially the same as paying 22 percent interest.

paper profits. As with cash inflows there are two factors of cash outflows that must be controlled: (1) the amount of cash being paid out and (2) the timing of cash being paid out.

Controlling the amount of cash being paid out is primarily a function of making good purchasing decisions and avoiding waste. By purchasing in the appropriate quantities with the appropriate quality at the appropriate times, the need to make cash payments can be aligned with the receipt of cash, to the extent that the nature of the business allows.

Every business that maintains inventory has an optimal level that minimizes the total cost of (1) carrying inventory, (2) processing orders, and (3) losing sales due to being out of stock. The optimum level of many other business resources can similarly be determined. Setting reasonable standards and carefully monitoring usage and stocking levels reduce the amount of cash required for these essential business resources while maximizing revenues. The determination of optimum stocking levels is fully discussed in the appendix of Chapter 16.

Waste also affects cash outflow. Resources that are wasted represent cash that was paid out with no economic benefit. Almost any resource can be wasted. You can waste the time of your employees by requiring procedures such as record keeping and reporting that are not useful for management. You can waste primary materials by inefficient cutting and by allowing materials to spoil, break, or be stolen. You can waste rent by maintaining space that does not produce revenue. The list of potential waste is endless.

Most of us become so accustomed to our ways of doing business that we often do not recognize waste when we see it. For years, restaurants paid people to haul away old cooking oils and grease. If there was no one to haul the oil, it was often dumped onto gravel parking lots or poured into solid waste dumps. The oil was indeed *scrap*—it had no further economic use in the restaurant. The oil was not *waste,* however, until it was poured out. There was an economically valuable use for the oil in making cosmetics, animal feed, paint, and chemicals. Today, the waste oil from restaurants and commercial food manufacturers is so valuable that not only is there an active market for waste oil, but organized bandits often steal the oil at night. Oil that once was considered trash is today a significant source of revenue.

It takes insight into your particular business to determine what constitutes waste.[16] Suppose you have a sizable store of the leftovers from cutting plywood to make your product. It is certain that the plywood pieces are scrap. But are they waste? To determine if these odd pieces of wood are waste, you need to find out (1) if there is a cutting pattern that will reduce the amount of leftover wood; (2) if you cannot reduce the amount of scrap, is there an economically valuable use for it; and (3) what it is costing you to keep the scrap pieces on hand. You may find that the wood is scrap, but the waste is the space that it occupies—space that you could otherwise put to productive use.

In addition to making wise purchasing decisions and avoiding waste of resources, there are several strategies that will provide savings in cash outflows, including:[17]

- Trade discounts.
- Noncash employee incentives.
- Use of temporary agencies.
- Consignment.
- Barter.
- Control of the timing of paying out cash.
- Negotiation of terms with suppliers.
- Timing of purchases.
- Gaming of the payment process.

Some of these should be familiar, because they are mentioned in the discussion of bootstrapping in Chapter 5, where bootstrapping is introduced as a way to make possible a part-time business operating on a very limited budget; but the ideas of bootstrapping, as we can see below, also apply to more established kinds of small businesses.

Trade discounts are given by suppliers and vendors to encourage customers to make timely payments on account. In effect, you are borrowing from the vendor at the discount rate for the number of days that you may wait to pay after the cutoff date for receiving the discount. The rule of thumb for trade discounts is that you should always capture discounts of 1 percent or greater, if the billing period is less than 30 days.

trade discounts
Percentage discounts from gross invoice amounts provided to encourage prompt payment.

If the supplier provides payment terms exceeding 30 days, then you must perform a quick analysis to determine whether taking the discount or delaying payment provides the greater value. To decide whether to take the discount, compare the annual effective interest rate of the discount to your cost of borrowing from other sources. Then choose the one with the lower annual effective rate.

Noncash incentives for employees is the most widely used technique to reduce the amount of cash that must be paid out of the business. The most common such incentive is to grant stock options, which give the employee the right to purchase company stock at a fixed price in the future. The hope of the employee is that the stock will go up significantly in price and, that upon either selling or exercising the option, the employee will realize large gains. Other noncash incentives

noncash incentives
Rewards that do not require payment of cash, such as stock options, compensating time off, or added vacation days.

THE THOUGHTFUL ENTREPRENEUR

Should I Take a Supplier's Discount for Payment?

Assume that MyLibros.com can borrow from the bank at 11 percent. The supplier of books provides credit terms at a 1 percent discount, if paid within 10 days of the receipt of the invoice, and the full amount must be paid in 30 days. To see if the heuristic ("take any discount of 1 percent or greater when the payment period is 30 or fewer days") holds in this case, calculate the annual effective interest rate:

Annual effective rate = discount/(100% − discount) × 365/(payment period − discount period)

$$AER = .01/(1.00 - .01) \times 365/(30 - 10)$$
$$AER = .01/.99 \times 365/(20)$$
$$AER = 0.01010101 \times 18.25$$
$$AER = 18.43\%$$

Yes, indeed, the heuristic holds. 18.43 percent is much greater than is 11 percent. MyLibros should pay within 10 days, taking the 1 percent discount on the goods.

Suppose, however, that the vendor's terms were 1 percent discount if paid in 10 days, due in full in 45 days after receipt. If you do the same arithmetic, the result is 10.53 percent. With the more generous terms, it is better for MyLibros to delay payment to the full 45 days.

include autonomy, a chance to be creative, flexible hours, telecommuting, praise, training, career opportunities, the chance to work with (or learn about) advanced technology, responsibility, benefits packages (health, vacation, retirement, etc.), a supportive or protective culture, and even small prizes and awards.[18]

Use of temporary agencies is another way to reduce the cost of employees. If you do not need a full-time, permanent employee, agencies can provide educated, trained, and skilled workers who will work only as much as you need. It is common today for small businesses to contract with agencies to provide all sorts of temporary employees, from unskilled labor to a chief executive officer.

consignment
The practice of accepting goods for resale, without taking ownership of them and without being responsible to pay prior to their being sold.

Consignment is the practice of accepting goods for resale without taking ownership of them and without being responsible to pay prior to their being sold. Consignment sales are the norm in the operation of art galleries. Living artists usually make an exclusive contract with a specific gallery to display their works. When a piece of art is sold, either by the gallery or by the artist, the gallery arranges for receipt of payment, delivery of the art, and guarantee of the provenance of the art, in return for a percentage of the sales price.

Lisa Fittipaldi (www.lisafittipaldi.com) provides an example of this type of arrangement. Lisa, who is completely blind, is a painter who produces remarkable, lifelike representational art. Her phenomenal visual memory allows her to work on several paintings at once, moving with assurance from one to another. Lisa has a contract with Gallery SOCO, of Austin, Texas, to display and promote her art, which she provides on consignment to the gallery.

Other industries that use consignment sales include the distributors of salty snacks (potato chips, corn chips, peanuts, etc.), specialty food items, used furniture and antiques, sporting goods, and used automobiles. The advantage of receiving goods on consignment is that they remain the property of the consigner and do not have to be paid for until sold, thus matching cash receipts with cash disbursement.

barter
The practice of trading goods and services without the use of money.

Barter is the practice of trading goods and services without the use of money. For example, an accountant may trade accounting services to a sign company in return for the sign company manufacturing and installing a sign at the accountant's place of business. Barter alleviates the need for cash by trading good for good, service for service, or service for good. Barter is legal in the United States and is widely practiced among small businesses.[19] Although money is not used in the transaction, the legislature, the IRS, and the courts have consistently ruled that barter is a taxable transaction, except in case of trades of "like-kind" goods or services. In other words, you may trade real estate for real estate, or machinery for machinery without creating a taxable transaction. However, if you trade your airplane for real estate or if you use any amount of money in the trade, the transaction is subject to tax.

Because of the provision for tax-free treatment of like-kind trades, barter transactions are susceptible to misuse to avoid paying taxes. As a result, the rules for reporting barter transactions are restrictive and quite complex. Misuse of barter is usually considered fraud by the IRS and can lead to criminal penalties.

There are numerous services, organizations, and Web sites that facilitate barter transactions. For example, the Open Directory Project, http://dmoz.org/Business/International_Business_and_Trade/Barter/, lists over 60 online barter clubs, organizations, brokers, exchanges, and for-profit companies that support barter, using the Internet. The Google directory, http://directory.google.com/Top/Business/International_Business_and_Trade/Barter/, returns 33 similar references. There are even trade associations for the barter industry such as the International Reciprocal Trade Association (www.irta.com) or the National Association of Trade Exchanges (www.nate.org).

Controlling the timing of paying out cash can be accomplished through a number of methods. The strategy is not to unnecessarily delay paying, but to arrange payment schedules in such a way that due dates match the times when cash is available.

Negotiating terms with suppliers is a common, acceptable method for controlling when payment must be made for goods and services. For example, many building contractors who build single-family houses expect to complete and sell a house in a 90-day period. Most builders negotiate with primary suppliers such as lumberyards and plumbing wholesalers to finance the materials needed to build a house. The suppliers are protected by having a lien on the house that must be paid before title of the house can be passed to the buyer.

Similar arrangements are made to finance many types of long-term projects, as well. Often the winning bidder on a large project will make the major suppliers subcontractors who agree to accept payment when the general contractor is paid.

Timing purchases is a method of controlling the timing of cash outflows that is invisible to suppliers and vendors. Your specific reason for placing any certain order on any certain day is not apparent. However, knowledge of the payment policies of suppliers can provide considerable leeway in when bills must be paid following delivery of goods. For example, it is common for wholesale suppliers to have payment terms that define an on-time payment as being any payment made on or before the tenth day of the month following purchase. Knowing this term, you can gain additional time to pay by delaying purchase until the first day of the month. This provides up to 41 days before payment must be made without being classified as late. Were you to purchase on the last day of the month, you would have only 10 days to make a timely payment.

timing purchases
A method of controlling the timing of cash outflows that is invisible to suppliers and vendors.

Gaming the payment process is a common, if a bit underhanded, method of controlling cash outflows. Methods range from simply not paying a bill when it is due to sending checks that you've "forgotten" to sign, to sending checks in payment and then stopping payment after the payment has been recorded, but the check has not yet cleared. Very few business owners and managers are proud of taking such measures, but most will, if promised confidentiality, admit to having done one or another in times of cash crises.

gaming the payment process
Using methods to appear to be paying bills on time, when in fact payment is being delayed or avoided.

Gaming payments can be quite costly, however. You may well get away with any one of these strategies with any single vendor one time. The more often you game payment, the more certain it becomes that your business credit rating and reputation will suffer as a result. Being consistently late in payment, regardless of gaming strategies, will cause a decrease in your business's credit worthiness. It is not uncommon for suppliers and vendors to refuse to do business with customers who regularly attempt to game the process.

Controlling Cash Shortages

LO7 Implement strategies for coping with cash shortages.

No matter how well you plan or how well you manage your business, sooner or later you will experience a significant cash shortage. Causes of cash shortages range from the obvious, a customer fails to make an expected payment or goes out of business without paying at all, to the obscure—an economic shock, such as a plant closing, natural disaster, or political turmoil like an oil embargo or war. During a time of economic shock, you may not attain your sales goals, *and* you may not be able to collect from customers as they suffer from the same bad economy. However, many, if not all, your bills go on, demanding payments that you no longer have the money to make.

Another often overlooked cause of cash shortages is a surplus of good news: Your business has proven to be wildly successful, and sales are growing at an exponential rate. This situation is often referred to as the **growth trap**.[20] Because of increased sales, you need more labor, more materials for your product, more factory space, and more warehouse space to store completed products until they can be shipped to your customers. All this growth requires money, and lots of it. However, as discussed above, sales take time to convert into money. The product must be made and shipped before any customer will pay. If you are offering credit to customers, you will have to wait even longer to receive that payment. You are in a "trap" made by growth: Growing will produce more money, but right now you need money to grow.

growth trap
A financial crisis that is caused by a business growing faster than it can be financed.

There are numerous strategies to handle cash shortfalls, including laying off employees, slowing payments for purchases, stepping up collection efforts, selling investment securities, or using your own money. A survey of small business owners (see Figure 14.7) found that there are at least eight strategies employed by small businesses for handling money shortages. These are, in the order of their frequency of use:

1. Use personal money.
2. Borrow.
3. Adjust scheduled purchases.
4. Adjust scheduled payments.

- The service provider will take up to five working days to make a deposit to your account.
- Credit card clearing services reduce the amount deposited in the event of fraud or customer challenge.

LO5 Develop a cash budget.

- A cash budget identifies when, how, and why cash is expected to come into the business, and when, how, and why it is expected to leave:
  - For businesses that make sales by cash or by credit card, the sales forecast *is* the cash receipts forecast.
  - If you provide credit to your customers, you will always wait some period of time for some of your money. You also, sooner or later, will have some customer who never pays.
- Cash receipts and cash disbursements budgets are used to put together a cash budget.
- All budgets are combined at this point to make the *comprehensive budget.*

LO6 Develop strategies for preventing and coping with cash flow problems.

- The best way to prevent cash flow problems is to pay attention to and understand your business's operations and patterns of cash flows.
- Five proven techniques to even out cash flows are:
  - Taking deposits and progress payments.
  - Offering discounts for prompt payment.
  - Asking for your money.
  - Taking on noncore paying projects.
  - Factoring receivables.
- Controlling the amount of cash being paid out is primarily a function of making good purchasing decisions and avoiding waste.

LO7 Implement strategies for coping with cash shortages.

- No matter how well you plan or how well you manage your business, sooner or later you will experience a significant cash shortage.
- Causes of cash shortages include a customer failing to pay or going out of business, and economic shocks, such as a natural disaster or war.
- The growth trap causes cash flow problems when the rate of growth is faster than the operating cycle.
- The three most common ways to handle cash shortages are (1) using personal money, (2) borrowing, and (3) adjusting scheduled purchases.

KEY TERMS

cash-to-cash cycle, 442
operating cycle, 442
payables, 443
receivables, 443
money, 445
profit, 446
cash, 446
cash equivalents, 446
currency, 446
demand deposits, 446
marketable securities, 447
commercial paper, 447
short-term debt, 447
bearer, 447
company book balance, 448
bank ledger balance, 449
bank available balance, 449
clearinghouse, 449
overdraft, 449
float, 449
reconciling, 450
nonsufficient funds, 450
charge back, 450
cash budget, 451
cash receipts budget, 452
cash disbursements budget, 455
comprehensive budget, 456
deposits and progress payments, 460
discounts for prompt payment, 460
noncore projects, 461
factoring receivables, 461
trade discounts, 463
noncash incentives, 463
consignment, 464
barter, 464
timing purchases, 465
gaming the payment process, 465
growth trap, 465

DISCUSSION QUESTIONS

1. Why is it important to plan for the amounts and timing of cash inflows and outflows?
2. What is money, and how does it differ from profits?
3. What are the primary purposes of money?
4. How do the economic and accounting definitions of cash differ?
5. What are the relationships among planning, budgeting, and forecasting?
6. Discuss five methods commonly used to increase cash inflows.
7. Discuss four methods to decrease cash outflows.
8. The text calls the practice of gaming the payment process, "underhanded." What is your opinion of this common practice? Does it have any ethical implications?
9. How does using the float as a cash management method differ from deliberately writing NSF checks?

EXPERIENTIAL EXERCISES

1. Make an appointment with a loan officer at your bank who handles small businesses. Conduct an interview to find out the following:
   a. Will the bank lend to small businesses, using receivables for collateral?
   b. Does the bank ever factor receivables or act as a collection agent for receivables?
   c. Present the example of the air-conditioning company on page 446 of this chapter. Ask what help from the bank would be available in such a situation.

   Write a report of your findings.
2. Form a group from your classmates who completed Exercise 1 above. Collect your findings into a chart. Compare and contrast bank offerings. Present your findings to your class with a recommendation of which banks in your area offer the best small business support.
3. WWW Do a Google search, using the name of your city and "online banking." Examine the sites returned to determine:
   a. How often is the account balance updated online?
   b. Are monthly account statements available online?
   c. How far back (one month, two months, one year) can you retrieve statements and transactions?
   d. Can you electronically transfer funds among your accounts?
   e. Can you electronically pay bills?
   f. Can you download bank account information into your small business computerized accounting system? If so, which systems are supported?
   g. What is the cost of online banking?

   Make a chart of your findings and report to your class.
4. Do a telephone survey of banks in your area. Ask:
   a. Do they use electronic check clearing?
   b. If they use a clearing bank to manually clear checks, ask what bank they use.
   c. Ask what the average period of float is for the bank.
   d. Ask what the bank's policy is for nonsufficient funds: Does it pay to the limit of ledger balance or to available balance?
   e. What other provisions does the bank make to help small businesses avoid having checks returned NSF?
   f. When does the bank make available funds from deposited checks?

   Write a report of your findings and present it to your class.
5. Form a group from your classmates who completed Exercise 4 above. Collect your findings into a chart. Compare and contrast bank offerings. Present your findings to your class with a recommendation of which banks in your area offer the best overdraft protection to small businesses.
6. WWW Use the resources of your library and the Internet to identify five credit card processing providers. Contact each and determine the following:
   a. The cost of equipment to be able to accept credit card charges.
   b. The transaction cost, if any.
   c. The amount of discount charged for:
      i. Physically swiped card charges.
      ii. Charges accepted over the telephone.
      iii. Online charges taken on the Internet.

d. How long does it take between accepting a credit card for payment and receiving the cash in your bank account?

Report your finding to your class.

7. Assume that you are preparing to open a new business. You need both an on-location sign and professional accounting services. Do a Web search and examine your local telephone book to find (a) a sign company and (b) an accountant who is willing to provide its product and services in a barter transaction for the product or service of your business.

MINI-CASE

BULLTUFF STOCK TRAILERS, INC.

Hal Carrier, of Bulltuff Stock Trailers, Inc., has asked you for help. In the last four months, he has had several checks written to suppliers that were refused by his bank because of nonsufficient funds. Now his main supplier, Alcoa Aluminum Supply Co., has cut off credit.

"We're sorry, Hal," Alcoa's credit officer said, "but we simply cannot keep accepting your checks. Every time one bounces, it costs us at least $100 combined in processing fees and our internal accounting. You simply will have to pay cash or bring a cashier's check for future purchases."

Hal simply cannot understand why his checks keep bouncing. "We've plenty of sales," he said, "and our customers pay pretty much as agreed. Right now, I have only one customer who is as much as 60 days past due. My accountant, Brill Yant, assures me that our cash balance never goes negative. So why are my checks bouncing?"

To try to understand Hal's problem and to advise him how to correct it, you have collected the following information about Hal's business:

1. Cash sales are 10 percent of total sales.
2. Credit card sales are 10 percent of total sales and are collected the week following the sale. The credit card provider deducts 2.5 percent of the gross amount of each credit card sale. (For example, on a $100 sale, $2.50 is deducted.)
3. Sales on account are 80 percent of all sales. All credit sales are to dealers. Terms for dealers are "30-30-30," that is, three equal payments made in each of the three months following the sale. Payments are considered late if they're not received by the tenth of the month in which they are due.
4. Direct materials, primarily aluminum, are 60 percent of the cost of building a trailer. Before credit was cut off, Bulltuff paid 30 percent on delivery and the remainder in 30 days. Now it must pay cash on delivery.
5. Total cost of direct labor is 15 percent of the cost of building a trailer. Workers are paid each Friday for work performed the previous week. Withholding and employment taxes are paid each Friday, also.
6. Variable costs combined (e.g., materials and labor) are 50 percent of gross sales. Fixed costs are *not* allocated to the cost of trailers but are expensed evenly across the year.
7. All other costs combined are treated as fixed costs, and total $1 million per year.
8. Bulltuff leases its building and equipment and has no depreciation.
9. Sales for the year were originally projected to be $2,450,000. However, given the current growth in sales, Hal now estimates that sales will be $5,000,000.

10. Sales for the first four months of the year have been:

January	$208,000
February	261,000
March	293,000
April	328,000

CASE DISCUSSION QUESTIONS

1. What is causing Hal's cash flow problems?
2. Develop a plan to address the problems.

SUGGESTED CASES AND ARTICLES

- Nate Mower & Son, Residential Plumber(s)

Available on PRIMIS:

- Patriot Electrical Manufacturing Corporation
- Le Parisien

SUGGESTED VIDEOS

Video Case:

- Credit Squeeze on Small Business, p. VC-6

eClips Videos:

- Aron Rosenberg Discusses Cash Flow and the Flame Date
- Richard Saltz Discusses Importance of Cash Versus Profitability

SBTV Videos:

- Credit Concerns
- eBay: Avoid Bad Payers

STVP Video:

- Importance of Cash Flow

APPENDIX

Completing a Bank Reconciliation

One very useful skill you can have for managing cash in your business is being able to quickly and accurately reconcile your own cash records with your bank's records.

To illustrate the process of reconciling a bank statement, we will use a fictitious company, Languid Lizard, Inc. Languid Lizard is a manufacturer of aluminum lawn furniture. Their primary material costs are for aluminum tubing and nylon webbing for the chairs and lounges.

Carefully examine the copy of Languid Lizard's December bank statement on the next page.

Of special interest are the amounts that are highlighted with the red labels. These are amounts added to and subtracted from the account directly by the bank. Languid Lizard's owner has no way of knowing these transactions have occurred, except to be informed of them by the bank. These amounts are one of the two reasons that the bank balance and book balance differ.

Now take a look at Languid Lizard's cash records: Notice five things: (1) According to Lizard's accounting records, there is a cash balance of $42,038.19. Compare this with the bank balance of only $34,220.22. This is an $8,000 difference. (2) Lizard made a deposit of $7,233.99 which the bank has not yet recorded. This may be because the deposit and the bank statement were both made on December 31. Normally, deposits made after 3:00 P.M. will not be recorded by the bank until the next work day. A deposit made at 3:01 P.M. on Friday will not show up as an addition to your bank account until the bank updates accounts *after 3:00 P.M. on the following Monday.* (3) Lizard has received a check from a customer that has been recorded in the company's books, but has not yet been taken to the bank for deposit. (4) Lizard has written two checks to suppliers that have not yet cashed them. (5) None of the items flagged in red that were added and subtracted by the bank show up in Lizard's books in any way.

No wonder that the bank and Lizard have very different opinions of how much money Languid Lizard has.

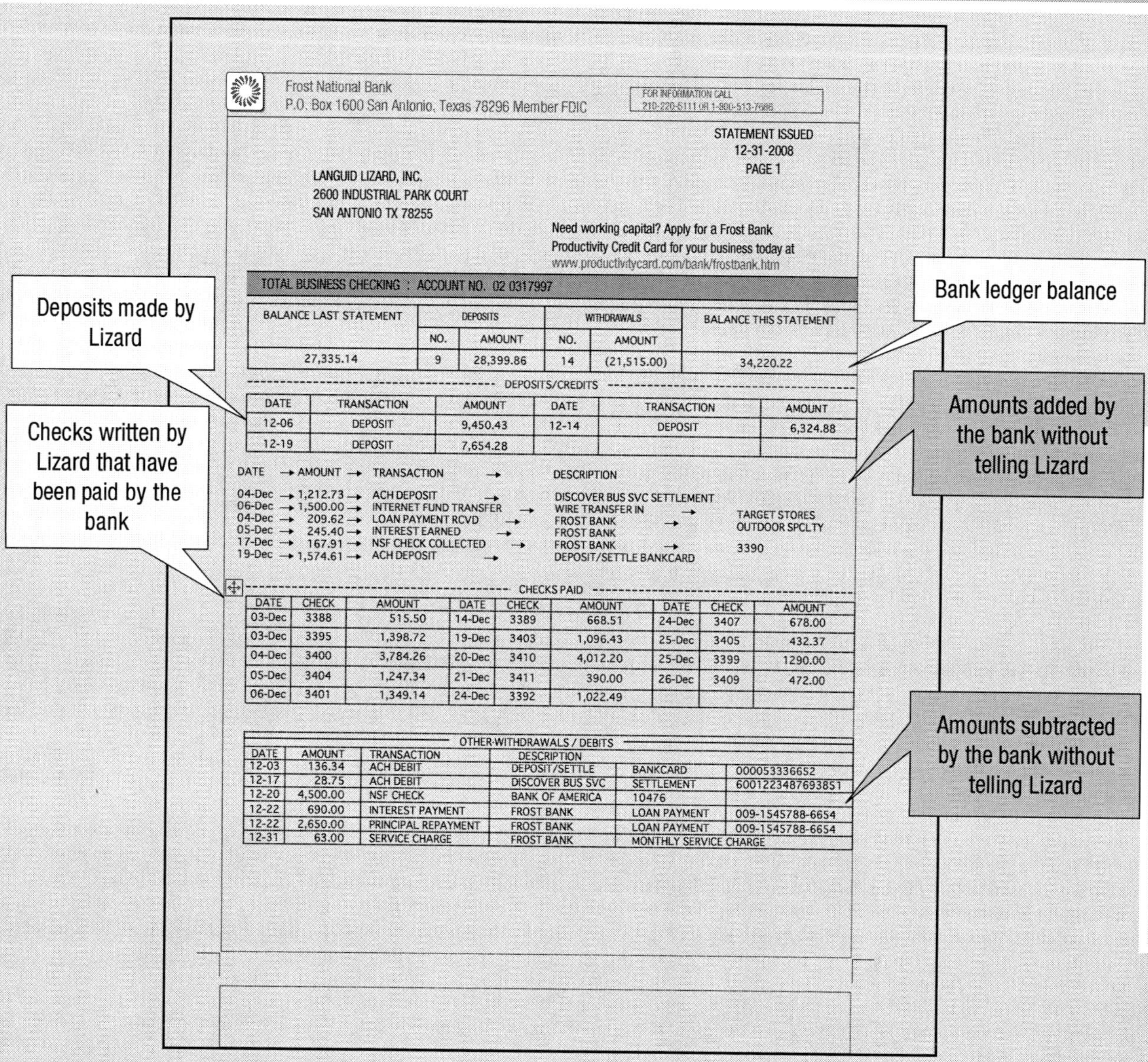

Frost National Bank
P.O. Box 1600 San Antonio, Texas 78296 Member FDIC

FOR INFORMATION CALL
210-220-5111 OR 1-800-513-7986

STATEMENT ISSUED
12-31-2008
PAGE 1

LANGUID LIZARD, INC.
2600 INDUSTRIAL PARK COURT
SAN ANTONIO TX 78255

Need working capital? Apply for a Frost Bank Productivity Credit Card for your business today at www.productivitycard.com/bank/frostbank.htm

TOTAL BUSINESS CHECKING : ACCOUNT NO. 02 0317997

BALANCE LAST STATEMENT	DEPOSITS		WITHDRAWALS		BALANCE THIS STATEMENT
	NO.	AMOUNT	NO.	AMOUNT	
27,335.14	9	28,399.86	14	(21,515.00)	34,220.22

DEPOSITS/CREDITS

DATE	TRANSACTION	AMOUNT	DATE	TRANSACTION	AMOUNT
12-06	DEPOSIT	9,450.43	12-14	DEPOSIT	6,324.88
12-19	DEPOSIT	7,654.28			

DATE →	AMOUNT →	TRANSACTION →	DESCRIPTION	
04-Dec →	1,212.73 →	ACH DEPOSIT →	DISCOVER BUS SVC SETTLEMENT	
06-Dec →	1,500.00 →	INTERNET FUND TRANSFER →	WIRE TRANSFER IN →	TARGET STORES
04-Dec →	209.62 →	LOAN PAYMENT RCVD →	FROST BANK →	OUTDOOR SPCLTY
05-Dec →	245.40 →	INTEREST EARNED →	FROST BANK	
17-Dec →	167.91 →	NSF CHECK COLLECTED →	FROST BANK →	3390
19-Dec →	1,574.61 →	ACH DEPOSIT →	DEPOSIT/SETTLE BANKCARD	

CHECKS PAID

DATE	CHECK	AMOUNT	DATE	CHECK	AMOUNT	DATE	CHECK	AMOUNT
03-Dec	3388	515.50	14-Dec	3389	668.51	24-Dec	3407	678.00
03-Dec	3395	1,398.72	19-Dec	3403	1,096.43	25-Dec	3405	432.37
04-Dec	3400	3,784.26	20-Dec	3410	4,012.20	25-Dec	3399	1290.00
05-Dec	3404	1,247.34	21-Dec	3411	390.00	26-Dec	3409	472.00
06-Dec	3401	1,349.14	24-Dec	3392	1,022.49			

OTHER WITHDRAWALS / DEBITS

DATE	AMOUNT	TRANSACTION	DESCRIPTION		
12-03	136.34	ACH DEBIT	DEPOSIT/SETTLE	BANKCARD	000053336652
12-17	28.75	ACH DEBIT	DISCOVER BUS SVC	SETTLEMENT	6001223487693851
12-20	4,500.00	NSF CHECK	BANK OF AMERICA	10476	
12-22	690.00	INTEREST PAYMENT	FROST BANK	LOAN PAYMENT	009-1545788-6654
12-22	2,650.00	PRINCIPAL REPAYMENT	FROST BANK	LOAN PAYMENT	009-1545788-6654
12-31	63.00	SERVICE CHARGE	FROST BANK	MONTHLY SERVICE CHARGE	

Languid Lizard, Inc.
Cash Account Summary for
The Month of December 2008

December 1 balance		30,045.14
December deposits		35,573.85
December checks		(23,580.80)
December 31 balance		42,038.19
Check from customer to be deposited at end of day		2,065.00
Deposit not recorded by bank		
Total deposits made in December	35,573.85	
Total deposits recorded by bank	28,339.86	
Total deposit in transit		7,233.99
Checks outstanding:		
Alcoa Aluminum Supply, Inc.	2,121.14	
Smurfit-Stone Container, Inc.	1,932.70	
Total checks outstanding		4,053.84

Account balance according to Lizard's books

Money yet to be deposited

Deposit not yet recorded by the bank

Checks written but not yet cashed by the bank

Fixing these differences is incredibly simple. We are going to do two little tasks. (1) We are going to add and subtract from the bank's balance those transactions Lizard has done that the bank currently knows nothing about. (2) We are going to add to and subtract from Lizard's balance those things the bank has done, that until now Lizard knew nothing about. When we are done, the *adjusted* bank balance and the *adjusted* book balance will be identical. This process is detailed on the next page.

We start on the bank balance by (A) entering the balance shown on the bank statement into our reconciliation worksheet. To the bank balance we add (B) the things Lizard added that the bank can't know—the undeposited check and the deposit which has not yet been recorded by the bank. Finally, we subtract (C) the checks written by Languid Lizard that have not yet gotten to the bank for payment.

We finish up on the book balance by (D) adding the items that the bank added, but Languid Lizard did not know until it received the monthly bank statement—deposits from the credit card provider, wire transfers in, collections on notes, interest earned, bad check collected, and a check that was incorrectly entered into Lizard's books. Then we subtract from Languid Lizard's balance (E) those things the bank subtracted that Lizard could not know—a bad check from a customer, charges made by the credit card provider, a payment on borrowed money taken directly from the account, and the bank service charge.

To complete the reconciliation, add each of the bank adjustments and the book adjustments, and as predicted, the resulting balances are identical.

Now Lizard's owner simply enters the adjustments into the accounting records. This brings the recorded book balance to $39,465.37, which is the amount of money the business really has.

This one business function, tracking and managing cash, is itself enough reason to buy and use a computerized accounting system. Although such systems cannot make reconciliations automatically, they have very powerful and very easy-to-use built-in functions to complete this important business task. With just a little bit of attention, you can always *know* just how much money your business has.

(A) Balance from statement

(D) Additions made by the bank

Languid Lizard, Inc.
Reconciliation of Bank and Book Balances at December 31, 2008

Bank Balance	
Ending bank balance, December 31	34,220.22
Additions:	
Undeposited cash on hand	2,065.00
Deposit in transit	7,233.99
Subtractions:	
Checks outstanding	(4,053.84)
Total	39,465.37
Correct cash balance	39,465.37

Book Balance	
Ending bank balance, December 31	42,038.19
Additions:	
ACH deposit	1,212.73
Wire transfer in	1,500.00
Note collected	209.62
Interest earned	245.40
NSF check collected	167.91
ACH deposit	1,574.61
Error: recorded check 3395 as $1,983.72	585.00
Subtractions:	
ACH debit	(136.34)
ACH debit	(28.75)
NSF check returned	(4,500.00)
Interest payment	(690.00)
Principal payment	(2,650.00)
Service charge	(63.00)
Total	39,465.37
Correct Cash Balance	39,465.37

(B) Unrecorded deposits

(C) Outstanding checks

(E) Subtractions made by the bank

books:	1,983.72
bank	1,398.72
error	585.00

Book balance is understated by $585.00

Same

CHAPTER

15

Small Business Finance: Using Equity, Debt, and Gifts

• Dr. Mary Pat Moyer, pictured here, began INCELL Corporation in 1993 with her husband, Jim Janowiak. Though continually challenged by the financial needs of their company, Mary Pat and Jim are slowly but surely reaping the benefits of their substantial personal investments. Why do you think INCELL has stayed away from enlisting venture capitalists, even knowing firsthand the significant personal responsibilities this course of action entails? In their shoes, would you do the same?

LEARNING OBJECTIVES

LO

When you complete this chapter, you will be able to:

LO1 Describe the three types of capital financing and their costs and trade-offs.

LO2 Explain the characteristics of a business that determine its ability to raise capital.

LO3 Determine the best type of financing for your business.

LO4 Describe the differing needs for financial management at each stage of business life.

Focus on Small Business: Dr. Mary Pat Moyer and INCELL Corporation

Doctor Moyer ("Call me 'Mary Pat,'" she says.) knows firsthand the availability and value of nontraditional financing sources for small businesses. She has used both nontraditional and traditional means to finance the founding and growth of her successful biotech business, INCELL Corporation.

"I've used my own savings, borrowed from banks and credit card companies, and obtained grants from both the U.S. government and the state of Texas. If I had depended solely on the traditional sources of investment for small businesses—angel, seed, and venture capitalists—INCELL would not have survived its first year." "In fact," Mary Pat continued, "INCELL may be the only biotech in the world to be bootstrapped."

In 1993, after 20 years as an academic scientist, Mary Pat resigned from her tenured professorship at the University of Texas Health Science Center at San Antonio to start INCELL Corporation in partnership with her husband, Jim Janowiak. Today, INCELL is a successful small business that has 14 full-time employees.

INCELL's success has come at a greater personal cost in both time and money than Mary Pat and Jim originally expected. As do many entrepreneurs who start firms based on prior successes as academics or executives, they initially underestimated the difficulties of managing the finances of a small business.

Mary Pat said, "After all, I reasoned, just how hard can financial management be for a Ph.D. in microbiology? Besides, I also had 'an ace up my sleeve.' Jim is a CPA with long experience in business management."

Jim agreed, "I'd worked with many businesses, both large and small. If I could do their accounting, prepare their financial statements, and provide business advice, certainly I could do these things for myself."

To their chagrin, they soon realized that financial management for an entrepreneurial business is very different from either academic microbiology or public accounting practice.

"At first, INCELL was 100 percent funded from our personal savings. From day one we bootstrapped growth by carefully using personal credit cards, accounts payable, and revenues from sales. We 'played the game' by collecting as fast as we could and paying as slowly as our personal ethics would allow. Still, we barely scraped by. Finally, about a year after INCELL was started, we received our first Small Business Innovation Research grant from the National Institute of Health. Since then, we have received over $2 million in seven additional grants. Although we've been able to keep afloat ever since, there have been those times that we've wondered whether or not we'd be able to meet the current week's payroll," Mary Pat said. "So far, with careful planning, the grace of God, and plain old good luck, we've managed."

Jim said, "Many times Mary Pat and I have worked a series of 60 hour weeks because we did not have the money to pay an employee. Still, we'd do it again. We've had to do without personally from time to time, but we've never missed a meal. Of course, when you own the business, you pay your employees first, your suppliers second, and then if there is anything left over, you might be able to pay yourself."

"Our problem right now is one of too much success, if there is such a thing!" Mary Pat said. "We have a product in human clinical trials in conjunction with Johns Hopkins, and we just signed a contract with the U.S. Air Force to begin the testing of our oral smallpox vaccine. Each of these projects will require that we raise significant additional funds. Where the business is right now, it either grows or it fails."

In an effort to meet INCELL's funding needs, for the last year Mary Pat has been making the rounds of venture capitalists. To date, she has not been successful in obtaining needed investment.

"I've been to Philadelphia, Orange County, San Francisco, even Ft. Atkinson, Wisconsin—pretty much everywhere in the U.S. where there are venture capitalists specializing in biotech and pharmaceuticals. And I've not raised a penny, at least not at a price we're willing to pay! We have given up on the venture capital route for now," she said. "While a venture capital investment seemed like an easy way to raise growth funds, the interest rates and amount of equity that were demanded were much, much too high. Instead, we are working with the Air Force, the Texas Department of Economic Development (www.tded.state.tx.us), the San Antonio Economic Development Department (www.sanantonio.gov/edd), and a regional commercial bank to put together a financing package. The package will include direct grants, tax abatement, tax increment financing, and commercial loans secured with buildings and equipment. The terms of the package will require that we create a specified number of new jobs, provide job training opportunities, and, of course, repay the loans with interest."

In the meantime, INCELL continues to increase sales of its current products and to work as both a contract research organization and as a development partner for other biotech firms. The revenue from these activities provides funds to pay rent, payroll, and the many expenses of an operating biotech business.

"Financial management is a daily, constant, on-going process for INCELL," Jim said. "We regularly remind ourselves that every dollar must be made to work. We do not tolerate any waste, because we quite simply cannot afford to do so."

"We work hard. We have fun. We hire wonderful people," Mary Pat said. "We try to keep a spiritual center and a sense of humor—and we never, never, never give up!" Visit www.incell.com to learn more.

DISCUSSION QUESTIONS

1. What did Dr. Moyer mean when she said, "INCELL may be the only biotech in the world to be bootstrapped"?
2. In what ways does financial management for small start-up businesses differ from that of academic organizations and businesses?
3. What problems are created by "too much success"?
4. What did Dr. Moyer mean when she said, "We've not raised a penny, at least not at a price we're willing to pay!"?
5. How can raising money from venture capitalists be said to be expensive?

Sources of Financing for Small Businesses

LO1 Describe the three types of capital financing and their costs and trade-offs.

Getting the money to start or grow a business seems like one of the greatest challenges, but in reality most people who try find the means to get their business going. There are two reasons for this. First, financing is often easier than people think, because most of us have many assets and financial resources that we take for granted. Second, the range of financing resources available to us is so varied that few people just starting out in business know more than a fraction of the options available to them. The more you learn about your personal finances and the financing options, the greater your chances of finding the financing you need to start your business.

However, getting money to start is only the tip of the iceberg of finance for small businesses. Once you have started your business, you must continually work to keep up a constant flow of money and capital assets to meet the strategic and operating goals of your business. As Jim Janowiak of INCELL Corporation said, constant, careful management of money and other capital resources is essential for success throughout the existence of any business. A business's needs for financial management change as the business develops, as economic conditions vary, and as your needs and goals change. Although the details of financial management are unique to each business, there are patterns that can be seen as a business develops from start-up to exit. We examine these patterns, first getting money for start-up and growth and second using strategic financial management to reach your goals.

Where *does* financing come from for most small businesses? The number one source is from the owners (or potential owners) themselves. The other major sources include family and friends, credit cards, trade credit, banks, and other commercial lenders. There are also a number of other sources that exist but are used very rarely. These include angel investors, government programs, community-based financiers, stock sales, and venture capital.

Table 15.1 lists sources of financing as debt, equity, and gifts. **Debt** can take many forms. A business may borrow money directly from banks, development agencies, governments, or individuals. When you sell part of your business, the money you receive is **equity capital**. Any valuable assets or services, including money, that are donated to your business without any obligation to repay or to give any ownership interest, is a **gift**. Each of these three types of financing requires a different approach, which we cover below.

debt
A legal obligation to pay money in the future.

equity capital
Money contributed to the businesses in return for part ownership of the business.

gift
Valuable assets or services donated to the business without any obligation to repay or give up any ownership interest.

Which of these financing sources is right for you? The answer depends largely on whether you are trying to start a new business or are trying to get financing for an existing business. Existing businesses have a track record of financial performance, which lets investors and lenders make better guesses about the firm's ability to pay back a loan or pay off an investment. This means that more forms of financing are available to existing firms than to start-ups. Even when the same form of financing is available to start-ups and existing firms, existing firms that are profitable or have made profits in the recent past are likely to get better terms for debt or equity. They may pay a lower interest rate on debt or give up a smaller part of ownership.

We start with equity capital because for most businesses the owner's own resources are the first source of funds. Then we consider **debt capital** and conclude with a look at gift capital. After that, we look at some of the decisions entrepreneurs make in the financing process.

debt capital
Money borrowed for the purpose of investment in a business.

Financing with Equity

Equity can come from the entrepreneur or from others. In general the entrepreneurs' own pockets are the first source of financing for most businesses. Because of this, understanding your own financial situation and the opportunities available to free up personal capital for use in your business become the foundation for any effort to finance using equity.

Personal Equity

How much are you worth? How is that value held? Often people underestimate their personal worth, because many parts of their wealth are seen or thought about only occasionally—such as retirement funds—or because they use it so much that they forget about it having value, like a car, home, or personal collection. But when starting a business, knowing your personal wealth is critical to your ability to fund yourself. Also, if you plan to get investments or loans from other people or banks, they may ask to see your personal financial statements to understand *your* commitment to the business. Skill Module 15.1 has you determine your personal financial situation.

TABLE 15.1 Financing for Small Business by Phase, Type, and Source

Phase of Business/ Financial Management Need	Sources of Capital Financing		
	Debt Financing	**Equity Financing**	**Gift Financing**
Financing for start-ups Profits are secondary to cash flow Need cash to pay employees Need cash to pay suppliers Need cash to live on	Consumer banks Commercial banks SBA insured loans Economic development agencies Small business investment companies Incubators Accelerators Leasing companies Personal credit cards	Friends, family, and "fools" Angels Venture capital Public stock offerings Direct public offerings	Institutional: Grants don't exist for start-ups Personal: Cash, picking up the tab, accelerated cash-outs, free use, free work/ unpaid labor, overpayment, favored status/ sweetheart deals, forgiveness, deferral, piggybacking
Financing for growth Profits consistent with risk levels Funds for investment in equipment Cash for marketing Cash for building inventory levels	Commercial banks Small Business Administration Private placement loans Economic development agencies Small business investment companies Suppliers Leasing companies Personal credit cards	Self-generated funds Venture capital Direct public offerings Mergers Acquisitions	Institutional: SBIR, STTR grants State grants Incubators, accelerators Donated capital Tax abatement Personal: Same as for start-ups
Financing for operations Profits consistent with risk Build owner wealth Cash flow "smoothing" Reinvestment for maintenance	Factor receivables Business credit cards Commercial banks Small Business Administration Private placement loans Suppliers Leasing companies	Self-generated funds Venture capital Direct public offerings	Institutional: Same as for growth Personal: Same as for start-ups
Financing for exit Investing to build equity and firm value Reinvestment to replace worn assets New technology Productivity Quality	Consumer banks Commercial banks Small Business Administration Private placement loans Economic development agencies Small Business investment companies Suppliers Leasing companies Lines of credit	Self-generated funds Venture capital Direct public offerings	Institutional: Same as for growth Personal: Same as for start-ups

Determining Personal Net Worth

SKILL MODULE 15.1

Use the worksheet below to determine your personal net worth. You may either copy the form or go to the Web site for this text, **www.mhhe.com/katzesb**, and download it in Excel format. Enter into the column labeled "Cash Value" the amount of money you could get if you were to sell what you own. Enter into the next column any amount that you owe to pay off your debt on the item. Then, in the third column, enter the difference between what you could sell it for and what you owe on it (the difference could be a negative number). After you have listed all that you own and all that you owe, the difference is what you are worth financially.

Lenders and investors usually require that you furnish a personal net worth statement. You can find two different common formats for the report on the text Web site.

	Cash Value (A)	Amount Owed (B)	Net Value (A − B)
Cash			
Your personal checking account		0	
Your spouse's checking account		0	
Other checking accounts you own		0	
Money in all savings accounts		0	
Cash value of money market account		0	
Total money in other accounts		0	
TOTAL CASH			
Cash Equivalents			
Cash value of stocks owned (net of selling commissions)			
Cash value of bonds owned			
Cash value of annuity			
Cash value of IRAs			
Cash value of other retirement funds			
Cash value of life insurance			
TOTAL CASH EQUIVALENTS			
Personal Property			
Automobile 1			
Automobile 2			
Motorcycle			
Bicycles			
Personal watercraft			
Boat and motor			
Airplane			
Guns and rifles			
Cameras			
Sports equipment (binoculars, skis, parachutes, etc.)			
Art and collectibles			
Antiques			
Jewelry			
Shop tools			
Furniture			

	Cash Value (A)	Amount Owed (B)	Net Value (A − B)
TOTAL PERSONAL PROPERTY			
Real Estate			
Primary dwelling			
Second or vacation home			
Lot at the lake			
Farms, ranches, development property			
Houses, duplexes, apartment buildings that you rent to others			
Business lots and commercial buildings			
TOTAL REAL ESTATE			
Intangible Assets			
Copyrights on books, songs, videos, movies, etc., that you own			
Patents you own			
Trademarks			
URLs			
TOTAL INTANGIBLE ASSETS			
Unsecured Debt			
American Express credit card		0	
Master Card 1		0	
Master Card 2		0	
Visa card 1		0	
Visa card 2		0	
Discover card		0	
Unsecured loan from credit union		0	
Unsecured loan from bank		0	
Loan from your brother-in-law		0	
TOTALS			

outside equity
Money from selling part of your business to people who are not and will not be involved in the management of the business.

partnership
Two or more people cooperating to conduct a business enterprise.

corporation
A legal "artificial" entity that is formed by filing specific documents with a state government.

limited liability company (LLC)
A legal form of business organization that is created by filing required documentation with a state government. LLCs have a choice, under federal tax law, of being taxed as either corporations or partnerships.

limited partnership
A legal form of business organization that is created by filing required documentation with a state government; within a limited partnership, one or more partners may have no liability for the debts and actions of the partnership.

Outside Equity

Outside equity is money from selling part of your business to people who are not and will not be involved in the management of the business. People who buy ownership rights in your business are considered *outside equity investors*.

- *Outside* because they are not part of the management of your business.
- *Equity* because they have legal ownership rights to your business.
- *Investors* because they are letting you use their money now in order to get wealth in the future.

You can sell ownership in your business only if your business is organized as one of three broad types of legal forms of business: a **partnership**, a **corporation**, or a **limited liability company**. We start the discussion of legal forms of business here, because the choice of legal form does make a difference in taxation, a critical issue in your efforts to secure financing. The other legal factors driving the choice of a form of organization are discussed later in Chapter 18 on small business law.

The decision of which type of business organization is best for you depends on a lot of factors, including tax treatment, business conduct, and legal liabilities. There are seven forms of organization commonly used by small businesses: sole proprietorship, general partnership, **limited partnership**, C-corporation, limited liability company, professional corporation, and S-corporation. You may need a different form of business organization at different times as your business grows and develops. A detailed comparison of the seven forms is given in Table 18.5 in Chapter 18, but two of the factors are introduced here because they are relevant to financing a business. (See Table 15.2.)

TABLE 15.2 Legal Forms of Business Organization

	Taxed as an Entity	Tax Passed Through to Owners
Owners personally liable for debts and actions of the business		Sole proprietorship General partnership
Owners *not* personally liable for debts and actions of the business	C-corporation LLC	S-corporation Professional corporation Limited partnership LLC

Businesses are either taxed as entities or the revenues and expenses of the business are "passed-through" to the owners who report them on their individual income tax forms. Limited Liability Companies (LLCs) are a relatively new form of organization whose primary advantage is that owners may easily choose whether to be taxed as an entity or have tax items pass through. Corporations, S-corporations, and partnerships have no choice of tax treatment.

In general, all the forms of business organization can be categorized along two dimensions: (1) how much responsibility owners have for the organization's liabilities, and (2) how the business is taxed. In business and in law, responsibility is called *liability*. In terms of the form of the organization, the amount of responsibility (liability) the owners personally face for the debts of the business can be all or "none." If the owners have *all* of the responsibility for business debts, they are *fully liable,* and they face the potential of having to pay business debts from their own wealth. If the owners bear *none* of the responsibility for the business debts, they have *limited liability,* and may lose only what they have invested in the business, and not any other assets they own. Business organizations that provide limited liability are corporations, limited partnerships, and LLCs. However, in limited partnerships, at least one partner, the *general partner,* is fully liable. In general partnerships all partners are fully liable as is the owner of a sole proprietorship, who is completely responsible for all debts of the business.

Sole proprietorships are not separate from their owners, and thus there is no specific documentation that creates their existence. The business and the owner are inseparable. Similarly, partnerships do not *have* to have a written agreement. If they don't, then they are assumed to be equally owned by the partners. However, partnerships should have a written partnership agreement covering key issues such as ownership, profit splits, buyouts, and other matters important to the partners. Thus partnerships may or may not be separate from their owners, depending upon the provisions in the written partnership agreement and the laws of the state in which they are formed. Corporations, and limited liability companies, are required by law to file specific forms with the state in which they are organized. Ownership of corporations is established by stock certificates. Ownership of partnerships is determined by partnership share agreements. Ownership of limited liability companies is shown by member share certificates.

sole proprietorship
A business owned by a single individual who is responsible for all debts and claims against the business.

interest
A charge for the use of money, usually figured as a percentage of the principal.

gain on investment
The percentage amount that the payout of an investment differs from original cost: calculated as (payout − investment + dividends)/ investment.

dividends
Payments of profits to the owners of corporations.

Getting Equity Investment for Your Business

LO2 Explain the characteristics of a business that determine its ability to raise capital.

Small businesses get started and stay in business because their owners want to make money. Investors want to make money, too. Lenders expect a return on this money from making loans, by getting back the amount they had plus more money in the form of **interest**. In the same way, people invest in a business to get back the money they invest plus extra money, a **gain on investment** or a **dividend**. Governments also expect their gifts of grants and tax abatements to make a return for the people they represent. The only difference is that governments expect to be repaid in the form of the owner creating more jobs and paying more taxes. When a business succeeds and grows, it contributes to the *economic development* of an area.

Equity Capital from the Investors' View

Look at it from the investors' point of view. They have money to invest. They may lend it or put it to work by buying a share in someone's business. They do this to make money, so they want to invest in a business that will succeed and thereby provide them with returns. But of course, all businesses are not equal. Every year thousands of people start new restaurants. Every year, thousands go out of business. Of all the businesses that they could invest in, how do they choose the right one?

One way to decide is by analyzing the business's prospects. Investors want to know just how likely the business is to succeed and produce a gain. In other words, they want to know the business's **risk**. Unfortunately, they can't see risk directly, so they have to look at other things that are associated with risk. Investors know that some of their investments will fail. They just don't know exactly which ones. To protect themselves from losing everything, they **diversify**—invest in several businesses so that the ones that do succeed provide gains that more than offset the losses from those that don't.

risk
The level of probability that an investment will not produce expected gains.

diversify
To invest in multiple investments of differing risk profiles for the purpose of reducing overall investment risk.

Thus to get money from other people, you've got to show them that your business probably can make gains for them. Of course, you're not the only one looking for those investment dollars. You have to convince them that your business is a better place for their dollars than some other business. You do this by promising high enough gains. The minimum potential gain necessary to get someone to invest in your business depends mostly on the amount of risk they are taking by purchasing part of your business. Your investors could put their money into a bank savings account earning 2 percent, a CD earning 5 percent, or a government bond earning 3.25 percent. For these there is no risk at all.[1] Corporate bonds might offer higher rates of return, but they also offer a higher risk of default—think of Enron, WorldCom, or other corporate failures. The riskier the business investment, the higher the return investors expect. Most investors, certainly those who aren't your parents, insist that they take no risk other than the potential loss of their investment. To ensure that nothing other than their investment is at risk, they will invest only if your business is organized to limit the liability of outside owners.

To estimate how much gain they might get from investing in your business, investors consider the growth potential of your business, how long it will take for them to see a return on their investment, and the options they have to receive back the original investment and their gains.

Growth potential is a primary concern for equity investors. Equity investors buy part of a "pie" of a known size. The more slices into which the pie is cut, the smaller each slice is, unless somehow the pie can be made larger. For this reason, it is much easier to get equity financing to develop a new factory to make flexible liquid crystal displays or to produce a treatment for obesity than it is to get someone to invest in a lawn care business in a city of 50,000 people. Lawn care in a small city has a limit to its growth, but there are millions and millions of computer users and of overweight people who want to be slim.

The time required to receive gains can be a deal killer for potential investors. The longer they have to wait, the greater their risk that the business will fail. Also, all other things being equal, an investment that pays sooner is more profitable than one that pays later. Consider two simple situations. You are going to sell 25 percent of your business for $100,000. Your deal with the investor is that you will buy his or her share back at the end of one year for $150,000. In the second situation, you agree to buy back the investor's share for $150,000 in two years. Investors in the first case realize a 50 percent gain on investment, but investors in the second realize only 22 percent.[2] Waiting an extra year reduces the rate of gain by more than half.

Arrangements for paying gains to owners is an essential, but often ignored, facet of small business finance. Once more than one person owns equity in a small business, it *cannot* be a sole proprietorship. By law, lacking any specific legal business filings, it instantly becomes a general partnership. By making a legal filing, the business entity may become a limited partnership, a corporation, or a limited liability company. Regardless of what business form you choose, the issue of how to pay the owners is suddenly much more complex. Issues arise because of tax considerations, fairness to investors, and compensation for manager-owners. There is certainly no one right way to provide for returning gains to owners. It can take the form of salaries, stipends for serving on the board of directors, dividends, or stock repurchases. In those few cases in which a small business becomes a large business, equity investors often realize their gains by selling stock. Having a plan in place greatly aids in the process of acquiring outside equity capital.

Equity Capital from the Owner's View

From the point of view of an existing owner, financing with equity is (1) expensive and (2) guaranteed to create problems of control and decision making.

Equity capital is not free, as many entrepreneurs think. Suppose you sell half your business to raise capital. You have just sold half of all your future profits, half of all your future growth, half of all your future wealth. If, on the other hand, you were to borrow the money, your cost will be only the cost of acquiring the loan and making interest payments. In addition, owners of your business (even those who own only a small part) have a legal right to know how you're managing *their* business. As a matter of fact, most equity investors in small businesses insist upon having the right to inspect the accounting records *at any time they choose.* Once you accept equity investors, you will find that you'll have to keep careful records of transactions, and you'll have to make regular reports to your investors. If those investors disagree with your running of the business, they can challenge your decisions, even to the point of suing you for supposed damages, or replacing you as manager. Many, many entrepreneurs have found themselves forced out of their own businesses by minority equity investors.

Why Use Equity Capital?

There are three primary reasons to use outside equity in your business: (1) you will reduce your own exposure to financial loss, (2) your business will not have increased costs in the form of interest, and (3) bringing outside investors into an existing business can often reenergize it by providing new ideas, procedures, and processes.

Financing with Debt: Getting a Loan for Your Business

The most common source of capital for established ongoing small businesses is borrowed funds. This is the case for several reasons, including all the reasons discussed above, and the simple fact that small businesses do not have easy access to equity financing. Additionally, national, state, and local governments all encourage small business borrowing. This is done in three ways: (1) direct loans of cash, (2) guaranteeing loans made by commercial banks, and (3) reducing taxes by allowing interest to be deducted. However, when it comes to borrowing significant amounts of money, all firms are not created equal. Established businesses that have valuable assets that are separable from the owners are able to borrow more easily than are start-up or knowledge businesses.

So, where can a small business actually get loans to start and grow? As you might expect, your best source is the bank where you are currently doing business. After all, it is in the business of making loans. You are a customer. As such, you are a known commodity—you pay your bills, you keep your account balance positive, you don't bounce checks. Start where you're known.

But if your bank turns you down, you are not out of luck. In fact, in the Small Business Administration guaranteed loan programs, you *must* be turned down by a bank before you qualify. So, maybe your bank did you a favor. Having been turned down, you can apply for an SBA guaranteed loan. Through this avenue, you will still borrow from your own bank, but the SBA will guarantee the bank that if your business fails, the SBA will pay off your loan. Other sources for SBA guaranteed loans include **community development organizations**, and for small loans, *microlenders.*

A third source of SBA guaranteed loans is the numerous **small business investment companies** (SBIC). A directory of SBICs is maintained on the SBA Web site: http://www.sba.gov/aboutsba/sbaprograms/inv/inv_directory_sbic.html. All SBIC's are listed by state. Click on the "hot link" to open the appropriate list. The directory provides not only a list of active SBICs, but also an outline of the business requirements.

community development organization
An organization authorized by the SBA to make insured loans to small businesses that are expected to increase economic activity within a specific geographic area.

small business investment companies
Private businesses that are authorized to make SBA insured loans to start-ups and small businesses.

FIGURE 15.1

The Four Cs of Borrowing

Character of the managers of the business.	**Capacity** of the business to repay both principal and interest on time.
Conditions of the industry and economy in which the business operates.	**Collateral** that can be used to secure the loan.

accelerator
An organization that supports start-up technology businesses by providing inexpensive office space, a variety of support services, and resources; most accelerators are associated with universities.

You may also have access to *incubators* or **accelerators** in your area. These organizations exist solely for the purpose of facilitating the start-up and growth of new businesses. They provide advice for finding loans, and, in some cases, have the ability to make loans to member businesses.

The main things that lenders want to see before they give businesses their money are the Four Cs of Borrowing, listed here and shown in Figure 15.1:

1. Character of the managers of the business.
2. Capacity of the business to repay both principal and interest on time.
3. Conditions of the industry and economy in which the business operates.
4. Collateral that can be used to secure the loan.

No matter how you have organized your business, the bank is going to look at it as an extension of you. The simple fact is that you have the power to make decisions, good or bad, about all facets of operation regardless of its form, whether sole proprietorship, partnership, or corporation. Thus, although technically the loan may be made to the business entity, from the point of view of the lender, a loan is not made to a small business, a loan is made to the *owner* of a small business. The owner's character and business reputation are important considerations for lenders when they decide whether or not to let a business have money.

Owner character is judged largely by the owner's personal credit rating and by that of the business. All lenders want some assurance that a loan will be repaid as agreed. There are several private agencies called consumer **credit reporting agencies** (CRAs) which exist solely to collect, collate, and report the credit histories of individuals and businesses. Lenders pay a fee to join a credit agency, and then pay for each report received. Lenders also promise to provide information about you back to the agency.

credit reporting agency
A business that collects, collates, and reports information concerning an entity's use of debt.

There are four primary CRAs: Equifax, Experian, Innovis, and TransUnion. There are also many specialized agencies that provide special services for landlords, medical providers, and resellers of information who create customized reports from data acquired from the four primary CRAs.

The information collected and reported by the CRAs is limited to three areas:

- Identifying information.
- Credit information.
- Public record information.

Race, religious preference, medical history, personal lifestyle choices, political affiliation, criminal record, or anything not related to credit is prohibited from being reported. Of course, for a price, all this information can be obtained from sources other than credit reporting agencies.

Fair Credit Reporting Act
U.S. federal legislation specifying consumers' rights vis-à-vis credit reporting agencies.

The **Fair Credit Reporting Act** requires that all information reported by CRAs be accurate. However, the law does not require that CRAs independently confirm any information. It is incumbent upon you, the consumer, to obtain a copy of your credit report and to notify the CRA in writing of any inaccurate information. The CRA has 30 days in which to investigate. The CRA must also forward copies of all relevant information that you provide to the source of the inaccurate information. The source must then make its own investigation and report any inaccuracies to all nationwide CRAs.

Eventually you will get a report of the outcome of the investigation. If the information is still inaccurate, you have to send a notice of dispute to the provider. The provider does not have to change the information, but a copy of your dispute must then be included with any future credit reports.

Obtaining Your Credit Report

SKILL MODULE 15.2

Under the Fair and Accurate Credit Transactions Act consumers can request one free credit report in every 12-month period from each of the three national credit reporting agencies, Experian, Equifax, and TransUnion. You must use the toll-free telephone number, (877) 322-8228, the **https://www.annualcreditreport.com** Web site, or a special mailing address—Annual Credit Report Request Service, P.O. Box 105281, Atlanta, GA 30348-5281. You will have to supply a Social Security number and date of birth and answer a few personal questions to get instant access online. Credit agencies have up to 15 days to send out reports that are requested by phone or mail.

Use one of the methods listed here to obtain copies of your credit report. Carefully examine each report for accuracy. If you find any incorrect information, contact the CRA and have it corrected.

Commercial credit reporting agencies began in the 1830s when a silk merchant, Lewis Tappan, began to collect extensive records concerning customers of the business. Tappan eventually offered credit reports to other merchants. Through a series of mergers, Tappan's business today is known as Dun & Bradstreet (D&B).

Providers of commercial credit reports are much more entrepreneurial and less rule-bound than are CRAs. For example, Dun & Bradstreet allows businesses to self report gross sales, profits, numbers and types of customers, numbers of employees, and so on. D&B does, however, make extensive efforts to confirm the accuracy of information and also makes independent investigations of midsize to large businesses, including interviewing management.

You can create a credit file for your business with D&B by filling out an online application and paying an initial fee of $500. Once your file is established, D&B maintains it, using a sophisticated computer system to confirm accuracy. Visit http://smallbusiness.dnb.com/manage-business-credit/get-duns-details.asp.

Although D&B is the best known provider of commercial credit reports, it is by no means the sole provider. Experian provides commercial reports as well as consumer reports. Additionally, there are numerous other commercial credit reporting agencies, including National Information Bureau, Ltd, Veritax Business Information, Inc., and Fair Isaac's® Small Business Scoring, to name a few. Finally, there are industry-specific reporting agencies; for example, Seafax provides credit reports for the seafood, poultry, meat, and associated food industries.

The capacity of the business is the most important single factor for being able to borrow significant amounts of money. Your capacity to repay loans is measured primarily by two factors: profitability and cash flows from operations. **Profitability** that has been maintained over time indicates that you are an effective manager who will produce future profits to repay the borrowed money. *Cash flows from operations* that have been constant and reliable indicate that you can reliably convert profits to cash.

profit, profitability
The amount that revenues exceed expenses.

Condition of the industry and economy includes such factors as technology, competition, and economic growth. For example, right now the telecommunications industry is undergoing huge changes. Cable providers are offering telephone service, and telephone companies are offering movies. Satellite operators are adding broadband to their television and radio services. Copper wire connectors are being replaced with fiber optic cable directly into businesses and homes. Cell phones have rendered pay phones obsolete. Now is not a good time to try to raise money for a telecommunications business.

Collateral value is simply the estimated market value of the assets of your business. Tangible, long-lived assets are the best **collateral**. Auction markets for automobiles, trucks, and commercial machinery provide both a source for estimating value and an immediate market in which they can be sold.

collateral
Something of value given or pledged as security for payment of a loan; collateral may consist of financial instruments, such as stocks, bonds, and negotiable paper, or of physical goods, such as trucks, machinery, land, or buildings.

Intangible assets, other than patents, copyrights, and trademarks, are not good collateral. For example, *goodwill,* the value of a business that exceeds the sum of the value of all individual assets, cannot be sold separately from the business. The same is true of other intangibles, such as experience, education, institutional knowledge, and customer relations. These things can be very valuable, but none can be transferred to a lender to satisfy debt.

Other factors affecting debt worthiness include why you want to borrow the money and just how much money of your own is invested in the business. Lenders eagerly loan money to purchase capital equipment. After all, if you default, they will just repossess your truck and sell it to someone else. If you are willing to pay high enough interest rates, they will even lend you money to finance marketing efforts or business growth. They will not, however, lend you money to make up for financial failure. They will not loan money to finance consumption or extravagance. In fact, it is quite difficult to even borrow working capital to finance ongoing operations of all types. Also, most commercial lenders will not make a loan in an amount greater than that which, when added to existing debt, will bring the debt-to-equity ratio above 50 percent. (See discussion later in the chapter for an explanation of debt to equity.)

Gift Financing

Gift financing has a special allure. It seems to many people as if they are getting something for nothing. The impression might be that a government or a foundation hands out money that never has to be repaid, or a family member magnanimously offers a present at just the right time. It is unfortunate that anything that seems too good to be true usually is. Gift capital is often anything but free. Often it costs time and money to obtain; and it often requires time and money for accounting and reporting to the granting agency, family members, and government. There are two general sources of gift financing: one is institutional, from government agencies and foundations, and the other is personal, from family or occasionally from friends.

Institutional Gifts

The most common form of institutional gift financing is in the form of reduced taxes, either through tax abatement or in the form of a credit against taxes payable. It does seem a misnomer to call reducing the amount taken from a business a gift, but as taxes are a cash cost to businesses, reducing tax burden has the same effect as receiving that same amount of cash would have.

Farmers receive gift financing from the U.S. government in the form of direct cash payments and price subsidies for not planting crops, for planting cereal grains, apples (but not peaches), cotton,

THE THOUGHTFUL ENTREPRENEUR

When Uncle Sam Is a Soft Touch

It is hard to even begin to grasp how many government tax abatement programs exist. They are provided to businesses both large and small.

Many small businesses have taken advantage of the U.S. government's program that encourages building low-income housing and rebuilding historic structures through reduced income taxes.

The city of Kansas City, Missouri, once forgave all property tax on Trans World Airlines' aircraft overhaul facilities.

Right now, the city of San Antonio, Texas, and Bexar County agreed to forego property taxes on a new Toyota pickup truck factory. In addition, the state of Texas, Bexar County, and San Antonio together contributed over $23 million for the building of an 8-mile-long railroad spur from the main railroad line to the Toyota factory site.

The city of Albuquerque, New Mexico, arranged a three-way trade for city property which resulted in Eclipse Aviation receiving the gift of 150 acres of land. It is most unfortunate that Eclipse went out of business in 2008, after delivering 259 airplanes.

Homestead, Florida, has established an enterprise zone in which there are property tax abatements, a direct refund of sales taxes, direct credits of property tax up to $50,000, as well as tax credits for job creation. Portland, Maine, offers tax increment and tax-exempt bond financing for firms that will relocate to the area.

Provo, Utah, is spending $7 million of tax money to build a new rendering[3] plant some distance from town. The city council explained this gift by pointing out that moving the plant would remove a source of unpleasant odors from the city, while keeping the taxes from the plant, which employs several hundred people.

tobacco, and a plethora of other crops, for raising mohair goats, and for producing lamb meat and dairy products. Payments for not growing crops are made through a program called "conservation reserve payments," in which farmers contract to not plant specified plots of erosion-prone land for a specific number of years. Direct subsidies and price supports are made through numerous programs, including payments for wetlands protection.

Tax abatements are provided by state and local governments, primarily to encourage specific activities that are expected to improve blighted areas or to provide additional employment. Most governments that impose a tax on real estate have some form of tax reduction to encourage rehabilitating old dwellings, providing housing for low-income citizens, and maintaining buildings that are deemed to be historic. Tax abatements can take many forms, depending upon the type of taxes that are imposed.

tax abatement
A legal reduction in taxes by a government.

Tax credits are provided by the U.S. government and some state governments for the purpose of encouraging investment in specific types of assets, to increase economic activity in specified disadvantaged geographical areas, increase the welfare of specific groups of citizens, or support industries that are held to be of national strategic interest. Credits provided include those for empowerment zone employment, employing (American) Indians, purchasing electric automobiles, or using ethyl alcohol for fuel. The list of available tax credits and the details of how to claim them is too voluminous to reproduce in this text. Also, the credits change with each Congress, and thus any specific information would be sorely out of date by the time this text is published.

tax credits
Direct reductions in the amount of taxes that must be paid, dependent upon meeting some legal criteria.

Grants of money are available from the U.S. government, most state governments, and semiprivate and private economic development agencies. The purpose of the grants varies with the entity that makes the grant. U.S. grant programs for small business are primarily a response to political pressure brought upon Congress. The stated purpose of the grant programs is to encourage development of small businesses, thereby increasing the economic activity of the country. Various states also have grant programs. As with the federal program, the rationale for providing grants to small business is to increase economic activity, provide job growth, and provide increases in the overall standard of living of the citizens of the state.

grants
Gifts of money made to a business for a specific purpose.

Grants from governments are highly structured and require very accurate record keeping and reporting. Agencies that issue grants first publish a request for proposal (RFP) that specifies the conditions of the grant. Interested small businesses may then create a proposal, which must be submitted by the specified date and time, in the *exact* format specified. Grant proposals are then judged in a "blind" process. Winning proposals receive notification within about 30 days and funding within 6 months.

The two largest governmental grant programs that are specifically intended for small business are (1) the Small Business Innovation Research (SBIR) program and the Small Business Technology Transfer (STTR) program. These two programs require that every U.S. agency that makes research grants provide a minimum of 2 percent of its grant budget to small businesses, as defined by the SBA. Two percent may not sound like much, but in 2002, the SBIR program resulted in over $1.5 *billion* in grants made to participating small businesses. These programs are each three-phase programs. A winning proposal will initially receive about $100,000 to conduct a feasibility study, as detailed in the grant proposal. Depending upon successful completion, additional funds, which can range up into millions of dollars, are provided for stage II and stage III activities.

Grant programs vary widely among the states. As with federal programs, the agency that provides the grant will publish a request for proposal. Proposals are competitively judged, and only the best written proposals, which meet each and every requirement of the RFP ever receive funding. Accurate record keeping and timely reports are essential to maintain the right to use the grant money.

Finding SBIR Grants

SKILL MODULE 15.3

What kind of business are you interested in? Do you have any new ideas or procedures for this business that might lead to better ways of solving problems of health, national security, threats of terrorism, or any other area in which the U.S. government has an interest?

If you do, there is probably an SBIR grant for you.

Assume that you have come up with an idea that might result in stopping would-be terrorists at airports outside the United States. Your idea, if it works, will stop terrorists from getting to the United States in the first place. Do a Google search using the search terms: SBIR grants "national security."

Follow the leads returned by Google (more than 10,000) to identify agencies and programs that will provide funds through SBIR grants for ideas that might help national security.

1. Write a report of your findings to be presented to your class.
2. Use the skill you have now developed to find an SBIR grant that would apply to a business that you are actually interested in starting.

economic development agency
A government organization that works to increase economic activity in the form of job opportunities within a specific geographic area.

foundation
An institution to which private wealth is contributed and from which private wealth is distributed for public purposes.

Economic Development Agency (EDA) grants are much less common than are those from general governments. Most economic development agencies prefer to provide loans rather than providing equity capital or gift capital. However, from time to time, EDAs will either provide direct grants or will assist small business owners in obtaining grants from other agencies.

Grants from foundations are rarely made to for-profit businesses. **Foundations** exist for the purpose of addressing some identified social need that cannot be adequately met by market forces. The Ewing Marion Kauffman Foundation supports *education* and *research* concerning entrepreneurship and small business. The Ford Foundation supports the arts, including public television programs. The Rotary Foundation supports efforts to eradicate hunger and polio worldwide. All these foundations were founded by successful entrepreneurs and business managers, but they do not specifically support the start up, expansion, or operation of for-profit enterprises. Rather, their (and those of about 30,000 other private foundations) missions clearly state that grants are made to nonprofit organizations.

However, occasionally private foundations will make grants to for-profit businesses, *if the purpose of the grant is to address some goal of the foundation.* If your business is such that it addresses a pernicious social problem, then you may be able to find private foundation grant funding for specific, limited projects.

Personal Gifts

While the type of gifts governments and foundations offer are relatively consistent, stable, and publicly known, the forms of personal gifts are as varied as human imagination and need can make them. Remember from Chapter 14 that not just money has value; goods and services can provide tremendous value to a start-up business. The most popular forms of gifts are shown in Exhibit 15.1.

Personal gift financing is tremendously popular. In the Panel Study of Income Dynamics,[4] fully one-third of the firms reported having unpaid labor contributed by family members. In business plan classes, the same one out of three ratio of personal gifts to start-ups in general is a fairly common occurrence. These gifts range dramatically in size, but the commonality of personal gifts as a major source of funding for start-ups is fairly well known.[5]

Gift giving seems so easy and straightforward that it is hard to imagine how complex it really is—for the giver and the recipient, as well as the business. Consider gifts from the standpoint of the recipient and then the giver.

You are trying to get your business off the ground, and your favorite uncle offers to provide you with start-up capital. Not just any start-up capital, not an investment, not a loan. He is going to *give* you that boost that you need to get into business. It is an entrepreneur's dream—capital without any strings.

Do you take the money? Not so fast. The simple fact is that although Freud may have believed that "sometimes a cigar is just a cigar"[6] you can bet that a gift is *always* much, much more than just a gift. Gifts are loaded with special meanings and hidden purposes. Robert Cialdini wrote that gifts "create and cement alliances, allegiances, and partnerships."[7] Are you ready to enter into an alliance or partnership with your beloved uncle?

Accepting money from family members and friends entails some real risks. That favorite uncle might really mean it when he says that he is *giving* you start-up capital. But gifts like this have a

EXHIBIT 15.1

Forms of Personal Gifts

Cash—always useful, but also the gift most likely to have tax implications.
Picking up the tab—when someone buys something on behalf of your business and lets you benefit from it.
Accelerated cash-outs—where you might be given the funds for your business from an account your family set up for your future education or first home. Some cash-outs come when family or friends cash out their retirements or home (often via taking out a mortgage).
Free use—your family has an empty storefront, apartment, van, car, or other useful product which they let you use for free, or at a severely reduced price, for your business.
Free work—you get family or friends to help you out in the business for free, or for pizzas and drinks, or for wages significantly below minimum wage. This is sometimes called **unpaid labor**.
Overpayment—where family or friends "hire" you at higher than market rates, to help you generate cash for your business. A variant of this is **favored status** or **sweetheart deals** where family or friends give you contracts to help you fund your business, instead of giving their work to the most qualified candidate.
Forgiveness—where family or friends give up on collecting debts you owe them, so you can use the money for the business. A variant of this is **deferral,** where the repayment of debts is delayed until the business is doing well.
Piggybacking—where family or friends let you add (i.e., piggyback) your purchases with theirs in order to get lower prices.

nasty way of morphing into very real expectations that you may quickly come to hate. Meanings, especially in spoken messages, are slippery little devils. Your uncle may well be saying "gift" but thinking "loan," or "investment." If you are successful, you may suddenly find that the "gift" has now transformed (at least in your uncle's mind) into something very different. So here you stand—you *accepted* a gift, but your uncle *gave* you a loan.

Lawsuits are made of just such differences of opinion.

Accepting gifts is difficult for many people. Especially when the gift is substantial. Before you accept your uncle's offer, you should examine your own feelings. Can you accept a gift? Or do you have some secret plan that you will repay the money when you become successful? If you do not like being beholden to anyone, you probably should think twice about accepting an outright gift. Taking one most likely will lead to guilty feelings and resentment.

No need to immediately refuse your uncle's offer, but you should be absolutely certain that both you and he understand just what is being given and just what is expected in return.

Now turn the example on its head. Assume now that you are the uncle who is going to give a gift of cash to your favorite niece to start her business.

Do you just write out a check and forget it? If you wish to keep your niece as a favorite, you probably shouldn't. Giving a gift is risky, just as is receiving one. Any gifts that you make had better be equitable among those who expect to receive from you. It is a simple fact that brothers, sisters, nieces, and nephews all expect to be treated fairly by their parents, grandparents, aunts, and uncles. Overtly favor one heir, and you will trigger resentment in all the others.

Giving a gift also has tax implications. Currently, any gift that exceeds $13,000 may be subject to U.S. Gift Taxes. Depending upon the size of the gift, and your own situation, current gift taxes can be as high as 47 percent of the amount given. So if you are planning to finance your niece's start-up with $500,000, you'll probably need some creative financial planning to avoid the tax implications.

You should carefully consider just why you want to make this gift. Perhaps you are one of those very rare people who are true Santa Clauses: You get real satisfaction from giving away your wealth. This is unlikely, however. Komter and Vollebergh showed that gifts given to extended kin are usually made because of feelings of obligation and rarely because of feelings of affection.[8] Probably, you are expecting to receive gratitude. If so, you'll more than likely be disappointed. Or do you think that your niece's business idea is the next Microsoft and that your support will result in untold wealth? In this case, you should not make your support a gift. Structure it as an investment in her business—make it a loan or a purchase of stock.

Given the many problems of gift giving, should you change your mind about supporting your niece's new business?

No, but you should understand exactly what you are giving, and what you expect in return. You should also be sure that your niece also understands.

For both of you to be certain that you agree, you should:

● Even when gifts are given to help a family member or friend's business, common sense and clear communication are essential. Make sure both parties understand and assent to what exactly is being given, under which conditions, and with what kind, if any, of repayment plan.

1. **Put your agreement into writing.** As is said in Mexico, "Words walk. Paper talks." This has the same message as the saying, "Oral agreements are just as valuable as the paper they're written on!" There simply is no better way to be certain that everyone understands a transaction than to write it out, then have each party read, sign, and date the document. When disagreements arise later, the written agreement provides a permanent, immutable record of your original intentions.
2. **If it is a gift, have the agreement specifically say so.** "This is a gift, freely given between uncle (grantor) and you (recipient). No repayment is expected, and none will be accepted."
3. **If it is a loan, have the agreement specify the exact interest and payment terms.** A good idea from the point of view of the recipient is to make repayment a percentage of positive cash flows. Ideally, payments will be made either (a) until the principal amount plus accrued interest has been paid or (b) until the giver has received a specified return on the original amount. In the real world, loans between family members often go unpaid. Be clear concerning the circumstances under which the loan will be forgiven.
4. **If it is an equity investment, consider nonvoting stock.** One common problem with family and friends as equity investors is that they want to have a say in the management of your business. This may be fine if they have appropriate talents and experience. It can be a kiss of death if they just want to meddle. Nonvoting stock provides the opportunity for capital gains, but pretty much precludes interference in business operations.

What Type of Financing Is Right for Your Business?

LO3 Determine the best type of financing for your business.

Consider the simplest case in which a small business owner has the alternatives of using personal equity funding or borrowing funds. The business may be 100 percent capitalized by either equity or debt, or any mix of equity and debt. Equity capital costs are estimated to be 20 percent per year—the investors expect $200 in interest or dividends for every $1,000 invested in the business. Debt capital costs are estimated to be a net of 6 percent after tax, or for every $1,000 borrowed, the entrepreneur owes the bank $60 a year (plus the $1,000 will need to be paid back as agreed).

If the owner chooses to use a capital mix of 70 percent equity and 30 percent debt, the weighted average **cost of capital** is approximately 16 percent. At a 50–50 mix of equity and capital, the **weighted average cost of capital** is 13 percent and at 30 to 70 percent equity, and debt is approximately 10 percent. The more debt that is included in the capital mix, the lower the weighted average cost will be. The lower your cost of capital, the more profits you can keep for yourself. The more money your business generates for its owners, the more the business is worth. Thus, firm value is inversely related to cost of capital at any level of operations.

cost of capital
The percentage cost of obtaining future funds.

weighted average cost of capital (WAC)
The expected average future cost of funds.

In reality, you will never have such alternatives. Although you may choose to use 100 percent personal funds for equity capital, no lender will agree to loan 100 percent. In fact, most lenders, without having some sort of guarantee such as collateral or Small Business Administration insurance, will not lend an amount that exceeds the amount you have invested. Even with guarantees, as the amount of debt increases, so does the risk of default. Because of the added risk, lenders will demand higher rates of interest for those later loans. For these reasons, the cost of both equity and debt capital changes as their relative percentages of total capital change.

A more realistic case is a small business that is 100 percent funded from the owner's own personal wealth. In this case, the value of the firm can be described as the amount of profit divided by the owner's cost of capital. For now, assume that your business is producing $100,000 per year and that the cost of capital is 20 percent. The value of the business is $500,000 ($100,000 cash flow divided by 20 percent). Now suppose you have an opportunity to purchase a productive asset which will return 20 percent per year for its life, such as a computer-controlled 5-axis milling machine. The asset costs $50,000, which you decide to borrow at 8 percent interest. Firm value will increase. Profits will increase to $106,000 [$100,000 + ($50,000 × .20) − ($50,000 × .08)]. The weighted average cost of capital will be 19 percent ($500,000 at 20 percent plus the additional investment of $50,000 at 8 percent). The value of the business is now $560,600.

A few weeks later, you have an opportunity to purchase another asset which will cost $50,000 and will also produce 20 percent returns. Again, you can borrow the money, but because of the added debt and greater probability of default, the lender requires 10 percent interest. Making the same set of calculations shows that profits will now be $111,000. The weighted average cost of capital is 18 percent, and the value of the business is now $611,000.

Notice that the first investment increased the value of the firm by $60,600 (12 percent), while the second investment increased the value of the firm by only $50,400 (9 percent). As debt increases as a percentage of total investment (called **financial leverage**), *the value of the firm increases at a decreasing rate.* At some debt-to-equity ratio, the firm value peaks and then begins to decrease as added debt is incurred. You may make a series of such calculations, each time increasing the interest rate to convince yourself. You will initially see firm value increase. It will eventually reach a maximum value, and then start to decrease as debt and the cost of debt increases.

financial leverage
A measure of the amount of debt relative to total investment.

Few, if any, small business owners, however, even attempt to estimate the **optimum capital structure** of their business. Making such calculations takes too much time for the value provided. If you understand the concept that having debt in your capital structure works to increase your profits and you know that interest rates do not increase smoothly as financial leverage increases, you can find that level of debt that works for you.

optimum capital structure
The ratio of debt to equity that provides the maximum level of profits.

A similar argument holds for obtaining outside equity investors. The difficulties and costs of obtaining equity capital are so great that most owners of small businesses don't even try. A study reported in 2003[9] found that so few small businesses raised capital by selling equity to outsiders that no statistical analysis could be done. Given these facts, it is reasonable for you to approximate cost of capital by examining only a few specific debt-to-equity ratios which are reasonable for your business and which you expect to persist for significant periods of time.

The owners and managers of small businesses are quite diverse. Entrepreneurs come from all social classes. They have different levels of education ranging from no formal schooling to those with advanced degrees. People of all major religions, of every race, and from every part of the world are represented among small business owners. As you would expect, such a diverse group of people have very diverse attitudes toward work, toward investing, toward management.

Some people gleefully jump out of airplanes; others are determined to "keep one foot on the ground." Business owners similarly differ in their response to financial risk. A few seek risk, thriving on the pressure of attempting to make the big strike. Most prefer to avoid business risk to the extent possible. In academic terms, some business owners are *risk seeking,* although most small business owners are *risk averse.* The personal preferences of each owner of a small business affect choices concerning financial risk, debt, sharing of ownership, and interaction with private and governmental foundations and agencies. Because of this, the optimal capital structure for one entrepreneur may well be anathema to another. Each owner of a small business must find the levels of equity, debt, and financial risk with which he or she is comfortable.

Financial risk is the probability of financial loss. Business opportunities, projects, and assets that have a greater chance of producing a loss are considered more risky than those that have a smaller chance. In a very real sense, risk is synonymous with uncertainty. If you purchase a 30-day

financial risk
Uncertainty of returns; the probability of losing money.

FIGURE 15.2

Interaction among Profitability, Control, and Risk

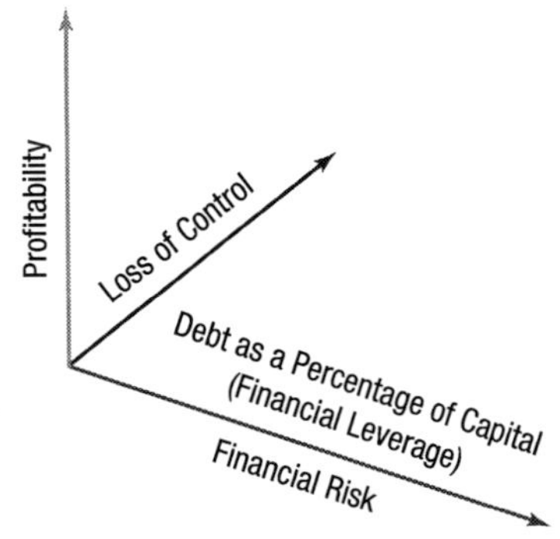

U.S. Treasury bond, the return is certain. On the thirtieth day the government will issue a check for the amount of the bond plus interest. Because the government has the power to create money, there is no uncertainty and thus no risk of financial loss. If, on the other hand, you use the same amount of money to invest in a business, the return is very uncertain. You might succeed greatly or the business might fail and you lose your entire investment.

Borrowing money increases financial risk. In effect, borrowing money for a business is very much like selling the business to an investor and simultaneously buying back an option to repurchase the business on specific terms of payment. If the terms of payment are not met, the lender has the right to keep the business. The lender may enforce this right through either repossession if business assets were pledged as collateral, or involuntary bankruptcy, mediated by the court system. Payments on debt must be made as agreed without regard to the cash position of the business.

Selling equity in the business provides neither the opportunity to repurchase nor the obligation to make payments to owners. If the business does not provide sufficient profits and cash flows, an equity investor must accept the situation and hope that future operations will be profitable.

So why should you borrow, if doing so increases the probability of financial loss? Borrowing money for capital investment provides two benefits: (1) Borrowing enhances the potential for higher rates of return for the owners. (2) Borrowing allows the owners to keep a greater level of control of the business. For these reasons, the majority of small business owners prefer to borrow over accepting outside equity investment.[10] The interaction of the effects of choosing between equity and debt capital results in a small business owner having to compromise among the levels of potential profits, financial risk, and control of the business. This is depicted graphically in Figure 15.2.

Borrowing increases potential profits by (1) lowering the weighted average cost of capital and (2) providing capital funds that allow the business to consider additional opportunities. To illustrate how this works, consider the following:

- Nucleodyne, LLC, is a biopharmaceutical start-up that owns intellectual property rights to a protein that will treat male pattern baldness. The science is sound, and the molecule grows hair on laboratory mice.
- The founders of the firm have already invested $1 million.
- To complete trials on human beings, the company must raise an additional $1 million. The owners have an agreement with a venture capital group to provide the money in return for 40 percent of the equity of the business.
- Alternatively, the money may be borrowed from a local investment bank at 10 percent annual interest.
- Based on projections of sales and expenses, the company expects to realize a profit of $300,000. Using these facts, compare the balance sheet and income statements in Figure 15.3.

It is immediately apparent that the business makes a greater profit if all capital is equity capital. What is not so apparent is the effect on the owners of the business. When investments are made, they are not evaluated by the number of dollars that are returned. Rather, investments are evaluated on the *percentage of return* that is realized. In this case, compare the **return on equity** (that is, the percentage of return on the amount actually owned) for each of the original founders of the business and new equity investors as we can see in Table 15.3.

return on equity
The ratio of profits to owner investment in a business.

FIGURE 15.3

Effect of Financing Sources on Financial Results for Nucleodyne, LLC

EFFECT OF FINANCING SOURCES UPON FINANCIAL RESULTS

100% Equity Financing		50–50 Debt-to-Equity Financing	
Balance Sheet			
Total assets	$2,000,000	Total assets	$2,000,000
Debt	0	Debt	$1,000,000
Equity	$2,000,000	Equity	$1,000,000
Total of debt and equity	$2,000,000	Total of debt and equity	$2,000,000
Income Statement			
Operating income	$300,000	Operating income	$300,000
Interest expense	0	Interest expense	100,000
Net income	$300,000	Net income	$200,000

If the *original* owners solely use their own funds, then they will realize a return of only 15 cents on each dollar invested. If they sell 40 percent of the business to outside investors, the *original* owners will realize 18 cents on the dollar (60% of $300,000 divided by $ 1,000,000). If, however, they borrow the additional funds, then they realize a 20 percent return on their investment. The total original owners' return on each dollar invested in the business is one-third greater if the needed capital is borrowed than if the business is 100 percent financed by owners' personal funds.

This analysis, of course, does beg the question, "If the owners have the additional personal funds, why not invest them into the business because the total profit realized will be greater?" There are two reasons that making the additional investment might not be the best alternative. First, obtaining equity investment from others reduces the potential loss for any single investor. Second, it is often possible to borrow at interest rates substantially lower than the opportunity cost of using the business owners' own resources. For example, you may have money invested in an IRA, 401(k), or other tax-sheltered retirement fund. Suppose your retirement is earning near the long-term market average of 10 percent. Interest rates for borrowing are currently about 8 percent. If you take money from your retirement funds, you are giving up a 10 percent tax-free gain. On the other hand, interest on money borrowed for your business is deductible for tax purposes. If you are in the 25 percent tax bracket, you will, in effect, pay interest of only 6 percent [(.08 × (1 − tax rate of .25)]. Thus, as a rule, even if you have enough money to finance your business solely with equity, you still should consider borrowing in order to get the greatest total profits.

TABLE 15.3 Owners' Return on Equity in Three Business Situations

$$\text{Owners' Return on Equity (ROE)} = \frac{\text{Net Income}}{\text{Owners' Equity Investment}}$$

Alternative 1 Use Personal Funds for Capital		Alternative 2 Issue Stock for 40% Equity		Alternative 3 Borrow Capital Funds	
Net income	$300,000	Net income	$300,000	Net income	$200,000
Original owners' equity	$2,000,000	Original owners' equity	$1,000,000	Original owners' equity	$1,000,000
New owners' equity	0	New owners' equity	$1,000,000	New owners' equity	N.A.
Original owners' ROE =	15%	Original owners' ROE =	18%	Original owners' ROE =	20%
New owners' ROE =	N.A.	New owners' ROE =	12%	New owners' ROE =	N.A.

Control issues arise under both alternatives of issuing equity to outsiders or borrowing funds. When outside investors acquire equity, they also acquire some level of influence over the operations and strategy of the firm. In the example above, Nucleodyne gave up ownership of 40 percent of the firm. The original owners retain 60 percent ownership. This provides majority voting control only so long as the original owners vote as a bloc. Should disputes arise, it is quite possible, depending upon the number of owners and their percentage of ownership, that disgruntled stockholders could form a coalition and take control of the firm from the original founders. Alternatively, disgruntled minority owners may sue majority owners. For these reasons, many owners of small businesses are loath to sell any ownership shares. They prefer to accept the added financial risk of borrowing rather than deal with stockholders.

Borrowing capital, however, is not without its own issues of control. Lenders have to trust your management to operate the business efficiently, generating sufficient cash flow to meet the repayment terms of the loan. It is common, therefore, for lenders to require borrowers to provide regular documentation of the financial condition of the business. Many banks require that a copy of each year's income tax return, income statement, and balance sheet be furnished during the term of the loan. Loan contracts may also impose restrictions on the operation of the business, such as requiring that a specific minimum net worth be maintained, a specific debt-to-equity ratio not be exceeded, no dividends be paid to stockholders, executive salaries not exceed a specified amount, no capital assets be acquired or disposed of without the concurrence of the lender, and so on. These types of restrictions, called *loan covenants,* can seriously limit management's freedom to operate the business and can make taking on shareowners seem like less of a burden. It could also make do-it-yourself funding more attractive.

Financial Management for the Life of Your Business

Tools for Financial Management

Financial management requires that you have some method to measure and compare your financial position and financial results. Your financial position is reflected on your balance sheet, your financial results on your income statement. The problem is how to interpret the information on these two reports.

As with any analysis, you must have something to compare with your position and results. The obvious comparisons are (1) with your planned position and results (your master budget), (2) with prior years' position and results, and (3) with the position and results of other firms. The difficulty is in how to understand the comparison. Suppose last year you had a net business profit of $50,000 and this year your profit was $55,000. Did you do well in the current year? You did make 10 percent more this year than last. But it is often misleading to compare dollars to dollars for a financial result. You did not do well for the year if you invested an additional $100,000 into your business: Your return on your added investment is only 5 percent: added income / added investment = 5,000 / 100,000 = .05.

For these reasons, most financial comparisons are made using ratios. You made $55,000 in profit. You have a competitor who also made a net profit of $55,000. So, were the two of you equally effective business managers? Perhaps so, perhaps not. You made the same profit, but what was your respective inputs to the business? Suppose you had $110,000 invested in your business. Your competitor has $550,000 invested. Your return on investment is $55,000 / 110,000, or 50 percent. Your competitor's return is $55,000 / 550,000, or 10 percent. It would certainly seem from this analysis that you are the better business manager.

There are four broad categories of financial ratios: (1) Activity ratios, (2) Profitability ratios, (3) Liquidity ratios, and (4) Leverage ratios. Activity ratios measure how productive a particular asset is in producing sales activity. Profitability ratios measure management effectiveness in creating wealth from sales and from invested funds. Liquidity ratios measure the business's ability to pay debts and expenses that are due in the current accounting period. Leverage ratios measure the relative risk that a business setback could cause bankruptcy. Commonly used ratios are explained in Table 15.4. The three most commonly used ratios are Return on Investment (ROI),

TABLE 15.4 Common Ratios for Financial Management Using Ratios to Analyze the Income Statement

Ratio Name	Interpretation	Decision Criterion	Formula
Activity ratios	Measures of how productive a particular asset was in producing sales activity		
Asset turnover ratio	Measures how efficiently a business uses all its assets to produce sales	A higher ratio is better than a lower ratio	Net Sales Revenue / Average Total Assets (Beginning assets + ending assets) / 2
Accounts receivable turnover ratio	Measures the frequency with which receivables are converted to cash	Higher turnover provides faster access to cash that can be used in the business	Net Credit Sales / Average Net Accounts Receivable
Inventory turnover ratio	Indicates how quickly inventory is sold and thus the relative efficiency of both the sales and purchasing functions	Higher turnover is preferred	Cost of Goods Sold / Average Merchandise Inventory
Average holding period	Indicates the same as inventory turnover, but is easier to understand	Shorter period is preferred	365 Days / Inventory Turnover Ratio
Profitability ratios	Measures management effectiveness in creating wealth from sales and from invested funds		
Gross margin ratio	Measures the percentage of sales revenue available to pay operating costs and to provide profits after paying for inventory	Higher is preferred	Gross Margin / Sales Revenue
Profit margin ratio, also called return on sales (ROS)	Measures management's effectiveness in managing all costs relative to sales	Higher is preferred	Net Income / Sales Revenue
Return on equity	Measures management's effectiveness in using investor funds to provide profits	Higher is preferred	Net Income—Preferred Stock Dividends Declared / Average Common Stockholders' Equity
Return on assets	Measures management's effectiveness in using the assets of the business to provide profits	Higher is preferred	Net Income / Average Total Assets
Return on investments (ROI) (Discussed on pp. 519–521)	Measures management's effectiveness in using the invested capital of the business to provide profits	Higher is preferred	Net Income / Average Investment
Earnings per share	Measures profitability per share investment	Examined over time, a trend of increasing per share earnings is preferred	Net Income—Preferred Stock Dividends Declared / Weighted Average Common Stock Outstanding
Liquidity ratios	Measures the business's ability to pay debts and expenses that are due in the current accounting period		

TABLE 15.4 (Continued)

Ratio Name	Interpretation	Decision Criterion	Formula
Current ratio (Discussed on p. 413)	Measures how much money can be made available to pay obligations within the fiscal year	Higher ratio is preferred	$\frac{\text{Current Assets}}{\text{Current Liabilities}}$
Acid test or Quick ratio	Measure of how much money can be made available very quickly to pay obligations within the fiscal year	Higher ratio is preferred	$\frac{\text{Current Assets} - (\text{Inventories} + \text{Prepaid Assets})}{\text{Current Liabilities}}$
Leverage ratios	Measures that indicate the relative risk that a business setback could cause bankruptcy		
Debt to assets ratio	Measures the extent to which the business can meet its obligations for the long haul	A lower ratio indicates greater solvency. A greater ratio indicates increased business risk	$\frac{\text{Total Liabilities}}{\text{Total Assets}}$
Debt to equity ratio	Measures the extent to which the business can meet its obligations for the long haul	A lower ratio indicates greater solvency. A greater ratio indicates increased business risk	$\frac{\text{Total Liabilities}}{\text{Total Owners' Equity}}$
Times interest earned	Measures the risk of being forced into bankruptcy for not meeting required interest payments	Higher is preferred	$\frac{\text{Operating Income before Interest and Income Tax}}{\text{Interest Expense}}$

Current Ratio, and Debt to Equity Ratio. The value of these ratios for management depends to a large extent on the type of business you are conducting and the stage of your business in the business life cycle.

The ratios are the key way businesses are evaluated. You have seen many of these key ratios in reports from BizStats.com, BizMincr.com, and the Risk Management Association *Annual Statement Studies* mentioned in Chapters 7 and 8. Sources like those can provide important comparisons to help you determine if your key ratios are better or worse than the norms for your industry. While you are in the start-up phase, there can be considerable volatility in your business, and looking over a month or two's results can lead to confusing results using ratios. That is why for start-ups ratios are usually based on annual figures, or at least a six-month period.

In addition, the kinds of ratios that add important information to your business decision making will change as the firm matures. As we have said, initially your concerns are less with profitability and more with having enough cash on hand to meet your immediate needs (what we call the "short term"). That is why initially Liquidity Ratios are the most important to you. As your firm gets past its initial trial-and-error period and develops its standard operating procedures, Activity Ratios help tell you if your use of the firm's assets in those standard operating procedures is giving your firm the kind of results it needs to be successful.

As the firm reaches its break-even point, profits become a reality, and Profitability Ratios become increasingly important to the firm. At this point, Leverage Ratios also become more important because they look at the longer-term success of the firm, as well as its ability to weather threats leading to bankruptcy. Table 15.4 provides the major financial ratios, and tells you how they are computed and interpreted.

financial management
A set of theories and techniques used to optimize the receipt and use of capital assets.

L04 Describe the differing needs for financial management at each stage of business life.

Financial Management for Start-Up

During the start-up phase of a small business the primary **financial management** need is to obtain sufficient funds to pay for equipment, buildings, inventory, and indeed, all the costs of starting and running a business. Generally, start-up businesses have a very limited ability to obtain funds from outside sources. Necessary funds for start-ups therefore are usually obtained through a mixture of the founders' personal resources, personal credit worthiness, and internally generated cash flows. Outsiders who provide funding during the start-up phase of a small business are often referred to as "3-F investors," that is, "friends, family, and fools." The emphasis of financial management at this stage is to obtain needed funds and to conserve scarce cash.

Figure 15.4 shows the forms of financing available to small businesses. According to the SBA, there is a pecking order of popular funding sources from most available to least.[11] Owner's capital is the most widely available source, while loans from commercial-grade lending institutions such as banks are the least available. Loan and finance companies are more likely sources of financing than banks because these lenders are "motivated" by the payoff from high-interest-rate loans. Figure 15.4 shows that the 3-Fs and trade credit are also fairly popular sources for funds. Once the firm gets going, a whole other source of financing becomes available as the owner uses the profits or cash generated by the business to pay for growth.

One other factor to consider in start-ups is the power of combined resources. Often solo entrepreneurs face greater pressure to use their own money in a start-up situation than do start-ups done by teams. In the Panel Study of Entrepreneurial Dynamics, teams generally reported having greater debt financing available for use at the time of start up.[12] Figure 15.5 shows from where the initial funding for team and solo start-ups comes. Solo entrepreneurs could raise only 47 percent of their start-up funds using debt, while teams could raise over 62 percent from debt sources. This means that solo entrepreneurs are more dependent on their own equity and that of the 3-F investors.

One small but important and growing source of external financing is the business angel. Angels are individuals who routinely invest in small businesses. They are often **accredited investors**[13] which is a term coined by the SEC to define an investor sophisticated enough to make (and know how to

accredited investors
The SEC's term for individuals with a net worth greater than $1 million or a personal annual income of at least $200,000 in each of the two most recent years, who are therefore qualified to make private equity investments in businesses.

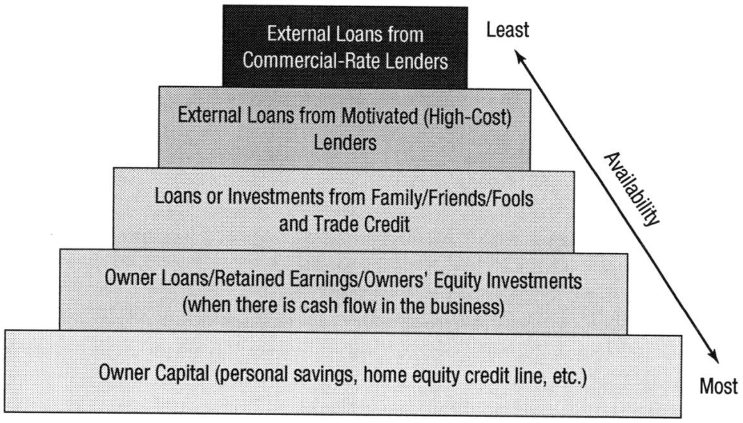

FIGURE 15.4

The Pecking Order of Funding Sources for New Firms

Source: Adapted from Charles Ou and George W. Haynes, "Uses of Equity Capital by Small Firms—Findings from the Surveys of Small Business Finances (for 1993 & 1998)." Presented at the 14th Annual Conference on Entrepreneurial Finance and Business Ventures at the De Paul University, Chicago, Illinois, on April 30–May 2, 2003, http://www.sba.gov/advo/stats/wkp03co.pdf, and from correspondence with Dr. Ou.

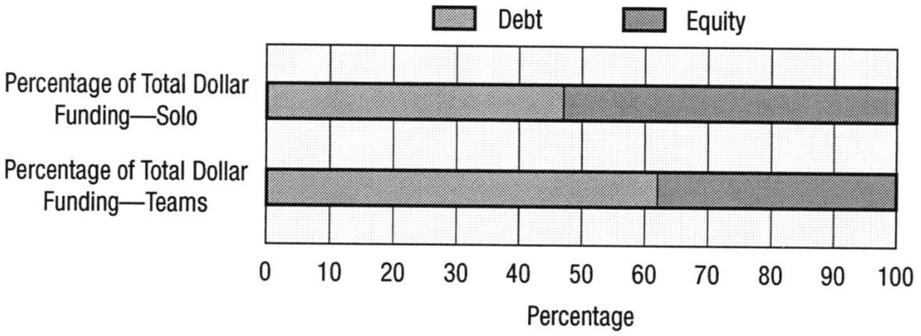

FIGURE 15.5

Use of Debt and Equity in Start-Ups from the PSED

Source: Adapted from Michael Stouder and Bruce Kirchhoff, "Funding the First Year of Business," in William B. Gartner, Kelly G. Shaver, Nancy M. Carter, and Paul D. Reynolds, (eds.), *Handbook of Entrepreneurial Dynamics: The Process of Business Creation* (Thousand Oaks, CA: Sage, 2004), p. 368.

TABLE 15.5 Types of Angel Investment

	Individual Angel	Angel Network	Angel Fund
Ease of Finding Angels	Hard to find	Formal networks public so easy to find; small private networks hard to find	Publicly known, so easy to find
Legal Form	Private individual	Formal networks, corporation; informal networks vary	Corporation
Source of Funds	Invests own money	Each angel invests their own money	Fund invests on angels' behalf
Typical Size of Investment	$50–100K	$50–$250K	$50–$500K
Geographic Proximity Preferences	Very close proximity is preferred	Very close proximity is preferred. May invest remotely via syndicate	Very close proximity is preferred. May invest remotely via syndicate
Why Invest?	Equity growth and personal interest	Equity growth and personal interest	Equity growth, sometimes regional development
Reporting Requirements	Varies by individual	Varies, set by investing angels	Formal, set by the fund
Involvement Level and Method	Low to extremely high; informal	Low to extremely high; informal	Low to extremely high; more formal
Angels Exit Expectation	Often unplanned, Trade sale	Cash-out when firm bought or VCs invest	Cash-out when firm bought or VCs invest

Parts of this table were adapted from Dirk De Clercq, Vance Fried, Oskari Lehtonen, and Harry J. Sapienza, "An Entrepreneur's guide to the venture capital galaxy," *The Academy of Management Perspectives, 20*, 2006, pp. 90–112.

correctly make) a major investment in a business. Accredited investors are millionaires in terms of assets they own (not counting their house), and have substantial annual incomes. They are a popular source of funding for cash-intensive firms at the earliest stages—seed and start-up. For a long time, most angels usually operated as individuals, but recently more and more angels have banded together into two kinds of groups—networks and funds.[14] These are compared in Table 15.5.

Angel networks are groups of accredited investors who operate together to prospect for investments. Usually the decision to invest in a business rests with each individual network member. The advantage to the network members is having a greater chance to see good investment opportunities, as well as having a group of potential co-investors and sources of needed expertise. These same reasons lie behind the creation of angel funds, but in funds the angels put in an amount to the fund, and the fund invests. Some of these angels funds look and operate a lot like venture capital funds, with professional staffs and elaborate reporting procedures. Others are member-managed, and are more varied in their approach to individual investments.

Angel networks can be informal, consisting of a group of friends or colleagues who help each other find businesses to invest in. These informal networks are very hard to find unless you have personal contacts to the wealthy individuals who are eligible to make up an angel network. Formal angel networks are generally more public, and angel funds are also easily found. The most complete directory of angel networks and funds is maintained by the Angel Capital Association (www.angelcapitalassociation.org).

Whether an individual, a network, or a fund, the interests of angels are the same. They invest first in order to make money, and then for other reasons. In order to protect their investment, they will invariably require such things as board membership and the business being incorporated so they can own shares of stock. This protection will also extend to the business's next stage, when you need even more money. If the angels cannot put more money into the business, new investors are needed.

Typically, new investors will want to dilute the ownership of the previous owners, including the angels, so that the new investment gets the best terms. This can cause fights between the original angel investors and the new investors. The resolution of these are often complex, involving advanced financial instruments like warrants. By the time these issues occur, you should be relying on

THE THOUGHTFUL ENTREPRENEUR

DIRECT PUBLIC OFFERINGS[15]

While initial public offerings (IPOs) are limited to those few start-ups with billions of dollars in potential sales and a powerful start-up team, there are other types of public offerings more accessible to more conventional types of small businesses. They are called direct public offerings or DPOs. These can be used for raising equity by selling stock (for C-corporations) or membership units (for LLCs), or for raising debt by selling a note (also known as a bond). There are four forms of DPO: Section 504 or SB-1 offerings (for under $1 million), a 505 offering (for up to $5 million), the more complex 506 or SB-2 offering (for more than $1 million), and the still more complex Small Corporate Offering Registration (SCOR) program for up to $1 million. These are designed for selling securities nationwide and over the Internet. There is a fifth DPO limited to sales within only one state (i.e., the entrepreneur offering the DPO and the investor both live in the same state) and is called an Intrastate, or Rule 147, Offering.

All five offerings depend on the creation of a private placement memorandum (a specialized type of business plan discussed in Chapter 8), a subscription agreement, and for a debt offering a promissory note. All five also require government filings, sometimes with the federal SEC, often with your own state's security regulations office (a good directory of state offices is given at the North American Securities Administrators Association Web site—**www.nasaa.org**—search the site for its "Directory of Securities Laws"). Not enough small businesses use this approach, but it is also one that requires involving a lawyer to make sure the filing is done correctly.

your own attorneys and accountants to help make sure your business gets the money it needs and you keep the power you need to run the business.

There is a world of debt and equity techniques available to the small business, with exotic sounding names like PIPEs and Regulation D 504s (for example, see the Thoughtful Entrepreneur: Direct Public Offerings). The types of investment vehicles given in Table 15.1 and Figure 15.4 just scratch the surface. However, virtually all of these are advanced financial techniques, and should only be approached with the support of a good lawyer specialized in small business financing, and the backup of a good accountant, since the accounting and financial record-keeping requirements for all of these advanced techniques are rigorous.

To be successful at using advanced financing techniques, the start-up usually requires a high-potential business idea, a solid and experienced start-up team, a professional approach, and evidence of your and your team's investment in the business. For most small businesses, it is far easier, simpler, and faster to cast farther afield for more family, friends, and folks, or dig deeper into their own pockets to fund the start-up.

Financial Management for Growth

Many small businesses successfully start up only to find that the need for financial management is greater than ever as the business enters a phase of rapid growth. This situation is like a lame "bad news-good news" joke. The bad news is that the business has greater capital needs than ever. The good news is that more sources of money are available to meet those needs. The emphasis of financial management during periods of growth is to obtain increasing amounts of cash inflows to pay for added inventory, productive assets, and employees needed to meet growing levels of business operations.

Financial Management for Operations

Most small businesses eventually reach a size that is relatively stable: not too small to generate sufficient profits, not too large for the preferences and abilities of the owners. At this stage of the business, the emphasis of financial management is to build owner wealth, to conserve assets, to match cash inflows to outflows, and to maximize the return on capital assets by making optimal investing decisions.

Financial Management for Business Exit

Eventually, you will face the necessity of leaving the active management of your business. This may be because you want to take advantage of a different opportunity, the business needs professional management, you want to pass ownership to family members, or you want to retire. You might become ill or disabled. Regardless why, successfully leaving your business requires maximizing the value of your business for your successors.

The goals of financial management in preparation for exiting the business depends, in part, on the nature of the exit that is planned. Business exit can entail a transfer to your heirs. Another common exit is to sell the business, either to outside investors or to the employees. Finally, business exit can come from terminating the business through bankruptcy, a "work-out," or simply closing the business and disposing of its assets.

If your plan is to transfer the business to family members, then you will want to ensure that the business is in sound financial condition. You should be working to minimize debt and to increase asset value. It is essential that you establish internal controls over assets by establishing policies and procedures that are clearly stated and understood by everyone involved in management.

If you plan to sell your business, your goals should be to optimize capital structure for profits. Investors usually will not pay to "buy" cash in your business. Therefore, you should be removing all surplus cash and tightening the cash-to-cash cycle to the shortest time possible. The condition and age of assets will greatly affect the final selling price, so now is the time to ensure that all equipment is in good working order, that the facilities are clean and organized, and that accounts receivable and accounts payable are up to date.

Termination of a business is also very common. Many small businesses are extensions of the owner. For example, CPA firms, beauty salons, real estate brokerages, indeed any business that provides personal services, often depend solely on the reputation and personality of the owner. In reality, there is no business to sell. In cases such as these, exit usually involves finishing all outstanding projects, collecting all money due, disposing of all business assets, and finally (if possible) paying off any outstanding debt. Thus, the goals of financial management are to recover all asset value possible, cover any indebtedness, and use the remainder for personal purposes.

Refer to Chapter 20, "Achieving Success in the Small Business," for a more comprehensive discussion of the many issues of business exit.

CHAPTER SUMMARY

LO1 Describe the three types of capital financing and their costs and trade-offs.

- Most people have many assets and financial resources that can be used to finance their business.
- Financing can be in the form of equity, debt, or gifts.
- An entrepreneur's own funds are the first source of financing for most small businesses.
- Forms of business organization can be categorized along two dimensions.
  - How the business is taxed.
  - How much responsibility owners have for the liabilities of the business.

LO2 Explain the characteristics of a business that determine its ability to raise capital.

- Investors put money into a business to make money for themselves.
- Lenders expect a return from making loans, by getting back the amount they loan plus more money in the form of interest.
- Equity investors expect to get back the money they invest plus extra money, a gain on investment.
- To get money from other people, owners must show them that their business probably can make gains for them.
- Financing with equity is expensive and creates problems of control and decision making.

- Other than the owner's own funds, the most common source of capital for established ongoing small businesses is borrowed funds.

LO3 Determine the best type of financing for your business.

- As debt increases as a percentage of total capital, total cost of capital declines.
- Lower cost of capital results in higher firm value, all other things being held equal.
- Borrowing money increases financial risk because payments on debt must be made as agreed without regard to the cash position of the business.

LO4 Describe the differing needs for financial management at each stage of business life.

- You can use financial ratios to evaluate your business.
- There are four broad categories of financial ratios: activity ratios, profitability ratios, liquidity ratios, and leverage ratios.
- During the start-up phase of a small business the primary financial management need is to obtain sufficient funds to pay for equipment, buildings, inventory, and indeed, all the costs of starting and running a business.
- During the growth phase, the need for financial management increases to pay for added inventory, productive assets, and employees to meet growing levels of business operations.
- During the mature phase of the business, the emphasis of financial management is to build owner wealth, to conserve assets, to match cash inflows to outflows, and to maximize the return on capital assets by making optimal investing decisions.
- Successfully leaving your business requires maximizing its value for your successors by creating effective internal controls and developing business systems to replace your specific skills and knowledge.

KEY TERMS

debt, 479
equity capital, 479
gift, 479
debt capital, 479
outside equity, 482
partnership, 482
corporation, 482
limited liability company (LLC), 482
limited partnership, 482
sole proprietorship, 483
interest, 483
gain on investment, 483
dividends, 483
risk, 484
diversify, 484
community development organization, 485
small business investment companies, 485
accelerator, 486
credit reporting agency, 486
Fair Credit Reporting Act, 486
profit, profitability, 487
collateral, 487
tax abatement, 489
tax credits, 489
grants, 489
economic development agency, 490
foundation, 490
cost of capital, 492
weighted average cost of capital (WAC), 492
financial leverage, 493
optimum capital structure, 493
financial risk, 493
return on equity, 494
financial management, 498
accredited investors, 499

DISCUSSION QUESTIONS

1. Why does a business require a constant flow of money and capital assets during its existence?
2. Explain how a sole proprietorship differs from a corporation.
3. What things do you need to do to convince an investor to make you a loan or purchase equity in your business?
4. In what ways does accepting outside investment change the ways you manage your business?

5. Why do you have to give up more ownership to get outside investment if your business is risky?
6. Explain why investors prefer investments that pay back sooner to those that pay back later.
7. Name four ways that an investor can receive payment from a business. Describe the advantages and disadvantages of each.
8. Many small business owners prefer to borrow money rather than sell equity. Why is this so?
9. In what ways do the Four Cs of Borrowing differ from the requirements for being able to obtain equity capital?
10. Explain why it is easier to borrow money to buy a semi truck than to purchase rights to a business process.
11. Explain how borrowing money (1) increases firm value and (2) makes more money for a business owner.
12. Explain the differing financial management needs of a small business during the start-up, growth, mature, and exit phases.

EXPERIENTIAL EXERCISES

1. Go to the SBA directory of SBICs (**http://www.sba.gov/INV/index.html**). Search through the directory, specifically looking for SBICs that will invest in businesses in the industry in which you are interested. Make a chart of the minimum and maximum investments that the SBICs will make, and their requirements to invest. Present your findings to your class.
2. Contact the owner of a business you would like to own. Arrange an interview. Ask how the owner arranged for start-up financing. What sources of financing does the owner use today? Report your findings to your class.
3. Find out if your city has an office of economic development. (Almost every city with a population greater than 100,000 does.) Contact the office and inquire about the programs that it supports. Ask specifically how the office would provide support to you for start-up and operations.
4. Find out if your city or county has any tax abatement economic development zones. What must you do to be able to take advantage of the tax abatement?
5. Make an appointment with a commercial bank loan officer who handles business loans. Ask about the bank's documentation requirements. Determine what commitment, if any, the bank has for making loans to local small businesses. Present your findings to your class.
6. Do a search of *Entrepreneur, Inc.*, and *BusinessWeek Small Business* Web sites looking for information about businesses that were successful in obtaining financing. Write a report detailing how the businesses arranged financing.

MINI-CASE

VIVID SKY IN 2008

Vivid Sky's sole product, SkyBOX, was designed to provide sports fans in a stadium with continual access to videos, sports statistics, info-graphics (e.g., pitch locations and hit/out locations), maps, chats and concession-ordering capabilities—giving the fan in the stadium "the best seat in the house."

To reach this point, Vivid Sky's founder, Tim Hayden, had achieved numerous developmental milestones since 2003 using nothing but bootstrapped help and his own cash (and very much his own credit cards). The software was ready for deployment on iPhones and other 3G cell phones and laptops/desktops. The back-end programs to run in stadiums to gather and tie together the many data streams and feed them to SkyBOX users were ready to go. What was needed now was $1 million to deploy the programs in the baseball, football, basketball, and hockey stadiums in North America starting with the 2009 baseball season.

Through an innovative product, a positive attitude, and tireless networking, Tim had convinced four Fortune 1000 companies to seriously consider investing $500,000 toward the million-dollar round. The companies were all in the entertainment business, and all saw the SkyBOX as a vehicle for selling content on a new platform, the cell phone. Tim still had to raise $500,000 before any of the big players would put their cash in.

Despite presentations from 2003 to 2007 to angels in St. Louis, Seattle, Chicago, Detroit, and Boston, and even a couple of presentations to Silicon Valley and Seattle venture capitalists, in the end his funding came from the people who knew him the longest and trusted him the most.

Tim's first investors were his parents, who invested $100,000 explaining to Tim that the money was his inheritance. That investment led to a friend of the family investing another $100,000, not based on the business plan, but on knowing Tim, the person. Once these two investors were aboard, a friend of the second investor wanted to get involved so an additional $130,000 was injected into Vivid Sky. When all was counted, Tim had raised $530,000 by the end of April 2008 from six partners who were all one degree separated from Tim.

Each $100,000 was set up as a convertible note (i.e., it starts as a loan, and when funding is complete, converts to stock) worth 2 percent of the stock, for 20 percent of the company total when all $1 million was raised. Twelve percent of the stock was held for the developers and executives, with Tim holding 68 percent. Those percentages put the valuation of the company at $5 million.

It was a great moment for Tim, with continuing successful deployments in baseball and hockey, international corporate sponsors signed up, iTunes Store sales exceeding projections, and four Fortune 1000 companies ready to do their due diligence now that they knew who their potential partners would be.

Sitting back, Tim started wondering, "What could go wrong now?"

1. Why might the investors want a convertible note instead of getting straight stock in a start-up?
2. From the standpoint of the smaller investors, what are the advantages or disadvantages of having a single large investor (like one of the entertainment companies) along with the smaller ones?
3. If the large firms decide not to invest, what are the options available to Tim and how likely will he be to raise the capital needed?
4. Finally, what do you think is the answer to Tim's question—What could go wrong now?

SUGGESTED CASES AND ARTICLES

- The Landlords: Investments in Commercial Real Estate

Available on PRIMIS:

- Fabricare, Inc.
- Circle Electronics Corporation

SUGGESTED VIDEOS

Video Case:

- Women Entrepreneurs, p. VC-7

eClips Videos:

- Mark Brandt Discusses Options for Funding When You Start as an Entrepreneur
- Mac Cummings Discusses Options for Funding a Start-up

SBTV Videos:

- Distributors of Seafood P&G Trading—Credit Line
- Raising Capital: Fundraising for the Risk Averse

STVP Video:

- You Need Too Little Money

Your Business Videos:

- Elevator Pitch: Sunshade
- Elevator Pitch: Entertainment Humvee Pitch

CHAPTER 16

Assets: Inventory and Operations Management

• Curtis Graf's company lost a significant amount in assets when a thief disguised as a worker literally walked onto a construction site and drove off in a backhoe. Managing your business's property can be a challenge. What are some of the security measures Curtis could have put into place that would have deterred this theft? What measures do you think you would need to implement for your dream business?

LO

LEARNING OBJECTIVES

When you complete this chapter, you will be able to:

LO1 Describe techniques to manage short-term assets.

LO2 Calculate the value of the assets in your business.

LO3 Describe techniques for managing fixed assets.

LO4 Calculate ratios used to analyze capital investment decisions.

LO5 Describe the advantages of renting or leasing capital equipment.

LO6 Describe techniques to manage and improve the operations of your business.

Focus on Small Business: Curtis Graf and the Nightmare on Construction Street

It's every contractor's nightmare. You arrive on a job site at six in the morning and find that hundreds of thousands of dollars of construction equipment was stolen overnight. Work comes to a halt. Expenses escalate as workers stand around while you make a frenzied effort to buy, borrow, or rent replacement equipment.

Curtis Graf in the Dallas suburb of Mesquite, Texas, encountered something even worse. A bold thief, in broad daylight, simply walked onto one of his construction sites, started up, and drove away in a $40,000 backhoe. A worker on the site saw the whole thing, but because the thief looked and acted as if he belonged, mistook him for another worker.

"I paid $3,000 to have it burglar-proofed," Curtis said, "but they stole it anyway!"[1]

Most unfortunately, equipment theft is a nightmare that all too often comes true. Despite all efforts—those of law enforcement, the owners, and industry groups—500 pieces of heavy construction equipment are stolen in the United States *each week*. Fewer than 15 percent of the machines stolen are ever recovered.[2]

Curtis did not get his machine back. He faxed a report to the local police and called numerous times to see if it had been found. Curtis said that the only reply from the police was, "We will call you when we find something." He added, "That's short for, 'We don't have time to talk to you anymore.'"[3]

His insurance company was little help, as well. It not only delayed payment as long as it could, but it also canceled his policy, which resulted in his changing insurance carriers for the third time in three years. He did finally receive a payment of $24,000 nearly a year after the machine was stolen, leaving him $16,000 shy of the cost of a replacement.

DISCUSSION QUESTIONS

1. Why do you think that thieves target heavy construction machinery?
2. To what extent do you think that Curtis Graf's negative experience with insurance coverage for theft is commonly encountered by small business owners?
3. Why do you suppose that fewer than 15 percent of stolen heavy machines are ever recovered when the FBI reports that 62 percent of stolen automobiles are recovered?
4. Think of the business that you own or would like to own. How and to what extent would the theft of machinery or equipment be a threat to your business?

Managing Short-Term Assets

LO1 Describe techniques to manage short-term assets.

In many ways, you can think of your business as a collection of assets: things you own that will provide value in the future. The things that you own include the obvious, such as cash, inventory, tools, machinery, buildings, and land. Less obvious things are also owned, such as legal claims to collect money from customers in the future, patents, copyrights, trademarks, expertise, and your reputation.

Because your business *is* its assets, if you allow them to be damaged, lost, stolen, or destroyed, your wealth diminishes. At some point, if your business loses enough value, it will cease to exist. It will be bankrupt, and you will have lost your investment.

Managing your business assets to obtain their maximum value is critical to ultimate business success. Chapter 14 is dedicated to the issues of managing cash, the most liquid of all business assets. This chapter discusses managing the critical short-term assets of accounts receivable and inventory, and managing the essential long-term assets of property, plant, and equipment.

Accounts Receivable

accounts receivable Money owed to your business by customers who purchased your product on credit.

Accounts receivable are money that is owed to your business by your customers. As was discussed in Chapter 14, relatively few small businesses today provide credit to customers. Current practice is for small businesses to provide credit only by accepting bank-issued credit cards. However, there are still some small businesses, especially those involved in wholesale distribution, that provide direct credit to customers. For these firms, managing receivables is an essential activity.

The Pros and Cons of Offering Credit to Customers

Credit is provided to customers for marketing reasons. Providing credit usually results in higher sales revenue because of increased repeat business. Providing credit also reduces the cost of selling, because it is much less expensive to obtain repeat business than it is to get new customers.

On the downside, selling your product and then allowing customers a month or two to pay has three negative effects that are often overlooked when business owners make the decision to extend credit. First, providing credit delays the receipt of cash. If your small business is like most, you exist in a state of constant cash shortages. Anything that delays receiving cash makes the problems of meeting payrolls and paying suppliers and vendors even worse. This causes the second problem: You must somehow replace the "missing" cash. Most often this means borrowing. Borrowing, of course, is expensive. You spend time to arrange a loan, and then must make regular payments of interest. Third, if you give credit to your customers, sooner or later one of them will not pay. Although you provide credit only to those customers who you believe will pay, despite careful monitoring and despite strenuous collection efforts, eventually someone won't. The reasons why people don't pay can be almost anything, from inability to pay because they have no money to low ethics to outright fraud. Regardless of the cause, your business loses when customers don't pay.

Managing Accounts Receivable to Receive the Greatest Benefit for Your Business

As stated above, providing customer credit usually results in increased sales revenues and lowered transaction costs, which usually more than offsets the costs of interest and uncollectible accounts, resulting in greater profits. To realize this benefit, you must establish and enforce efficient and effective policies and procedures for extending credit. Your goals are to: (1) minimize the time that passes between when a credit sale is made and when the cash is received, and (2) keep the number of bad accounts as low as possible. Exhibit 16.1 provides a list of standards that should always be followed if you provide credit to customers.

Using Your Accounts Receivable as a Source of Financing

You can often get immediate cash from third-party finance companies if you have established and enforced policies to maintain a high quality of receivables. Having high-quality receivables lets you quickly get cash to meet unexpected needs.

You can use your receivables in two ways to quickly lay your hands on cash. First, you can pledge your receivables as collateral for a commercial loan. Depending on the finance company,

EXHIBIT 16.1

Policies for Managing Accounts Receivable

If you want to collect the money owed you from credit sales, you must be very careful to give credit only to those customers who are likely to pay. To make credit work for your business, you must work consistently to collect what you are owed. The following nine policies are *minimum standards* for managing customer credit:

1. Make an extensive credit check prior to authorizing credit sales to any individual customer.
2. Promptly bill each customer following each credit purchase.
3. Provide cash discounts for making timely payments.
4. Enforce significant late fees and interest on past due accounts.
5. Maintain constant "aging" of accounts to quickly identify customers who become delinquent.
6. Make consistent, vigorous efforts to collect from customers, including dunning letters and phone calls.
7. Discontinue credit sales to customers who become significantly late in paying.
8. File suits and liens against the assets of customers who default on payment.
9. Use your bank as a **lock box** for the receipt of payments.

lock box
A locked receptacle for money, the keys to which are not available to those who physically handle the receptacle; a common example of a lock box is the coin receptacle for parking meters which cannot be opened by the workers who are responsible for collecting the deposited coins.

SMALL BUSINESS INSIGHT

PUT YOUR BILL ON THE TOP OF THE PILE

Dwight Cooper, CEO of PPR Travel,[4] a nurse-staffing firm in Jacksonville, Florida, was in a quandary. Average time to collect payment on accounts was a crippling 60 days from the time the bill was sent. For two months, Cooper had to cover all the costs of his nurses—wages, benefits, and tax withholdings—as well as his own operating expenses. In effect, Cooper was financing the operations of his customers. On the other hand, if he pressed his clients for payment, he risked creating bad will and perhaps even losing business.

"What should I do?" he asked himself.

Owners of small businesses commonly face the same dilemma. A recent study by REL Consultancy Group of Purchase, New York, found that fully one-third of big businesses are habitually late paying vendors' bills.[5] Sooner or later, if you provide credit to customers, you too will have difficulties in collecting what is due. Customer accounts will slip ever farther into arrears. Past due accounts will accumulate: 90 days, 120 days, even 6 months in arrears. Cooper took a unique approach to his problem. He *asked* his customers why they paid late and what he could do to help them speed payment.

Dwight Cooper shaved 15 days off his company's average time for collection of bills receivable. Which of his steps could you see yourself imitating in your own business? What ideas might you add in improving your company's collection process?

Even more unusually, he *acted* to implement the things that his customers said would help them pay more quickly. First, he established procedures to ensure that every bill was accurate. Second, he issued a single invoice to each hospital for all nurses provided, rather than sending multiple invoices, one for each nurse provided. Third, he started printing his invoices on blue paper, making them immediately recognizable. Fourth, he began sending a reminder when a customer was only one day late. To take the sting from the reminders, each is addressed by hand.

The results of Cooper's efforts is that average collection time has been reduced from 60 days to 45.[6]

customer payments on pledged receivables may be collected either by you and forwarded to the lender, or may be directly collected by the lender. Second, you can *sell* your receivables to a finance company in a process called **factoring**. A factoring company will usually pay you about 75 to 80 percent of the total amount that can be collected. The factor then collects the receivables. The difference between the gross amount of the receivables and the amount that is ultimately collected is the factor's profit margin. Skill Module 16.1 gives you a chance to work through the ways a factor might structure a deal for you.

factoring
Selling the rights to collect accounts receivable to an entity outside your business.

pledging receivables
Giving a third party legal rights to debts owed your business in order to provide assurance that borrowed money will be repaid.

Pledging receivables to a commercial lender is usually less expensive than factoring. When you pledge receivables, your business is liable only for the borrowed amount and accrued interest on the loan, regardless of the amount that is subsequently collected from your customers. You have the opportunity to collect it all. On the other hand, a commercial lender will loan you only one-half of the amount that can be collected. When you factor receivables, you immediately get 75 to 80 percent of the amount due. But, you forever give up all rights to the factor's discount. Of course, for this amount, the finance company assumes your bad debt risk. If a factor does not collect enough to make a profit, it's the factor's problem, not yours.

SKILL MODULE 16.1

Using Receivables to Raise Immediate Cash

Suppose that you need $50,000 immediately in order to purchase welded steel roof trusses for a building that you have contracted to construct. Normally, you would simply purchase the materials on account from an established supplier, but two things prevent this. First, you have reached your credit limit with your supplier, and the supplier refuses to provide more. Second, your regular supplier is operating at maximum possible output and cannot deliver the trusses within the time required by your contract.

You have found a supplier who will manufacture and deliver the trusses when you need them. However, this supplier does not offer credit. Further, the supplier demands an immediate deposit of one-half of the cost of the trusses, $25,000, with the remaining $25,000 paid on delivery. You have approached your bank, but the bank has refused you a loan because (1) you are at your borrowing limit, and (2) the business with which you have contracted is embroiled in a lawsuit with the bank, and the bank therefore will not accept the contract as collateral.

You have current receivables of $67,000. You have contacted a factor in your area that has proposed two financing deals.

1. The factor will purchase your receivables for 75 percent of their collection value. You will receive 95 percent of the cash immediately, and the factor will retain the remaining 5 percent until all the receivables are collected. If the entire $67,000 is collected, then the remaining money will be paid to you. However, the money being held will be reduced by any amount uncollected at the end of 120 days from the date of the factoring contract.
2. The factor will lend you $54,000 discounted at 12 percent interest for 90 days. You must pledge 100 percent of your receivables as collateral for the loan. The factor will collect your receivables, applying 100 percent of the amount collected against the $54,000 until it is completely repaid, dollar for dollar.

What should you do? Show calculations to support your decision.

Managing Inventory

inventory
Products that are held for sale to customers.

Inventory is a constant, everyday problem for most small businesses. It is the largest current asset that most manufacturing, wholesale, and retail firms have. Manufacturing firms, wholesalers, and retailers simply cannot operate effectively without a minimum level of inventory on hand. Even service firms such as restaurants, beauty shops, automobile garages, plumbing businesses, electrical contractors, sign companies, and so on also have to have some inventory to function efficiently. It is a rare business, indeed, that has no inventory at all.

The amount and type of inventory held for resale is important for small businesses because (1) the supply of inventory and demand of customers cannot be precisely matched at all times, and (2) holding inventory requires a nonproductive cash investment. While inventory sits on your shelves, the money required to buy it is tied up and is not making a return for you.

Determining the Appropriate Level of Inventory

The *right* amount of inventory to keep on hand and the *right* amount of inventory to order at one time is determined by (1) the cost of processing an order, (2) the cost of keeping merchandise in inventory, (3) the cost of lost sales if you run out, and (4) the time it takes to receive inventory after it's ordered. These factors vary widely with the location and type of business. Small retailers and service firms that also sell products (such as a beauty shop) and are located in urban areas usually have easy access to wholesalers and can make frequent small purchases. If the business is in a small town or if it needs hard-to-get resources, then it may have to keep a lot of merchandise on hand. For example, our manufacturer of fine wooden desks, from Chapter 9, may well need hardwood, such as mahogany, teak, or burled maple, which is produced in only a few places and for which there are only a few wholesalers, worldwide. The distribution system for hardwoods is such that, except in very large cities, you have to buy a lot of it at one time and then keep it in stock until it is used.

There is a way to know how much you need to order so that you have an adequate supply of inventory on hand. It is called **economic order quantity (EOQ)**, and it helps you think in terms of ordering costs and carrying costs.

economic order quantity (EOQ)
A statistical technique that determines the quantity of inventory that a business must hold to minimize total inventory cost.

The total cost of keeping inventory is the sum of:

- The cost to buy the inventory.
- The cost to store, protect, and maintain inventory.
- The cost of making an order to purchase inventory.[7]

(See Exhibit 16.2.)

If the cost of carrying inventory were the only factor in making the decision of how much inventory to obtain, it would make the most sense to purchase the smallest number of units possible at any single time. On the other hand, if ordering costs were the only consideration, you would order the largest number that you expect to sell. But if you consider both these *and* purchase price, as we do in Figure 16.1, you get the economic order quantity (EOQ)—the quantity at which the total cost of inventory is minimized.

You do not have to derive the EOQ equation to use it. You can simply substitute your business's projected annual sales demand, cost of placing one order, and cost of holding one unit in inventory

EXHIBIT 16.2
Inventory Costs

Costs of Carrying Inventory	Costs of Ordering Inventory
1. The opportunity cost of the funds invested in inventory	1. The transaction costs of preparing and transmitting the order
2. The cost of keeping inventory secure and in sellable condition	2. Investigating and selecting an appropriate vendor
3. Cost of warehouse or other storage facilities a. Utilities b. Physically moving inventory into, within, and out of the storage area c. Security guards, fencing, access control, etc.	3. Receiving inventory
4. Insurance and taxes on inventory	4. Time required to travel to suppliers to pick up inventory
5. Inventory shrinkage, i.e., loss from waste, spoilage, and theft	5. Inspecting shipments
6. The transaction costs for counting and record keeping	6. Record keeping

FIGURE 16.1

Economic Order Quantity Graph

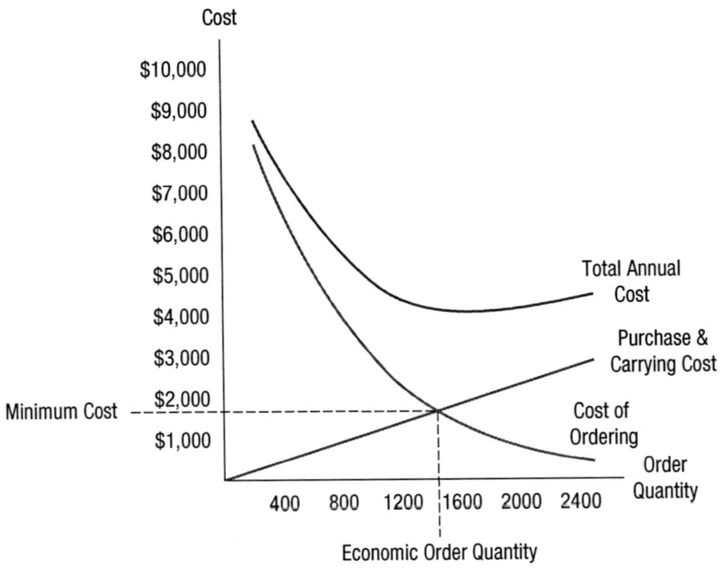

to calculate your unique optimum order quantity and the number of orders that you should place each year. If you are interested, Appendix A of this chapter, entitled "Economic Order Quantity," provides a detailed explanation of how the EOC equation can be used.

Scheduling Ordering and Receipt of Inventory

Determining the right quantity to order is only part of the problem of inventory management. You also need to know *when* to place each order. The EOQ tells us only how many units to order and how many orders to make. It does not tell us *when* to place each order. Deciding when to place an order is determined by (1) the rate of sales and (2) the time required to receive new stock.

optimum stocking level
(Also known as the *reorder point*.) The amount of inventory that results in the minimum cost, when considering the cost of lost sales resulting from running out of stock, the number of units sold per day, and the number of days required to receive inventory.

The **optimum stocking level** (also called *reorder point*) is the amount of inventory that results in the minimum cost, considering (1) the cost of lost sales resulting from running out of stock, (2) the number of units sold per day, and (3) the number of days required to receive inventory.

If everything worked perfectly, you would receive new inventory just as you sold the last unit from the prior order. But in business as in most things in life, things are never perfect. Delivery times vary. Sales volumes are not constant. Sometimes demand exceeds your estimate. Sometimes your estimate exceeds demand.

If you know how demand for a particular product or part changes, you can calculate the probability of being out of stock, given any initial level of inventory and time between receipts of inventory. Computing the reorder point tells you the minimum stock level at which you would place an order. Ordering at that time would ensure that you do not run out of inventory before you run out of customers, and at the same time would minimize your holding unnecessary amounts of stock.

In practice, managers of small businesses rarely attempt such statistical analyses. Rather, they use a heuristic (rule of thumb) developed from experience. Unless you are selling a product that has very high unit costs, such as automobiles, tractors, or airplanes, the effect of having too little inventory is worse than the effect of having too much. For this reason, most businesses deliberately time the placement of orders to keep some extra amount of inventory on hand as **safety stock** to provide for the possibility that sales might be greater than forecast, or that deliveries might be delayed.

safety stock
An amount of inventory carried to ensure that you will not run out of inventory because of fluctuating levels of sales.

One interesting use of optimum stocking levels comes when an entrepreneur starts to use it as a sales tool directed toward customers. If you compute customers' reorder point, you start to have an added reason to contact them and check to find out whether it is time for them to reorder your product.[8]

Just-in-Time Inventory Systems

The cost of owning and holding inventory is far greater than the cost of ordering inventory. As a result, most businesses try to acquire and keep on hand the minimum amount of inventory possible while still being able to meet customer needs. At the extreme, a few businesses hold no inventory at all. Rather, these businesses order and receive inventory only after a customer purchase has been made.

The practice of acquiring inventory only in response to a completed sale is called a **pull-through system**. Once a customer sale is made, an order is placed to either obtain or produce the product. Each stage of the production process operates in response to this order, ultimately reaching back to the acquisition of the raw materials from which the product is made.

pull-through system
A term for just-in-time inventory systems in which product is ordered and placed into production only after a sale has been completed.

The ultimate extension of pull-through processing is **just-in-time inventory** management. A just-in-time (JIT) inventory system attempts to reduce inventory levels to the absolute minimum by (1) accepting inventory only as it is sold, (2) assembling product in the absolute minimum time possible, and (3) shipping product to the customer immediately upon completion. In this way, the three primary inventories of manufacturing, (1) raw materials, (2) work in process, and (3) finished goods, are all kept at the minimum levels possible.

just-in-time inventory
The practice of purchasing and accepting delivery of inventory only after it has been sold to the final customer.

One of the best-known examples of just-in-time manufacturing is Dell Computers,[9] but small businesses use the approach too. Consider Alienware, a maker of high-end PCs for game enthusiasts started by two lifelong friends in Miami, Alex Aguila and Nelson Gonzalez. Their model is simple: "First you pay. Then we build." Having started with only $13,000, they could not afford to spend a lot on inventory. When Alienware receives a computer order from its Web site, a work order is generated that specifies each individual component to be assembled. Alienware maintains a just-in-time delivery system for needed parts, and leverages its relations with suppliers to ensure speedy delivery. With the parts together, the computer is assembled, tested, and then sent to the packing and shipping department. The use of the JIT approach originally meant that Alienware had no receivables to underwrite, no inventory to depreciate, and no bad debt.[10] Today Alienware still gets the same benefits, but it has grown to over $100 million in annual sales, and even has an arrangement with Best Buy.

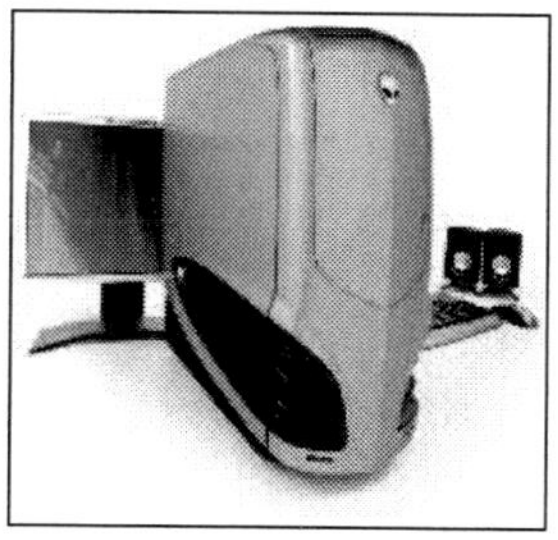

Alienware uses just-in-time inventory management in order to keep costs of its high-end PCs at a reasonable level

Adoption of just-in-time inventory management requires an extreme degree of cooperation with your vendors. The location, scheduling, and transportation of inventory must be as carefully choreographed as is a Broadway dance routine. A single misstep in process can result in the shut down of production and in lost sales. To ensure against this, most businesses that adopt just-in-time inventory management compromise between the theoretical "best way" and the exigencies of real-world business management and maintain some level of safety stock.

The development and growth of the eBay online auction service has provided many small businesses with the ability to practice just-in-time inventory management. Buyers on eBay know that there will be a period of a few days between winning a bid and receiving the product. Numerous eBay sellers use this time to obtain the product. Often, it is shipped directly from the wholesaler to the buyer. This practice is the ultimate just-in-time process: The eBay seller never owns or handles the products being sold. It is called **microinventory** and is a very special form of JIT found in Internet-based businesses[11] such as Alienware.

microinventory
The purchase of inventory only after a sale is made; very typical with Internet firms.

Other Approaches to Inventory Control

There are three approaches to maintaining records of inventory which are very common in small businesses: (1) periodic inventory, (2) perpetual inventory, and (3) point-of-sale systems. Any one of these, applied conscientiously, can help control inventory and inventory costs.

Periodic inventory is the process of physically counting business assets on a set schedule. The time between counts is usually one business year, although periodic inventories may be conducted twice per year, quarterly, monthly, or as often as your business needs require. Most small businesses use the periodic inventory method because it is relatively inexpensive and meets the requirements of both local and federal taxing agencies.

periodic inventory
The process of physically counting business assets on a set schedule.

Perpetual inventory is a system of recording the receipt and sale of each item as it occurs. A perpetual inventory system maintains a constant record of the amounts and value of inventory that has been sold and the amounts and value of inventory on hand. Perpetual inventory systems provide

perpetual inventory
A system of recording the receipt and sale of each item as it occurs.

FIGURE 16.2

The Stock Card

Stock Card					
Type of product:			Unit of measurement:		
Date	Reference	Designation	Receipts	Disbursements	Stock in hand
Total to be carried forward					

you with instant access to accurate inventory records, thus greatly easing the problems of managing inventory levels. The main drawback to using perpetual inventory systems is the high cost in time needed for constant record keeping. (See Figure 16.2.)

bar coding
Obtaining a Universal Product Code number and scan-ready visual tag, and printing it on the product or its packaging. Bar codes can then be scanned and recognized by others.

Bar coding is one method used to reduce the cost of perpetual inventory systems. Bar codes are computer readable tags that are unique to each item of inventory. The most common bar codes (those that are used every time your grocery purchases are scanned at the register) are called UPCs or universal product codes.

UPCs are registered with and controlled by a private company, GS1 US (www.gs1us.org). Manufacturers pay an annual fee to participate in the UPC system. Each member of the system makes an application for codes for its products. In return, the company issues a six-digit code for each member, and an additional, unique five-digit code for each registered product. The 12-digit UPC comprises the manufacturer identification number plus the product number plus a check sum to allow for computer error checking.

Each UPC is therefore unique to the product for which it is issued. As a member of GS1 US, you have access to the database of all codes and the corresponding product information. The company maintains an extensive Web site that explains the system, the use of bar codes, and information necessary to join.

You may also create private bar codes of any number of digits for your internal use. Because the private codes are for your internal use, they do not have to be registered with GS1 US.

To use bar codes effectively in your business, you need (1) a method to create bar codes, (2) a means to print the codes on the items that you wish to track, (3) a scanner that can read the codes, and (4) a computer software program that can interpret the codes and update a database of information associated with each code. There are hundreds, if not thousands, of businesses that provide all the elements necessary for you to use bar codes internally in your business. A search of the Internet's open directory (DMOZ) on the term "bar codes" returned 229 individual listings for firms that provide bar code software and hardware.

point-of-sale (POS) system
Hardware and software combinations that integrate inventory management directly into accounting software.

Point-of-sale (POS) systems comprise both hardware and software to integrate inventory management directly into your accounting system. You are very familiar with POS, whether or not you are aware of being so. The familiar supermarket scanner and the multibutton registers at fast food restaurants are examples of point-of-sale systems. In these systems, every sale is immediately recorded in the accounting system. Revenue is increased and inventory is decreased simultaneously.

Point-of-sale systems have recently become inexpensive enough to be used by small businesses. Today, you may acquire complete systems, including a cash drawer, credit card scanner, bar code scanner, computer, monitor, and software for less than $2,000. There are numerous providers of POS systems, including such well-known companies as Intuit, Hewlett Packard, Sony, and Panasonic.

If it is important to you that your product be recognized universally, be sure to apply with GS1 US in order to receive your product's UPC.

Value of Assets in Your Business

LO2 Calculate the value of the assets in your business.

There are two fundamental kinds of assets in a business—short-term, which includes inventory and accounts receivable, and operating or **capital assets**. The methods for determining the value of each are similar in many respects. Many small businesses need little in the way of capital assets. However, transportation, manufacturing, automobile repair, mining, ranching, and farming businesses all require the use of substantial capital assets in the form of land, buildings, and machinery. The value of such businesses is largely determined by the value of the physical capital assets that they own.

capital assets Assets that are expected to provide economic benefits for periods of time greater than one year.

The value of assets for use in your business usually far exceeds the value that you might realize if you were to sell them. An example of such an asset is fencing for a ranch or farm. A four-strand barbed wire fence on steel posts can easily cost $4,000 per mile. However, no rancher can ever realize the value of the fence by selling it. At least half the cost of fencing is in the labor required to install it. Once installed, it would cost a similar amount to uninstall. Used barbed wire and posts will bring only a fraction of their cost new. In fact, farmers and ranchers often cannot even give away old fencing; rather, they incur significant costs to safely dispose of it.

Similar situations exist in other businesses such as manufacturing, in which equipment, especially custom-made machinery, is much more valuable as an operating asset than can ever be realized from disposal. Even restaurant equipment such as deep fryers, cooking grills, and ventilation hoods have a much greater value being used in a restaurant than they do sitting in a restaurant supply store.

Determining the Value of Your Operating Assets

The value of operating assets is a function of their utility. In other words, your assets are worth the sum of the future benefits that the assets will produce. It is this definition that is the source of the discounted cash flow methods discussed in Appendix B of this chapter. Discounted cash flow valuation methods define *utility* as being the net cash inflows that the asset will produce. The value of the asset is the sum of these cash flows discounted for time and cost of capital.

Just as estimating future cash flows is highly problematic for small businesses, predicting future utility of capital assets is so uncertain that it is largely a waste of time. Therefore, most small businesses determine the value of capital assets using some combination of the four common accounting methods of assigning asset value.

The four accounting methods to value capital assets are (1) book value, (2) disposal value, (3) replacement value, and (4) fair market value.

book value
The difference between the original cost of an asset and the total amount of depreciation expense that has been recognized to date.

Book value is an accounting term that describes the difference between the original acquisition cost of capital assets and the amount of depreciation expense that has been recognized for them. Even a superficial consideration of book value discloses that it is simply an accident if book value even approximates the asset's economic value. This is true for two reasons: (1) Purchase price is not an indicator of the current value of any asset, and (2) depreciation is not, nor is it intended to be, any measure of the consumption through use of an asset's value.

Depreciation is an arbitrary, but regular and systematic, method used to take asset value as an expense for the purpose of calculating net income or loss. Depreciation is based on three assumptions: (1) that the asset has a fixed, determinable period of utility (called useful life), (2) that the asset has a fixed, determinable value that will exist when the depreciation process is complete (called *salvage value*), and (3) that the value of the asset will decline in a continuous and predictable manner over the period of utility (e.g., straight line, declining balance, etc.). In fact, none of these assumptions necessarily holds for any capital asset. Thus, depreciation is arbitrary. Book value is generally considered to be not very useful for any purpose other than accounting and income taxes, each of which, through law, regulation, and practice, require its use.

disposal value
The net amount realized after subtracting the costs of getting rid of an asset from its selling price.

arm's length transaction
A business deal where the parties have a prior relation or affiliation, but where the business is conducted as if they were unrelated. This approach is done to help guard against potential conflicts of interest.

Disposal value is a method of estimating asset value by calculating the net amount that you would realize were you to sell the asset in an **"arm's length" transaction**. This is accomplished by subtracting from the estimated sale price the estimated costs of selling, disassembly, shipping, indeed, all costs necessary to dispose of the asset. Disposal value is the residual of many estimates. At best, you must consider the value to be a rough approximation. At worst, the value may hold no relationship to the asset's unknown, "true" economic value.

replacement value
The cost incurred to replace one asset with an identical asset.

Replacement value can be determined with much greater confidence than can be given to either book value or disposal value. In effect, you are estimating the value of a currently owned capital asset by determining the cost that would be incurred to replace it with an identical asset. Unlike disposal value, in which you must estimate an essentially unknowable selling price for a used asset, replacement value is based on determining the price of either a new asset or a used asset for which there is an organized market. For many assets, such as machine tools and vehicles, this is done quite easily by obtaining quotes from dealers. Custom-made assets require a bit more work, but still can be accurately priced through an engineering approach.

The primary advantage of replacement value is that you can be quite confident of its accuracy. The disadvantage is that the price of a new asset is often much greater than the price of an essentially identical asset already in your business.

fair market value
The price at which goods and services are bought and sold between willing sellers and buyers in an arm's-length transaction.

Fair market value lies somewhere between disposal value and replacement value. Fair market value is an attempt to determine the price that the asset would bring, in its current location and condition, in an arm's length transaction between a willing buyer and a willing seller. In contrast to disposal value, fair market value is assigned from the point of view of the buyer, and thus includes the selling price and all costs to install, test, and prepare the asset for productive use.

The appropriate valuation method is largely determined by the purpose for which the valuation is being made. As stated above, laws, regulations, and the requirements of GAAP require that book value be used for financial reporting and income tax purposes.

For any other purpose, you may use the valuation method that best meets your needs. If you are offering assets as collateral, lenders are most interested in disposal value, as that best approximates the amount that would be realized if the asset were repossessed. If you are considering an investment opportunity, disposal value provides an estimate of the timing and amounts of cash flows that can be used for net present value and internal rate of return calculations. If you are offering your business for sale, as the seller of a business you would view disposal value as a "lower limit" for the selling price because it approximates the amount that would be realized were the business to be liquidated. On the other hand, potential buyers and investors are most interested in replacement value. Replacement value sets an "upper level" for the value of your business assets as an approximation of the cost that would be incurred to equip a start-up business.

Determining the Value of Inventory

If your business holds inventory for sale, you are faced with the problem of determining its value. The value that you assign to inventory sold and on hand affects (1) the amount of profit that you recognize and (2) the value of your business.

Inventory valuation begins with knowing *how much* of *what* you are holding. All too often owners of small businesses purchase inventory items which are stored out of sight. These items somehow never get used or sold. Over time such "forgotten" items accumulate, tying up scarce funds. At the minimum, you should conduct a **physical inventory**—a type of periodic inventory—at least once each year, identifying and counting all items that your business owns. Items that have not been sold or used for significant periods of time should be disposed of to free their value for productive use. Slow-moving and dated inventory may be disposed of by discounting or "dumping" it to overstock resellers such as Big Lots, Dollar Stores, or junk dealers.

inventory valuation
Determination of the amount of assets held by the firm for sale or production.

physical inventory
A count of all the inventory being held for sale at a specific point in time.

SMALL BUSINESS INSIGHT

JAMES P. SMITH OF SIGNGRAPHICS, INC.

James P. Smith, owner of Signgraphics, Inc., of Blue Springs, Missouri, had just learned that a contract to produce signs for a chain of convenience stores had been lost to a competitor. As a result, Signgraphics was now stuck with twenty 8 ft × 12 ft polycarbonate plastic sign faces. The faces could not be used for any other purpose because they were vacuum molded and internally painted with the logo and name of the store chain. Each sign face, molded and painted, cost over $1,300. That meant Signgraphics had $26,000 of scrap.

Signgraphics, as would most small businesses, would be severely damaged by such a loss. Something had to be done, and done quickly.

Biting the bullet, James called the competitor who had just won the contract. The competitor quickly agreed to purchase the faces for $22,000. Although still a painful loss, $4,000 was not great enough to threaten the survival of the business. In fact, Signgraphics continued to be successful for an additional four years until the business was sold to yet another competitor in the area.

Sooner or later, you are likely to be stuck with surplus, slow-moving, or obsolete inventory. If you are like most entrepreneurs, you'll be tempted to keep the inventory, "just in case you find a use for it." Over time, such surplus inventory can build up to astonishing levels, tying up money that could and should be used in the business.

A better strategy is to constantly monitor the use of inventory and quickly dispose of any "dated" items before they become obsolete or otherwise unsellable. Such inventory items may, as in the case of Signgraphics, find a ready buyer in a competitor. If you are a wholesaler or retailer, you can offer steep discounts to existing customers. You may sell to a company that specializes in buying surplus and distressed items. Finally, you may, as a last resort, scrap such inventory, and take its acquisition cost as a business deduction against profits.

Signgraphics had to make a tough call on selling their extra sign faces inventory to a competitor. Having an inventory handling approach that allows for quick and easy adaptation is key to successfully managing your small business. What are some ways you think owners can build flexibility into their inventory management procedures?

Once you know what inventory you have, you can then assign it a value. One of the unpleasant surprises that many small business owners experience is the discovery that inventory is often worth far less than it cost to acquire. Inventory loses value in many ways. It can lose value because of changes in fashion or changes in technology. Some inventory items, especially food items, spoil with the passage of time. Some things get broken, dented, scratched, dirty, or otherwise shopworn. Determining the value of items being held for sale is essential to efficient inventory management.

The value of inventory items held in stock is highly problematic, especially when prices are rapidly changing. You must answer the questions, "Is inventory worth what I paid for it? Is it worth what I must pay to replace it? Or is it worth only the amount for which I can sell it?" Any of these methods, **acquisition cost, replacement cost**, or fair market value, respectively, can reasonably be used to determine the value of your inventory. However, your choice of valuation method affects the profit you recognize and thus the amount of taxes you must pay.

acquisition cost
The total cost of acquiring an asset, including such costs as purchase price, transportation, installation, testing, and calibrating in order to ready it for its first productive use.

replacement cost
The total cost of replacing an asset with an essentially identical asset.

If you assign a high value to inventory, you increase the amount that you deduct for cost of goods sold which results in decreased sales margin and reported profit. Less reported profit means less will be paid in income taxes. However, lowered reported profits makes your business worth less to investors, lenders, and potential buyers. On the other hand, if you assign the lowest acceptable value to inventory, you will make the results of operations of your business look better, but at the price of paying increased income taxes.

Property, Plant, and Equipment

LO3 Describe techniques for managing fixed assets.

The importance of the issues of the acquisition and maintenance of real estate, buildings and machinery varies among businesses. If your business is wholesale or retail merchandising, the issues of **property**, **plant**, and **equipment** (PPE) are most likely of relatively minor importance to your success. If your business is manufacturing, mining, farming, ranching, or transportation, your greatest investments and your greatest costs are consumed by land, buildings, and machinery. Obtaining, maintaining, and efficiently using these expensive capital assets is critical to your success.

property
A general term for real estate, but it can also be applied as a legal term for anything owned or possessed.

plant
A general term for the facilities of a business.

equipment
Machinery, tools, or materials used in the performance of the work of the business.

whole of life costs
The sum of all costs of capital assets, including acquisition, ownership, operation, and disposal.

cost of owning
Cost incurred in financing, insuring, taxing, or tracking an asset.

cost of operating
The direct cost incurred in using an asset for the purpose for which it was intended.

cost of disposition
Cost incurred in the activities necessary to get rid of an asset.

All capital assets cause you to incur four costs over time: (1) the cost of acquiring the asset, (2) the cost of owning the asset, (3) the cost of operating the asset, and (4) the cost of disposing of the asset.

It is common for owners of small businesses to consider only the first of these costs in making an investment decision. This narrow focus on acquiring an asset is unfortunate because although you make such decisions infrequently, the ramifications of the decisions are critical to your success. Making a correct decision will increase the value of your business, and thus your wealth. Making an inappropriate decision will lead to suboptimal returns, even to your business going bankrupt. The probability of making a good capital investment decision is greatly increased when all the costs of the asset, called **whole of life costs**, are included in the decision process. In Skill Module 16.2 you will analyze the whole of life costs for one asset.

Acquisition cost of a capital asset is the sum of *everything* that you spend to acquire and prepare the asset for its first productive use. Thus, the cost of engineering to specify the details of the asset, purchase price, shipping, insurance during shipping, setup, testing, and interest on any borrowed funds are all accumulated to determine the cost of the asset.

Costs of owning an asset include interest on funds borrowed and the opportunity costs of funds invested to acquire it. Costs of ownership also include insurance on the asset, property taxes, value of the space that the asset occupies, and the cost of record keeping and security for the asset.

Costs of operating the asset include the energy the asset consumes, maintenance, loss of economic value resulting from wear and obsolescence, and any necessary training of operators.

Costs of disposition are composed of the value of the activities necessary to get rid of the asset. Such costs include meeting environmental regulations, disassembly, advertising, commissions, shipping, insurance, and fees. The cost of meeting environmental requirements can be huge for some assets. For example, it is nearly impossible to find affordable means to dispose of radioactive tools, anything that contains mercury or lead (e.g., computer monitors), electric motors and transformers that contain polychlorinated biphenyls (PCBs),[12] and personal computers which contain significant quantities of several poisonous heavy metals.[13]

Understanding Whole of Life Costs for Capital Budgeting

SKILL MODULE 16.2

You are the owner of the Real Wood Furniture Company. Business has grown to the point that a bottleneck has formed at the point where the 4-ft × 12-ft lumber-core plywood sheets are cut to finish size. You have identified two automated panel saws that have identical capacity sufficient not only to eliminate the bottleneck, but also to be able to keep up with projected growth for the next 10 years.

Each machine has a useful life of 10 years. However, each will have to be rebuilt at the end of the seventh year to be able to get the final three years of use. At the end of 10 years, either machine will be technologically obsolete, and thus you will have to dispose of it at that time. Estimated cost data for each saw are shown in the chart at the left.

Real Wood Furniture Co.
Manufacturers of Fine Wood Desks
Data Concerning Automatic Panel Saw

	Kyrobi	**Delta**
Purchase price	$110,000	$80,000
Shipping	3,500	1,000
Installation	6,500	4,000
Testing	3,500	4.500
Total acquisition cost	$123,500	$89,500
Maintenance cost per year	$12,000	$14,900
Energy costs per year	8,500	13,000
Rebuilding in seventh year	25,000	35,000
Disposal cost end of tenth year	4,850	6,000

1. Examine the data in the chart. Without doing any specific mathematical analysis, state which saw you would purchase, and why you made your choice.
2. Assume that every desk to be produced for the next 10 years will be made from wood that is cut by the saw that is purchased. Sales for the year the saw is purchased are projected at $260,000 and are expected to increase by 15 percent per year for the next 10 years. Use Real Wood Furniture Co.'s cost of capital to perform a discounted cash flow analysis of purchasing each saw. Now which saw would you choose, and why?
3. **Advanced topic:** Assume that Real Wood Furniture Co. is profitable and will pay 30 percent income taxes each year of the life of the saw purchased. Repeat the discounted cash flow analysis, only this time make adjustments for the effect of income taxes. Now which saw would you choose, and why?

The Capital Budgeting Decision

capital budgeting
The process of deciding among various investment opportunities to create a specific spending plan.

LO4 Calculate ratios used to analyze capital investment decisions.

Eventually small businesses get to the point where they can begin to make investment choices—do you open a new location or expand the one you have? Do you buy new machinery or invest in real estate? The process of deciding among various investment opportunities to create a specific spending plan is called **capital budgeting**. The goal of capital budgeting is to improve the quality of decisions about how to best use the scarce resources of the business. Capital budgeting works by determining the costs and benefits of each alternative investment, such as machinery or real estate. The question that must be answered to make a decision is, "Which of the available investment alternatives provides the greatest benefit relative to the cost of the investment?"

To do this, the alternatives are simultaneously compared by examining various financial ratios or by applying the concepts of the time value of money. The time value of money is the concept that a dollar received today is worth much more than is a dollar to be received at some time in the future.

The two most commonly used financial ratios for comparing investment alternatives are (1) **payback period** and (2) **return on investment (ROI)**. There are also two significantly more complex approaches called *net present value (NPV)* and *internal rate of return (IRR),* which are discussed in Appendix B of this chapter. Each of these measures has both advantages and disadvantages. Not one of them is appropriate in all circumstances, although each can be useful in the capital budgeting process.

payback period
The amount of time it takes a business to earn back the funds it paid out to obtain a capital asset.

return on investment (ROI)
A capital budgeting equation used to measure the relationship between initial investment and the profits that are expected to be received from making the investment.

To illustrate each of these investment analysis tools, consider the following: The owner of a sign shop has the opportunity to contract with a rapidly growing franchise operator to install signs at all new locations. To be able to complete this contract, she will need to invest in a heavy truck and a truck-mounted crane. She has reduced the decision alternatives to two different truck-crane combinations: a Skyhook 85-foot heavy-duty crane with a service ladder mounted on a Ford diesel truck and a Sponco 87-foot medium-duty crane with a service bucket and remote controls mounted on a GMC diesel truck. The cost of the Ford-Skyhook combination, ready for use, will be $150,000. The cost of the GMC-Sponco combination will be $185,000. Each truck and crane will have a useful life of 10 years.

Each crane has certain advantages and disadvantages. The Skyhook crane can lift 2,000 pounds to its full extension height. However, it does not have remote controls, and thus requires a crew of two people. The Sponco can lift only a 950-pound load, but its service bucket with remote controls allows it to be used by a single operator as a "cherry picker" to lift the operator into position, obviating the need (and dangers) of working from a ladder. Based on these facts, the owner has estimated future cash flows that will be provided by each alternative.

The owner has determined the following criteria to aid in making a decision:

1. The business's weighted average cost of capital is 20 percent.
2. The maximum acceptable payback period is four years.
3. Depreciation is recognized using a **straight line for a useful life of 10 years**.
4. Salvage value of each combination will be $0 (zero).
5. Cash flows and profits will differ by the tax effect of depreciation recognized.[14] Depreciation for the Ford-Skyhook is $15,000 a year, for the GMC-Sponco $18,500 a year.

straight line for a useful life of 10 years
Depreciation is computed using a straight line method over 10 years, so an asset would lose 10% of its value each year.

Payback Period

The payback period measure is a statement of how much time must pass before your business receives back the same number of dollars in cash flow as you must pay out to obtain a capital asset. Only cash flows are considered.

Two decision rules are applied in choosing from among alternative investments:

1. Accept only those alternatives for which the time required to recoup the original investment is equal to or less than a maximum allowable time determined by management.
2. Accept the alternative with the shortest payback period among those that meet the first criterion.

Consider the following example: Using the data in Table 16.1, we can calculate that the Ford-Skyhook combination pays back in 2 years and 11 months. In the first year, $35,000 is paid back. Another $60,000 is received in year 2, leaving $55,000 to be recovered. If we assume that the money is received evenly across the year, then it will take 55,000/60,000, or 0.917, of one year to recoup the final $55,000.

Using the same method, we find that the GMC-Sponco combination will require 3 years and 2.7 months to pay back its initial investment.

Following the decision rules, we find that both alternatives meet the minimum hurdle of paying back in four or less years. However, the Ford-Skyhook alternative payback period is 3.7 months shorter, and thus we would choose this alternative.

The main advantage to using the payback period analysis is its simplicity. Also, it allows easy comparison of alternatives that are dissimilar in magnitude of cash flows and overall project life. The primary disadvantages of the payback method are that (1) it disregards the time value of money and (2) it disregards all cash flows that occur after the payback period. These disadvantages often result in managers making suboptimal investment decisions.

Rate of Return on Investment

Rate of return on investment (ROI) is a measure of the relationship between the initial investment and the profits that are expected to be received from making the investment. The calculation is straightforward:

$$\text{ROI} = (\text{average annual profits})/(\text{average investment})$$

TABLE 16.1 Data for Capital Budgeting Decisions

Estimated Cash Flows and Accounting Profits of Each Alternative

	Ford-Skyhook		GMC-Sponco	
Years	Cash Flows	Accounting Profits	Cash Flows	Accounting Profits
0	$ (150,000)		$ (185,000)	
1	35,000	20,000	45,000	26,500
2	60,000	45,000	62,500	44,000
3	60,000	45,000	62,500	44,000
4	65,000	50,000	67,500	49,000
5	70,000	55,000	77,500	59,000
6	75,000	60,000	87,500	69,000
7	75,000	60,000	92,500	74,000
8	80,000	65,000	95,000	76,500
9	80,000	65,000	95,000	76,500
10	80,000	65,000	100,000	81,500

As with the payback method, two decision rules are applied to choose from among alternative investments:

1. Accept only those alternatives for which the return on investment is equal to or greater than the business's weighted average cost of capital, which is the expected average future cost of funds and is discussed in Chapter 15.
2. Accept the alternative with higher ROI among those that meet the first criterion.

We can then calculate the ROI of each alternative:

	Ford-Skyhook	GMC-Sponco
$\dfrac{\text{(Sum of profits/length of project)}}{\text{(initial investment + salvage value)/2}}$	$\dfrac{(530{,}000/10)}{(150{,}000 + 0)/2}$	$\dfrac{(600{,}000/10)}{(185{,}000 + 0)/2}$
	$= 0.707$	$= 0.649$

Both alternatives meet the first decision rule as the ROI of each exceeds the business's weighted average cost of capital of 20 percent. We accept the Ford-Skyhook alternative because it has the greater ROI of the two.

Return on investment analysis has two advantages: (1) It is easy to calculate, and (2) it relies on accounting information with which business owners, lenders, and investors are comfortable. ROI's disadvantages are (1) profits are not the same as cash, and (2) the method ignores the time value of money.

Net Present Value

Calculation of net present value (NPV) and its application to this investment decision is explained in Appendix B, beginning on page 533.

Rent or Buy

LO5 Describe the advantages of renting or leasing capital equipment.

It is often not necessary, or even advisable, to purchase capital assets. Many capital assets for which there is an active market, such as real estate, trucks, tractors, and airplanes, can easily be obtained through rental agreements.

Renting such assets provides several important advantages. First, renting requires little or no cash investment on your part. Purchasing, however, often requires that your business be able to pay cash of 20 percent or more of the purchase price in order to be able to borrow funds to finance your purchase. Second, renting usually does not require an extensive (and expensive) application process as does borrowing money. Third, renting usually protects you from unexpected costs of repairs. If you are renting a truck for your business and it breaks down, you can quickly obtain a replacement vehicle. Fourth, renting capital equipment provides an easy method to avoid ongoing costs if business conditions change. If a sudden loss of business makes the asset uneconomical, you can return it to its owner, thereby avoiding the costs of ownership, operation, and disposal.

Making the decision to rent rather than to buy an asset provides a partial answer to the problem of projecting future cash flows. You may make the same analysis that you would in order to decide to buy. However, in making this analysis, renting provides two advantages over buying: (1) The exact amount and timing of cash **outflows** is specified in the rental contract, and (2) renting provides a fallback position should your projections prove to be incorrect. If actual cash flows fall short of your projections, you may be able to return the rented property, avoiding future rent payments. If you still wish to pursue the opportunity despite lower cash flows than expected, you can make provisions for a less expensive alternative. Should actual cash flows exceed your projections, you have the options of either purchasing the rented asset or returning the asset and purchasing a higher-capacity replacement.

outflow
Funds being paid to others by the firm.

The disadvantages to rental are, first, you do not have an ownership position. The value of a rented asset does not ever show up on your business's balance sheet. Should you need capital, rented assets cannot be used as collateral to obtain borrowed funds. Second, rental requires that you make regular, timely payments. If you own an asset, you may be able to exercise some control over cash outflows for costs of ownership and operations, such as maintenance and upgrades. These options do not exist for rented assets. Third, the number of dollars paid in rent usually exceeds the number of dollars you would spend to own the asset. The owner of the asset you are renting bears the risk of breakdowns, obsolescence, and disposal costs. Because of these risks, the owner must receive a premium over the costs that you would incur if you were to buy the asset.

Financing with Leases

A lease is simply a rental agreement that specifies a minimum period of time for which you must make rental payments. Lease periods range from as short as a few days to 99 or more years, and leases can include other sorts of provisions or specifications for how the business deal or the leased property is to be handled. Thus, as lessee, you may agree to bear the costs of maintenance, insurance, and taxes on leased assets. Alternatively, any of these costs may be born by the lessor. Leases provide a middle ground between renting and owning assets.

There are two basic types of leases, operating leases and capital leases. The two types of leases differ primarily in how the property is disposed of at the end of the lease period.

Operating leases are leases that are similar to renting. In an operating lease, ownership of the asset never passes to you as the lessee. At the end of the lease period, you either return the asset to its owner, or you may purchase the asset at its then current fair market value.

operating lease
A long-term rental in which ownership of the asset never passes to the person paying for the lease.

All other aspects of maintaining and operating the asset can be negotiated between lessor and lessee. Either party may be contractually responsible for maintenance and operating costs.

Capital leases are leases that are essentially the same as buying the asset. At the end of the lease period the asset becomes property of the lessee, either without any additional payment or by the lessee paying a nominal amount. The test to determine if a lease is a capital lease, rather than an operating lease, is the existence of provisions for title of the asset to pass to the lessee at a price less than the asset's fair market value.

capital lease
A lease in which at the end of the lease period the asset becomes the property of the lessee, possibly with an additional payment.

The benefits of leasing are numerous. First, you can usually obtain a very low down payment. Second, the process of negotiating and closing a lease is usually less complicated and expensive than making a purchase and obtaining borrowed funds. A third benefit is that it is usually much easier for you to replace leased assets than it is to replace assets you own.

Because actual ownership of the asset remains with the lessor until the provisions of the lease contract are fulfilled, the owner is not faced with the expensive and time consuming process of repossession. As owner of the asset, the lessor may simply take it back, should you default on the contract. Because of this, a lessor is less concerned with your ability to pay than is a lender and is willing to accept a lower initial investment from you in return for higher periodic lease payments. Similarly, because the lessor is in the business of acquiring and disposing of assets, the lessor assumes the responsibility of disposing of obsolete assets and providing new ones.

The primary disadvantage of leasing is that it usually costs more than would purchasing. A secondary disadvantage is that leased assets are usually subject to numerous restrictions on how they may be used, maintained, and disposed of. Restrictive lease covenants are intended to provide protection to the owner by preventing the lessee from allowing the asset to lose value through misuse, neglect, or abuse. A typical lease restriction is a prohibition on driving or flying leased transportation equipment across an international border. Were you the lessee of a business airplane, such a provision could become a serious inconvenience should you develop business that requires you to regularly travel to Monterrey, Mexico, and no airline offers such service from your home city.

Fractional Ownership and Other Forms of Joint Ventures

A less used method of reducing the costs and risks of acquiring capital assets is the process of joint venturing. A joint venture is simply a formalized partnership between two or more businesses for some specific purpose. Joint ventures are quite common among medium to large businesses and are growing among small businesses.[15]

Joint venturing makes economic sense when each party to the venture has limited use of an expensive asset or faces major investments that could be sidestepped by partnering with another firm that already has made that investment. One area in which joint ventures are relatively common among small businesses is the ownership of airplanes. Airplanes are quite expensive. Even a 30-year-old Beech King Air turbo prop airplane can easily sell for $1 million. Although old, and by some standards obsolete, a King Air can still produce more than 6 million seat miles per year: the equivalent of 1,600 transcontinental trips. Very few small businesses need even a fraction of the transportation capacity produced by such an airplane. Because of these facts, it is common for airplanes to be owned by partnership arrangements among several businesses that share the costs proportionate to their use of the plane.

Recently, some leasing companies have created an ownership structure similar to joint ventures, called *fractional ownership*. These companies offer buses, airplanes, and yachts under arrangements in which a small business may buy only that share that it can reasonably use during the course of business. In this manner, many small businesses now have access to business jets by having purchased as little as one-sixteenth of the ownership rights.

"Once bought, forgotten" might be the sort of saying that reminds all entrepreneurs about why managing assets is critical to being successful in managing a small business and its finances. Whether inventory or operating assets, most firms have substantial value tied up in the assets of the business. It is possible to make sure that these assets are being managed to be financially useful, and this chapter outlines the techniques—ranging from simple to complex—to do that. The simple techniques of inventory tracking and management can be easily grasped and implemented in a wide variety of settings. The more statistically driven approaches are increasingly workable, because they use functions built into spreadsheets or accounting programs' inventory routines. Like so much in small business, asset management works if you take the time to do it or have it done for you.

Managing Operations

LO6 Describe techniques to manage and improve the operations of your business.

No matter what your business is, the functions of management are always the same: planning, organizing, staffing, directing, and controlling. You and your managers must establish the goals and objectives of your business. Once you have a set of coherent goals, you must make plans on how to attain them. You must organize and direct your business to attain the desired goals. You must also analyze the working of your business to be able to control it and to correct any variations from the planned procedures in order to reach the predetermined goals. These functions interact and it takes skill to coordinate them so you can accomplish your business goals, often through the efforts of others.

Although the preceding paragraph was easy to write, and is easy to read, putting it into practice is far from easy. You must be able to determine which management functions are most important and be able to organize them by priority. Although all five functions are important parts of a manager's job, just how imperative each is varies with changes in the business, such as during the stages of a product life cycle. One simplifying fact for operations management is the fact that operations management is concerned primarily with directing and controlling. Planning, organizing, and staffing are primarily the responsibility of executive management.

Operations management is focused on all of the activities of the business, such as producing product and moving it to customers. Throughout the book, you have seen examples of the operations management decisions small business owners must make. These include managing your time in Chapter 5, optimizing your business's value chain in Chapter 7, managing the product and service life cycles in Chapter 9, and optimizing the location and physical layout of your business in Chapter 11. Similarly, much of this chapter deals with optimizing the use of your assets, like inventory and property. Along the way we have mentioned the kinds of strategic operational choices owners have to make about product design, process choice, capacity, quality, productivity, technology, workforce, and job design. The overriding goal of operations management is to be constantly improving the organization, through a more efficient use of resources and through improved or expanded service to customers, where "customer" means the next process as well as the final, external user. Because there is an operations element in every function of your business, people in all jobs should work together to improve their own operation efficiency.

Inputs into Your Business

inputs
The materials, labor, and energy put into the production of a good or service.

The **inputs** of a business are determined by its objectives. Your business objectives establish which raw materials are needed in what quantities. Your objectives will determine whom and how many people you must hire. For you to keep your business running smoothly, you must have information (feedback) concerning the essential processes that comprise your production system. This is as true for service industries, as it is for retail and manufacturing.

Business Operations Comprise Converting Time and Materials into Service and Products

operations
The process of transforming materials, labor, and energy into goods or services.

Business, to a great degree, comprises **operations,** or taking materials, the time of workers, and the investment of owners and changing these things into a desired product or service. This is illustrated in Figure 16.3. The specifics of your manufacturing, marketing, and distribution must be known in

FIGURE 16.3

The Operations Process

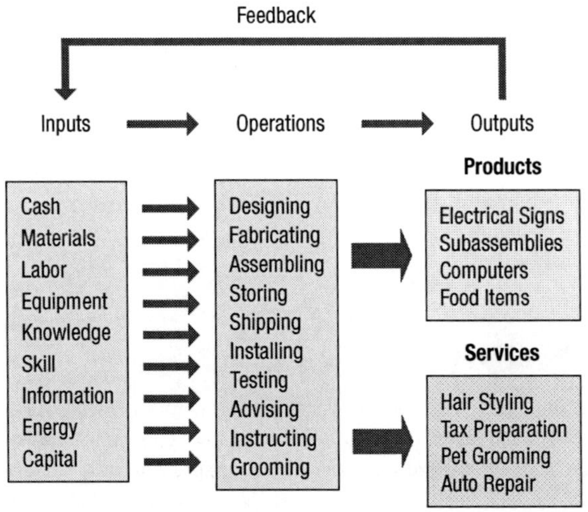

detail. You must also have some understanding of the ways your employees act and react. Some people will be interested in all the fine details. Others will be indifferent to the details as long as the desired result is obtained. For example, a manager may not know or care about the details of how a report is created and circulated. He or she is interested only in the information that the report contains. On the other hand, your accountant will be concerned with the details of each step: gathering data, preparing the report, and communicating it to those who need it.

Business Outputs

What constitutes the **outputs** of your business depends upon what your business is. The output for a Liberty Tax franchise is completed income tax returns. The output for an automobile garage is properly repaired cars. Generally speaking, output is the quality and quantity of goods and services produced, those things that produce revenue for your business. The entire system of your business should be designed to produce something that is desired in a market. Business customers of all types want goods and services that will make them more efficient, more effective, or more profitable. Individuals as customers will buy those things that provide greater comfort, improved health, enhanced entertainment, etc.

outputs
The service or product that is produced for sale.

Feedback

Any control system must have **feedback.** All inputs, material and labor, must be compared with a predetermined standard. If there is variation between the output and the standard, management action can be undertaken to correct the situation.

feedback
The process of communicating within or to the organization about how the outputs worked or were received.

A business that has multiple systems requires complicated feedback. Information must be communicated among all managers and employees who are part of the system. Operations control depends upon three types of feedback: (1) informational feedback, (2) corrective feedback, and (3) reinforcing feedback. Informational feedback is just that: information about the processes of your business. Corrective feedback is evaluative and judgmental. It comprises a value judgment about processes and behaviors. Inefficient work processes and undesirable employee behaviors are provided with various correctional actions. The manufacturing line may be redesigned. Misbehaving employees may be given training or punishment. Punishment ranges from a "dressing down" to termination of employment. On the other hand, reinforcing feedback rewards efficient processes and desired employee behaviors and can range from a simple statement, "Good job," to tangibles such as money or paid time off.

Measuring and Improving Productivity

The essence of production management is to ensure that the factors of production, materials, labor, machinery, land, and capital, are used efficiently to produce your business's product or service. Simply put, the major outcome of operations and production management is improved **productivity**. Productivity applies what you have just learned about inputs and outputs, because productivity is simply the ratio of outputs to inputs, or:

productivity
The ratio measure of how well a firm does in using its inputs to create outputs, literally, productivity is outputs divided by inputs.

$$\text{Productivity} = \frac{\text{Outputs}}{\text{Inputs}}$$

If you are creating a product (a.k.a. the output of your production process) that you can sell for \$10 and it costs you \$2.50 to make, your productivity ratio is 4:1. If you can cut your production cost to \$2, you have increased your productivity to 5:1. That increase is hard dollar proof you have improved your productivity. You might have done this by saving money on energy or raw materials or labor. In short, you have increased productivity by improving the **efficiency** of your production process—where efficiency means doing the same with less.

efficiency
The comparison of productivity ratios to see the extent that an organization has generated more outputs with fewer inputs.

There is another way to improve productivity, and that is through improving **quality**. Quality is a product's or service's fitness for use. It is usually measured by characteristics such as durability (how long it lasts), reliability (how consistently does it work), serviceability (how easily can it be repaired), style (how attractive is it), ease of use, and overall dependability (how much you can rely on it). If you can make your product so much better that a customer is now willing to pay \$11 for the new improved product, your gain is 11:2.50 or 4.4:1. That is a 10 percent gain in productivity due to quality improvements.

quality
Quality is a product's or service's fitness for use, measured as durability, reliability, serviceability, style, ease of use, and dependability.

Operations Management Challenges for Product-Based Firms

In talking about productivity above, the examples were primarily of product-based firms. Product-based firms take some sort of materials—groceries for a restaurant, crude oil for a refinery, or wood and pen parts for a high-end pen manufacturer like Michel Perchin ($1,000 and up) or David Oscarson ($4,000 and up) and add labor and technology to create a product. There are places for efficiencies all along the production process (or as we saw in Chapter 7, along the entire value chain, for that matter).

Consider high-end pens. One way to improve the efficiency of the production process is to use advanced technologies like lasers to help cut and drill quickly and precisely. Or using computerization with the laser to combine several steps into one, making it possible to produce more perfect pens faster. Another approach is to get the latest raw materials first when they are "hot" in the market. If moon rocks became commercially available, imagine what a pen made from moon rock would be worth. As more moon rocks would enter the market, the price would drop, so the best profits would come to the pen maker who gets the moon rock first into production and first into the hands of rich status-conscious buyers.

From this you can see the two major sources of efficiencies for product-based firms. One is to increase the amount, speed, or accuracy of work done for every day of operations. This can be done through scheduling improvements within the firm like those seen in the time management approach described in Chapter 5 or in this chapter's approach to inventory management. The other approach is to improve parts of the **supply chain** outside the firm so that raw materials get into production faster and that finished products get into customers' hands faster too.

supply chain
Like the value chain, the line of distribution of a product from its start as materials outside the target firm to its handling in the target firm to its handling by sellers into the hands of customers.

best practices
Activities identified by authoritative bodies as examples of optimal ways to get things done in a particular industry, profession, or trade.

How do you figure out ways to improve operations? There are several sources of expertise you can use. Our reliable friends at the SBA and SCORE can offer help, much of it low-cost or even free. Other major and relatively inexpensive sources are trade and professional associations. They often publicize "**best practices**" which represent the most productive ways found in your industry.

Often, top-performing firms will share their secrets of success with the rest of the industry to help improve the overall quality. It also does not hurt in advertising to say that "our procedures are now the industry standard, but we know more about them than anyone else!"

Another interesting source of free advice can be your vendors. For example, UPS, DHL, and FedEx will be glad to consult to you (for free) on ways to improve your supply chain. Although many of the answers will end with "we will be glad to do it for you" followed by a price quote, the analyses they can offer, as well as information about how other companies like yours have benefited from supply chain efficiencies, can help open new ideas to you. Similarly, raw material suppliers or equipment vendors will also be glad to consult with you on ways you could improve your productivity in areas where they have expertise—and possibly some equipment or supplies to sell you. The advice is often free and very current. Get it from competing firms to make sure you get the best ideas, and in case you are thinking about buying, also get the best price.

Operations Management Challenges for Service Firms

Service firms face several challenges in obtaining and maintaining efficient processes. Three characteristics of services—intangibility, inseparability, and perishability—impact operations choices and decision making, creating challenges for the managers of service operations. These characteristics confound and limit strategic choices and tactical decisions available to you.

The intangibility of services is a fundamental difference from goods. Services cannot be seen, felt, or tasted in the manner that goods can be. In contrast, tangible goods are produced, shipped, sold, and consumed in separate places. Another characteristic of a service is its inseparability: a service is produced and consumed at the same time. This exposes the entire production process to customer examination. In the manufacturing processes, the customer is rarely present. When producing services, however, the customer is usually present, preventing any clear distinction between the production stage and the consumption stage. Services are also perishable. In services, unused capacity is lost forever. Empty airline seats, vacant motel rooms, and unfilled theater seats not sold cannot be stored and sold later. Because of the characteristic of perishability, providers of services face great difficulty in managing capacity, and scheduling personnel.

However, despite intangibility, inseparability, and perishability, services can be improved. Part of the answer is deciding on a part of the service on which to focus. Services (let's use bowling as an example) tend to have differing degrees of four components. One component is called the explicit service. In bowling, rolling the ball and counting the pins dropped is the explicit service. The bowling takes place in a bowling alley, and that building with its balls and pins and equipment is what is called the supporting facility.

Part of the bowling experience depends on how you are treated—the friendliness of the staff, the process for which you are charged, and the cleanliness of the alley are examples. These aspects of what we usually think of as customer service are called implicit service. The fourth element, called a supporting good, refers to some tangible material outcome (remember that products were called "goods" in Chapter 9) you get from the service. In bowling, there are no tangible outcomes, unless you ask for a receipt. Because there is no real supporting goods in bowling, it is an example of a nearly pure service. Recall that in Chapter 9 we talked about pure services, pure goods, and the hybrids that include elements of both.

With these four elements in mind, it can become easier to target a way to improve the service. For a bowling alley, the owner could improve the supporting facility by getting faster pin-setting equipment, or adding more parking. The owner could add lights and sound equipment for "cosmic bowling" to improve (or at least expand) the explicit service. Improving cleanliness of the facility or getting the staff to be friendlier are ways to improve the implicit service, while a supporting good could be offered by giving bowling related tangibles, such as coupons for future games.

Also take a moment to consider innovative ways to improve service. For example, you could use the Internet to expand service delivery. Offering to post bowlers' pictures and high scores online, or sending them an e-mail with their scores, or letting customers network online for scheduling, or offering video analysis of a person's bowling stance are all implicit services which could add value to the customer and improve (as well as expand) the bowling experience.

The techniques for learning more about how to improve services are identical to those discussed for product-based firms. And if you have employees, there is one more great resource for improving productivity—asking them and putting their ideas into action. Employees of your business each have unique skills and knowledge. As your business grows, you most likely will find that certain employees have a greater understanding of certain functions of your business than do you. By including these people in the management process, you (1) ease your own work burden and (2) gain the advantage of expert input into the management process.

The point is that almost every service (and product) can be improved. In the long run, desirable operational improvements make your customers more loyal and your company more able to withstand competitive pressures. Operations management can add to the bottom line through efficiencies, through revenue growth, and when done right, to both at the same time.

CHAPTER SUMMARY

LO1 Describe techniques to manage short-term assets.

- Two short-term assets other than cash are critical to the success of most small businesses: accounts receivable and inventory.
- Offering credit can benefit a business in many ways, if the credit process is well thought out and carefully managed.
- High-quality receivables provide a means to quickly get cash to meet unexpected opportunities and problems.
- Inventory management is critical because for many small businesses inventory is the single greatest asset.
- Inventory requires significant cash investment that ties up capital that could be used for other business purposes.
- Careful management of inventory involves keeping the right amount of inventory available for sale and ordering the right amount of inventory at the right time to avoid both having too much on hand and running out of inventory, and thus losing sales.
- Techniques of inventory management include economic order quantity, just-in-time inventories, optimum stocking level, periodic inventory, perpetual inventory, bar coding, and point-of-sale systems.

LO2 Calculate the value of the assets in your business.

- Assets in use usually have a value greater than can be realized by selling them because of the value present in the assets' future use.
- Because the value of future use is very difficult to determine, accounting methods used to value capital assets are (1) book value, (2) disposal value, (3) replacement value, and (4) fair market value.
- Of these four methods, only book value and replacement value can be accurately determined.
- Each of the four accounting methods is useful in different situations:
  - Book value is used for financial reporting to outsiders.
  - Lenders prefer disposal value for the purpose of accepting collateral for a loan.
  - Disposal value is useful for estimating cash flows for discounted cash flow analysis.
  - Replacement value is useful for estimating sales prices for individual assets and for the business as a whole.

LO3 Describe techniques for managing fixed assets.

- Capital assets create four costs across their useful lives: (1) the cost of acquiring the asset, (2) the cost of owning the asset, (3) the cost of operating the asset, and (4) the cost of disposing of the asset.
- Better decisions result when all the costs above, called *whole of life costs,* are considered in the investing analysis.

LO4 Calculate ratios used to analyze capital investment decisions.

- The two most commonly used financial ratios for comparing investment alternatives are (1) payback period and (2) return on investment (ROI).
- There are also two significantly more complex approaches called net present value (NPV) and internal rate of return (IRR).
- Discounted cash flow methods (NPV and IRR) are the most complete, because they include the greatest amount of data in the analysis.

LO5 Describe the advantages of renting or leasing capital equipment.

- Renting requires little or no down payment. It therefore preserves cash.
- As a renter, you usually do not bear the costs of maintenance and repair.
- Leasing provides the same advantages as renting, but also provides assurance the asset will remain available for your exclusive use.
- Joint venturing for assets that have limited use allows you to obtain the benefits of the asset, but reduces the cost of ownership by sharing with other businesses.

LO6 Describe techniques to manage and improve the operations of your business.

- Operations management seeks ways to improve productivity.
- Increasing efficiency and increasing quality are the two ways to improve productivity.
- Product-based firms can improve the amount, speed, or accuracy of work, or improve the supply chain.
- Service-based firms can improve their explicit service, implicit service, supporting facility, and supporting good.
- You can get operations management advice from a variety of high-quality free and for-fee sources, as well as your own employees.

KEY TERMS

accounts receivable, 508
lock box, 509
factoring, 510
pledging receivables, 510
inventory, 510
economic order quantity (EOQ), 511
optimum stocking level, 512
safety stock, 512
pull-through system, 513
just-in-time inventory, 513
microinventory, 513
periodic inventory, 513
perpetual inventory, 513
bar coding, 514
point-of-sale (POS) system, 514
capital assets, 515
book value, 516
disposal value, 516

arm's length transaction, 516
replacement value, 516
fair market value, 516
inventory valuation, 517
physical inventory, 517
acquisition cost, 518
replacement cost, 518
property, 518
plant, 518
equipment, 518
whole of life costs, 518
cost of owning, 518
cost of operating, 518
cost of disposition, 518
capital budgeting, 519
payback period, 519
return on investment (ROI), 519
straight line for a useful life of 10 years, 520
outflow, 522
operating lease, 522
capital lease, 522
inputs, 524
operations, 524
outputs, 525
feedback, 525
productivity, 525
efficiency, 525
quality, 525
supply chain, 526
best practices, 526

DISCUSSION QUESTIONS

1. Discuss the pros and cons of providing credit to customers. If you do decide to provide credit, what policies should you establish and enforce?
2. Discuss how the use of economic order quantity (EOQ) and reorder calculations can benefit a retail business. What are the drawbacks in using these calculations?
3. Which of the asset valuation methods (book value, disposal value, replacement value, and fair market value) is the best for determining the value of your business's assets? Explain your choice, detailing how your preferred method is better than the other three.
4. How would you estimate the whole of life costs of an expensive capital asset, such as an executive airplane?
5. Discuss the advantages and disadvantages to payback period and to return on investment (ROI) as analysis tools for making capital investment decisions. Which do you prefer and why?

EXPERIENTIAL EXERCISES

1. Choose a local business in the industry in which you would like to own a firm. Visit the business that you choose, and walk about to observe the amounts and types of inventory on display. Interview the owner or manager. Determine the approximate value of inventory kept on hand. Find out the average time that any single item stays in inventory before it is sold. Also find out the minimum order quantities and delivery times of inventory. Use this information to estimate the amount of working capital necessary to maintain inventory. Make a report to your class.
2. WWW Make a search, using your library, the Internet, and your business contacts, to find factors in your area. Interview the factor and determine the terms offered. Ask what things about the receivables are considered in pricing the factor contract. Contact a commercial banker in your area and find out the bank's policy for lending against receivables. Report your findings to your class.
3. Contact a dealer who sells expensive capital assets, such as earth-moving or transportation equipment. Find out the costs of acquiring, owning, operating, and disposing of the asset. Use a spreadsheet program to estimate the amounts and timing of the whole of life costs of the asset. Estimate the cash inflows that the asset will produce. Use your estimates of costs and cash inflows to calculate the NPV, IRR, ROI, and payback of the asset. Make a presentation to your class, detailing the calculations you have made.
4. Assume that you have a plumbing business that requires the use of a backhoe. Contact equipment rental businesses in your area and find out the rental cost and terms for a suitable machine. Contact leasing companies to find out the cost of leasing a similar backhoe. Assume that, on average, you need the machine for 12 hours weekly. Which is more advantageous, renting or leasing? How would your answer change if you needed the machine an average of 20 hours per week? At what level of usage would renting and leasing not matter?
5. Assume that you own a 2005 Ford F750 Super Duty truck. The truck has been driven 32,000 miles. What is a reasonable disposal value for this truck? (Be sure to reduce your estimate of sales price by the costs of selling the asset.) What is the replacement value of this truck (in other words, how much would another F750 with 30,000 miles cost to find, buy, finance, deliver, and license?) Peruse newspaper ads, search the Internet, and talk with truck salespeople to estimate the truck's fair market value. Make a report to your class of your findings.

MINI-CASE

QUALITY SIGN COMPANY

The Quality Sign Co. of Visalia, California, provides credit to customers. The firm is currently averaging receivables of $34,500. The business needs an additional truck-mounted crane to keep up with its rapidly growing business. Quality's owner, George McElroy, has worked up an estimate of the cost of a suitable crane, which is presented in the chart below. Quality's bank is willing to loan 90 percent of the purchase price of the truck, crane, and equipment. All of Quality's currently available cash is needed as working capital and is not available to invest in this project. As a result, Quality must find a way to finance the 10 percent that the bank will not loan, plus the other costs of acquisition.

Quality has contacted a factor who has offered to pay 80 percent for all accounts that are less than 60 days past due. The factor is also willing to act as a collection agency for those accounts that are 60 or more days past due for a fee of 25 percent of the amount collected. Alternatively, Quality's bank has agreed to make a 90-day loan discounted at 12 percent interest in the amount of $32,100, secured by 100 percent of outstanding receivables. The sum of $32,100, which includes accrued interest, is due on the 90th day after the loan is made. During the 90 days, all new receivables will be pledged to the bank as they are incurred. Quality will continue to collect the receivables in the normal course of business. Examine the financial information provided below and prepare a recommendation to Mr. McElroy.

Cost of Acquiring Mobile Crane

Ford F750 Tandem truck	$ 73,000
120-ft heavy-duty crane	67,000
Hydraulic outriggers	12,500
Hydraulic pump	8,000
30-ft truck bed	5,000
Installation of bed	1,500
Delivery	1,500
Sales tax	12,338
License	1,000
Total acquisition cost	$181,838

Accounts Receivable

Current	$34,500
>30 days	6,000
>60 days	5,000
>90 days	4,000
Delinquent	4,000
Total receivables	$53,500

SUGGESTED CASES AND ARTICLES

- Richard Harris and Harris Homes LLC

Available on PRIMIS:

- Meyers & Morrison

SUGGESTED VIDEOS

Video Case:

- Wine Entrepreneurs, p. VC-7

eClips Videos:

- Cheryl Francis Discusses Aspects for Measuring the Value of the Company
- Malia Mills Discusses Importance of Creating a Budget, Monitoring Inventory and Cash Flow

STVP Video:

- Owning Your Product Formula

APPENDIX A

Economic Order Quantity

To solve for the quantity at which total inventory costs is minimized, consider the following definitions:

EOQ	=	economic order quantity in units (quantity that minimizes total inventory cost)
Q	=	quantity in units to be ordered at one time
P	=	price of one unit of inventory
O	=	cost of placing one order
C	=	cost of carrying one unit in inventory for one year
D	=	number of units to be sold in one year (demand)
D/Q	=	number of order cycles per year
Q/D	=	length of one order cycle as a fraction of one year

The total cost of making a single order is calculated as:

$$\text{Total cost of one order} = O + P \times Q$$

The total cost of holding inventory is the cost of holding one unit in inventory times the average number of units held during one order cycle times the number of order cycles in one year. If the number of units at the beginning of an order cycle is Q, and the number at the end of the cycle is 0, and sales are made at a constant rate, then the average number of units held is (Q + 0)/2, or simply Q/2. The length of one order cycle, as a fraction of one year, lies between 1 and 1 divided by the number of units to be sold in one year.

Holding cost per order cycle =
$C\,(Q/2)\,(Q/D)$ which can be simplified to:
Holding cost per cycle = $C\,Q^2/2\,D$

The total cost of ordering and holding inventory for one order cycle is the sum of these two equations. The total cost of inventory for one year is the cost for one cycle times the number of order cycles per year:

$$\text{Total annual cost} = [(O + P \times Q) + (C\,Q^2/2\,D)] \times D/Q = (O\,(D/Q) + D\,P + C\,(Q/2)$$

The purchase price of inventory (DP) is independent of how many units are ordered at any one time and how many orders are made, and thus may be disregarded. This provides the total cost of ordering and holding inventory:

$$O\,(D/Q) + C\,(Q/2)$$

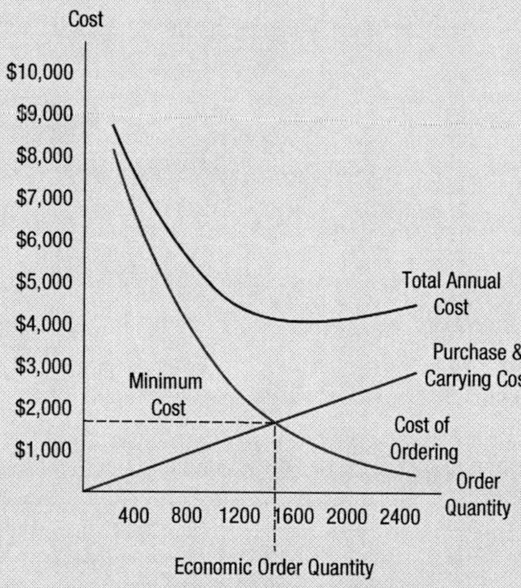

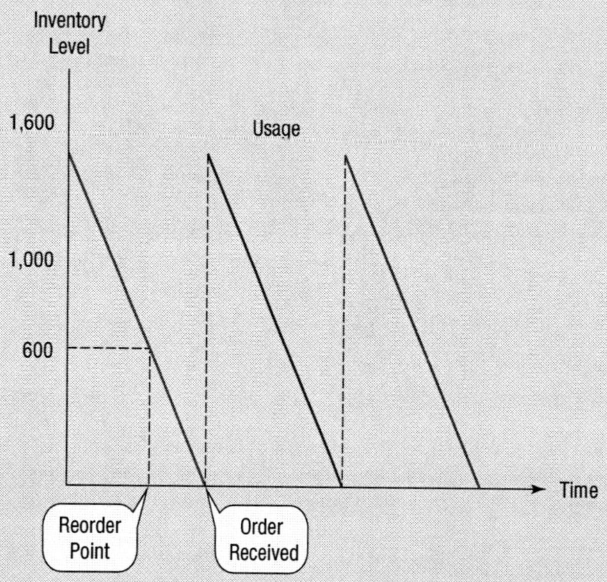

The minimum value of this equation is found by setting the first derivative equal to zero and solving for Q:

$$Q = (2OD/C).5$$

The EOQ calculation indicates how much to order at one time. It does not tell you when to order, however. To make this decision, you have to know how much time will pass between when the order is placed and when the inventory will be received. Suppose that the lead time is one month and that your business uses 600 units of inventory each month. You, therefore, must reorder when inventory levels fall to 600 units, leaving you with one month's supply on hand.

But what if your usage fluctuates, say, between 400 and 700 units of product each month? If you wait to reorder until inventory drops to 600 units and you then have a high-sales month, you could run out of inventory long before you run out of month. To protect from this, you can set a policy of maintaining a safety stock of surplus inventory over the minimum. You will reorder when inventory drops to 700 units. This will increase the cost of carrying inventory, but for almost all businesses, the cost of carrying inventory is a fraction of the cost of lost sales. Thus, for you, the cost of holding safety stock is offset by the advantages of not having a stock-out situation.

As you can see from this explanation, deriving the economic order quantity equation requires the use of calculus. Additionally, there are two simplifying assumptions that are unrealistic:

1. Ending inventory quantity is zero for each order cycle.
2. The purchase price of inventory is not affected by the number ordered at one time or by the number of orders placed.

In reality, neither of these assumptions is likely to be true. However, providing for a positive ending inventory and for a price that varies with changes in order quantity and number of orders complicates the solution so much that nobody bothers to do so.

Thus, EOQ determination is another example of an accounting or finance calculation that is approximately true, but precisely wrong. This is why it is necessary to apply common sense to the mathematical solution.

APPENDIX B

Time Value of Money and Discounted Cash Flow Analysis

Which would you prefer? One dollar right now, or one dollar to be received one year from now?

Certainly, you'd prefer to have the dollar today. Anyone would. But consider this: Suppose you were offered the choice between one dollar now or a U.S. savings bond that will pay you $10 one year from now. Which of these would you prefer? Most people immediately see the savings bond as being more valuable.

Now ask yourself, "Why is a dollar right this minute preferable to receiving a dollar in the future, but an iron-clad guarantee of 10 dollars one year from now is preferable to one dollar now?"

Almost everyone, even young children, have an instinctual grasp of the concept that waiting for a benefit somehow lessens the immediate value of that benefit. Given the alternatives of a benefit to be received immediately and a benefit to be received later, the delayed benefit must be of significantly greater value if it is to be chosen. This simple concept is the basis of the concept of the time value of money.

Suppose you knew for a fact that to save your life, you would need to have exactly one dollar one year from today. You can make an arrangement with a bank to deposit any amount of money. The bank will pay 10 percent interest. How much must you deposit to have the one dollar when it is needed?

Let "x" represent the amount that you will deposit. Then $10\%x$ is the amount of interest that the deposit will earn in one year. The sum of the amount you deposit plus the interest earned must equal one dollar:

$$x + 10\%x = \$1$$
$$1.1x = \$1$$
$$x = \$1 / 1.1$$
$$x = \$.91$$

In finance terms, we would state that the *present value* of one dollar, *discounted at 10 percent for one year,* is $0.91. Alternatively, we could say that the *future value* of 91 cents, *compounded at 10 percent for one year,* is $1.00. The term *present value* simply refers to the amount of money that would have to be deposited now to grow into a specified amount, given an interest rate and period of time. *Future value* is the inverse: the amount that a specific amount of money would grow to be, given a specific interest rate and period of time.

With just a little bit of effort, this concept can easily be expanded to calculate the amount that you must deposit now, at any stated interest rate, to accumulate any amount desired to be received at any time in the future. For example, consider the problem of accumulating for four years:

Value at the End of Year 1	Value at the End of Year 2	Value at the End of Year 3	Value at the End of Year 4
$(1 + r)X$	$(1 + r)(1 + r)X$	$(1 + r)(1 + r)(1 + r)X$	$(1 + r)(1 + r)(1 + r)(1 + r)X$

Where X = amount to be deposited
r = interest rate to be earned

The property that in years 2, 3, and 4 interest is being earned on interest from the prior years is called *compounding.*

PRESENT VALUE AND FUTURE VALUE OF 1

Notice that the value at the end of each year is equal to the amount deposited multiplied by 1 plus the interest rate, raised to the power of the number of the period. This allows us to develop an equation that can be easily solved for any amount deposited, any interest rate, and any number of compounding periods:

$$FV_n = PV\,(1 + r)^n$$

Where:

FVn = future value of the investment at the end of n years

PV = present value (the amount to be deposited)

r = annual interest rate (also called *compounding rate, or discount rate*)

n = number of periods that the deposit is compounded

By solving the equation for PV, we can develop a general equation that will answer the original question, "How much must you deposit now, at a stated interest rate, to accumulate a desired amount at a specified time in the future?"

$$PV = FV_n \times 1/(1 + r)^n$$

Thus, if you need one dollar four years from now, and you can earn 10 percent compounded annually, you must deposit $1/(1.1)^4$ dollars, or 1/1.4641, which equals 68.3 cents.

The calculated value of $(1 + r)^n$ is called the *future value of one,* and can be calculated for any discount rate, r, and any period of time, n. Similarly, the calculated value of $1/(1 + r)^n$ is the *present value of one.* You can easily calculate either the future value or present value of any amount by simply multiplying that amount by the appropriate future value or present value of 1. Thus, if you needed to have available $68,301.50 five years from now and you can earn an interest rate of 8 percent, you would multiply 68,301.50 times the present value of 1 for five years at 8 percent:

$$68{,}301.50 \times 1/(1.08)^5$$
$$68{,}301.50 \times 1/1.4693$$
$$68{,}301.50 \times 0.6806$$

The amount that you would have to deposit today is approximately $46,485.75.

PRESENT VALUE AND FUTURE VALUE OF AN ANNUITY

As the owner of a small business, you will often need to know information about the value of a series of equal payments over time. A series of equal payments made regularly over a set period of time is called an *annuity.*

For example, suppose you know that in three years you will have to replace an essential piece of equipment for your business. Your best estimate is that you can deposit $500 per month for three years at 8 percent interest in order to have sufficient money to make a down payment. How much would you have at the end of three years? The answer to this question can be easily, but tediously, solved by making a series of calculations. First, you must calculate the *monthly* compounding rate by dividing 8 percent by 12 months. Then, you use this monthly rate of .00666 to calculate the *future value of each payment,* then simply sum all 36 values:

$$FV = \$500 \times (1 + .00667)^{36} + \$500 \times (1 + .00667)^{35} + \$500 \times (1 + .00667)^{34} + \ldots + \$500 \times (1 + .00667)^{1}$$
$$635.119 \quad + \quad 630.912 \quad + \quad 626.734 \quad + \ldots + \quad 503.333$$

There is, however, a much less tedious, although slightly more difficult, means to calculate the future value of an annuity. The above summation equation can be solved algebraically, providing the following:

$$FV = C\left[\frac{(1 + r)^n - 1}{r}\right]$$

Where:

C = cash payment per period

r = number rate

n = number of payments

Substituting values into this equation provides:

$$FV = 500\left[\frac{(1 + .00667)^{36} - 1}{.00667}\right] = \$20{,}403$$

rounded to the nearest whole dollar.

The present value of a series of equal payments may be similarly solved by discounting each payment and summing all the payments. However, this summation equation has also been reduced to a formula:

$$PV = C\left[\frac{(1 - (1 + r)^{-n}}{r}\right]$$

Thus, by substituting in the appropriate values, you may easily calculate the present value of an installment contract, a lease, indeed, any series of equal payments.

DISCOUNTED CASH FLOW ANALYSIS

These simple concepts and calculations are the basis of all discounted cash flow analyses. Estimated current cash expenditures and net future cash inflows are discounted by some appropriate rate to derive *net present value* and *internal rate of return.*

NET PRESENT VALUE

To perform a net present value analysis, you must:

1. Estimate the *amount* and *timing* of all cash flows of the project.
2. Select an appropriate discount rate.
3. Discount to present value each cash flow using the selected discount rate and timing.
4. Sum the discounted cash flows.

As you can see from the steps above, net present value (NPV) is simply the sum of all cash flows, both negative and positive, discounted by an appropriate discount rate. The difficulty of NPV analysis lies first in accurately estimating future cash flows and second in selecting an appropriate discount rate. Performing the calculations is trivial.

Estimating future cash flows is basically a process of guessing the revenues and expenses that the project will create. Revenues and expenses are then netted for each time period, usually by month, quarter, or year. The estimating process can be as simple or as complex as you believe necessary to produce reliable numbers and dates.

Selecting an appropriate discount rate is absolutely essential to the utility of the analysis. If you select too high a discount rate, desirable projects will be rejected. Select too low a discount rate and money-losing projects will be accepted. Arguments can be made for using any of three very different discount rates: (1) cost of capital of your business, (2) the incremental cost of capital (or marginal cost of capital), and (3) a management-selected minimum acceptable rate of return.

The computation of NPV is accomplished by the following algorithm:

$$NPV = -CF_0 + \frac{CF_1}{(1 + r)^1} + \frac{CF_2}{(1 + r)^2} + \frac{CF_3}{(1 + r)^3} + \ldots + \frac{CF_n}{(1 + r)^n}$$

Where:

NPV = net present value of the project

CF_0 = initial investment in the project

CF_n = cash flow at period n

r = discount rate

To illustrate the calculation of *NPV,* consider the following: You are thinking about purchasing for your restaurant a pressurized fryer that will allow you to rapidly prepare spicy deep-fried chicken wings. You believe that the demand for this product will peak within a year, then decrease to zero over three years. The total cost of the fryer, installed and ready for service, is $25,000. The cost of disposing of the fryer at the end of its useful life will be equal to its value at that time. In order to make an NPV analysis, you have determined that your weighted average cost of capital is 24 percent. You estimate that the fryer will provide the following cash flows to your business:

Cash flows	($25,000)	$20,000	$8,000	$4,000	$2,000
Time period	Right Now (t_0)	One Year from Now (t_1)	Two Years from Now (t_2)	Three Years from Now (t_3)	Four Years from Now (t_4)

Net present value of these cash flows is calculated thusly:

$$\text{Cash flows / Discount factor:}\quad \frac{(\$25{,}000)}{(1+.24)^0}+\frac{\$20{,}000}{(1+.24)^1}+\frac{\$8{,}000}{(1+.24)^2}+\frac{\$4{,}000}{(1+.24)^3}+\frac{\$2{,}000}{(1+.24)^4}$$

You may easily calculate the present value of the individual cash flows by using a financial calculator, any calculator that does powers, or a computer spreadsheet such as Lotus 123, Quattro Pro, or Excel.[16] The calculated NPV is ($724.16). Because the NPV is less than zero (a negative number), you should reject this project because it would not provide a return as great as your business's weighted average cost of capital.

Although the decision rule for NPV indicates that the project should be rejected, remember that all the numbers on which the analysis is made are estimates. No matter how carefully you attempt to estimate future results, you can never do so with certainty. In fact, were you to purchase the fryer, you might find that the product was either much more successful or much less successful than you would ever have expected.

There are several ways to deal with this inevitable uncertainty. You can change your estimates slightly up or down, a process called *sensitivity analysis,* to determine the effects of small changes in your estimates. For example, if you were to increase your estimate of the first year cash flows by just $898, the decision would change to "accept." If you enjoy doing math, you could adjust each of your estimates for the probability of their being correct, then use the *expected* values in the analysis. You might reconsider using weighted average cost of capital for the discount rate. Perhaps you should consider using the cost at which you can borrow funds. Or you might consider using a discount rate that is the sum of the cost of borrowing and some minimum return that you are willing to accept. In fact, in this example, reducing the discount rate by less than 3/10 of one percent reverses the decision.

INTERNAL RATE OF RETURN

Another way of dealing with the uncertainty of NPV analysis is to ask the question, "If this project does not provide a return equal to the discount rate, then what rate of return does it provide?" Internal rate of return (IRR) provides the answer to this question by disclosing the actual rate of return, based on the amount and timing of the cash flow.

The internal rate of return of a project is that rate at which NPV = zero. In other words, IRR is the discount rate at which the present value of the cash inflows of the project exactly equals the present value of the cash outflows. Thus, in this example, you must solve the following equation for the value of the discount rate (IRR):

$$\frac{(\$25{,}000)}{(1+\text{IRR})^0}+\frac{\$20{,}000}{(1+\text{IRR})^1}+\frac{\$8{,}000}{(1+\text{IRR})^2}+\frac{\$4{,}000}{(1+\text{IRR})^3}+\frac{\$2{,}000}{(1+\text{IRR})^4}=\$0$$

It is unfortunate that there is no way to directly solve this equation for IRR. The only way to find the value of IRR is to try different numbers in a reiterative process until you find a number that provides a solution sufficiently close to zero. Financial calculators, such as those provided by Hewlett Packard and Texas Instruments, all provide an automated means to derive the answer. Computer spreadsheet programs also provide functions to find the IRR of any series of cash flows.

If you do solve the above equation, you will find that the IRR is approximately 21.59 percent. Compare this number with your estimate of your cost of capital, 24 percent. The question you must answer is, "How confident am I that my cost of capital actually exceeds 21.6 percent?" If you are confident, reject the project. If, on the other hand, you are not so sure, perhaps you should reconsider the assumptions and estimates that you have made.

APPLYING THESE APPROACHES TO THE TRUCK AND CRANE PROBLEM

Earlier in the chapter we discussed the problem of deciding whether to buy a Ford-Skyhook or GMC-Sponco truck and crane combination. We worked through two simple methods for making a capital budgeting decision—the payback period approach and the ROI or rate of return on investment approach. We noted then that NPV and IRR approaches could also be used.

Using either NPV or IRR will avoid the shortcomings of both the payback period and the return on investment methods. Discounted cash flow methods make specific numeric adjustments to approximate the lower value of money to be received as compared to the value of money received now.

Net present value (NPV), like the payback period method, is based upon estimates of the cash flows that an investment will cause and utilizes your business's weighted average cost of capital. It is like ROI in using the weighted cost of capital, but unlike ROI because NPV uses cash flows, not profits. When Warren Buffett is deciding if he will buy a company, he uses this technique. In his case he looks at the cash flow the business generates in a year and then figures how much it would be worth—after being discounted—at some point in the future. For buying businesses, he uses a U.S. Treasury long-term bond rate[17] for the period of time that he decides is appropriate. The final result of NPV calculation is a single dollar value, which can be of any magnitude, even a negative number, although the more positive the number, the better.

For our truck and crane example, the time period is the 10 years the truck and crane would be used. We know from the owner's earlier calculations that her weighted cost of capital is 20 percent, and we saw the cash flows in Table 16.1. The computations are complex, but spreadsheets like Excel can do them quickly and easily.

As with payback period and ROI, two decision rules are applied to decide among alternative investments:

- Accept only those alternatives for which the net present value is equal to or greater than zero.
- Accept the alternative with the greatest value among those that meet the first criterion.

Ford-Skyhook	GMC-Sponco
Net present value = $108,112	Net present value = $107,544

Both alternatives meet the first decision rule. Applying the second, you would accept the Ford-Skyhook alternative because it provides the greater positive net present value.

Internal rate of return (IRR) is a special case of net present value. IRR focuses on the return to the company, but also factors in the cost of the project. What is distinctive about the way IRR does this is that it statistically makes the net present value equal to zero, so the discount rate is thrown out as a consideration.

The decision rules for using IRR are:

1. Accept only those alternatives for which internal rate of return is equal to or greater than the business's weighted cost of capital.
2. Accept the alternative with the greatest IRR among those that meet the first criterion.

Ford-Skyhook	GMC-Sponco
Internal rate of return = 36.5197%	Internal rate of return = 33.37265%

As with net present value, both alternatives pass the first decision test. Of the two, you would choose the Ford-Skyhook alternative because it has the greater IRR.

It is important to note that NPV and IRR are considered some of the most complex of financial equations. The advantages of discounted cash flow analyses for evaluating investment alternatives are (1) all cash flows of each investment are explicitly included in the analysis, and (2) the time value of money is specifically calculated. Discounted cash flow methods do have serious drawbacks, however. First, a discounted cash flow analysis has the appearance of being extremely accurate. This appearance is highly deceiving, however. Every number in the calculation is, at best, an estimate. The weighted cost of capital, the amounts, and the timings of cash flows cannot ever be known with certainty. Second, the calculation uses a single estimate for each projected cash flow. Although cash flows that will occur soon may be reasonably accurately estimated, the longer the period of time over which projections are made, the greater the uncertainty of each estimate. Third, making good estimates of future cash flows requires considerable expertise and effort. Few owners of small businesses have either the time or the resources to do the necessary projections. All in all, discounted cash flow analyses are theoretically sound but are empirically highly problematic.

CHAPTER 17

Small Business Protection: Risk Management and Insurance

● Chimney sweeping is an example of an industry that is risky to insure. Read the chapter opening scenario to learn how two chimney sweeps catalyzed change by motivating a large group of fellow workers to get involved with the insurance company. Why do you think it is so important that small business owners and workers belong to a guild or similar industry group?

LEARNING OBJECTIVES

LO

This chapter will help you:

- **LO1** Explain the meaning and nature of business risk.
- **LO2** Describe the specific types of risks associated with different aspects of business operations.
- **LO3** Describe techniques to manage risks to stay within your level of risk tolerance.
- **LO4** Explain how insurance can be used to manage business risk.
- **LO5** Describe techniques for sharing risk with other businesses and organizations.

Focus on Small Business: The Massachusetts Chimney Sweep Guild[1]

Faced with paying twice as much for liability insurance as last year, Mike and Michelle Elliott decided to take action. Instead of simply paying the rates demanded and then griping about it, the couple prodded their industry group, the Massachusetts Chimney Sweep Guild, to use its bargaining power to get better rates for its members.

Chimney sweeps, like roofers, rough-in carpenters, and house movers, are difficult businesses to insure. Many large insurance companies do not want to deal with small businesses at all. Others will insure small businesses, but do not want to deal with businesses that involve heavy physical work, climbing ladders, and the presence of hazardous materials such as the soot and creosote that sweeps remove from flues. Such businesses have high risk of employee illnesses and injuries and high risk of damage to customers' properties—characteristics that are great disincentives for insurance companies.

The Elliotts sent a questionnaire to each of the 35 small business owners who comprised the Guild, asking for information concerning past claims, their volume of business, number of employees, and so on. Armed with the results of the survey, their own independent insurance broker, Tom Coonan, went to work to find appropriate insurance.

"Standard companies won't touch the Guild, because they have so few members. The total premium has to be over $1 million before the larger insurance companies will underwrite a group," Coonan says.

Coonan was able to find an insurance carrier that combined the desired coverages with affordable premiums. Overall, members of the Guild are highly satisfied with the insurance package. Plans are being made to obtain the group policy as an ongoing contract.

Operating a risky business such as chimney sweeping without the security of good insurance is a recipe for financial disaster. The cost of care for just one seriously injured worker or of repairing just one seriously damaged building can easily bankrupt a small business owner. On the other hand, if insurance coverage itself is excessively costly, the business cannot be profitable. By banding together, the members of the Guild were able to use their combined bargaining power to obtain appropriate coverage at affordable prices.

DISCUSSION QUESTIONS

1. The case mentions two kinds of risks faced by chimney sweeps. Name some others.
2. What is the risk to the small business owner of operating without insurance?
3. Why do you think the data on claim experience were useful for the insurance broker in negotiating the deal?

Risk in Small Business

LO1 Explain the meaning and nature of business risk.

We have discussed two kinds of risk in the previous chapters—financial risk that comes from your capital structure and investment risk caused by accepting or providing debt, and by holding debt or equity funds. Here we discuss other kinds of risk that small business owners face.

People define risk in many different ways, depending upon their unique situations and upon their own tolerance for uncertainty. You might define risk as the likelihood of getting an A in this course. A smoke jumper might consider risk the possibility of being trapped by a rapidly advancing forest fire. A surgeon who is to perform an operation might consider risk to be the level of probability that the patient will be no better after the surgery and will sue for malpractice. The person facing major surgery might think of risk as the chance that the operation will result in death.

For business owners, risk is the very real likelihood that the business may not succeed, that they may not only *not* become wealthy, but that they may well lose part or all of their investment in the firm.

We all know that people vary widely in their response to risk. Some people gleefully jump out of airplanes, while others are determined to "keep one foot on the ground." As we pointed out in the previous chapter, business owners similarly differ in their response to business risk. Some seek risk. Most prefer to avoid risk to the extent possible. In academic terms, some business owners are *risk seeking,* although most small business owners are *risk-averse.*

To the extent that small business owners are risk-averse, as part of every business decision, they consider what they could lose. If they can't reduce the level of risk to where they're comfortable, then they make arrangements to either insure against future losses or to spread the risk among other people or businesses.

Thinking about Risk

Generally speaking, risk is the probability that future states of being will be worse than you expect. For example, folks who build houses on or near the San Andreas fault expect those houses to survive the inevitable earthquakes. However, there is a small, but measurable, probability that an earthquake will be violent enough to destroy any building that can be built. The risk of building in an earthquake area is the *level of likelihood,* or the *probability,* that a strong earthquake will damage or destroy the house, an outcome that is definitely a worse state of being than the homeowner expects.

business risk
The level of probability that the future economic state of the business will be worse than expected.

Business risk is the probability that the future state of the business will be less successful than planned, resulting in the loss of value of business assets. No person enters a business for the purpose of losing money, but it can and does happen. The next quarter's business does not meet expectations. Investments go bad. Sales projections are not met. Products do not meet specifications. All of a sudden, investors find themselves the owners of assets that are worth much less than expected. The likelihood of this bleak outcome is the essence of business risk.

Among the most commonly identified sources of risk are:

- Financial risk that is a result of choosing among sources and types of capital investment.[2]
- Nonpayment of debts owed to the business.
- Changes in technology that render the business's product or service obsolete.
- Injury and illnesses suffered by employees as a result of their employment.

- Injury from accidents incurred by customers, vendors, and others while on business property.
- Loss or harm incurred because of the use of the business's product or service.
- Natural events, such as storms, floods, fire, and earthquakes.
- Violation of any of the multitude of laws and regulations that apply to small business.
- Theft of business property.
- Misbehavior by employees.

Risks Associated with Specific Business Operations

There are three general types of events that cause business risk. These are (1) events related to the property of the business, (2) events related to personnel, and (3) events related to customers and others.

LO2 Describe the specific types of risks associated with different aspects of business operations.

Property of the Business

Every business owns things of value. A retail or wholesale business owns inventory. A manufacturing business owns production machinery. A consulting company owns reputation, skill, and experience. Many businesses own furniture, office equipment, vehicles, buildings, and land. Some businesses own valuable patents, copyrights, trademarks, or trade secrets.

Each and every one of these types of property involves specific forms of risk. Inventory can be stolen, spoiled, or become obsolete. Production machinery can break down. Institutional skill and experience can be diminished or lost as key employees die, retire, quit, go to work for competitors, or start their own competing businesses. Furniture, office equipment, vehicles, and buildings can be damaged or destroyed by vandalism, accidents, fire, flood, or wind. Land may become contaminated by spills of hazardous materials or rendered unsafe by cave-ins or landslides. Patents may be infringed upon. Trademarks and brand names that are not properly protected may pass into the public domain. A trade secret may be disclosed.

Events Related to Personnel

There are three main types of risk related to events involving personnel: (1) theft, (2) violation of governmental regulations, and (3) loss of key employees.

Employee Theft

Employee theft is a fact of life for almost all businesses. Theft by personnel may involve direct stealing of money or other assets of the business, or may be the conduct of an illegal act that is intended to provide personal benefit at a cost to the business. The most common form of employee theft is the pilfering of items of small value, such as office supplies and small hand tools, or actions such as making copies for their children to use at school or otherwise using company resources to make personal items. Thought of this way, some experts estimate that 95 percent of small businesses face at least some of this sort of loss annually.[3] Losses of these types are usually insignificant in their effect upon the financial results of your business. However, theft losses of cash and inventory can be of such magnitude that your business is significantly damaged or even fails. As we discussed in Chapter 14, large losses usually arise from embezzlement or fraud.[4]

employee theft
Misappropriation of business property by employees of that business.

Violation of Governmental Regulations

Violation of government regulations has become a source of significant business risk over the last 30 years. **Regulation of the workplace** has increased, resulting in employer violations that range from having an employee one time "forget" to use required safety equipment to failing to provide required accommodations for handicapped employees and others to discrimination against a protected class (race, religion, color, national origin, age, disability, or gender). The cost of violating any of the many workplace regulations can range from as little as losing a few hours of your time completing paperwork, up to huge dollar fines and judicial awards.

regulation of the workplace
Laws and governmental rules that limit the freedom of business owners to manage their businesses as they please.

Violation of some of the regulations is probably inevitable, given the complex, ambiguous, and sometimes contradictory nature of the regulations. The federal rule making agencies of which employees may run afoul are countless, including the U.S. Food and Drug Administration, the Environmental Protection Agency, the Securities Exchange Commission, the National Transportation Safety Board, the Federal Aviation Agency, the U.S. Coast Guard, the Federal Drug Agency, and the Department of the Interior, to name only a very few. In addition, most states have similar business-regulating agencies that promulgate rules which often conflict with federal standards. The Small Business Administration estimated in 2001 that small businesses had to spend roughly $1,200 per employee per year to file and keep up with all the regulatory requirements. This rate was twice what large businesses had to spend.[5]

Although there are numerous government agencies that issue business regulations, those small businesses find most problematic are the rules from three agencies: the Internal Revenue Service, the **Equal Employment Opportunity Commission (EEOC)**, and the **Occupational Safety and Health Administration (OSHA)**. The problems arise because each agency has rules that are so complex that compliance problems are almost a certainty, if enough aspects of the business are reviewed. For example, the Americans with Disabilities Act has rules that govern the furnishings, size, placement, and clear space of public toilets and those run to over four pages and include more than 10 architectural drawings to specify exact maximums and minimums to the inch. Any violation of any of the specific accessibility measurements can result in civil fines or litigation awards. We discuss the IRS and the problems of tax code compliance later in this chapter.

Equal Employment Opportunity Commission (EEOC)
A commission established to enforce the provisions of the Equal Employment Opportunity Act.

Occupational Safety and Health Administration (OSHA)
A government agency created to enforce safety in the workplace.

The risk of noncompliance with OSHA and EEOC regulations is further increased by the continual growth in the scope of government regulations. For example, the Equal Employment Opportunity Commission's rule-making authority has grown from the agency's start in 1964. At that time, EEOC established five **protected classes**: "race, color, religion, sex or national origin."[6] Since then the authority of the EEOC has grown through the passage of (1) the **Age Discrimination in Employment Act** of 1967 (ADEA), (2) the **Rehabilitation Act of 1973**, (3) the **Americans with Disabilities Act of 1990** (ADA), and (4) the **Civil Rights Act of 1991**, all of which grant additional rule-making and enforcement powers. The commission has made thousands of rules that are ambiguous and, at times, contradictory.

protected classes
States of being that are expressly prohibited from suffering discrimination: race, color, religion, sex, national origin, gender, age, or disability.

Age Discrimination in Employment Act
An act of Congress that makes it illegal to discriminate against people who are older than 40 years of age.

Rehabilitation Act of 1973
An act of Congress that provides training for workers who are injured on the job.

Americans with Disabilities Act of 1990
An act of Congress that requires that businesses make provisions for access by disabled people.

Civil Rights Act of 1991
A series of acts by Congress that prohibit discrimination on the basis of race, color, religion, sex, or national origin.

Strategies for Dealing with Compliance

One strategy many small businesses use in coping with these rules is to stay small enough to remain below the thresholds for which these agencies' rules apply. For example, if there are no employees, there cannot be any discrimination in hiring. OSHA rules in most industries[7] do not apply to firms with fewer than 10 employees.

Some firms take the ultimate in risky strategies—indifference. Some owners figure it makes more sense not to spend time on compliance, and when they face government action, close the business. This sounds fine in theory, but government agencies can come after the owner of a business for damages and fines even after the business itself is bankrupt or closed. More often, the owner is fined and required to comply. The fines and time spent dealing with the agency are often said to cost more than complying ahead of time. You can see why indifference is the riskiest of strategies.

Another strategy is being proactive. Government agencies must post their rules and most make available summaries focused on the concerns of small business. For example:

EEOC's Small Business Page: http://www.eeoc.gov/employers/smallbusinesses.html.

EEOC's Americans with Disabilities Act Handbook: www.eeoc.gov/ada/adahandbook.html.

OSHA's Small Business Page: http://www.osha.gov/dcsp/smallbusiness/index.html.

OSHA's Small Business Handbook: http://www.osha.gov/Publications/smallbusiness/small-business.pdf.

A great listing of government small business resources can be found on the IRS's small business page, at http://www.irs.gov/businesses/small/content/0,,id598864,00.html. Perhaps the key resource for entrepreneurs trying to be proactive is www.reginfo.gov, the combined national Web site for federal, state and local regulation.

While many government agencies offer free reviews of a business for compliance, many small business owners are leery of such efforts, because they will be obligated to quickly fix any problems identified. A useful alternative is to have private contractors do assessments to check for compliance. Lawyers, especially labor lawyers, have experience in preventing EEOC compliance problems. Many consulting engineers can perform OSHA checks. In addition some of the major small business trade associations such as the NFIB and even local Chambers of Commerce offer classes on compliance for OSHA, EEOC, and other regulations.

One other strategy, which is not for the faint of heart or short of cash, is to fight for what you believe to be right. This usually entails first dealing directly with the agency's representative. Often this direct dealing is best done with an attorney present or only after being prepared by the attorney about how to handle your side of the meeting. If that meeting does not lead to a resolution, there are administrative reviews and even court actions at which the firm can stand up to the government. One famous example is that of Clint Eastwood (see Small Business Insight, below).

The Eastwood situation hints at one other strategy, what the original lawyer suing the hotel hoped to achieve—capitulation. In capitulation, often unscrupulous people use the threat of bringing a charge of noncompliance against a firm as a means of getting a cash settlement not to file. This type of person actively looks for minor violations of OSHA, ADA, or other laws. They then write the owner of the "offending" business, demanding a cash settlement for the alleged damage. The business owner is placed into an untenable situation: Either pay the "complainant" as demanded, or be stuck with the costs of litigation, and the risk that a jury will award even more. Many small business owners choose to pay rather than face the risk of losing. Because these payments are never recorded in any central location, it is possible for the individuals to repeat the process.

Loss of Key Employees

Loss of **key employees** is a particularly acute risk for small businesses. Because of the simple fact that there are only a few employees in a small business, invariably one person or a very few

key employees
Employees whose experience and skills are critical to the success of a business.

SMALL BUSINESS INSIGHT

It's More than a Fist Full Of Dollars[8]

Clint Eastwood may not quite match your idea of a small business owner, but in fact, Mr. Eastwood owns the 32-room Mission Ranch Hotel in Carmel, California.

In early 2000, the Mission Ranch was sued for alleged violations of the Americans with Disabilities Act. Unlike many owners of small businesses, however, Mr. Eastwood is wealthy, politically savvy (he had been mayor of Carmel), and willing to bear the costs of litigation. *The Wall Street Journal* quoted him:

> These "sleazebag lawyers," the veteran actor says, his voice constricting, messed with the wrong guy when they "frivolously" sued him and hundreds of other small-business owners for failing to comply quickly enough with the Americans with Disabilities Act.

Mr. Eastwood states that he is not in any way against the ADA. Rather, he will not "roll over" for trial lawyers whom he believes are using the ADA to extort money from small businesses by filing unwarranted lawsuits. Not only is he vigorously defending the suit against the Mission Ranch, but he has joined with U.S. Representative Mark Foley of Florida in an effort to insert a requirement into the law that would provide businesses with 90 days to come into compliance before any suit could be filed. Representative Foley stated that some lawyers have exploited the ADA and targeted stretches of small businesses, such as strip malls in south Florida.

Representative Foley, who is disabled himself, claims that there is no intent to reduce the effectiveness of the ADA. Rather, he said, "I just think for the benefit of everybody, they should cut out this racket because these are morally corrupt people who are doing this."

people are essential to the successful operation of the business. If such a key employee quits, retires, becomes disabled, or dies, the business faces a crisis. In many cases, the loss of a key employee has led to the bankruptcy and dissolution of the business.

Competition from former employees is also a constant risk. Good employees who understand the business, who successfully sell products and services, and who are skilled at the operations of the business are often tempted to become competitors. This can happen several different ways. A key employee may be "hired away" by an existing competitor who offers a higher salary and greater perks. A key employee may start her or his own business, using the knowledge and skills gained from working in your business. Customers may offer to back a key employee to establish a competing business in order to obtain lower prices and greater negotiating leverage. Vendors may offer a key employee dealerships or exclusive sales territories in a bid to increase sales of their specific products.

This risk is especially acute in knowledge and service businesses, such as accounting practices, medical practices, barber and beauty shops, and restaurants. All of these businesses have relatively low barriers to entry for qualified people. Each type of business depends upon personal relationships engendered with customers. When a key employee of a knowledge firm leaves, it is common for several customers to change to the new firm.

Events Related to Customers and Others

Although customers are, by definition, the "reason for being" of any business, they also are the source of considerable business risk. In addition to customers, you are also at risk from vendors and even trespassers on your property. This risk from customers and others primarily arises from (1) injuries suffered while upon business property and (2) injury or damage that is caused during the use of the business's products. These risks are, of course, in addition to the familiar risk of customers, who are sold products or services on credit, not paying as they have agreed.

Injuries suffered while on business property may or may not be your fault. People at times do stupid things, such as climb on shelves to get items that are "just out of reach." If the shelf collapses and dumps the customer onto the floor, you're going to pay twice: once for the broken shelf and spoiled merchandise, and once for the "pain and suffering" of the customer. A reasonable person might believe that the customer was responsible for his or her own acts and the business should not be liable. It is most unfortunate that juries are composed of "peers" and not of "reasonable persons."

Injuries on business premises may also arise from the actions of trespassers. In many cases, a business has been held responsible for harm experienced by a trespasser, as well as harm inflicted by

Retailers can be held responsible for damages caused by goods that have been tampered with and placed on the store's shelves. Constant vigilance is required to assure that inventory is free of any impairment.

the trespasser upon employees, customers, and vendors. An extreme example of this type of event is robbery and assault that occurs on business property. In many cases, injuries suffered by employees and customers at the hands of the criminals have been held to be the fault of the business. The rationale given has been that the business didn't provide good enough security. Again, the business pays twice: once when the robber steals money and other assets; again when the robber, employees, and customers are paid for pain and suffering caused by the robbery.

Payment for injury or damage that occurs during the use of the business's products is referred to as *product liability*. The magnitude of losses resulting from product liability claims has increased greatly in recent years with an increase in class action lawsuits. This is an issue that you must take very seriously if you are a manufacturer. Although individual customers usually get very little money from class action suits, the lawyers who pursue them often receive payments of millions of dollars, as occurred in the case of asbestos producers and tobacco companies. Certainly, the smaller your firm is, the less exposure you have to class action product liability suits. This is true for two reasons: A small business has fewer customers who can claim harm, and a small business does not have the "deep pockets" of cash and other assets that can be raided by rapacious law firms.

Individual lawsuits may also be filed when a single user claims to have been harmed by the product. Such lawsuits are actually more common than class action suits. Although the amount paid in settlement is usually a tiny fraction of that of a class action suit, a manufacturer must still take the issue very seriously. In the 1970s a rash of individual lawsuits against manufacturers of small (under 12,000 lb. gross weight) airplanes resulted in the demise of the industry. Many small businesses that either made small airplanes or made parts and subassemblies for airplanes were forced into bankruptcy. The production of small airplanes did not resume in the United States until Congress passed a law that limited the exposure of manufacturers to product liability suits.[9]

Risk of nonpayment by customers is experienced by all businesses that offer credit. This is true whether you directly provide credit or it is provided through a third party. You have to balance two conflicting things when you decide to offer credit: (1) giving credit to customers will increase your sales, and (2) offering credit guarantees sooner or later some customer will not pay as promised. How big this risk is depends on how many customers you give credit to and how much you let any single customer charge.

Restaurants, clothing retailers, barbers, and beauticians face relatively low risks of loss from nonpayment. First, most of these businesses provide credit only by accepting credit cards, which reduces the risk of nonpayment. Second, the amount that any one customer charges is unlikely to be big enough to threaten your business if it is not paid.

If you sell large-ticket items, such as signs, house remodeling, boats, and the like, you incur large risks by offering credit to customers. Few people have credit cards that have charge limits big enough to buy such things. Therefore, you have to give credit directly to your customer. When the inevitable default occurs, the amount of the unpaid debt can be large enough to threaten the survival of a business.

Managing Risks

Although none of the risks discussed above can be completely avoided, there are strategies you can use to minimize the likelihood and magnitude of losses. The best strategy is to develop a business environment that minimizes (1) the probability of the event occurring and (2) the amount of loss that can be experienced if the event does occur. You do this by (1) making specific plans for and arrangements to deal with foreseeable events, (2) creating and enforcing an appropriate code of conduct for yourself and all employees, (3) ensuring that valuable assets are physically secure, and (4) actively working to get rid of any physical hazards in your workplace.

LO3 Describe techniques to manage risks to stay within your level of risk tolerance.

You should develop disaster plans for events which are unlikely, but that have a finite probability of happening. For example, those businesses that are located in the Missouri and Mississippi River flood plains near St. Louis have a very real probability of significant flooding in any year. Prudent business management for these firms includes creating a plan of action to remove valuable assets to high ground, making plans for temporary business locations, and creating provisions for subcontracting work in order to minimize the effect of business interruption from the inevitable flood.

Disaster planning like this can also work to minimize the effects of fires, storms, and earthquakes upon business operations.

A written code of ethics and business conduct (like those discussed in Chapter 2) make explicit what you expect of your employees. By obtaining employee acceptance of the code, you can create an environment in which peer pressure works to discourage inappropriate behavior and works to encourage desired behavior. To be effective, it is essential that you abide by the code, leading your employees by your example of integrity and honesty.

Valuable assets of the business must be kept in secure areas. When valuable assets must be used, access to them should be carefully controlled and monitored by management. Only those employees who have a business need should be allowed access to valuable assets at any time.

Working proactively to ensure that your physical place of business is (1) free of potential hazards and (2) secure from intruders will prevent on-premises injuries and violations of EEOC or OSHA rules. It is easier and much less expensive to anticipate and prevent potential lawsuits than it is to defend yourself against them once they have been filed.

Managing Risk to Tangible Property

Managing risk to the tangible properties of your business depends upon the nature of the property. Land and buildings aren't subject to theft, but they can be damaged or destroyed by a variety of events. Equipment can be stolen, vandalized, or allowed to fall into disrepair. Small items of high value may be stolen by employees, customers, vendors, or others. The specific measures to control for each type of risk are particular to the specific asset at risk.

Managing Risk to Buildings and Land

Protection from fire for buildings may be obtained through such measures as installing smoke alarms and sprinkler systems and having a fire plug nearby. Other control measures include removing flammable ground cover such as brush, leaves, and fallen branches from proximity to all buildings.

Protection from flood can, first and foremost, be accomplished by not locating on a flood plain. Although this seems like a common sense directive, unimaginable numbers of businesses are built on flood plains, and new construction continues. In 1993, the entire flood plain of the Missouri and Mississippi Rivers in the St. Louis area, from Kansas City on the west, Hannibal, Missouri, on the north, to the confluence of the Mississippi and Ohio Rivers on the south, was inundated with water up to 50 feet deep. Hundreds of businesses in the areas around St. Louis and St. Charles, Missouri, were destroyed. Despite this experience and despite a second round of severe flooding in 1994, the flood plain of the Missouri River from St. Louis upstream for over 30 miles is the site of extensive building. It is only a matter of time until the river again rises, the levees fail, and hundreds of businesses are flooded with tens of feet of muddy water.

Flooding also occurs for reasons other than streams and rivers overflowing their banks. Floods often occur from breaks in water supply pipes, from accidental activation of fire suppression sprinklers, from blockages in storm and sanitary sewers, and from runoff of water that is sprayed upon burning buildings. You may protect yourself from these hazards through performing regular inspection and maintenance of the plumbing and fire suppression systems of your buildings.

Protection from storms can be accomplished by rigorously enforcing building standards concerning attachment of buildings to foundations, types and construction of roofs, and by choice of building materials and construction techniques. The specifics of storm proofing a building depends upon the geographical location of the building. Specific storm hazards, wild fire, wind, flood, or snow load are determined primarily by geography. Each geographic area has its own risk. California has frequent floods and mud slides. The mountains of the West are subject to winter snows, spring floods, and summer wild fires. The Gulf and Eastern shores south of New York are subject to frequent hurricanes. The Midwest, especially Oklahoma, Kansas, Nebraska, Iowa, Missouri, Illinois, Indiana, and Ohio, experiences thousands of tornados every year. The upper Midwest, including northern Ohio, western Pennsylvania, and western New York, is annually buried under tons of snow. Specific building techniques to withstand tornado winds are useless against five feet of snow on the roof, just as structure to withstand snow loading is useless when the entire building slides down the hillside.

Managing risks to tools, equipment, inventory, and other physical assets is largely a function of developing and enforcing appropriate business policies and procedures. Tools and equipment should be maintained on a schedule that prevents serious wear or damage. Frequent inspections should be made to ensure that any problem is detected as soon as possible, allowing repairs to be made in a systematic manner.

Physical assets that can be stolen must be kept in locked storage areas when not in use. Small items of high value should not only be kept locked away, but a procedure should be rigidly enforced that requires employees to sign for removing them from storage. A manager's signature should be required to confirm that the item has been returned to the proper storage when it's no longer needed.

Managing Risk to Computers and Data

One of the riskiest areas of business today involves computers, especially those connected to the Internet. Today hackers use programs which seek out unprotected computers connected to the Internet, and once identified, take them over through spyware programs. Some spyware may use your computer to send out advertising spam on behalf of the hacker's clients. Other spyware lets the hacker actually see and even steal data on your PC, including passwords and credit card information. If you have your business data on the computer, your customer lists (including *their* credit card numbers and identifying information) can get hacked.

The best way to think of protecting your PC is a lot like how you think about protecting your car. Locking the door and taking the keys with you prevents the vast majority of car thefts, those done by kids who find keys in the ignition or open an unlocked door and hot-wire a car. What is the equivalent for a PC?

1. A firewall: Firewalls are programs or pieces of equipment called routers which serve as a barrier between your PC and the Internet.
2. An antivirus program: Viruses are malicious programs designed to damage PCs.
3. Antispyware programs: Spyware are programs designed to report on your keystrokes or data, or give remote control of your PC to others.

The simplest answer is to buy an all-in-one collection of security programs like Norton Internet Security or ZoneAlarm Internet Security Suite. You can often find good deals on these packages (usually via rebates) at discounters like Office Depot or Office Max. The advantage of these programs is that all their installation and updating is done at the same time, so it is easier to maintain.

The least expensive alternative is to find a free stand-alone program. However, to be ethical in protecting your computer, you need to select programs that are free for use in business (profit-making) situations. Some great programs, like the free version of the ZoneAlarm firewall or AVG's free antivirus are not free for business use. One company which makes a complete set of programs (firewall, antispyware, and antivirus) available is Comodo (www.comodo.com). These can be used by businesses for free. The disadvantage of stand-alone programs is that each needs to be installed and updated individually (although many programs can be set to update themselves automatically).

Going back to our car thief analogy, if a professional car thief sets out to steal your car, the lock-and-take-keys approach will not deter them. Here you step up to a higher level of deterrence such as the use of an alarm system. The same is true for determined hackers. You may not be able to stop them from getting around a firewall or antispyware program, but you can protect your data by encrypting it. Encryption is the recoding of your data so that only people who know the unlocking code can see the data correctly. Windows comes with a way to encrypt data, but its approach does not let you move or share an encrypted file. A better approach is to use an encryption program like AxCrypt (http://axcrypt.sourceforge.net/) or Inferno (http://inferno.sourceforge.net), both of which are free. One caution though—if you encrypt a file, make sure you use a password for your encryption that you can easily recall. Once encrypted, if you lose the password, you lose the ability to decode the file!

That brings us to the final issue in Internet security—the human element. Many people reading about the problem of password loss probably think, "I'll write my password down." The problem is that most data theft comes from *inside* businesses. Writing your password down and leaving it where others can see it is the equivalent of leaving your keys in the car. Even with all the programs running, a computer can only be secure if the people using it practice safe surfing—using complex passwords, changing them frequently, and keeping passwords to themselves (or written down and hidden away from others), not opening downloads from unknown, unexpected, or untrustworthy sources, and having your PC set to lock itself up after a few minutes of inactivity (as when you leave your desk), so others cannot use your computer when you are not there.

Remember the car analogy? If your car is broken, it is of as little use as when it is stolen. That brings us to one other type of concern you should have about your data—preserving it. We have all heard the line, "my computer crashed and took my project." As your contact list in Outlook or your customer database or inventory and accounting records become more important to your business, the cost of a loss of data to *your* business increases. The cost is not just lost revenues—since you cannot charge people if you lost the information on what they owe—it is also lost time. Imagine how long it would take to recreate your complete list of contacts? Now repeat that for all the data files generated by your business. The result is frightening.

The solution is called backup. These days it is easier than you might expect. If you have Internet access, you can use Mozy (www.mozy.com), which gives you 2 gigabytes of backup space for free, and unlimited space for $50 a year. Their software can be set up for automated backup of key files when you are online. You can find other services by Googling "online backup." Many offer a mix of free and for-fee services like Mozy. Figure 17.1 graphically details this process. Another alternative is to use an external hard drive that gets its connection and power through a USB cable. Get an external drive which comes with backup software. With these drives, you plug it in once a day to your PC and back up your files. Then disconnect the hard drive. This protects your data from electrical storms or other failures of your PC's power system or motherboard. If the PC does not work, you still have your current (or at worst, day-old) data to work with, and your business can operate almost normally from another computer with the right software.

Today the biggest risk to most businesses comes when using computers, and as more and more of your business's most valuable information are in the files on your computer, the importance of

FIGURE 17.1

How Online Backup Systems Works

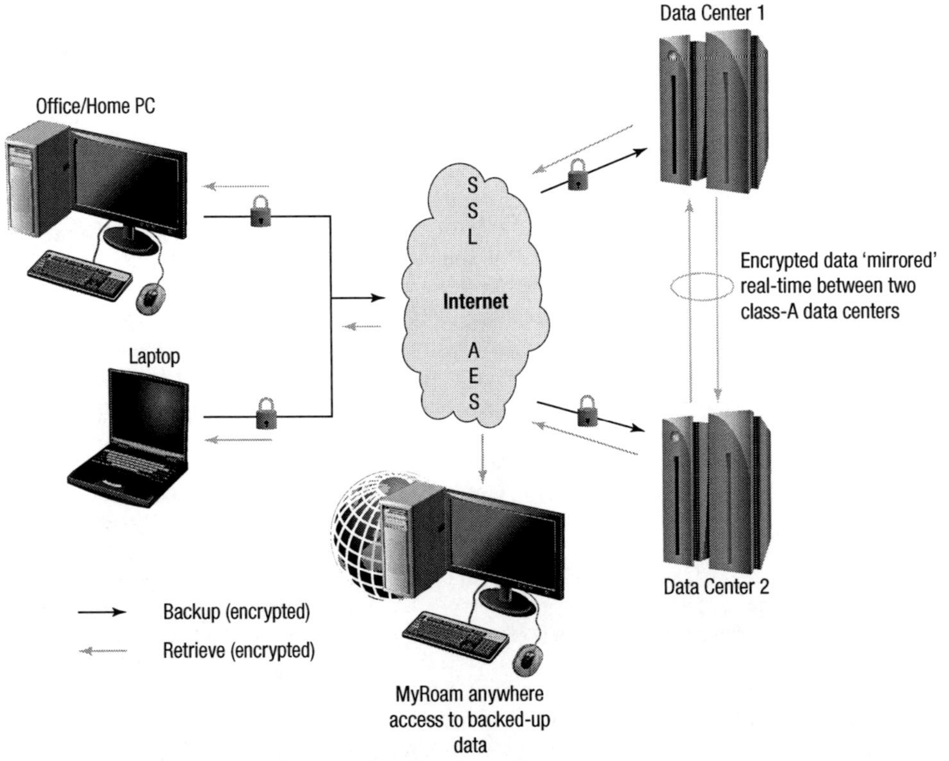

protecting it grows. The basics are relatively simple, but the quality of the protection depends on following through on the basics, and backing them up with behaviors that don't undermine your other efforts to secure your computer and data.

Managing Risk to Intangible Property

Intellectual property rights comprise the legal rights to use unique features of products or services that provide competitive advantage. The rights to use unique features may be legally protected in several ways, including establishing precedence, keeping the process secret, filing for a copyright or trademark, or obtaining a patent. However, if the feature is successful, competitors will eventually find a way to either lessen its competitive advantage or even to render it worthless.

The problem with legal protection methods for intellectual property is that there is no governmental agency that will assist you, as the owner of a small business, in maintaining your legal rights. Copyrights, trademarks, and patents do not automatically provide any protection. Anyone may copy any of these items at any time. If, and only if the holder of the intellectual property rights promptly reacts to infringement by making written objections to any and all infractions, can the legal rights be maintained. In other words, holding legal rights to intellectual property provides the owner solely with grounds to pursue lawsuits against infringement. Immediately upon learning of any infringement, a certified letter should be sent to the suspected violator, clearly specifying the nature of the intellectual property rights held and demanding an immediate cease and desist of the infringement. If the infringement continues, a lawsuit is your only recourse. If you do nothing, you get nothing, as was the case for Harvey Ball, the inventor of the smiley face (see Small Business Insight, below).

Guarding against obsolescence is best accomplished by maintaining a diligent watch on business intelligence concerning developments within the industry. If you own a small business that depends

SMALL BUSINESS INSIGHT

Harvey Ball and the Smiley Face[10]

• Does the story of Harvey Ball's design surprise you? Why do you think Harvey doesn't mind missing out on receiving royalties from use of the smiley face he invented?

You see them everywhere—yellow circles with a smiling caricature on them. The amazing thing is that as much of a cultural icon as the smiley face is, its inventor never got any money for it. Harvey Ball was a freelance designer working at state Farm Mutual Insurance in Worcester, Massachusetts, in 1963. He was asked if he could provide a design to boost morale after a merger had left some people upset. He designed the circle and smile, and he added the eyes so disgruntled employees couldn't easily turn the smile into a frown by wearing the button upside down. Ball was paid $45. He did not trademark it (which, as the designer, he could have done), nor did State Farm. State Farm gave them away—first to the employees, but then to customers who clamored for them. As the buttons spread, it got copied and copied. Franklin Loufrani of France registered the design in 1971 in over 80 countries and did receive royalties, and eventually Ball registered a version with his name on it. In the end, Loufrani made the money from the design, while Ball never got anything else for it, except a lot of satisfaction. As he said, "Never in the history of mankind or art has any single piece of art gotten such widespread favor, pleasure, enjoyment, and nothing has ever been so simply done and so easily understood in art."

upon valuable intellectual property, you should regularly read the journals and magazines that are unique to your industry. You also should subscribe to clipping services, such as those provided by WestLaw (www.westlaw.com) and Dow Jones (www.wsj.com).

Additionally, you should carefully listen to customers and vendors for information concerning developments in your industry. Although it sounds paranoid, the truth is that intellectual property is constantly under attack. Very smart people are diligently working to develop better products and processes from which they will gain wealth at your expense if you move too slowly reacting to threats to your business.

Protection from theft of business property also depends upon the type of property held. Although land is not subject to being physically stolen, you can lose your property rights through a process called *adverse possession.* Adverse possession occurs when the owner of real property does not enforce property rights and allows a nonowner to use the property as if it were his or her own. Just as land cannot be stolen, buildings and large equipment for which there is no ready market are similarly free from theft because of their physical nature. The property most at risk is cash and small items of high value that can be quickly and easily sold.

You need to do two things to protect yourself from theft: (1) physically protect your property, and (2) develop and enforce rules that prevent the employee responsible for the asset from being able to account for the asset. This is called **separation of duties**, and is a core management technique to safeguard money and other valuable assets of a business.[11]

separation of duties
A type of internal control that separates the physical control of an asset from the person accounting for that asset.

Although separation of duties will keep any single employee from stealing, nothing will keep two or more employees who decide to cooperate from stealing company property. Employee collusion is the source of the largest amount of employee theft.[12] When employees agree to defraud, "one lies, and the other swears to it!" This is the way that common frauds are perpetrated, such as sales of nonexistent advertising, payments to nonexistent vendors, and purchases of inventory and supplies from a vendor who will pay a kickback to the dishonest employees. As Figure 17.2 shows, employees account for the single largest source of business theft.

Managing Risk Resulting from Events Involving Personnel

Managing risks created by personnel starts with the hiring process, as is discussed in Chapter 19. Efforts must be made to identify people of high moral character and ethical standards. Owners of small businesses are well advised to use employment services to screen potential employees. Employment services can perform background checks, administer drug tests, and conduct psychological tests that are designed to measure an individual's level of integrity.

When potential applicants have been identified, they should be brought into the business to meet the people with whom they will be working. Current employees can participate in an informal interview with the job candidate. The purpose of these practices is to hire honest people who will become active and enthusiastic employees who consider themselves to be part of a team.

However, no hiring process is 100 percent foolproof. For that matter, no human being is 100 percent reliable. Ultimately, no one is able to withstand all temptation, regardless of ethical standards.

FIGURE 17.2

Sources of Theft

Source: Richard C. Hollinger and Amanda Adams, 2008 National Retail Security Survey, University of Florida, 2008, page 7.

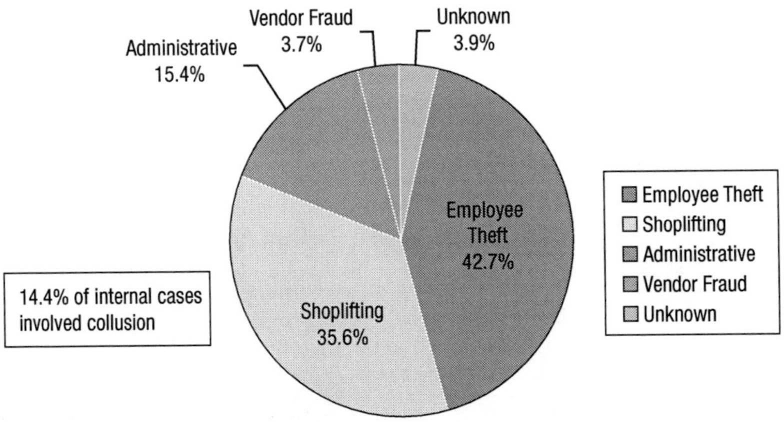

Because all people are fallible, owners of small businesses have an obligation to employees to make theft difficult and honesty easy and rewarding. If you tempt employees with easy access to valuable property and with little likelihood of theft being detected, sooner or later most employees will succumb to temptation in ways great or small.

The Association of Certified Fraud Examiners found in a 2004 study (the Wells Report[13]) that the most costly employee frauds compared to total business assets occur in businesses with fewer than 100 employees. The median loss to these businesses was a staggering (for the owner of a small business) $98,000. This finding is interesting for two reasons: (1) The vast majority of small businesses have fewer than 100 employees, and (2) it contradicts the belief that people do not steal from people they know. The fact is that thieves come from all social classes, all levels of education, and all ethnic backgrounds. It is an unfortunate fact that the difference between many a thief and many an honest citizen is only that the citizen has not yet been caught. For these reasons, all owners and managers of small businesses must be aware of and guard against dishonesty in employees.

internal control
A set of rules and procedures that work to limit the opportunity for employee theft or malfeasance.

Internal control is the primary method of ensuring honesty in employees. Internal control is a matter of establishing policies and procedures that work to make dishonesty difficult and honesty easy. The most basic technique of internal control is to separate the duties of maintaining the security of assets from the duties of maintaining records of those assets.

While internal control will reduce the opportunity for employee fraud, it is not sufficient to disclose frauds that are currently taking place. The Wells Report found that internal controls were the fourth most likely method to discover fraud, following accidental discovery. As Figure 17.3 shows, nearly 40 percent of all frauds that were detected were found because of a tip. About one-fourth of frauds were detected by an internal audit, and one-fifth were found by accident. Internal controls were responsible for disclosing only 18 percent of the frauds that were detected during the study period.

Separation of duties is most important for intangible assets—those things of value that have no physical "reality," such as money, accounts receivable, patents, and licensing agreements. Consider the problems of keeping money secure. Money exists primarily as an entry in the accounting records of your bank. The employee who has authority to write checks and to make deposits has free access to the things related to embezzlement. All that person needs to do is write a check made payable to a fake entity, and then cash the check and pocket the money. If one employee both writes checks and keeps accounts receivable records, theft is even easier to commit and harder to detect. The employee merely mails an invoice from a fake entity. When the fake invoice is received, the employee creates a payable account for the fake vendor. Subsequently, during the ordinary course of business, the employee writes and mails a check which will be delivered to an address held by the employee. The accounting records of the business are in perfect order. The only problem is that you are out the money that was stolen.

Such simple frauds can amount to huge amounts of money over time. The 2004 Report to the Nation on Occupational Fraud and Abuse reports on 508 cases of fraud that combined resulted in over $761 million in losses to the defrauded companies. Nearly 93 percent of the frauds detected

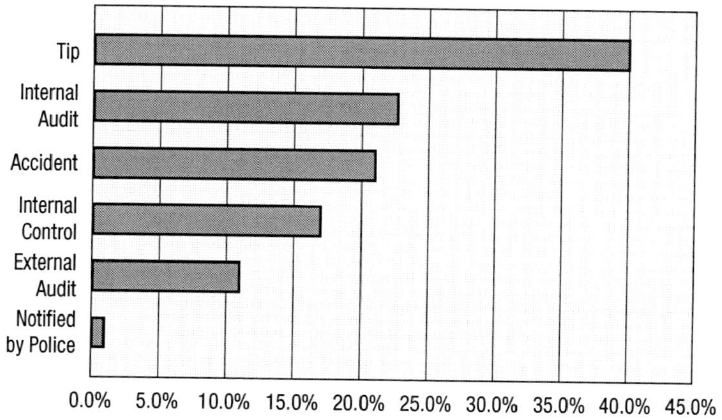

FIGURE 17.3

Percentage of Frauds by Method of Detection

Note: Total exceeds 100 percent because of multiple responses.

Source: Association of Certified Fraud Examiners, 2004 Report to the Nation on Occupational Fraud and Abuse, 2004.

involved misappropriation of business assets, but fewer than one-fourth of those involved assets other than cash. Fraudulent disbursements of cash comprise 74 percent of all misappropriations with an average loss to a business of $125,000.

The greatest threat of loss from employee dishonesty occurs when two or more employees *collude:* agree together to defraud your business. Employee collusion is both very common and very difficult to detect. The most common form of employee collusion is the theft of cash and inventory. Cash is most usually stolen by making false disbursements. Inventory is stolen through false employee sales.

Many small businesses allow employees to purchase inventory at cost for personal use. When two employees agree to steal, one purchases merchandise from the other. The employee who is "selling" records the sale as being less expensive items. For example, Andrew wishes to buy a complete computer from his employer's business. Brenda makes the employee sale, but records the merchandise as a hard drive. Andrew pays only the $40 cost of a hard drive, not the $400 cost of a complete computer. The owner is out the $360 difference. Of course, at some point the computer will show up as an inventory shortage. But by the time inventory is taken, there is no way to determine if the missing computer was taken by an employee or stolen by a shoplifter.

Securing valuable property is a commonsense, but often overlooked method, of keeping honest employees honest. If your business involves small items of high value, such as precision tools, jewelry, laptop computers, data projectors, computer chips, gold, platinum, and so on, those items should be kept locked in secure areas, except when being used. Employees who use such items should be required to sign for removing them from storage and obtain a manager's signature when the item is returned to storage. All items of high sensitivity, such as trade secrets, formulas, and employee and customer records, should be protected with locks, access cards, and passwords.

Risk from loss of key personnel and former employees setting up competition against your business can be managed through the contracting process. When a key employee is identified, an employment contract should be negotiated. The contract should include provisions that (1) limit the employee's freedom to go into competition, (2) contain the employee's specific promise not to disclose sensitive or secret information, and (3) offer rewards for providing adequate termination notice and a smooth transition for replacements.

Additional protection from harm resulting from loss of key employees can be obtained by cross training among employees. Although any specific employee may not be able to be directly replaced, the needed skills and talents can certainly be found within a group of employees. If employees are cross trained, the loss of one individual can be alleviated by drawing upon the diverse abilities of other employees. Finally, any truly key employee, including yourself as the owner of a small business, should be actively grooming his or her own replacement to be able to step in on an instant's notice.

Managing Risk from Violations of Tax Regulations

tax codes
Laws and regulations that specify the requirements of taxation.

It is a rare business that has never run afoul of a taxing agency. Small businesses are subject to taxation from cities, counties, states, and the U.S. government. The **tax codes** of all levels of government have become ever more complex, placing more and more responsibility on businesses for calculating, collecting, and paying various taxes. Taxes imposed on small business include franchise or corporation taxes, income taxes, employee taxes, sales and use taxes, and property taxes. The regulations that relate to all these taxes are so voluminous that it is impossible for any individual to know them all. In fact, the regulations are so complex that even the enforcement personnel of various taxing agencies are often ignorant of the myriad details of the code and regulations. Perhaps then it is not surprising that the government estimates that 15 percent of taxpaying businesses are not complying with the rules.[14]

Although there is no magic formula that will prevent financial loss that arises from being the subject of a tax audit, there are some fairly simple techniques that will work together to limit your exposure. First, you must keep complete, *accurate* accounting records. If you use a computerized accounting system, be certain that the audit trail function is enabled. Control access to the functions of the accounting system by issuing and regularly changing passwords. File all source documents, such as purchase orders, bills of lading, requisitions, and invoices, in a systematic manner that will

SMALL BUSINESS INSIGHT

When Careful Planning and Preparation Aren't Enough

"Neither Rex nor I expected any problems when we found out that the Texas Sales Tax Commission was going to conduct an audit," said Jay Hall.

Rex said, "When the auditor came, we set up a desk for him. We kept him in coffee and gave him every record he requested. He worked for about three days checking through the last five years of our business."

"We were cool with it. After all, we have always kept our taxes squeaky clean. We knew that we had nothing to worry about."

"Little did we know," said Jay.

Rex Stone and Jay Hall are the owners and managers of Rex Stone Associates. Their business comprises planning, producing, and managing events, primarily in the San Antonio, Texas, area. They have a highly diverse client list, including businesses, unions, academic associations, and church groups. In the last few years, they have conducted training sessions, provided trail rides and chuck wagon dinners, conducted motor tours of the Hill Country, and put on numerous balls, dances, and hops for their clients.

"We were stunned when he told us that we owed the state over $125,000 in unpaid taxes, penalties, and accumulated interest. It just couldn't be so!" said Jay.

Rex continued, "When he left, we immediately called our lawyer. The issue boiled down to taxes on the services of bands and combos we had furnished for events. The auditor claimed that we had to collect sales tax on the amount that we charged our client for the music group."

"The problem was," Jay said, "we had already gotten an opinion from the Tax Commission that held that if we did not sell tickets to the event, no sales tax was due. In our business, we never sell tickets. We charge our client a fixed bid price, and only members and guests of the client group attend. Thus, no tax was due, and we had never collected for any music group."

"It took a year and cost us over $24,000 in legal fees, but finally we got a ruling that we had complied with Texas law. We did not owe the tax."

"Of course," Rex said, "we were out the twenty-four thousand. But you know, it could have been a lot worse."

provide easy access if you are called upon to "prove" any transaction. Carefully document all cash transactions. Ensure that employees properly enter all cash sales into the cash register, and then reconcile the cash register tape to the cash register contents every day. Insist on receiving a *signed* receipt from vendors when you pay in cash.

The simple fact is that many, if not most, owners of small businesses "skim" in ways small and large by taking cash from their businesses before it is recorded as a revenue. Many owners also inappropriately charge personal expenses to the business as a way of extracting money without paying income taxes. Tax agents know these facts very well. As a result, when your business is audited, the agent will assume that you have understated your revenues and overstated your deductible expenses. It is your responsibility to prove that you have not.

Second, you should establish a relationship with both an accountant and a lawyer who are expert in tax issues. Although attestation by an accountant or lawyer is not evidence of lack of criminal activity (think Enron), an accountant or lawyer whose practice comprises issues of small business taxation will most likely do a much better job of representing you than you can ever do for yourself.

Third, and most important, make paying your taxes your first financial priority. The temptation to "borrow" from tax money is at times overwhelming, especially when you are being hounded by creditors for payment. Do not give in to this temptation. You can go to prison for not paying

You won't go to jail for failure to pay your creditors, but you will spend some time behind bars if you do not pay your taxes. Keep your business in financial shape by making timely payment of taxes your first top priority.

employee withholdings, for not paying sales taxes when they are due, for not paying your income taxes. If you do not pay your creditors, your credit rating will suffer. Your business may fail. But you won't go to jail for not paying your bills.

Managing Risk from Employee Violation of Government Regulations

Reducing risk from events involving employees who violate business regulations is best accomplished through a proactive program of training and enforcing appropriate policies and procedures. The courts have consistently ruled that it is the responsibility of the employer to police employee compliance with regulations. Ignorance of either the regulations or of employee violation of regulations is not a defense against administrative action. You are financially responsible for employee violations, intentional or inadvertent. Those few cases where the employer has been held harmless all involve employers who (1) have a written policy provided to each employee, (2) have conducted training of managers and employees concerning those policies, and (3) have immediately and consistently acted upon receipt of any complaint.

Risks from violating the requirements of Equal Employment Opportunity Commission are best managed, as with risks from violations of any government regulation, by the owners being proactive:

- Know the EEOC rules that apply to your business.
- Obtain assistance from experts in EEOC regulations to assess the level of your compliance.
- Establish policies and procedures designed to prevent violations.
- Educate and train employees to know the policies and procedures and to understand the importance of following them explicitly.
- Enforce the policies and procedures by immediately dealing in a systematic manner with any employee complaint.

Knowing the EEOC rules is a daunting task for any business owner. As stated above, the rules are voluminous, ambiguous, and arcane. There are, however, many sources of information that are written to be easily understood. Most such third-party information is provided by industry associations, and thus is usually specifically written for the problems you are most likely to encounter.

Assistance can be obtained from experts in several different ways. One source that is often overlooked is the employment agency that you use to screen applicants. Employment agencies must be highly knowledgeable of the EEOC rules in order to remain in business. Often, such agencies can provide sample policy manuals and advice concerning compliance. Other sources of expert help include SCORE (www.score.org) and the EEOC, itself.

The EEOC maintains a Web site that contains myriad resources for small business owners. The commission also publishes numerous books and pamphlets that are available from http://www.EEOC.gov.

Alleged violations of the Americans with Disabilities Act are best handled through a proactive threefold approach: (1) Determine if you are subject to any of the provisions of the ADA. (2) Obtain the services of experts on the ADA to evaluate the level of your compliance. (3) Work diligently to meet the requirements to which you are subject. Although these actions will *not* prevent you from being the target of frivolous lawsuits, you may use records of your actions as evidence of your intent to comply. This is often sufficient to persuade a mediator to pressure the complainant to either reduce the amount demanded or to withdraw the complaint entirely.

The Department of Justice maintains an ADA Technical Assistance Program which provides help directly to interested parties. By using these services, a small business owner can be assured of having current information. The Technical Assistance Program provides specific advice for your business concerning how to comply with the pertinent requirements. This program is specifically aimed at the needs of hotels, motels, restaurants, and other affected small businesses. The program provides an information hot line, printed materials, and a speakers bureau. It does not provide any inspection or affirmation services. Visit www.usdoj.gov/crt/ada/adahom1.htm for more information.

Managing risk from violations of OSHA standards and regulations is also best accomplished through proactive efforts. As with risks from EEOC and ADA enforcement, you should first ascertain the standards to which your business is subject. The OSHA Act covers all employees except those in mining, transportation, state and local governments, and self-employment. If your business is in any other industry, you are subject to the standards of OSHA for employee health and safety. Also remember that while *you* are self-employed, anyone you hire is not. Thus, while OSHA standards and regulations do not apply to you, they do apply to your employees.

The best way to meet the basic laws of OSHA is to provide a place of employment that is free of recognized hazards and to:

1. Maintain tools and equipment in good condition.
2. Provide appropriate safety equipment and training in its proper use.
3. Provide medical examinations.

OSHA also offers free consultation services to employers who want help in identifying any deficiencies and in developing appropriate solutions. Consultations begin with a conference among the consultants and managers of the business where the scope of the consultation is set, and all parties agree on a set of working rules for the engagement. The conference is followed by an on-site inspection for hazards. The business's health program is also assessed. A final conference is held during which all findings are presented, along with suggested solutions to each identified problem. No report of any deficiency is made to OSHA for enforcement. However, if significant hazards are found, you can count on a follow-up inspection by OSHA after a reasonable time during which you must remedy the problems.

A directory of OSHA-funded consultants can be obtained by requesting OSHA Publication No. 3047, *Consultation Services for the Employer.*

You must also keep accurate records of all employee job-related illnesses and injuries. You must report within eight hours any accidents that result in a fatality or in the hospitalization of three or more employees. If your business has fewer than 10 employees or if your business is in one of the OSHA-defined "low- hazard" industries, you are exempt from the record keeping requirements of the regulations. Low-hazard industries include automobile dealers, apparel and furniture stores, eating and drinking establishments, finance, insurance, real estate, and legal, educational, personal, and business services, as well as cultural and membership organizations.

Using an Internal Audit as a Tool to Manage Risk

A valuable process that can greatly help you with the issues of keeping risks at acceptable levels is completing an internal audit. You probably are somewhat familiar with public business's external audits, which are conducted by CPA firms and which must comply with a set of standards called Generally Accepted Audit Standards (GAAS). An internal audit is similar in conduct; however, because it is strictly a management tool which is not provided to outsiders, it can be structured and conducted in any systematic manner you find acceptable.

It is unlikely that you (or any owner of a small business) have the time, experience, or inclination to attempt to conduct an internal audit on your own. Rather, you should consider outsourcing the conduct of an audit to an expert in the process. Your own accountant may be able to conduct such an audit. But if not, he or she will, in any case, be able to recommend a reputable and reliable firm that can do so at a reasonable cost.

A properly conducted, independent internal audit will give you:

- An evaluation of your overall level of business risk.
- An objective evaluation of your risk control structure.
- A systematic analysis of your business processes and controls.
- Information on irregularities detected during the audit process.
- Review of your firm's compliance with relevant regulations.
- A review of the existence and value of the assets of your business.
- Review of operational and financial performance.
- Recommendations for more effective and efficient use of resources.
- Assessments of how well your business is accomplishing your goals and objectives.
- Information about your employees' adherence to the organization's values and code of ethics.

As the owner of a small business, you must assume much of the task of conducting oversight of all aspects of your business. Activities that make up oversight include listening, asking questions, assessing and challenging answers. This is exactly what an effective internal audit will do for you. To be sure that the audit effectively meets your goals in having it conducted, you should:

1. Meet (without the presence of other members of your management) with whomever is going to conduct the internal audit.
2. Establish with the auditor that you and your board of directors (if you have a board) have the final authority to review and approve the audit plan.
3. Write an engagement agreement with the auditor that clearly establishes the scope of work to be done.
4. Provide sufficient authority to the auditor to ensure that he or she can accomplish the goals of the audit.

Once the audit is completed, you must make positive steps to address any findings that indicate an unacceptable level of business risk.

Insuring against Risks

LO4 Explain how insurance can be used to manage business risk.

Although it is impossible for the owner of a small business to avoid all business risks, it is possible, through the use of insurance, to minimize the damage that such risks can cause. However, insurance can be expensive. Because of its expense, many small business owners choose too little insurance. When the inevitable occurs, an underinsured business may well face bankruptcy and liquidation.

The key to using insurance is to obtain the "right" amount of insurance at an affordable rate. Having too little insurance leaves the business open to unsupportable losses. Carrying too much insurance wastes money.

Using Insurance to Manage Risks

insurance
A contract between two or more parties in which one party agrees, for a fee, to assume the risk of another.

Insurance is a contract between two businesses in which one, the insurance company, for a fee, agrees to indemnify the other for specific losses that are likely to occur in the future. In other words, the insurance company contracts to pay money to your business if a specific "covered" event occurs that causes your business to suffer financial loss.

Not all risks are insurable. Insurance provides a benefit by requiring a relatively small fee compared to the amount of loss that is possible. The insurance company makes a profit by collecting premiums for coverage from many businesses for the same set of risks. In effect, you and the insurance company are taking opposite gambles. You are betting that your business will be damaged or destroyed. The insurance company is betting that it won't. The insurance company wins by collecting more from all the covered companies combined than it has to pay out to those few businesses that do, indeed, suffer damage. You win (if it can be considered a "win") by having the insurance company pay when your business suffers a covered loss. Thus, the more likely an event is to occur, and the greater the potential amount that the insurance company must pay, the higher the price that you must pay for coverage. For this reason, insurance coverage is either not available or is excessively expensive for common events.

Developing a Comprehensive Insurance Program

Developing an appropriate insurance program for your business requires that you understand the risks to which your business is vulnerable. You must then know the amount of loss that your business could suffer as a result of the adverse events. Finally, you must obtain appropriate rates from reliable insurers, rates that are not too high for your business to pay but that do provide sufficient payouts if the insured event occurs.

Identifying risks is the first task to be completed before a comprehensive insurance program can be developed for your business. Risks, as discussed above, vary with the nature of your business. Risks that are common to most small businesses include fire, flood, storm, theft, business interruption, and loss of key personnel. Business-specific risks include product liability claims for manufacturers, malpractice claims for dentists and physicians, and errors and omissions claims for lawyers and accountants.

Determining which risks are to be covered is the next step. Not all identifiable risks can be or should be covered by insurance. The risk of events that are certain to occur cannot be insured at any price. Risks of events that are highly likely to occur but that have indeterminable payouts can be insured, but only at a very high price. Extremely unlikely events (being struck by a meteorite, for example) can be insured, but why would anyone do so?

Events that should be insured are those that are likely, and the economic cost of which would create a severe burden upon the finances of the business. Such events include natural disasters, liability to others, and the death or disability of key employees.

Coverages required by law exist to provide social protection from harm caused to employees, customers, and uninvolved individuals. The most common mandatory insurance coverages are liability for damages caused by vehicle accidents and illness and injury caused by employment. Most businesses are also required to pay for unemployment insurance for employees to help defray the personal cost of having one's employment terminated.

coverages
Contractual provisions of insurance policies that specify what risks the insurance company is assuming.

THE THOUGHTFUL ENTREPRENEUR

WHAT RISKS CAN BE INSURED?

Not all business risks can be covered by insurance at a reasonable cost. Insurance companies, just like you, are in business to make profits. An insurance company must charge competitive prices to be able to sell policies. At the same time, the insurance company must charge enough to be able to pay legitimate claims of its policyholders. To be able to balance these conflicting needs, an insurance company must be able to accurately predict the amount of payments that will be made to settle claims for insurable events.

The amount that an insurance company must pay out in claims is a function of (1) the frequency with which an event occurs, (2) the amount that must be paid according to the terms of the contract, and (3) the number of policies that have been issued.

- **The risk must be calculable:** An insurance company estimates the amount of potential claims payments by performing statistical analyses of the number and frequency of the occurrence of the event for which the insurance is being provided. For example, the probability of an individual business being flooded can be calculated from information concerning its location relative to sources and frequencies of floods. Although a specific flood may not be predictable, the number of businesses that will encounter floods in any one year can be predicted with reasonable statistical confidence, which allows an insurance company to determine the appropriate price for a flood policy.
- **The value of any loss must be measurable in dollars:** Insurance companies contract to pay only specific amounts of money for specific types and amounts of losses. In order to determine the amount that will be paid, it must be possible for the loss to be stated in a dollar amount. Thus, an insurance company will insure you for physical damage from fire. It will not insure you for the loss of your beautiful view, should the fire burn your neighbor's property across the road.
- **The policyholder must have an insurable financial interest:** Insurance companies will not insure losses for individuals who do not suffer a financial loss from what is being insured. This requirement acts to prevent fraud by persons deliberately "creating" the event in order to profit from it. In the same vein, an insurance company will not pay more than the actual amount of the loss, regardless of the amount of the policy terms.
- **The pool of potential policyholders must be of sufficient size:** Insurance works because the insurance company diversifies its risk by insuring numerous businesses in widely separated locations. This ensures that no single disaster will result in the insurance company having to pay an excessive number of claims at any one time. Of course, this strategy occasionally fails. In August 2005 Hurricane Katrina became the most costly catastrophe on record. The extensive damage to a relatively large area has seriously tested the ability of several insurance companies to pay required claims and to remain in business.

Vehicle liability insurance is mandated by the legislatures of all the states and territories of the United States. Minimum amounts of coverage are specified for property damage caused by the vehicle and for injury suffered by anyone other than the driver of the vehicle.

Workers' compensation insurance is mandatory in some states. In others, it is discretionary. In all states, the workers' compensation laws provide fixed monetary awards to employees who are injured or disabled on the job. Workers' compensation is enforced through administrative procedures which preclude employees suing their employers. Federal statutes are limited to workers who are employed in some interstate commerce.

Unemployment insurance is collected by the IRS and state agencies as a percentage of tax upon payroll. The amount collected varies among industries and among businesses within an industry. Industries and businesses that have frequent seasonal layoffs pay higher amounts of unemployment premiums than do those that have stable employment.

Desired coverages beyond mandatory insurance include general liability, product liability, catastrophe, and various types of malpractice coverage. Liability insurance protects your business against claims from harm caused by inadvertent consequences of actions of the business or its employees. The list of potential causes of harm to customers, vendors, or others is nearly endless. Customers fall while on business premises. A careless worker can splatter paint on a stranger's automobile. Sparks from welding can start fires on others' property. A faulty valve can release noxious or even deadly fumes into the atmosphere. Your sewer can plug and cause flooding in your neighbor's place of business. Commercial liability insurance covers losses that are the result of such mishaps and accidents.

Product liability insurance covers losses resulting from claims made by persons who use the products of your business. The risk of customers and others being harmed by your product is largely a function of (1) the nature of your product and (2) the intended users. Those products that have historically given rise to the largest claims for injury and illness are (1) transportation equipment, such as automobiles, airplanes, and bicycles, (2) health products, such as pharmaceuticals and body implants, and (3) appliances, such as toasters, vacuum cleaners, and kitchen ranges. However, examples of huge cash settlements for product liability exist for a multitude of products that would seem to be harmless by nature. Examples of such cases include insulating foam that was discovered to emit formaldehyde, asbestos-containing products that are believed to be carcinogenic, and a multitude of toys that are alleged to cause choking and other hazards to children.

Errors and omissions insurance and malpractice insurance are examples of special types of liability insurance that cover losses from harm caused during the performance of your profession. Errors and omissions insurance covers claims made by clients of attorneys, accountants, and other consultants. Malpractice insurance covers claims made by patients of physicians, dentists, nurses, and other medical practitioners. The primary value of this type of insurance is the access to highly competent specialist lawyers that is provided by the insurance company. The insurance companies employ cadres of lawyers to represent professionals who are accused of incompetence or wrongdoing. These lawyers are usually successful in negotiating reasonable settlements with clients who have been harmed. Should a settlement be impossible, the same lawyers will vigorously defend the accused professional in the subsequent court action. Of course, in the event that the professional is held responsible for a client loss, the insurance company will pay the claim, up to the limit of the insurance contract.

You, as an individual owner or manager of a small business, can obtain a general liability insurance, which is often called an *umbrella policy,* or a *success protector policy.* General liability policies exist to pay losses that are not covered by other liability insurance. It is a sad fact of our current legal climate that actual culpability is irrelevant to many damage claims. If you are successful in your business, your success makes you a target for lawsuits because you are considered to be able to pay a judgment, either through your personal wealth or through seizure of your business property. Claims against general liability policies are usually a result of such litigation.

Insuring the Property of the Business

Commercial property insurance covers losses to the business property from causes such as fire, storm, vandalism, and theft. Other property insurance exists to pay losses resulting from floods or earthquakes. The cost of property insurance is determined largely by (1) the property's insurable value, (2) the amount of deductible loss, (3) the amount of co-insurance required, and (4) the loss limits of the policy.

All the value of a property does not have **insurable value**. For example, as a general rule, the value of land, excavation, and basement is not insurable. This is because even when a disaster occurs, the land remains. Only a very few types of disasters, such as earthquake or landslide, can change the nature and topography of land.

insurable value
The amount of an asset for which a company will write an insurance policy.

Additionally, some property has value that cannot be stated in dollar amounts. The value of the historical significance of a building often cannot be determined. For example, in Clarksville, Tennessee, the Hachland Hall Bed and Breakfast has a log cabin that was the home of President Andrew Jackson during the time that he was building the famous Hermitage. Were this cabin to burn to the ground, its replacement cost for logs, timber, and finish lumber could be no more than a few tens of thousands of dollars. However, no matter how carefully rebuilt, the replacement would be a replica, not the actual cabin. As such, it might be interesting, but it would not have the special character that now makes it unique. Placing a dollar amount on the historical value of this cabin is highly problematical.

A **deductible** is an amount of loss that is specifically excluded by the insurance contract. It is common for vehicle policies to specify that in the event of loss, the insurance will pay the amount of the loss, less a deductible of $250 to $1,000. Policies on buildings and equipment usually have similar deductibles ranging from $1,000 to $10,000 or more. As a general rule, the higher the deductible, the lower the policy premium payments will be.

deductible
An amount of loss that will not be paid by an insurance company.

THE THOUGHTFUL ENTREPRENEUR

HEIDI KLUM'S UNIQUE INSURANCE POLICY[15]

In 2004, the model Heidi Klum had her legs insured for $2 million.[16] This may seem a little strange, but it is not unprecedented. During World War II, the then-famous actress and pinup girl, Betty Grable, received widespread publicity from insuring her legs for $1 million. More recently, the soccer player, David Beckham, had his legs insured for a cool $70 million.[17]

Given that the loss of a leg is not a common occurrence, why would a model, an actor, and a sports star seek such insurance?

Given that there is not a sufficient pool of models, actors, and athletes to allow an insurance company to diversify its risk, why would an insurance company write such a policy?

In actuality, such policies are not as unusual as you might think. Insurance companies routinely write policies that place a dollar value on the loss of a person's appendages. While the occurrence of the maiming of actors is low, nationwide a significant number of people lose arms, legs, hands, feet, and eyes in a variety of accidents and illnesses. Thus, the risk of such loss is well understood by insurance companies, and the cost of paying claims for such policies can be reliably predicted. Provisions for specific dollar payments for the loss of appendages is commonly included in insurance policies that cover disability.

Despite the ordinariness of disability insurance, it is clear that the purpose of these insurance policies for Ms. Klum and Ms. Grable was the publicity value to be gained. In both cases, they and the insurance companies all received lots of press coverage. It is interesting to note that while the amount of the insurance coverage is reported, no mention is ever made of the cost of the premium or of the term of the insurance contract.

There is a popular perception that any risk can be insured. This perception has arisen because of highly publicized events that were not actually insurance transactions but were publicity stunts. While it might be comforting to be able to insure against any loss, the fact is that businesses must constantly weigh the cost of insurance coverage. In many cases, the cost of insurance coverage greatly exceeds any benefit for small business.

● When disasters hit, like this fire, most small businesses depend on insurance to make up for the loss. What factors should you consider when seeking insurance?

co-insurance
A contract stipulation that requires a policyholder to carry insurance in an amount equal to a stated minimum percentage of the market value of the property insured.

fidelity bonds
Bonds, also called *dishonesty bonds,* that repay employers for losses caused by dishonest or negligent employees.

surety bonds
An agreement with an insurance or bonding company that will pay a specified amount in the event that the entity bonded fails to comply with specified contractual requirements.

Co-insurance is a contract requirement that works to prevent property owners from deliberately underinsuring. Co-insurance requires that the owner carry insurance in an amount equal to a stated minimum percentage of the market value of the property, most usually 80 percent. If the owner allows insurance coverage to fall below this amount, then the amount that the insurance company will pay in the event of loss is reduced by an amount proportional to the amount of underinsurance.

The reason for such arcane provisions is to increase the amount of premium that the insurance company collects relative to the risk that the insurance company is taking by insuring the property. The higher the value a property has, the greater the likely payout an insurance company will have to make in the event of loss.

Consider that property losses are highly correlated with the value of the property. At one extreme, the loss can never exceed the market value of the property. At the other extreme, loss cannot be less than zero. In between the two extremes, losses are often a function of the value of the property. For example, suppose two businesses each experienced a fire that destroyed the roof of a warehouse. A 43,000-square-foot warehouse worth $3.5 million has a much more expensive roof than does a 10,000-square-foot warehouse which is worth less than $750,000. Similarly, losing your 1,600-square-foot retail space will be a much greater dollar loss if the store is located on Rodeo Drive in Beverly Hills, California, than if it is located on Main Street in Beckwourth, California.

Business interruption insurance provides funds to pay the ordinary operating expenses of your business should it be forced to close temporarily because of an insured event. Although business interruption insurance can be purchased as a stand-alone policy, it is most usually acquired as a provision of commercial property insurance.

Crime insurance offers protection against losses from crimes committed against your business. It is an unfortunate fact that the greatest number of crimes of which you are likely to be victim are committed by trusted employees.

Theft insurance is normally included in insurance on physical assets. However, the greatest threat of loss because of employee dishonesty is the misappropriation of cash, as was discussed earlier. Cash cannot be insured. An approach to obtaining insurance against employee theft of money is to require all employees with access to money or to accounting for money to be *bonded.*

Fidelity bonds, also called *dishonesty bonds,* repay employers for losses caused by dishonest or negligent employees. Fidelity bonds cover losses from employee fraud, theft, forgery, and embezzlement. Unlike **surety bonds**, fidelity bonds are purchased only for the employer's benefit.

If you have any employee who handles large amounts of cash or other valuable assets, you should consider bonding that person. Some businesses, including insurance companies, securities brokers, real estate brokers, and businesses that hold escrowed cash are required by law to carry fidelity bonds. All employees who have direct access to a company's cash, securities, and accounting records, or who handle investment or retirement funds, should be bonded. Bonds are available to cover individual specific key employees, or as blanket bonds that cover all employees.

When obtaining fidelity bonds, you should consider the following:

- The scope of coverage.
- All exclusions.
- Types of employee dishonesty not covered (e.g., salary, benefit, or computer fraud).
- Coverage for employee actions off-premises.

Credit insurance covers abnormal losses from credit customers not paying their bills. Abnormal losses are carefully defined within the insurance contract. Typical covered events include customers who cease business because of bankruptcy or business interruptions caused by fire, storm, wind, floods, and earthquakes. Less common and more expensive coverage exists that will pay for losses that arise from general economic conditions such as recession, war, or trade embargos.

Credit insurance can be obtained that covers all credit accounts or that covers only specific accounts. General credit insurance is expensive, and it is common to choose to cover only very large accounts, the loss of which would threaten survival of the business.

All credit insurance requires the merchant to provide co-insurance in the amount of 10 to 20 percent of the credit loss. The co-insurance provision works to prevent both frivolous claims and to provide a disincentive to companies to issue credit indiscriminately.

Credit insurance companies provide mandatory collection services. The insured business is required to promptly report all past due accounts. When an account is determined to be delinquent, usually after 90 days of no payment, then the account must be assigned to the insurance company which will make vigorous efforts to collect.

Credit insurance is available only for manufacturers and wholesalers. At this time no insurance company will write coverage for retailers who offer credit to customers.

Retailers who provide credit are protected in two ways. First, those few retailers who offer credit directly to customers usually have a large number of relatively small accounts receivable. This provides a greater diversification of the risk of loss than is available to wholesalers who usually have a relatively small number of large value receivables. Second, most retailers today provide credit only through credit cards, including Master Card, Visa, Discover, and American Express. Credit card

THE THOUGHTFUL ENTREPRENEUR

BRING IN THE CLOWNS

Imagine a fair without a midway. Can a fair even be a fair without a carousel, a roller coaster, or a Ferris wheel? Carnivals are hugely popular entertainments. Over 500 million people attend amusement parks, fairs, and carnivals in the United States each year (which is quite impressive, given that the entire population of the nation is only 300 million).

As you might expect, carnivals experience numerous accidents each year, ranging in severity from bruises and abrasions to permanent maiming and death. According to the U.S. Consumer Product Safety Commission (CPSC),[18] approximately 11,000 people are injured on amusement rides each year. Of these, about five die.

There are approximately 500 carnivals that travel the United States each year, ranging in size from 1 to over 100 portable amusement rides. The vast majority of carnivals are small family-owned businesses with second and third generation members involved in management and operation.[19]

If your carnival is large enough and you expect to have about 1 million riders in a year, then you should expect to experience approximately 20 to 25 injuries, based on CPSC statistics. If the people injured are representative of the national experience, all of them will be younger than 16. Not one will have an injury severe enough to require more than outpatient treatment. However, there is a small, but measurable risk that you will be among the unfortunate carnival operators who have patrons seriously injured to the point of maiming or death.

As the owner of a carnival, what insurance should you carry to cover the injuries of customers on your rides? Insurance to cover the potential medical expenses for twenty-some minor injuries would be prohibitively expensive. It would, on the other hand, be quite risky for your business to carry no insurance at all. A reasonable strategy is to obtain insurance that will cover only serious injury and death. Your carnival will then absorb the cost of treating minor injuries, the number of which can be reduced by a safety program that prevents customer horseplay, requires operator training, and enforces regular rigid safety inspection of the rides. Taking such measures not only reduces the probability of serious injury, but also reduces the cost of accident insurance.

companies perform credit checks before issuing cards, and thus limit the risk of nonpayment. Additionally, the credit card companies have developed rules which include checking cards for customer signatures, requiring a government-issued picture ID, and obtaining a transaction authorization prior to providing the credit sale. Retailers who follow the rules are not liable for any future nonpayment by the credit card holder.

Personnel insurance is available to protect both you and your employees from specific risks. Personnel coverages include key person insurance, life, disability, and medical coverage insurance.

Key person insurance protects you in the event that a key employee dies or is disabled and cannot work.

Life insurance is the most common kind of coverage on key persons. Usually key person insurance names you, as the owner, or your business as the beneficiary of the policy. Life insurance also is often provided to employees to provide security for their families. Life insurance provided by you, the employer, is usually term insurance. *Term insurance* is a form of insurance that does not accumulate any value over the contract term. Rather, only specific events, including disability, dismemberment, and death, are insured events. Term insurance is very inexpensive for healthy young people. The premiums increase with age, and with specified risk factors such as obesity, heart problems, and a history of driving while intoxicated.

Disability insurance is usually provided as part of life insurance, although it can be obtained as either a stand-alone policy or as part of medical coverage. You as the owner of a small business should carefully consider obtaining disability coverage not only for key persons but also for yourself. Statistics provided by the American Association of Retired Persons (AARP) show that between the ages of 22 and 65, there is a greater than 25 percent probability that you will be disabled for a period of 12 months or more.[20] Statistics provided by the Social Security Administration indicate that the greatest probability of becoming disabled for this period of time occurs between ages 50 and 65.[21] The probability of shorter periods of disability is, of course, much higher. Given the high probability of temporary disability and the devastating effects it can have upon a small business, it is becoming ever more common for disability coverage to be included in business insurance plans.

Disability insurance can take several forms. The most common disability coverage provides the insured person with funds to replace income lost because of the inability to work. While this coverage is important to the disabled person, it provides no direct benefit to your business.

Some insurance companies now offer disability coverage that provides direct benefits to small businesses and to owners of small businesses. The most common of such disability coverage is **buyout insurance** which provides funds to the business to purchase the ownership position of a disabled partner. Less common, but of similar value for small business owners, is disability coverage that will pay specific fixed costs of the business, such as rent, salaries, and utilities, in the event that the owner or other named key person becomes disabled. Even less common is disability coverage that will pay specific dollar amounts to the business to replace lost revenue caused by the disability of a key person.

buyout insurance
Insurance that provides money to owners of a business to buy the shares of any deceased owner from that owner's heirs.

Medical coverage is the most highly desired form of insurance for most employees. Medical coverage is quite expensive, and the cost has been increasing rapidly in recent years. There are many reasons, however, that you, as the owner of a small business, might wish to provide such coverage for your employees. First, receiving medical coverage is a strong retention incentive for employees. Second, if you provide medical insurance for all employees, you can obtain reduced rates and can include yourself and your family. Third, the least expensive way to obtain key person insurance is as a part of a comprehensive medical insurance plan that covers all employees.

Sharing Risk

LO5 Describe techniques for sharing risk with other businesses and organizations.

One very effective method to reduce and to control business risk is to share that risk with other entities. As discussed above, one way to share risk is through insurance programs which, in effect, diversify risk across industries, businesses, and geographical areas. Additionally, risk can be directly shared without the intermediary of an insurance company, by forming joint ventures, by joining industry groups, and by obtaining government grants and guarantees.

Joint Ventures

Joint ventures are partnerships through which two or more businesses combine to undertake a specific economic activity. Each business involved in a joint venture keeps its own identity and conducts its own business separately from that of the other partners. The businesses are partners only for the activities specified in the joint venture contract.

joint venture
An agreement between two or more entities to pool resources in order to complete a project.

Joint ventures are most usually formed and taxed as partnerships. This allows for disproportionate allocation of revenues and expenses among the partner businesses. The ability to assign tax items to the partner for which they are most advantageous eases the problems of dissimilar businesses forming a partnership. A relatively large, profitable partner can be assigned the deductible costs of the joint venture, while revenues are simultaneously assigned to the smaller, less profitable (or even unprofitable) partner who will pay taxes at a lower rate.

Another advantage of joint ventures is that each partner can lose no more than its investment in the venture. The joint venture is a separate entity from any of the partners that own it. Thus, if the joint venture fails, only the resources of the joint venture are lost. The partner companies can continue in their individual businesses.

Industry Groups for Insurance Coverage

One of the primary reasons that there is at least one organized group for every conceivable industry is that joining in groups provides benefits of scale to members. The most common benefit is low-cost group insurance. The cost of insurance, as discussed above, is partly a function of the risk that the insurance provider assumes. Insurance companies diversify risk by insuring large numbers of similar businesses. It is obvious that the National Electric Sign Association can provide a much larger pool of people to be insured than can any single sign shop member. Because of the larger pool of potential insured people and because of its greater bargaining power, the NESA can obtain much lower insurance rates for its members than the members can obtain individually.

Government Funding of Risky Ventures

The final source for sharing risk is governments. Townships up to the federal government have programs to encourage economic activity. Governments do not have the profit-making requirements of businesses, but they do have the power to extract money from citizens. As a result, risk for a government is very different from risk for private business. Governments often subsidize very risky ventures that private companies would otherwise never attempt.

One example of government subsidizing risky ventures can be seen in the building of sports arenas, convention centers, and convention hotels. Cities across the nation have imposed taxes upon citizens and tourists to subsidize the building of such facilities. St. Louis has three such publicly funded arenas: one for the Cardinals baseball team, one for the Rams football team, and a half-million-square-foot convention center. Houston recently demolished an old facility and built a new one for the Houston Oilers football team. The City of San Antonio, Texas, and Bexar County recently enacted one of the nation's highest taxes on hotel rooms and rental cars to finance a new arena for the Spurs basketball team, despite having the largely unused Alamo Dome.

It is important to realize that the cities do not directly profit from these facilities. Nationwide, arenas, convention centers, and convention hotels operate at losses, which are covered by taxes imposed on nonusers of the facilities. In those rare instances in which the facilities are profitable, the profits go to private businesses which lease or operate the facilities on contract. Absent government subsidies, few, if any, of these facilities would exist.

Small businesses can obtain their share of government subsidies through direct contracting and grants. Opportunities exist for small businesses to obtain government funding for recycling of waste materials, for research and development of products for health, security, and defense, and for providing services directly to government entities.

All businesses operate in varying states of risk. The most careful planning and the best management in the world cannot remove all uncertainty from business operations. Storms, earthquakes, tsunamis, famines, recessions, and wars are facts of life with which you must sooner or later cope.

Although business risk cannot be eliminated, it can be controlled. Management techniques including security devices and internal controls can reduce the risk of misappropriation of business assets. Those risks that cannot be controlled can be insured. Insurance works to reduce the amount of loss that any individual business experiences because of natural events, dishonesty, or negligence. Because the environment in which business operates is constantly changing, you, as the owner and manager of a small business, must constantly reassess your risk controls, your exposure to disaster, and your insurance coverage.

Ben Franklin said long ago "A penny saved is a penny earned," and that adage is truly important for small businesses. Money saved means more flexibility and more profit. The point of spending time on risk, insurance, and protecting yourself and your business is to help you identify the ways to minimize your losses. Often, thinking about the potential sources of risk and loss ahead of time makes it possible for you to take action to minimize the risk or handle the loss should it come. The whole concept of insuring against risk works best when you can think objectively about the potential risk, loss, and cost to your firm. Only then can you be sure that you are spending your insurance dollars wisely. Despite all the talk about financial loss, it is important to note the human and emotional cost of loss. Whether through injury or criminal action, loss focuses our attention and can make us sad, angry, guilty, or a combination of the three. When it causes harm to employees or customers, it can derail a business and its owner. For all these reasons, taking the time to protect your business, its assets, and people always makes sense.

CHAPTER SUMMARY

LO1 Explain the meaning and nature of business risk.

- Business risk comes from many sources, including financial risk from capital structure, economic risks from business decisions, and the environment.
- Business risk is the probability that the future economic state of the business will be worse than is projected.

LO2 Describe the specific types of risks associated with different aspects of business operations.

- Economic risks arise from events related to the property of the business, to the personnel of the business, and to the customers, vendors, and visitors to the business.
- Violation of government regulations has become a significant business risk due to the many laws, rules, and regulations of the ADA, OSHA, the EEOC, and various tax agencies.
- Businesses are usually held liable for injuries suffered on business property, regardless of the cause.

LO3 Describe techniques to manage risks to stay within your level of risk tolerance.

- The loss from various events can be reduced by making specific plans and arrangements to deal with them, should they occur.
- Disaster plans can reduce losses by reducing the time that business operations are interrupted when the event occurs.
- Following building codes, locating away from flood plains, and keeping property clear of flammables can reduce loss from natural events.
- Risk to computers and data can be controlled by protection software, backups, and password use.
- The best control for risks from personnel is to hire qualified people of high integrity.
- Conducting an internal audit can provide an independent analysis of the levels and types of business risk.

LO4 Explain how insurance can be used to manage business risk.

- Keeping the right types and levels of insurance can minimize a business's loss from adverse events.
- You should not try to insure against all risks, rather only those that have economic consequences great enough to threaten the survival of your business.
- Some insurance coverages are required by law.

LO5 Describe techniques for sharing risk with other businesses and organizations.

- Risk may be reduced and insurance made affordable by joining with other similar businesses.
- The risky activity can be separated from the main part of your business through joint ventures and placing the risky activity into a separate legal entity.
- Industry groups can obtain lower insurance rates than can a single business.
- Government agencies can provide protection from risk by limiting the potential loss and by subsidizing risky ventures.

KEY TERMS

business risk, 540
employee theft, 541
regulation of the workplace, 541
Equal Employment Opportunity Commission (EEOC), 542
Occupational Health and Safety Administration (OSHA), 542
protected classes, 542
Age Discrimination in Employment Act, 542
Rehabilitation Act of 1973, 542
Americans with Disabilities Act of 1990, 542
Civil Rights Act of 1991, 542
key employees, 543
separation of duties, 550
internal control, 551
tax codes, 552
insurance, 556
coverages, 557
insurable value, 559
deductible, 559
co-insurance, 560
fidelity bonds, 560
surety bonds, 560
buyout insurance, 562
joint venture, 563

DISCUSSION QUESTIONS

1. Discuss the types of risk encountered by small businesses. Are these risks different in any way from risks facing big business?
2. What are the risks to small businesses caused by personnel issues?
3. How are the risks from personnel affected by government business regulations?
4. How does disaster planning help a small business cope with risk?
5. The text discusses methods to protect against weather. What might a business do to protect itself against an earthquake?
6. Which is easier to steal, money from an employer's bank account or secret business processes? Why?
7. What types of insurance should a small business have? Give your reasons for maintaining each type of coverage.
8. Suppose you are in the business of making ladders. A customer places a board plank between two of your ladders as a scaffold. One of the ladders fails, causing your customer to fall and break a leg. Are you responsible for your customer's losses? How can you protect yourself from lawsuits in such cases?
9. You are considering offering credit to good customers to increase sales. What things should you consider to limit your risks if you do?
10. One of your partners has special skills that would be very difficult to replace. His great joy in life is single-track bicycle racing. How can you protect yourself from the probability that he will be injured and unable to work?

EXPERIENTIAL EXERCISES

1. Identify a business you would like to own. Make a list of the risks that are specific to that business. Contact an insurance broker to find out what coverages are available and what they would cost. Make a report to your class of your findings.
2. Identify a business you would like to own. Go to the OSHA Web site and find out what rules and regulations apply to this business. Create a chart of hazards of this business and the applicable OSHA rules. Make a report to your class of your findings.
3. Suppose you are going to open a consulting business. You are going to finish half of your garage to use as an office. Go to the ADA site and determine what accessibility requirements you must meet. Make a report to your class of your findings.
4. Identify a specific location (street address) where you would like to operate a business. Visit your city's planning and zoning office (or its Web site, if it has one) and determine if this site is in a flood plain. Make a copy of the city's map of flood plains. Make a report to your class of your findings.
5. Identify a business you want to own. Use the resources of your library and the Internet to identify what insurance you are legally required to carry. Contact an insurance broker to determine how and for how much you can obtain the required coverage. Make a report to your class of your findings.

MINI-CASE

RISKY BUSINESS

Vicky Volare fell in love with motor scooters on her vacation trip to Aruba. "They're a blast!" Vicky said, "They are convenient, safe, inexpensive, and fun to ride." Now she is planning to buy 30 Vespa Scooters to provide scooter rental in Vail, Colorado. Vicky will need four employees, in addition to her own services. She has completed a business plan, except for determining what types and amounts of insurance coverage she should have. As soon as she completes the insurance planning, she can complete the financial section of her business plan. Vicky will invest $50,000 of her own funds and is borrowing $230,000. $180,000 of the loan will be secured with the 30 scooters. The other $50,000 is a personal note to her from her bank. She hopes to start her business within 90 days, to catch the beginning of the summer.

CASE DISCUSSION QUESTIONS

1. What financial risks is Vicky assuming?
2. What are the risks that are specific to renting motor scooters?
3. What are the risks specific to motor scooters as physical assets?
4. What risks will Vicky face because she is hiring four people?
5. What regulatory risks will Vicky face in operating a vehicle rental service in the state of Colorado?
6. What insurance coverage will Colorado require Vicky to have?
7. What insurance must Vicky have for her employees?
8. How should Vicky structure her business to minimize the potential loss she can suffer if a customer or bystander is injured or killed by one of her scooters?

SUGGESTED CASES AND ARTICLES

- The House of Wine (Revisited)

Available on PRIMIS:

- Daniel Dobbins Distillery, Inc.
- Play Time Toy Co.

SUGGESTED VIDEOS

Video Case:

- New Orleans Biz, p. VC-8

eClips Videos:

- Kathy Koultourides Discusses Importance of Taking Small Risks
- Alison Gerlach Discusses Different Risks That Face Companies

SBTV Videos:

- Stopping Employee Theft
- Legal Protection for Business Owners

STVP Video:

- Fail Fast Forward: Appreciating Risk

Management and Organization in the Small Business

PART FIVE 5

Management and Organization in the Small Business

CHAPTER 18

Legal Issues: Recognizing Your Small Business Needs

● A top-notch turntable scratcher, like B-Money Hughes, could make a good royalty income from getting one of his tracks included on a commercial CD. But in order to get that royalty, you need a good lawyer negotiating on your behalf. How could you tell if a lawyer is right for the negotiation you face?

LO

LEARNING OBJECTIVES

This chapter will help you:

LO1 Know when you need legal information and how to get it.

LO2 Understand legal structures in setting up a new business.

LO3 Learn how to master the process of negotiating.

LO4 Recognize potential legal liabilities for your business.

LO5 Know contract terms and when a contract is needed.

LO6 Understand the basics of intellectual property.

Focus on Small Business: Brian "B-Money" Hughes[1]

Brian "B-Money" Hughes has a tip for budding hip-hop producers: "The best advice I can give to anyone that's coming up: Make sure you get yourself a good lawyer." He knows of what he speaks.

B-Money was a turntable scratcher good enough to get credits on Jennifer Lopez and Murphy Lee CDs. He scored big in street cred when he produced 50 Cent's "Hustler's Ambition," the lead track to the soundtrack of *Get Rich or Die Trying*. This did not translate into much money, though. Two weeks before the film's release, 50 Cent's team offered a small flat fee rather than a larger royalty. B-Money was told to take it or leave it, but do it now. An experienced lawyer would have realized that the cost to 50 Cent to redo the film's soundtrack without B-Money's contribution would have been a lot more than what was offered. But as B-Money put it, "I had way more leverage, but my lawyer wasn't poised and let it slide."

B-Money took the flat fee offered, but he replaced that lawyer with an industry veteran. So later, when Jay-Z's producer asked for a B-Money-produced track called "The Prelude," this time the artist and lawyer were ready to negotiate. The track was the lead for Jay-Z's *Kingdom Come* CD. The new lawyer delivered, and B-Money finally came into some of the money he deserved for his work.

DISCUSSION QUESTIONS

1. Given B-Money's experience, if you were interviewing a potential lawyer, what sort of questions would you want to ask?
2. Can you think of anything you could have said to your lawyer to get a better outcome during the negotiation with 50 Cent?
3. Did B-Money have any recourse when it turned out his first lawyer was just not very good at the music business?

You and the Law

LO1 Know when you need legal information and how to get it.

Business and law are inseparable. For B-Money, the two predictably merged when he was negotiating a deal for his tracks. At other times, the merger is unpredictable, like when your business faces an unexpected auto accident, product recall, or government regulation change. In either type of situation, when business owners know the law, they can better protect themselves and sometimes even avoid the problems completely. This chapter will help you spot important legal issues for small businesses and provide guidance for dealing effectively with those issues.

The United States is one of the most *litigious* (from the word *litigate,* meaning to sue) societies in the world, along with countries such as Germany, Sweden, Israel, and Austria.[2] On the other hand, in a 2002 National Federation of Independent Business poll of small businesses, less than 1 business in 10 had been sued in the prior five years. No matter what the perception, the law affects everything about business. Despite all the negative comments about attorneys, attorney jokes, and general resentment of the legal profession, the fact remains that if you are going to start a small business, you are going to be stuck with the legal system—virtues and faults both.

Because of that, it is important for you as a prospective small business owner to understand our legal system. Understanding the legal system will help you be less intimidated by attorneys and the law. And that knowledge can help move you from being a passive victim of the legal system, merely reacting to legal threats, to an empowered owner able to use the law to your advantage in a proactive way. Starting a business is risky enough. With the right knowledge about the law and the use of legal counsel, many of those risks can be significantly reduced or eliminated altogether.

It is easy to underestimate the number of laws that apply to a new small business because it is hard to believe how many laws apply—federal laws, state laws, even county and city laws. Let us take a moment and get an overview of the laws most likely to apply.

Table 18.1 provides an overview of some major federal laws in the areas of taxation and environmental health and safety. Intellectual property laws are considered later in this chapter, and labor and employment laws will be considered in Chapter 19. Even so, what Table 18.1 does not consider are state laws. There are some areas which only states legislate, for example, workers' compensation and employment security, which we will cover in Chapter 19. There can also be areas where there are overlapping state and federal laws, most typically in civil rights, and in such cases, the more demanding law is the one you should obey.

While the scope can be overwhelming, the good news is that not all laws apply to your business on the day you open. Many laws only start to apply as you reach certain thresholds. For example, tax laws tend to focus on financial thresholds, while environmental laws look at how much waste you produce.

Meanwhile, the state laws applicable to a small business are extraordinarily varied. It is truly a case where one size does not fit all. In Chapter 19 you will see the additional state laws that apply to labor and employment. For any category of laws, it is important to check what is applicable in your state. The Online Learning Center shows how to begin your check on the Internet. State laws can vary dramatically, so Missouri's laws are unlikely to be of much use anywhere else.

There is no central online starting point for finding the relevant state laws. One of the best ways to get a complete rundown of the relevant laws is to contact your closest state Small Business Development Center (to find it, type "SBDC Locator" into the search box at the SBA Web site, www.sba.gov). Also, your local SCORE chapter (www.score.org) should be able to help, or at least point you to the right resources. Obviously, you can also work with an attorney to get expert help personalized for your business.

In the next portion of this chapter we start with your key legal expert—your attorney. We talk about how to select and work with an attorney. We also cover how to make some key legal decisions, such as choosing a legal form for your business, how to negotiate, liability issues, and contracts (in person and online), that come up in business. We conclude the chapter with a discussion of the latest hot topic in law—intellectual property.

TABLE 18.1 Selected Laws Applicable to Growing Businesses

Benchmark	Law/Regulation	Ramification
Business and Taxation		
Employer's portion of federal employment taxes plus federal income and employment taxes withheld from employees' total wages: ● Less than $2,500 during a quarter. ● Under $50,000 during the four quarters in the "lookback period" applicable to the calendar year of withholding. ● More than $50,000 during the "lookback period." ● $100,000 or more during a monthly or semiweekly period.	Circular E-Employer's Tax Guide	Employer must deposit withheld taxes: ● Quarterly (if paying with Form 941) ● Monthly ● Semiweekly ● Next banking day after $100,000 threshold is reached
Gross receipts up to $5,000,000.	Section 448 of Internal Revenue Code	The business may qualify for an exception that allows it to compute taxable income using the cash method of accounting rather than the accrual method.
More than 100 shareholders of a corporation, more than one class of stock, certain prohibited shareholders.	Section 1361 of Internal Revenue Code	Corporation could lose or be ineligible to elect "Subchapter S" status.
Filing requirements for an employee benefit plan with: ● One participant (with plan assets more than $100,000) ● 2–99 participants ● 100 or more participants ● Reporting to participants: Summary Annual Report	Internal Revenue Service/ Department of Labor Reg. §2520.104(b)-10	● Generally must file form 5500EZ annually with IRS. ● Form 5500 must be filed annually with IRS, with some exceptions if the plan is unfunded or insured. ● Form 5500, with some exceptions, must be filed annually including a report by an independent qualified accountant. ● Annually provide to participants no later than 8½ months after the end of plan year.
Qualifying depreciable tangible personal property (and certain computer software) purchased for use in the active conduct of a trade or business in excess of $450,000.	Section 179 of the Internal Revenue Code	Reduction of the $112,000 maximum amount of qualifying property that can be expensed in the current year instead of depreciated over several years.
Environmental/Health & Safety		
Conditionally Exempt Small Quantity Generators of Hazardous Waste: ● Generators of less than 1 kilogram of acute hazardous waste in a month, may accumulate up to 1 kilogram of acute hazardous waste before accumulation period begins. ● Generators of up to 100 kilograms of hazardous waste in a month, may accumulate up to 1,000 kilograms of hazardous waste before accumulation period begins. Small Quantity Generators: ● Generates at least 100 kilograms but less than 1,000 kilograms of hazardous waste in a month, may accumulate 6,000 kilograms of hazardous waste before accumulation period begins.	Hazardous Waste Regulations under RCRA (Resource Conservation and Recovery Act)	Exceptions for the small quantity generator relax handling requirements. Allows the generator to accumulate hazardous waste on site until the amount of accumulated waste exceeds the small quantity exclusion limits. After this amount is exceeded, the time period allowed for accumulation of hazardous waste begins to run (90,180 or 270 days). If the generator does not exceed this time period, the generator need not obtain a RCRA Part B permit to store the waste.

Benchmark	Law/Regulation	Ramification
Environmental/Health & Safety		
• Part 70 Source: Facility has the potential to emit 10, 25, 50 or 100 tons per year of certain air pollutants (depends on nonattainment status of area for the pollutant emitted). • Intermediate Source: Facility has the potential to emit at Part 70 source levels but has voluntarily agreed to enforceable limits on the rates of production, or greater control efficiencies to reduce potential emissions below Part 70 source levels. • Basic Source: Facility has potential to emit greater than de minimis levels but no the potential to emit Part 70 source levels.	Missouri's Operating Permit Rule—CSR 10-6.065	Required the owner or operator of a Part 70 facility to apply for an operating permit and intermediate facilities to notify within 60 days after EPA approved Missouri's permitting program. (Final Interim EPA approval was effective May 13, 1996, so first year permit applications were due July 15, 1996.) Required all other Part 70 facilities and all intermediate facilities with actual emissions less than 50% of the Part 70 thresholds to apply by May 13, 1997. Basic facilities were to apply by May 14, 1998. A Small Business Environmental Compliance Assistance Program has been established in both Missouri and Illinois to provide assistance to small businesses for permitting and technical matters. In Illinois call 1-800-252-3998. In Missouri call 1-800-361-4827.
Facility has hazardous chemicals present at the facility at any one time in amounts equal to or greater than 10,000 pounds, or extremely hazardous substances present in an amount greater than or equal to 500 pounds, 55 gallons, or the threshold planning quantity (if lower).	Hazardous Chemical Inventory Reporting under §312 of the Emergency Planning and Community Right-to-Know Act	Requires owner or operator to submit reports on inventories of various chemicals based on certain threshold levels.
The Clean Air Act imposes stringent emissions limits on various air contaminate sources and also adds several new provisions to address acid rain, ozone depletion, and federally enforceable operating permits.	Clean Air Act Amendments of 1990	Missouri and Illinois have been delegated the authority to administer the regulations and permitting of air contaminant sources.
Own or operate petroleum underground storage tanks.	State Underground Storage Tank Programs (Illinois and Missouri)	Requires owner or operator to provide proof of financial responsibility to cover costs of corrective action and liability to third parties resulting from releases from existing underground petroleum storage tanks. All tanks not meeting "new" UST standards were to have been upgraded by December 22, 1998, or be removed from service and closed.
Process involves one of over 130 listed chemicals in an amount exceeding a listed threshold level or involves any flammable gas or liquid in a quantity of 10,000 pounds or more.	Process Safety Management Rule under the OSH Act 29 CFR 1910.119	Requires owners to perform a process hazard analysis and develop written operating procedures, employee training, emergency action plans, evaluation of mechanical integrity of critical equipment and written procedures for managing changes in process or procedures.
Employs 100 or fewer individuals on a companywide basis.	EPA's Interim Policy on Compliance Incentives for Small Businesses	EPA will eliminate or mitigate its settlement penalty demands against small businesses based on: (1) good faith effort to comply with applicable environmental requirements; (2) this is the business's first violation of this requirement (no previous enforcement of that requirement within last 3 years); (3) the violation has not caused or does not pose a serious harm or threat to health or the environment; (4) the violation does not involve criminal conduct; and (5) the violation is corrected within a specified period.
An employer with more than 10 employees on a company-wide basis (except those in Standard Industrial Classification codes 52-89).	OSHA's Recording and Reporting of Occupational Injuries and Illnesses	Employer is required to record occupational injuries and illness on a log with a separate supporting record for each injury or illness and post in the workplace the log for the previous calendar year during the following month of February.

The chart is not, nor is it intended to be, a comprehensive summary of the threshold levels at which the statutes and regulations cited therein take effect, and it is qualified in its entirety by reference to the appropriate statute and regulations.

Chart compiled in March 2007 by: Joseph Demko, Robert A. Kaiser, Julie O'Keefe, Guy Schmitz, and Larry Sewell, all with the law firm of Armstrong Teasdale LLP.

You Need a Good Attorney

Setting up a business requires some familiarity with several areas of law—forms of organization, contracts, and licensing, for example. Usually with legal issues, as with health issues, it is best to confront potential problems before they have a chance to get serious. Timely decisions and action may avoid a problem altogether or may make solving the problem much easier and cheaper. Think of legal knowledge as a form of insurance. The key is finding the right lawyer.

First, look for an attorney who is experienced in forming new business entities and handling the needs of small businesses.[3] Where can you find such a person? If you do not have someone in mind, get suggestions from small business owners you know and respect. Bankers involved in commercial financing on a regular basis often know which attorneys handle small businesses well. In addition, a trade association for your industry may have suggestions.

These days, it is typical to be involved with more than one attorney. As with doctors, where you might work with one generalist and several specialists, today most businesses need to depend on one general purpose lawyer and several specialists. The law is so complex that no one can be an expert in all areas. Beware of the attorney who tells you he or she can handle all your legal needs. However, if the attorney is in a group practice, there may well be others in the firm who specialize in the other areas where you need specialized help. Ask about the legal specialties covered within the firm when you call to make an appointment. You may make several calls and visits. If one attorney does not meet your needs in terms of qualifications, work ethic, or pricing, there are many others who would like to have your business.

Again, like with physicians, once you have chosen an attorney, having an ongoing relationship helps him or her to know you and your situation when something comes up and you need legal advice on short notice.

Clients and attorneys start with a natural conflict of interest. The attorney wants to make money for the services, and you would like the services for as little cost as possible. In reality, all entrepreneurs know they will have to pay, so the key issues are how and how much you will be charged for legal services.

Typically you and the attorney will discuss and decide on the type and rate of charges up-front, before you engage his or her professional services. The attorney-client agreement should definitely be in writing and signed by both parties.[4] Take the time to read the agreement before signing. Ask for it to be sent to you to review. If the agreement is hard to understand, think about what other work from the attorney will look like, and consider whether that attorney is right for you. There are four ways attorneys typically charge:

1. **Hourly fees:** **Hourly fees** can vary greatly from one part of the country to another, as well as from firm to firm and even within a firm. Attorneys with more experience often charge more than new law school graduates. Prestigious law firms often charge more than smaller, less recognized firms.
2. **Flat fees:** **Flat fees** are a fixed amount paid for a certain task. For example, an attorney may have a flat fee for handling all the paperwork to establish a corporation.
3. **Retainers:** When using a **retainer**, the attorney will be paid a specified amount every month regardless of the workload for that month. Usually there is a retainer agreement which specifies what types of work that monthly fee covers and when and how much additional fees are when circumstances change.
4. **Contingency fees:** You have seen the attorney ads on television announcing, "I don't get paid unless you get paid." That ad is describing a contingency fee. **Contingency fees** are typical in accident (especially personal injury) situations, but are not usually used in everyday contract and business-related matters. With a contingency fee, the attorney will take a percentage of your recovery (if your side wins) as his or her fee.

Just like anything else, pricing of legal services is based on supply and demand, especially your negotiating demands. Do not be intimidated by having to negotiate price with an attorney. Regardless of what the attorney says, the attorney's fee schedule in all four types of pricing of services may be negotiable, particularly if the attorney is a more senior member of the firm with the authority to negotiate. Diplomacy is recommended in these negotiations because once the original issue of pricing is resolved, it is in your best interest for you and your attorney to have a positive working relationship.

hourly fees
A basis for legal charges in which the rate is based on a price per hour. Often lawyers will charge for fractions of an hour.

flat fees
A method of billing for lawyers in which a fixed amount is paid for a certain task.

retainer
A fee paid by a client to an attorney to engage the attorney's services.

contingency fee
Fee paid by a client to an attorney for legal services that is dependent upon the outcome of a case.

Can I Do This for Free?

There are three elements to most aspects of business law—finding the right information, negotiating the specific outcome you want, and then taking care of the paperwork associated with it. The three elements are what you pay your lawyer to do, but when you look at paying lawyer's fees, you probably want to know if there are things you can do yourself. The good news is that you can.

These days there are many sources of reliable legal information on the Internet for small business owners who want to do the legal work themselves. Also be aware that your local library and bookstores are brimming with titles on business law and how to start your own business.

There are two basic categories of information available to small business owners: free and paid. If you are paying a nonattorney for legal services, such as using an Internet company to set up your business as a corporation, you may not be saving that much money over what an attorney would charge. Consider whether you would be better served in seeking out an attorney and getting individual, custom-tailored advice. Falling between free and paid are the do-it-yourself products. Nolo (www.nolo.com) is one well-known company that has been established for some time and offers do-it-yourself products.

Of the free information available, some are more reliable than others. Government Web sites, such as www.business.gov (the general business site), www.reginfo.gov (the regulatory information site), www.dol.gov (for labor laws), and www.sba.gov (the Small Business Administration site), provide information to business owners that is reliable, and the government does not have the conflict of interest of wishing to make money from the business owner. State government sources can be very valuable in helping you choose a business entity; check your state's secretary of state Web site. You can easily find the sites by searching Google with the term "secretary of state" followed by a comma and your state's name, or you can go to www.business.gov/states/ to find your state's offices, as shown in Skill Module 18.1 and on the Online Learning Center.

Visit **www.business.gov** to take advantage of the government's free legal resources. Looking at this and related Web sites can help you determine which legal aspects you can manage on your own and which require a paid attorney's involvement.

Getting Started on Legal Issues Online

SKILL MODULE 18.1

The Internet can be a great source of information in helping you determine which various governmental requirements apply to a business. On the state level you can go to the Web site for the state and obtain all sorts of information on starting a business in that state, required licenses, and the like.

Pretend that you wish to start business as a debt collector in the state of Washington. You have questions on professional licenses required of debt collectors, and you are considering hiring a high school student to work parttime after school. In addition, you have concerns about safety and health rules that apply to businesses in Washington.

There are two easy ways to find the information on **www.business.gov**. Click on "Register, Licenses & Permits" and in the "Enter City/State or Zip Code" box type "Washington." The drop-down box shows "Debt Collection Agency." Select that and click "Search."

Another way to do it is to click on "State & Local" on the **www.business.gov** home page, select "Browse the Map," then select Washington State, and from the resulting page select "Get a Business License" under the "How do I . . . ?" section, and then select "Professional Licenses" and "Collection Agencies."

On each state page inside **www.business.gov** you will find a section on "Starting a Business" which will link you to the key resources for new firms in each state. Most states have a start-up guide. For Washington State, it is the "New guide for doing business in Washington (PDF)" and you can find it by clicking "Starting a business" from the Washington State page in **www.business.gov**, then clicking "Washington Business Portal," and then "Plan a business." You can also see this demonstrated on the Online Learning Center.

States vary in where they put their guide, but the business.gov Web site's "Starting a Business" hotlink usually gets you within a click or two of your goal. Now go to your state's Web page at **www.business.gov** and see if you can find the state start-up guide and the licensing requirements for your business. If you don't have a business idea at this point, see what kind of license a debt collector would need in your state.

Trade associations are another source of information for business start-ups. Many trade associations compile legal information for their members, including laws particularly applicable to certain types of businesses in various jurisdictions and proposals for changing the laws that affect your industry. As you may be aware, these organizations also hire lobbyists to push the agenda of an industry or trade group within the various branches of government, both federal and state. Because of the limited resources of small businesses, membership in one of these organizations can be particularly valuable in informing the business owners and giving them more power as a group to influence legislation that affects them. In addition, through these trade associations it is possible to meet others in your industry and make noncompetitive connections that help you network and keep up with industry trends. Remember that you learned how to find your relevant trade, industry, or professional association in Skill Module 2.1 in Chapter 2.

Be wary of legal information on matters such as statutes or agency regulations offered by individuals who seek to profit from doing business with you. For instance, if you are looking for space to locate your business, be wary of what real estate agents tell you regarding the law. Never forget, these folks make their money when you buy something or if they arrange some lease agreement for you. It may not be in your best interest to buy property, but real estate agents are not likely to tell you that because they will make money by getting a percentage when you buy.

For example, in the issue of zoning, go to your local governmental unit and check on the zoning of the property before you seriously consider it.[5] Do not take the real estate agent's word on the zoning. Be sure that the business you plan may be legally operated in that location. If the building will need any remodeling to suit your purposes, be sure to contact the local government regarding safety standards, exits, entrances, and so on so that the property will pass inspection once the remodeling is done. In the contract with your remodeler, it is best to insert a provision that the remodeling has to be done according to applicable building codes before the contractor is fully paid.

In the contract to purchase or lease the property, insert a provision that the property has to be zoned such that your business can be legally operated in that location. By contacting the local

One key legal issue for small business owners is the matter of real estate. Before you purchase a space for any of your business's activities, make sure the site is zoned appropriately and that you can legally undertake any planned remodeling, expansion, or re-zoning of the area.

government, you should be able to get guidelines on zoning, placement, and size of signage, parking, property tax, and other matters related to the location.[6] Also, be sure to inquire about future plans regarding street repairs, expansions, and closures in the area, which could affect your ability to do business. Do not rely on the real estate agent for any of this information.

As noted at the start of this section, there are three elements to the law—finding the right information, negotiating the specific outcome you want, and then taking care of the paperwork associated with it. Often as businesspeople become familiar with the legal specifics of their business, they take on more of the responsibilities. Most often they do the negotiating themselves (you will see how later in this chapter), and where the paperwork is standardized (as we see below with standard contracts) even handle aspects of the paperwork themselves. Even some legal research can be done, especially when the business owner is made aware of new legal concerns by the trade or professional association. But for all of these things you can eventually do for yourself, when learning the business or when facing a new or unusual situation, it makes sense to go with the pro. When in doubt, call your lawyer.

Small-Claims Court

There is also a legal option available to entrepreneurs that does not involve an attorney. It is typically called small-claims court. Despite the name, many of these courts will accept cases where the stakes are as large as $10,000. Most are designed so that ordinary citizens can bring their cases in. Yes, this is the sort of court you see on afternoon television—*Judge Judy, The People's Court, Judge Joe Brown*, and the like include a lot of small-claims court cases.

Believe it or not, you can learn something about preparing yourself for small-claims court by watching the television shows: (1) evidence helps, (2) have everything ready and with you when you go to court, (3) practice your explanation, (4) be on time, (5) stay calm, and (6) above all, stay respectful to the judge and court.

Small-claims courts work only when you are owed money, can prove it (proof you did the work, and that your customer did not pay—think of purchase orders, contracts, invoices, past-due letters, etc.), and have exhausted other procedures like calls and letters to the customer. If there is a reason the other party did not pay—for example, they said your work was late, shoddy, or not as promised—you need to prove you are in the right, otherwise you will have a tough day in court.

The typical next step starts with finding the right court—either where your business is located or where the person (or business) you want to sue lives or works. Realize this means small-claims court is not really useful for problems in other states, unless it is a short drive for you. To find the right court for your state, look at nolo.com lists of small-claims courts on their Web site. Go to nolo.com, select "Rights & Disputes," and then select "Go to court or mediate." Look for "Small Claims

Court" to find the listing and help by state on the process. Most state bar associations also have pamphlets on small-claims courts. There is a video showing this on the Online Learning Center.

Contact the court to find out the specifics and costs of filing. These fees are typically less than $50, and are something you can charge the customer for if you win. You will probably have to fill out a form and give a written explanation of the problem. Make copies of your evidence to include in the packet. If you have potential witnesses, list them and get their testimony written down. Take the packet and the originals of your evidence to court to file the complaint with the clerk.

When you get to court, the TV lessons apply. Look the judge in the eye as you talk. Speak up and sound confident. Stick to what you wrote. Answer questions directly, briefly, and politely. Don't get angry at the other party, especially if they get angry or they insult you or the court. If you have a court date, be there no matter what. In case of emergency, it might be possible to get one postponement (called a continuance)—if the other party agrees. Otherwise, the case will be thrown out and you cannot refile it.

If you win, the court will give you official support to get your money; however, it remains mostly up to you to collect payment. The customer will have a fixed amount of time to pay up. If they don't, you can get the clerk to serve the losing party with a certified letter reminding them of the court order. A personal delivery can often be arranged for an additional fee. If that doesn't get the job done, the court can help garnish the loser's income or attach assets of the losing party, making them yours until you get the payment the court ordered. But realize that a defendant with little income and few assets will be difficult to collect from, regardless of the decision, so it only makes sense to go to small-claims court if you think you will be able to collect, should you win.

Choosing a Business Name

As we saw in Chapter 4, some entrepreneurs start out with the goal to start a business, others with an idea they want to commercialize. The legal issue for either approach is protecting the business's name or idea from copycats. Both of these are issues of intellectual property. At this point, we will consider the ways you can protect the identity of your business, while later in the chapter we will consider the other forms of intellectual property that can protect your idea.

The name of your business is called its **trade name**. It can also be called an **assumed name** or a **doing business as (dba) name**. If you use something other than your own name (e.g., The Jerome Katz Company), then the trade name must be registered in the states in which your firm does business. The filing is typically called an **assumed name filing** or a **fictitious name filing**. In most states, this filing is made with the Secretary of State's office. You can find these at Business.gov (http://business.gov/register/business-name/dba.html). The same office usually offers a public database to see the names of the people behind other businesses using trade names.

trade name or assumed name or doing business as (dba)
The name under which a business is operated.

assumed name filing or fictitious name filing
Filing made with a state(s) in which the business operates disclosing the trade name or assumed name of the business along with the owners of the business.

There may be more than one business using the same name within a state. Most states allow several firms to use the same trade name, as long as the firms are in different parts of the state, or are in different lines of business (e.g., Courtesy Cleaners, Courtesy Pharmacy, etc.) in the same town, and as long as none of the firms have received a trademark or service mark in that name. You can check this using the Secretary of State database mentioned above, as well as the trademark search at the U.S. Patent Office (www.uspto.gov).

When selecting a trade name, you want to find one that is memorable and descriptive. "Social Networking Experts, LLC" tells customers who you are, better than "Darlene Jones, LLC" does. If you have plans to grow, factor that in too. Since St. Louis is known for baseball and beer, but not bread, the founders of the St. Louis Bread Company had to create a new name when they left their home market. Now the country knows them as Panera Bread. Given how Panera's menu has grown, it is possible that "Bread" may someday get dropped from the title, too.

In the end, the other key element in picking a trade name is your own goals. It can be very satisfying to have your name on a successful business—think of Donald Trump! But also realize that it can make it hard to sell the business. Imagine the Trump Companies without Trump. On the other hand, for a family-owned business, having the family name visible can be a benefit. Part of what makes Ford a bit more personal brand compared to General Motors is that there are members of the Ford family who own stock, sit on the board, and occasionally even run the place. The Ford family stands behind the Ford line, even today.

St. Louis Bread Company® really did start out in St. Louis, but when they wanted to expand outside the region, they felt they needed a name that was place-neutral. They came up with Panera Bread, which is what the company is known as everywhere except St. Louis, Missouri, where the original name is still used.

Choosing a Business Form

LO2 Understand legal structures in setting up a new business.

legal entity
A being, human or nonhuman, such as a corporation, that is recognized as having rights and duties, such as the right to own property.

plaintiff
Person or other entity filing a lawsuit.

defendant
Person or other entity being sued.

Most often choosing the *form* of your business is the next legal decision you need to make. Except for sole proprietorships, business forms are types of separate, legal entities. A **legal entity** is a unit recognized as having rights and duties apart from the owners of the company. Legal entities can own property, sue, and be sued.

The original type of legal entity recognized in England, the source of United States law, was the individual. An individual may hold property ownership and be a **plaintiff** (the party who files a lawsuit) or a **defendant** (the party who is sued) in a lawsuit. As time passed, the law recognized other legal entities that were not human beings. For example, about 1600 the corporation was recognized as a separate entity in England. In other words, a corporation itself, without its shareholders (or owners), could hold title to property and could sue or be sued in its own name, without its owners being sued.

Today there are seven general types of business form—sole proprietorships, general partnerships, limited partnerships, C corporations (commonly known as just "Corporations"), S corporations (also known as Subchapter S corporations), professional corporations, and limited liability companies (commonly known as LLCs). Each general form has advantages and disadvantages, which are outlined in Tables 18.2, 18.3 and 18.4. For start-ups, the most popular form is the sole

TABLE 18.2 Advantages and Disadvantages of Corporations

Advantages	Disadvantages
Can have representative management	Impersonal
Ease of raising large amounts of capital	Owners have limited interest in firm's activities—except profits
Legal entity separate and distinct from its owners as individuals	High incorporation fees and high taxes, especially double income taxation
Relatively permanent, since life of firm not affected by loss of any shareholder	Burdensome procedures, reports, and statements required by governments
Owners' liability for the firm's debt limited to their investment in it	Powers limited to those stated in charters—may be difficult to do business in another state

Source: Adapted from Megginson/Byrd/Megginson, *Small Business Management* 5th edition, 2006, p. 61. Copyright © 2006 by The McGraw-Hill Companies, Inc.

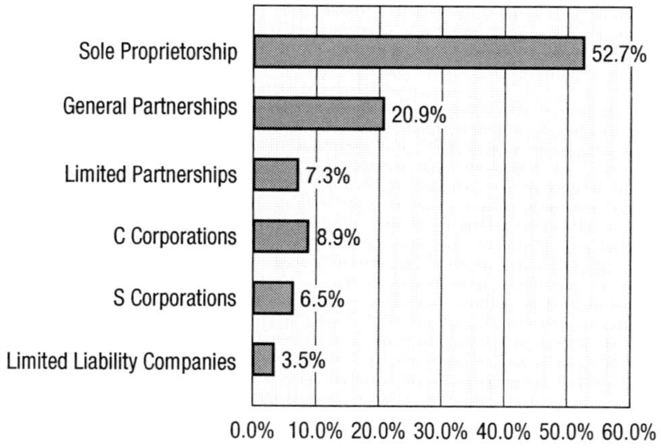

FIGURE 18.1

Legal Forms of Start-Ups from the PSED

Source: Paul D. Reynolds, "Nature of Business Start-ups," in William B. Gartner, Kelly G. Shaver, Nancy M. Carter, and Paul D. Reynolds (eds.), *Handbook of Entrepreneurial Dynamics: The Process of Business Creation*, p. 250. Copyright © 2004.Reprinted by permission of Sage Publications, Inc.

proprietorship, although the approach is not always optimal for a small start-up, as we see below. General partnerships are the second most popular, and C corporations are third. These results are shown in Figure 18.1.

Unless you are going to see a lawyer for advice on what legal form of business makes sense in your situation, or you are using an interactive guide (like the "Formation Assistant" at http://www.bizfilings.com/la/assistant.html) to get a general idea about the best type of business form to use, the best choice for a new small business is a limited liability company (LLC). This is because LLCs are simple to set up and relatively easy to maintain once started. They can be used for an individual or a group of partners. If you have partners, it makes sense to create an agreement specifying ownership, profit splitting, buyouts, and the like, called **articles of organization**. In addition, an LLC offers legal protection to owners for assets they personally hold outside the LLC. It also gives the owners the benefits of single taxation, if they choose to go that route. (See Table 18.5.)

articles of organization Document setting forth information about a limited liability company that is filed with the state to establish an LLC.

The major advantage of the sole proprietorship is that it is extremely easy to set up. There are no forms to file; you just start doing business. The problem is one mentioned in Chapter 17 when discussing risk. In a sole proprietorship, the owner and the firm are one and the same. If an employee has an accident while at work, the business is liable for the damages—*and the owner is personally responsible too.* This means the sole proprietor's home, stocks, savings, and even personal property could be taken to pay damages. (See Table 18.3.)[7]

TABLE 18.3 Advantages and Disadvantages of Sole Proprietorships

Advantages	Disadvantages
Secrecy	Limited capital
Unique tax advantages	Difficulty in obtaining credit
Owner doesn't have to share profits	Inadequate management and employee skills
Relative freedom of action and control	Unlimited liability for the firm's debts
Easiest and simplest form to organize, operate, and dissolve	Limited life because business and owner are legally the same

Source: Adapted from Megginson/Byrd/Megginson, *Small Business Management* 5th edition, 2006, p. 58. Copyright © 2006 by The McGraw-Hill Companies, Inc.

TABLE 18.4 Advantages and Disadvantages of Partnerships

Advantages	Disadvantages
Easy to form	Limited life
Division of labor and management responsibility	Unlimited liability for debts of the firm
Can use ideas and plans of more than one person	Each partner is responsible for the acts of every other partner
Specialized skills available from individual partners	An impasse may develop if the partners become incompatible
Can raise more capital since good credit may be available	Death of any one of the partners terminates the partnership
Obtains financial resources from more than one person	A partner cannot obtain bonding protection against the acts of the other partner(s)

Source: Adapted from Megginson/Byrd/Megginson, *Small Business Management* 5th edition, 2006, p. 59. Copyright © 2006 by The McGraw-Hill Companies, Inc.

articles of partnership
Agreement between the partners of a firm on matters pertaining to the formation and operation of the partnership.

Partnerships can vary dramatically. They can be set up quickly with nothing more than with a handshake or with a formal legal agreement called **articles of partnership** (the latter is usually safer). They can be set up so all partners are equally and fully responsible for the business's obligations (called a *general partnership*) or where most partners are liable only for the amount they invested in the partnership (called a *limited partnership*—but every limited partnership has at least one general partner). The total liability issue in general partnerships is like that of sole proprietorships, so although easy to start, partnerships are something to avoid. (See Table 18.4.)

Maybe you are not sure that an LLC is right for your situation, or your lawyer has suggested another form. How do you go about thinking through the issues? There are six major factors at play in the decision on the form of a business organization to set up:

1. Personal liability of the business owner—how much the owner can lose if there are problems arising from the business.
2. Taxation of both the entity and its owners—do owners get taxed as well as the business?
3. Complexity and organizational costs in setting up the business and maintaining that entity—how difficult and costly is it for the owner to maintain the legal form of the business?
4. Control of the business—who runs the business and how is decision making split among various people?
5. Continuity of the business—how long that particular form of business can continue and under what conditions the business could end.
6. Ability of the business to raise capital—can the business borrow money, issue stock, or issue bonds?

Table 18.5 provides a simple summary of how the forms of legal organization differ on the six issues. After going through the characteristics of these various entities, you can easily see how some of the newer and nontraditional business forms, such as S corporations and LLCs, can offer the best of both worlds, that is, limited liability of owners as well as single taxation. Of these newer forms, the easiest to form and the most user-friendly is the LLC or limited liability company. As a result, LLCs should be viewed as a default of sorts, so select an LLC unless there is a compelling reason to choose another form.

TABLE 18.5 Forms of Legal Organization

Factors	Sole Proprietorship	General Partnership	Limited Partnership
Personal liability of owners	Unlimited personal liability.	Unlimited personal liability of partners if partnership has insufficient assets to cover partnership liabilities.	A limited partnership has to have at least one general partner and one limited partner. The general partner has unlimited personal liability. The limited partner can lose "only" his or her investment in the business.
Taxation	Single taxation of income to sole proprietor.	Single taxation of income to individual partners.	Single taxation of income to individual partners.
Control or management of business	Complete control by sole proprietor.	Authority shared equally between partners unless otherwise stated in articles of partnership.	Written articles of partnership generally are required for limited partnerships. Authority of various partners is set forth in the articles.
Continuity of business	Ends at death of sole proprietor.	Whenever mix of partners is changed, that partnership is dissolved.	Whenever mix of partners is changed, that partnership is dissolved.
Raising capital	Dependent upon assets and credit of sole proprietor.	Dependent upon capital contributions of the partners, credit of the partnership, and credit of the individual partners.	Dependent upon capital contributions of the partners, credit of the partnership, and credit of individual partners.
Complexity of setup and maintenance of business form	No government permission required, few (if any) legal costs.	May be formed by conduct of the parties, no government permission required, optional cost of articles of partnership.	Limited partnerships have to meet state statutory requirements which may vary from state to state. Filings with the state are generally required. In addition, states usually require that the business always identify itself to the public as a limited partnership.

single taxation
Earnings of the business are taxed once with the owners paying the taxes.

double taxation
Earnings of the business are taxed twice with the business as well as its owners being subject to tax.

pass through (taxation)
Earnings of the business are distributed to the business owners and those owners (rather than the business) pay individual tax on the earnings.

check the box taxation
A choice LLCs can make on their tax returns to be taxed as a corporation or a partnership.

Corporation	S Corporation	Professional Corporation	Limited Liability Company
Shareholders are not responsible for debts of the corporation. If the corporation fails, the shareholders can lose, at most, the value of their investment in the corporation.	Shareholders are not responsible for debts of the corporation. If the corporation fails, the shareholders can lose, at most, the value of their investment in the corporation.	Shareholders are not responsible for debts of the corporation. If the corporation fails, shareholders can lose, at most, the value of their investment in the corporation.	Members (owners) are not responsible for debts of the LLC. If the LLC fails, the members can lose, at most, the value of their investment in the LLC.
Double taxation of earnings generated by the corporation. Corporation is taxed on its income at the corporate rate, and shareholders are taxed on dividends at their individual rate.	There is no taxation of the S corporation, itself. The earnings are **passed through** to the shareholders who are taxed at their individual rate on their individual tax returns.	There is no taxation of the professional corporation (PC) itself. The earnings are passed through to the shareholders who are taxed at their individual rate on their individual tax returns.	**"Check the box taxation"** An LLC can choose whether to be taxed as a corporation or as a partnership (pass through taxation).
Shareholders elect directors who set broad corporate policy. Directors appoint officers to carry out that policy, aided by employees.	Shareholders elect directors who set broad corporate policy. Directors appoint officers to carry out that policy, aided by employees.	Shareholders elect directors who set broad corporate policy. Directors appoint officers to carry out that policy, aided by employees.	Members enter into an operating agreement under which the division of management rights, e.g., committees, voting, is established.
The corporate entity can continue indefinitely if the corporation is properly formed, regardless of changes in ownership of shares.	S corporations may continue as long as the business qualifies under the Federal Tax Code and the rules and regulations of the Internal Revenue Service.	PC can continue as long as the business qualifies under state law.	Depends upon state statute creating LLCs. Some states allow perpetual existence.
Corporations may issue securities such as stocks and bonds, and/or borrow money based upon the corporation's credit.	S corporations may issue securities such as stocks and bonds, and/or borrow money based upon the corporation's credit.	PC may issue stock although ownership may be limited by state law.	In addition to the capital contributions paid in by members, the LLC can borrow money as a separate entity.
Corporations are created by the state. Incorporators must submit articles of incorporation and pay appropriate fees to the state.	S corporations are created by the state. Incorporators must submit articles of incorporation and pay appropriate fees to the state. In addition, the S corporation must elect this tax status with the Internal Revenue Service.	Professional corporations are created by the state. The incorporators must qualify under state law. An application and fees are submitted to the state.	In some states a single individual may form an LLC. In other states two or more members are required. To form the LLC, articles of organization must be filed with the state. The members also need an operating agreement. There will be minimal state filing fees.

If you choose any of the forms other than the sole proprietorship, please be careful to treat your legal form of business as if it were a being separate from the owner(s). When you keep the business separate from you personally, that business entity can have liability apart from its owners. If you fail to keep them separate, such as using personal funds for business purposes or using the business's car or equipment for personal purposes, there is a chance that a court may hold that there is no distinction between the entity and its owners in practice. If this happens, called **piercing the veil**, the court may hold that the owners have some personal liability for debts of that business entity. A good place to start in this area is to keep the finances of the business entity and those of its owners entirely separate. Company bills should never be paid from the owners' personal accounts using an owner's personal check. An asset of the business, such as a car, should not be used for personal use without accounting for that nonbusiness use.

piercing the veil
The dissolution of a corporate form, making it back into a sole proprietorship or general partnership, if the court finds that the owner carelessly mixed up personal and business assets or finances.

Another essential caution comes from recognizing that *no* form of LLC or corporation will make the owner(s) bulletproof. No matter what form of business a person owns, if he or she causes a traffic accident or accidentally hurts another person in some way (causes a tort), that person may be found "personally liable" in a lawsuit. That person may have to sell his or her car, home, or other assets (including the business) to pay the judgment. On the other hand, if the owner's employee causes the loss, as mentioned before, the business may be held liable. This is when it makes a huge difference what the structure of the business is in terms of what the owner can lose. If the business is a sole proprietorship or a partnership, the owner may lose personal assets as well as business interests. If the business is a corporation or an LLC, the owner can "only" lose what he or she has in that business.

Similarly, for a newly created LLC or C corporation going to the bank for a loan, it is unlikely that the new corporation will have the collateral base, asset base, or cash flow to convince a banker to issue a loan to the corporation. Regardless of your efforts to shield yourself from liability, the likelihood is that a bank giving a loan to your new corporation will require that you *personally* sign for the loan, in addition to the corporation's signing for it. From a banker's view, a corporation is only as strong as its balance sheet.

Taxation Issues

As you can see in Table 18.5 (and saw in Table 15.2 earlier), the legal form of organization you choose can have an impact on the taxes you pay. For every type of legal form except the C corporation and limited liability company, the taxes are paid by the owner on the basis of the income received from the business. This income can consist of a salary you pay yourself and any profits made by the firm. In these cases, you are being taxed at the applicable personal rate, shown in Table 18.6.

For C corporations, as a shareholder, you get taxed on the income you receive from the firm. This income can be in the form of dividends and profits. The good news is that tax rates for these are lower than for individuals. The bad news is that those profits face double taxation. The C corporation files taxes as an entity, and pays taxes on its profits and dividends. When the remaining posttax profits are paid to you as the owner or shareholder, you personally pay taxes again on the income, again at your individual rate. Dividends have a rate fixed at 15 percent. But for dividends or profits you are looking at the double taxation mentioned in Table 18.5.

For the other forms of organization (except the LLC), the money you take out of the business is taxed at your individual rate. The firm itself does not pay taxes. This is the idea of single taxation. The good news here is when your business is unprofitable, these losses can also be applied to your personal taxes. So if you are employed somewhere else full time, and run your own business part time, the loss you have from your small business can be used to reduce your overall taxable income for the year.

One thing to watch for is the issue of paying yourself a salary. In a C corporation and S corporation, the IRS expects you to pay yourself a salary that is roughly at market rates. Why would you pay yourself less in salary? Because salary has the added costs of Social Security and Medicare taxes. But paying no salary is one of the red flags that draws IRS auditor attention.

The LLC has been curiously absent in this discussion, but it can operate using either of the approaches described here. To use the C corporation taxation approach, you need to file a Form 8832 with the IRS. Otherwise, a one-person LLC is taxed as a sole proprietorship and a multiperson LLC

TABLE 18.6 Tax Rates

Sole Proprietors, General Partnerships, Limited Partnerships, S Corporations, Professional Corporations, and LLCs Not Filing Form 8832	C Corporations and LLCs Filing Form 8832
10% < $8,350 (single) < $16,700 (married)	15% up to $50,000 15% on all dividends
15% on $8,350–$33,950 (single) $16,700–$67,900 (married)	25% on $50,000–$75,000
25% on $33,950–$82,250 (single) $67,900–$137,050 (married)	34% on $75,000–$100,000
28% on $82,250–$171,550 (single) $137,050–$208,850 (married)	39% on $100,000–$335,000
33% on $171,550–$372,950 (single) $208,850–$372,950 (married)	34% on $335,000–$10,000,000
35% on $372,950 and up (single) $372,950 and up (married)	35% on $10,000,000–$15,000,000
	38% on $15,000,000–$18,333,333 35% on $18,333,333 and up

like a general partnership. Once a Form 8832 is filed, you can't change it for 60 months, unless the business changes ownership and the IRS agrees.

Because the legal form of organization can make a difference in the taxes you (and the firm) pay, it makes sense to think about which legal form can make the most difference in your annual income. For many small businesses in their first years, losses are typical and profits are not, so it helps to have a form that provides for single taxation. As the firm becomes profitable, the advantages of the C corporation or LLC organized with Form 8832 as a check-the-box corporation can make a lot of sense.

Everything Is Negotiable, and Negotiation Is Everything

LO3 Learn how to master the process of negotiating.

Some people argue that business is all about negotiation. While customers go into stores, find price tags, and pay the amount all the time, deals between businesses and even deals between businesses and consumers are often handled through a negotiation. Negotiations are discussions aimed at coming to an agreement about a particular outcome.

The ideal goal in a business negotiation is for each side to feel it got what it wanted. Leaving one side feeling a loss, particularly if someone thinks he or she lost and the other side won, only paves the way for future bad feelings, bad reputations, and bad negotiations. Often small businesses entering into negotiations worry that their youth, lack of experience, lack of track record, or lack of resources mean that there is no way they can win. Experience has shown that small businesses, even *new* small businesses, can do well in negotiations.

Use these four steps to structure a negotiation to achieve a winning solution for you and the other party: prepare, position, propose, and pounce.[8]

- **Prepare** what you need to achieve, what you are ready to give up, and what it takes to close rapidly once agreement is reached. Learn as much as you can about the other side, its track record, current situation, and possible needs.

- **Position** by putting your best foot forward, show confidence in yourself, your firm, and your prospects. Don't lie or mislead, but do not apologize. All businesses started small. With the right deals some small businesses grow large and bring their trading partners along with them. Talk about where you see your business in a couple of months or years. Position your firm as a good partner with which the other firm can ally.
- **Propose** solutions that provide value and balance for both you and the other party. This is often the hardest part of the negotiating process, but it is also the aspect which has received the most attention. Consider using these techniques for finding mutually winning propositions:
    - **Seek to create value:** Listen to what *drives* the other side's needs and seek alternative ways to solve the problem. For example, it says it needs money, but it may be able to work with more time, more flexibility, or a preferred treatment later. Adding new acceptable factors enlarges the negotiated pie.
    - **Seek long-term solutions:** Today you are small, but tomorrow you may be bigger, so think longer term.
    - **Seek balance:** Ideally, each side's contributions should closely balance. Where close balance is not easily achieved initially, structure contingent contracts to ensure balance later. For example, pay a small amount now to get started, but agree to pay a larger amount (e.g., a balloon payment) or a percentage of sales when sales reach a higher level.
    - **Seek mutual safety:** Where risk is faced, consider sharing risks and rewards so each party is providing some of the safety net for the other, and each shows commitment to the deal working out.
    - **Seek outcomes commensurate with investment:** Scale returns or considerations according to the size of the contribution of the party to your success. Aim to satisfy people or organizations that are major factors in your business, and realize you cannot accommodate every small contributors' every need.
- **Pounce** when agreement on any part of the negotiation appears at hand; move to close the deal on that issue. When you have an agreement, even on small issues, pounce on it as a positive outcome, an indicator of future deals to be made. Then get the deal down in writing. When stalled, ask the other party how to move forward.

One fear some people have is being dealt a dirty trick by the other side. Preparation and a long-term view help here. A dirty trick only works when the other party can be confident you will not be able to retaliate or tell others about the dirty trick, since publicizing it will ruin negotiations with others. One-time deals are more prone to dirty tricks; long-term arrangements make them harder to sustain. Also, knowing if the other party has done dirty tricks in the past can help you prepare for them. Being well networked (and letting the other party know you are) can also help since if you are tricked, you can let others know, making the chance of the other party playing dirty tricks on others much less.

What makes all negotiations work is honesty. No one expects you to give up your secrets, but to build trust, you need to offer some information that helps the other side determine where to start negotiating. The optimal strategy is called *tit-tit-tat.*[9] Give up one piece of information on what you need or are willing to offer. Wait for an equal response. If you get one, your negotiation is off to a good start. If you do not get a response, offer one more piece of information. Wait for a response. If you do not get one, bring up the point that so far in the negotiation you have made all the overtures. If the other side is serious about coming to a fair deal, it needs to step up to the table and start talking seriously. If not, then it is clear it is not interested in striking a fair deal, and the negotiation must obviously be over.[10]

Along these lines, another negotiating tactic that lets you be open about your goals without giving away your secrets involves prioritizing your goals. Let us say you know three key goals you hope to achieve. Go into the negotiations asking for 5 or even 10 goals. In the bargaining process, you can "give up" some of your demands to show the other side you are willing to compromise. As long as you gain some or all of the three key goals you wanted, you are ahead of the game by negotiating.[11]

Always keep issues of legality in the back of your mind when negotiating without a lawyer present. Let's say you negotiate a trade of services with another business—you print its ad brochure, it waterproofs your parking lot. Legal? Yes, *but* in barter arrangements, you are trading something of value. That means you need to count it when tax time rolls around. If you fail to account for it, you *have* done something illegal. Twists like that are a good reason to get lawyerly advice until you know enough to go solo.

Legal Liabilities

LO4 Recognize potential legal liabilities for your business.

A huge concern for business owners is liability arising from the business. The simplest form of liability is direct liability. Simply put this means the business entity is responsible for something the entity has done. For example, when a customer goes into a fast-food restaurant and places an order, the restaurant employee is there representing the restaurant. The contract formed is between the customer and the restaurant, not between the customer and the employee. The employee is an agent of the entity, in this case the restaurant. The employee represents the entity. Through that employee's actions, the restaurant is now bound in contract to provide certain food at a certain price. Failure of the restaurant to honor its contractual obligations will bring direct liability upon the restaurant. The liability could apply through contract or tort law, each of which is described below.

Torts: Responsibility for Your Actions and the Actions of Employees

Torts here are not fancy French desserts, but are civil, not criminal, wrongs. Torts can arise when a person's legal rights are violated in ways other than from a breach of contract. For example, where a person is hurt in a car accident caused by your driver, the tort issue is that the victim's right to travel down the road was impaired by the wrongful actions of your driver. Often when this happens, the driver faces direct liability for causing the accident, but the employer can also be sued by the injured party for what is called **vicarious (indirect) liability**. Vicarious liability against a business is possible if the employee involved was an agent of the business and at the time of the accident doing work for the employer.

vicarious (indirect) liability
Indirect liability or responsibility for the actions of another.

If your business is facing vicarious liability, there are two typical arguments you can try to deflect the liability: (1) the actor is not an employee, but an independent contractor, and (2) the actions were outside the scope of agency/employment. If you can prove that either one applies, your firm is not likely to be held for vicarious liability. The employee as an individual would face the liability alone.

The Independent Contractor Argument

independent contractors
Persons working to achieve a certain goal without being subjected to substantial controls by another.

Sidestepping the problem of agency is one of the reasons businesses often use **independent contractors**. If your firm publishes a cookbook series, and you sell it door-to-door through independent contractors, and one of those contractors accidentally damages a person's home while doing the sales pitch, your publishing company is not responsible for the damages—the independent contractor is.

That kind of distancing makes independent contracting attractive to small businesses. The fact that the entrepreneur doesn't pay benefits for an independent contractor makes it even more attractive still. It is so attractive that the IRS takes claims of independent contractor arrangements very seriously. According to the IRS, to be an independent contractor the person has to display three characteristics:[12]

1. **Behavioral:** The contractor solely decides how the work is to be done.
2. **Financial:** The contractor pays his or her own expenses (e.g., benefits, tools, purchases) directly rather than having the employer pay them.
3. **Relational:** The independent contractor is employed for a project or a distinct term and the service the contractor provides is not central to the operation of the business.

There are many ways to show these three characteristics, and the IRS can look beyond the three. For example, if the entrepreneur is not paying the contractor benefits, but also pays no or almost no benefits to employees, the contractor could look to the IRS like another employee. If the IRS classifies the independent contractor as an employee, the firm becomes responsible for damages, but also for benefits not paid, and for the taxes and workers' compensation sidestepped—the latter two with penalties possibly added. Checking with a lawyer ahead of time to make sure you are going to use independent contractors correctly is most often the right way to go to make sure you can benefit from using independent subcontractors.

Another approach to protection against liability is to train employees to avoid problems. Training employees on diverse issues such as safety measures, including spotting hazards at the business and how to treat customers, can drastically lower the exposure to liability for a business.

● Protect yourself and your business from unnecessary lawsuits, which can quickly cripple your best-laid plans. The very first step in doing so is to develop clear guidelines for your employees to follow in regulating their conduct on the job and give them complete training programs on how to apply the guidelines.

The Scope of Authority Argument

Another important part of agency law involves the amount of authority given to each agent. Employees differ in their job descriptions and responsibilities, so it is common for them to also differ in the amount of authority they have to handle their jobs. In practice this relates to the activities an employee can do and make decisions about without checking with their boss for approval. If employees make a decision requiring more authority than they really possess, the business can argue it was not liable for the problem.

For this argument to work, the firm needs to show that it fully trains or informs the employees of the exact authority they possess—when they can decide for themselves, and when they need approval from higher-ups. It also helps to include informing employees that they may face personal liability for problems which arise from their exceeding their authority. The business also ought to take steps to convey to its customers what the authority level of an employee is. For example, calling a sales clerk a "retail manager" would give the wrong impression of how much authority the clerk possesses.

Similarly it is important that management take appropriate steps to listen to employees. This is because one of the rules of agency law is that notice to an agent can serve as notice to the business itself. For example, if a customer comes into a retail store and announces to the employees that sleet has started falling on the steps outside, the business itself is now on notice that there is a hazard. If someone subsequently falls on that slick, frozen surface, the question may arise as to whether the business was negligent in clearing the icy area. The business will be unable to argue that it was unaware of the hazard. The court will be looking at what would be reasonable to expect of the business in terms of how quickly the area was cleaned up after any member of the business had notice of this problem. It is important to note that these issues work only where the concerns revolve around civil law. If it is a case of criminal law (see Thoughtful Entrepreneur: Dealing with Criminal Companies on the next page), another, tougher standard applies.

If you have involved business dealings with a publicly traded company, or are subcontracting with one, partnering with one, or being bought by one, or if you have plans to become a publicly traded company, or even if you have government contracts, you need to be aware of the **Sarbanes-Oxley Act** or SOX for short. SOX is legislation resulting from the Enron and other scandals, and its purpose is to make the financial activities of companies more visible to the shareholders, government, and public.

Sarbanes-Oxley Act
A federal law describing the steps publicly traded businesses must take to protect and provide their key financial information.

SOX has requirements for preserving data and tracking its use, as well as extensive financial reporting requirements and external checks on all of these. Since its inception in 2002, the SEC (Securities and Exchange Commission) has focused its enforcement of SOX on large publicly

THE THOUGHTFUL ENTREPRENEUR

Dealing with Criminal Companies

Here's an example to think about. Suppose a business markets some sort of medical device used to close wounds. Assuming this device is widely sold and used, many thousands of patients may come in contact with the device. If the device is poorly designed or manufactured, one can imagine situations in which infections could result from the use of this product. Assume further that employees of the business know of the problem and do nothing to improve the product or to warn the users of this product. Perhaps the company has even been issued a warning of some sort from a governmental agency on this matter.

Even though the business entity itself cannot form criminal intent like a human being, if that entity produces or sells a product that is widely used, the potential to harm a great number of people is certainly present. The prevailing thought is that such businesses are subject to criminal prosecution in order to protect the public from harm and secondarily as a warning to others who might contemplate similar actions.

In other words, nowadays, there are cases in which the business itself (e.g., the corporation, partnership, or LLC) or management can be held *criminally* liable for damages caused by the actions of its employees. If management directs, encourages, knows of, or in some cases should have known of criminal behavior of others in the organization, the company and management may be held criminally liable. Of course, a nonhuman business form cannot be put in jail, but in such cases the business can be, and often is, fined a substantial amount of money as punishment.

There are also specific statutes which provide criminal penalties against businesses (as well as managers and under certain circumstances, owners) if those statutes are violated. Examples of these statutes are laws that protect the public health and environment, certain tax laws, and certain employment laws protecting employees from sexual discrimination and harassment.

traded businesses. While the SEC has considered giving exemptions for publicly traded small businesses, this is far from a done deal. Small businesses that are not publicly traded are not covered by SOX.

However, many large businesses are requiring their subcontractors to meet SOX standards, so all of the actions of the larger firm are seen as in compliance. Similarly, big businesses thinking about buying smaller firms look at the SOX liabilities they will be taking on when they buy the smaller firm, so compliance helps make a firm more saleable. Right now, at a practical level, SOX officially applies only to the small group of publicly traded small businesses, but if you find you are being asked by big corporate partners or investors to start operating under SOX rules, the only way to handle it is to get legal and accounting advice on how to do it correctly. It is not something that works as a do-it-yourself project.

Litigation vs. Arbitration vs. Mediation

litigation
A formal dispute resolution method that operates using the court system, typically with a lawyer representing each party.

Problems of contract or tort law can be handled either through litigation, through arbitration, or through mediation. **Litigation** uses the court system to settle differences. Whether you go to a small-claims court or go through a lawyer and the regular courts, the litigation approach is draining, both financially and emotionally, on both sides in a lawsuit, so before pursuing the litigation route, think through these issues to decide if litigation is right for you.

Either form of litigation means that prior efforts—letters, calls, or even visits—have failed. That will increase the emotional stakes for the entrepreneur and the defendant. While small-claims court is lawyer-free, it is not stress-free. It is a rare entrepreneur who really wants to play attorney when his or her own money and reputation is on the line. It is true that litigating going the lawyer route in the regular courts will cost money, time, and aggravation. It can cost to have the attorney handle correspondence and recovery efforts. If these don't solve the problem, you will pay additional fees for your attorney to take the case to court. And if you lose in regular court, you can be responsible for both sides' attorney's fees.

Our approach here is to recommend using an attorney from the start when creating contracts and setting up major deals or deals new to you and your firm. Why? There are four good reasons. First, in litigation, the only guaranteed winners are the attorneys. That is how they make their living, and particularly in business litigation, the case is not emotionally draining for them. Second, remember that good attorneys keep their clients *out* of court by writing better contracts and negotiating on behalf of their clients. If you are going to court, it means you have failed to win at the bargaining table. Third, remember that since litigation is so expensive, large, well-funded companies have a definite advantage over small businesses. And finally, beware of any attorney who guarantees a certain outcome in a case, particularly a jury trial. Human beings are not always predictable, and it is not all that unusual for a case to be decided in an unforeseen way. Of course, litigation can have wonderful outcomes for participants, but the point is that litigation can be risky, it often is expensive, and it always is emotionally demanding for the small business owner.

Given these cautions, if litigation does not make sense, a growing alternative is called *arbitration*. **Arbitration** is a way of settling disputes in place of going to court. Often it involves the two sides of a case presenting their perspective, facts, and materials to a private judge. If you agree to submit your dispute to arbitration, you are giving up a legal right to sue if you do not like the result. For that reason, an agreement to arbitrate should be in writing and should be given in exchange for something (a contract) if it is to be enforceable. Many of us unwittingly sign such agreements all the time. In a standard contract, such as an agreement with a brokerage firm to open an account, a contract for wireless service, and even in employment agreements, a closer look at the written contract terms may show that the parties have agreed, as part of the contract, to settle their disputes by the use of an arbitrator rather than by litigation.

arbitration
A dispute resolution process held instead of court cases in which both sides present their case to a legal professional.

A third choice is *mediation,* in which the dispute is put to a neutral third party who is not a judge. While arbitration and court cases have decisions that are binding, mediation works only if the two sides agree to the decision and settlement. If mediation fails, arbitration and litigation are still possible. Mediations are generally much faster to complete than either arbitration or litigation, and it is the least expensive of the three approaches. Mediation can even be used with the government, based on the rules set out in the Administrative Dispute Resolution Act, which is handled by the Federal Mediation and Conciliation Service (www.fmcs.gov). Outside of government, mediators and arbitrators generally come from the same sources, such as the American Arbitration Association (www.adr.org).

A comparison of the three approaches is given in Table 18.7. Generally, the optimal situation is to include a clause in your contracts requiring binding arbitration. If an issue arises, you can see if you can handle it yourself. If you cannot get satisfaction, think about asking for mediation, since it is the fastest and cheapest of the procedures. If mediation does not work, exercise the binding arbitration clause. If there was no clause, the route is negotiate on your own, mediate if possible, and then go to litigation.

Commonsense Ways to Avoid Torts

In addition to the obvious ways of avoiding being sued, such as making sure there are no hazards on your property, not infringing upon another's trademark, and impressing upon your employees the importance of safe driving, there is another method to avoid a lawsuit that is rarely mentioned. When it comes right down to it, transactions between businesses and customers are an interchange of communications between people.

You know from personal experience that there are various ways of dealing with conflicts besides suing, the most obvious being communication and negotiation. You might think that lawsuits come as the result of a careful decision-making process, since they are so costly and time consuming, but in reality lawsuits are often filed out of frustration or anger. It sounds simplistic, but people are less likely to sue someone they like or someone they perceive to be willing to work the problem out with them.

TABLE 18.7 Litigation versus Arbitration versus Mediation

Litigation		Arbitration	Mediation
Regular Courts	**Small-Claims Court**		
Uses court system	Uses court system	Works outside the court system	Works outside of the court system
Both parties represented by attorneys	Both sides represent themselves	Both sides represent themselves	Both sides represent themselves
Formal	Informal	Informal	Informal
Public judges	Public judges	Private judges	Attorneys or mediation specialists
Multiple levels of postdecision appeal	Appeal to regular court possible (varies by state)	Limited appeal possibilities	Full range of appeals
Can force the other party into court	Can force the other party into court	Occurs by agreement or accepting clause to arbitrate	Occurs only by mutual agreement
Binding decisions	Binding decision	Binding decision if agreed to beforehand	Nonbinding decision
Public	Public	Confidential	Confidential
Most costly	Least costly	Costly	Less costly
Slowest	Moderately fast	Moderately fast	Fastest
Favors those with more money for legal help	Friendly format for small businesses	More balanced than courts	Friendly format for small businesses

Adapted from John R. McGinley, Jr., "Arbitration or Litigation? Having Trouble Choosing between the Two? Here Are Some Factors to Consider when Making Your Decision," *Entrepreneur*, April 01, 2002, http://www.Entrepreneur.com/article/0,4621,298318,00.html. Steven C. Bahls and Jane Easter Bahls, "Stuck in the Middle: You're Jammed between a Court and a Hard Place. Get Free with Third-Party Mediation," *Entrepreneur*, November 2000, http://www.Entrepreneur.com/article/0,4621,281851,00.html.

Take a moment to think about the actor Tom Hanks and *American Idol* judge Simon Cowell. Both are wealthy. Imagine each caused a car wreck. Which one do you think is more likely to be sued? If Hanks and Cowell are at all like their screen personalities, Hanks is much less likely to be sued. Being perceived as a likable and genuinely concerned person can sometimes save you from an angry reaction. How do you achieve this? Try to develop client loyalty and give personal service. Listen to your customers. Besides helping the bottom line of your business, developing such relationships can keep you out of court.

Contracting

LO5 Know contract terms and when a contract is needed.

The vast majority of business law in the everyday operations of a business is contract law. Contracts are essentially agreements in which the parties exchange promises. Not all contracts have to be in writing to be enforceable. For example, one neighbor wishes to buy a snowblower from the other neighbor who is relocating to Hawaii. The two discuss the purchase agreement and decide on a price of $800. Nothing is put in writing. It is a spoken promise to pay $800 in exchange for a spoken promise to give possession and title to the snowblower. If it works out as described, fine. But if there is a problem, how can it be resolved? There is likely to be a difference of opinion on what was intended. Without a written contract, there is no way to be sure what should have happened.

Oral agreements are as legally binding as written ones, but when the two sides disagree, how can a court decide which of the two versions to believe? In reality, it is very difficult to enforce oral agreements (also called handshake agreements). Sometimes oral agreements are unavoidable, but even in those cases, you can make the oral agreement written.

It works best if you specify you will write up the agreement and send it to the other person as you are shaking hands on the deal, but even if you did not mention it, write up what you thought the two of you agreed to and mail (use certified mail if possible), fax, or e-mail it to the other person. Mention in a note or letter accompanying the written form of the agreement that if the other person's recollection of the agreement is different, you would like to clarify what they thought was agreed to before either of you go further on the business deal—putting a deadline on the response can help move the work along. Follow up with the other person (preferably by certified mail or e-mail so there is a record of your sending it) if you don't hear back by the deadline. Should you continue the business if the other person does not respond? That is up to you, but at least you know that the situation is risky, and you have also taken the initiative to clarify what the responsibilities are for you and the other person.

In business, there are several kinds of situations in which you want a lawyer to take charge in making things work, for example:

- **Standard contracts:** If you are going to use one type of contract over and over, such as a purchase order, have your attorney draft that contract so that agents of the company can just fill in the blanks as needed.
- **Specialty contracts:** Unique contract terms and/or large dollar amounts at stake usually require careful drafting and legal counsel.
- **Interstate contracts:** When doing business outside your home state, it makes sense to have your lawyer draw up the contract because state laws vary. Charging 20 percent interest on financed purchases may be all right in your state, but this rate may be illegally high in another.
- **Noncompete clauses:** In a **noncompete clause** someone promises not to open a competing business or to go to work for a competitor.[13] Such clauses are tricky because they need to be part of another agreement and cannot stand alone. They also have to be reasonable. You cannot keep people out of their line of business forever, nor can you force them to leave town to practice their business. A lawyer can tell you what is reasonable for the kind of situation you face.
- **Exculpatory clauses:** **Exculpatory clauses** say that a party to the contract will not be responsible for certain things. An example of an exculpatory agreement is the statement on the claim check for dry cleaning that says that the dry cleaner will not be responsible for any damages to clothing. This may not be true, but such statements are "cheap" to make, just the cost of the ink and paper. The only chance for having one that works is to have a lawyer draft it.
- **Hold harmless agreements:** By agreeing to a **hold harmless** clause in a contract (also called a **waiver**), one party is agreeing not to hold the other responsible for his or her actions. In other words, one party is giving up legal rights to sue or otherwise enforce his or her rights. Courts tend not to like such agreements, so again the best chance to have an agreement that holds up in court is to have a lawyer draft it. If you see such a clause in a contract, let *your* lawyer advise you what to do. A workable clause makes it possible for Ann Williams to run a children's gym (see Small Business Insight: Ann Williams and Head Over Heels).

Contracting often seems intimidating, with all the small print and often official sounding language. But the point in contracting is to make sure *your* needs and goals are covered. Three ways to help take some of the fear out of contracting includes:[14]

- Putting in a binding arbitration clause to minimize the possibility of court expenses (and because small businesses often do better before arbitrators than judges).
- When sued, call your insurance agent first. Your business liability insurance may not only cover the settlement costs, but often even your legal fees.
- Consider getting extra liability insurance if you fear you will be facing added business risks. For example, if you expand your business into a wealthy neighborhood, you might want to have an extra $1 million in insurance coverage.

Subcontracting

As the term indicates, a **subcontract** may be necessary to fulfill the promises of a "larger" contract. Particularly in small businesses, many support types of tasks such as human resources and

In the photo above, a park district has attempted to warn all park users of a potential hazard while denying responsibility for any eventual damages. Do you think this sign is effective? Why or why not?

noncompete clause
Part of a contract in which a person agrees not to open a certain type of business or seek employment doing certain things in a particular area for a period of time.

exculpatory clause
Part of a contract in which a party to the contract states that he or she will not be responsible for certain actions.

hold harmless
A type of waiver in which a party agrees not to hold another party responsible for certain events.

waiver
Part of a contract in which a party intentionally gives up legal rights or claims.

subcontract
A contract by which a new party agrees to perform a duty that one of the original parties to a contract was already legally obligated to perform.

SMALL BUSINESS INSIGHT

ANN WILLIAMS AND HEAD OVER HEELS[15]

Ann Williams and her husband Craig bought Head Over Heels, a children's gym in Birmingham, Alabama, in 2000. Ann had been a gymnast at Auburn University and had worked for another gym in town gaining experience. A key problem facing any gym—but especially one that focuses on children—is liability. Young bones and muscles are easily hurt, and while children are resilient, parents often are not.

The Williamses have liability insurance, but to keep it reasonably priced and to provide assurance to the parents (which is far more important in the long run), Ann makes sure parents know that every instructor is trained on safety issues and puts the safety of the children first. Additionally the gym has only the finest equipment. With all these in place, it is easier for Ann to get parents to sign a lawyer-drafted agreement, in which parents recognize the possibility of injury to their child and hold the business harmless for injuries.

marketing are often subcontracted, thereby allowing for fewer employees and thus lower salary and benefit costs to the business. Generally speaking, the same contract principles apply to both regular and subcontracts.

Subcontracting has one unique aspect: Saying that the subcontractor did not perform does not get you off the hook. Imagine you get a contract from Ford to make rearview mirrors. You subcontract out making the glass, while you concentrate on the housing. Your subcontractor does not deliver. Who gets sued? It is you. Your firm signed the Ford contract, so you are responsible. You can sue the subcontractor, but you still have obligations to Ford, and can be sued by Ford.

Internet Issues in Contracting

Small businesses have blossomed through the Internet. They have taken their place in commerce alongside brick-and-mortar establishments. Contract law that has existed for hundreds of years is now being applied to Internet transactions. Courts are being asked to apply this old, standard, contract law to new situations arising in e-commerce as legislatures try to enact new statutes specifically addressing contract law as applied to e-commerce. In the meantime certain problems can be anticipated.

B2B
Business-to-business transactions.

In business to business (**B2B**), contracts are often transactions involving electronic data interchange (EDI). These systems link suppliers of raw materials and components with wholesalers and retailers, often using dedicated lines or satellites. In this way, for example, an order for new inventory may be submitted electronically. B2B systems are generally used in situations in which repeat transactions are entered into and there is generally a master contract or umbrella contract that states the terms of the transactions covered, leaving for example, quantity and prices to be determined in each transaction. These master agreements between the parties are known as *trading partner agreements.* You need to have your lawyer review these before you enter into any major EDI effort.

B2C
Business-to-consumer transactions.

Another type of Internet contract is the business-to-consumer (**B2C**) contract. This is commonly used by small businesses to sell over the Internet. Here are a couple of pointers for setting up the Web sites. First, if you want to ensure control over the selling process, make it very clear on the Web site that the representations of merchandise or services are not actual offers to the buyer. Direct wording to that effect is common on many Web sites. The reason for this is so that the seller is not tied into a certain price and that the buyer cannot create the contract simply by accepting in the form of placing an order. In setting up a Web site, in addition to stating that information on the Web site is merely informational and not an offer, the Web site might also contain a statement to the effect that the seller reserves the right not to sell to everyone and that the Web

EXHIBIT 18.1

Sources of High-Technology Alternatives to Signatures

Digital Certificates (also called SSL Certificates)	**Encryption Programs**
Entrust: www.entrust.com	OpenSSL (a free open source program): www.openssl.org
GeoTrust: www.geotrust.com/	PGD: www.pgp.com
Thwate: www.thawte.com	Comodo: www.comodogroup.com
Verisign: www.verisign.com	eOriginal: www.eoriginal.com
	And the digital certificate companies

site seller need not accept the buyer's offer. This gives the seller some control over pricing and also in this new world of terrorism allows the seller to not sell certain merchandise if he or she considers it a risk.

Another issue with online contracting is how to handle contracts that are required to be in writing to be enforceable. For a contract written on paper to be enforceable, it must contain the "wet signature" of the party to be held to his or her contract promises. An alternative is to use technology such as encryptions, third-party certificates, or passwords to guarantee that the parties to the contract are who they say they are. The law does not yet dictate what precise technology must be used, just that there be protection from imposters purporting to be someone else. See Exhibit 18.1.

Although not an issue in business contracting, there is one other Internet-related issue with legal overtones—how a business handles e-mail. As business e-mail becomes more important, more problems have arisen with employee misuse of these tools. For that reason, it is very important that businesses, big and small, establish policies for employees on usage of the Internet and e-mail.

LO6 Understand the basics of intellectual property.

If your employees have access to the Internet at work, make it very clear how that access can be used both in terms of amount of time spent and sites visited. Employees should be informed (ideally through a written communication such as an employee handbook or written notice) about the company's policy regarding usage of the Internet for personal business. For example, are employees allowed to access Internet sites for sports scores, sexually explicit materials, stock quotes, and online shopping while "on the clock"? If not, you need to specify this.

For e-mail, the essential message that must be conveyed (again, ideally through a written communication such as an employee handbook or written notice) to employees is that the business owns the e-mail system and has full rights to monitor that system. This even includes e-mail in outside ISPs (like a personal e-mail account) that is accessed from work. In fact, over 50 percent of U.S. companies monitor employee e-mail, and 22 percent of companies have terminated an employee for misuse.[16]

Employees should be informed of policy regarding personal use of the e-mail system at work. For example, are employees allowed to send e-mails at work informing co-workers that their children are selling cookies for scouts or candy bars for the baseball team? In addition, employees should be told explicitly what is considered inappropriate content of e-mails. Clearly, unauthorized transfer of trade secrets is a huge concern of business owners and should be prohibited as well as e-mail that contains offensive sexual, ethnic, or racial messages. Besides monitoring e-mail for misuse by employees, it can be very beneficial for a company to monitor its system as a way to ensure proper customer service. A good rule of thumb is that nothing should be sent by e-mail that you wouldn't be embarrassed to read on the front page of the newspaper. Once that send button is clicked, it may be impossible to limit access to that message.

Intellectual Property

intellectual property
Property coming from some sort of original thought; for example, patents, trade secrets, trademarks, and copyrights.

intangible property
Property that has no value of its own but that represents value, such as a stock certificate.

patent
A grant by the U.S. government to an inventor for an idea that is new, useful, and nonobvious, giving the inventor the exclusive right to make, use, or sell his or her idea.

trade secret
Confidential information within a company that gives that company a competitive advantage.

copyright
Exclusive right given to the creator of a literary or artistic work to make use of that work.

trademark
Distinctive word, slogan, or image that identifies a product and its origin.

design patent
A 14-year patent for a new, original, and ornamental design for an article of manufacture.

utility patent
A 20-year patent covering a process, machine, article of manufacture, composition of matter, or any new or useful improvement of an existing one.

plant patent
A 20-year patent that covers new strains of living plant organisms, algae, or macro fungi.

infringer
Someone who uses intellectual property without the permission of the owner.

When you worry about making copies of books or songs, you are dealing with issues of **intellectual property**. Intellectual property is a type of **intangible property** in which what is being protected is an idea or a form of expression. This includes the law of **patents**, **trade secrets**, **copyrights**, and **trademarks**. It also touches on the creation of a trade name for a business. Businesses may deal with one or more of the forms of intellectual property. Intellectual property laws are most active at the federal level, although trademarks and service marks can be registered with any state also. A partial listing of the major federal intellectual property laws are given in Table 18.8. We also include an example of a Missouri law protecting trade secrets so you can get an idea of the kinds of state laws you could use. Remember, state level laws vary dramatically, so check what laws apply (and how) in your state.

Patents and Trade Secrets

New ideas can be protected from being used by others by the owner obtaining a patent issued by the U.S. Patent Office (www.uspto.gov) or by keeping the information as a trade secret. A **design patent** (which lasts 14 years) covers the look of a product and those parts that are essential or a part of the design. **Utility patents** cover processes and functions and last 20 years. There are even **plant patents** for newly created strains of living matter, which last 20 years from when the patent application is filed. A great first stop at the Patent Office Web site (http://www.uspto.gov) is the Inventor Resources page, at http://www.uspto.gov/web/offices/com/iip/index.htm. It can tell you most of what you will want to know.

Patents are essentially monopolies granted to inventors by the U.S. government giving patent owners the exclusive rights to make, use, or sell that invention for a certain period of time. Once the patent is issued, anyone can have access to the information covered by the patent, but people cannot make use of that information without the consent of the patent holder. Persons doing so are known as **infringers** and are subject to being sued by the patent holder. Because of the complexity in this area of the law (starting with the question of whether an idea *is* patentable), it is highly unlikely that an inventor could obtain a patent without the services of a patent attorney. See Figure 18.2.

Whether an idea is patentable and whether it should be patented or whether an idea can or should be protected as a trade secret are questions for a patent attorney. There are certain ideas that can be patented and also would be suitable for protection as a trade secret. Once again, a patent attorney is the appropriate source to help the business owner make that determination.

Here is an important word of warning: Be extremely wary of companies stating that they will assist you in finding financial backers to develop your new idea or that they will assist you in patenting your new idea. Do not deal with these "companies." They are often out there to steal unprotected, new ideas from inventors. Before sharing information on a new idea to obtain financing or marketing assistance, that idea must first be protected as a trade secret or by a patent.

Also be aware that the United States and the rest of the world run with different laws regarding patents. One of the key differences between the two approaches is when you need to file your patent applications in order to qualify for patent protection if and when a patent is granted. In the U.S. you have one year from the first time you publicly disclose your idea, while in the rest of the world, you need to file your patent application *before* you disclose it publicly. So if you plan to file patents in Europe, Asia, Africa, or South America, start your patent filings before you disclose to the public. Also check the World Intellectual Property Organization's database at http://www.wipo.int/ipdl/en/ to see if your idea has popped up elsewhere. Outside the United States, patent applications are publicly available, while in the U.S. only granted patents can be searched.

In general, it makes a lot of sense to file before you talk about your idea to anyone, regardless of the year U.S. patent law gives you after that first disclosure. Anyone to whom you disclose an idea could beat you to a filing, and then you would find yourself trying to prove you had an idea first—not easy and unnecessary if you file before speaking. Filing a provisional patent application electronically with the U.S. Patent Office is a good way to start—*after* you talk to a patent attorney (the U.S. Patent Office lists them). Do not worry, talking to your attorney does not count as a public disclosure. While there are books showing patent filing as a do-it-yourself project, in reality the vast majority of patents granted to individuals are those filed by professional patent attorneys and patent agents. To give your patent the best chance of surviving, this is a case where you want to go with the pros.

US00D472245S

(12) **United States Design Patent** (10) **Patent No.:** **US D472,245 S**
Andre et al. (45) **Date of Patent:** ** **Mar. 25, 2003**

(54) MEDIA PLAYER

(75) Inventors: **Bartley K. Andre**, Menlo Park, CA (US); **Daniel J. Coster**, San Francisco, CA (US); **Daniele De Iuliis**, San Francisco, CA (US); **Richard P. Howarth**, San Francisco, CA (US); **Jonathan P. Ive**, San Francisco, CA (US); **Steve Jobs**, Palo Alto, CA (US); **Duncan Robert Kerr**, San Francisco, CA (US); **Matthew Dean Rohrbach**, San Francisco, CA (US); **Douglas B. Satzger**, San Carlos, CA (US); **Calvin Q. Seid**, Palo Alto, CA (US); **Christopher J. Stringer**, Pacifica, CA (US); **Eugene Anthony Whang**, San Francisco, CA (US)

(73) Assignee: **Apple Computer, Inc.**, Cupertino, CA (US)

(**) Term: **14 Years**

(21) Appl. No.: **29/164,950**

(22) Filed: **Aug. 2, 2002**

Related U.S. Application Data

(63) Continuation of application No. 29/153,169, filed on Oct. 22, 2001.

(51) **LOC (7) Cl.** **14-03**
(52) **U.S. Cl.** **D14/496**
(58) **Field of Search** .... D14/400, 401, D14/435, 454, 474, 446, 483, 217; D21/332, 333; 273/148 B; 463/43–47, 1; 206/308.1, 308.3, 307; 369/2, 24, 25; 370/342, 343, 344

(56) **References Cited**

U.S. PATENT DOCUMENTS

D264,969	S	*	6/1982	McGourty	D14/496
4,976,435	A	*	12/1990	Shaford et al.	345/156
5,192,082	A	*	3/1993	Inoue et al.	463/44
5,661,632	A	*	8/1997	Register	345/905
5,964,661	A	*	10/1999	Dodge	463/24
D430,169	S	*	8/2000	Scibora	D14/496
D450,713	S	*	11/2001	Masamitsu et al.	D14/496
D542,250		*	12/2001	Chan	D14/496

* cited by examiner

Primary Examiner—Prabhakar Deshmukh
(74) *Attorney, Agent, or Firm*—Beyer Weaver & Thomas, LLP

(57) **CLAIM**

We claim the ornamental design for a media player, substantially as shown and described.

DESCRIPTION

FIG. **1** is a perspective view of a media player in accordance with the present design.
FIG. **2** is a front view for the media player shown in FIG. **1**.
FIG. **3** is a left side view for the media player shown in FIG. **1**.
FIG. **4** is a right side view for the media player shown in FIG. **1**.
FIG. **5** is a bottom view for the media player shown in FIG. **1**.
FIG. **6** is a top view for the media player shown in FIG. **1**; and,
FIG. **7** is a rear view for the media player shown in FIG. **1**.
The broken lines in FIGS. **1** and **2** are for illustrative purpose only and forms no part of the claimed design.

1 Claim, 5 Drawing Sheets

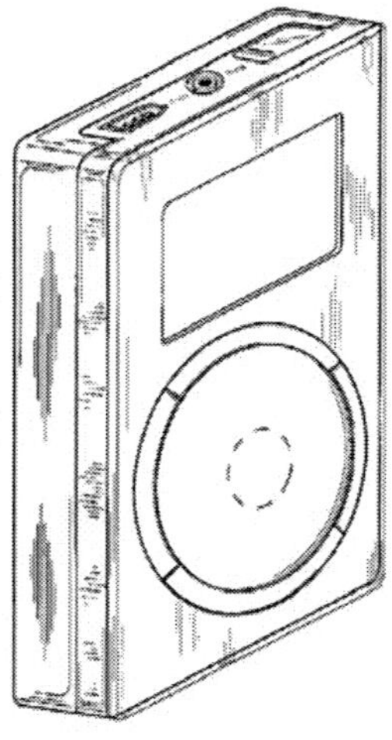

FIGURE 18.2

Section of a Patent Application

Patents protect designs, processes, or plants but are complex documents which should be handled by a patent attorney.

Source: http://patimg1.uspto.gov/.piw?Docid=D0472245&homeurl=http%3A%2F%2Fpatft.uspto.gov%2Fnetacgi%2Fnph-Parser%3FSect1%3DPT02%2526Sect2%3DHITOFF%2526p%3D1%2526u%3D%2Fnetahtml%2Fsearch-bool.html%2526r%3D44%2526f% 3DG%2526l%3D50%2526co1%3DAND%2526d%3Dptxt%2526s1%3DWKU-D%2526s2%3D'apple%252Bcomputer'ASNM.%25260S%3DPN%2FD%252BAND%252BAN%2F%252522apple%252Bcomputer%252522%2526RS%3DPN%2FD%252BAND%252BAN%2F%252522apple%252Bcomputer%252522&PageNum=&Rtype=&SectionNum=&idkey=E0AFABE9F82D.

Table 18.8 Intellectual Property Laws Applicable to Growing Businesses

Benchmark	Law/Regulation	Ramification
Intellectual Property—Patents & Trade Secrets (continued)		
Develop a trade secret protection program. Consult counsel to implement such a program by which trade secrets are identified, cataloged, and carefully protected.	Missouri Trade Secret Act	Employees or others who have unnecessary access, or permit others to have access to trade secrets, may jeopardize protection of trade secrets. Use non-disclosure and noncompete agreements to protect trade secrets outside of and within a company. Companies must take reasonable measures to maintain secrecy of competitive information.
Develop an outside inventions submission program. Consult counsel to implement such a program to avoid inadvertently receiving confidential disclosures.	Case Law	Absent a written confidential disclosure waiver, outside submissions can raise an issue of whether confidential information is being disclosed and possibly jeopardize use of internally developed intellectual property.
Use employment agreements or other technology agreements by which employees agree to disclose and protect company technological developments and other confidential information.	Case Law	In some states, including Missouri, the laws do not always entitle companies to ownership rights in employees' inventions unless there is a prior agreement so providing.
Maintain patent "watches" to stay abreast of patents of competitors and competitive technologies.		Patent counsel can assist in establishing patent "watches" and other investigations to develop awareness of competitors' patented technology and to determine a state-of-the-art for potentially patentable inventions. Such investigations can often identify areas for common activity.
Intellectual Property—Trademarks		
Trademarks and trade names: Prior to use, an investigation should be conducted to determine if the proposed trademark or trade name is available for use.	The Lanham Act	Failure to conduct a search of at least the federal records contained within the United States Patent and Trademark Office can result in costly conversions and potential damages for infringement.
New trademarks used or planned for use in interstate commerce should be registered in the United States Patent and Trademark Office.		Federal trademark protection is an important asset.
Maintain trademark and trade name "watches" to stay abreast of any infringements.		Exclusive right to use a trademark, service mark, or trade name may be lost if considered abandoned. Abandonment may result from lack of use over an extended period of time, failure to protest unauthorized use by others, or improper use by authorized users.
If the client receives notice of trademark infringement from a third party, such notice should be promptly brought to the attention of intellectual property counsel.		Failure to timely respond to a notice of infringement can result in damages and payment of attorneys' fees.

Intellectual Property—Trade Dress		
Distinctive packaging, product design, decor, building designs, etc. including colors and shape should be protected.	The Lanham Act	Trademark protection should be obtained for all nonfunctional features; design patent protection should also be considered.
Intellectual Property—Copyrights		
Client should promptly place copyright notice on all original works it creates, including Internet Web page content. (©<year of first publication><owner of copyright>)	Title 17 US Code	Without a copyright notice, an infringer can assert an innocent infringement defense in mitigation of actual or statutory damages.
Client should file an application with United States Copyright Office for all of its valued and/or critical copyrighted works. Client should file applications to cover each version of its copyrighted works and retain copies in their records of each such version.		A presumption of validity is only attributed to copyrighted works registered with the United States Copyright Office. Statutory damages in the amount of not less than $750 or more than $30,000 per infringement (which may be increased to $150,000 by a court) and attorney's fees may be available for infringing activities that occur after registration.
Client should file an application with United States Copyright Office within three months after publication of the work.	Title 17 US Code	If application is not filed within this time frame, client cannot obtain an award of statutory damages or attorney's fees for an infringement of copyright commenced after first publication of the work and before the effective date of its registration.
Client should seek "special relief" when filing a copyright application to protect software, which allows up to 50% of any proprietary source code deposited with the United States Copyright Office to be kept secret.		If special relief is not sought, client's complete source code will become a public record.
To the extent client uses nonemployees to create copyrightable works, client should obtain written assignment of all rights in and to such works **before** the works are created and preferably before the independent contractor is paid to create such works.	Title 17 US Code Case Law	If a work is "made for hire," title automatically vests in commissioning party. Many types of works, which can include computer software, do not qualify as for treatment as a work "made for hire," and without a written assignment of the work, the independent contractor owns all rights in and to the works he or she is commissioned to create.
Client should have all of its employees sign an agreement prior to employment in which they agree to assign all rights in and to any works created by them within the scope of their employment.	Title 17 US Code Case Law	Without such an express agreement, the ownership of any such works may be left open.
Client should record all transfers of copyright ownership of its works with the United States Copyright Office.	Title 17 US Code	If a transfer of copyright is not recorded, a later transfer to a good faith, bona fide purchaser of rights in and to the works without notice of the previous transfer prevails.
The copyright in a compilation or derivative work extends only to the material contributed by the author of such work, as distinguished from the pre-existing material employed in the work, and does not imply any exclusive right in the preexisting material.	Title 17 US Code	If client has not obtained rights to the preexisting work, its compilation or derivative work based on the preexisting work may infringe same.

Intellectual Property—Domain Names		
Clients should consider registering their company name or key product names in the following top-level domains (TLDs): .com, .biz (businesses), .us (requires U.S. nexus), and .net. Other TLDs that may be available to client include: .aero (air-transport industry), .coop (cooperatives), .edu (U.S. educational institutions), .gov (U.S. government), .info, .int (organizations established by international treaty), .mil (U.S. military), .museum (museums), .name (individuals), .org, .pro (accountants, lawyers, physicians, and other professionals). Multiple TLD registrations are possible for a given name and, in many cases, are recommended. Prior to registering a TLD, an investigation should be conducted to determine if the domain name is confusingly similar to a U.S. registered trademark, and if the goods or services offered in connection with the domain name are the same or similar to those associated with the registered trademark.	ICANN Dispute Resolution Policy The Lanham Act Anticybersquatting Consumer Protection Act	Rights in domain names could be lost—for example, the client could be forced to transfer the domain name pursuant to an order resulting from a domain name arbitration proceeding. In addition, there may be potential trademark infringement liability. Do not use competitors' trademarks as domain names or metatags.

The chart is not, nor is it intended to be, a comprehensive summary of the threshold levels at which the statutes and regulations cited therein take effect, and it is qualified in its entirety by reference to the appropriate statute and regulations.

Chart compiled in March 2007 by: Joseph Demko, Robert A. Kaiser, Julie O'Keefe, Guy Schmitz, and Larry Sewell, all with the law firm of Armstrong Teasdale LLP.

A *trade secret* is not created by the government but is information known to certain people in the company that makes that company more competitive. Trade secrets include more than patents. A trade secret can be a formula (e.g., the formula for the KFC "13 herbs and spices" chicken coating), the name of the company's top salesperson, or details of (or even acknowledgment of) the upcoming ad campaign. One rule of thumb when considering whether certain information is a trade secret is to ask whether a competitor would be willing to pay for that information. If the answer is yes, then you may have an idea that is protectable as a trade secret.

To protect a trade secret, the secret must literally be kept a secret from all except those who need to know to operate the business. The most famous example of a trade secret is the formula for Coca-Cola Classic. Had that recipe been patented back in the late 1800s, the company would have had exclusive rights to it for 17 years under the patent laws in effect at that time (today it would have had the rights for 20 years). Then, after 17 years, anyone could follow the recipe and make the beverage known to us as Coca-Cola. However, by treating the formula as a trade secret and successfully keeping the formula a secret from outsiders for all these many years, Coca-Cola still has exclusive rights to its use. There is no expiration date for trade secrets. There are five steps to protecting trade secrets:[17]

1. **Trade secrets must really be secrets:** They cannot be shared with others or be likely to be known by others.
2. **Use warning labels:** Put "confidential" on *every* page that contains trade secrets. The full legal version can go on the front page of the document, and it looks like this:

> *This item/document/material contains CONFIDENTIAL TRADE SECRET INFORMATION owned by [THE LEGAL NAME OF YOUR COMPANY] and/or its affiliated companies. This information is protected by applicable state law and may be protected by the federal Economic Espionage Act of 1996 (18 U.S.C. Sec. 1831), which provides for criminal penalties of up to 15 years in prison and/or a $5 million fine for stealing, receiving, possessing and/or duplicating any information contained herein.*

3. **Restrict physical access:** Coca-Cola has a big vault. You can get by with a locked cabinet or a password protected file, but if you have a secret, it should be locked up when not in use.
4. **Confidentiality agreements:** Only people who sign one of these (have your lawyer draft it) get to handle, see, or hear the trade secret material.
5. **Keep doing Steps 1 through 4:** A trade secret is enforceable only as long as you take positive steps to protect it. If you get lazy, the secret may get out, and you have no protection.

Wrongful acquisition of a trade secret is a tort and if certain behavior, such as trespassing or bribery, is involved in getting the information, criminal violations may also have taken place. Concern over protection of trade secrets can justify use of a noncompete agreement to help protect against former employees taking that information to new employers.

Copyright

Copyright involves the expression of ideas, not (as with patents and trade secrets) the ideas themselves. For example, if a greeting card company creates a picture of a single sunflower for use on a greeting card, what can be copyrighted is that particular rendition of a single sunflower. Copyright does not mean that no one else can create a card with a single sunflower (which would use that idea). That *particular* image of a sunflower is protected, so another person or company cannot use that same image without permission. Copyrights for new works last for the creator's life plus 70 years. If it is a "work for hire" bought from the creator, the copyright lasts for 120 years after creation or 95 years after its first publication, whichever is less.

Writers, artists, and others who create unique expressions of ideas automatically copyright those expressions by creating their work. Even though it is not now required, it is a very good idea to place a notice upon your original creation such as a book, painting, sculpture, computer program, or musical score that the work is copyrighted. Placing a notice on the work is done by using the word "copyright," "copr.," or "©," the creator's name, and the year of creation. Because original works are automatically copyrighted, this notice does not create the copyright, but it puts others on notice that the materials cannot be copied without permission of the copyright holder and will prevent any infringer from successfully arguing that he or she didn't know the materials were copyrighted.

The government does not create copyrights. However, copyrights on works can be registered with the federal government (www.copyright.gov) for more complete protection of the work(s). Registration with the government of copyrighted materials will establish a presumption as to ownership of the work. However, registration is not generally done unless wide distribution of those materials is planned.

One of the recurring issues for self-employed professionals, Web designers, and artists is who owns the work they do for others. Unless there is a contract giving the hiring individual rights to the material (making the project into a "work for hire" in copyright law), the creator owns the material. Often freelancers have developed a set of materials, templates, or designs which they adapt for a variety of clients. If that is your plan, you need to make sure you retain the intellectual property rights to the materials you develop. You can grant the client rights to the specific products from your project, while retaining the rights to the underlying intellectual property for use in other projects. In these work-for-hire contracts, the typical approach is to license to the hiring party the particular creative materials produced. The license can be limited by duration (it is yours for a year), territory (you can use it in your city), media (you can use it only on the Web), or exclusivity (others may not have a logo similar to the one made for you). There are work-for-hire templates available, and it is a good idea to get with a lawyer early in your business to sort out how to create a standard contract to protect your ideas and your business.

Trademarks

One last area of intellectual property, *trademark,* can be of particular significance to small business owners. Trademarks identify certain goods. A trademark will indicate the source of particular goods, for example, a Mini Cooper automobile, and not just any automobile. A related concept using the same law is a service mark. Service marks identify services. Some words or groups of words such as Weight Watchers® can be both trademarks (applicable to foods sold under this name) and service marks (identifying services such as programs of instruction on dietary management).

SMALL BUSINESS INSIGHT

PEACEABLE PLANET AND "NILES"[18]

Peaceable Planet is a very small toy maker from Savannah, Georgia, that makes a line of plush toy dolls. In 1999 it created a camel it called "Niles," named for the Egyptian river. Niles had a name card with information on it about Egypt. Peaceable Planet trademarked the name, and it sold a few thousand in the first year. The next year, Ty, Inc., the maker of Beanie Babies bean bag dolls, introduced its camel, who also happened to be named Niles, and sold more than one million of them in the first year.

Peaceable Planet sued for trademark infringement, and lost in the U.S. district court. Peaceable Planet appealed and won. In the complex world of intellectual property protection, what this meant was that Peaceable Planet got another chance to prove in district court that Ty took advantage of the Niles name. Peaceable Planet faced another round in court, with the attendant legal fees and time spent on depositions and briefings. Like so many stories about small firms versus large in intellectual property, it may be awhile for this issue to have an ending. However, in pursuing the case to the appeals court and getting a favorable ruling, the chance of getting an out-of-court settlement increases. In reality, sometimes that is what a "win" in intellectual property lawsuits looks like.

Once a mark is established as identifying certain goods or services, the owner of the mark can keep others from using a similar or identical mark to identify similar or identical goods. As with other intellectual property, anyone using the mark without permission is an infringer and is subject to legal action such as Ty, Inc., learned in 2004 when it was sued by a small business (see Small Business Insight: Peaceable Planet and "Niles"). A trademark once granted lasts for 10 years and can continue to be renewed for another 10 years at a time.

Trademark issues can come up at the very beginning when a name is being chosen for a new business. It is very important to check to see what marks are already being used to identify goods and services similar or identical to yours, *before* a mark is selected. Skill Module 18.2, "Checking Out Trademarks Online," can help you get a start on this.

SKILL MODULE 18.2

Checking Out Trademarks Online

Before you settle on a name for your business or product, it is very important to determine how that word or group of words is already being used in the United States to avoid trademark infringement challenges. Assume you are starting a business doing detailing work on vehicles. You are considering the name "Clean as a Whistle." In checking the name, one source of information is the U.S. Patent and Trademark Office listing of federally registered trademarks. While that list shows only federally registered marks and there may be an identical or similar name used that is not registered, this listing is a start. Go to the U.S. Patent and Trademark Web site, **www.uspto.gov**, then to "trademarks," then to "search," then to "new user form" and search for "Clean as a Whistle." According to the information in this site, is this name currently being used for a car detailing business?

All too often with small businesses, a name is chosen and used, and the business incurs all sorts of expenses in terms of labels, signs, and even advertising without considering trademark issues. Before selecting a business name, an Internet address, or the mark for products or services, an attorney should be consulted. An attorney can do a trademark search to determine what use is being made of the words or groups of words a business may want to use. Researching the desired name(s) ahead of time can avoid liability for infringement in which someone already using or having rights to that name sues the business, as well as financial costs (including loss of goodwill) in changing names. Once an attorney has established that it is unlikely that your choice of name is infringing on another's, consideration can be given to obtaining state or federal trademark registration to get additional rights for your mark.

Any size business may own valuable intellectual property such as patents, trade secrets, copyrights, and trademarks. Understanding and protecting these assets by seeking qualified, professional counsel cannot be overemphasized.

Whether you think we have too many laws or not enough, the stability and success of the United States' business community is based, in large part, upon our legal system. Laws guarantee rights to individuals and companies. Those rights are upheld every day in courtrooms across America. Caveat emptor (let the buyer beware) is *not* the motto in twenty-first century America. Knowing the law or even knowing when to ask for advice concerning the law gives business owners more power in pursuing their dreams. Knowledge is power. After reading this chapter, you should have a greater understanding of our legal system and particular areas of interest for business owners. This should give you more confidence in pursuing those dreams.

CHAPTER SUMMARY

LO1 Know when you need legal information and how to get it.

- There are many federal, state, and local laws applicable to any small business.
- Get a good attorney with experience in your areas of concern. You may need more than one attorney for various issues that arise over time.
- You can use online sources from the government or trade associations for certain legal information.

LO2 Understand legal structures in setting up a new business.

- Trade names exist when a firm uses something other than the owner's name as the name of the business.
- The most common business forms are sole proprietorships, general partnerships, limited partnerships, C corporations, S corporations, professional corporations, and limited liability companies.
- Each of various types of business entities has pros and cons in terms of personal liability of the owners, creation and maintenance of the organization, management of the organization, continuity of the organization, the raising of capital, and taxation.
- Unless there is a compelling reason to do otherwise, an LLC is probably the best choice of business entity because of its ease of formation, limited liability of owners, and flexibility in taxation.

LO3 Learn how to master the process of negotiating.

- Nearly everything in business is negotiable.
- Negotiating successfully depends on mastering four steps: prepare, position, propose, and pounce.
- The goal is to create outcomes where you and the other party win.
- Be honest in your presentation and balanced in your approach.

LO4 Recognize potential legal liabilities for your business.

- You and your business may be held responsible for the actions of agents, including employees.
- Avoid lawsuits by properly training employees, using independent contractors, or submitting disputes to arbitration.

LO5 Know contract terms and when a contract is needed.

- You are free to contract for anything that is not illegal or unethical.
- Put agreements in writing and have them reviewed by legal counsel.
- Make use of special contract terms such as noncompete clauses, exculpatory clauses, and hold harmless agreements to avoid litigation.
- The primary contractor is responsible for a subcontractor's failure.
- On the Internet make sure to specify that your site is informational and arrange for secure alternatives to "wet signatures."
- Design and implement a company e-mail policy.

LO6 Understand the basics of intellectual property.

- Intellectual property is composed of patents, trade secrets, copyrights, trademarks, and trade names.

- Ideas can be protected as patents or trade secrets.
- Expression of ideas can be protected as copyrights.
- Trademarks uniquely identify products and their origin.
- Intellectual property is a business asset and can be extremely valuable. For that reason protection of intellectual property should be taken seriously.

KEY TERMS

hourly fees, 575
flat fees, 575
retainer, 575
contingency fee, 575
trade name or assumed name or a doing business as (dba), 579
assumed name filing or a fictitious name filing, 579
legal entity, 580
plaintiff, 580
defendant, 580
articles of organization, 581
articles of partnership, 582
single taxation, 583
double taxation, 584
pass through (taxation), 584
check the box taxation, 584
piercing the veil, 585
vicarious (indirect) liability, 588
independent contractors, 588
Sarbanes-Oxley Act, 589
litigation, 590
arbitration, 591
noncompete clause, 593
exculpatory clause, 593
hold harmless, 593
waiver, 593
subcontract, 593
B2B, 594
B2C, 594
intellectual property, 596
intangible property, 596
patent, 596
trade secret, 596
copyright, 596
trademark, 596
design patent, 596
utility patent, 596
plant patent, 596
infringer, 596

DISCUSSION QUESTIONS

1. How would you go about finding a lawyer for your business?
2. Which form of business structure would be best for your new business and why?
3. In what ways could the owner of a parking lot limit his or her potential liability?
4. How could you keep your employees from going to your competitors after you have trained them?
5. How can you protect your company's trade secrets?
6. What issues should be addressed in a company policy on e-mail?

EXPERIENTIAL EXERCISES

1. WWW Find your state's Secretary of State home page on the Internet. Find information on forming LLCs. Can the form(s) be submitted online? If not, can the form(s) be downloaded or filled in using the computer?
2. WWW In most states you can contact the state bar, the state supreme court, or a state commission to check on whether a particular attorney has been disciplined for professional conduct violations. To find out whom to contact in your state, go to the American Bar Association Web site at **http://www.abanet.org/cpr/regulation/directory.pdf** and check it out.
3. WWW You may be able to represent yourself on small matters by going to small claims court. These courts of limited jurisdiction have different names in different states. Go to **http://business.gov**, click on "regions," and select the state of Indiana as an example. Select "legal assistance," and there you will find information on small-claims courts in Indiana.
4. WWW Would you like more information on LLCs? Go to **http://nolo.com**, click on "business and human resources," and then "Ownership Structures."

MINI-CASE

VIVID SKY AND MAJOR LEAGUE TROUBLE

Entrepreneur Tim Hayden had created a service called SkyBOX which could stream videos and statistics to sports fans over their 3G cell phones (like the iPhone). It had taken four years to launch the service, which originally was going to require military-grade hardened wireless PDAs and wiring stadiums for Wi-Fi, but had been reconfigured to run on Internet-ready cell phones.

Professional teams in baseball, football, basketball, and hockey had seen SkyBOX and were enthusiastic about its deployment. However, there were competitors to the SkyBOX. One of the largest was Major League Baseball, who was developing their own iPhone application to tie fans into MLB video feeds and statistics.

Executives at Apple liked the SkyBOX so much they made it their Feature Product on the iTunes home page.

It wasn't clear if MLB's team saw this or not, but it was at that moment that they served Vivid Sky with a cease-and-desist claiming that the SkyBOX used content that was copyrighted. In addition, MLB contacted Apple and demanded that the SkyBOX application be pulled from the iTunes Store. Executives from Apple refused to pull the SkyBOX application. However, they wanted Vivid Sky to work out a solution with MLB.

While Tim knew that Vivid Sky conformed to all copyright issues and were legally within their rights, he suspected that MLB might be going this route to disrupt Vivid Sky and the sale of their applications in the iTunes Store. He could make a stand and hire lawyers, which would cost a small business like his lots of money. Or he could look for a mutually agreeable solution.

Tim thought, "What is an entrepreneurial way to handle this?"

CASE DISCUSSION QUESTIONS

1. What are Tim's choices at this point?
2. What do you think Tim means when he asks if there is an "entrepreneurial way to handle this"?
3. If there is no infringement, but the injunction was brought to slow down a fast-moving new competitor, would it make any difference in the strategy Tim should employ?

SUGGESTED CASES AND ARTICLES

- Theresa Murray and In the Eye of the Beholder

Available on PRIMIS:

- Integral Vision Ltd. (A)
- Jack Schofield, Fast Food Franchisee (A)

SUGGESTED VIDEOS

eClips Videos:

- Kevin McGovern Defines Concept of Piercing the Corporate Veil
- Paul Joseph Discusses Dissolving the Partnership

SBTV Videos:

- How to Choose the Right Business Structure—LLC or C-Corp or LLP
- Protecting Your Company or Product Name
- Get It in Writing (Simple Letter of Agreement, 1 of 2)

STVP Video:

- When and How are Patents Important?

CHAPTER 19

Human Resource Management: Small Business Considerations

● Chris Perkett switched from part-time, virtual employees to full-time ones to staff her firm PerkettPR, Inc. What do you think she could do to ease that transition?

LEARNING OBJECTIVES

LO

This chapter will help you:

- **LO1** Explore the decision to hire full-time or part-time help.
- **LO2** Understand how to recruit good employees on your budget.
- **LO3** Know how to match the right person to the job.
- **LO4** Learn about employee training methods and resources.
- **LO5** Gain insight in meeting employees' needs and expectations.
- **LO6** Learn how to develop a fair compensation and benefit plan.
- **LO7** Understand the complexities of managing family within your business.

Focus on Small Business: Chris Perkett and PerkettPR, Inc.[1]

As a former consultant herself, Chris Perkett had a fairly easy time deciding whether to hire independent contractors when she started her Marshfield, Massachusetts, virtual public relations agency in 1998. "I wasn't ready to hire employees because there's so much involved with doing that," says the CEO of PerkettPR, Inc. "I wanted to make sure I was [building the company] right and wasn't biting off more than I could chew."

Perkett admits she initially appreciated the temporal nature as well as the flexibility of having independent contractors, but as she began to increase her client base, those very aspects began to concern her. "I needed more of a commitment from my staff," she explains. "The knowledge that they could leave at any time was always looming over my head. I needed to show my client base that I had a staff that was as committed to serving them as I was."

So at the end of last year, Perkett decided to switch to an employee-based staff, hiring many of her former consultants as full-time employees. Since then, Perkett says there's been an increase in the level of excitement in the company's projects, and her clients now feel the company is growing and stabilizing, two things that weren't happening with the contractors.

Still, employees aren't necessarily the only way to achieve a common vision and commitment for a business, according to Jennifer Johnson, principal of Johnson & Co., The Virtual Agency. With 15 contractors and only 2 employees on board, Johnson encourages dedication to her Salt Lake City public relations firm by requiring all contractors to attend regular business meetings and retreats and to meet with a senior consultant mentor. "I think it's a myth to believe that because someone is an employee, it means they're more dependable," says Johnson. "In today's fast-moving, competitive market, the best talent needs to stay motivated and driven whether they're a consultant or an employee."

According to Johnson, the ever-changing nature of today's business world has left traditional job descriptions by the wayside and forced companies to have a more flexible structure. "Consultants are used to change; they thrive on [that]," she says. "They understand they're getting paid to deliver tangible results as opposed to just punching a clock."

As for Perkett, although she's had to adjust to the variety of personalities that now exist in the core of her company, she's confident that hiring employees was the right choice for her growing business. "If you're not sure where or how you want to grow, then it's a lot to take on," she says. "But I think it helps our clients feel like we're growing, we're adding clients, and we're committed to this business."

DISCUSSION QUESTIONS

1. What are some potential advantages as well as drawbacks of having contractors in Jennifer Johnson's firm attend meetings, retreats, and be mentored by senior consultants?
2. Do you agree with Johnson's assertion that "In today's fast-moving, competitive market, the best talent needs to stay motivated and driven whether they're a consultant or an employee"? Why or why not?
3. What do you think Chris Perkett means when she mentions that "I wasn't ready to hire employees because there's so much involved with doing that"? As a small business owner, what do you think is involved in hiring that first employee to your firm?
4. How does Chris Perkett's hiring and retaining employees perspective compare or differ from Jennifer Johnson's perspective?

The Bigger Small Business: Hiring Employees

LO1 Explore the decision to hire full-time or part-time help.

Of all the decisions that differentiate the types of small businesses, no decision is as important or complex as the decision to hire an employee. Many small businesses never do. Of the more than 25.4 million businesses in the United States in 2004, over 19.5 million had no employees at all—only the owner. Another 5.8 million firms had one or more employees.[2] For the economy, those firms that hire employees are an important source of job generation.[3]

For the owner, adding employees is important for several reasons. Adding employees increases the amount of work that can be done—serving more customers, producing more, or staying open longer. It also increases the demands on the owner. Now sales need to be made to cover the employee's wages or salary, and, when adding employees, the owner and business become responsible for the safety and well being of the employee, as well as face legal requirements as an employer. Some owners look at the pluses and minuses and decide to stay a solo operation for as long as possible, like Chris Perkett in the early stages of her business. Others take on the opportunity and responsibility, as Chris did later. For those entrepreneurs, the next key decision is what work should be done, who the best person is to do that work, and how the firm should take care of them. Those areas are where the field of human resource management comes into small business. In this chapter we look at those three areas.

Let's start with the decision of what kind of work needs to be done. Generally we start by thinking about how much work we want to cover. As a small business owner, you can hire either part-time or full-time employees. Which one will be best for you? You need to consider the pros and cons and expand with care. Full-time employees make it possible for you to take significant time away from the business. They get to understand the business sooner, and often are willing to take on more responsibility. They provide the ability to dramatically increase your hours open, material produced, or sales. But there are many additional expenses to having a full-time employee on staff as opposed to a part-time employee. The cost of adding an employee includes compensation, training time, and employee tax and accounting costs. Presumably, such costs are outweighed by greater productivity, but you need to carefully balance the ledger. "Probably the biggest mistake I made in my early hires was hiring too early," says Louis Gudema, president of Magic Hour Communications, a marketing agency in Watertown, Massachusetts (www.magic-hour.com). "As a result, we were not as profitable as we might have been if I had been slower to hire."[4]

"While every business has its own rhythm, it's usually wise to go through the first year without hiring. Get a feel for the sales cycle and the downturns. Measure the 'just right' temperature of income and outgo. Experts suggest squirreling away at least a year's worth of expenses and overhead before hiring in order to see you through any rough patches," says Joanna Krotz, co-author of the *Microsoft Small Business Kit*.[5]

employee fit
The match between the needs, expectations, and culture of the small business with the expectations and the skills of the individual employee.

Not only are there additional expenses to consider, but also **employee fit**.[6] You can ease into an employment contract by first hiring part-time help and if he or she works well and the demand for additional help is present, you can ease into a full-time position weighing the additional expense.

Before making a full-time offer, let the applicant work part time for awhile so you can see how she or he fits. Likely as not, this will be learning period for you, too. You can ease someone into the business as a part-time worker. Or, if you go ahead and hire a full-time applicant, set up a **probationary period** or set up the job as an internship or a temporary one.[7] Usually, state law dictates how long such trials may last, so check with your state employment office. Typically, a probationary period lasts 90 days. You can find this information for your state at www.business.gov/states/. A trial period can be important, and if your first choice turns memorable in all the wrong ways, chalk it up to experience and keep recruiting.[8]

probationary period
Trial period in which an employee has temporary status before a formal offer to work full time is presented.

Whether you hire a part-time or full-time employee, it is important that each type of employee values your company's mission. Don Dymer, a former Scotland Yard police inspector, started his preemployment screening business in Jacksonville Beach, Florida, in 1995. He emphasizes the need for "employees to take on the mission and values that you want the business to take on." You do that by setting an example and making sure to define those values for every new hire.[9]

One of the challenges facing entrepreneurs who want to grow is understanding the many laws that apply to small businesses as their number of employees grows. Figure 19.1 provides a simple graphic to see which employment laws begin to apply at what size of firm, while Table 19.1 gives a quick rundown of the major Federal laws.

There is some help for determining if the federal employment laws will or do apply to your business. The U.S. Department of Labor has created a set of interactive online exercises to help you determine which laws apply in your situation, and they have gathered them all in one location—www.dol.gov/elaws. In particular, use the FirstStep Employment Law Advisor to get

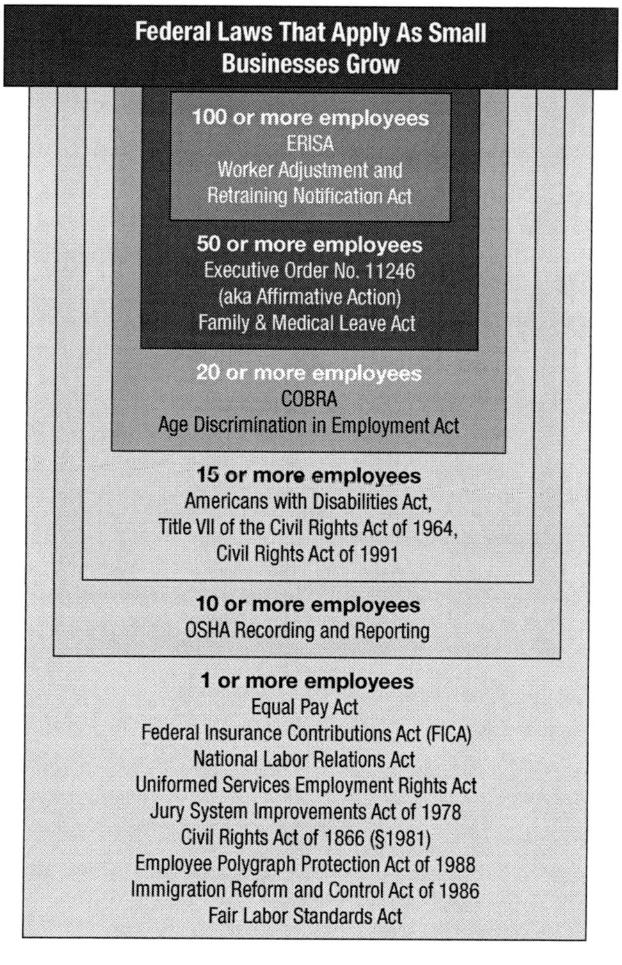

FIGURE 19.1

Federal Laws That Apply as Small Businesses Grow

TABLE 19.1 Federal Employment and Labor Laws Applicable to Growing Businesses

Labor and Employment		
Employers engaged in interstate commerce or engaged in the production of goods for interstate commerce (almost all employers).	Fair Labor Standards Act	Requires payment to most hourly employees of minimum wage and time and a half for overtime hours. Requires payment of same wage to males and females for work requiring equal skill, effort, and responsibility in similar working conditions. Notice posting requirements.
Employers who have 15 or more employees for each workday in each of at least 20 calendar weeks in the current or preceding calendar year (federal).	Title VII of the Civil Rights Act of 1964	Prohibits discrimination with respect to any condition of employment based on race, color, sex, religion, or national origin, except where religion, sex, or national origin is a bona fide occupational qualification which is reasonably necessary to the conduct of a particular business. Includes a prohibition on harassment, including sexual harassment. Notice posting requirements.
All employers.	Immigration Reform and Control Act of 1986	Prohibits hiring of unauthorized aliens. Prohibits employment discrimination based on national origin or citizenship status. Requires employers to complete I–9 forms for each employee. Notice posting requirements.
All employers.	Employee Polygraph Protection Act of 1988	Prohibits employers from using polygraph results as basis for employment action with limited exceptions. Notice posting requirements.
Employers with 20 or more employees for each working day in each of 20 or more calendar weeks.	Age Discrimination in Employment Act	Prohibits employment discrimination against individuals 40 years old and older. Notice posting requirements.
Employers with 15 or more employees.	Americans with Disabilities Act	Employers must have nondiscriminatory application procedures, qualification standards, selection criteria, terms and conditions of employment. Employers must make reasonable accommodation for limitations of qualified applicant or employee unless to do so creates undue hardship. Also governs confidentiality of medical information. Notice posting requirements.
Employers with 50 or more employees (within a 75-mile radius) each working day for 20 weeks in the current or preceding calendar year.	Family and Medical Leave Act	Requires employers to give employees up to 12 weeks leave, paid or unpaid, without loss of position, seniority, or benefits, for a qualifying condition or event. General notice requirements, including posting requirements.
Employers with 100 or more employees.	Worker Adjustment and Retraining Notification Act	Requires 60 days advance notice prior to a plant shutdown or layoff of 50 or more employees. Notice posting requirements prior to action.
50 or more employees and contracts or subcontracts of $50,000 plus.	Executive Order No. 11246	Requires employers to implement an affirmative action plan for hiring and promoting females and minorities.

The chart is not, nor is it intended to be, a comprehensive summary of the threshold levels at which the statutes and regulations cited therein take effect, and it is qualified in its entirety by reference to the appropriate statute and regulations.

Chart compiled in March 2007 by: Joseph Demko, Robert A. Kaiser, Julie O'Keefe, Guy Schmitz, and Larry Sewell, all with the law firm of Armstrong Teasdale LLP.

an overview of which laws apply. eLaws also provides a host of other interactive advisors to help you determine eligibility for more than two dozen laws and programs.

To be fair, there are always more laws that apply. In addition to those detailed in Table 19.1, there are related laws that apply to small businesses. For example, the Civil Rights Act of 1991 kicks in at 15 employees. Some of the other laws applicable as soon as you hire one employee include at least two big issues—the Federal Insurance Contributions Act (FICA) which is the Social Security and Medicare withholding law, and the Uniformed Services Employment and Reemployment Rights Act of 1994 (USERRA) which gives veterans the right to the jobs they left behind when called up for service.

Meanwhile, the state laws applicable to a small business are extraordinarily varied. For example, in Missouri, there are laws such as the Missouri Genetic Testing Law, jury-release laws, a Voting Leave Act, the Political Activities of Employees Act, the Final Wage Payment Statute, Missouri's own Equal Pay Act, an Indoor Clean Air Act, and at the other extreme a Smokers and Alcohol Users Rights' Law. This is by no means a comprehensive list, but it gives you an idea of the range of laws that apply to businesses.

When it comes to state law, it is truly a case where one size does not fit all. Even when two states use similar names for laws, the specifics of the law in each state are likely to differ. Being in the same region doesn't mean two nearby states will be similar. To give you an idea of the laws you might have to deal with, take the example of two adjoining states, Missouri and Illinois. There are a lot of firms in either state that might consider expanding into the adjoining state, but the laws to run firms in the two states differ. Table 19.2 shows laws from the two states for three types of human resource practices a small business would typically need to consider.

Remember, most states have laws protecting citizens in the same general ways. But the names of these laws can differ—and more to the point—have slightly different starting sizes, requirements, processes, and penalties. You want to be sure to determine the laws that apply to you as you start hiring.

To find this out, as noted in Chapter 18, you can get help from you local Small Business Development Center (remember, to find it, type "SBDC Locator" into the search box at the SBA Web site, www.sba.gov), your local SCORE chapter (www.score.org), the local chamber of commerce, or the local branch of the trade or professional association for your line of business. Probably the best source for employment law questions is the state employment security office for your area. While the Federal government no longer provides a comprehensive national online listing of state sites, you can find a very well done list of state offices at the Job-Hunt.org Web site (www.job-hunt.org/state_unemployment_offices.shtml).

The point is that hiring more employees makes your organization a more professional one, and with that professionalism comes a need to deal with more laws and regulations. While the best way is to work with a lawyer to make sure all issues are covered, these days you can get much of the work done at little or no cost by yourself, using the resources and free advice available to you. With the legal side under control, you are ready to go out and find those employees who will help you grow.

TABLE 19.2 Differences In State Laws: The Case of Two Adjoining States

	Illinois	Missouri
Legal holidays	President's Day; Casimir Pulaski's Birthday; Good Friday	Washington's Birthday; Truman Day
Minimum wage	$8.00 (7/1/09–6/30/10) $8.05 (7/1/10 on)	$7.25 (as of 7/24/09)
Wages must be paid	Monthly (for executive, administrative, and professional personnel) or bi-weekly (for everyone else)	Bi-weekly

Source: www.findlaw.com.

Attracting Employees

LO2 Understand how to recruit good employees on your budget.

A lot of the time a smaller firm can actually outperform large businesses in attracting high-quality employees.[10] To attract and hire new talent into a medium to large growing organization, help wanted ads in regional newspapers or the use of an employment service have been traditional methods. For small business owners, these methods tend to be expensive and have a long turnaround time. Today there are less expensive alternatives to consider.

Networking is a relatively low-cost, although time-intensive, method of recruiting. There are many benefits such as receiving a credible critique of a potential candidate's work experience and personal character. People to network with include colleagues, business professionals (your attorney or accountant), friends, vendors you have strong relationships with, alumni, and advisory board members. You can also use online social networking sites like LinkedIn (introduced in Chapter 2) to recruit, either by directly posting for a job or asking if people on LinkedIn know someone who might want the job you are offering.

Internet recruiting
Method of recruiting that allows you to search a résumé database or post a job description to the Web; a small business owner who knows exactly what he or she wants can use filters to search vast numbers of résumés with pinpoint accuracy.

employee referral
An underused, low-cost method for finding workers that rewards your employees for recommending potential candidates that would be a great employee fit.

Internet recruiting allows you to search a résumé database or post a job description to the Web. The main contribution of a recruiting Web site, such as Monster.com, has been to speed up hiring and vastly increase the accuracy of the job-search process. You can post a job at 2 P.M. and get your first response a minute later. An employer who knows exactly what he or she wants can use filters to search vast numbers of résumés with pinpoint accuracy.[11]

Employee referral is an underused, low-cost method which rewards your employees for recommending potential candidates that would be a great fit. Even for small businesses, to work successfully, referrals should be handled formally, with guidelines such as following up on all leads within 24 hours.[12]

Company Web sites can be used to post job openings. This method would be effective if your site receives a fair amount of traffic, and it would incur only a small incremental cost to your Web site budget.[13] If your business does not have a company Web site, the investment of Web site development and maintenance may be a limiting factor, but when a Web site can cost $50 a year, it is a worthwhile investment. Search Google for "cheap web hosting" and you will find plenty of services offering template-based design and hosting services. The Online Learning Center showed how to do this.

Many universities have *career service offices* that encourage companies to post openings to their job bank to recruit at both the undergraduate and the graduate levels. This service is commonly offered at no cost to companies and allows businesses to set up an account to manage résumé selection. Universities can often help you evaluate if it makes sense to offer an internship to their students. Internships are jobs in businesses like yours, arranged through the university. Some internships are done as a for-credit class, some are not. Some internships are paid by the employer, some are not. Interns usually work for only one semester, and the best internships involve a mix of simple and challenging work as well as time to talk with you, the entrepreneur, about what they are learning and what is the best way to do things. If you feel like teaching a little and working a little, an internship could work for you.

Attracting the best talent to your company can be encouraged by the strategic use of networking. Spend time in conversation with colleagues in the field, friends, vendors, and others to learn of possible employee leads.

Professional groups can be a resource for recruiting new talent. Many associations publish newsletters or post openings online or at their meeting locations. Try sending a one-page job description to associations to which you belong.[14]

Outsourcing may be the answer if your small business is not ready to hire employees, but you have a growing need to meet workload demand. Consider, as an example, outsourcing to an assistant who is an independent entrepreneur and provides administration, creative, or technical support. The assistant works on a contractual basis online and handles such functions as keeping your schedule, customer intelligence, or database up to speed.[15] Assistants can be people from your neighborhood or city, or virtual assistants working over the Internet. The nonprofit Virtual Assistant Association can be found at www.ivaa.org, and the major Web sites for outsourcing are eLance Online (www.elance.com) and Smarterwork (www.smarterwork.com).[16] Advice for hiring and managing **virtual employees** can be found in the accompanying Small Business Insight: Go Virtual.

virtual employees
Independent contractors who provide specialized business services or support from a distance, through the Internet, telephone, fax, or another method of communication.

Employee leasing is a hybrid between outsourcing and having a paid staff. In employee leasing, your "employees" actually work for the leasing company, who handles recruiting, training, compensation, and government filings. You lease employees from the leasing company, paying a fixed amount for the employee as well as an annual fee, usually 2 percent to 7 percent of the dollar value of your annual payroll. Leases can be set for periods of a few weeks to a year or more. For employing the same people part time but repeatedly over a long period of time, or keeping the total number of full-time employees low, this can be a good way to handle the complexities of employment.

SMALL BUSINESS INSIGHT

GO VIRTUAL

Virtual employees or assistants can change the way many small businesses are operated and managed. This field is growing tremendously and is offering employers and small business owners alike an attractive new alternative to hiring and managing employees. Virtual employees are independent contractors who provide specialized business services or support from a distance, through the Internet, telephone, fax, or another method of communication. A virtual assistant can assist a small company that needs extra people to meet seasonal demands; step in to meet the demands of business growth, locally, domestically, or globally; or provide unique skills for a special project.

In the small business, virtual employees are not hired as full-time employees. They can be business owners themselves and are hired on a contract basis. Small business owners who work with a virtual employee have the distinct advantage of not having to deal with taxes, unemployment insurance, sick leave, vacation pay, or benefits. Rather than having to provide additional office space and be responsible for the development and supervision of an employee, they can enjoy the support and assistance of a professional without the headaches of hiring and managing employees.[17]

Here are some guidelines and methods for managing and fostering productivity among virtual employees:[18]

- Hire virtual employees who have experience with being self-motivated and disciplined, including former consultants, freelancers, and salespeople who are accustomed to dealing with deadlines and working independently. As a small business owner, this is critical, given that you already have multiple deadlines and responsibilities.
- As you manage your virtual employees, make sure to spend time developing a system of task lists, schedules, and goals with varying time frames and clear deadlines. Invest in spreadsheets and project scheduling software that will help your virtual employees organize tasks. Be sure to consistently review status reports with virtual employees to ensure that tasks are completed on time and on budget.
- Maintain communication with virtual workers via voice, fax, and other electronic methods. Don't become reliant on e-mail since it is too easy to misinterpret or misunderstand the written word. Speak on the phone and schedule face-to-face meetings occasionally.
- Micromanagement is nearly impossible with a remote staff, and it will unnerve anyone who attempts it. Trust that your employees are doing the right thing until evidence proves otherwise. If you are paranoid about slacking, hire salaried, rather than hourly, workers or pay per project.

THE THOUGHTFUL ENTREPRENEUR

LOW-COST AND NO-COST EMPLOYEES

If your budget does not allow for a paid employee, consider three alternative methods to hire an employee at no cost.[19]

1. **Barter:** Trade your products or services for those of another business, for example, a maid service trading its house-cleaning services to a designer in return for a new logo. For this method of recruiting, you must be flexible in services rendered and received. Bartered services may add great value to a particular function of your small business and can be particularly useful when money is in short supply.
2. **Internships:** Hiring students to work at no cost in exchange for work experience may be a great way to get the assistance you need. Generally, students who intern are looking to use specific skill sets or be exposed to a particular functional area of a business. If you can provide valuable work experience, offering internships may be an appealing way to attract temporary help.
3. **Volunteers:** Volunteers are a wonderful resource if your business is strapped for cash, although the search process may be time consuming. Who will work for free? Family members are always the first source, with friends a close second, although people who need relevant work experience might give a few hours to have an entry on their job applications, such as stay-at-home spouses who are looking for work experience while children are at school. Also, individuals committed to your company's mission are possible candidates. If your firm is doing a promotion for a charitable organization (like operating a stand at a fair), you may be able to get customers or members of the charity to contribute their help.

Other traditional and nontraditional hiring sources to consider include:

- Contact *local churches* and the pastors and see if they have parishioners who are looking for a new job.
- Visit local *high schools* for entry-level jobs, local *community colleges* for those interested in management or a technical career.
- Finally, *state unemployment offices* are a great resource, with no cost to the employer.

Matching the Worker to the Work

LO3 Know how to match the right person to the job.

Even before your first hire, you will need to know what your basic needs are and what roles this new employee will fit into. Ultimately, you would like to "match" the job with the ideal individual who can fulfill the responsibilities of the job and grow with the business. Your first step is to define and describe all the work that will be part of the new job. Then you'll need to know how to evaluate the potential employees to see how well they match your ideal set of requirements.

Writing a Job Description

job description
Defines and discusses all the essential knowledge, skills, and abilities that are needed to fill a position.

Your **job description** needs to define and discuss all the essential knowledge, skills, and abilities that are needed to fill the position. In addition, you will need to describe what kind of personality, experience, and education you believe a person who performs the job should have. To determine some of these attributes, sit down and do a job analysis covering the following areas:[20]

- The reason the job exists (including an explanation of job goals and how they relate to your position and other positions in the company).
- The mental or physical tasks involved (ranging from judging, planning, and managing to cleaning, lifting, and welding).
- How the job will be done (all of the methods and equipment to be used).
- The qualifications needed (what kind of training, knowledge, skills are necessary).

If some of these questions are difficult to answer, consider talking to other small business owners in your area. You may also discuss these issues with employees and supervisors at other noncompeting small businesses that offer similar positions.

JOIN THE REVOLUTION: BUSINESS/ENTREPRENEURSHIP/MANAGEMENT INTERNSHIP

Company or Recruiter	Make Me Heal	Position Level	Entry Level
Industry	Health Care	Position Type	School Year Internship
Function	Corporate Business Development	Intern Paid	Yes
Location	Los Angeles, CA	Intern Type	Undergraduate

BUSINESS/ENTREPRENEURSHIP/MANAGEMENT/FINANCE INTERNSHIP

Make Me Heal Internship Associate Program

Please e-mail your resume and cover letter to: interns@makemeheal.com

We offer paid internships during the entire year (summer, fall, winter, spring) in all areas of the company, from business, marketing/press relations, to writing, journalism, and research. The nationally renowned The Princeton Review has honored our Internship Program by selecting it for inclusion in its prestigious Internship Bible, the book profiling the top U.S. internships.

Join The Revolution: The Internship Associate Program and the people who make part of this important team at Make Me Heal are an essential part of our "revolution." We are proud to have created internship positions that will not involve brainless tasks and will not only serve to try to impress or fill space on your resume. Rather, our internships are designed to actually educate, empower, challenge, inspire, and accelerate your growth before you join the workplace.

Exposure and Growth in Several Disciplines: An important element of our Philosophy is to enable our team members to acquire expertise in a number of areas of our business. If we were to align together, you would be exposed to and learn about a number of disciplines. So during the scope of the Internship, team members can be expected to delve into various facets of our business as they grow with us.

Leap from an Internship to a Full-Time Career: Due to our philosophy of cultivating long-term connections with everyone in our team, it is entirely possible that an internship may evolve into a full-time career with us if the internship experience proves to be meaningful, productive, happy, and fun for you and all of us at Make Me Heal.

We're Family: Whether one is an Internship Associate or a full-time employee with us, we care about all of our MMPeople and are dedicated to offering everyone incredibly rewarding, meaningful, and fun career opportunities. Indeed, when you become an Internship Associate with us, you also become a part of our extended family.

Selected for Inclusion in the Internship Bible: It is worthwhile to note that the nationally renowned The Princeton Review (the U.S. leader in the educational/school services industry) has selected our Internship Associate Program to be included in its prestigious Internship Bible, which is indeed the "bible" profiling the top internship opportunities in the United States.

We're looking to connect with highly entrepreneurial, ambitious individuals who thrive in an ever-changing, multibillion dollar industry where rewriting the rules is the law.

Roles involve researching, analyzing, and formulating innovative business strategies and implementing them, conceiving strategies to build our brand name to a national/international scale, creating strong operational infrastructure, assessing financial issues, among other functions. Work directly with CEO (former investment banker and Wharton Business School alum) to formulate business strategies and plans, implement new product and service lines, initiate supplier relationships with multinational cosmetics companies and leading manufacturers, devise innovative marketing and publicity initiatives, devise financial forecasts, strengthen quality of consumer experience, develop financial statements and forecasts, participate in deal-making, make presentations to institutional/high-net worth individuals and strategic business partners, and create quality controls, accounting, and legal structures for transacting with consumers.

FIGURE 19.2

Sample Job Description

Source: Copyright © 2005 Vault.com: Item posted by an employer, job/internship listing on the Vault.com Job Board.

To get started, write down the job title and whom that person will report to (define how the job relates to you or other positions in the small business). Next, develop a job statement or summary describing the position's major and minor duties. List any educational requirements, desired experience, and specialized skills or knowledge required. Include salary range and benefits (see "Compensation" later in this chapter). Finish by listing any physical or other special requirements associated with the job.

Figure 19.2 gives you an example of a job description for an internship in a growing small business. For a one-person business hiring its first employee, these guidelines may seem unnecessary. But remember, you are laying the foundation for your personnel policy, which will be essential as your small business grows. Keeping detailed records from the time you hire your first employee will make things a lot easier when you hire your tenth, twentieth, and so on.

Also, writing the job description will help you determine whether you need a part-time or full-time employee, whether the person should be permanent or temporary, and whether you could use an independent contractor to fill the position. The specifics for crafting a job description are given in Skill Module 19.1.

SKILL MODULE 19.1

Crafting a Job Description

In this skill module, you have the opportunity to write job descriptions for a student worker and for an instructor on your campus. Write a job description for the role of student worker, and ask one of your instructors about his or her job and write a description. In your instructor interview or when thinking about the student job, cover many of the areas and questions discussed to get a full view and perspective of the positions. Write a half-page job description using the following how-to steps:[21]

1. **Start with a Title:** Provide a job title for the position (two–three words). Beneath the title, you want to include important information related to the job such as the status (exempt vs. nonexempt) and to whom the employee reports.
   Example:
   Intern: A nonexempt summer position reporting to the CEO.
2. **Give a Job Overview (or Summary of the Job):** Be sure that this section is not more than three to four sentences long and that it explains the level and basic nature of this job position. You will be outlining details of the job in the following sections.
   Example:
   An entry-level job position providing administrative support to a technology business with three employees.
3. **Define the Duties and Responsibilities:** Write down all the tasks that the employee will be doing in this position. Be flexible in writing the duties and responsibilities to accommodate growth of the position. Be clear, concise, and complete.
   Main duties include: scheduling appointments, giving information to callers, and generally relieving staff of clerical work and minor administrative and business detail.
4. **Knowledge, Skills, and Abilities:** These are basic qualities that the employee should possess. They could include:
   Knowledge of computer software, including: PowerPoint, Excel.
   Skilled at performing multiple tasks simultaneously.
   Ability to relate to people and make them feel comfortable.
5. **Credentials and Experience:** List the level of educational and professional experience the person should have (possibly allow for additional experience to make up for the lack of an educational degree).
   Minimum two years of college with coursework in business or related fields. Prior business experience desirable.
6. **Special Requirements:** Anything that may not have been covered up until this point should go here. For example:
   Frequent travel required to other universities and conferences.
   Job includes some evening and weekend hours.
   Ability to lift 15 lbs or more.

Then compare the descriptions with those of other students. You might also try to find the official job description for an instructor from your school. When comparing your description with the other ones, consider the following:

1. How difficult was it to define and narrow the many responsibilities of the position?
2. Were there differences between your description and the actual description?
3. How many similarities were there between your description and the actual description?
4. If there were discrepancies, where were the "gaps" between the two?
5. As a small business owner, what can you do to ensure there is a mutual understanding between you and the employee in describing the job/position as your business grows?
6. How can you get both formal and informal feedback from employees regarding the job on a continual basis?

Evaluating Job Prospects

Once you have a job description, you can use it to help you evaluate whether an individual would be the right match for the position and your small business. So what can you do to make sure you hire the right person for the job? This is probably one of the most difficult decisions you may be faced with making, especially since we are all not trained in the art and science of hiring employees. In making successful hiring decisions, rely on the information developed in your job description to identify the most important knowledge areas, skills, and abilities the ideal candidate should possess. Next, create the same specific questions that you will ask of all candidates that will clearly and behaviorally demonstrate to you that they have these critical factors. Do not simply accept the candidate's word that he or she possesses a certain skill or knowledge base. Ask that person to demonstrate the skill, solve a problem, or write or create something that clearly and concretely provides you with the proof you need to make an informed decision.

We recommend the behavioral-interviewing approach because it is one that entrepreneurs can do a good job on by themselves, and because the kinds of information it generates is something an entrepreneur can directly understand and relate to the applicant and the job in question.

You have heard of selection tests for jobs, and there are a variety of tests and simulations that can be used. However, these techniques usually require major up-front costs for training, validation, and the materials themselves. Work simulations hold many of the same issues, but are even more complex and costly. Either approach usually accounts for no more than 50 percent of the variation in performance among multiple candidates, and in real-world situations, often can account for only 10 percent of performance.[22] So we focus on using a behaviorally based interview (along with application forms and references) as the centerpiece of the selection process.

Develop questions structured like those shown in Figure 19.3. These use slightly different techniques to obtain descriptions of situations the interviewee had encountered before. You will notice that the questions are designed so a "yes" or "no" answer is not applicable, and that most questions lend themselves to follow-up questions from you about the specifics of the experience. In the process, you are observing how the candidate analyzes situations, how rationally or logically the situation is presented, and whether or not, to the best of your judgment, the person is being truthful.

If at all possible, consider involving one or two other interviewers (if possible from within your small business) to look at a candidate who seems promising. This helps you be sure that you understand the individual as well as possible. In that way, you can all share your insights and impressions of the candidate. Furthermore, one interviewer can add an aspect to a question that another one (or even you as the owner) may have overlooked.

Finally, make sure you know enough about a candidate before you hire that person, and never, ever hire even a moderately qualified person just because you need someone now. You want to be sure you haven't hired a problem. It can be long and painful to terminate someone and advertise, screen, interview and hire another person. Take your time to make sure you have the best person that best matches the position for your small business.

Interviewing can be a nerve-wracking experience for both interviewer and candidate. As an interviewer, be prepared as fully as possible, with specific questions to ask and a clear communication of job details. See Figure 19.3 to glean sample interview questions and start you thinking of additional questions you might want to ask in your own company setting.

Selecting the Right Person

Imagine you have crafted the job description, sought candidates from several sources, and interviewed the candidates using the same set of basic questions. If you are hiring your first employee,

FIGURE 19.3

Typical Types of Behaviorally Based Interview Questions[23]

These help match the right person to the job based on questions tied to the demonstrated knowledge, skills, abilities, and experiences of the applicant.

1. *Tell me about a time when:*

   You worked effectively under pressure.
   You were creative in solving a problem.
   You had to deal with an irate customer.
   You were unable to complete a project on time.

2. *Describe:*

   One of your strengths and one of your weaknesses.
   Your three most important work-related values (and an example of where you demonstrated each value at work).
   A decision you made that was unpopular and how you implemented it.
   A time when you were tolerant of an opinion that was different than your own.

3. *Give an example of:*

   A goal you reached and tell me how you achieved it.
   An occasion when you used logic to solve a problem.
   A time when you anticipated potential problems and developed preventive measures.
   A time when you had to make an important decision with limited facts.

4. *The last time it happened, how did you:*

   Adapt to a difficult situation?
   Persuade team members to do things your way?
   Overcome a major obstacle at work?
   Preserve your integrity when it was put to the test at work?

Remember: (1) You can replace "work" with "school," "church," "club," or "dorm" depending on the experience you think the interviewee is likely to have. (2) Questions that ask what they have done give a better indication than questions asking what they would do.

you probably learned a bit about yourself, your business, and your employee needs as you went through this process. You run a consulting business that helps local companies identify promising markets overseas. You split your time between your clients' offices, learning about their businesses, and your own office, where you work up prospects using the Internet and phone.

You started looking for someone to handle the office phone and e-mail when you were out, and to prepare reports for clients and sales catalogs for overseas customers from the templates you've developed. As you started talking to prospective employees, you realized that you could go any one of several ways: (1) Since you have an orderly process, you could hire someone relatively

SMALL BUSINESS INSIGHT

MAVENS & MOGULS, A MARKETING STRATEGY CONSULTING FIRM[24]

I feel like my role is to connect the dots . . . I'm a conductor of a world class orchestra.

—Paige Arnof-Fenn

Paige Arnof-Fenn, founder and CEO of Mavens & Moguls, launched her company in 2001. Paige had worked with companies at all stages that needed expert marketing advice, including projects for start-ups, authors, professional service firms, the Sundance Film Festival, Merrill Lynch, Sprint, and Delta Airlines. With Mavens & Moguls she has assembled a team of marketing all-stars, the best people that she has encountered in her career across all marketing disciplines. They are spread across the United States and as far away as Bangkok.

As the sole business owner of Mavens & Moguls, Paige relies on her virtual employees to knit together the network of experienced professionals who have actually "done it" for the top companies across a variety of industries. Working from their own offices, homes, or other private work spaces, they provide marketing strategy, planning, and execution. The real mavens and moguls specialize in promotion, PR, direct marketing, media, pricing strategy, positioning, customer acquisition, and new product launches. In many ways, all the areas of the marketing mix are covered that can be used to build a brand and grow a client's business.

inexperienced (and inexpensive) and quickly get them up to speed doing the above tasks or (2) you could hire someone with more experience in international sales (and would need higher pay) who could actually handle finding overseas customers and negotiate pieces of deals while you are soliciting more business. You have a top candidate for either approach. How do you decide?

Recall the idea of fit introduced earlier. As the owner, you decide how the firm should be run and what will be important. Both people seem nice enough and you think you could get along well with either one. So look at something different. Do you like your current pace of business? If yes, the inexperienced person should help take off some of the stress you're facing now, and will cost you less in wages, so is less of a burden. You should be able to grow your business at your own rate, but you will also be responsible for training and checking up on this person until she or he gets experienced in the job and your approach to it.

If you want to grow the business more quickly, the experienced person can be of more help. The experienced person should be able to do more things upon starting and learn new ways more quickly because he or she understands the underlying ideas of your industry, but that person will require more money from you and may have ideas about the best way to do something that do not match your preferred way.

Notice that a lot of the decisions about hiring really involve the entrepreneurs' realization of what they want to see happen in the business. Sometimes this becomes apparent only by going through the hiring process. In fact, for first-time hiring situations, it can be a good thing to try someone in the job part time in order to have a chance to refine what you want to see in the job description and in the business. In other situations, making use of the probationary period mentioned earlier can help define the job's potential end point, leaving you a graceful way out of having the wrong person in the job, or the wrong job described.

Training Your Employees

Of course, it would be great if employees came to work fully prepared to meet your business needs. However, most employees (even the most ideal new hires) need training. The time and money you spend teaching employees how to do their jobs could turn out to be your small company's wisest investment.

LO4 Learn about employee training methods and resources.

To begin, you should first assess your small firm's training needs from the perspective of the business, the job itself (job description), and the needs of the employees. This assessment will provide answers to the following questions:

- *Where* is training needed? What key areas need the most attention?
- *What* specifically must an employee learn in order to be more productive?
- *Who* needs to be trained?

Once you have answered these questions, you can then design your training program. There are two different types of training: initial training and ongoing training. When employees first join your small business or start a new role, offering them the training they need to handle the position makes them feel valued, challenged, and rewarded.

Initial and Ongoing Training Methods

There are two broad types of training available to small businesses: on-the-job and off-the-job techniques. Individual circumstances and the where, what, and who of your training program determine which method to use.

On-the-job training is delivered to employees while they perform their regular jobs. In this way, they do not lose time while they are learning. After a plan is developed for what should be taught, employees should be informed of the details. On-the-job techniques include orientations, job instruction training, apprenticeships, internships and assistantships, job rotation, and coaching.[25]

on-the-job training Delivered to employees while they perform their regular jobs; techniques include orientations, job instruction training, apprenticeships, internships and assistantships, job rotation, and coaching.

For on-the-job training in a small business, you need to stay abreast of all the jobs that need doing and define them so others can be trained in doing parts of the job. It is critical to design a job to make sure that nothing important is missed. To give you an idea on how to design on-the-job instruction that gives an employee a method to complete a certain task in a job, consider Skill Module 19.2, "Writing Instructions and Procedures."

SKILL MODULE 19.2

Writing Instructions and Procedures[26]

- Give the instruction/procedure a clear heading that summarizes the task.
- Show clearly who does what.
- Start each step or instruction with a verb that tells the reader to do something: "Open the valve ..." "Press the emergency button . . . ." "Tell your supervisor . . . ."
- Use a numbered list when the order in which tasks are to be performed is important. Use a bulleted list (like this one) when the order is not important.
- Put notes, warnings, and prerequisite conditions at the start, or *before* the list item to which they refer.
- Don't mix instructions with conceptual information. Present any necessary background information before the instructions.
- Use a level of detail that is appropriate to your employees' skill level and will ensure they will be able to know how to complete the job task.

Along with on-the-job training techniques, off-the-job methods such as lectures, special study, videos, television conferences or discussions, case studies, role-playing, simulation, programmed instruction, and laboratory training are all possible. Most of these techniques can be used by small businesses, although some may be too costly.[27] Other affordable and ongoing training methods can be less formal. In fact, training can be as simple as encouraging employees to meet regularly to discuss issues and share new ideas and perspectives. If your firm is large enough, you can also assign mentors to junior employees. Mentors give less experienced employees the opportunity to learn from seasoned veterans. Employees will be more comfortable in the face of new challenges if they know where to go for help. Mentors can inspire employees to strive for greater levels of success, help them channel their ambitions, and teach them new ways of handling ongoing problems more effectively.

Three Guidelines for Training[28]

1. **Give your employees opportunities to use their new skills:** Many small business owners complain that it is sometimes useless to train employees. Owners may argue that employees will take the knowledge and leave for a higher-paying job at another firm. While this may happen, small business owners can help prevent it. Once your employees are trained, give them opportunities to use their new skills.
2. **Make training an ongoing process:** Good employees want to learn, and you should provide them with opportunities to do so. Give employees encouragement to talk to you when their learning curve goes flat and then find ways to provide them with challenges and the knowledge to meet them successfully.
3. **Think of training as an investment (as opposed to an expense):** Many small business owners hesitate to invest too much energy, time, or money in training employees. Feeling that the expense does not justify the end results, they choose instead to give new hires a crash course and then put them right to work. Results of that sink-or-swim approach include costly mistakes, unhappy workers, and low productivity.

Rewarding Employees

LO5 Gain insight in meeting employees' needs and expectations.

Congratulations! Your business is growing and you have hired your first employee(s), either full time, part time, or on a virtual basis. Most likely the hiring process was time consuming to ensure a perfect fit between your new employee and your company. So how are you going to retain your first employee and ensure you are meeting his or her needs? To retain productive employees and increase their job satisfaction, the simplest answer is to ask them what their needs are. Next, create an environment that appeals to them.

But when you do not have employees to ask, where do you start? Jill Kickul studied 23 owner promises, including everything from salary and health care to workload and opportunities for

TABLE 19.3 **23 Rewards Offered Employees of Small Businesses**

Factors	Psychological Contract Items
Autonomy and growth	Meaningful work Challenging and interesting work Participation in decision making Freedom to be creative Opportunity to develop new skills Increasing responsibilities A job that provides autonomy and control Recognition of accomplishments Career guidance and mentoring
Benefits	Health care benefits Vacation benefits Retirement benefits Tuition reimbursement
Rewards and opportunities	Opportunities for promotion and advancement Opportunities for personal growth Pay and bonuses tied to performance Job training Continual professional training
Job security and work responsibilities	Well-defined job responsibilities A reasonable workload Job security
Work facilitation	Adequate equipment to perform job Enough resources to do the job

Source: Jill Kickul, "Promises Made, Promises Broken: An Exploration of Employee Attraction and Retention Practices in Small Business," *Journal of Small Business Management* 39, no. 4 (October 2001), p. 325, based on factor scores. Reprinted with permission.

advancement, and distilled them down to five underlying factors, in order of most important to least important: autonomy and personal growth, rewards/opportunities, job security/responsibilities, benefits, and facilitating work.[29] The full list is given in Table 19.3.

Salary rewards, bonuses, and perks were not as important to employees as autonomy and personal growth; job security and responsibility were less important than benefits. But small business owners often implicitly or explicitly communicate conflicting terms when making **psychological contracts** with employees. To avoid this, denote strict limits on what you promise employees and how and when those promises will be delivered. Put what you agree to in writing to prevent problems when it comes time to evaluate whether you've delivered on the contract.

Entrepreneurs need to make job offers and manage based on an **open-book policy**. If you work this way and your company hits a downturn and promises cannot be met, employees are less likely to react badly since they have a better understanding of the firm's situation. Five factors are most valuable to employees:

1. **Teamwork:** Fostering a sense of teamwork allows people to interact with one another on a professional level. Sharing ideas, working toward a common goal, analyzing one another's work, and communicating cross functionally help build stronger professional bonds which increase a sense of belonging and company fit.
2. **Recognition:** Showing appreciation for a job well done or giving credit to an employee who introduced a great idea can go a long way in making your employee feel valued. Recognition

psychological contract
Refers to employees' beliefs about the promises between the employee and the firm. These beliefs are based on the perception that promises have been made (e.g., competitive wages, promotional opportunities, job training) in exchange for certain employee obligations such as giving of their energy, time, and technical skills.

open-book policy
Concept that key employees should be able to see and understand a firm's financials, that they should have a part in moving the numbers in the right direction, and that they should have a direct stake in the strategy and success of the firm.

can be given in person, by voice mail, through e-mail, or written in a memo or letter. You can also incorporate a reward system. Do you have star performers? Increase their motivation by recognizing their accomplishment with a certificate, plaque, or personal bonus such as a dinner or movie gift certificate. This will help them to feel valued for their hard work and dedication and encourage them to continue this behavior.[30]

3. **Training:** A common reason people leave a company is if they feel they are not developing professionally. Providing learning opportunities at every level of the organization through on-the-job training or professional training will increase your employees' capabilities, allow them to expand their job responsibility, and help to increase job satisfaction. Commitment to employees' development and growth is one way to ensure an employee is growing and will stay longer.[31]
4. **Empowerment:** This means letting employees make on-the-spot decisions for the companies' best interest. Making empowerment work requires giving employees permission to act, the knowledge to act, and the skill to act.[32] When empowerment works, it increases employees personal feelings of responsibility and increases their commitment to the company.
5. **Contribution:** Providing meaningful work for employees gives them the feeling or belief that the day's work was a valuable contribution to the company and that they made a difference.[33] Employees have to believe that the decisions they make and the work they perform have a direct impact on the product or service you provide.[34]

Although not included in the study, another key element on which the other factors depends is communication. Open communication is vital for new employees. Share your vision and the mission of the business. To be sure your employees feel valued, it is important to make time to talk about the direction of the company. Make sure *you* understand how they see what you have said and what they think you have promised.[35] To do this, you can have a casual conversation while working side by side. Or find time to schedule brief one-on-one meetings to make sure the conversation takes place and the message is understood. Employees want to know what the company is trying to do, where it is going, and what it stands for.[36] After you have communicated the goal of the position and your expectation of their performance during the hiring process, follow up with feedback on a consistent basis regarding their performance. And ask how they personally prefer to communicate and what they need in their work environment to maximize their productivity.

Increasingly, small entrepreneurial companies are implementing formal performance appraisals. Reviewing employees' performance is an ongoing process. Owners and managers need to communicate with employees and give year-round feedback to employees on the job regarding performance and company goals. Before conducting a formal review, it is important to understand that there are two parts to a review: (1) the performance review and (2) the pay review. These reviews should be held at different times of the year. The performance review typically occurs once a year to monitor your employees' job satisfaction, overall performance, and set career objectives. The goal of the performance review is to identify employee strengths, formally recognize performance, set goals to utilize the skills identified as strengths, and set direction for the upcoming year. It is also a time to identify areas of development and communicate with employees concerning how you will support them and the necessary steps they need to take to develop identified areas. It is a time to plan and set goals for the year ahead and to review work from the year past. The goal of the pay review is to reward your employees if they have performed all duties and met general requirements as discussed in initial job description conversations.

Small business owners with fewer than five employees may find formal performance reviews unnecessary or impersonal—taking away the strength of a small firm. But it is a good idea to conduct written reviews to track employee performance. This gives you an out if their performance becomes unsatisfactory after coaching or retraining. To successfully conduct an employee review, you should have a clear understanding of the position.[37] Next you should create a list of questions and issues that will be discussed in preparation for creating an evaluation sheet.[38] This list can include what the current responsibilities are, how well they are performing in the identified responsibilities, what needs to be improved or learned to be successful in position, and where employees are headed in their career. The evaluation sheet should include open-ended questions for the employees to fill out regarding job performance, strengths, areas of development, and what gets in the way of accomplishing the job.[39] For a sample appraisal and type of questions you may want to begin with, go to www.bizhelp24.com.

An appraisal form should be filled out and returned to you before the scheduled performance review so that you can learn the employees' goals, interests, and self-evaluation when you are crafting your comments.[40] Your comments during the review should address how the employee can grow, improve, and build on his or her current set of successes to contribute to the company, what you can do as a leader to provide resources, guidance, and opportunities, and what the individual needs to do on his or her own to continue to grow and succeed.[41]

Compensation, Benefits, and Perks

LO6 Learn how to develop a fair compensation and benefit plan.

One of the first steps in developing a compensation plan is to determine your organization's salary philosophy. Do you believe in raising the level of base salaries in your organization or do you appreciate the flexibility of variable pay? A small business, with variable sales and income, may be better off controlling the levels of base salaries. When times are good, the business can tie bonus dollars to goals achieved.

The next step is to find comparison factors for salary. Research the salary range for similar positions and job descriptions. Determine whether you are competitive with organizations of similar size, sales, and markets. If you can find companies in the same industry, especially in your area or region, that is another good comparison source. You can check salary surveys and want ads, and scout out competitors to see if they are underpaying or overpaying their employees. You can get a start by searching Google for "salary comparison." Probably the best-known site for comparison information is Salary.com shown in Skill Module 19.3 and on the Online Learning Center. You can get the same report without registering by using hotjobs.yahoo.com. Paying too much is an unnecessary drain on your resources, but paying too little will make it difficult for you to find and keep the best people.[42]

Finding Local Salaries and Benefits Information Online

SKILL MODULE 19.3

There are two possible sources of online information on salaries and benefits specific to your locality. One is the state employment security office for your area. The best list of state offices is found at the Job-Hunt.org Web site (**www.job-hunt.org/state_unemployment_offices.shtml**). When looking at the state sites, the information you want is typically under "Employers." You will be looking for salary data. If it is not apparent, and the site has a search function, enter "salary data" in the search box to track it down.

Salary.com offers a wealth of information on salary and benefits, organized by type of job and locality. Over the years, more and more of its information has become available only for a fee, but basic information remains free and useful. Let's pick Provo/Mammoth, Utah (zip 84601) as our location and "retail cashier" as our position of interest.

The resulting page gives you several job positions. Choose the one which says "Retail Cashier—Full-Time." Below the description are four choices. As a potential employer, you want the report "For Employers: Base Salary Range (Free)." The resulting report has three panels. The first one gives you the range of the salary by percentile (a 90th percentile means 90 percent of people have lower numbers, and 10 percent have higher). To get the median (50 percent of people above, 50 percent of people below this level) salary for the position, look at the tab labeled "Benefits." Click on this and you will find the median salary as well as the median additional amount of money spent by the employer to provide the benefits typical in that zip code.

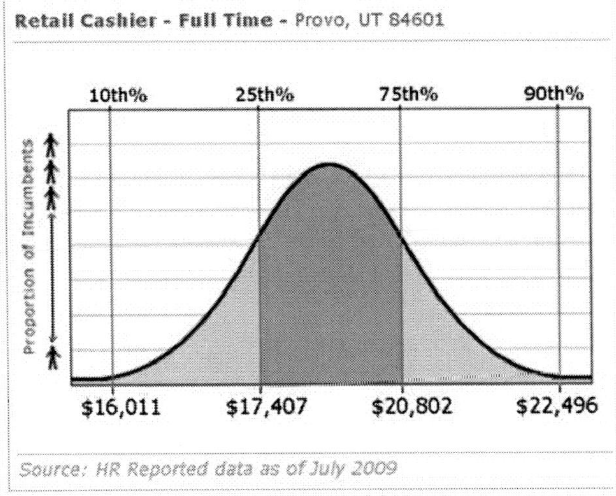

Retail Cashier - Full Time - Provo, UT 84601

Benefit	Median Amount	% of Total
Base Salary	$18,941	62.3%
Bonuses	$54	0.2%
Social Security	$1,453	4.8%
401k / 403b	$684	2.2%
Disability	$190	0.6%
Healthcare	$5,722	18.8%
Pension	$874	2.9%
Time Off	$2,484	8.2%
Total	**$30,402**	**100%**

Source: HR Reported data as of July 2009

As a potential employer, you need to keep both the base salary and the total salary in mind. Often potential employees screen jobs based on the base salary, so it is important to offer a competitive wage. But as an employer, that position can cost you as much as the total wage, which can be from 25 percent to even 50 percent higher than the base wage.

The last place to check online is the Living Wage Calculator at the Pennsylvania State University (**www.livingwage.geog.psu.edu**). A **living wage** is the amount needed for a person (or family of a particular size) to meet the basic necessities of life from a single job. In Provo, Utah, the 2009 living wage for one person was $16,783, so the median salary for a cashier given above does put the person about $180 a month above the poverty level. That is around $6 of spendable cash a working day over basic needs. For a person just starting out, with no family responsibilities, the median cashier's job may not be a bad one, for awhile.

living wage
The amount needed for a person (or family of a particular size) to meet the basic necessities of life from a single job.

When deciding on a wage, it is important to remember that some benefits are required, like Social Security and Disability, while others may be up to the entrepreneur's choice, like health care or retirement plans. If you expect the job you offer to be the employee's full-time job, it is important, and when you think about it, only fair, to make sure you cover their basic needs.

Provo City, Utah County, UT

Population 105,166

Typical Expenses

These figures show the individual expenses that went into the living wage estimate. Their values vary by family size, composition, and the current location.

	One Adult	One Adult, One Child	Two Adults	Two Adults, One Child	Two Adults, Two Children
Monthly Expenses:					
Food	$232	$378	$448	$594	$740
Child Care	$0	$572	$0	$572	$1,012
Medical	$76	$151	$152	$227	$302
Housing	$571	$667	$571	$667	$667
Transportation	$232	$397	$464	$629	$794
Other	$188	$369	$376	$557	$738
Monthly After-Tax Income That's Required	$1,299	$2,534	$2,011	$3,246	$4,253
Annual After-Tax Income That's Required	$15,588	$30,408	$24,132	$38,952	$51,041
Annual Taxes	$1,195	$2,158	$1,808	$2,839	$3,628
Annual Before-Tax Income That's Required	$16,783	$32,566	$25,940	$41,791	$54,669

Moreover, salary should be tied to a person's skills and experience. Subsequent increases need to be based on an employee's performance, value, and contribution to the small business. Use the information from the employee's performance appraisal form to help you determine the appropriate increase. You will also want to consider percentages of increase in salary in similar jobs in your local area.[43]

Bonuses and Long-Term Incentives[44]

Employee bonuses, usually paid in a single lump at the end of the year, are one way of providing performance incentives. Profit-sharing plans, stock options, or stock grants not only provide long-term incentives to employees, but they can also help retain valuable team members through your small business start-up phase. However, you also may want to consider these options once you are beyond the start-up phase and have stability in your business earnings overall.

Health Insurance[45]

Employer-sponsored health insurance is fairly standard among medium-sized companies, but not among small businesses. While an employer-sponsored plan saves employees money and gives them peace of mind in knowing that they won't be denied coverage, it is not always affordable to the small business owner. However, providing insurance to your employees sends the message that you care about their health and the health of their families. To minimize costs, consider having employees pick up part of the tab. Employees who have coverage through a spouse may want to opt out of a plan, particularly if there's a cost associated with it.

THE THOUGHTFUL ENTREPRENEUR

LABOR UNIONS

Today a tiny percentage of small business employees are members of labor unions. A labor union is an organization of employees that usually work for the same employer at the same workplace. Labor unions try to get a "collective" contract for their members. The labor laws governing unions can be very complicated. If you are faced with a union organizing drive, you should contact a labor lawyer immediately to make sure that your response to the organizing drive is legal.

If your employees belong to a labor union, they probably already made a "union contract," which is also called a "collective bargaining agreement" with you. This agreement and contract covers wages, working conditions, and procedures for complaining about problems on the job.

Union contracts usually provide that employees cannot be fired, suspended, or disciplined without "good cause." This rule is usually found in a section of the contract titled "Grievance Procedure" or "Discipline." If an employee thinks you didn't have "good cause" to fire or discipline, he or she generally contacts the union. The union may decide to file a grievance for the worker against you. If the union files a grievance against you, you should see an attorney who specializes in labor law, who should help you decide how to defend against the grievance. If you have questions about labor unions, contact a business lawyer near you, or you can start some of the research yourself by contacting the U.S. Department of Labor, **http://www.dol.gov/compliance/**. Its main goal is to help employers and employees comply with Department of Labor laws and regulations as well as to give you additional information related to your state's laws and compliance issues specific to managing and operating your small business.

Retirement Plans[46]

401(k) plans have become popular because they are relatively easy to administer and are less expensive than traditional pension plans. Many employees like these plans because they maintain some control over the amount of their contribution and how the money is invested. Most small companies try to put some kind of savings or 401(k) plan in place, even if they don't contribute money to them. Other incentives that you may want to consider include time off and flexible schedules such as holidays, vacations, sick days and personal days. An employer unable to offer competitive salaries may close part of the gap by offering more time off or flexible work hours. Some employers make no distinction between sick, vacation, and personal days and allow employees a set number of days off each year to be used at their discretion. This prevents employees from abusing sick days and keeps employees from feeling that they need to lie when a child is ill or a personal emergency arises.

Perks

Perks is short for perquisites, and refers to the privileges, services, or even tangible items given to employees as part of the overall compensation and benefits package. Perks is a great way to provide short-term boosts in motivation—in effect a psychological pick-me-up. Good perks do not have to cost a lot; in fact, some perks can be powerful, even if free. Consider the list of perk ideas given in Table 19.4.

The rule of thumb is that perks like these should take no more than 3 percent of the annual personnel budget. That said, a bagel and coffee breakfast for your staff may be a very inexpensive way to say you care about them, as well as being a great way to position them for a more productive day, and in the long term, that is what compensation and benefits are supposed to achieve.

TABLE 19.4 **Innovative Low-Cost and Free Perks for Your Employees[47]**

- Time-off and flexible scheduling (esp. for families with children and elderly at home).
- Arrange discounts with local merchants for your employees.
- Offer free seminars onsite (your insurers, banks, and HMOs will often do this for free).
- Arrange pickups and deliveries at your location for your employees (like dry cleaning, auto cleaning, etc.).
- Offer supplemental services administered through payroll—but paid for by the employee (e.g., supplemental health insurance or retirement programs, prepaid legal services, etc.).
- Offer credit union memberships.
- Let employees buy excess inventory at a big discount.
- Special days (work from home days, family days, community service days, bring your dog days, pizza lunch day, etc.).
- Offer a group perk like two tickets to a movie that weekend.
- Free car washes in the lot (detailers will charge around $5 per car for external washes bought in bulk).
- Let employees expense work clothing bought for sales efforts.
- After-work party.
- Bring a continental breakfast for all.

Entrepreneurial Leadership

In most general management and business classes, when we talk about "leadership," what we really mean is administration. In fact, the two key factors in traditional leadership theories are task and person. If you are getting the job done, and you are keeping your people happy with each other and the firm, then you have achieved the primary goals of "leadership." Neither one of these key factors does much to explain what we commonly think of when we talk about leaders like Washington or Iacocca or Jobs. The disconnect is exactly the difference between everyday administration of your team and project, and that beyond the regular increment of energy that we imagine around people with entrepreneurial leadership.

Leadership is essential to the growth of any small business. If you intend to have employees, you need to be able to provide the skills of the entrepreneurial leader. In any year, about 75 percent of the businesses in the United States consist of only their owner. There are no employees. This remains true for most one-person businesses, and when larger small businesses are studied, we often find that businesses freeze their employee growth at particular levels. Some of this can be explained by a desire to avoid ever-increasing levels of federal and state laws, with their complexities and costs, but an even more powerful reason is that many entrepreneurs realize that there is an optimal size of firm for them to manage. It is central to your evaluating your potential for entrepreneurial leadership.

Entrepreneurial leadership looks at how you operate as the chief executive of your business. It has three key components over and above task and person—innovation, operation, and inspiration. Innovation is the idea that we look to the leader of a small business as its key visionary. The owner should be the person thinking about the future of the business, how to compete better, how to grow, what next new thing should be tried. Employees can contribute ideas, but in the end, the boss is the key to innovation. If you spend all your time worrying about today and spend no time thinking about tomorrow, eventually your business will lose.

Operation is often the scariest of the three components—although it is the one most closely related to the task and person elements of administrative leadership. Operation refers to the ability to manage the business as it grows. Some people have trouble delegating. Those people often feel out of control when they start to employ others, and the business suffers as a result. They may not know how to delegate, or even if they do, they want to rush in and take over when things "go bad" (i.e., "It was not done the way *I* would have done it."), and thus undermine the employees. Some bosses are just so personally disorganized that it can be difficult to explain or find or share with others the key information of the business, and so the business is locked inside their heads or on their piled-high desktop. If you have employees and they are unhappy, the most likely problem is one of operation.

Inspiration is the third component, and stems from the very reasonable expectation among employees and customers that the entrepreneur should be the business's biggest booster and champion. If you do not have 100 percent iron-clad belief in your business, its product and services, its people, and your ability to make it all work, how can anyone else? While the ability to deliver a stirring speech is an admirable inspirational skill, it is not necessary. Speaking quietly from the heart can work just as well, as long as it is apparent that it *is* from the heart, and it is backed by your own passion. Think of basketball coaches Phil Jackson and Bobby Knight. Both inspire, but one is quietly intense, and one is loudly bombastic.

How do you know if you have what it takes in terms of entrepreneurial leadership? Your past experience is the best indicator. If you have been a leader of teams, study groups, shifts at work, or church projects, and people seemed to get the job done and liked each other and you—you probably have what it takes to cover the operation. If you could keep them working when problems arose or times were tough, then you probably have what it takes in terms of inspiration.

If you have not had these sorts of opportunities, college is a great place to get them—in classes, in student organizations, and at work. If you have had these opportunities and they have not been positive, then you want to enroll in workshops and classes on leadership and supervision, and develop the behaviors you need to be successful. You can test out how well you are learning by volunteering to lead on and off campus. Innovation, the third component, is often easy for entrepreneurs because the process of creating and growing a business is a natural application of the innovative component of leadership.

Human Resource Issues in the Family Business

LO7 Understand the complexities of managing family within your business.

Family business is a catchall covering tens of millions of firms. In fact, some researchers estimate that 95 percent of all businesses are indeed family businesses.[48] From a one-person business with occasional infusions of free help from family members to larger family firms employing multiple generations of family members along with nonfamily employees, there are two key human resource management issues that continually surface in family businesses: striking a balance between nepotism and meritocracy as well as managing privilege. There are basic human resource management "best practices" that help whether the business is a family firm or a business with no family ties which get covered next, with a moment spent revisiting the issues of managing compensation and benefits within the family business and the family.

Nepotism, Meritocracy, and the Family Business

nepotism
A management philosophy of selecting and promoting people based on family ties.

meritocracy
A management philosophy of selecting and promoting people based solely on their being the most capable person for the job.

As a family business owner, you need to make a decision about how you feel about two ideas that at first do not fit easily together—nepotism and meritocracy. **Nepotism** is the management philosophy of selecting and promoting people based on family ties. Nepotism's advantages are involving people you know and hopefully trust in your business, being able to involve the person more completely (in terms of work time and family time) in the business, and having loyalty and support from your worker and their family in return. **Meritocracy** on the other hand is the management philosophy of selecting and promoting people based solely on their being the most capable person for the job.

When the family member is also the most capable person for the job, the two philosophies live in harmony. But what if you want to hire your son as manager and hopefully heir to the business, but there is a more capable person available to you? If you can afford to employ and use both, you may be able to eventually create a strong top management team using both people. If you can only afford to hire one person, this is when you have to make a hard decision as to which philosophy wins out.[49]

If you are extremely lucky, your family member might make life easy by saying that you hired the best person and that is the best for all in the long run. But it is just as likely that hiring meritocratically is seen as showing no loyalty to kin, and results in estranged relationships in the family. In a family business, if the family is stressed out, it almost always spills over into the business in negative and sometimes disastrous ways.

Sometimes it is important to recognize that "good enough" may well be just that. If the family member is good enough to do the job well (but perhaps not <u>as well</u> as the nonfamily candidate), hiring from the family may well make the most sense in the long run, to build the family and the family business. It is one situation where it might make sense to favor a slightly nepotistic philosophy over a strictly meritocratic one.

If you make that nepotistic decision, what you as the decision maker must do is avoid comparisons of the family member you hired to the "one that got away." It is your job to make every employee, including family members you hire, best able to contribute to the business. Part of being the boss is taking responsibility for your decisions, especially when that is difficult.[50]

The nepotism vs. meritocracy issues also comes up when the child of a family business owner considers coming into the family business. If this happens right after graduating, the nagging question for the owner, the potential heir, and the employees is whether the young person gets ahead because of his or her skill or family tie. The answer to this is simple and often highly beneficial to everyone—work somewhere else first.[51]

In particular, seek a job in a related industry, or with a customer, or even with a competitor with whom your family's business is friendly (e.g., a similar company operating in a different market). A job in one of these areas will give you insight into groups important to your business. It can expand your contacts in key areas like new customers or suppliers, and it can help you learn new ways of getting things done to bring back to the family business.

If you take a job elsewhere, and do a good job there, you return to the family business a proven winner in a more objective situation. You know you have done well, your new fellow employees know it, and your boss knows it. It helps by giving you a stronger basis for what you say, and what you say you are worth.

Managing Privilege

Nepotism has the potential to play a role in the everyday operations of your business and its human resources activities. In fact, many entrepreneurs purposely create a family business in order to give their family members jobs, a sense of purpose, incomes for now with the possibility of future ownership, and the privileges of flexibility. Part of the advantage they imagine for a family business is that it can accommodate family needs better than an impersonal, nonfamily business. So the boss's son, who works in the family business, needs time off to coach the grandson's hockey team. In a family business, a doting grandparent can give the time off. You can see how this could be great for the family, but come across as unfair to nonfamily employees.[52]

There is a way to handle this which is easy to say and hard to do—separate family and business. In those everyday occurrences at work, family members should be treated just like anyone else, with no special status or privileges. Making decisions based on what is best for the firm (a meritocratic philosophy) and what is fair to other employees (the basic idea of equality) is a great way to operate if you can do so without totally alienating your family.

Giving all employees similar privileges, or denying favorable treatment to your family are the options most likely to work overall. When looking at "similar privileges," realize that they do not have to be identical. Letting family and nonfamily members pick and choose from a set of privileges or benefits helps create a situation where people in the firm can opt for working (or not working) in a way that best fits with their needs.

Sometimes, the opposite can happen. Some owners hold expectations that their family should work longer and harder than anyone else, because, after all, it is the family's business.[53] If the family members are working harder without the promise of eventual ownership, they are unlikely to upset nonfamily members. If those family members are believed to be making a down payment of sweat equity for future ownership of the firm, there is a greater possibility of negative employee reaction, since the family members' harder work looks like it could have a large payout in the future. Realize that such situations reflect the creation of a type of career ladder—a sequence of increasingly responsible positions—for family members, with ownership at the top.

In the end, while employee ownership is a possibility (and is discussed as one of the options for firm endings in Chapter 20), it is a rare event. Family firms most often stay in the family. But to treat family and nonfamily as similarly as possible, it becomes especially important to create career ladders for nonfamily members. These may not lead to ownership, but can lead to increased skills, responsibilities, and income. Having career ladders for all employees is a way to help minimize the differences and show how important every employee's contribution is seen to be.

● When it is working well, having multiple generations together in a family business is a great experience. What sort of HR actions are most likely to minimize problems in a family business?

While talking about handling employees, let us jump from the best to the worst. Have you heard the phrase "With privilege comes responsibility"? Where that applies in a family business is when other family members want to saddle your firm with family members who are not a good fit to your business.[54]

If you can find a place where their skills would be a good fit, then you may be able to sidestep a problem. There is another old saying that "For every pot, there is a lid," and that may be the best solution. If you end up saddled with this person, consider putting them to work where they can do the least harm to the business and to your employees. Also, since the family may have guilted you into hiring the person, don't be shy about reversing the process to guilt those same people into helping you make the new family employee toe the line. Obviously, if mentoring, coaching, or training can work to help them do well, those are great ways to resolve a tricky problem.

In the end, disciplining and even firing the relative may be necessary. "Sometimes people think just because they're family, they can take advantage of the rules," says Leon Eastmond, president of A. L. Eastmond & Sons Inc., a second-generation, family-run boiler/tank manufacturing and repair company in New York City. "But I won't tolerate such foolishness. Business is business, and I tell them that I don't dictate the terms of their behavior; the business does. If they don't act properly on the job, they'll be on a slippery banana with this company—even if they're members of the family."[55]

Good Human Resource Practices for All Businesses

As you have seen, there are times when a family business may need to reflect a bit of nepotism but that we recommend a general philosophy of meritocracy in handling employees, both family and nonfamily. This is true for most of the key elements of a good Human Resource (HR) approach. The professional way to craft a consistent HR process depends on a set of key elements:[56]

- Transparent procedures with consistent application: There should be procedures in place to handle the major human resource activities of a firm. They should be publicly known and they should be consistently and fairly applied.
- Job basics: The basics for every job should consist of the job description, which we talked about earlier in the chapter. The version of that job description used after the hire should also explain how this position relates to other jobs, so all people in the firm can be sure what is (and is not) the individual's responsibility.
- Job metrics: It should be possible to objectively evaluate how well someone is doing their job. It is ideal if the metric is clear enough for the employee to be certain that they did the job well or poorly. Note that metrics are not just for after the job. Knowing the metrics to be applied help employees know what is expected on the job.
- Task repair: People will make mistakes. That is true of everyone in business. When that happens, are there processes in place to help the mistake-maker learn what went wrong, and how to do a better job the next time? Knowing that learning (even trial-and-error learning) is a part of the job helps them feel less threatened and helps employees take the initiative when needed.

- Lines of communication: Even good employees can have a valid complaint about something in the firm and need an outlet to express their views. This can be as simple as a suggestion box (wooden or electronic), an open-door policy to hear complaints and suggestions, a special time set aside with your people to talk about their ideas and issues, or an ombudsperson or go-between who confidentially receives the complaints and suggestions and forwards them to the owner.
- Clear termination rules: Mistakes can happen, and will. Some will repeat, and if they do, it may be necessary to fire someone. Other mistakes will be so enormous that firing the person responsible may be the only way to save the firm. When firing is necessary, are the reasons for it clear to all? Are the rules and procedures used known to all, and applied the same way to all people, family and nonfamily alike? Firing is emotionally difficult for everyone, but having procedures that are known, known to be fair, and followed consistently help the process go more smoothly.
- Lines of appeal: Lines of appeal means having a way for the person who has failed to meet a metric, or made a mistake, or is facing firing to have their side of the story heard. In small businesses this can be tough since the owner might be the disciplinarian. In such cases, having a trusted employee (or even an entrepreneur outside the business who knows the business and people and is trusted by the owner) serve as the go-between can help.

Dividing Up Ownership and Dividends

Family businesses can also add complexity to compensation and benefit packages. This typically occurs when family members working in the business receive a compensation or benefits package which looks like it was modeled after the owners' packages instead of the other employees' packages. For example, owners of corporations often receive the base of their compensation as a salary as the CEO of the corporation. In addition, they receive a dividend from the corporation based on company profits and amount of stock owned.

Family members working in the business may also receive a similar package, which raises their annual salary above nonfamily employees in similar positions. The best ways to handle this are to create profit sharing plans or a bonus system for nonfamily employees based on performance.[57] These approaches help give everyone in the firm a stake in the outcome and a tangible benefit for good performance. There is often a temptation to declare salaries and dividends secret and assume you are done with the problem, but in reality few pay plans are secret, and HR-related secrets in most businesses are usually counterproductive.

The benefits problem is tougher to solve. Today, with health benefits so costly and so important to people, family businesses can end up with different levels of health care benefits for owners and employees. That type of difference is a bit easier to take than differences between family and nonfamily employees, since the health of the business directly depends on the health of the owner, not necessarily the other family members.

Obviously the best solution is treating family and nonfamily members the same. There are several possible ways to do this. Offering the higher level of benefits to all employees at a subsidized rate may make it easier for family members to get a superior benefits package without discriminating against other employees. Along these lines, the cost of these higher level of benefits can be paid for employees who are family members using money from the owner's or family's stock dividends.

You may notice that a recurring theme in this section is to treat people as close to the same as possible, and to be transparent and open in policies and communications in general.[58] That open, transparent, equal, and communicative approach is essential to a successful HR policy in the small business or family business. The natural human resource and competitive advantage of a small or family business is realized when the firm treats all of its people "like family." That usually reflects a personal touch, a focus on personal needs, and the flexibility to treat people equally well, even if that does not mean treating each person identically (which is how big businesses end up applying the idea of "equal treatment"). Small businesses and family businesses, especially in their early years, may not be able to afford the compensation and benefit packages of larger businesses, but they often have exceptionally loyal and hard-working employees. Why? Because that "like family" atmosphere in the small or family business makes a tremendous difference for good in a lot of employees. That atmosphere is driven more by open communication and personal concern than through other policies or payouts. That is why the key to successful human resource management in <u>every</u> type of small or family business rests with open communication.

CHAPTER SUMMARY

LO1 Explore the decision to hire full-time or part-time help.

- There are many additional expenses to having a full-time employee as opposed to a part-time employee. You need to consider the pros and cons and expand cautiously.
- The cost of adding an employee includes compensation, training time, employee taxes, and accounting costs.
- Whether you hire a part-time or full-time employee, it is important that the employee values your company's mission.

LO2 Understand how to recruit good employees on your budget.

- For the small business owner, there are inexpensive, alternative methods to consider in attracting and recruiting key employees.
- Networking, Internet recruiting, employee referrals, and company Web sites are several ways to look for talent for your small business. Also consider bartering and internships for part-time employees.
- Hire virtual employees that have experience with being self-motivated and disciplined, including former consultants and freelancers who are accustomed to dealing with deadlines and working independently.
- As you manage your virtual employees, make sure to spend time developing a system of task lists, schedules, and goals with varying time frames and clear deadlines.

LO3 Know how to match the right person to the job.

- The first step in hiring is writing a job description that discusses and reveals all the essential knowledge, skills, and abilities that are needed to fill the position.
- Use the job description to help you evaluate whether an individual would be the right match for the position and your small business.
- Use the information developed in the job description to identify the most important knowledge areas, skills, and abilities the ideal candidate should possess. Next, create specific questions that you will ask of all candidates that will clearly and behaviorally demonstrate to you that they have these critical factors.

LO4 Learn about employee training methods and resources.

- To begin, you should first assess your small firm's training needs from the perspective of the business, the job itself (job description), and the needs of the employees.
- There are two different types of training: initial training and ongoing training.
- There are two broad types of training available to small businesses: on-the-job and off-the-job techniques. Individual circumstances and the where, what, and who of your training program determine which method to use.

LO5 Gain insight in meeting employees' needs and expectations.

- Factors conducive to a positive and rewarding work environment include communication, teamwork, recognition, training, empowerment, and contribution.
- Increasingly, small entrepreneurial companies are implementing formal performance appraisals. Reviewing employees' performance is an ongoing process.
- The performance appraisal sheet should include open-ended questions for the employee to fill out regarding job performance, strengths, areas of development, and what gets in the way of accomplishing the job.

LO6 Learn how to develop a fair compensation and benefit plan.

- One of the first steps in developing a compensation plan is to determine your organization's salary philosophy. The next step is to find comparison factors for salary. Subsequent increases need to be based on employee performance, value, and contribution to the small business.
- Employee bonuses, usually paid in a single lump at the end of the year, are one way of providing performance incentives (consider also profit-sharing plans, stock options, or stock grants early or later on).
- While an employer-sponsored medical insurance plan saves employees money and gives them peace of mind in knowing that they won't be denied coverage, it's not always affordable to the small business owner.

LO7 Understand the complexities of managing family within your business.

- The family business owner needs to strike a balance between nepotism and meritocracy with which they can live.
- Treating everyone in the business the same is the best approach for minimizing the problems arising from favoring family members.

- Having open and transparent human resource policies and practices can help family and nonfamily businesses run more effectively.
- In all businesses, open communication is the key to effective human resource management.

KEY TERMS

employee fit, 608
probationary period, 609
Internet recruiting, 612
employee referral, 612
virtual employees, 613
job description, 614
on-the-job training, 619
psychological contract, 621
open-book policy, 621
living wage, 624
nepotism, 628
meritocracy, 628

DISCUSSION QUESTIONS

1. As a small business owner, you will most likely have the opportunity to hire either part-time or full-time employees. What do you need to consider in determining which one will be best for you and when to hire the first or another employee for your business?
2. Whether you hire a part-time or full-time employee, in what ways can you ensure that each type of employee knows and values your company's mission?
3. While a smaller firm can actually outperform large businesses in attracting high-quality employees, how can you communicate to the job market the multiple benefits of working within your firm? How can you get the word out about these advantages in a cost-effective manner?
4. What are the multiple benefits of hiring virtual employees for your small business? What are some of the ways to manage and foster productivity among your virtual employees? Are there any drawbacks to these methods?
5. What recommendations or suggestions would you give Paige Arnof-Fenn, founder and CEO of Mavens & Moguls, on how to manage and "orchestrate" her multiple virtual employees?
6. What are some of the different ways small business owners can write a job description for the first time? How can they ensure that they cover all the essential knowledge, skills, and abilities that are needed for the position? Why is this important?
7. As a new small business owner, what can you do to make sure you hire the right person for the job? This is probably one of the most difficult decisions you may be faced with making, especially since we all are not trained in the art and science of hiring employees.
8. What specific training guidelines would you incorporate into your business? What inexpensive techniques (on-the-job training) can you use after you make the first hire? Did the owner of the business where you are employed use any of these techniques with you? If so, how beneficial were they to your own development and learning?
9. What are creative ways that you can retain your first employee and ensure you are meeting his or her needs? Consider how you can meet or exceed the employee's "psychological contract."
10. Consider your previous employment position; did the firm have an open-book philosophy? How much information was shared regarding the strategy and financials of the business? What are the advantages and disadvantages of sharing too much or too little information with employees, particularly from a small business owner perspective?
11. Managing health care costs is one of the biggest concerns for small business owners; what are some creative ways that they can minimize some of these costs? In your own community, how have owners confronted these concerns and costs? Be specific with types and the size of the small firms you believe are being innovative in how they manage health care costs.
12. As mentioned by Dr. David Gage, clinical psychologist, "Families don't need written guidelines to operate, but family businesses do." What are some initial guidelines that should be defined in the family business?
13. As mentioned, one of the most common problems in a family business is the hiring of relatives who do not have talent to fulfill the necessary job responsibilities. What can you do if you are "stuck" with an unproductive family member to ensure that he or she does not disturb the work and interfere with the operations of the business?

EXPERIENTIAL EXERCISES

1. At ReCellular, Inc., a cellular phone remanufacturing company in Ann Arbor, Michigan, the small business owner put together a list of interview questions that immediately improved the hiring process. The owner first defined the qualities, characteristics, and basic aptitude he wanted to find in a potential remanufacturing employee. The owner wanted to find people who shared these characteristics:

    - Excellent attendance and dependability
    - Flexibility
    - Integrity and honesty
    - Motivated and dedicated
    - Detail-oriented
    - Team-oriented
    - Strong work ethic
    - Positive, polite, and approachable
    - Continuous improvement oriented
    - Good communication skills
    - Actual hands-on demonstration of capability to sort phones and identify cosmetic problems with phones

    The owner then worked with several online resources to structure questions that would indicate whether candidates had these characteristics. No list of questions is totally comprehensive; however, these questions are helping the interviewers find better candidates:

    - What made you decide to apply at ReCellular?
    - Tell me about yourself and your last/current job/class.
    - When we call your previous employer for references, what are they likely to tell us in regard to your dependability/attendance?
    - Tell me about a time when you demonstrated your trustworthiness or integrity in school or at work.

    This is, of course, a start—your job is to think of other questions that the small business owner may want to ask a potential employee (either for a full-time, part-time, or virtual assistant position).

2. WWW You have just been asked by a small business owner to uncover U.S. and state laws that are relevant to managing people (in the future, when the small business owner is interested in hiring). Go to Businesslaw.gov and obtain three to four critical areas of information about specific laws within your state regarding: hiring issues, wage laws, taxes, health and safety, and termination.

3. WWW Small business owner Jeff Birdsell opened Shauncey's Gourmet Ice Cream, Inc., in Battlefield Shopping Center in Springfield, Missouri. Like any small business owner, Jeff Birdsell realized that starting this venture would entail a tremendous commitment of time and energy. He had expected to work 60–80 hours a week indefinitely, and finds he works at least that. He estimates that he and his parents frequently tally up to 250 hours per week in the organization. Employee turnover at Shauncey's runs at 100 percent per year. What creative and innovative hiring and retention recommendations would you give Jeff as he manages both his family and part-time workers (especially with 100 percent employee turnover)?

MINI-CASE

VIVID SKY EMPLOYEE WAVE 3

It was 2006 and Vivid Sky's sole product, SkyBOX, had survived its pilot test. Designed as an in-stadium information service for fans, SkyBOX offered video feeds, statistics, infographics (like graphics of the last 10 pitches, last 10 hits, etc.), maps, live chats and voting, and in-seat ordering. All of this was delivered by wireless PDAs (think of a Palm Pilot) "hardened" to withstand dropping and spilled liquids.

SkyBOX got to this stage because of three different waves of employees. Founder Tim Hayden was tech savvy, but lacked the skills to write the code that would meld all of these different streams of data into one application. The first wave of programmers worked with Tim at his full-time employer. They shared Tim's love of sports and passion for using technology to revitalize the stadium experience. Together they created the overall design of the program and an interactive demo to show potential investors. These employees worked nights and weekends with no expectations. Since they couldn't put more time (and money) into the project, they decided to move on to other projects once Tim had a working model.

Tim used the local network he built as SkyBOX developed to recruit the next group of programmers. This group was even more skilled, and they were able to dedicate the time to build a "basic" application. For this, Tim was able to pay them a small amount as he continued to bootstrap the company. Unfortunately, they found that they lacked the time to take the SkyBOX to the level of refinement customers and investors were asking for. Lacking equity in the business, they left on their own when Tim asked them to.

The third wave of programmers had more time and wanted to take the "basic" SkyBOX to the next level. This group, recruited from across the country based on Tim's SkyBOX promotional trips, created a highly interactive application that was used for Vivid Sky's first stadium deployment. Because of their dedication, Tim decided to give the developers a bonus in the form of equity.

But the third wave of programmers faced two major challenges. Vivid Sky was receiving requests from numerous sports properties for national and international events, and the current development team couldn't keep up with the new opportunities. Also the current programmers were untested developers for the iPhone and iPod touch platform, which was the future of the company.

Tim faced the prospect of asking the third wave of programmers to leave Vivid Sky and give up their salaries and equity. He wasn't sure all of them would do this voluntarily, and he wasn't sure he could afford to share more of his own equity with a fourth wave of programmers. On the other hand, he knew his current programmers couldn't handle the conversion to the new platform. If he fires the programmers who don't go voluntarily, will it hamper efforts to recruit the fourth wave of programmers?

CASE DISCUSSION QUESTIONS

1. What were the differences in the sources of employees for Vivid Sky as it developed?
2. What are the benefits and problems of using equity to compensate employees? What about using pay?
3. How could Tim have managed the third wave of employees if he had hired them right off the bat?
4. Should Tim replace the third wave of programmers? If yes, how do you recommend he go about this doing this? Can you find a way for him to protect his share of the equity he has in the business?

SUGGESTED CASES AND ARTICLES

- Alaska Wildland Adventures

Available on PRIMIS:

- Compensation at Carrington: The New Pay Plan

SUGGESTED VIDEOS

Video Case:

- Unique Vacation Policy, p. VC-8

eClips Videos:

- Jessica Bibliowicz Discusses Managing People and Getting the Best from Employees
- Michael Crooke States Importance of Hiring People Who Have Passion

SBTV Videos:

- Keeping the Employees Happy
- Should Your Small Business Hire Illegal Aliens?
- How to Fire a Problem Employee
- Help Wanted for the New First Time

STVP Videos:

- Take Care of Your Employees
- Defining Company Culture
- Attracting People in the Early Stages

CHAPTER 20

Achieving Success in the Small Business

● From tires to wholesale foods to sporting goods, Shoppers' Service evolved spinoffs, grew larger and smaller, and changed hands over the 42 years of its existence. By remaining flexible, creative, and committed, the owners enjoyed these changes—and made good profits, as well. How are you encouraged about small business ownership as a result of reading this story?

LEARNING OBJECTIVES

LO

This chapter will help you:

- **LO1** Know how to recognize the stages of the small business life cycle.
- **LO2** Understand the four types of firm-level growth strategies.
- **LO3** Understand the options for harvesting or closing the small business.
- **LO4** Know the firm-level critical success factors for small business.
- **LO5** Understand what success means with the quadruple bottom line.

Focus on Small Business: The Many Lives of Shoppers' Service Store

From 1962 to 2004, Shoppers' Service was an entrepreneurial company serving a variety of customer needs. Originally founded as a discount department store—sort of a mini-Walmart—in Memphis in 1962, its original owners, three European immigrants to Memphis—Morris, Sol, and Karl—combined their money, skills, and energy to start the business. Each had prior experience in small business ownership, and with their combined savings, contacts, and experience, Shoppers' grew to encompass the mini-discount store, a second store branch in the suburbs, a sporting goods wholesaling warehouse, a food wholesaling company, a tire store, and three pharmacies.

Along the way, the partners decided to go their separate ways. First Karl asked to leave, and he was given the pharmacies and tire store as his share of the assets. A few years later Sol left, taking with him the suburban branch discount store. Working solo, Morris sold off the warehouse and the original store, keeping the food wholesaling company going as his major source of income.

At each change in the business, the partners obtained expert assistance, working with attorneys, accountants, and industry consultants to make sure the valuations of the businesses were fairly determined. They also worked with the experts to minimize tax burdens on each of the soon-to-be separated firms and owners.

When Shoppers' closed with the death of Morris in 2004, the business had gone through three owners, five changes of its legal structure, over one dozen additions and deletions of subsidiary business entities, and forty-two years of profitable operations. Along the way it supported more than a dozen members of the three owners' families, and, at its peak, nearly twenty other employees. For all of that, the story of Shoppers' Service is like millions of other small businesses that start, grow, survive, and eventually succeed.

DISCUSSION QUESTIONS

1. How would you describe the stages in the life of Shoppers' Service Store?
2. How did Shoppers' Service make use of outside help?
3. How do you imagine long-term customers would describe Shoppers' Service over the years?
4. How successful would you say Shoppers' Service was as a business?

Small Business Life Cycle

LO1 Know how to recognize the stages of the small business life cycle.

business life cycle
The sequence or pattern of developmental stages any business goes through during its life span.

Like every person, every small business is unique. But just as we all go through childhood and adolescence on the way to adulthood, as we saw with Shoppers' Service, so do small businesses. There is a lot of predictability in this growth process, and knowing the developmental stages of the **business life cycle** can help you better understand your business and your career as a small business owner. The small business life cycle is shown in Figure 20.1.

Several models exist for the life cycle of the small business firm.[1] Each divides the stages a bit differently. But all models have the same general ideas: (1) there are multiple stages, (2) the key issues, actions, and lessons at each stage are different from the other stages, and (3) the level of risk the business faces changes from stage to stage.

For most small businesses, though, the usual sequence of stages is emergence, existence, survival, success, and resource maturity. Let's look at each of these stages to see what they involve for the small business and the key issue you can expect to face in each. These stages and business growth patterns are shown in Figure 20.1.[2]

Emergence

Morris, Sol, and Karl were friends before they opened the business, and over several years they talked about a variety of business prospects before finally settling on Shoppers' Service. They were engaged in the stage called *emergence,* in which a person thinks about and takes actions toward starting a firm. Typically a lot more people think about starting a firm than actually take steps to do so. In 2002, 50 percent of the general population expressed an interest in owning their own firm, and among young adults, the rate was an even higher 80 percent. But in 2002, only 7 percent of the population was actually taking steps to start a firm.[3]

Getting from entrepreneurial thinking to entrepreneurial action is the challenge of the emergence stage.[4] Two techniques discussed earlier in the book can help you move from thought to action. One is using the BRIE behaviors from the Chapter 1 checklist to start on the road to creating a firm. The other is to get into business part time (as discussed in Chapter 5) as a way to lay a foundation for future entrepreneurial action.

Existence

When Shoppers' Service opened in 1962, the three partners had a lot of ideas, a fair amount of merchandise, an absolutely certain set of overhead costs, and no guarantee of sales. Sales did come, but it was a rocky first couple of years. This is typical of the *existence* stage, which is defined by having the business in operation, but not yet stable in terms of markets, operations, or finances. In 2002, according to the GEM study, about 4.5 percent of Americans were involved with businesses in their existence stage. Existence is the second riskiest period after emergence. The reason risk is so

FIGURE 20.1

The Small Firm Life Cycle

Sources: Adapted from Churchill and Lewis (1983), Baumol (1968), Chandler and Hanks (1994), and Katz and Gartner (1988).

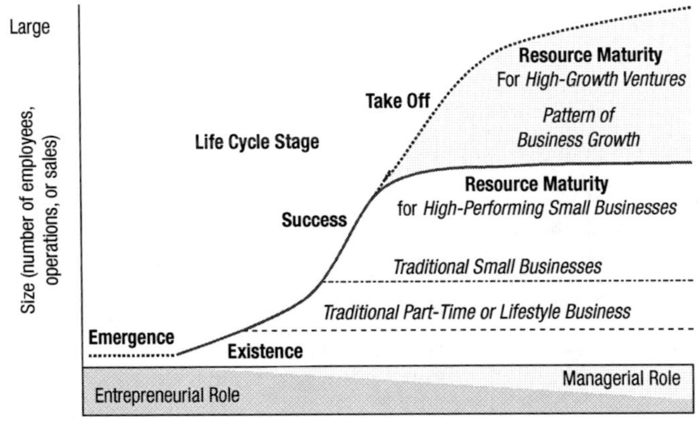

high is that many business owners lack the key information or experiences they need in marketing, production, and management.[5] The problems of mastering these three areas form what are called the **liabilities of newness** for small businesses in their existence stage.

liability of newness
The set of risks faced by firms early in their life cycles that comes from a lack of knowledge by the owners about the business they are in and by customers about the new business.

The solutions for liabilities of newness come from getting expertise as quickly as possible. For most owners of firms, personally getting more experience is risky because it takes too long. The safer way is to obtain help from others. As noted in Chapter 2, developing an extensive social network is essential for the success of any firm. Whether you use family, friends, industry contacts, or free or paid advisers, getting help helps you survive.

Success

Woody Allen once said that "Eighty percent of success is showing up,"[6] and it seems to be particularly true for small businesses transitioning from existence to success. The success stage occurs once the firm is established in its market. For Shoppers' Service, success came in the 1970s, when it was well known in the local market and started to have the profits for expansion. Success stage firms show consistently growing financial performance, usually with slowly rising sales.

Firms at this stage develop the information, skills, and most importantly the routines to grow the business's profits. Those profits aren't always taken in the form of money. Time off from work, a slower pace at work, or hiring additional personnel to take on more of the tasks of the owner are all ways that these profits can be used to make the owner's life easier. Used that way, the extra profits are called **slack resources** by economists, because they can be rechanneled into the business if needed. For most owners, though, these profits are called *flexibility.* All new businesses—from small businesses to high-growth firms—go through this stage. For most small business owners, this is a stage that lasts a long time. For the owners of high-growth businesses, this is only a chance to catch their breath and lay the groundwork for the period of takeoff.

slack resources
Profits that are available to be used to satisfy the preferences of the owner in how the business is run.

Resource Maturity

For most small businesses, resource maturity will follow the success stage. This stage is characterized by a stable level of sales and profits over several years. At this stage, the functional areas, the market, and the products or services are all being dealt with consistently and efficiently. The challenge of maturity is to avoid complacency. Shoppers' Service was able to sidestep that problem because of its changes in what would have been the maturity years, as the partners broke up and took pieces of the business with them, requiring adaptation. After years of consistency, customers and businesses can begin to take each other for granted. For your business, that can be deadly, because a competitor can come to your customer, show personal interest and competitive products or services or prices, and take your customer away. Since the rule of thumb is that getting a new customer costs five times as much as keeping an existing customer,[7] every lost customer is important. How do you avoid customer complacency?

Supersalesman Zig Ziglar says he learned from Australian psychologist Joseph Braysich the four key components for staving off customer complacency—recency, frequency, potency, and recommendation:[8]

- **Recency:** Be among the people your customers have seen in the past few days. Do this through magnetic business cards on their file cabinet, a phone call or e-mail to make sure they have everything they need, or a thank-you note saying that you appreciate their business.
- **Frequency:** You never know when your competitors will show up, so to make recency work, you have to stay in touch with customers on a frequent basis. This might be on a quarterly or monthly basis in cases where customers buy only a few times a year, but contacts can even be on a daily basis if that is how often customers buy from you. All forms of contact count here—visits, phone calls, e-mails, newsletters, business letters, and so on.
- **Potency:** Did you ever see a funny TV advertisement but a few days later could only recall the joke, but not the company being advertised? The problem was the potent part of the ad—the joke—was not related to the important part of the message—the business. When you contact customers, your message has to remind them that your firm values their business. A potent message is one that is remembered, and remembered for the right reasons.

- **Recommendation:** We all seek recommendations. It is a powerful way to get help and advice. Your customers hopefully see you and your firm as experts in certain areas of business. After all, you've been in business for years at this point. Making clear recommendations that can help your customers provides a memorable way to show that you think about, understand, and care about your customers and their business.

Takeoff

Although rare among small businesses, one possible complication is when the success stage leads into takeoff rather than resource maturity. Takeoff happens if a business embarks on a period of exceptional growth. For small businesses, it might come from landing an unexpectedly gigantic contract, expanding into multiple locations, or just being in the right place at the right time, as was the case for Sun-Hill Industries when it created the Stuff-a-Pumpkin.

The challenge Sun-Hill and other firms face in the possible takeoff stage is to understand the nature and demands of growth and get some control over it. Managing takeoff involves working extensively with potential sources of funding and other key resources, as well as working with markets outside and employees within the firm. It also often entails relearning the processes that led to this level of success, as a growth-oriented firm often needs to do things differently from one content with maintaining a stable state. One example of this is outsourcing or subcontracting for the growth-oriented firm to let the firm stay focused on its own key competencies. A growing nursery might subcontract out its bookkeeping and human resources functions so the managers at the nursery can focus on increasing sales and managing the expansion.

It is important to remember that most small businesses never go through the takeoff stage, and for those that do, the takeoff path often moves them into the high-growth firm model (discussed next) and away from small business. For firms that don't reach a possible takeoff stage situation, the jump is from the success stage to the resource maturity stage.

The lesson of the life cycle model of business is that much of your firm's development as a business is predictable within some broad terms. Knowing the stages of the life cycle and where your firm is among those stages can serve as a powerful reminder of the kinds of issues for which you need to watch. Knowing the different possible life cycle paths for the resource maturity stage makes it possible to clearly choose when to grow, and what to expect if a higher-growth approach is in the cards for your firm.

SMALL BUSINESS INSIGHT

SUCCESS = OPPORTUNITY + DANGER

Stuff-a-Pumpkins are the pumpkin-colored leaf bags you see on lawns around Halloween. You know the ones—they have a jack-o-lantern's face on them. They were the brainchild of Anita Dembiczak and Ben Zinbarg. Zinbarg's company, Sun-Hill Industries, had been operating consistently for 17 years in Stamford, Connecticut. When he came up with the idea, he spent his own money to get the first run of bags made. They sold out instantly at the discount stores where he tried them out. The stores clamored for more and demanded immediate delivery! But Dembiczak's, Zinbarg's, and Sun-Hill's finances were tapped out, and the discount stores were months away from paying for the bags they'd sold. Zinbarg went to his business banker, who refused to extend credit, even though Ben had contracts from big retailers. Twenty-three other banks also turned Ben down. He got the money needed to get out the next order by investing all his remaining personal money, securing a loan from a friend, and convincing suppliers and employees to delay receiving money owed them. He got the bags made and out to the retailers. But competitors meanwhile started to copy his bag, so he took the remaining money and started legal proceedings against these concept pirates.[9] Eventually he succeeded in getting the pirates on the run, but Zinbarg probably came to a new understanding of why the Chinese term for crisis consists of the symbols for opportunity and danger.[10]

Growth Strategies

As entrepreneurs come to develop an understanding of their firm, from the planning process or from getting into the business itself, they usually find that they have the chance to decide the overall growth strategy for their firm. The *overall growth strategy* describes the kind of business the owner (or owners) would like to have, from the perspective of how fast and to what level they would like the firm to grow. There are four generic growth strategies that account for nearly all businesses. They are:

LO2 Understand the four types of firm-level growth strategies.

- **Lifestyle or part-time firms**: These typically have sales of $25,000 a year or less, which provides enough profit or salary to supplement an income but usually not enough on which to live. These businesses start and stay very small, often operating seasonally or when the owner wants to work in the business. Growth in these firms tends to quickly level off after the owners operate long enough to learn the basics of making money in their industry and setting. About 53 percent of all small businesses fall into this category. (See Figure 20.2.)
- **Traditional small businesses**: These are the smallest full-time businesses, with schedules defined by customer, not owner, needs. Most often, these are one-site businesses with sales of between $25,000 and $100,000. Growth levels off after operations settle into a consistent, money-making pattern, generating enough income to provide a living for the owner and family. Around 22 percent of small businesses fall into this category.
- **High-performing small businesses**: These tend to level off after the success stage, with sales of between $100,000 and $1,000,000, depending on the industry. These firms grow at rates more like 5 to 15 percent a year, adding employees, and often growing through multiple locations and higher levels of professionalization, in order to maximize their profitability over a long term, while reaching a plateau that lets them remain manageably small. Many of the millionaires Stanley and Danko described in *The Millionaire Next Door* had businesses in this range. About 20 percent of businesses fall into this category, including Shoppers' Service.
- **High-growth ventures**: These aim to achieve growth rates of 25 percent or more a year, with sales of more than $1 million. These businesses typically go through all the stages, but include takeoff before going through resource maturity. These firms aim to become big businesses and pursue high levels of professionalization and external funding. Such firms represent about 5 percent of all businesses.

For many entrepreneurs, the milestone of financial success comes when they can call themselves millionaires. Usually this reflects having $1 million in assets over and above their home. Entrepreneurs in surviving high-growth ventures and high-performing small businesses achieve these levels of wealth within 5 to 15 years. For owners in traditional small businesses, it is a rarer event, and even for those who achieve millionaire status, it comes after 25 to 30 years of work.

lifestyle or part-time firm
A small business primarily intended to provide partial or subsistence financial support for the existing lifestyle of the owner, most often through operations that fit the owner's schedule and way of working.

traditional small business
A firm intended to provide a living income to the owner, and operating in a manner and on a schedule consistent with other firms in the industry and market.

high-performing small business
A firm intended to provide the owner with a high income through sales or profits superior to those of the traditional small business.

high-growth venture
A firm started with the intent of eventually going public, following the pattern of growth and operations of a big business.

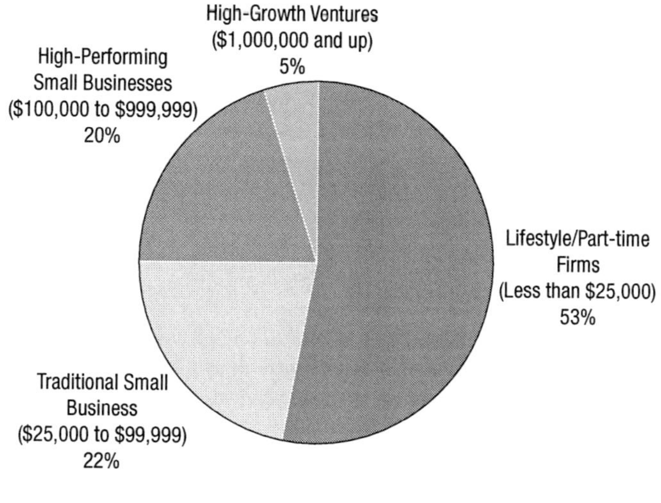

FIGURE 20.2
Types of Firms

The lesson of *The Millionaire Next Door* was that wealth is achieved more often by frugality, saving, and careful investment over years than by windfall profits from the business. That said, it is possible to purposely grow a business. The two key approaches to doing this is by either growing the sales or by introducing new technologies.

Sales growth can come from any of several ways. The most straightforward is by increasing sales to existing steady customers—by selling more of the same or by expanding your offerings. If you have a good relationship with your customers, they may well tell you what other items they would like to buy from you instead of other vendors. A related way is to return to occasional customers and see what you can do to make them into steady customers. If you can afford it, expanding into areas where you may have a small customer base is another way to grow sales, counting on the established customers to help you improve sales through word-of-mouth.

Technological growth can take two forms: using technology to improve efficiencies and profits, or by using technology to create new products or services. Just as the personal computer dramatically dropped the cost of getting aspects of business done, such as designing and printing flyers or maintaining a real-time inventory, moving aspects of business to the Internet can facilitate another wave of innovation as more sophisticated business procedures become economically and procedurally accessible to you as an entrepreneur. Meanwhile, technology continuously offers new products and enables new services, both of which offer new opportunities for sales, and even new markets. Whether we are talking about complex approaches like nanotechnology or basic technologies like those behind gasohol, there is a constant stream of new ideas coming out of universities as well as your customers, employees, and other individuals with ideas about new ways of doing things. The trick is being open to these and knowing how to analyze the many ideas you will find to identify the one which you can add value to, and from which you and the idea's inventor can benefit. We talked about analyzing ideas in Chapter 4, and as you think about finding the idea which can make you a millionaire, the lessons of feasibility should always be in the back of your mind.

It is also worthwhile to note that most of the individuals who do find that successful market or technological expansion continue to work even after they become millionaires. For most entrepreneurs, achieving the million dollar milestone is not an end in itself, it is just a benchmark along the way. They continue to work because most often it is easier to work than to think about what they would do without the business. As we will see in the rest of this chapter, sometimes, successes may be easier than endings.

Closing the Small Business

LO3 Understand the options for harvesting or closing the small business.

As we note in Chapter 1, about 1 million businesses start each year, or about 1 million firms move into the existence stage of the life cycle each year. This sounds like a lot of activity, and it is important for our economy, but the really high levels of activity happen farther along in the life cycle. Every year, nearly 4 million firms go through changes in ownership or existence.

The type of exit is important not only for the entrepreneur, but also for the larger community. About half of all workers in the United States work in small firms, and when firms close down, small business employees lose jobs. There are also ripples throughout the community as other firms lose the business they got from the closing firm and its employees and as the larger community has one less source for goods or services. Entrepreneurial exits which transfer ownership have a greater chance of continuing the jobs, purchases, and product/service deliveries on which the community and its members depend.

harvest
Recover value through a sale of a firm or its assets.

initial public offering (IPO)
Transfer method describing the first-time public sale of a stock listed on a public stock exchange.

The ideal goal for most entrepreneurs is to be able to **harvest** from the firm some of the value of the hard work they put into it over the years. For the owners, a central goal of a harvest is to get the maximum value they can for their business.[11] Often the harvest will represent their last major return from the firm and a key pool of money for retirement or further businesses.

Some of the ways harvests take place are so well known they have become part of our everyday language. For example an **initial public offering** or IPO is where a business sells its stock to the public on a major stock exchange. Google's IPO in 2004 was a famous example, but there were only 71 IPOs in 2004 out of 4 million firm transitions.

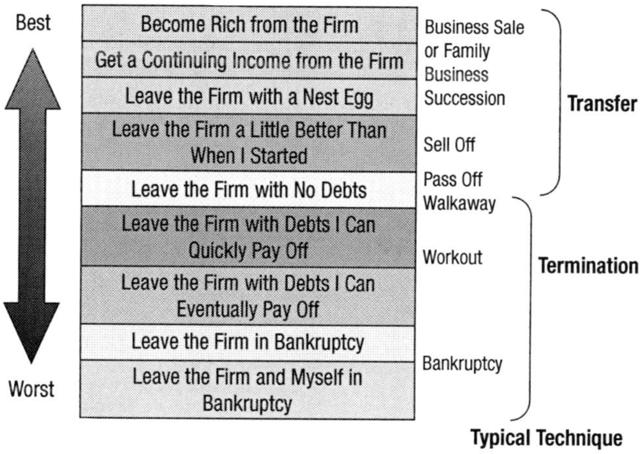

FIGURE 20.3

The Hierarchy of Business Outcomes

Other techniques are similar and nearly equally rare. *Mergers and acquisitions* are where one firm combines (i.e., merges) or absorbs (acquires) another through a purchase. In 2006, there were 9,235 mergers and acquisitions in the United States,[12] with most of these involving multibillion dollar companies like NBC and Vivendi. A similar approach is called **consolidation** and involves a company buying up many smaller competitors to form a giant firm, such as the case of how Blockbuster Video was originally created, but consolidations account for only a few thousand purchases all year. An **employee stock ownership plan** (ESOP) is a special tax-protected way to sell a firm to its employees, but these are very rare, accounting for around 11,000 businesses in the United States[13] altogether, and fewer than 100 are done in any year.[14]

So what does happen to the other 4 million businesses? There are two general possibilities for most small businesses. About half of the changes are **transfers**, which involve moving ownership from one legal entity, person, or group to another. Examples of transfers include selling a business in whole or in part, or arranging a succession of the business between family members, or giving the firm as a gift to someone who will keep the business a going concern. The other half are **terminations**, which refer to the methods for closing down a business, and include three major methods—walkaways, workouts, and bankruptcies.

As mentioned above, the goal of the owners is ideally to obtain value from the firm when they transfer or terminate it, but that goal sits at the top of a hierarchy of business outcomes that are a part of the way every owner thinks about their firm. The hierarchy is shown in Figure 20.3. The top of the hierarchy describes situations in which the owner leaves the firm with substantial funding, while the other extreme has situations of bankruptcy. Obviously owners would prefer to end up as high on the hierarchy as possible, and transfers are the technique that yield those results.

consolidation
A transfer method in which a small business is bought by a larger firm for the purpose of quickly growing the larger firm.

employee stock ownership plan
A formalized legal method to transfer some or all of the ownership of a business to its employees.

transfer
An endgame strategy in which ownership is moved from one person or group to another.

termination
An endgame strategy in which the owner closes down a business.

Transfers

In 2003, around 860,000 firms were transferred within the family, a process called *family business succession*. That year nearly 1 million *business sales* took place, where the business was transferred to people other than family. Successions and business sales generally occur only among the largest small businesses, such as high-performing small businesses and high-growth ventures, because only these firms generate the kinds of cash flows and profits that make paying the former owner possible.

Regardless of the method used for transferring or harvesting, the key issue remains the same—doing it well. All transfers are legally, financially, and operationally complex, but need to be done well. Because, between the federal and state taxes on transfers, on portions of larger estates, and on capital gains, a business can lose as much as half its value to the government.

There are three classes of strategies for managing transfers within a family.[15] One strategy is called **liquidity enhancement**, arranging (usually through a life insurance policy in your name held by your heirs) to generate cash to cover the estate taxes. A second strategy is called **tax management**, in which you structure your transfer to make tax payments as small and as manageable as possible. This includes selling small portions of your business to your heirs for cash or promissory notes (with

liquidity enhancement
An estate planning strategy which focuses on generating cash to cover likely estate taxes.

tax management
An estate planning strategy which focuses on minimizing estate tax payments.

the lowest legal interest rate possible). If done the right way (which requires a lawyer's help), this results in giving the heirs 14 years to pay for the shares with only interest payments necessary for the first five years. There are literally dozens of other tax management methods. The third strategy is called an **estate freeze** and depends on moving assets from the entrepreneur to the heirs when they are worth less. There are several methods for doing this including family limited partnerships and grantor retained annuity trusts (GRAT).

estate freeze
An estate planning strategy which focuses on transferring assets to heirs when the asset costs are low.

Strategies can be combined as in the case of a charitable bailout where the entrepreneur puts the business into a tax management technique called a charitable remainder trust, getting income from the trust. After the entrepreneur dies, a life insurance policy on the entrepreneur held by the heirs—the classic liquidity enhancement approach—generates the cash to buy the business from the trust, with the purchase price going to a charity.

Current federal laws governing estate taxes on business transfers are changing on a yearly basis until 2011.[16] Meanwhile many states are decoupling their own estate tax laws from the federal approach.[17] In estate planning the best advice is to enlist the aid of lawyers and accountants with expertise in estate planning and in business buying and selling, and leave time to let the transfers take place in ways that minimize the tax burden on everyone.

bankruptcy
An extreme form of business termination which uses a legal method for closing a business and paying off creditors when debts are substantially greater than assets.

walkaways
Business terminations in which the entrepreneur ends the business with its obligations met.

For most part-time businesses and traditional small businesses, the firm cannot easily be sold because it does not generate enough profits to pay a current owner and a former owner. In such cases, the original owner must decide if it makes sense to close the business down and lose all invested value, or transfer the business in a way that lets some of the value be realized.

Several approaches are available. For small firms these include approaches such as a *pass off,* which happens when the owner realizes there is little chance of being able to sell the firm, but in the interest of keeping the firm going, or providing employees with a source of income, the owner gives the firm to someone as a gift, without compensation. In a 1998 survey of family business transfers, around 38 percent of firms used gifts as a major way to transfer ownership.[18] For pass offs, legal and accounting advice is necessary to make sure that the owner leaves all financial and tax obligations with the firm, permitting a clean exit.

Another typical form is the *sell off.* In this approach the assets of a firm—perhaps including the customer list, real estate, and even the inventory—are sold to another business, with the proceeds used to pay off the firm's remaining debts, and perhaps leaving the owner some small profit. Often the purchasing firm absorbs the assets, so the customers or real estate appear to move to another business. Transfers are estimated in the tens of thousands annually, but reliable statistics are hard to come by. The key to a successful sell off is finding customers for the assets and determining a price for the different assets. For assets that lead to revenue, such as customer lists or working real estate, it is typically possible to get an amount ranging from one-half year to two years profits from the asset, with more possible for negotiators with information on comparable deals.

Bankruptcy is the most extreme business closing situation, which occurs when the business has such high debt that it cannot reasonably expect to earn back the funds required by its creditors. A lawyer's involvement can help owners protect as much of their personal assets as possible throughout the process and eventually recover their financial standing.

Terminations

There are nearly as many terminations as transfers—around 1.8 million a year. Terminations are more likely for young firms, those four years old and less.[19] As noted, there are three types of terminations—walkaways, workouts, and bankruptcies. In a walkaway the entrepreneur ends the business with its obligations met. In a workout the firm's legal or financial obligations are not fully met at closing,[20] while **bankruptcy** refers to a legal method for closing a business and paying off creditors in extreme situations, and is quite rare with less than 50,000 in 2008–2009.[21]

Walkaways

A **walkaway** describes the single most typical way businesses close down. Walkaways are businesses that close down with all debts paid. The entrepreneur might consider the business successful or unsuccessful at closing. About one-third of closing firms, around 600,000 a year, are considered by their owners to be successful, with the business ending voluntarily, often due to illness, old age, family moves, and choosing new opportunities.[22]

A successful walkaway depends on the owner having completed meeting all the firm's financial and organizational obligations. The goal in closing a business is "doing it right"—being able to walk away from the business with a sense of satisfaction.[23] The factors that lead to this include:

- All bills are paid off (or scheduled).
- All taxes are paid up, and the various levels of government are informed of the closure.
- Contracts, leases, and the like are fulfilled or formally terminated.
- Employees are let go as they find other jobs.
- Assets or inventory are depleted.
- No lawsuits consuming money and time.
- Customers placed so they get needed goods or services.
- If needed, insurance is continued to cover unexpected claims after the firm closes.

Workouts and Bankruptcy

In a **workout**, the entrepreneur feels that the business was less than successful, usually because of the result of poor use of the firm's human or financial assets, with an unsatisfying business experience (e.g., not enough leisure time, not enough time for family needs, too much conflict, not good at selling, etc.) the second most likely reason.[24] In a workout the entrepreneur arranges to pay off all debts, often doing this after the business is officially closed. This approach accounts for about one-half of all business closings, or roughly 1 million closings.

workout
A form of business termination in which the firm's legal or financial obligations are not fully met at closing.

In preparing the workout, the owner personally makes arrangements to pay off creditors. Often this involves asking for extended terms and smaller payments. The money for these payments might come from the sale or refinancing of a home, through selling business and personal assets, cashing out pensions or stocks, money from personal bank loans, or credit card advances. Most often, the funds come from a mixture of these efforts as well as from paychecks as the former owner becomes an employee for someone else.

In walkaways and workouts, a key goal for entrepreneurs is to maintain their goodwill and reputation in the business community, often as a means of maintaining trust for future entrepreneurial efforts. All small businesses face tough times, and entrepreneurs are often willing to extend terms to a former entrepreneur (and customer) who has fallen on hard times. As long as they feel confident they will get their money from the former owner and their own cash situation is not life-or-death tight, they are likely to accept extended terms.

When facing severe difficulties in arranging a payback, one worthwhile strategy is to enlist the aid of a consumer credit bureau. These agencies provide low-cost debt reduction advice and have experience in negotiating repayment schedules and making credit bureaus aware of debt remediation efforts. A good source for finding these bureaus in your area is to use the Web site of the National Foundation for Credit Counseling (http://www.nfcc.org/), which is the professional association for nonprofit credit counseling agencies. Your local Small Business Development Center can also refer you to local credit counseling agencies with small business experience.

In the more extreme cases of closing, entrepreneurs are so far in debt at the business's end that they have little or no chance to earn the money to pay back all the major debts. In such cases owners and firms need to declare bankruptcy. Because bankruptcy is a formal legal situation and one handled in the courts, it is important to involve a lawyer early in the process. The lawyer will not only help you work out the legal papers but will advise you on restructuring your debt and taking other actions to protect as much of your personal assets as possible.

Bankruptcy, you will recall from Chapter 13, is the legal form of insolvency, where liabilities are greater than assets. There are three forms of bankruptcy: Chapter 7, Chapter 11, and Chapter 13. Chapter 11 bankruptcy is the type you hear about big businesses declaring. It allows the firm to reorganize its operations and renegotiate with creditors to forgive some of the debt (desirable, but not legally required of the creditors) and lengthen payments for the remaining debt. Small firms can apply for Chapter 11, but the high costs of administering a Chapter 11 bankruptcy makes it rare in small businesses.

reorganization
The popular name for a Chapter 13 bankruptcy in which a bankrupt firm continues to operate while paying off debts identified by the bankruptcy trustee.

liquidation
The popular name for a Chapter 7 bankruptcy in which a bankrupt firm's assets are sold by the bankruptcy trustee and the proceeds used to pay the firm's debts.

A more common variant for smaller firms is **reorganization** using a Chapter 13 bankruptcy. Like Chapter 11, the firm stays in business, and the remaining debt gets renegotiated so that a portion of it is forgiven if the remainder is paid off from your income over a set period of time. The bankruptcy court has to approve your filing Chapter 13 before you can, and there are several limits as to the amount and type of debt you face.

If you don't qualify for Chapter 13, you will face a Chapter 7 bankruptcy. It is the well-known example of **liquidation** where all of your assets—business, cars, home—can be sold with the proceeds given to your creditors. You get to keep your clothes and household goods, but little else. That said, if your home or business does not get bought, it reverts back to you. The liquidation is in the hands of a bankruptcy trustee appointed by the court, and the trustee handles all issues. Once a Chapter 7 is completed, all remaining debts are declared discharged or wiped out by the court. In Chapter 11 and 13, you continue paying off debts for years as part of the agreement.

Simply put, if you think your firm is facing bankruptcy, it is important to find and work with a lawyer who specializes in bankruptcy. The area is too complex and specialized for do-it-yourself approaches to work. Also, a bankruptcy specialist can help with workarounds like a workout, which is often a reorganization done contractually without your declaring bankruptcy.

Why try to avoid bankruptcy? Going bankrupt will destroy your credit rating for anywhere from 6 to 10 years. It is public record, so everyone will know you declared bankruptcy, and in many communities it carries a negative social stigma. If you are at heart an entrepreneur, bankruptcy will make it hard for potential investors or creditors to trust you or your business. That said, realize that only a very small minority of all business closings are bankruptcies. That is good news for all of us because the low number of small business bankruptcies sends a message that most entrepreneurs do pay off their debts, which makes it easier for all of us to start businesses with other peoples' money on the line.

serial entrepreneurs
People who open multiple businesses throughout their career.

For entrepreneurs, the message of harvesting is an upbeat one. Of the 4 million firms that will change hands or close down this year, almost half will make the entrepreneurs richer, through sale and succession. Another quarter will have benefited from their businesses, and walk away ready to start their next firm. And start them they do. There is a special term for those owners who start multiple businesses in their careers—**serial entrepreneurs**. What do these entrepreneurs know? For those who are determined not only to survive but also to truly do well, the key is recognizing and building a firm along the lines of the critical success factors for small business.

The Not-So-Secret Secrets of Success

LO4 Know the firm-level critical success factors for small business.

Ask entrepreneurs what they hope to achieve and the universal answer is "success." But what is the measure of success for a business firm? One of the most famous models for success was offered by Daniel Katz and Robert Kahn. They suggest that the measure of success for any organization in the short term is profit, and in the long term is survival. In practice however, new businesses often face challenges in the reverse. In the short term their greatest need is to survive, even if there is no profit. For example, the typical mail order business will not show a profit for three to five years, according to John Schulte, chairman of the National Mail Order Association (NMOA).[25] The key for new firms is to do those things that will help them survive so that they get to the longer term, when to prove their legitimacy as a business, they need to show a profit.

Over the years the experience of small business consultants, experts, and researchers has converged on a set of critical success factors for small business.[26] Critical success factors (CSF) are processes, benchmarks, or components of the business that are essential for the business to be profitable and competitive in its market. They are by definition best practices for a given industry.

CSFs are important because they come from sources external to entrepreneurs, who are prone to biases in assessing the causes of success and failure in their businesses.[27] CSFs fall into two broad types—outside help and entrepreneurial experience. The CSFs below will seem familiar to you because they have been some of the major pieces of advice we have offered throughout the book. As we conclude our thinking about small business, it makes a lot of sense to bring together some of the most important CSFs that are under the control of the entrepreneur and give the firm the greatest possible chance of success.

EXHIBIT 20.1

How to Get Help

- Contact your local SBDC or SCORE or economic development office.
- Join the trade or professional association for your industry and get help or referrals from it.
- Ask successful entrepreneurs for advice and referrals.
- Talk to a lawyer or accountant or other for-profit expert.

To put it simply, help helps. People who get help from experts are far more likely to survive and achieve profitability than those who do not. Consider this. While the SBA has reported that 50 percent of owner-only firms fail in four years, 81.5 percent of clients of Small Business Development Centers are still going strong five years after starting.[28] As noted in the first chapter, 87 percent of incubator based start-ups are still going after five years.[29] See Exhibit 20.1 above for a listing of good sources for help. Time and time again similarly positive results are reported for students taking entrepreneurship and small business courses,[30] proving that small business education works.

The more you know, the better the chances for your firm to succeed. This can come from formal education past high school[31] (like this course) or from working in the industry or market. Anything that gives you the kinds of entrepreneurial or managerial competencies[32] (discussed in Chapter 3) or social[33] or networking[34] skills (discussed in Chapter 2) needed to start and run a business is useful.

But there is also a collection of other CSFs that have been repeatedly shown to be important. These CSFs help identify those businesses more likely to survive. These include:

- **Being incorporated:** Because incorporation usually involves a lawyer, who is likely to give small business owners advice and help them avoid some of the major pitfalls of a new firm.[35]
- **Employees:** Because employees are a way to get more done, to appeal to a larger market, a great source of expertise and feedback, as well as a larger responsibility, which usually means the owner has to make more sales to pay wages.[36]
- **Extreme start-up capital:** Businesses starting with no start-up capital and those starting with more than $50,000 are among those most likely to survive long term.[37] For those with the higher amounts, getting those funds implies prior hard work, and funds that size indicate a major investment, one an owner is more likely to work hard to protect. On the other hand, bootstrap entrepreneurs, who start with nothing, are likely to keep overhead low, live on a shoestring, and build their business over the long term, or change tracks quickly when new opportunities arise. The folks in the middle are those most likely to be undercapitalized for their industry and start-up situation.
- **Protectable intellectual property:** Such as patents or trademarks show preparation for the business, a potential asset, and implied expert assistance.[38]
- **Brand name affiliations or partners:** Having a major brand name shows that you have been checked out and found to be acceptable. It also increases the chances of favorable customer response.[39]
- **Optimal strategies:** Picking to start a business in a growing industry offers above average prospects of business growth.[40] Pursuing an imitator strategy shows a lower risk and greater learning from the mistakes of pioneers.[41]
- **Presales:** Perhaps the strongest benchmark is to have proven your idea through sales—in a pilot test, or through contracts, orders, or letters of intent from customers.[42]

Few businesses achieve all CSFs, but they provide a checklist for running your business in a way that increases its chances for survival. In addition, many of these CSFs are visible to customers, suppliers, and financiers, and convey the idea that you are running your business in a manner likely to lead to continued success.

Measuring Success with Four Bottom Lines

LO5 Understand what success means with the quadruple bottom line.

Originally, the *bottom line* referred to the profitability of a business, figured from the financial statements. For more than a hundred years in the thinking of economists, financiers, and accountants, it had been the ultimate and sovereign criterion of business success.

Today entrepreneurs and consultants realize that success can no longer be measured solely in terms of profits.[43] Financial success in business with a miserable family life or profits at the expense of public approval represent forms of "success" that leave a lot to be desired. There are four domains in which balanced entrepreneurs need to achieve success to be truly happy: the firm, the community, the family, and their own life.

But the bottom line concept, with its implication of some sort of adding up of pluses and minuses, still makes a lot of sense as a way for entrepreneurs to think about their business and life. In this section we talk about the four bottom lines of business—the firm, the community, the family, and the entrepreneur.

The Firm

Once started, it often seems that a firm takes on a life of its own. That is not surprising. Social systems researchers tell us that firms, as well as other types of groups, are living systems. Just as we think of a nation or culture as a living, growing entity, businesses are too.[44] As noted earlier, Daniel Katz and Robert Kahn suggest that the short-term measure of success for any organization is profit with survival the long-term measure, but in reality these are probably reversed for small businesses just starting out because new firms need to survive long enough to generate a profit. In effect, in order to succeed, you need to survive.

Entrepreneurs have the opportunity to define the level of profit that they seek. There are generally three levels: **supplemental profits** are intended as a secondary income for the entrepreneur, who has another job which provides his or her main income; **substitution profits** are intended to equal and replace the salary or wages the entrepreneur could draw working for someone else; **success profits** represent income levels higher than the person could make working for others.

supplemental profits
Returns above costs intended as a secondary income for entrepreneurs (where self-employment is secondary to their main job).

substitution profits
Returns intended to equal and replace the salary or wages the entrepreneur could draw working for someone else.

success profits
Returns at levels higher than the entrepreneur could make working for others.

The other measures of firm success can come from leadership of the industry. This can come through inventions and patents the business holds, which show its thought leadership, or from positions in professional and trade associations or in the marketplace, which make the firm distinctive in the eyes of customers and competitors.

For small businesses with employees, employee satisfaction and well being become a big part of the measure of success. Typically owners and employees in small businesses become a business family, with the owner taking on the parental role and responsibility. Making sure that the employees are taken care of becomes a key measure of success. In the opening vignette, at Shoppers' Service one of the key goals before closing down the firm was to first find a job for the one remaining employee.

Community

In the end, every small business is a part of its larger community, and one of the ways success gets measured is how the business relates to its community. Simply put, is the community better off for having the business present? In businesses operating for the long term, managing this bottom line is important to some extent. Few businesses operate to maximize the social bottom line over the profit one, but taking steps to be seen as a net benefit to the community is an expenditure worth making in the long run.

In small business, doing good takes many forms. In Chapter 2, we talk about five areas in which firms want to do good:

- Community impact, such as providing jobs to employees, business for other firms, and goods and services to customers.
- Building trust, such as through dependability and "doing the right thing."
- Promoting a positive culture, such as through promoting hard work, fair treatment, and developing the industry, market, and community.
- Enhancing flexibility by increasing the firm's and community's ability to respond to changes in the marketplace, economy, and environment.

- Fostering innovation, which is the basis for increasing profits, services, or goods offered, and competitive ability.

But many small business owners find themselves taking a more active role in the community, through charitable works, sponsoring others as they do good, and taking steps to ensure that the community remains a good place to be. This can range from picking up trash around the business to promoting professional standards and self-monitoring in the trade or industry association to taking a stand on issues important to the community.

Family

Time and time again, family has been shown to be the area that entrepreneurs worry about the most.[45] Running a business is time consuming, and often the demands of customers mean that the entrepreneur cannot control the schedule. Often that time comes out of family time. Making sure that you spend the time with your family and tackle the issues of communication and commitment that often underlie family problems is the key to success in this factor.

It is not easy. Reflecting on her years as founder and president of Tocquigny Advertising, Interactive and Marketing, in Austin, Texas, Yvonne Tocquigny observes, "I sometimes had a difficult time adjusting to the slower, gentler pace of home and was impatient and less nurturing than I should have been."[46]

Often the key is to leave personal time to make the transition from work to family—clearing your work list and your mind. It also helps to declare certain times as ones when you are unavailable, either letting others fill in, or letting voice mail take the messages.

Another key factor is keeping a portion of family time free of business issues, especially when other family members are involved in the business. Family time needs to be focused on the family, not the family business.[47]

Note that some entrepreneurs work best when combining family and work, while others work best when each is separate.[48] While you might quickly recognize which type you are, the measure of success is not based on your preference, but on that of your family. If your family complains that you do not seem to "be all here," then you are integrating too much and need to segregate business and family life more.

Yourself

So far, the domains discussed—the firm, the community, and the family—are external environments for the entrepreneur. You and your personal goals and desires count, too. They deserve the same chance for success that you strive for in the other settings. Part of what makes owning a small business rewarding to the entrepreneur is the possibility of personal returns—the fourth bottom line. Returns to the entrepreneur reflect the kinds of outcomes that the individual values. In Chapter 1, you learned about the rewards mentioned by most entrepreneurs—flexibility, income, and growth—as well as a collection of rewards that crop up occasionally, things like admiration, recognition, wealth, product creation, power, and family.[49]

The returns to the entrepreneur can include these and much more. Consider fun as an outcome. Sergey Brin and Larry Page of Google actually delayed growing their business to the IPO stage because they were afraid of having less fun when they became a public company.[50]

In the end, entrepreneurs go into business with a variety of expectations, dreams, and goals. A large reason for much of what we do—schooling, marrying, raising children, helping the community, and perhaps most of all, working—is to help us achieve those dreams. Entrepreneurship is one area in which, because you create the business and its goals, you have your best chance of capturing or creating your dream. Because of that, to be a successful entrepreneur, you need to be able to achieve those things in your life that are important to you.

Often the biggest risk to achieving that dream is getting caught up in the thousands of immediate demands on your time, attention, and life. Keeping track of your personal bottom line requires two key actions from yourself—keeping the dream alive and occasionally assessing yourself from the perspective of your dream.

Keeping the dream alive starts with giving a name to your dream and putting that name somewhere where you can remind yourself about your own personal ultimate goal. The other part is to schedule a meeting with yourself every once in a while—perhaps quarterly for a start—to assess how you are doing in achieving your dream and what you should do to help yourself.

Simply put, when you talk with entrepreneurs who consider themselves completely successful, you will find that they talk about what they were able to accomplish in their business, their community, their family, and their personal life. Knowing the four areas where success is critical, you can begin to think about how well you are achieving in each and begin the process for working up a plan to maximize your achievement of all forms of success. The procedure for doing this is discussed in Skill Module 20.1.

SKILL MODULE 20.1 Assessing the Four Bottom Lines

As discussed in this chapter, the four bottom lines of business refer to yourself, your family, your firm, and your society or community. In planning a business or evaluating it every once in a while (say once or twice a year), it makes sense to think about how well you and your business are doing at meeting the four bottom lines. Here is how to do it:

1. For yourself, pick the two or three personal goals you have for the business. Ask yourself what it is that you want to achieve through running your business or what you would miss the most if it were gone. List these.
2. For your family, ask what family members want from you personally (time with you, money to support their efforts and needs, etc.). List these.
3. For your firm, there are always three items of critical importance—profits, how well the firm does its job (making or selling products or services—this is based on customer and industry information), and how satisfied are the people involved in the business (owners and employees).
4. For your community, there are also clear indicators of outcome—economic contributions (profits, salaries, taxes), quality of life contributions (lack of pollution, providing needed products or services, supporting civic betterment), and industrial contributions (supporting the industry, operating responsibly, developing the industry through innovation and improvement).

In the matrix in Table 20.1 you can see that to evaluate these goals you need two pieces of information for each. The first is some sort of metric—a way to measure the degree of achievement. Despite the name, metrics do not have to be "hard" measures like dollars or customers. Opinions are acceptable, and behaviors are even better. With a metric in hand, you are ready to get the second piece of information, the achievement level. This is how you have scored on the metric. To really understand how well your firm is doing on all four bottom lines, you will want to ask others for their assessment on relevant goals. In the end, the evaluation of your business is your opinion, but checking your perceptions against those of knowledgeable others can help you identify areas for improvement and reinforce your recognition of areas of achievement.

TABLE 20.1 The Four Bottom Lines

Area	Goal	Metric	Achievement Level
Yourself	Feel in control of my life	Personal opinion	Achieved
Family	Have time for spouse and children	Their opinions	Spouse—Not Achieved Child (Ann)—Achieved Child (Roger)—Not Achieved
Firm	Profits or take outs	Practical income of $75,000 in cash or services a year	$71,000
Community	Satisfied employee Support local charities	Her opinion 5% of sales minimum	"Generally yes" 4.88%

Conclusion

The quadruple bottom line does a wonderful job of showing how starting and running your own small business can reward not only you, but your family, your firm, and your community. It is a means to gain control over the working portion of your life, and perhaps even all of it. It offers communities services and goods, employment, and innovations that make all our lives better. Doing a small business well is not easy. Even knowing the critical success factors for small firms does not mean that you can develop or achieve them. That means that in every small business effort there is always an element of risk.

But millions look at the prospects and decide to take those risks—nearly 40 million people in 2003, with 27 million already self-employed and another 13 million who have been, or are planning to be again. Why do so many do this? The answer is simple—because they want to and they can! Today, with the ready availability of help and the many ways to get into small business with less financial and personal risk than ever before, the chances for success in small business have never been higher.

And the returns from small business have never been greater. The opportunity to work your own way, with flexibility and support, increases as more different types of people, technologies, and businesses remake entrepreneurship for the twenty-first century. The chance for people to learn the right way to run businesses, whether part time or full time, local or global, has never been greater. Classes like the one you've taken and resources like the ones in this book are just the start. Having the right help can help, and now you know the kind of help available to you. You can do this. The time to do it is right now.

CHAPTER SUMMARY

LO1 Know how to recognize the stages of the small business life cycle.

- Every firm goes through a similar sequence of developmental stages.
- Emergence comes before the firm starts, followed by existence.
- Survival happens to most firms, as does resource maturity.
- Some firms experience the takeoff stage, but most do not.
- Each stage poses a distinct challenge to the small business and owner.

LO2 Understand the four types of firm-level growth strategies.

- Every owner has a chance to decide on his or her firm's approach to growth.
- Lifestyle/part-time firms start and remain small and centered on the owner's needs.
- Traditional small businesses are more customer-driven, but remain small and simple, providing an income for the owner.
- High-profit businesses add employees and locations in order to provide a substantial income to the owner.
- High-potential ventures attempt to grow enough to become a big business.

LO3 Understand the options for harvesting or closing the small business.

- Harvests reflect an owner's efforts to take value out of a firm.
- Firms get transferred through sales or family succession.
- Terminations can be walkaways, workouts, or bankruptcies.
- The terminations that have legal repercussions, like bankruptcies, and almost any sort of transfers are complex enough that expert assistance is necessary.
- IPOs, ESOPs, mergers and acquisitions, and other specialized transfer techniques exist but are relatively rarely used.

LO4 Know the firm-level critical success factors for small business.

- Critical success factors are processes, benchmarks, or components of the business that are essential for the business to be profitable and competitive in its market.
- CSFs fall into two broad types—outside help and entrepreneurial experience.
- Specific experience factors that lead to success include being incorporated, having employees, having large or no start-up capital, protectable intellectual property, brand name affiliations, an optimal strategy, and preopening sales.

LO5 Understand what success means with the quadruple bottom line.

- Today entrepreneurs and consultants realize that success can no longer be measured solely in terms of profits.
- There are four domains in which balanced entrepreneurs need to achieve success to be truly happy: the firm, the community, the family, and their own life.
- Auditing the four bottom lines requires specifying the goal, the metric, and the achievement level.

KEY TERMS

business life cycle, 638
liability of newness, 639
slack resources, 639
lifestyle or part-time firm, 641
traditional small business, 641
high-performing small business, 641
high-growth venture, 641
harvest, 642
initial public offering (IPO), 642
consolidation, 643
employee stock ownership plan, 643
transfer, 643
termination, 643
liquidity enhancement, 643
tax management, 643
estate freeze, 644
bankruptcy, 644
walkaways, 644
workout, 645
reorganization, 646
liquidation, 646
serial entrepreneurs, 646
supplemental profits, 648
substitution profits, 648
success profits, 648

DISCUSSION QUESTIONS

1. What is the difference between a lifestyle business and a traditional small business?
2. What are some of the differences between a lifestyle business and a high-performing small business?
3. What are the stages of the small business life cycle? What stage do high-growth ventures go through that other forms of small business do not?
4. What is the difference between a transfer and a termination?
5. From the entrepreneur's perspective, what is the major reason for preferring a transfer of the business to a termination?
6. What are the key business characteristics needed for a successful walkaway?
7. Identify and compare three critical success factors for small businesses.
8. What are the four bottom lines of small business?
9. Why are separate bottom lines broken out for the family and the firm, rather than just including it in the "yourself" category?
10. In assessing the four bottom lines, what is the difference between the goal and its metric? Why is each needed?

EXPERIENTIAL EXERCISES

1. Look up businesses for sale in an industry of your choice (or the industry assigned you by your professor), at a site such as www **www.bizbuysell.com**. What kind of information does the Web site provide you? List three additional pieces of information you would most want to get. Can you think of other online or print resources you could use to find this information, such as online business databases your library has? Try and find at least one of these key pieces of information using these other resources.
2. Make your list of your personal goals for the "yourself" assessment in the quadruple bottom line exercise. Compare this list to the major reasons people give for going into business

(covered in Chapter 1). Which of your goals overlap the popular reasons and which are unique to yourself?

3. One of the most common ways to evaluate firm success is by profitability. Use a financial database such as the Risk Management Association's *Annual Statement Studies* to find out target profitability levels for your business.

MINI-CASE

TIM HAYDEN, VIVID SKY AND SKYBOX IN JULY 2009

It was the summer of 2009 and Tim had to make a decision. He had started with an idea of using advanced electronics to make any seat in the stadium "the best seat in the house." To do that he created SkyBOX, a program for displaying game videos, sports statistics, and interactive fan-focused social networking (like votes, chats, etc.) inside sports venues. In 2003 SkyBOX was imagined as a rental fleet of PDAs "hardened" against spills and drops and fed data through a Wi-Fi installation put into participating stadia. By 2009 the idea morphed into an application which could be run on 3G cell phones like the iPhone as well as personal computers equipped with cellular Wi-Fi.

SkyBOX was a darling of DEMO 2006, and could point to over 80 articles and news segments extolling the idea, the technology, and the charismatic founder behind it. *Inc.* magazine had profiled Vivid Sky in their 2006 valuation story. Pilot tests with the St. Louis Cardinals (Tim's hometown team), the Detroit Tigers, and the Detroit Redwings in 2007 and 2008 had been very successful. Since 2008 SkyBOX was on sale online at the iPhone Applications Store and had sold several hundred copies. In terms of buzz and media appreciation, SkyBOX was a winner.

The financial situation was the problem. Tim had sunk all his own money into Vivid Sky to bring it to market. He had advertisers lined up and ready to buy visibility on SkyBOX. He had access to the baseball, football, basketball, and hockey stadia, but he needed $1,000,000 to deploy the system. He had gotten half the funding from his family, local friends, and friends of friends, but the economic downturn meant he had been unable to get the remaining $500,000 investment from any of the Fortune 1000 firms looking at SkyBOX.

Tim had run out of money, again (he refused to use the $500,000 from family and friends unless he had the match). Tim pledged to keep looking for a way to get SkyBOX operational but, in the meantime, he found his four programmer employees jobs with firms he had dealt with along the way. One of those firms, a local sports conglomerate, called Tim with an offer—chief marketing officer of the conglomerate reporting to the CEO, and sporting a six-figure salary of his own. They needed an answer tomorrow.

Meanwhile, a group from the advanced technology team at one of the biggest media companies was asking Tim if he would be willing to sell them the SkyBOX technology so they can incorporate it into their cell phone offerings. No hard numbers have been given yet, but they are also interested in hiring back the four programmers and would be giving Tim ongoing consulting contracts. But try as he might, Tim couldn't get a go/no-go date from this group. He had just hung up on another one of those exhilarating and frustrating calls.

As he had so often in the six years shepherding SkyBOX to reality, Tim sat back and asked himself, "What's the entrepreneurial thing to do?"

CASE DISCUSSION QUESTIONS

1. Should Tim use the $500,000 raised to keep SkyBOX going until he can find other funding? Explain your reasoning.
2. In terms of the business outcomes shown in Figure 20.3, which outcomes is Tim's firm facing at this point?
3. Is there an entrepreneurial solution to dealing with both the chief marketing officer job offer and SkyBOX? Explain your reasoning.

SUGGESTED CASES AND ARTICLES

- Joseph Shaughnessy, BSI Constructors, St. Louis

Available on PRIMIS:

- Dice, Inc.

SUGGESTED VIDEOS

Video Case:

- Entrepreneurs and Failure, p. VC-9

eClips Videos:

- Debbie Mace States Importance of Finding a Balance between Work, Family, and Fun
- Carushka Jarecka Discusses Business Growth during the First Year
- Frank Farwell Discusses Exit Strategy and the Process of Leaving the Business

SBTV Videos:

- Dissolving a Corporation
- A Living Trust for the Small Business Owner
- Retirement Considerations Interview

STVP Videos:

- Exit Strategies Now and Then
- Difficult Negotiations
- Seeing Failure as Opportunity

Back Matter

CASES

CASE 1

BROTHERS GOING SEPARATE WAYS OR NOT?

Derrick and Kevin Petersen, twin brothers from a small town outside of Chicago, will soon graduate from a local business school. The boys have remained inseparable throughout their lives, including sports, hobbies, friends, and work. Decision time is now facing the young men in terms of career choices and tracks. While the brothers have always shared an interest in becoming business owners, their individual goals and newly acquired management training and vision may very well have them going separate ways after all these years.

The Petersen family owns and operates a very successful auto repair and towing business. Each of the five children in the family has worked for their parents throughout high school and during summers throughout college. The boys' parents took over the one-man business nearly 30 years ago. Since that time, they have purchased and now maintain a fleet of seven tow trucks and have expanded the garage to include four bays that provide a wide range of auto and truck repair services. The business generates about $4,000,000 in sales, a higher than industry average profit margin, and has provided the once poor family with a very good life.

The elder Petersens are approaching retirement and would love to see one of their kids continue the tradition. Kevin and his three other siblings have come and gone and made it very clear that they want no part of the business. Derrick remains as the lone ranger and is seriously considering the opportunity.

The elder Petersens are well known and respected for their quality work and service and for their active role in the community. They are set in their ways and have a hard time dealing with new ideas and with letting go. Derrick has many new ideas as to how he would grow the next generation of the business.

There is unused space above the garage that Derrick has talked about turning into a custom auto parts showroom. There is unused space on the property that Derrick would like to convert into self-service gas pumps and an automated car wash. Derrick has also commented on the great success that area competitors enjoy through the addition of a convenience store.

This has all resulted in a family-business conflict of sorts, as the parents want to work something out and get out, but continue to resist the changes that Derrick has offered. Derrick appreciates the knowledge, experience, and success that his parents have, but wants to be his own man and build his own empire if he is to stay on and make this his career. Derrick wants to take on his own new challenges and achieve his own personal rewards. A close friend of the family has recommended bringing in an objective outside consultant and attorney to work up a formal contract that everyone can live with.

Derrick's parents want the business to provide them with retirement income and would like the option of staying on as seasonal employees, as they plan to winter in the south and come home for the summer.

Derrick has many questions that need answering. He is unsure about the best legal form for the business to have. He is not sure how to best deal with his parents. He is not sure about the particulars for the best financial package, one that will reward his parents accordingly, and at the same time provide him with the best opportunity for continued success.

Brother Kevin has a very different mind-set. He wants to start up and own several businesses, but he does not want to be tied down or committed to any single one. He has $200,000 of seed money available to him through the family. He has taken the time to build a relationship with three of the bankers that the family has worked with for many years. He participated in an internship through the SBA while in school in order to familiarize himself with the programs and opportunities that that organization has to offer. He also spent a semester in London in order to learn more about the way business is conducted in Europe.

Kevin is interested in franchising. He envisions himself starting and perfecting a number of service businesses that he can eventually take national and international. He is interested in going public in order to raise large sums of capital and to expedite his expansion plans. Kevin is interested in e-commerce. He views that industry as being in the early growth stages of the product life cycle and feels that the time is right to enter that industry. There appears to be many opportunities to buy low and sell high to worldwide markets. Kevin is interested in real estate development. The family lives in the urban/suburban area of Chicago, which is the site of very active construction of new homes, condo units, and commercial developments. Kevin knows that there are many other such venues around the country and world with plenty of room for new developers.

Kevin is also interested in other parts of the world. He wants to live and work in China and South America and possibly eastern Europe. While he greatly enjoyed the people, activities, and surroundings of his childhood, he really does not want to go home. At the same time, graduation is just three months away, and Kevin does not have a job.

Derrick is encouraging Kevin to come home for a year and help him take over and grow the family business. Derrick feels that this will be an exciting and fun challenge and that it will give his brother time to put together a more specific plan for his own endeavors. That choice also comes with an immediate source of income and a free place to live.

QUESTIONS

1. Profile the brothers. Are they typical "small business" people or "entrepreneurs" or both? Is there really a difference?
2. Advise the brothers. Develop a strategic and tactical plan that best fits their goals and aspirations and that has the highest likelihood for success.
3. How would each brother make a contribution to the family, community, and economy if their efforts were successful?

CASE 2

G & R GARDEN CENTER: LAWN CARE SERVICES DIVISION

Rick and Gloria Ash started a new business in 1986 on the outskirts of Columbus, Ohio. Their original retail store with greenhouse attachment featured fresh-cut flowers, annuals, vegetables, and perennials. The building is on the grounds of Gloria's family farm, which enables the Ashes to grow some of their retail products from scratch. Gloria's parents gave the couple several acres of commercially zoned land as a wedding gift in 1982. The building and greenhouse construction were completed by Rick with a little help from his brothers. This combination of land acquisition and building construction resulted in a very low overhead situation that contributed to their start-up success.

An addition to the building was completed in 1991 and included several new and related product lines such as garden tools, soil and mulch products, gifts, seeds, and related accessories.

Gloria earned a horticulture degree at the local community college prior to the establishment of the business, and in 1997 she was able to fulfill a lifelong dream of starting a landscape design and installation service that became the company's next and newest product line. Gloria set up a small studio and office in the couple's nearby home and was able to acquire some new clients. Her timing was good, as the Columbus area experienced a housing boom during that period. New houses and new developments sprang up in every direction from the city. Their garden center was able to supply the plant materials that each new job required. Soon after, the Ashes expanded their product lines to include a new and wider variety of trees, shrubs, landscape terraces, patios, and walkways as a means to generate new sales and to complement Gloria's new service line.

The original start-up business and each expansion project (building addition, new products, design and installation service) have more than covered their costs but have only generated fair to moderate profit margins according to the Ashes. They attribute this mostly to the presence of their competition, which always seems to be growing. As a result, they have been reluctant to raise prices even though some product costs have risen.

One year later, the Ashes completed the final phase of their original long-range business plan with the addition of another new service—Big Rick, The Lawn & Garden Doctor. This new product line was added because of its very high profit projections coupled with the fact that the Ashes would (temporarily at least) have a monopoly on this market, as none of their competitors currently offer the service.

This new division specializes in the treatment and eradication of lawn and garden pests. There are many insects and diseases that affect plant life, some of which are fatal. In spite of the fact that the Ashes and other local garden centers offer high-quality plants to consumers, Mother Nature has a way of wreaking havoc on lawns, gardens, shrubs, and trees over time.

The start up of this division required a tremendous amount of time, effort, and expense as a result of the environmental and safety-related hazards of some of the products such as insecticides and fungicides.

The Ashes were required to train and license two of their employees as certified applications technicians. A custom built, high-security storage facility was required and built to house all hazardous materials. The building was secured with a locked, barbed-wire fence, an alarm system, and a hazardous material runoff-proof partition. A special liability insurance policy was purchased as well.

As expected, the new division turned out to be very profitable. Demand was strong, and the technicians' work was professional and effective. In fact, at the end of its first full year of existence, Big Rick, The Lawn & Garden Doctor turned a profit that almost matched that of all other divisions combined. At the company's monthly staff meeting, it therefore came as quite a surprise to everyone when Rick announced that he was seriously considering dropping the division entirely.

Rick Ash is a local native of the area. He has very strong family and community values and has always felt responsible for the welfare and happiness of his friends, neighbors, and especially his customers. He was always nervous and apprehensive that something bad would happen as a result of the pesticide or fungicide applications.

And then it happened. A customer's dog died as a result of eating some grass from a recently treated lawn. Big Rick's technician had taken every precaution. The area was properly treated, marked, and roped off, and the customer was instructed as to the after-care safety precautions which included a well-written handout and a signed liability waiver form. While the company was clearly not negligent, Rick was clearly upset.

Two months later, a lawsuit was filed against the company, claiming that the water runoff from the property of one of their customers had tainted a neighbor's well. The Ashes were forced to hire an attorney, and following a full and costly investigation were found to be not guilty of that charge. In fact, the case never even made it to court.

Gloria feels that Rick is overreacting. She points out that the company is in full compliance with every regulation and that Rick has gone out of his way to ensure the safety of all. Gloria also noted that no business can control the behavior or responsibility of its customers or of the population in general and that incidents beyond their control will naturally and always occur. In addition, the high profitability of the division will allow the Ashes to embark upon an aggressive advertising campaign aimed at improving the sales and profits of their other divisions.

Rick is losing sleep over all of this and is not sure what to do. He is worried about the image and reputation of his family and their business. He feels that the conditions surrounding the lawn and garden doctor business are in conflict with his values and conscience.

QUESTIONS

1. Present an argument in favor of retaining the new division that considers and incorporates the ethical and moral conflicts that Mr. Ash is experiencing.
2. Present an argument in favor of eliminating the new division, and make recommendations to improve overall company profits through means that will be socially and morally acceptable to Mr. Ash.
3. Aside from compliance with the law, just how much additional responsibility does a business owner have to his or her customer base, employees, suppliers, and the community at large? How do you feel about the old saying, "buyer beware"?

CASE 3

REAL ESTATE MILLIONAIRES OF MEMPHIS

The one sure way to make money in Memphis, Tennessee, has always been through real estate, but the kinds of people who became millionaires this way defied a single, simple description. Consider five people who became millionaires within a few years of each other. All were in their early 30s when they struck it rich, but otherwise, they were a very varied group.

For example, Abe was the local "do it right" guy. He went to college, got his start in real estate working for a successful firm (he was one of the few African Americans in the local industry who specialized in commercial real estate), and built a nest egg. He left the firm after about five years to start his own, and he kept up his conscientious ways. He made a profit in his first year of operations through frugality and careful money management. He studied the market, the competition, and how and where the city was growing. He negotiated tirelessly but fairly to get the best price on land, and he developed it for the commercial market because that was where the money was.

Cal was the promoter. He was college-educated but seemed to have majored in partying. He was always talking up one big deal or another, developing major projects for tourists. More than anyone else in town, he sold visions of a future Memphis. He built his deals from the downtown out, looking for opportunities near the Mississippi River, which he saw as Memphis's key tourist attraction. He was always putting together consortia, but often forgot or failed to cover key details. His relationships with people were emotional roller coaster rides, and he likewise led a life of financial feast or famine, depending on where he and his latest project was. Just after his 30th birthday, one of his projects "came in," and he became a millionaire.

Lee went to college in engineering and joined her father's construction company right after graduation. She knew business as well as engineering and made the family firm a major force in home construction. She had a keen eye for where new subdivisions should go and was able to get the best work out of local architects and subcontractors. She was considered not only sharp, but kind to people and careful about the details of her homes and her firm. She prospered because her subdivisions were the best in town.

Dave ran a grocery on the outskirts of Memphis and said he "dabbled" in real estate. Self-educated, he largely limited his real estate dealings to when one came across the butcher shop refrigerated case in his grocery. All the locals knew him, and he knew every piece of property and its history from experience and listening to his customers. When someone needed to move or sell a deceased parent's farm, Dave was there with his checkbook, financed through the grocery. He did not prospect, and he resold land rather than developing it.

Frank also lived on the outskirts of town. Never graduating from high school, he apprenticed himself to a gas station owner as a teen. When the company needed to open a gas station just outside of Memphis, Frank agreed to do it, and the company financed his purchase of the gas station. At his gas station, Frank mostly sat outside in a rocking chair by the gas pump. He became a millionaire when gravel was discovered on his land and was mined by local gravel and building companies. Armed with serious money, Frank always said he was looking for his next deal, but he never found one.

QUESTIONS

1. In terms of the five types of entrepreneurial personalities mentioned in the chapter, do any of them fit the description of the Memphis real estate tycoons?
2. What role in their development as entrepreneurs would you think special conditions had—for example, Abe being African American, Lee being a female in a male-dominated industry or working within a family business, or Frank or Dave going into serious business without a college education?
3. What kinds of competencies do you see these real estate entrepreneurs bringing to their business?
4. Are there any conclusions you can draw about there being an entrepreneurial personality type for the real estate business? What does it say about the kind of entrepreneur *you* can become with the personality you have?

CASE 4

BIG BUSINESS IN A SMALL RURAL CITY

Bud Collier grew up "smack in the middle of a 100 mile-long hay field," as he puts it, near central Kansas. That part of the country features a lot of land, a lot of cattle, very large farms, agricultural processing centers, and relatively few people. The region has a number of very small farm towns, with populations of less than 1,000 located as much as 30 to 50 miles apart, and a much smaller number of small cities, with populations of 10,000 to 30,000 widely scattered throughout the state. There is an ongoing effort by state and federal agencies to support the development of commerce in those regions. Outside of farming and the few small retail shops that serve those small towns, there is not much happening in the way of new employment opportunities. The farm base continues to shrink, and natives of the area continue to move to other parts of the country after high school, college, or a hitch in the military.

Bud's small family farm is located near one of those small cities. He has earned a degree in marketing and graphic arts and now faces a dilemma and turning point in his life. He very much wants to go home and settle down in the community that he loves, wants to start a career related to his newly acquired skills and knowledge, but has no idea as to what or if that area has to offer him.

He developed a great interest in market research and data analysis while in school. Bud has studied national and international trends in business in an attempt to discover where the opportunities and connections lie between future product and service demand, his graphic arts and marketing skills, and his desired home base. He is trying hard to be creative and innovative and to "think outside the box" as he was often encouraged to do while in school. Bud is also trying to "make the data work for you" as his statistics professor often spoke about.

He has thought about and studied the data regarding food production and world hunger. His area of the country is capable of producing additional and abundant quantities of much needed agricultural products. The only thing standing in the way seems to be governments and politics. His area of the country is a national hub for the transportation and distribution of products from coast to coast and includes a number of major interstate highways. Bud has learned that health care and wellness and its many related industries are projected to become the number one source of jobs and opportunities to the new generation of college graduates. That industry offers options ranging from traditional forms of health care, to fitness, recreation and leisure, diet and nutrition, and nontraditional programs and practices. From a global perspective, Bud knows that China and the Pacific Rim and all of the so-called "Latino Nations" represent two gigantic and growing markets for virtually all consumer goods and services. His mind continues to race with thoughts and ideas as to how to connect these opportunities with his desired home base.

Bud also gained skills in the process and art of new product development while in school. He was often assigned to work with small groups of classmates to brainstorm ideas, to shrink the list to the best and most feasible, to conduct research and analysis, and to finally develop prototypes and test marketing strategies. Bud is now ready to do this for real; he also wants to incorporate his graphic arts skills into the mix. Bud has become very proficient in desktop publishing, computer animation, and video production. He is familiar with and proficient in current multimedia marketing software.

Soon after his return home, Bud learns that an old friend of the family is about to retire and sell his printing and stationery business. That business is located in the downtown of a nearby small city, population 26,000, near Bud's home and has provided a nice income and lifestyle for the proprietor. The shop sells greeting cards, office supplies, and other complementary paper products and includes a small warehouse and processing center where the owner is able to produce custom business cards, office stationery, and a limited line of brochures and flyers. Most of the equipment is old and labor-intensive with limited capabilities.

QUESTIONS

1. Use your imagination and creativity along with the information provided to identify a short list of the best opportunities for Bud to consider.
2. Should Bud consider purchasing the printing and stationery business, and if so, what do you see as his goal for the business, especially how could he expand production and sales given the limited opportunities that the location offers?
3. Business ideas are easy to come by. The more difficult task is determining the feasibility of business success. How would you go about doing that? What kind of information does Bud need in order to make an informed decision? What types and sources of data are available to assist you in determining your best opportunities?

CASE 5

THE AMBITIOUS COLLEGE KID WHO JUST CAN'T WAIT

Lyle Wong has been carrying a briefcase everywhere he goes since the age of 12 and has always been glad to let anyone and everyone know that he is an up and coming entrepreneur. At the age of 14, Lyle started and ran a flea market on weekends on a field next to his house. He rented space to vendors and sold his own merchandise on consignment for a commission. He then started and ran his own landscaping company during the following three summers. This required Lyle to first persuade his older brother to use his truck and become an employee, as Lyle was not yet old enough to drive. He then started and ran a DJ business during his last two years of high school. By the time Lyle graduated from high school, he had more than $75,000 in savings and mutual fund investments.

His parents had all they could do to keep him in high school. Although he earned straight A's, Lyle considered high school to be a waste of time and nothing but an obstacle to earning his first million. He was offered a full scholarship at a Michigan college. Thanks to some friendly and persistent convincing from his parents and from his already established business associates, Lyle agreed to give college a try as long as he could continue to conduct business.

Lyle is now a 19-year-old sophomore, majoring in computer science, with minors in business and international marketing, and lives in a dorm. He started a T-shirt business during his freshman year, which he says pacifies him for now, earns him spending money, and allows him to continue investing in his retirement portfolio.

He is ready to take it to the next level. Lyle has set a goal of accumulating $1,000,000 by the time he graduates from college. He is willing to do this "part time" since he is in school. Lyle has discovered that college takes up much less time than high school. He figures that he needs only about 30 hours a week to attend class, study, complete all assignments, and continue to earn straight As. He has decided to dedicate an additional 40 or 50 hours per week, his version of part time, to the next venture in order to earn him his first million.

Lyle is still undecided as to which direction to go with his next venture. He is thinking about setting up and running an entire operation from his dorm room. He views this as a location with free overhead. As a full-time student, Lyle also has access to many other on-campus resources. Those resources include an abundance of cheap help if needed, access to all computer technology, access to most on-campus buildings and facilities, free public transportation, and access to the student newspaper and radio station.

Lyle is thinking a lot about e-commerce. He knows that this gives him access to a worldwide customer base. Unlike his previous ventures, which were all very small and localized, Lyle is excited about the prospect of selling merchandise on a global basis. He has always liked the concept and role of the middleman, and is searching for product lines that he can buy low and sell high in volume. Lyle knows that the necessary infrastructure is already well established. There are an abundance of manufacturers, shippers, and consumers throughout the world. Lyle figures it is just a matter of putting together the right mix of those entities with him properly placed to reap the benefits.

Lyle's current and past ventures have given him a lot of good experience in key areas of business. Those include customer and employee relations, handling merchandise, and managing cash and the many details and tasks that arise from the normal day-to-day operations of most any business. He is now very computer literate, and in spite of his passion and drive for business success, Lyle has lots of friends, good social skills, and enjoys and participates in many hobbies, social events, and extracurricular activities.

QUESTIONS

1. Do you believe that Lyle can achieve his goal of earning $1,000,000 by graduation? Why or why not?
2. Help your colleague. You are familiar with the resources available to students on a typical college campus. Consider those resources and Lyle's goals, and develop a short list of the best products or services to consider. Include an outline and action plan to make it all happen.
3. Trying to start up a part-time business while being a full-time student in college could pose some problems for Lyle. What are the ones you think are most likely? How could he minimize their impact?
4. Do you see yourself taking a route similar to Lyle's? Could you do it? Will you do it?

CASE 6

THE GRANDE GENERAL STORE, EST. 1948—IT'S TIME TO SELL

Three generations of Grandes have dedicated their lives and careers to a small general store located on the outskirts of Denver, Colorado. Rocky and Anita Grande, the current owner-operators, have decided to sell the family business. They have declared themselves "tired, burned out, and ready to get out." Their two adult children have no interest in the business, and Rocky and Anita want to spend more time with their three young grandchildren.

They need help with setting a fair price for the business, with finding a qualified buyer, and with preparing a formal prospectus for use by investors, bankers, and others. The Grandes want the highest price possible and at the same time sincerely wish to see the business survive and prosper. It has been in the family for a long time, is a well-established part of the community, and has a dedicated workforce. Most of the employees have been with the company for more than 10 years. The Grandes will allow a buyer to continue to use the family/business name if desired.

What began as an old-fashioned general store (1940s–1960s) carrying everything from food and clothing, to tools, farm supplies, penny candy, and train tickets evolved into a traditional hardware store (1970s–present). The current 4,200 square feet of floor space is divided into four major departments: lawn and garden, paints, electrical and plumbing, and general hardware.

Sales and profits are divided equally between consumers and contractors. The store is located adjacent to a railroad siding with a storage building that allows for large shipments of merchandise to be received, stored, and sold. Building materials of all types (lumber, roofing, siding, Sheetrock, and so on) are picked up and delivered to local construction sites, which represent the mainstay of the contractor business.

The Grande family is well respected by all. Their honesty, loyalty, hard work, and community involvement have come back to bless them on many occasions. During tough economic times, suppliers often extend credit terms far beyond the norm. Customers and contractors are fiercely loyal to the Grande's business even with the presence of modern-day giant warehouse outlets that offer a wider variety of the same products for less money.

While the main buildings date back to 1948, the Grandes have upgraded their fleet of delivery trucks and forklifts. The inside of the store is a mix of the old and the new. State-of-the-art computers, paint processing equipment, and landscape machinery rentals are scattered around the old wooden building that still sports some original display fixtures and the wormy chestnut paneling that Rocky's grandfather Jeb installed during construction of the original building.

The principals have compiled the following summary financials for the past five years of operation:

Income (Profit and Loss) Statement Summary: 1998–2002 (in 000s)

	1998	1999	2000	2001	2002
Sales	$1,100	$1,215	$1,500	$1,800	$2,200
CGS—Cost of Goods Sold	550	600	732	822	995
GM—Gross Margin	550	615	768	978	1,205
Operating Expenses:	500	520	600	720	795
• Payroll					
• Mortgage/Debt					
• Insurance					
• Utilities					
• Supplies					
• Transportation					
• Depreciation					
Net Income before Taxes	$ 50	$ 95	$ 168	$ 258	$ 410
Taxes	15	29	50	77	123
Net Income	$ 35	$ 66	$ 118	$ 181	$ 287

Net Cash Flow from Operations: 1998–2002 (in 000s)

	1998	1999	2000	2001	2002
Cash In	$1,014	$1,098	$1,360	$1,617	$1,996
Cash Out	945	1,014	1,250	1,430	1,760
Net Cash Flow from Operations	$ 69	$ 84	$ 110	$ 187	$ 236

Balance Sheet Summary: January 1, 1998–2002 (in 000s)

	1998	1999	2000	2001	2002
Cash	$ 12	$ 19	$ 22	$ 23	$ 21
Inventory	41	47	59	65	80
Accounts Receivables	80	102	124	148	187
Land	$ 35	$ 35	$ 35	$ 35	$ 35
Buildings	612	567	505	459	414
Equipment	84	190	171	241	214
Accounts Payables	$ 36	$ 46	$ 51	$ 61	$ 71
Notes Payables	21	6	7	9	6
Long-Term Debt	$121	$225	$211	$278	$261
Owner's Equity/Net Worth	$686	$683	$647	$623	$613

Suburban Denver is considered a moderate- to high-growth region of the state and is projected to stay that way for years to come. New housing, new neighborhoods, new schools, new malls, and the like are under construction and in the planning stages throughout the area.

The Grande business sits on seven acres of land and includes room for growth, in terms of new buildings, increased parking, and other business options. The business was recently appraised by certified professionals. The assessed values are as follows:

• Land	$110,000
• Buildings	515,000
• Equipment	155,000
• Inventory	70,000
• Total Current Assessed Value	$850,000

The Grandes have compiled all their data into a prospectus and are about to formally put the business on the market. They have yet to settle on an asking price.

Two local area banks have indicated a willingness to offer a 15-year note to a qualified buyer for a maximum of $624,000 (which represents 80 percent of the assessed value of the land, buildings and equipment).

QUESTIONS

1. Use your entrepreneurial skills to evaluate this investment opportunity. Is this a business worth buying? If so, why? How much would you be willing to invest? Why?
2. Given the economic outlook in the Denver area, the land and physical plant, and the competition, what short- and long-term operational and growth strategies would you consider?

CASE 7

THE COMPUTER GURU: A ONE-MAN SHOW OR AN EMPIRE?

Juan De Jesus, of San Antonio, Texas, earned a computer science degree from The University of Texas in 1994. Upon graduation, Juan was hired as a sales and service technician for one of the large national computer corporations. That job provided him with a tremendous amount of experience in the small business sales and service sector. Four years later, he left the company, deciding to go it alone as an independent computer consultant.

Juan set up an office and computer-testing lab in his home and worked hard to grow the business. He was able to take advantage of some of the relationships and contacts that he established during his tenure at his last job that resulted in several immediate clients. His wife Conchita helps with some of the office work on a part-time basis.

The business grew rapidly thanks to Juan's excellent work and reputation. He has the ability to install hardware and software systems, including industry-specific software, is very effective at training, can fix almost any computer, and is readily available by phone to answer questions and solve problems that occur after the installation and training.

Four years into the business, Juan finds himself charging $100 per hour and earning nearly $150,000 per year for his services. He is good at what he does, and people want him—his phone is ringing off the hook. He also feels that it is time to take a step back to reevaluate his current position, his business options, and his personal goals.

Juan recalled the internship program that is offered at his alma mater and arranged to have three current business students conduct a feasibility study on his behalf. The project began with an interview at his home office. The highlights and key points of that interview follow.

Juan reported that he is making a good living, currently billing about 1,500 hours per year at $100 per hour. He actually works about 60 hours per week, however, with the addition of travel time, seemingly endless phone calls, searching for and ordering parts, office paperwork, and attending classes and seminars to remain current with new technology. Conchita works about 20 hours per week in the office. She indicated this to be her limit, as she has another part-time job and is expecting the couple's first child in a few months. She plans to give up the second job and to continue working with Juan at their home office.

Juan is concerned about the fact that his entire business is just Juan. He gets paid only when he works. He sells no actual products, just services. If he is sick or if he takes a vacation, he earns nothing. He wondered out loud whether he had already reached his maximum potential. He is worried about the fact that there are no growth opportunities under his current setup. He is not sure whether he should just keep doing what he is doing or whether he should change.

The conversation then turned to "the building of an empire" as Juan put it. He wants the student team to take a close look at some other business options that include:

- Hire an additional computer technician or two and grow the existing business.

- Open a retail computer store as a complement to his current services. If he were to establish a retail store, should he rent, lease, or buy the building?
- Hire an outside salesperson or two to generate new business either as part of the retail store or as an extension of his current business.
- Establish a Web site rather than a retail store as a complement to his current services.
- Consider new and related ideas generated by the student team.
- Do nothing.

Juan indicated to the students that he likes the idea of building an empire, but that he feels as if he is wading into new waters that he is unfamiliar with. For example, if he were to open a retail store, could he possibly compete with the Circuit Citys and Best Buys of the world? He wants his success story to continue and wants to make more money while working fewer hours. He also wants to earn money when he is not working.

Juan is not sure about the best product mix and about the pricing of those products. He is very concerned about the very rapid product life cycle that is inherent to the computer industry and is afraid of getting stuck with suddenly obsolete products. Juan is also accustomed to getting paid very quickly for his services and has not had to deal with credit and cash flow issues.

QUESTIONS

1. Form small groups and brainstorm and develop a strategic plan for Juan. Compare and contrast each group's plan and gain consensus as to the best.
2. Using that best plan, return to your original group and develop a tactical plan for Juan.
3. Having now developed a tactical plan, what are the major challenges facing Juan if he were to go forward with your plan? Include a SWOT analysis as part of your assessment.

CASE 8

THE EARLY STAGES OF PAINT CHECK SERVICES

Randy Bunge grew up in his grandfather's family business, inspecting paint jobs for a market mostly made up of businesses and government agencies who were having contractors paint their buildings and public works. He had some ideas about how to modernize the business, but his grandfather was content with the old ways of working. Still, his grandfather encouraged Randy to pursue his dream, so, with his father's support, Randy set out to create a new business called Paint Check Services (PCS).

In his entrepreneurship class, one of the first things Randy was required to do was create an elevator pitch for his business to help explain it to potential investors, suppliers, customers, and professional supports like accountants and lawyers. His first version of the pitch is given below.

Elevator Pitch—Paint Check Services

Mr. Customer, I know that you have recently decided to have your structure repainted. I would like to offer my third party inspection service to you. A third party inspector will ensure that the job is done correctly and eliminate a lot of headaches for you.

Hiring a painting firm on time and material gives them the incentive to drag the job out. So you are left with having to hire them on a contractual basis. The only problem is that this sets up an incentive to cut corners or use inferior materials. The most commonly cut corner in the painting industry is using PCS instead of the required thinner. In most cases the PCS will still allow the paint to go on nicely and everything will look nice when they are finished, but instead of getting a 10-year service life out of the coating, you will only get five to seven years. Having our inspectors on the job to watch the whole process will ensure you get the 10-year service life that you are expecting.

Our inspectors are highly qualified in the coatings field with several years of experience and NACE* training. The inspector we put on your job will watch every stage of the painting process to make sure it is being performed correctly and will report to you as often as you would like. Some customers want to see the inspector once a week to see how the job is going. Others like to see the inspector every morning for a progress report. The inspector will also create an electronic inspection report every day that will be e-mailed to you at the end of the day for you to keep in your records.

Bottom line, you can be confident that the job is being done correctly and that you will not have to spend any more time than you want to supervising the project.

* NACE is the professional organization for paint inspectors.

QUESTIONS

1. Using the description of the elevator pitch given in Chapter 8's "How to Write Your Elevator Pitch,"

evaluate this pitch. How does it do on the four parts of the pitch? How could it do better?

2. Would this pitch be equally effective with the four audiences mentioned (investors, suppliers, customers, and professional supports)? Did it "play favorites" with one or more audiences? What could be done to make it more universal in appeal?

CASE 9

THE HOUSE OF WINE—GRAND OPENING

CASE PERSPECTIVE

Fred and Larry Butts are excited and a bit nervous about their new wine and specialty store that is scheduled to celebrate its grand opening in about four months. Fred and Larry have spent the past year choosing a location for their new venture and completing a market research and business plan.

The couple purchased a lakeside parcel of property in the heart of the lakes region of upstate New York. Their newly built structure includes a 7,200-square-foot retail showroom (72 × 100) with a below-ground wine and inventory storage area of the same dimensions. The retail showroom is very elegant, featuring wood floors, a large number of beautiful windows, many of which overlook a scenic lake vista, bright stucco walls adorned with works of art and a high-end surround-sound system. The building is located on a busy road, and the parcel includes plenty of room for parking and possible building expansion.

Fred and Larry's market research indicates that the area is evenly divided between an upper-middle-class population of second home seasonal and year-round retirees, a white-collar population of insurance and banking people, and a blue-collar population of factory workers. The total population of the multitown region nearly doubles between Memorial Day and Labor Day each year (from 50,000 to 100,000+), as there are a large number of summer cottages and campgrounds that surround the many small lakes within their market radius. The region also enjoys a "leaf-peeping" tourist season in the fall and a pass-through and nearby ski market during the winter months.

Tourism is the area's major industry, followed closely by the manufacturing sector. There are no major cities nearby. The area consists of several small towns surrounded by beautiful hardwood forests, fresh water lakes and ponds, and several nearby small mountain ranges.

Fred and Larry's market research also revealed that there is currently very little direct competition in the area and that the fine wine and related products markets are growing steadily. Wine is currently available only in local convenience stores and supermarkets. Those establishments typically carry the lower-priced, lower-end, faster-moving selections. Fred and Larry are very optimistic about their chances for success, but are still faced with several important decisions to make prior to their grand opening.

Highlights of the financial section of Fred and Larry's business plan include the following:

- A budget of $150,000 for store fixtures, furniture, and other equipment.
- A budget of $250,000 for merchandise inventory.
- A beginning working capital balance of $100,000 (they expect this and their initial sales to support the net cash flow from operations for a period of six months, at which time the business is projected to support itself).
- A break-even sales volume of $650,000.
- All sales are for cash or credit.
- About half of their wine inventory must be paid for up front; the other half is purchased under 2/10/ net/30 terms.
- All complementary products (described below) are purchased under 2/10 net/30 and/or 2/10 net/ 45 terms.

Fred and Larry's major remaining unfinished business and related decisions revolve around their specific product mix, the specific layout of the store and warehouse, and their short-, medium-, and long-range marketing and promotion plan. Each is described below in more detail.

PRODUCT MIX

While wine is obviously Fred and Larry's major product line, there are a very wide range of products and prices to choose from. A single bottle of wine can sell from as little as $5 to as much as $10,000 or more. Wines are generally grouped into categories that sell from $5 to $8, $9 to $17, $18 to $30, $30 to $75, and $100+. There are red wines and white wines, small- to standard- to large-sized bottles, champagnes, after-dinner wines, and dessert wines. Wines can be sold by the case, as part of a gift set, on site and through the mail. The major producers of wine are found in France, Italy, Germany, South America, Australia, and California.

Fred and Larry need to select the "right" mix of complementary products. They already find themselves with vendors offering more products than they can possibly handle. Those products include but are not limited to assorted glassware; wine racks and storage units; corkscrews; cookbooks; party platters; serving utensils; coasters; dry, fresh, and frozen food products; tablecloths and napkins; newspapers and magazines; and so on.

Their goal is to operate an upscale, classy establishment and to make as much money as possible. They must pay attention to cash flow and store image. The cheaper wines move fast but generate a smaller profit per unit and portray a "lower-class image." The more expensive wines move more slowly, generate a much larger per unit profit, and portray an image of "upper-class elegance." They must also consider services as well as products. Those include but are not limited to delivery, catering, wine-tasting parties, wine classes, and so on.

STORE LAYOUT

With building construction nearly complete, Fred and Larry keep staring at their (now empty) 72 by 100 feet of retail/showroom space that they must soon fill with equipment, fixtures, products, and other accessories. The lower level must soon be filled with storage equipment, inventory, supplies, and other operational necessities. How should each level be laid out? What kind of display cases should they buy? How should they incorporate light, music, and other presentation aspects into their business? Where should the cash register be? What about an office? How should inventory be received, stored, and handled?

They must design their layout in a way that will maximize sales and profits; maximize their customer's buying experience; maximize the use of wall, floor, ceiling, and window space; minimize shoplifting; maximize safety; and minimize liability.

Outdoor presentation and layout decisions must be made as well. Those include but are not limited to road and building signage, lighting, parking lot design, trash and snow removal, landscaping, traffic flow, and safety.

SHORT-, MEDIUM-, AND LONG-RANGE MARKETING AND PROMOTION PLAN

Fred and Larry envision a three-phase marketing and promotion plan. In the short term (first six months), they want to maximize exposure by having as many people learn about and visit the store as possible. They want people to show up and have an experience that makes them want to come back soon and often. They want to generate enough sales to establish and sustain a positive cash flow within six months of their grand opening.

Their medium-range (six months to one year) goals call for the establishment of a never-ending positive cash flow from operations, a year-round local clientele to support that cash flow, and the beginning of a long era of word-of-mouth referrals.

Their long-range goals are focused on sales and profit stability and flexibility. Fred and Larry's first, second, and third year sales projections are $1,000,000, $1,500,000 and $2,000,000, respectively. At that point, their goal is to achieve an annual increase in sales of 5–10 percent. By the end of their fifth year, they want to be in the position of being able to sell the business for a substantial profit ($1,000,000 or more) or continue to run and grow the business if they are having fun.

QUESTIONS

1. Fred and Larry raised several issues regarding the product mix for their business. What product strategy do you think makes the most sense for The House of Wine? Why?
2. Given the market and product line options for this new business, what kind of pricing strategy do you think makes the most sense for the business?
3. Prepare a time line of strategies and actions that will help the principals achieve their short-, medium-, and long-term goals.

CASE 10

BUSINESS DEMISE

When you look at a page of a textbook chapter, you see a carefully organized grouping of body matter text lines, text boxes, photos with captions, and figures. For more than 200 years, the process of arranging material to be printed (called typesetting) was the same, with hundreds of small mom-and-pop businesses doing this type of work under contract for major publishers. Often, the shops were near the publisher's major installations, and the business relationships were based on personal contacts between publishers and typesetters. By the 1980s, Asian companies (primarily in India and China) came into the business, seeking work from the large American and British publishers.

Donald Sontag was a 32-year-old New Yorker who had been in the business and had the idea to buy a large number of the small mom-and-pop typesetting shops (called a *rollup*). He started by buying the 100-employee Carter Typesetting Company, an Iowa typesetter and one of the larger such companies, as a basis for the rollup. He had roughly 70 people employed in small shops in the

Northeast. He also bought a 30-person Manila, Philippines typesetter to take advantage of the lower costs of Asian typesetting shops. His vision was on target. Carter soared to $10,000,000 in annual sales and profits of $1,000,000. His own bank account grew to over $2,000,000.

In the world economy of the 1990s, outsourcing from the United States to Asia was a growing phenomenon, and one from which Donald thought he was positioned to benefit. But even as he was taking the lead in this, and promoting this approach to his customers as a competitive advantage, his customers were themselves looking for Asian typesetters to forge direct business relations.

Ironically, the growth of the Internet made outsourcing easier for the large publishers. Originally, the graphic transfer machine needed for remote typesetting cost $45,000 and the slow data line cost $10,000 a year at least. Since typesetting was an industry composed of many small shops, it was uneconomical to try and equip all of them with the equipment. However, with the advent of digital typesetting programs and the growth of personal computers and the Internet, the graphic equipment dropped to a cost of $200, while a fast data line cost $1800 a year. Suddenly it was cost-effective for the major publishers and all typesetters to have the equipment and fast Internet hookups that made worldwide outsourcing feasible.

While the American typesetters like Carter originally had an edge on quality, the Asian shops were faster at adopting the new lower-cost technologies, which decreased their costs. As the Asian typesetters got more opportunities for business from the major publishers, they quickly improved their quality to keep these lucrative customers. Soon the American typesetting industry was losing market share to their Asian competitors.

At Carter, the employees were resisting the new technologies and were very protective of their good pay and perks. The workers (mostly women who were second breadwinners in their families) were more interested in protecting a lifestyle they valued than in meeting the economic and technological challenges of a newly competitive industry. In addition, they had trouble letting work go overseas, keeping it in Carter even when it made financial sense to send it overseas. The company's profitability was dropping quickly. Donald's partner Dan believed in "benevolent capitalism" (an idea about treating employees in as fair and considerate a way possible pioneered at IBM in the 1950s and 1960s) and was reluctant to press the employees for faster changes or cost-cutting activities.

Donald could see business moving overseas at an even faster rate. He could see the quality of the Asian typesetting improving dramatically and quickly. He saw the costs of the technology for outsourcing (and managing outsourced projects) improve in completeness and drop in cost at the same time. The all important question was, what should he do about this and what could he get the Carter Company to do?

QUESTIONS

1. How would you describe the problem the Carter Company is facing? What is causing it?
2. What strategy would you recommend Donald take to solve this business problem? Why?
3. How can Donald entice his customers at the big textbook publishers to use Carter instead of cutting their own deals with Asian typesetters?

CASE 11

S & Z EAST COAST IMPORTERS

OVERVIEW

Herbie Shapiro has worked as a retail footwear salesman in the New York City area for nearly 20 years. The New York City native has always worked for someone else but knows the business and its people very well. Herbie has always felt that the supply side of the retail footwear business is poorly organized, and that few if any distributors provide good service to the hundreds of retail outlets in the metropolitan area.

Mei Zhao, a native of China, is a longtime acquaintance of Herbie, and a manufacturer's rep for several of the Pacific Rim footwear manufacturers. Mei functions primarily as a foreign agent and freight forwarder for the Asian manufacturers, overseeing the unloading and trucking of container ship cargo.

Mei shares many of the same views as Herbie when it comes to the distribution and supply side of the retail footwear business. Both men are at the midpoint of their careers, have built a solid business and personal relationship with each other, and following several meetings, have decided to form a partnership. S & Z East Coast Importers has the opportunity to lease a 60,000-square-foot warehouse with a buy option in northern New Jersey for purposes of establishing a distribution center for the metropolitan area retail footwear business.

Mei already has many good links and relationships with the major suppliers and shippers of retail footwear. The partners plan to import a wide range of products including casual shoes, athletic footwear, fashion and outdoor boots, slippers, socks, laces, pads and inserts. Mei has access to all the major national brands as well as the bargain priced no-name lines.

In addition to his long association and membership in local and national footwear organizations, Herbie knows many store owners and employees within the New York–New Jersey metro area. Herbie is well liked and well respected. The partners believe that their strong combination of supply side and retail experience will provide them with access to many good markets.

As is the case in many industries, there are a very small number of large suppliers of manufactured products coupled with a very large number of small retail stores. One of the major keys to success therefore is the existence of an efficient, well-organized system of distribution. Herbie and Mei are focusing their efforts on doing a better job than the competition and on filling that niche in the footwear market.

LOGISTICAL ISSUES AND CHALLENGES

Most of the aforementioned footwear products arrive at the West Coast on giant container ships. After clearing customs, the containers are off-loaded onto tractors for local (western) delivery and onto railcars for Midwestern and East Coast distribution. Herbie and Mei plan to set up their building as a warehouse and distribution center.

Warehouse and distribution centers must purchase virtually all their products in large quantities. Herbie and Mei will be faced with buying stock shipments ranging from no less than 1,000 to as many as 50,000 to 100,000 units of laces, shoes, socks, running shoes, and so on.

Retailers on the other hand typically must purchase very small quantities of mixed loads of products, primarily because of a lack of retail and storage space. Herbie and Mei will be faced with orders that call for 50–150 pairs of laces, shoes, socks, running shoes, and so on.

Warehouse and distribution centers must therefore be set up to receive, unload, and store large shipments of product (railroad cars/tractor trailers), to "break bulk" (unpack, count, inventory, and repack), and to load and deliver small mixed loads to retail establishments. Many metro area retailers are located on cramped and busy streets with limited access.

The financial side of Herbie and Mei's business looks very promising. Thanks to Mei's connections with suppliers and Herbie's connections with the New York-New Jersey metro market, the partners anticipate an average markup of 30–40 percent for their products. That is about twice as much as Mei earns as a manufacturer's rep.

In order for their business to succeed, several variables and logistics must fall into place and be properly managed. Their warehouse and distribution process, quality of service, and financial management must operate at maximum efficiency. In addition to in-house efficiency and cost control, the company must also buy and sell enough volume of product to cover all costs and generate profits.

Retail customers are looking for timely and frequent deliveries of small quantities of very specific products. Some of those customers may need merchandising help as well. If their products are not selling, the distribution centers and manufacturers will soon be backed up with product as well. Retail sales are the key to avoiding a "bottleneck" in the process and flow of manufacturing and distribution.

The financial side of this business requires close and careful management of receivables and payables. Many manufacturers expect and receive payment for their products in about 10 days. This is essential to the sustained cash flow of their operations (primarily for payroll and raw materials purchases). Some manufacturers are in a position to offer credit terms of up to 30 days. Retailers on the other hand often require accounts payable terms ranging from 30 to 60 days. This is essential to the sustained cash flow of their operations, as customer sales are the primary source of funds.

So while the prospect of a 30–40 percent markup is clearly attractive, there is a cash flow situation and challenge that must be met.

Herbie and Mei are unsure about the best way to facilitate and manage trucking and insurance. They have the option of buying or leasing their own trucks on both the supply and delivery side and also have the option of using independent trucking companies. They could select some combination of those two options. In addition, merchandise must be insured, but who exactly is responsible for that coverage and when does that "ownership" change hands?

The partners project monthly warehouse operating expenses of $55,000 (building, payroll, administration, and salaries). This does not include merchandise, trucking, or insurance. The partners have conservatively projected first year sales to be $3 million.

Their warehouse inventory capabilities are in excess of $30 million. Herbie and Mei realize that it will take some time to approach that level from both a sales and cash flow perspective. Their facility and market base clearly present the potential to achieve sales of $40 million or more. Cash flow is the current obstacle. They have just over $4 million in cash and working capital (line of credit) for their start-up and believe that that will accommodate first year sales of $3 million given their logistics of inventory purchase, sales, and cash flow.

From a distance, the prospect of success is promising. The partners have the opportunity to buy low and sell high in large volume. There is a market niche to fill. The partners have the experience and the connections on both the supply and sales sides of the business.

QUESTIONS

1. What model for distribution does S & Z plan to pursue? What does its distribution channel chain look like?
2. Does its site selection make sense for the kind of business S & Z plans to pursue?
3. How should Herbie and Mei go about figuring the right mix of using their own trucks and using independent trucking companies?
4. How can the principals use technology to achieve success in their new venture? Be sure to address each of the major categories presented, i.e., purchasing, transportation, operations, distribution, and financial management.
5. Select a specific business or industry that you may become a part of; how would you incorporate the technological aspects described in the text into your day-to-day operations?

CASE 12

THE WALLINGFORD BOWLING CENTER

A group of 12 lifelong friends put together $2 million of their own funds and built a $13 million, 48-lane bowling alley near Norfolk, Virginia. Two of the investors became employees of the corporation. Ned Flanders works full time as general manager, and James Ahmad, a licensed CPA, serves as controller.

The beautiful, modern-day facility features a multi-level spacious interior with three rows of 16 lanes on two separate levels of the building, a full-service bar, a small restaurant, a game room (pool, video games, pinball), and two locker rooms. The facility sits on a spacious lot with plenty of parking and room to grow.

The bowling center is located in the small blue-collar town of Wallingford. There is no direct competition within the town. The surrounding communities include a wide-ranging mix of ethnic groups, professionals, middle- to upper-middle-class private homes, and several apartment and condominium complexes ranging from singles to young married couples to senior citizen retirement units. Nearly 200,000 people live within 15 miles of Wallingford.

The bowling center is open 24 hours per day and has a staff of 27 part- and full-time employees. After four years of operation, the partners find themselves frustrated with the low-profit performance of the business. While sales are covering expenses, the partners are not happy with the end-of-year profit sharing pool. The most recent income statement follows:

Wallingford Bowling Center
Income Statement—2004

Sales		$3,844,000
Cost of Goods Sold		1,315,000
Gross Margin		$2,529,000
Operating Expenses:		$2,381,000
Mortgage	$960,000	
Depreciation	195,000	
Utilities	138,000	
Maintenance	125,000	
Payroll	700,000	
Supplies	127,000	
Insurance	136,000	
Taxable Income		148,000
Taxes		54,000
Net Income		$ 94,000

The bowling center operates at 100 percent capacity on Sunday through Thursday nights from 6:00 P.M. until midnight. Two sets of men's leagues come and go on each of those nights, occupying each lane with mostly five-person teams. Bowlers from each league consistently spend money at both the bar and restaurant. In fact, the men's leagues combine to generate about 60 percent of total current sales.

The bowling center operates at about 50 percent capacity on Friday and Saturday nights and on Saturday morning. The Friday and Saturday "open bowling" nights include mostly teenagers, young couples, and league members who come to practice in groups of two or three. The Saturday morning group is a kid's league, ages 10 through 14.

There are four women's leagues that bowl on Monday and Wednesday afternoons.

Business is extremely slow at the bowling center on Monday through Friday and Sunday mornings, and on the afternoons of Tuesday, Thursday, Friday, Saturday, and Sunday. It is not uncommon to have just three or four lanes in operation during those time periods.

The owners have taken a close look at the cost side of their business as a way to improve profitability. They concluded that while the total operating expense of $2,381,000 might appear to be high, there was in fact little room for expense cutting.

At a recent meeting of the partners, James Ahmad reported on the results of his three-month long investigation into the operating cost side of other bowling alleys and discovered that The Wallingford Bowling Center was very much in keeping with their industry. James went on to report that bowling alleys were considered to be "heavy to fixed cost operations" and that the key to success and profitability lies in maximizing capacity and sales dollars.

QUESTIONS

1. Develop a complete short marketing plan for this company. The goal of the plan is to increase capacity to as close to 100 percent as possible.
2. Given the particulars of this case, develop a list of the five best target market groups and the distinct features of the "4Ps" for each of those groups.

CASE 13

PARKER MOUNTAIN PRODUCTS, INC.

COMPANY HISTORY

The New England region of the United States includes a beautiful coastal stretch that extends from Maine to Rhode Island, through the states of New Hampshire, Massachusetts, and Connecticut. The area is famous for its summer tourism, which includes beaches, quaint villages and towns, restaurants, shops, historic sites and landmarks, and lobsters. Tens of thousands of people from around the world vacation in the area each year, especially during the summer season, which extends from Memorial Day to Labor Day.

Shortly after World War II, Ernest Parker returned to his hometown of Rochester, New Hampshire, and built a small factory that produces low-end glass and ceramic regional souvenirs. These products include wine glasses, general glassware, ceramic cups and bowls, and small platters. Each of these is decorated with a variety of painted images and words related to the specific coastal tourist towns and markets, that is, pictures of lobsters, seagulls, ocean waves, famous towns, and famous sites.

Ernest has provided steady employment for 35 production and support staff. The business has grown at a rate of about 5 percent per year (in sales). The most recent profit and loss statement is shown:

Parker Mountain Products, Inc.
Profit and Loss Statement—2001

Sales	$2,000,000
Cost of sales*	990,000
Gross profit	$1,010,000
Expenses	930,000
Net income	$ 80,000

*Includes direct materials only.

The entire production is sold through a small number of manufacturer's reps, wholesalers, and brokers. While the opportunity was always there to sell direct, Ernest chose to focus all his efforts on the production side of the business, allowing others to market, sell, and distribute the products to retail shops, hotels, and other vendors. The industry average or norm for profits is between 5 and 7 percent (net income to sales).

CURRENT SITUATION

Having now reached the age of 75, Ernest has decided to retire and turn the business over to his grandsons Chris and Ben, two young and ambitious entrepreneurs who recently graduated with honors from the renowned Applied Business Management program at the University of New Hampshire's Thompson School.

Chris and Ben are anxious to improve efficiency on the production side and to develop a variety of direct niche markets to complement their wholesale distribution on the marketing and sales side. The opportunity to add, drop, or shift the product mix, and to increase production and sales exists. In order to properly analyze and act on this, they have asked their bookkeeper to provide more specific production and cost data.

This information is presented below:

Product Line	No. of Units Produced	Selling Price per Unit	CGS per Unit	Total Variable Costs per Year
Platter	300,000	$2.00	$ .60	$240,000
Cups	200,000	2.50	1.50	160,000
Bowls	100,000	2.00	.20	80,000
General glassware	100,000	1.00	.70	80,000
Wine glasses	300,000	2.00	1.40	240,000

The total variable costs of $800,000 are assigned or charged to each product line based on the number of units produced. Total fixed costs for the factory are $80,000; selling and administrative costs for the total company are $50,000.

Chris and Ben have determined that the factory is now at 85 percent of capacity. They are certain that production can be increased without incurring any extra expense beyond direct materials.

They also know that the selling price could be increased by 15 percent as a result of a direct sales program. Their only uncertainty or fear is in disrupting the long-standing relationships that exist with the various manufacturers' reps, wholesalers, and brokers who have been able to sell all of the company's production for many years. They are afraid of "biting the hand that feeds them" by selling to an end user who currently buys from one of their own distributors.

QUESTIONS

1. As a first step, conduct a financial analysis of current operations by reformatting the income statement to include individual product lines as well as the total company. Analyze those data.
2. Use the information provided along with any assumptions you wish to make and construct a balance sheet and cash flow statement. Analyze those data.
3. What specific goals and standards of performance would you recommend for the new managers? What control process or audit system would you include for follow-up purposes?

CASE 14

NATE MOWER & SON, RESIDENTIAL PLUMBER(S)

Nate Mower has worked as a plumber in the Minneapolis area for 20 years. Nate has operated his business as a one-man show and has also had as many as six employees working on two or three jobs at a time.

During the winter months, Nate traditionally works alone, servicing local residents with routine plumbing repairs, furnace maintenance, and frozen pipes. During the summer months, Nate takes on a few new home construction plumbing and heating installations that call for the help of additional workers.

Nate has an excellent reputation for honesty and high-quality work. He has never had to advertise, as the work requests seem to be endlessly lined up and waiting. Nate works long hours, yet has managed to earn only a modest living for his wife Jessie and son Brett. In fact, Jessie has been heard to comment out loud to friends and family that Nate is "always busy and always broke." Several years back, Jessie had to take on a part-time cashier position at the local supermarket "just to put groceries on the table." The Mowers inherited Nate's grandparent's old farmhouse and have no mortgage. Nate drives around in his grandfather's old panel truck that he converted into the company work vehicle.

Nate is from the old school. He is a down-to-earth, hard-working country boy who loves to hunt and fish in his spare time. As Nate puts it, "I love my job and don't want to charge people too much for my work." Nate charges $25 per hour for his time (while onsite only) and provides all parts at cost. Nate believes that "it would be stealing" to mark up the price of parts that he buys from a nearby wholesale distribution center. Nate mails out bills when he gets around to it, usually late at night if he's not too tired.

Brett Mower has learned a lot about the trade from his father. He often went along with Nate on jobs when he was young, and worked for his father throughout high school, mostly during the summers. Brett has returned home from a tour of duty in the military and is thinking about becoming a partner in the family business. He has several serious concerns, however, and is not sure which way to turn.

Although Brett would never say so out loud, he acknowledges that his father does seem to be always busy and always broke. He wonders why his mother is forced to work to put groceries on the table and help pay the bills. The family has no mortgage and no car payments. His folks have never taken a vacation, rarely go out, and still don't own a personal computer.

Brett recalls many incidents of receiving angry letters from creditors and parts suppliers over past-due bills. There have also been a few bounced and delayed paychecks over the years. Nate is currently on "COD—only" status with his suppliers who also expect some payment toward outstanding payables.

Brett wonders whether the business could ever support two families. He is planning on marrying his childhood sweetheart within the next year and has dreams of a house, family, and career of his own.

And yet, business is booming. The phone never stops ringing, especially during the long winter months, and Nate has barely scratched the surface of the new home installation market. The Minneapolis area is booming with new home construction. There have been reports in the local papers that several jobs have been delayed because of a shortage of contractors, including plumbing and heating. The short- and long-term market outlook is excellent.

Brett has been anguishing over his next move. Nate is thrilled at the prospect of forming a partnership with his son. Brett wants to start a new life and career in his hometown but has serious concerns about the condition and future of his father's business. Jessie suggested that perhaps someone in the know should take a look at their books and point them in the right direction.

Nate's most recent IRS returns reveal the following:

Schedule C—Profit and Loss Statement—2007
Nathan Mower, Residential Plumber

Sales		$221,250
CGS		135,000
GM		$ 86,250
Expenses:		$ 49,500
Outside		
Labor	$39,500	
Truck	2,000	
Supplies	4,000	
Insurance	4,000	
Taxable income		$ 36,750

Balance Sheet Accounts—12/31/2007
Nathan Mower, Residential Plumber

Cash	$ 600	Accounts payable	$ 98,000
Accounts receivable	97,500	Notes payable	14,000
Inventory	143,400		
Land	0	Long-term debt	0
Buildings	0		
Equipment	36,000	Net worth	$165,500
	$277,500		$277,500

QUESTIONS

1. Using the above statements, provide specific recommendations that will alleviate Nate's cash flow problems.
2. Given the history of the company, is it possible for Brett to come on board, earn a living, and successfully grow the company? If so, how?

CASE 15

THE LANDLORDS: INVESTMENTS IN COMMERCIAL REAL ESTATE

Greg, Chris, and Nancy are midcareer high school teachers in the Pittsburgh area. They love their jobs, are very dedicated, and plan to stay on until they are eligible for retirement in about 15 or 20 years. The three teachers and friends have met on several occasions to brainstorm ideas for an outside business partnership. With kids about to enter college and a somewhat pessimistic outlook toward their retirement pensions, the three want to make some extra money.

Their financial goals are to supplement their annual incomes by $10,000 to $15,000 each for college tuition purposes and to build an equity base of about $300,000 each for retirement.

Following several meetings, some consultation with friends and advisers, and some local market research, they have settled on the business of commercial real estate investment, more specifically, multiunit rental properties.

The Pittsburgh and surrounding communities are currently experiencing and are projected to sustain above-average growth in both jobs and housing. In fact, there is a current shortage of both rental units and single-family housing in the area. As a result, rents have increased steadily during the past three to five years and currently average:

1-bedroom apartment	$750–$900 per month
2-bedroom apartment	$1,000–$1,200 per month
3-bedroom apartment	$1,200–$1,400 per month
4-bedroom apartment	$1,400–$1,800 per month

Tenants are responsible for heat, hot water, and electricity. Landlords provide parking and maintenance.

Interest rates are very low at this time and are therefore very attractive for borrowing and investing purposes. Greg has learned that local banks will finance commercial properties for up to 25 years at 6 percent interest. In addition, those banks will provide loans for up to 85 percent of assessed property values.

Multi-unit apartment buildings in the area range from $300,000 to $600,000 depending on size, condition, and neighborhood location. Most buildings include three to six separate units ranging from one to four bedrooms in size.

Greg, Chris, and Nancy want to locate and purchase enough buildings to meet their financial goals. Each building must therefore generate enough rental income to offset all costs and generate an after-tax profit. The buildings must also be carefully selected with regard to their expected growth in appreciation.

In addition to building and outside maintenance, the landlords are responsible for mortgage payments, city water and sewer bills, insurance, and local taxes. The IRS requires that depreciation be spread over a 28-year period.

The landlords each have $30,000 to invest for down payments on properties. One of their advisers urged them to set aside a portion of that amount for working capital depending on their cash flow outlook.

QUESTIONS

1. Greg, Chris, and Nancy could do their real estate rental business strictly self-financed or with bank loans. Which do you recommend and why? What are the monthly financial obligations under each approach?
2. Given their starting funds and loan opportunities, how large a real estate deal can they handle their first time out if they go the bank loan route?
3. One adviser mentioned putting aside a portion of their money for working capital. How much would you recommend they put aside? On what do you base your suggestion?
4. What are the typical cash flow problems that people in real estate rentals face? How can Greg, Chris, and Nancy prepare themselves to meet these?
5. Many real estate investments or projects are of a much greater magnitude than those in this case. How would you go about organizing and financing a project that required an investment of say $300 to $350 million?

CASE 16

RICHARD HARRIS AND HARRIS HOMES LLC

Many people who thought the devastation from 2005's Hurricane Katrina would be a golden opportunity for the Gulf Coast construction industry were sadly mistaken. Consider the situation of Richard Harris.

Harris had owned Harris Homes LLC about ten years when Katrina hit Ocean Springs, Mississippi. By 2004, his sales had grown to $3.5 million and his 2005 sales were on track for $5 million when the storm hit. Before the storm, he had $3 million in projects and $300,000 worth of vacant property. Before the storm, he was building 24 houses, and 12 of them were already under contract. When Katrina hit, those homes sustained damage, and even with insurance, Harris' out-of-pocket expenses to cover his deductible were around $100,000. The bad news was that paying those deductible expenses would eat up all of his working capital.

That money problem fed into another problem—people. Harris was employing 60 to 80 subcontracted workers, but now he couldn't make competitive offers to get the workers back. FEMA (the Federal Emergency Management Agency) was spending money for their Blue Roof emergency repair program, out-of-state contractors with fat bank accounts were hiring local workers at premium rates to help them start repairing and rebuilding, and the area's worker base was still depleted because of the people who evacuated the area and had not yet returned. Just as workers were scarce and going for premium prices, so were lumber and all building materials, as an entire region tried to rebuild at the same time.

Those 12 homes under contract were sold at pre-Katrina prices, in effect "locking-in" low prices the region will not see for months, perhaps years to come. Harris was obligated to finish those homes. However, the cabinetmaker, plumber, and electrician he had favored all had businesses underwater after Katrina, and may be out of business.

It is now about three weeks after Katrina (and the glancing blow from Hurricane Rita) hit. Looking at his immediate future, Harris knows he needs to get to work on the other nearly finished homes, which would get some new cash flowing into his business. He has applied for SBA disaster relief, but has been told it would be 90 days before any money became available—if he qualifies. He needs to move to get some of the potentially lucrative government contracts for rebuilding that are being offered. But even here, it is hard to know how to bid when prices are so unpredictable. For example, the cost of dumping debris from cleared land jumped from $1 a cubic yard to $4 after Katrina.

Harris had done several things right. He had insurance. He kept a set of records where they would be safe, making it easier to apply for government relief and insurance after the storm. He even had kept ready cash for expenses. Despite all of that, Katrina hit, and Richard Harris is looking at the possible loss of his business, right at the moment when the construction industry in his area appears about to enter a golden age of rebuilding.

QUESTIONS

1. What do you think are the two greatest risks facing Richard Harris's business? Why?
2. What actions can Richard take now to manage the risks you mentioned above?
3. From this experience, what recommendations would you make to Richard Harris to do an even better job of preparing for future hurricanes?

Source: Jackie Larson, "Gulf Coast Entrepreneurs Face Reality," Entrepreneur.com, September 22, 2005, http://www.entrepreneur.com/article/0,4621,323569,00.html.

CASE 17

THE HOUSE OF WINE (REVISITED)

Please refer back to Case 9. The focus now shifts to inventory management. The proprietors have a somewhat limited start-up budget for inventory and working capital. It is very important for them to buy the right quantity of the right products (part of asset management).

Inventory may be purchased with cash, through short-term loans from a bank (notes payable/line of credit), or through a credit arrangement with suppliers (accounts payable). There are also a variety of shipping and receiving programs and systems available.

QUESTIONS

1. Use the information from this case, Case 9, and your classroom discussions to create a detailed inventory management program for the proprietors.
2. How would you recommend they pay for the inventory?
3. What milestones in the House of Wine's operations do you think should occur in order to signal when a different approach to inventory might make sense?
4. When thinking about the House of Wine's inventory, will it make any difference that some inventory is time-limited (i.e., can spoil), other parts of it are seasonal, and some can be sold or held for long periods of time? If it is an issue, how do you propose to handle it?
5. Will the House of Wine face much in the way of accounts receivable problems? Why or why not?

CASE 18

THERESA MURRAY AND IN THE EYE OF THE BEHOLDER

Theresa Murray started a new business called In the Eye of the Beholder about two years ago. Her business is a retail store that sells art work and does framing. Theresa purchased an old house for her business. The house is in an older neighborhood in the city which is back on the "upswing" because young professionals are moving into the area. The houses in the neighborhood are all small by today's standards and have small lots. In the Eye of the Beholder is on the corner of a street that has been zoned as commercial, so Theresa's business is in full compliance with zoning regulations. The houses on that street are in the process of being or have been modified for use as businesses such as an insurance agency, a dental office, a chiropractor's office, a lawyer's office, a hair salon, and retail stores. There is on-street parking as well as three to four parking spaces in the former backyards of each house accessed by driveways running beside the houses.

The street behind In the Eye of the Beholder, however, is still zoned for single-family residences. The house directly behind Theresa's place is owned and occupied by an elderly gentleman, Elmer Ferguson. Elmer has been nothing but trouble to Theresa from the beginning. He has complained about everything, including traffic, noise, lighting, her trash bin—you name it. Theresa has tried to be cordial to him and has met all legal requirements for parking, lighting, signage, and the like. In an attempt to keep Elmer calm, she even had a privacy fence built between the parking area behind her house and Elmer's backyard, although there was no legal requirement for the fence.

Theresa knew when she bought the house that it would need a new roof in the near future. The time has come to replace the roof and she would like to go ahead and get the job done. Theresa has a can-do attitude and is fully capable of roofing the small house herself. She worked construction during summers when she was in college and looks forward to being outside in the sunshine. Clearly, she could save money by doing the work herself. She has one lingering doubt, however. The house is close enough to the ocean that there is always a breeze, and, not infrequently, it is downright windy. Theresa is concerned that no matter how careful she is, something could blow off the roof onto Elmer's property and cause damage, or at least infuriate Elmer. In launching his tirades against her in the past, he has threatened to sue her for various aggravations, both real and imagined. Theresa has a real concern that Elmer may sue her should nails, roofing materials, or even tools blow off the roof onto his property.

QUESTIONS

1. If Theresa's personal negligence, not that of an employee, causes damage to Elmer's property, will it make any difference what her business structure is in terms of her personal liability and how much money she could lose, should Elmer sue her and win damages?
2. If one of Theresa's employees causes damage to Elmer's property while doing his job, would it matter what business structure Theresa has in terms of what Theresa could lose?
3. What would be the arguments, pro and con, for hiring a professional roofer to do the roof repairs on the house?

CASE 19

ALASKA WILDLAND ADVENTURES

Between August 10 and 11, 2003, a 500-acre fire raged across Alaska's Kenai Peninsula. Caught in the path of this blaze was a small lodge owned by Alaska Wildland Adventures, a Girdwood, Alaska-based ecotourism company. The facility was situated in a remote area inaccessible by car, and owner Kirk Hoessle feared firefighters would not reach it in time. What's more, it was the height of the company's peak season and the majority of his staff were occupied with running tours in other parts of the state, leaving him short on help. Hoessle assembled as many of his people as he could, but with the fire fast encroaching on the lodge, the situation was growing dire. It was at this point that help came from a most unexpected source: his former employees.

Dennis Weber, a former camp manager and owner of his own construction business, received word of Hoessle's emergency around midnight on August 10. He immediately packed up some equipment and made the three and a half hour trek from his home, about a mile north of Anchorage, to the Kenai Peninsula. He arrived in the early morning hours and joined a group of 15 people, about half of whom were former employees, in fighting the blaze. The group cleared trees and brush from the lodge's perimeter. "The firefighters didn't arrive until around evening," says Weber. "By that time we had the fire ring cut." With the help of Weber and other former employees as well as some assistance from Mother Nature—the winds shifted, diverting the fire—the lodge was spared.

The incident was a testament to the goodwill Hoessle has garnered over the years with his employees. "It was truly a beautiful thing," he says. "We would've struggled to keep the business intact had the fire gone through."

Hoessle attributes the loyalty of his former and current employees to creating a work environment grounded in trust and open communications. "I don't like to make decisions in a vacuum," he says. The majority of the company's workers are seasonal tour guides, and every year they are given an employee survey. Hoessle addresses his seasonal people's concerns and communicates all improvements at the beginning of each season. Hoessle also delegates a lot of decision making to employee committees. At times, these committees serve a strictly advisory function. On other issues, such as the company's holiday schedule, the employees are empowered to make the final decision. In order to avoid giving his people false expectations, Hoessle tells employees when their deliberations will be taken on a strictly advisory basis.

Not only does the company engage employees in the decision making process, but it practices open-book management. Alaska Wildland Adventures has a revenue sharing plan, and Hoessle believes that sharing the company's financial information helps to instill trust in the program. What's more, practicing open-book management has helped engage the employees. "Knowing the financials helps me understand the big picture," says sales manager Alicia Foster. "I know what we can afford and can make decisions from the perspective of my job."

Foster says that creating a good workplace has benefited the organization in a number of ways. For example, the company is involved in ecotourism, which entails providing an educational experience that does not disturb wildlife and other natural resources. It is a complex operation that requires heavy training for new guides. The company, however, has been able to keep its training expenditures at a reasonable level because many of its seasonal employees return year after year.

Sales representative Glenda Denny first heard of the company when she worked at a nearby hotel. There she had the opportunity to come in contact with its guides, and she says meeting them convinced her to join the company. "They were all so knowledgeable, and you could tell that they loved their jobs," she says. This stable and knowledgeable staff has helped to create a loyal clientele, as evidenced by the fact that about 40 percent of the company's business comes from referrals. What's more, it has fishing guests who have been returning for 15 years.

Most importantly, Alaska Wildland Adventures' inclusiveness and open-book management style has helped the company survive during tough economic times. The August 2003 fire wasn't the first time the company's viability was threatened. The travel industry has struggled since the terrorist attacks of September 11, 2001. And unlike its competitors who offer a more diversified catalog of vacation spots, Alaska Wildland Adventures is home grown and solely dependent on travel to the state.

The downturn in business has forced the company to make some difficult choices over the last couple of years. Faced with dwindling revenues, the organization needed to cut costs. Ultimately, Hoessle decided to reduce work schedules rather than lay people off. Everyone would take off 30 days without pay. Hoessle sought the insight of employees on how they would like to handle their schedules. Some chose to take their time off all at once; others chose to work four-day weeks. Hoessle extended loans to people who were struggling to get by on the new schedules.

Understanding the sacrifices his employees made, Hoessle found inexpensive ways to reward them. For example, the company has tried to give employees greater flexibility in their scheduling. Marketing coordinator Heather Dudick is a mother and she says that working a reduced, flexible schedule has made it easier to care for and spend quality time with her eight-year-old child. The company operates several lodges and encourages employees to make use of them during the off-season. The organization also owns a transferable ski pass, which staff members can use on their downtime.

It appears that Alaska Wildland Adventures has weathered the worst of the downturn. According to an Associated Press article the adventure travel industry was rebounding. Hoessle said that the company appeared poised for a good year. And the importance of his employees' loyalty, both past and current, in surviving the tough times is not lost on him. "People work here because they are attracted to our mission and environmental beliefs," he says. "They stay because they are treated well." The loyalty and the rebound paid off. Alaska Wildland was voted the world's top eco-tour operator by Condé Nast travel magazine in 2005.

QUESTIONS

1. How would you characterize Hoessle's open-book management style?
2. How do you think this style motivates and retains key staff and employees?
3. In what ways has Hoessle been able to reward employees despite slower growth and having to cut costs throughout the small business?
4. What additional recommendations would you make to Hoessle if he needed to bring in new employees, especially as the adventure travel industry begins to heat up?

Source: Reprinted from Todd Luchik, "Survival of the Fittest," Winningworkplaces.com, http://www.winningworkplaces.org/library/success/survival of the fittest.php. Used with permission.

CASE 20

JOSEPH SHAUGHNESSY, BSI CONSTRUCTORS, ST. LOUIS

To his family and friends, Joseph "Joe" Shaughnessy became a local TV star at age 68, appearing on screen with a new Fox TV sportscaster as honorary co-chair of the 2004 United Negro College Fund's Annual St. Louis Walkathon. How many construction company executives would be so well known that they would be used as a local charitable pitchman? Not many, and that speaks volumes about Joe Shaughnessy's career.

Joe's firm, BSI Constructors, shows the unexpected paths one entrepreneur's life can take. After graduating in Civil Engineering from Saint Louis University, Joe and friend Lorry Bannes went to work for St. Louis's Gamble Construction Company, where over 10 years they rose to executive positions. Wanting to get out on their own, they formed Bannes-Shaughnessy Incorporated in 1972 with carpenter and field supervisor Ed Clinard as the third owner, and a grand total of $27,500 in capital between them. Despite their prior experience, it took five years before they received their first million dollar contract. But once that milestone was passed, their firm grew. Clinard retired in 1980 and Bannes in 1988, so by 1989 Joe was the sole owner of the firm, now called BSI Constructors, Inc.

Throughout its life the firm was innovative, pioneering the building of the region's first earthquake proof building at the Missouri Botanical Garden. The company also had a reputation for high-quality building. Churches, hospitals, universities, and companies looking to build for the long term turned to Joe Shaughnessy's firm.

The firm was also compassionate. In 1975, it won the first national Build America award given by the

Associated General Contractors of America for promoting minority subcontractor participation in the building industry. In 1989, Joe's firm would renovate a statue commemorating the first Jewish settlers in the New World on a no fee basis. In 1999, Joe (a devout Catholic) would give up weeks of his time and use of company facilities to organize the transportation for the St. Louis visit of Pope John Paul II.

Even when Joe solely owned BSI, he knew it was important to transition the ownership. He hoped to involve his children in the company and eventually pass it on to them. It was a close-knit family, and the company was like the eighth child for all seven. Many of the children worked in the company doing summer jobs, and helped on projects when needed. Eldest son Paul worked his way up through the ranks of the firm after working in mortgage banking for five years. Son Jim, who originally intended to pursue medicine, came back to the company after being successfully cured of leukemia and realizing he wanted to be productive immediately after graduating from Saint Louis University's Business School. Youngest son Dan, a Washington University Architecture School graduate, went into the business after six years with an international architecture firm. To set things straight, Joe started his transition process by writing a letter to all seven children explaining his view about the company and its need for clear management and control. Paul, with the most experience, would become president, with Jim and Dan continuing to work as executives of the company and being involved in business development and all company operations.

Today, Joe is the chairman of the board of BSI, and Paul is the president. The firm's revenues have reached $200 million a year and it continues to get many of the premier building contracts in the St. Louis region. Joe's involvement in civic activities makes him one of the best known entrepreneurs in St. Louis, and winner of the area's Ernst & Young Constructor Entrepreneur of the Year award in 1998.

QUESTIONS

1. How did Joe Shaughnessy seem to do in achieving the four bottom lines?
2. Did Joe balance with the four bottom lines at the same time, or did some come before others?
3. How did Joe use the business to promote beliefs he felt were important?
4. Some folks would say the solution to balancing the four bottom lines is to never sleep. How do you think Joe Shaughnessy would respond? Do you agree with that approach for yourself?

VIDEO CASES

VIDEO CASE 1-1

DO-GOODERS WHO SPREAD THE DOUGH

Summary

Julius Walls, Jr., CEO of Greyston Bakery and practicing minister, created a shining example of social responsibility in the business world. Greyston produced a unique business model from its human resources methods to community involvement through its foundation. While some might mistake it for a nonprofit, Mr. Walls makes it clear that his goal is to be successful and profitable.

The bakery employs approximately 60 people and produces nearly 20,000 pounds of DoGoodie brownies per day. DoGoodie brownies are currently found in select retail establishments and online. The brownies also are used in ice cream mixes for Ben and Jerry's, Stoneyfield Farms, and Häagen-Dazs.

Many of the employees are hired through the open hire program. Essentially, the job seeker signs up on a simple sheet located in the front office. Greyston Bakery gives hope to potential employees by providing opportunities to those that are labeled "unemployable" by other employers. The employee opportunities range from job advancement to education reimbursement to housing.

Unlike most businesses looking to provide its shareholders with returns each year, Greyston gives 100 percent of its profits to its Greyston Foundation, a foundation designed to provide job training, youth services, and housing for HIV/AIDS patients within the Yonkers community. Clearly, Greyston's social mission is not hurting its bottom line, with a value of over $6 million. With its strong performance, Mr. Walls hopes Greyston will be a model for others to understand how success can also include socially responsible actions. In an effort to strengthen his message, Mr. Walls is partnering with Jerry Greenfield of Ben and Jerry's in a speaking tour across college campuses to promote and inspire future generations of entrepreneurs to think and act socially responsibly.

DISCUSSION QUESTIONS

1. Name the ways that Greyston Bakery is important to the economy and its community.
2. What key concepts make Greyston Bakery socially responsible?
3. Would the Greyston model work well for other companies? Explain.
4. Give an example of a company that could integrate social responsibility.

VIDEO CASE 3-1

SMALL BUSINESS VOLUNTEERING

Summary

Milestone, a small financial services group in New York, has taken team building outside the office and into the classroom. However, this is not the typical learning classroom with pencil and paper but with paint and paintbrushes. In an effort to promote teamwork, the company encouraged the employees to arrange such events as painting a gym and classrooms at a local public school in Brooklyn. Grace Yeh, a senior consultant, felt a sense of appreciation that a firm small in size was willing to engage in community outreach much like the corporations she had worked for earlier in her career.

Milestone understands that charitable giving creates a positive corporate image, but also that staff volunteering together breeds an excellent opportunity to work on team building elements. Peter Bond, a partner in Milestone, states that consultants need to sharpen their team skills to produce a better end product through shared knowledge and resources.

NYCares, a philanthropic organization that helps companies give back to the community through different avenues, helped organize Milestone's volunteer efforts as well as those of hundreds of companies throughout New York. In fact, the organization submits that companies that give back to their community will see many returns and benefits such as positive company image and employee retention.

DISCUSSION QUESTIONS

1. Why is team building important?
2. Should a small business with only two people invest time in team building activities? Explain.
3. What elements of charitable team building differ from traditional team building exercises such as games?

VIDEO CASE 4-1

FROM GRANNY'S KITCHEN TO TESCO

Summary

Fraser Doherty, founder and CEO of Super Jam and winner of the GSEA competition, took time to learn jam making from his dear granny at the age of 14. He caught the entrepreneurial bug early as he took his jams to sell to his neighbors, and at churches, fairs, festivals, and farmer's markets.

Two years later, Fraser decided to quit school and devoted his time to capitalizing on the growth of his jams. He now produced over 1,000 jars a week in a tiny kitchen at his parent's house. Knowing his production would be limited there, he had to consider his next options. Fraser devised a plan to make jams solely from fruits and fruit juice. He started approaching large manufacturing firms looking for an agreement to produce his jams for supermarket shelves.

While Fraser believed in his jams and his ability, many large food companies he approached were far more cynical of a 16-year-old CEO. Undeterred, he pressed on to find a manufacturer willing to fill underused capacity created by the slumping economy. He managed to qualify for a small loan and convinced suppliers to give extended credit terms. Super Jam is very lean in its payroll with only the CEO and a few contract employees; nevertheless, the company's jams are on the shelves of Tesco, a major UK grocery chain. Additionally Super Jam is in initial talks with supermarkets in the United States, Australia, and other countries throughout Europe.

Super Jam has many competitors with similar ingredients and a similar price point but it offers an imaginative story of a youngster taking his granny's jam recipe all over the world.

DISCUSSION QUESTIONS

1. What method of coming up with an idea did Fraser Doherty use? How did he use SCAMPER to come up with a particular niche?
2. Do you think Fraser Doherty displayed entrepreneurial alertness? Explain.
3. How did Fraser test the feasibility of Super Jam?
4. Should the commercial buyers of Super Jam have conducted a pilot test before purchasing a large inventory? What would be the advantages and disadvantages?
5. Use SCAMPER to help Fraser come up with spin-off ideas for Super Jam.

VIDEO CASE 5-1

MAGNO-GRIP

Summary

Andre Woolery, founder of Magno-Grip, had an unusual inspiration for his innovative work gear. In fact, Andre created a utility armband three years ago for his brother-in-law, a makeup artist, to help keep the important accessories close while working with a client. The makeup utility belt sparked the thought of what other professions might require such a tool to organize their craft efficiently. His thought process led him to construction and repair services. His first product was the utility wristband called the Magno-Grip, which is equipped with a magnetic strip over the entire circumference of the wrist.

Andre bootstrapped Magno-Grip with $5,000 of personal savings and $40,000 of funding from his family. He learned through bootstrapping how to become more resourceful, such as developing marketing initiatives. Magno-Grip didn't want to be a one-product wonder and Andre created a line of products that he hopes will work well in the market. While Andre took the time to develop the collection, he was not able to focus on the other full-time task of fund-raising. He feels that this is the crux of the problem for other start-up and existing companies because the act of fund-raising is quite tedious. It requires extra meetings that can take away much-needed attention from the day-to-day business.

DISCUSSION QUESTIONS

1. What bootstrapping techniques did Andre Woolery use? What other ones could he use?
2. What recommendations would you make to balance the day-to-day business with the fund-raising?
3. Assuming Magno-Grip started as a part-time venture, which of the five major categories do you feel Magno-Grip would best start in? Why?

VIDEO CASE 6-1

BLUE MAUMAU

Summary

Many entrepreneurs may turn to franchises as a way to ensure success since the franchiser has already established the business. However, most franchisees soon find that buying in does not guarantee success at all. A Web site that hopes to provide industry information as well as support and advice for the franchise community is an independent community called BlueMauMau.org.

Don Sniegowski, founder and CEO of Blue MauMau, named the business after a New Zealand Polynesian fish that groups together in large schools to network and provide protection against predators. Sniegowski heard from many franchisees that had made serious mistakes even after extensive research and understanding the uniform franchise agreement. One key situation that prompted the start of BlueMauMau.org was a businessperson who had already started a franchise only to learn that three stores before his did not survive. The franchisee was in disbelief that the salesperson or the area stores did not know about or chose not to tell him about the closed businesses. In order to relieve the information disconnect, Blue MauMau was launched in November 2005.

The site combines investigative reporting, bloggers, and expert advisers that tackle all types of occurrences in the franchising industry. All contributors to the site are volunteers who feel passionate about the industry and want to dispel any myths or trouble within the industry. Paul Steinberg, current Blue MauMau blogger and former franchise lawyer, writes about the common misconceptions of franchising and how to fully investigate entering the marketplace. Fortunately, Blue MauMau has been well received by franchisers, who often provide quality feedback on the site.

DISCUSSION QUESTIONS

1. What are the advantages and disadvantages to franchising?
2. When researching a potential franchising opportunity, what should the researcher do to determine if the opportunity is good?
3. What is the difference between a start-up business and a franchising business?
4. How can a site like Blue MauMau be beneficial to those already in business and those looking to enter a franchise business? Could the site also be beneficial to start-ups and existing businesses?
5. Can you envision another type of service that could work using the Blue MauMau model?

VIDEO CASE 8-1

FINANCING FOR ENTREPRENEURS

Summary

Starting a business with adequate financing in a sluggish economy is tough for a seasoned entrepreneur, but try being a college student with just a hope and dream. Many universities have attempted to offer a solution to keep hope alive by hosting business competitions with a cash prize of start-up capital. Columbia University is just one of those universities that created a path for up-and-coming entrepreneurs through its Outrageous Business Plan Competition.

The competition starts with a preliminary elevator pitch to introduce the business idea submitted by video. Some students really channel creativity by dressing up in costumes, playing videos, and acting. The judges then select the students who move to the second round where their business plans are presented to potential investors. During the presentation, students have to demonstrate their understanding of the market, justify the start-up capital, and express how long before the investors start to see a return.

Michael Dwork won the top prize of $6,000 in the 2007 Outrageous Business Plan Competition. The business plan for Greenware, now known as verTerra, an ecofriendly dishware with biodegradable properties, really caught the attention of the panel of judges. Michael's pitch demonstrated that not only did he have a good product, but also an understanding of the market and practical strategies of the business. Dan Burstein of Millennium Technology Ventures, venture capitalist and panel judge, felt that Greenware might revolutionize the disposable goods industry.

Dan Burstein stated that Michael had the major attributes that venture capitalists look for from up-and-coming entrepreneurs—understanding the competition, passion and self-confidence, and financial savvy. Burstein found that many entrepreneurs try to generalize or estimate the cost of a business, which is a real red flag for any investor.

DISCUSSION QUESTIONS

1. Why are business plans important?
2. Why would a business need an elevator pitch?
3. Write a potential elevator pitch for Greenware. (You may invent details not given in the video.)
4. In terms of focusing the business plan, what would be the focus of Greenware's business plan out of the four situations?

VIDEO CASE 9-1

CRAFT BEER BOOM

Summary

Beers have been around for over 6,000 years, but only recently have many Americans brewed up interest in beers made the old world way. The brewers of this yesteryear beer or "craft beer" are more concerned with the quality through the taste, texture, and aroma than mass production. Scott Vaccaro, owner of Captain Lawrence Brewing Company, began brewing beer in his parents' home in Westchester, New York, at the age of 17 and later worked for craft beer legend Sierra Nevada. After gaining this experience, Scott felt Westchester needed a local brewery in his home town. He noticed that the wine list varied at local restaurants, but the beer taps had the "usual suspects." Now, Captain Lawrence Brewing Company sells four different types of beer and has developed a local fan base in Westchester.

While many small brewers continue to develop their local brews, some well-known breweries took their craft beer to the masses. Jim Koch of Samuel Adams developed his craft beer in his kitchen in 1984 and become one of the first craft brewers. Samuel Adams was a leader in a market that had few competitors over the years. Today, craft beer is the fastest-growing segment in the beer industry with a growth of 18 percent in 2008. Jim Koch and Scott Vaccaro have been joined by nearly 1,400 craft brewers in the United States.

Even though Samuel Adams, Sierra Nevada, and Anchor Steam Brewery are giants in the craft beer segment, the overall sales of the niche are tiny compared to the overall sales of beer. Mass-production brewers, now, have taken notice of the growing interest and have developed their own line of craft beers.

DISCUSSION QUESTIONS

1. Where would beer be on the product life cycle? How about craft beers?
2. Using Exhibit 9.1, how would a small brewery such as Captain Lawrence rank versus a large brewery like Anheuser-Busch with the developing craft beers?
3. Why would branding be important for Captain Lawrence and Samuel Adams?

VIDEO CASE 10-1

ANTIPRENEURS

Summary

A new wave of business rebels is taking on the mainstream business model, the newly coined "antipreneurs." Bill Goldsmith stepped away from mainstream radio in an effort to make a statement that is not about the music but about ad sales. Bill wanted to create a different business platform that alleviates the dependency on ads by creating a listener-sponsored radio site, Radioparadise.com, with his wife in Paradise, California. He has more than 50,000 listeners worldwide and brings in approximately $1 million in revenue each year.

Antipreneurs are thought to be cynical about big business and big brand advertising and have essentially created a niche market for those consumers that feel the same. Antipreneurs create antibrands that depend largely on word-of-mouth and selling on the brand attributes and not the brand itself.

The message from the antibrand is strong and sometimes political. MooShoes, a vegan shoe store in New York, sells shoes that are leather-free and ecofriendly. Aside from selling products, MooShoes positioned itself to provide educational materials and partnerships with organizations such as the Humane Society. Erica Kubersky of MooShoes feels that consumers identify with their message of saving the environment, fair business practices, and preventing animal cruelty. She also feels that consumers want to shop where their personal beliefs and practices are mirrored. MooShoes has grown to over a million dollars in sales per year and has created its own brand of shoes.

As more consumers find the antibrand, the antipreneurs will begin to thrive and grow. While the antipreneurs welome the growth, they do not welcome the desire to change to more mainstream business practices.

DISCUSSION QUESTIONS

1. What is MooShoes' value proposition?
2. How can antipreneurs use contemporary marketing approaches to reach their target audience?
3. How can Radioparadise.com and MooShoes use publicity?

VIDEO CASE 11-1

FRESH-BAKED ENTREPRENEURS

Summary

Shane Colton, VP and director of marketing for HomeMade Pizza Co., understands the importance of location for the bake-at-home pizza business. A unique twist on the typical pizza parlor was inspired by a business in California that used the same bake-at-home concept. However, HomeMade Pizza wanted to capture a niche audience by using high-quality, all-natural ingredients free of preservatives and chemicals with organic elements. The creators spent countless hours conducting taste tests in their basement to create the standout product. However, the HomeMade Pizza team understood that it would take more than a unique take on an American classic to create business success.

Like most budding businesses, the ability to find the perfect location often requires diligence and lots of research. The process is even more daunting when expansion is considered. HomeMade Pizza looks for high-traffic areas, but even more so foot traffic. The hope is that individuals walking by the establishments during their daily routine will create awareness and, more important, repeat customers. With most customers still unaware of the bake-at-home concept, the locations also serve as informative and educational sites for the different method of creating the perfect pizza. Shane Colton states that high-traffic areas have been consistently rewarding for the business.

DISCUSSION QUESTIONS

1. Would HomeMade Pizza be as successful in an area that had little to no foot traffic? Explain your answer.
2. What other components should HomeMade Pizza consider when selecting a location other than a high traffic area?
3. How important is the factor of location to this type of business?

VIDEO CASE 14-1

CREDIT SQUEEZE ON SMALL BUSINESS

Summary

Small businesses often struggle to secure financing in good times, but bad times offer little hope. With the credit issues rising, most small businesses are starting to sink from lack of funding. Carol Conolly has run a successful nursery school called Discovering Me in New York for over 20 years. Discovering Me was growing to the point that expansion was necessary and needed funding. Most would consider two decades in a business as a proven track record that should be comforting for a bank. In fact, the search for lending proved difficult even at the bank Discovering Me had used for the past 18 years. Luckily, the New York State Small Business Development Center was able to assist Carol in securing financing for the construction cost.

Many small businesses have faced similar financing woes like Discovering Me since the global credit crisis struck and banks stopped lending. Tom Morley of the NY State SBDC notes that the credit situation has been dire for many small businesses since working capital has become increasingly difficult to acquire especially for businesses with seasonality. Individuals looking to buy a business are also meeting substantial roadblocks. Ronnie Jagoda was looking to purchase a delicatessen and was willing to put down a third of the purchase price, borrow less, and forgo some remodeling, but was turned down numerous times.

Recent estimates claim that there are approximately 27 million small businesses in the United States and those businesses employ roughly 40 percent of the national workforce and earn over 50 percent of the economy. With the credit freeze creating havoc, the situation has heightened the possibility of further job cuts and closings for small businesses.

DISCUSSION QUESTIONS

1. Why is cash flow important to a small business?
2. What incentives could be used by small businesses to prevent cash flow problems?
3. What can small businesses do to protect their cash when lending is tight?

VIDEO CASE 15-1

WOMEN ENTREPRENEURS

Summary

As the number of women entering the world of entrepreneurship continues to rise, their success still falls below men. It is estimated that 10.4 million women started and are operating small businesses. However, the benchmark for successful revenue of $1 million has been obtained only by 3 percent of the women entrepreneurs as compared to 6 percent of men entrepreneurs. The million dollar mark makes a statement to the lending community that the business is dependable, focused, and growth oriented.

In an effort to ramp up the number of successful women entrepreneurs, an initiative to provide business counseling and financial services was created by Count Me In. One of their initiatives is the Make Mine a Million contest. The goal of the Make Mine a Million program was that 1 million women business owners reach the million dollar milestone by 2010. Nell Merlino, founder of Count Me In, states that women entrepreneurs need key attributes of good overall management, financial responsibility, and the willingness to learn to reach the million dollar mind-set.

One of the winners of the Make Mine a Million program in 2007 was Doreen Zayer, proprietor of Relax on Cloud 9; she received consulting services from top corporations such as AIG, Cisco, FedEx, and a guaranteed $50,000 investment from Count Me In and OPEN from American Express. Relax on Cloud 9, a health and wellness spa, seemed a model of success. She moved from a small storefront to a large establishment on Staten Island, a second location at a Hilton Hotel, and a mobile spa. However, all of her growth had to be financed by personal methods such as refinancing her home and maxing out credit cards because small business loans or other financing were very difficult to obtain. Doreen's recognition has solidified her business and she no longer has difficulty receiving credit lines from banks.

DISCUSSION QUESTIONS

1. Why do you suspect that few women entrepreneurs are reaching the $1 million mark?
2. What other programs are available for women or other underrepresented groups of entrepreneurs? For entrepreneurs in general?
3. What types of other financing are available for small businesses?

VIDEO CASE 16-1

WINE ENTREPRENEURS

Summary

When picturing a sophisticated wine drinker, a classy upscale wine retailer may be the place many assume they would find their perfect palate match. COSCO would probably not come to mind; however, COSCO is setting the standard for fine wines and is currently the number one wine retailer. One entrepreneur, Cameron Hughes of Cameron Hughes Wine, created a unique business model that reaches the average COSCO consumer. He devised a plan to take the distributor out and provide high-quality wines for low prices. Cameron buys quality excess quantity in bulk from large wineries, either bottled or ready to be blended.

The business model is structured to eliminate most of the overhead and he acts as a virtual company. The process starts with receipt of samples from brokers and then creating his own blend with his winemakers. The final blend is transported to a central facility and bottled using a mobile bottling truck. The bottles are then boxed, stored, and shipped out to COSCO. Cameron states that he does not own a tank, a truck, or wine barrel, but rents time, space, and winemakers. The majority of the wines are from Californian vineyards, but he hopes to expand into South African, French, and Italian wines in the future.

As far as pricing, the wine retails for approximately $8.99 to $9.99 with all of the quality of its higher-dollar competition. He notes that the average cabernet sells for about $30 but only costs approximately $5 to manufacture. He is able to achieve the lower price point through high volume and a lower markup since COSCO caps markups at 14 percent.

COSCO is primarily interested in constantly rotating products and Cameron Hughes created a program that fits their objective. Since the wine is produced in lots, there may only be a few hundred cases or a few thousand cases of a lot and once it has sold out, that lot is complete.

Cameron Hughes's wine created a cult following in its primary California market. In 2003, Hughes produced about 3,000 cases and has grown to producing over 37,000 cases in 2008. He projects to sell 100,000 cases in 2010. The growth is largely anticipated by expanding into other COSCO markets other than just California. Not bad for a guy that started selling wine out of the back of his station wagon to his parents' friends.

DISCUSSION QUESTIONS

1. What are the costs of inventory that Cameron Hughes is and is not incurring?
2. What are the advantages and disadvantages of renting and not buying equipment, owning facilities, and employing staff? Are there other advantages to being a virtual business?
3. What type of inventory system would you suspect Cameron Hughes has in place?

VIDEO CASE 17-1

NEW ORLEANS BIZ

Summary

Ralph Brennan, president of the Ralph Brennan Restaurant Group and former president of the National Restaurant Association, has certainly met his share of challenges while rebuilding New Orleans after Katrina. From renovating to staff, he was determined to reopen quickly to help motivate others to bring life back to the French Quarter.

Unlike most of the heavily hit parts of the city, the French Quarter sustained relatively minimal damage. However, it was not an easy task to bring the life back to one of the most noted tourist attractions in the southeastern United States. Ralph decided to reopen The Red Fish Grill only 10 days after the storm. While Ralph was eager for back to business as usual, many issues had to be dealt with such as the remaining storm water. The restaurant underwent cleaning and repairs to meet health standards and regulations but the main trouble that prevented approval was the lack of clean water for the bar, cooking, and restrooms. Undeterred, Ralph sought the help of the National Restaurant Association in changing the regulation to allow the use of bottled water for all aspects. Staffing the restaurant would present other challenges since many of the locals were displaced and the population of the city was decreased by hundreds of thousands. Some creative hiring practices were put in place not often used in the restaurant industry, such as higher wages, signing bonuses, and flexible scheduling. Creativity was also used in bringing back business though specials and festivals that brought locals and tourist alike back to the French Quarter.

Ralph Brennan was clearly eager to get back to life as it was before Katrina but many businesses in other parts of the city did not fare as well. Nearly two years after Katrina, most businesses in the harder-hit areas have yet to rebuild and the hope of government assistance is dying. Through word-of-mouth and advertising campaigns, the French Quarter has begun to see some activity again. Ralph noted that he is working twice as hard for less business and it is certain that most businesses in New Orleans feel the same way.

DISCUSSION QUESTIONS

1. What different risks does a business strongly based on tourists have from a business not based as heavily on tourism?
2. Could some of the difficulties this restaurant experienced have been reduced or eliminated with a disaster plan?

VIDEO CASE 19-1

UNIQUE VACATION POLICY

Summary

What comes to mind when hearing the word unlimited? Unlimited refills or unlimited talk time is what typical Americans may think of when hearing the word. However, at Bluewolf, an IT consulting company with headquarters in New York City, employees may have a different reference when using unlimited. Forget the seniority or hour accumulation per month for vacation time, Bluewolf employees have unlimited vacation time.

In business, it is crucial to retain great employees to help further growth and sustainability in any industry. Aside from salary, many employees have become more savvy about and demanding of benefits that provide more freedom and create more value than casual Friday. The founders of the company wanted to create a culture that allows the employees the freedom and independence of flexible hours with the understanding that goals and objectives are met. Bluewolf employees have used the vacation time to travel, consult for another industry, or volunteer for a charity.

DISCUSSION QUESTIONS

1. How do you think creating a benefit such as unlimited vacation can increase productivity and retention? What would be some of the drawbacks to adding the unlimited vacation?
2. Do you think a small business can use unconventional benefits in lieu of a high salary to recruit and retain a good employee?
3. What other unusual benefits have you heard of or do you think could make a business attractive to potential employees?

VIDEO CASE 20-1

ENTREPRENEURS AND FAILURE

Summary

Being an entrepreneur and taking risks often go hand in hand; however, present-day economic changes and general uncertainties may be leading potential entrepreneurs away from taking the leap and starting their own businesses. Paul Ofman, psychologist and managing director of RHR International, found that entrepreneurs need to take risks and even experience some amount of failure to sharpen their reactions to change.

While some entrepreneurs have experienced success throughout their business life cycle, Paul notes that failure is unavoidable at some point and such situations are necessary for better strategy development. Even businesses that have failed can learn valuable lessons in reevaluating their business planning and market observation.

All in all, Paul Ofman sees an upside to entrepreneurial failure and parallels the occurrence to immunizations in the medical realm. He suggests a stronger business inclination and valuable life lessons can be attributed to exposing oneself to certain amounts of failure.

DISCUSSION QUESTIONS

1. What can entrepreneurs do to decrease the effect of liability of newness?
2. In what areas are most entrepreneurs weak and how can they improve these areas?
3. What are the critical success factors (CSFs) that can positively impact the chance of success?

GLOSSARY

A

Accelerator An organization that supports start-up technology businesses by providing inexpensive office space, a variety of support services, and resources; most accelerators are associated with universities.

Access The opportunity to find and obtain opportunities offered to others.

Accounting equation The statement that assets equal liabilities plus owners' equity (assets = liabilities + owners' equity).

Accounts receivable Money owed to your business by customers who purchased your product on credit.

Accredited investors The SEC's term for individuals with a net worth greater than $1 million or a personal annual income of at least $200,000 in each of the two most recent years, who are therefore qualified to make private equity investments in businesses.

Acquisition cost The total cost of acquiring an asset, including such costs as purchase price, transportation, installation, testing, and calibrating in order to ready it for its first productive use.

Activity-based cost estimates An accounting method which assigns costs based on the different types of work a business does in order to sell a particular product or service.

Advertising Advertising is often used to support the corporate identity and value propositions that are established through public relations efforts. Part of conveying your message to your customers, advertising outlets include newspapers, magazines, billboards, television, and Internet banner ads, to name a few.

Age Discrimination in Employment Act An act of Congress that makes it illegal to discriminate against people who are older than 40 years of age.

Agent A middleman business which represents a manufacturer's product or service to other business-to-business middleman firms.

Aggrandizing Attempting to make your business or yourself seem more accomplished or grander than reality.

Ambitious firm sector Consists of franchises and multi-site firms, with low to moderate innovation and high levels of growth.

Americans with Disabilities Act of 1990 An act of Congress that requires that businesses make provisions for access by disabled people.

Arbitration A dispute resolution process held instead of court cases in which both sides present their case to a legal professional.

Arm's length transaction A business deal where the parties have a prior relation or affiliation, but where the business is conducted as if they were unrelated. This approach is done to help guard against potential conflicts of interest.

Articles of organization Document setting forth information about a limited liability company that is filed with the state to establish an LLC.

Articles of partnership Agreement between the partners of a firm on matters pertaining to the formation and operation of the partnership.

Articulate The concept that information flows from the income statement through the statements of retained earnings and owners' equity to the balance sheet.

Asset Something the business owns that is expected to have economic value in the future.

Assumed name filing or a fictitious name filing Filing made with a state(s) in which the business operates disclosing the trade name or assumed name of the business along with the owners of the business.

Auction A business setting in which products consigned from multiple sellers are available for bidding by customers.

Augmented product Core product plus features that tend to differentiate it from the competition.

B

B2B Business-to-business transactions.

B2C Business-to-consumer transactions.

Balance sheet A statement of what a business owns (assets), what it owes to others (liabilities), and how much value the owners have invested in it (equity).

Baldrige Award The Malcolm Baldrige National Quality Award is given by the U.S. government to businesses and nonprofit organizations that have been judged outstanding in seven measures of quality leadership; strategic planning; customer and market focus; measurement, analysis, and knowledge management; human resource focus; process management; and results (see http://www.quality.nist.gov).

Bank available balance The sum of money that has actually been received and paid out of a depositor's account.

Bank ledger balance The sum of deposits and withdrawals recorded in a bank's accounting records.

Bankrupt The financial state of having more debt than assets, such that net worth is negative.

Bankruptcy An extreme form of business termination which uses a legal method for closing a business and paying off creditors when debts are substantially greater than assets.

Bar coding Obtaining a Universal Product Code number and scan-ready visual tag, and printing it on the product or its packaging. Bar codes can then be scanned and recognized by others.

Barter The practice of trading goods and services without the use of money.

BATNA Best Alternative to a Negotiated Settlement is the strategy or action a person or firm would pursue if the current negotiation fails.

Bearer Any person or business entity who possesses a security.

Benefits Characteristics of a product or service that the target customer would consider worthwhile.

Best practices Activities identified by authoritative bodies as examples of optimal ways to get things done in a particular industry, profession, or trade.

Billboard principle An ethical model that asks whether someone would be comfortable having his or her decision and name advertised on a billboard for the public to see.

Blog A Web page in which entries are posted in reverse chronological order (i.e., the most recent at the top of the page).

Book value The difference between the original acquisition cost and the amount of accumulated depreciation.

Boom A type of life cycle growth stage marked by a very rapid increase in sales in a relatively short time.

Bootstrapping Using low-cost or free techniques to minimize your cost of doing business.

Born international A new firm that opens a Web site immediately, thus being exposed to customers from around the world.

Bot A Web-based program that uses artificial intelligence techniques to automate tasks such as searches.

Brainstorming A group discussion in which criticism is suspended in order to generate the maximum number of ideas.

Breakeven point The point at which total costs equal gross revenue.

Brochure A sales document, typically consisting of multiple panels (when folded) or multiple pages, describing your business or specific products or services.

Budget A financial plan for the future, based on a single level of operations; a quantitative expression of the use of resources necessary to achieve a business's strategic goals.

Bundling Combining two or more products in one unit and pricing it less than if the units were sold separately.

Business cards A 2- × 3½-inch cardboard card with your personal and company contact information; the key way of leaving information about yourself.

Business entity concept The concept that a business has an existence separate from that of its owners.

Business format franchising An agreement that provides a complete business format, including trade name, operational procedures, marketing, and products or services to sell.

Business life cycle The sequence or pattern of developmental stages any business goes through during its life span.

Business plan A document designed to detail the *major* characteristics of a firm—its product or service, its industry, its market, its manner of operating (production, marketing, management), and its financial outcomes on the firm's *present* and *future*.

Business risk The level of probability that the future economic state of the business will be worse than expected.

Business stationery A standard 8½- × 11-inch page of blank paper typically imprinted with your company's name and contact information.

Business-to-business (B2B) Business-to-business transactions. Sales of products or services that one firm sells to another firm.

Business-to-consumer (B2C) Business-to-consumer transactions. Sales of products or services directly to individuals.

Buyers People who purchase an existing business.

Buy-in The purchase of substantially less than 100 percent of a business.

Buyout The purchase of substantially all of an existing business.

Buyout insurance Insurance that provides money to owners of a business to buy the shares of any deceased owner from that owner's heirs.

C

Cannibalizing Taking business away from your employer.

Capital assets Assets that are expected to provide economic benefits for periods of time greater than one year.

Capital budgeting The process of deciding among various investment opportunities to create a specific spending plan.

Capital lease A lease in which at the end of the lease period the asset becomes the property of the lessee, possibly with an additional payment.

Captive pricing Setting the price for an item relatively low and then charging much higher prices for the expendables it uses.

Career A lifelong series of jobs or occupations.

Cash Money that is immediately available to be spent.

Cash budget A cash budget identifies when, how, and why cash is expected to come into the business, and when, how, and why it is expected to leave.

Cash disbursements budget A schedule of the amounts and timings of payments of cash out of a business.

Cash equivalents Assets that may be quickly converted to cash.

Cash flow The actual receipt and spending of cash by a business.

Cash flow statement A statement of the sources and uses of cash in a business for a specific period of time.

Cash receipts budget A schedule of the amounts and timings of the receipt of cash into a business.

Cash-to-cash cycle The time that is required for a business to acquire resources, convert them into product, sell the product, and receive cash from the sale.

Categorical questions Questions that are answered by selecting the proper category; for example, "What is your ethnicity? White, African American, Hispanic, Asian, American Indian, Other."

Caveat emptor Latin: let the buyer beware.

Certification An examination based acknowledgement that the firm is owned and operated as specified.

Charge back A reduction in the bank account of a merchant by a credit card company.

Check the box taxation A choice LLCs can make on their tax returns to be taxed as a corporation or a partnership.

Civil Rights Act of 1991 A series of acts by Congress that prohibit discrimination on the basis of race, color, religion, sex, or national origin.

Clearinghouse An entity that processes checks and electronic fund transfers for banks and other financial organizations.

Cognitive dissonance Doubt that occurs after a purchase has been made. An inconsistency between experience and belief.

Co-insurance A contract stipulation that requires a policyholder to carry insurance in an amount equal to a stated minimum percentage of the market value of the property insured.

Collateral Something of value given or pledged as security for payment of a loan; collateral may consist of financial instruments, such as stocks, bonds, and negotiable paper, or of physical goods, such as trucks, machinery, land, or buildings.

Combinational competencies Organizational capabilities that come from combining tangible and intangible resources in ways superior to the competition.

Commercial paper Notes issued by creditworthy corporations.

Community development organization An organization authorized by the SBA to make insured loans to small businesses that are expected to increase economic activity within a specific geographic area.

Company book balance The sum of cash inflows and cash outflows recorded in the firm's accounting records.

Competencies Forms of business-related expertise.

Competitive advantage The particular way a firm implements customer benefits that keeps the firm ahead of other firms in the industry or market.

Competitor Any other business in the same industry as yours.

Comprehensive budget Comprehensive budgets, also often referred to as *master budgets,* are sets of budgets that detail all projected receipts and spending for the budget period.

Concentrated strategy A marketing strategy in which a marketer selects one specific group of consumers and designs a marketing mix specifically for that group.

Conflict of interest A situation in which a person faces two or more competing standards or goals.

Consignment The practice of accepting goods for resale, without taking ownership of them and without being responsible to pay prior to their being sold.

Consignment shops Retail stores in which customers can come and buy products placed in the shops by a wide variety of sellers.

Consolidation A transfer method in which a small business is bought by a larger firm for the purpose of quickly growing the larger firm.

Consumer A private individual or household that is the end user of (the entity that "consumes") a product or service.

Contingency fee Fee paid by a client to an attorney for legal services that is dependent upon the outcome of a case.

Contract manufacturing An existing firm with the correct manufacturing capabilities makes your product for you.

Conversion franchising An agreement that provides an organization through which independent businesses may combine recourses.

Conversion rate The measure of how many visitors to your Web site (or people who click on your online advertisement) actually make a purchase from you.

Copyright Exclusive right given to the creator of a literary or artistic work to make use of that work.

Core competency The main work of a firm in a particular line of business.

Core product The very basic description of what a product is—a bar of soap, a house-cleaning service.

Corporate entrepreneurship The form of entrepreneurship which takes place in existing businesses around new products, services, or markets.

Corporation A legal "artificial" entity that is formed by filing specific documents with a state government.

Cost The value given up to obtain something that you want.

Cost of capital The percentage cost of obtaining future funds.

Cost of disposition Cost incurred in the activities necessary to get rid of an asset.

Cost of goods sold budget A schedule that shows the predicted cash of product actually sold during the accounting period.

Cost of operating The direct cost incurred in using an asset for the purpose for which it was intended.

Cost of owning Cost incurred in financing, insuring, taxing, or tracking an asset.

Cost strategy A generic strategy aimed at mass markets in which a firm offers a combination of cost benefits that appeals to the customer.

Cost to start-up The amount of money it takes to start a new business.

Cost-volume-profit analysis A managerial accounting technique which looks at the fixed and variable costs of a business to arrive at a number of unit sales (volume) to maximize profits.

Covenants The limitations imposed on an individual's property by their neighborhood group.

Cover letter A one-page document on business stationery (also called *letterhead*) that introduces the business plan and the business owner to the recipient and indicates why the recipient is being asked to read the plan.

Coverages Contractual provisions of insurance policies that specify what risks the insurance company is assuming.

Creation The entrepreneurial focus which looks at the making of new entities.

Creative destruction The way that newly created goods, services, or firms can hurt existing goods, services, or firms.

Creativity A process producing an idea or opportunity that is novel and useful, frequently derived from making connections among distinct ideas or opportunities.

Credit reporting agency A business that collects, collates, and reports information concerning an entity's use of debt.

Cultural resonance A concept in public interest which alludes to events with a broad appeal within the market or population.

Culture A set of shared norms, values, and orientations of a group of individuals, prescribing how people should think and behave in the organization.

Currency A concept in public importance which alludes to the degree to which the issue is immediate in its impact. (Ch. 10)

Currency The bills and coins printed by governments to represent money. (Ch. 14)

Current ratio The value of current assets divided by current liabilities.

Customer-focus The entrepreneurial focus which refers to being in tune with one's market.

Customer relationship management (CRM) The process of tracking the customer's different contacts with the firm, and using this data to help improve sales as well as the customer's experience.

Customer segment A group or subgroup of potential purchasers that can be approached in a coherent manner.

Customer vector A type of CRM report which segments by customer (or customer group) on purchases or dates of purchase.

D

Debt A legal obligation to pay money in the future.

Debt capital Money borrowed for the purposes of investment in a business.

Decline stage A life cycle stage in which sales and profits of the firm begin a falling trend.

Deductible An amount of loss that will not be paid by an insurance company.

Defendant Person or other entity being sued.

Degree of similarity The extent to which a product or service is like another.

Delegation The assignment of work to others over whom you have power.

Demand deposits Money held in checking and savings accounts.

Deposits and progress payments Cash payments received before product is completed or delivered.

Depreciation Regular and systematic reduction in income that transfers asset value to expense over time.

Design patent A 14-year patent for a new, original, and ornamental design for an article of manufacture.

Determination competencies Skills identified with the energy and focus needed to bring a business into existence.

Dichotomous questions Questions that have only two possible choices; for example, "Have you shopped here before?"

Differential advantage The characteristic that separates one company from another in product, price, promotion, and/or distribution.

Differentiated strategy A marketing strategy in which a marketer selects two or more distinct groups of consumers and designs specific marketing mixes to meet their needs. (Ch. 12)

Differentiation strategy A type of generic strategy aimed at clarifying how one product is unlike another in a mass market. (Ch. 7)

Difficult to imitate A resource characteristic which enhances value through offering uniqueness to the buyer.

Direct competition Other companies that make a similar product or provide a similar service; for example, direct competition for Coca-Cola includes all other soft drink providers.

Direct exporting Exporting using no middlemen.

Direct mail A method of selling in which catalogs, brochures, letters, videos, and other pieces of marketing materials are mailed directly to customers from which they can mail, call, or e-mail an order. Direct faxing and direct e-mailing are more modern forms of direct mail.

Direct response advertising Placing an advertisement in a magazine or newspaper, on television or radio, or in any other media. The ad contains an order blank with a phone number and e-mail or regular mail address with the intent of having the customer place an immediate order.

Direct sales Methods of going directly to your customer in order to sell your product. Vending machines, door-to-door salespeople, leasing space at a craft fair, farmer's markets, party sales, and most industrial sales are methods of direct selling.

Discounted cash flows Cash flows that have been reduced in value because they are to be received in the future.

Discounts for prompt payment A reduction in sales price provided to credit customers for paying outstanding amounts in a timely manner.

Disposal value The net amount realized after subtracting the costs of getting rid of an asset from its selling price.

Diversification A strategy whose goal is growth based on adding new products or services to the firm's existing collection of offerings.

Diversify To invest in multiple investments of differing risk profiles for the purpose of reducing overall investment risk.

Dividends Payments of profits to the owners of corporations.

Documentary draft A draft which can be exercised only when presented with specified shipping documents.

Donations Monetary or other gifts to organizations or people who are in need.

Double taxation Earnings of the business are taxed twice with the business as well as its owners being subject to tax.

Due diligence The process of investigating a business to determine its value.

Dynamic Capitalism Typology A model of an economy categorizing businesses based on their innovativeness and growth rate.

E

Early adopters A customer adoption segment that purchases after pioneers.

Early majority Customer adoption segment that purchases after early adopters, and whose demand creates a mass market.

Earnings multiple The ratio of the value of a firm to its annual earnings.

E-commerce The use of the Internet to conduct business transactions.

Economic core sector The most numerous and most widely available type of firm, also called small business, ranging from low to moderate levels of innovation and growth.

Economic development agency A government organization that works to increase economic activity in the form of job opportunities within a specific geographic area.

Economic order quantity (EOQ) A statistical technique that determines the quantity of inventory that a business must hold to minimize total inventory cost.

Economy of scale The idea that it is cheaper (per item) to make many of an item than few.

Efficiency The entrepreneurial focus which refers to doing the most work with the fewest resources. (Ch. 1)

Efficiency The comparison of productivity ratios to see the extent that an organization has generated more outputs with fewer inputs. (Ch. 16)

Efficiency-driven economies Nations with a largely industrialized economy.

Elastic product Product for which there are any number of substitutes and for which a change in price makes a difference in quantity purchased.

Elasticity A term from economics which describes the relationship between changes in two variables; for example, a small change in price (variable 1) resulting in a large change in sales (variable 2) would reflect high elasticity.

Electronic malls A group of companies—usually with a common target market—selling via the Internet through a specific site.

Elevator pitch A 30-second (100 words or less) action-oriented description of a business designed to sell the idea of the business to another.

Employee fit The match between the needs, expectations, and culture of the small business with the expectations and the skills of the individual employee.

Employee referral An underused, low-cost method for finding workers that rewards your employees for recommending potential candidates that would be a great employee fit.

Employee stock ownership plan A formalized legal method to transfer some or all of the ownership of a business to its employees.

Employee theft Misappropriation of business property by employees of that business.

Entrepreneur A person who owns or starts an organization, such as a business.

Entrepreneurial alertness A special set of observational and thinking skills that help entrepreneurs identify good opportunities; the ability to notice things that have been overlooked, without actually launching a formal search for opportunities, and the motivation to look for opportunities.

Entry wedge An opportunity that makes it possible for a new business to gain a foothold in a market.

Environment The sum of all of the forces outside of the firm or entrepreneur.

Equal Employment Opportunity Commission (EEOC) A commission established to enforce the provisions of the Equal Employment Opportunity Act.

Equipment Machinery, tools, or materials used in the performance of the work of the business.

Equity Ownership of a portion of a business.

Equity capital Money contributed to the businesses in return for part ownership of the business.

ESOP Employee stock option plan: a method for employees to purchase the business for which they work.

Estate freeze An estate planning strategy which focuses on transferring assets to heirs when the asset costs are low.

E-tailer An electronic retailer; a store that exists only on the Internet.

Ethical dilemma A situation that occurs when a person's values are in conflict, making it unclear whether a decision is the right thing to do.

Ethics A system of values that people consider in determining whether actions are right or wrong.

Ethics planning A process used to better consider issues of right and wrong.

Ethnographic research Data gathered by simple observation—seeing what consumers do, rather than asking them.

Exculpatory clause Part of a contract in which a party to the contract states that he or she will not be responsible for certain actions.

Executive summary A one- to two-page (250–500 words) overview of the business, its business model, market, expectations, and immediate goals. It is typically put at the start of a business plan and is the most popular summary form for a business plan.

Expense A decrease in owners' equity caused by consuming your product or service.

Expert business professionalization A situation that occurs when all the major functions of a firm are conducted according to the standard business practices of its industry.

External environment The entire world outside of the firm's boundary.

External (cost) factors Aspects of the world outside the business which could cause the business's costs to change.

External legitimacy The extent to which a small business is taken for granted, accepted, or treated as viable by organizations or people outside the small business or the owner's family.

External reference price An estimation of what a price should be based on information external to a consumer, such as advice, advertisements, or comparison shopping.

External relations The process of managing relations with the environment.

F

4 Ps of Marketing The four major components of a marketing effort—product, price, promotion, and placement.

Factor-driven economies Nations with little manufacturing and largely farming and raw material extracting industries.

Factoring Selling the rights to collect accounts receivable to an entity outside your business.

Factoring receivables Borrowing money secured by a firm's accounts receivable.

Fair Credit Reporting Act U.S. federal legislation specifying consumer's rights vis-à-vis credit reporting agencies.

Fair market value The price at which goods and services are bought and sold between willing sellers and buyers in an arm's-length transaction.

Family business A firm in which one family owns a majority stake and is involved in the daily management of the business.

Famous faces A concept in public recognition which alludes to connections of your event or firm to individuals the general public would recognize.

Favorable/unfavorable variance A label applied to variances to indicate their effect upon the income statement; favorable variances would result in profits being greater than budgeted, all other things being equal; unfavorable variances would result in profits being less than budgeted, all other things being equal.

Feasibility The extent to which an idea is viable and realistic and the extent to which you are aware of internal (to your business) and external (industry, market, and regulatory environment) forces that could affect your business.

Feedback The process of communicating within or to the organization about how the outputs worked or were received.

Fidelity bonds Bonds, also called *dishonesty bonds,* that repay employers for losses caused by dishonest or negligent employees.

Financial accounting A formal, rule-based set of accounting principles and procedures intended for use by outside owners, investors, banks, and regulators.

Financial flexibility A business's ability to manage cash flows in such a manner that the company can respond appropriately to unexpected opportunities and needs.

Financial leverage A measure of the amount of debt relative to total investment.

Financial management A set of theories and techniques used to optimize the receipt and use of capital assets.

Financial risk Uncertainty of returns; the probability of losing money.

Financial statements Formal summaries of the content of an accounting system's records of transactions.

Financial strength The ability of a business to survive adverse financial events.

Financing activities Activities through which cash is obtained from and paid to lenders, owners, and investors.

Fixed costs Those costs that remain constant regardless of quantity of output, for example, rent.

Flat fees A method of billing for lawyers in which a fixed amount is paid for a certain task.

Flexibility rewards The ability of business owners to structure life in the way that suits their needs best.

Float Delays in the movement of money among depositors and banks.

Flyers A sales document to be posted or handed out, typically printed on a 8½- × 11-inch sheet of colored paper (or printed in color on white stock to increase visibility).

Focus group A form of data gathering from a small group led by a moderator.

Focus strategy A generic strategy that targets a portion of the market, called a *segment* or *niche.*

Focuses of entrepreneurship The key directions the organization intends to pursue.

Forms of entrepreneurship The settings in which the entrepreneurial effort takes place.

Foundation An institution to which private wealth is contributed and from which private wealth is distributed for public purposes.

Founders People who create or start new businesses.

Franchise A prepackaged business bought, rented, or leased from a company called a *franchisor.* (Ch. 1)

Franchise A legal agreement that allows a business to be operated using the name and business procedures of another firm. (Ch. 6)

Freight forwarders Firms specializing in arranging international shipments—packaging, transportation, and paperwork.

Fulfillment center A company that will warehouse your products and fill your customers' orders for you.

Full (or classic) business plan Contains a maximum of 25 single-spaced pages of text and 15 pages of financials and appendixes.

Full-time self-employment Working for yourself for more than 35 hours a week.

G

GAAP Generally Accepted Accounting Principles are the standardized rules for accounting procedures set out by the Financial Account Standards Board and used in all audits and submissions of accounting reports to the government.

Gain on investment The percentage amount that the payout of an investment differs from original cost: calculated as (payout − investment + dividends)/investment.

Gaming the payment process Using methods to appear to be paying bills on time, when in fact payment is being delayed or avoided.

General environment The major forces or sectors outside the firm which have impact on the lives of people, businesses, institutions, and nations.

Generic strategies Three widely applicable classic strategies for businesses of all types—differentiation, cost, and focus.

Gift Valuable assets or services donated to the business without any obligation to repay or give up any ownership interest.

Glamorous sector Consists of firms with high growth and high innovation. These are among the most visible firms in the media.

Going concern concept The accounting concept that a business is expected to continue in existence for the foreseeable future.

Golden Rule An ethical model which suggests you treat others in the manner you wish to be treated.

Good story A concept in public interest which alludes to an incident with good triumphing.

Grants Gifts of money made to a business for a specific purpose.

Green entrepreneurship Starting or running a firm in a manner which saves or improves the environment. (See *Sustainable entrepreneurship.*)

Gross profit Funds left over after deducting the cost of goods sold.

Growth rewards What people get from facing and beating challenges.

Growth stage An industry life cycle stage in which customer purchases increase at a dramatic rate.

Growth trap A financial crisis that is caused by a business growing faster than it can be financed.

Guerilla marketing The use of creative and relatively inexpensive ways to reach your customer. Examples include doorknob hangers, flyers under windshield wipers, T-shirts, balloons, and messages written on sidewalks.

H

Harvest Recover value through a sale of a firm or its assets.

Heir A person who becomes an owner through inheriting or being given a stake in a family business.

Heterogeneity A quality of a service in which each time it is provided it will be slightly different from the previous time.

Heuristic A commonsense rule, a rule-of-thumb.

High-growth venture A firm started with the intent of eventually going public, following the pattern of growth and operations of a big business.

High-performing small business A firm intended to provide the owner with a high income through sales or profits superior to those of the traditional small business.

Highly fragmented industries Collections of similar businesses in which virtually all firms have small market shares.

Hold harmless A type of waiver in which a party agrees not to hold another party responsible for certain events.

Home-based business A business that is operated from the owner's home.

Hourly fees A basis for legal charges in which the rate is based on a price per hour. Often lawyers will charge for fractions of an hour.

Human interest A concept in public interest which alludes to a character to whom the public can relate.

I

Identity The basic description of the firm, its "who, what, where, and why."

Imitative Characterized by being like or copying something that already exists.

Imitative strategy An overall strategic approach in which the entrepreneur does more or less what others are already doing.

Income rewards The money made by owning one's own business.

Income statement A statement that lists revenues and expenses and shows the amount of profit a business makes for a specified period of time.

Incremental innovation An overall strategic approach in which a firm patterns itself on other firms, with the exception of one or two key areas.

Incremental strategy Taking an idea and offering a way to do something slightly better than it is done presently.

Incubator A facility which offers subsidized space and business advice to companies in their earliest stages of operation.

Independent contractors Persons working to achieve a certain goal without being subjected to substantial controls by another.

Independent entrepreneurship The form of entrepreneurship in which a person or group own their own for-profit business.

Independent small business A business owned by an individual or small group.

Indirect competition Companies that provide alternatives that are dissimilar to your product/service that consumers might choose to meet a similar need; for example, indirect competition for Coca-Cola includes any other company providing items to quench thirst.

Indirect exporting Exporting using middlemen such as agents, export management companies, or export trading companies.

Industry The general name for the line of product or service being sold, or the firms in that line of business.

Industry analysis (IA) A research process that provides the entrepreneur with key information about the industry, such as its current situation and trends.

Industry dynamics Changes in competitors, sales, and profits in an industry over time.

Industry life cycle The stages an industry goes through from its birth to its ending. There are five stages: introduction, growth, maturity, decline, and death.

Industry specific knowledge Activities, knowledge, and skills specific to businesses in a particular industry.

Inelastic product Product for which there are few substitutes and for which a change in price makes very little difference in quantity purchased.

Informal capital Sources of funding from noninstitutional sources such as family, friends, and other individuals.

Informational plans Give potential customers or suppliers information about the company and its product or service.

Informational Web site An Internet site designed to introduce and explain a business to others.

Infringer Someone who uses intellectual property without the permission of the owner.

Initial public offering (IPO) Transfer method describing the first-time public sale of a stock listed on a public stock exchange.

Innovation The entreprenurial focus which looks at a new thing or a new way of doing things.

Innovation-driven economies Nations with high-value-added manufacturing and large service sectors.

Innovative strategy An overall strategic approach in which a firm seeks to do something that is very different from what others in the industry are doing.

Innovativeness The extent to which a product, service, or individual's thinking process is novel or an improvement over existing choices.

Inputs The materials, labor, and energy put into the production of a good or service.

Inseparability A quality of a service in which the service being done cannot be disconnected from the provider of the service.

Insurable value The amount of an asset for which a company will write an insurance policy.

Insurance A contract between two or more parties in which one party agrees, for a fee, to assume the risk of another.

Intangible assets Things of value that have no physical existence, for example, patents and trade secrets.

Intangible property Property that has no value of its own but that represents value, such as a stock certificate.

Intangible resources Capabilities, organizational processes, information, or knowledge of a firm that are not clearly evident.

Integrative view An ethical overview which involves considering what is best for everyone involved in a situation.

Intellectual property Property coming from some sort of original thought, for example, patents, trade secrets, trademarks, and copyrights.

Interest A charge for the use of money, usually figured as a percentage of the principal.

Intermediary Firms that assist in getting your product to your end customers, distributors, retailers, and so forth.

Internal control A set of rules and procedures that work to limit the opportunity for employee theft or malfeasance.

Internal environment The people (owners, employees, and board members) inside the boundary of a firm.

Internal (cost) factors Aspects of or choices within the business which could cause the business's costs to change.

Internal reference price A consumer's mental image of what a product's price should be.

Internal understanding The extent to which employees, investors, and family members involved in the business know the business's purposes and operations.

Internet recruiting Method of recruiting that allows you to search a résumé database or post a job description to the Web; a small business owner who knows exactly what he or she wants can use filters to search vast numbers of résumés with pinpoint accuracy.

Introduction stage The life cycle stage in which the product or service is being invented and initially developed.

Invention plan A business plan that provides information to potential licensees. Invention plans focus on the details of an invention, including intellectual property rights.

Inventory Products that are held for sale to customers.

Inventory valuation Determination of the amount of assets held by the firm for sale or production.

Investing activities The purchase and sale of land, buildings, equipment, and securities.

ISO Stands for the International Standards Organization, and refers to certification for having met a standard of quality that is consistently evaluated around the world (see http://www.iso.org).

Issue recognition A concept in public recognition which alludes to the extent to which the public is familiar with the issue or problem at hand.

J

Job description Defines and discusses all the essential knowledge, skills, and abilities that are needed to fill a position.

Joint venture An agreement between two or more entities to pool resources in order to complete a project.

Just-in-time inventory The practice of purchasing and accepting delivery of inventory only after it has been sold to the final customer.

K

Key business functions Activities common to all businesses such as sales, operations (also called *production*), accounting, finance, and human resources.

Key employee/partner plans Provides information on the company, product/service, market, and critical risks to prospective business or marketing partners or to prospective key employees.

Key employees Employees whose experience and skills are critical to the success of a business.

Keyword and description tags Terms included in the hidden portion of a Web page (called the *document head*) which are used by search engines such as Yahoo! and Google to describe your Web site and evaluate its focus and category placement.

Keyword optimization The selection of words that describe a Web site ad that results in the site being displayed toward the beginning of a search engine's (e.g., Google, Yahoo!, etc.) listing for that term.

L

Laggard A customer adoption segment that holds off buying new products or services until either they are forced to or prices reach rock-bottom.

Late career entrepreneurs (also known as *second career entrepreneurs*) People who begin their businesses after having retired or resigned from work in corporations at age 50 or later.

Late majority A customer adoption segment describing people who wait until the technology has stabilized and the costs have begun to drop.

Legal entity A being, human or nonhuman, such as a corporation, that is recognized as having rights and duties, such as the right to own property.

Legitimacy The belief that a firm is worthy of consideration or doing business with because of the impressions or opinions of customers, suppliers, investors, or competitors.

Letter of credit A document issued by a bank that guarantees a buyer's payment for a specified period of time upon compliance with specified terms.

Liabilities Legal obligations to give up things of value in the future.

Liability of newness The set of risks faced by firms early in their life cycles that comes from a lack of knowledge by the owners about the business they are in and by customers about the new business.

License A legal agreement granting you rights to use a particular piece of intellectual property.

Licensee The person or firm which is obtaining the rights to use a particular piece of intellectual property.

Licensing Documented permission from the government to run your business.

Licensor The person or organization which is offering the rights to use a particular piece of intellectual property.

Lifestyle or part-time firm A small business primarily intended to provide partial or subsistence financial support for the existing lifestyle of the owner, most often through operations that fit the owner's schedule and way of working.

Limited liability company (LLC) A legal form of business organization that is created by filing required documentation with a state government. LLCs have a choice, under federal tax law, of being taxed as either corporations or partnerships.

Limited partnership A legal form of business organization that is created by filing required documentation with a state government; within a limited partnership, one or more partners may have no liability for the debts and actions of the partnership.

Liquidation A popular term for a Chapter 7 bankruptcy in which a bankrupt firm's assets are sold by the bankruptcy trustee and the proceeds used to pay the firm's debts.

Liquidity A measure of how quickly a company can raise money through internal sources by converting assets to cash.

Liquidity enhancement An estate planning method in which cash is generated (usually through a life insurance policy) to cover the estate taxes.

Litigation A formal dispute resolution method that operates using the court system, typically with a lawyer representing each party.

Living wage The amount needed for a person (or family of a particular size) to meet the basic necessities of life from a single job.

Lock box A locked receptacle for money, the keys to which are not available to those who physically handle the receptacle; a common example of a lock box is the coin receptacle for parking meters which cannot be opened by the workers who are responsible for collecting the deposited coins.

M

MACRS rate An Internal Revenue Service acronym for the Modified Accelerated Cost Recovery System. The MACRS approach lets taxpayers depreciate more of the cost earlier in the life of a capital expense.

Mail order Sales made from ads in newspapers or magazines, with purchases taken online or by phone as well as by mail.

Managerial accounting Accounting methods that are specifically intended to be used by managers for planning, directing, and controlling a business.

Manufacturer The entity which produces a product or service to be sold.

Margin The amount of profit, usually stated as a percentage of the total price.

Market The business term for the population of customers for your product or service.

Market expansion A strategy whose goal is growth, based on selling in areas or to groups previously not served by the business.

Market penetration A strategy whose goal is growth, based on selling more of the firm's product or service to the existing customer base.

Market research Research conducted to uncover market and customer needs and opportunities; it exists at two levels, primary and secondary.

Market segmentation The process of dividing the market into groups that have somewhat homogeneous needs for a product or service.

Marketable securities Stocks and bonds that are traded on an open market.

Marketing plan A systematic written plan of all phases of marketing for a business, including information on the product, price, distribution, and promotion strategy, as well as a clear identification of the target market and competition.

Marketing research Systematic collection and interpretation of data to support future marketing decisions.

Mass market A customer group that involves large portions of the population.

Master budget A budget, also referred to as a *comprehensive budget*, which consists of sets of budgets that detail all projected receipts and spending for the budgeted period.

Mat release A news release that is typeset and thus may be photographically reproduced for inclusion in a newspaper.

Maturity stage The third life cycle stage, marked by a stabilization of demand, with firms in the industry moving to stabilize or improve profits through cost strategies.

Me-too products Products essentially similar to something already on the market.

Meritocracy A management philosophy of selecting and promoting people based solely on their being the most capable person for the job.

Microinventory The purchase of inventory only after a sale is made; very typical with Internet firms.

Mindshare The degree of attention your target market pays to your idea or organization.

Minimalized business professionalization A situation that occurs when the entrepreneur does nearly everything in the simplest way possible.

Mission statement A paragraph that describes the firm's goals and competitive advantages.

Money An accepted medium of exchange.

Moonlighting Working on your own part time after your regular job.

Multichannel marketing The use of several different channels to reach your customers, for example, a Web site, direct mail, and traditional retailing.

Multiple or bonus pack Combining more than one unit of the same product and pricing it lower than if each unit were sold separately.

Mutuality The action of each person helping another.

N

Nepotism A management philosophy of selecting and promoting people based on family ties.

Net profit The amount of money left after operating expenses are deducted from the business.

Net realizable value The amount for which an asset will sell, less the costs of selling.

Network marketing An approach to selling in which the salesperson recruits customers to become distributors of the product or service to others.

Networking Interacting with others in order to build relationships useful to a business.

New entrant business A firm whose product or service is established elsewhere, but is new to this market.

Newsworthy events To garner serious attention from the media and the public, a news story needs to deliver certain essentials that will hold their attention and keep your news in their thoughts. It should have public recognition, importance, and interest.

Niche market A narrowly defined segment of the population that is likely to share interests or concerns.

Noncash incentives Rewards that do not require payment of cash, such as stock options, compensating time off, or added vacation days.

Noncompete clause Part of a contract in which a person agrees not to open a certain type business or seek employment doing certain things in a particular area for a period of time.

Noncore projects Revenue-producing tasks and activities related to, but not part of, the primary strategy of a business.

Nonsufficient funds A situation that occurs when a check is returned to a depositor because the writer of the check did not have a bank available balance equal to or greater than the amount of the check.

Novelty Characterized by being different or new.

O

Occupational Safety and Health Administration (OSHA) A government agency created to enforce safety in the workplace.

Occupational structure The sequence or organization of jobs and careers in the economy.

Odd-even pricing Setting a price that ends in the number 5, 7, or 9.

Off-peak pricing Charging lower prices at certain times to encourage customers to come during slack periods.

On-the-job training Delivered to employees while they perform their regular jobs; techniques include orientations, job instruction training, apprenticeships, internships and assistantships, job rotation, and coaching.

Open-book policy Concept that key employees should be able to see and understand a firm's financials, that they should have a part in moving the numbers in the right direction, and that they should have a direct stake in the strategy and success of the firm.

Open-ended questions Questions that allow respondents to express themselves as they choose; for example, "What do you like about this book?"

Operating activities Activities involved in producing and selling goods and services.

Operating cycle See cash-to-cash cycle.

Operating lease A long-term rental in which ownership of the asset never passes to the person paying for the lease.

Operational plan Business plans designed to be used internally for management purposes.

Operations The process of transforming materials, labor, and energy into goods or services.

Opportunity competencies Skills necessary to identify and exploit elements of the business environment that can lead to a profitable and sustainable business.

Opportunity cost The value of an economic activity or event that is foregone in order to be able to undertake a different, specific activity or event.

Opportunity recognition Searching and capturing new ideas that lead to business opportunities. This process often involves creative thinking that leads to discovery of new and useful ideas.

Optimum capital structure The ratio of debt to equity that provides the maximum level of profits.

Optimum stocking level The amount of inventory that results in the minimum cost, when considering the cost of lost sales resulting from running out of stock, the number of units sold per day, and the number of days required to receive inventory.

Organizational capabilities The abilities, skills, and competencies used by the firm to make profits from tangible and intangible resources.

Organizational culture A set of shared beliefs, basic assumptions, or common, accepted ways of dealing with problems and challenges within a company that demonstrate how things get done.

Outflow Funds being paid to others by the firm.

Outputs The service or product that is produced for sale.

Outside equity Money from selling part of your business to people who are not and will not be involved in the management of the business.

Outsourcing Contracting with people or companies outside your business to do work for your business.

Overdraft A negative balance in a depositor's bank account.

Owner-manager The individual who owns and runs a business.

Owners' equity The difference between assets and liabilities of a business.

P

Parallel competition An imitative business that competes locally with others in the same industry.

Partitioned pricing Setting the price for a base item and then charging extra for each additional component.

Partnership Two or more people cooperating to conduct a business enterprise.

Part-time self-employment Working for yourself for 35 or fewer hours a week.

Pass through (taxation) Earnings of the business are distributed to the business owners and those owners (rather than the business) pay individual tax on the earnings.

Patent A grant by the U.S. government to an inventor for an idea that is new, useful, and nonobvious, giving the inventor the exclusive right to make, use, or sell his or her idea.

Payables Amounts owed to vendors for merchandise or services purchased on credit (see *Receivables*).

Payback period The amount of time it takes a business to earn back the funds it paid out to obtain a capital asset.

Periodic inventory The process of physically counting business assets on a set schedule.

Periodic or random discounting Sales conducted at either predictable or nonpredictable intervals.

Perishability A service exhibits perishability in that if it is not used when offered, it cannot be saved for later use.

Permanance The impression of long-term continuity a business gives others.

Perpetual inventory A system of recording the receipt and sale of each item as it occurs.

Personal selling The process of selling your products and service; includes prospect and evaluate, prepare, present, close, and follow-up.

Physical inventory A count of all the inventory being held for sale at a specific point in time.

PICS Model of Entrepreneurship An acronym for the four forms of entrepreneurship—*P*ublic, *I*ndependent, *C*orporate and *S*ocial.

Piercing the veil The dissolution of a corporate form, making it back into a sole proprietorship or general partnership, if the court finds that the owner carelessly mixed up personal and business assets or finances.

Pilot test A preliminary run of a business, sales effort, program, or Web site with the goal of assessing how well the overall approach works and what problems it might have.

Pioneering business A firm whose product or service is new to the industry or is itself creating a new industry.

Plaintiff Person or other entity filing a lawsuit.

Plant A general term for the facilities of a business.

Plant patent A 20-year patent that covers new strains of living plant organisms, algae, or macro fungi.

Pledging receivables Giving a third party legal rights to debts owed your business in order to provide assurance that borrowed money will be repaid.

Point of indifference The price at which a buyer is indifferent about buying or not buying the business.

Point-of-sale system Hardware and software combinations that integrate inventory management directly into accounting software.

Poisoning the well Creating a negative impression among your employers' customers.

Potential for growth Refers to the potential market size.

Power A concept in public importance which alludes to potential shifts in control or influence.

Preselling Involves introducing your product to potential customers and taking orders for later delivery.

Press kit A type of sales kit sent to media outlets which is focused around a press release.

Press relations Activities used to establish and promote a favorable opinion by the media.

Press release A written announcement intended to draw news media attention to a specific event.

Prestige or premium pricing Setting a price above that of the competition so as to indicate a higher quality or that a product is a status symbol.

Price lining The practice of setting (usually) three price points: good quality, better quality, best quality.

Primary research Information collected to solve a problem at hand or answer current questions.

Private placement memorandum A specialized legal form of business plan crafted by lawyers for the purpose of soliciting formal investments.

Probationary period Trial period in which an employee has temporary status before a formal offer to work full time is presented.

Process of personal selling The process of selling your products and service; includes prospect and evaluate, prepare, present, and the close.

Product distribution franchising An agreement that provides specific brand name products which are resold by the franchisee in a specified territory.

Product expansion A strategy whose goal is growth, based on selling existing customers a product or service they have never bought before.

Productivity The ratio measure of how well a firm does in using its inputs to create outputs. Literally, productivity is outputs divided by inputs.

Professionalization The extent to which a firm meets or exceeds the standard business practices for its industry.

Profit, profitability The amount that revenues exceed expenses.

Profit before taxes The amount of profit earned by a business before calculating the amount of income tax owed.

Pro forma Latin for "in the form of" when used to describe financial statements, indicates estimated or hypothetical information.

Promotional mix How much of each message conveyance you will use to sell your product as well as your objective in using each one.

Proof-of-concept Web site An Internet-based type of business plan providing information or demonstration of a product or service designed to solicit information on customer interest.

Property A general term for real estate, but it can also be applied as a legal term for anything owned or possessed.

Proprietary technology A product or service or an aspect of one that is kept as a trade secret or is protected legally using patent, copyright, trademark, or service mark.

Protected classes States of being that are expressly prohibited from suffering discrimination: race, color, religion, sex, national origin, gender, age, or disability.

Proximity A concept in public recognition which alludes to the impact level of the issue being discussed.

Psychological contract Refers to employees' beliefs about the promises between the employee and the firm. These beliefs are based on the perception that promises have been made (e.g., competitive wages, promotional opportunities, job training) in exchange for certain employee obligations such as giving of their energy, time, and technical skills.

Public entrepreneurship The form of entrepreneurship that involves revitalizing government agencies.

Public importance (1) Things that are considered important to large numbers of otherwise unrelated people, (2) things that are of civic importance, as opposed to private or corporate entities.

Public interest (1) Things that are generally considered to be beneficial to large numbers of people, (2) civic causes and benefits, as opposed to private and corporate benefits.

Public recognition Being recognized or acknowledged by large numbers of people, similar to "fame."

Public relations Activities used to establish and promote a favorable opinion by the public.

Publicity Information about your company and its activities that is disseminated to the public in order to gain their good opinion.

Pull-through system A term for just-in-time inventory systems in which product is ordered and placed into production only after a sale has been completed.

Pure innovation The process of creating new products or services, which results in a previously unseen product or service.

Q

Qualitative research Techniques for gathering information that rely on opinions expressed without a numerical basis ("real good" instead of "4 on a 5-point scale"). Popular techniques for qualitative research include interviews, small groups discussions, and observation.

Quantitative research Techniques that depend on categorizing responses into numbers, enabling statistical analysis of opinions. Examples include surveys and focus groups.

Quality A product's or service's fitness for use, measured as durability, reliability, serviceability, style, ease of use, and dependability.

R

Radical innovation strategy Rejecting existing ideas, and presenting a way to do things differently.

Rare resource An asset, capability, organizational process, information, or knowledge that is not generally available to competitors.

Receivables Amounts that are owed to a business for merchandise that was sold on credit (see payables).

Reciprocal link A listed, live connection to a different Web site, which in turn displays a similar link to the first Web site.

Reconciling An accounting process that identifies the causes of all differences between book and bank balances.

Referral discount A discount given to a customer who refers a friend to the business.

Registration Information provided to the government concerning the existence of, name of, nature of, and contact information for your business.

Regulation of the workplace Laws and governmental rules that limit the freedom of business owners to manage their businesses as they please.

Rehabilitation Act of 1973 An act of Congress that provides training for workers who are injured on the job.

Reorganization The popular term for a Chapter 13 bankruptcy in which a bankrupt firm continues to operate while paying off debts identified by the bankruptcy trustee.

Replacement cost The total cost of replacing an asset with an essentially identical asset.

Replacement value The cost to acquire an essentially identical asset. (Ch. 6)

Replacement value The cost incurred to replace one asset with an identical asset. (Ch. 16)

Research and development (often abbreviated R&D) The part of a business (and a business plan) that is focused on creating new products or services and preparing new technologies, ideas, products, or services for the firm's market.

Reserve price A minimum acceptable selling price in an auction. If the bidding does not exceed the price, the sale will not go through.

Resource Any asset, capability, organizational process, information, or knowledge that contributes to the firm's performance.

Resource competencies The ability or skill of the entrepreneur at finding expendable components necessary to the operation of the business such as time, information, location, financing, raw materials, and expertise.

Resource constrained sector Consists of firms high in innovation but low in growth rate due to a lack of resources.

Retailer A middleman business which sells to consumers or end users of a product (typically in single or small quantities).

Retained earnings The sum of all profits and losses, less all dividends paid since the beginning of the business.

Retainer A fee paid by a client to an attorney to engage the attorney's services.

Retrenchment An organizational life cycle stage in which established firms must find new approaches to improve the business and its chances for survival.

Return on equity The ratio of profits to owner investment in a business.

Return on investment (ROI) A capital budgeting equation used to measure the relationship between initial investment and the profits that are expected to be received from making the investment.

Reverse auction An auction in which the low bid gets the business or wins.

Revolving credit A credit agreement that allows the borrower to pay all or part of the balance at any time; as the loan balance is paid off, it becomes available to be borrowed again.

Risk The level of probability that an investment will not produce expected gains.

Risks The parts of a business or business plan that expose the firm to any kind of loss—profits, sales, reputation, assets, customers, and so on.

Role conflict The kind of problem that arises when people have multiple responsibilities, such as parent and boss, and the different responsibilities make different demands on them.

Royalty A payment to a licensor based on the number or value of licensed items sold.

RSS feed An Internet messaging service that pushes (sends) whatever Web material you specify to subscribers to that feed.

S

Safety stock An amount of inventory carried to ensure that you will not run out of inventory because of fluctuating levels of sales.

Sales promotion A form of communication that encourages the customer to act immediately, such as coupons, sales, or contests.

Sarbanes-Oxley Act A federal law describing the steps publicly traded businesses must take to protect and provide their key financial information.

Scalar questions Questions that are answered by some sort of scale; for example, "On a scale of 1 to 5, how do you like this book?"

Scale A characteristic of a market that describes the size of the market—a mass market or a niche market.

SCAMPER A creativity tool that provides cues to trigger breakthrough thinking. The letters stand for substitute, combine, adapt, modify, put to other uses, eliminate, and rearrange.

Scope A characteristic of a market that defines the geographic range covered by the market—from local to global.

Screening plan Also called a *mini-plan,* gives the basic overview of the firm and a detailed look at the financials.

Search engine optimization A general approach to Web site design intended to result in the site being displayed toward the beginning of a search engine's (e.g., Google, Yahoo!, etc.) listing for that term.

Secondary research Information already collected for some other purpose than the current problem or questions.

Self-employed Working for yourself.

Separation of duties A type of internal control that separates the physical control of an asset from the person accounting for that asset.

Serial entrepreneurs People who open multiple businesses throughout their career.

Set-asides Government contracting funds which are earmarked for particular kinds of firms, such as small businesses, minority-owned firms, women-owned firms, and the like.

Shake-out A type of life cycle stage following a boom in which there is a rapid decrease in the number of firms in an industry.

Sheltered workshop A nonprofit organization or institution that provides business services by using handicapped or rehabilitated workers.

Short-term debt Any debt that must be paid in less than one year from the date of the financial statement on which it is reported.

Single taxation Earnings of the business are taxed once with the owners paying the taxes.

Skimming Setting a price at the highest level the market will bear, usually because there is no competition at the time.

Slack resources Profits that are available to be used to satisfy the preferences of the owner in how the business is run.

Small and medium enterprise The international term for small businesses.

Small business Involves 1–50 people and has its owner managing the business on a day-to-day basis.

Small Business Administration A part of the United States government which provides support and advocacy for small businesses.

Small Business Development Center Offices co-sponsored by states and the Federal government that offer free or low-cost help to existing and potential small businesses.

Small business investment companies Private businesses that are authorized to make SBA insured loans to start-ups and small businesses.

Social capital Characteristics of a business, like trust, consistency, and networks, that represent potential social obligations which are an asset of the firm or entrepreneur.

Social entrepreneurship The form of entrepreneurship involving the creation of self-sustaining charitable and civic organizations, or for-profit organizations which invest significant profits in charitable activities.

Social network The entrepreneur's set of relationships and contacts with individuals and institutions.

Sole proprietorship A business owned by a single individual who is responsible for all debts and claims against the business.

Specialized business professionalization A situation that occurs when businesses have founders or owners who are passionate about one or two of the key business functions, such as sales, operations, accounting, finance, or human resources.

Spin-off A business that is created by separating part of an operating business into a separate entity.

Sponsored link A form of paid advertising that gets your company's Web site at the top of a search list.

Sponsorships Paying for a local organization's needs in exchange for recognition.

Standard business practice A business action that has been widely adopted within an industry or occupation.

Start-up A new business that is started from scratch.

Straight line for a useful life of 10 years Depreciation is computed using a straight line method over 10 years, so an asset would lose 10% of its value each year.

Strategic direction The conceptualization of how a business might best move in response to the findings of a SWOT analysis—Flaunt, Fix, Fight, Flee, Find, or Fire-up.

Subcontract A contract by which a new party agrees to perform a duty that one of the original parties to a contract was already legally obligated to perform.

Substitution profits Returns intended to equal and replace the salary or wages the entrepreneur could draw working for someone else.

Success profits Returns at levels higher than the entrepreneur could make working for others.

Succession The process of intergenerational transfer of a business.

Succinct message Your key point in as few and as memorable words as possible.

Supplemental profits Returns above costs intended as a secondary income for entrepreneurs (where self-employment is secondary to their main job).

Suppy chain Like the value chain, the line of distribution of a product from its start as materials outside the target firm to its handling in the target firm to its handling by sellers into the hands of customers.

Surety bonds An agreement with an insurance or bonding company that will pay a specified amount in the event that the entity bonded fails to comply with specified contractual requirements.

Survey A data-collection method using a questionnaire—in person, on phone, on paper, or on the Internet.

Sustainable entrepreneurship Starting or running a firm in a manner which saves or improves the environment. (See *Green entrepreneurship*.)

Synergy A combination in which the whole is greater than the sum of its component parts.

T

Tagline (also known as a slogan) Memorable catchphrase that captures the key idea of a business, its service, product, or customer.

Takeover Seizing of control of a business by purchasing its stock to be able to select the board of directors.

Tangibility An item's capability of being touched, seen, tasted, or felt.

Tangible resources Assets of a firm that can be easily and concretely identified.

Target market The group of people on which a marketer focuses promotion and sales efforts.

Task environment Those parts of the environment outside of the firm which directly and consistently touch on the firm.

Tax abatement A legal reduction in taxes by a government.

Tax accounting An accounting approach based on specific accounting requirements set by governmental taxing agencies.

Tax codes Laws and regulations that specify the requirements of taxation.

Tax credits Direct reductions in the amount of taxes that must be paid, dependent upon meeting some legal criteria.

Tax management An estate planning strategy which uses structured transfers of the business to make tax payments as small as possible.

Telemarketing Contact via telephone for the express purpose of selling a product or service. Telemarketing can either be inbound (customer calls company) or outbound (company calls customer).

Termination An endgame strategy in which the owner closes down a business.

Test marketing Selling your product or service in a limited area, for a limited time.

Time management The organizing process to help make the most efficient use of the day.

Time to start-up How long it takes to start a new business.

Timing purchases A method of controlling the timing of cash outflows that is invisible to suppliers and vendors.

Total product The entire bundle of products, services, and meanings of your offering; includes extras like service, warranty, or delivery, as well as what the product means to the customer.

Trade association (also known as *professional association*) A group of people in the same industry who band together to gather and share information and present and represent the industry to the public and government.

Trade discounts Percentage discounts from gross invoice amounts provided to encourage prompt payment.

Trade magazines The magazines that target specific industries and professions.

Trade name or assumed name or a doing business as (dba) The name under which a business is operated.

Trade name franchising An agreement that provides to the franchisee only the rights to use the franchisor's trade name and/ or trademarks.

Trade secret Confidential information within a company that gives that company a competitive advantage.

Trademark Distinctive word, slogan, or image that identifies a product and its origin.

Traditional small business A firm intended to provide a living income to the owner, and operating in a manner and on a schedule consistent with other firms in the industry and market.

Traffic generators Other businesses that bring customers (generate traffic) to the area.

Transfer An endgame strategy in which ownership is moved from one person or group to another.

Transformational competencies The abilities of a firm to make its product or service in a way that enhances value or efficiency compared to other firms.

Trendiness A concept in public recognition which alludes to the fit of the topic to current fashion or public interest.

Trust A feeling of fairness in all business transactions in which the firm engages, such as financial transactions, employee matters, regulatory compliance, and complaint resolution.

Tweet A 140-character or less message sent using the Twitter Web service.

U

Undercapitalization Not having enough money available to the business to cover shortfalls in sales or profits.

Undifferentiated strategy A marketing strategy that uses no segmentation; assumes that all consumers have virtually identical needs and can be reached by the same marketing mix.

Universalism An ethical model that suggests that there is a code of right and wrong that everyone can see and follow.

Utilitarianism An ethical model that supports seeking the greatest good for the greatest number of people.

Utility patent A 20-year patent covering a process, machine, article of manufacture, composition of matter, or any new or useful improvement of an existing one.

V

Valuable resource An asset, capability, organizational process, information, or knowledge that lets a firm take advantage of opportunities or lock out competitors.

Value proposition Small business owners' unique selling points that will be used to differentiate their products and/or services from those of the competition.

Variable costs Those costs that change with each unit produced, for example, raw materials.

Variance Permission from a government organization to act differently than the laws state. (Ch. 5)

Variance The difference between an actual and budgeted revenue or cost. (Ch. 13)

Variance analysis The process of determining the effect of price and quantity changes on revenues and expenses.

Viability The preliminary assessment of the potential for a business to be created or, once created, to survive.

Vicarious (indirect) liability Indirect liability or responsibility for the actions of another.

Viral marketing Any electronic equivalent of word-of-mouth advertising, in which the advertiser's message spreads quickly and widely via e-mail, Web site, blogs, and other online tools.

Virtual employees Independent contractors who provide specialized business services or support from a distance, through the Internet, telephone, fax, or another method of communication.

Virtual instant global entrepreneurship (VIGE) Deploying a business internationally using the e-commerce capabilities of the Internet.

Vision statement A very simple 5–10 word sentence or tagline that expresses the fundamental idea or goal of the firm.

Visuals A concept in public interest which alludes to the graphic interest held by an event.

Volatility The frequency of business starts and stops.

W

Waiver Part of a contract in which a party intentionally gives up legal rights or claims.

Walkaways Business terminations in which the entrepreneur ends the business with its obligations met.

Weighted average cost of capital (WAC) The expected average future cost of funds.

Whole of life costs The sum of all costs of capital assets, including acquisition, ownership, operation, and disposal.

Wholesaler A middleman business which buys (typically in large quantities) and sells (typically in smaller quantities) to businesses rather than consumers.

Word-of-mouth A means of spreading information about your business through the comments friends and customers make to other potential customers.

Workout A form of business termination in which the firm's legal or financial obligations are not fully met at closing.

Z

Zoning laws Government specifications for acceptable use of land and buildings in particular areas.

END NOTES

Chapter 1

1. David Astor, "Boom in 'Boondocks' Client Papers as Comic Strip Sets Start-Up Record," *Editor & Publisher* 132, no. 16 (April 17, 1999), p. 53. David Astor, "'Boondocks' Artist Still Living on the Edge of Controversy," *Editor & Publisher* 132, no. 41 (October 9, 1999), p. 47. David Astor, "High-Profile Year for 'Boondocks,'" *Editor & Publisher* 132, no. 33 (August 14, 1999), p. 29. F. Romall Smalls, "Blowin' Up in 'The Boondocks,'" *Black Enterprise* 30, no. 12 (July 2000), p. 64. John Simpkins, "The Equal-Opportunity Offender (Cartoonist Aaron McGruder's 'Boondocks')," *The New York Times Magazine,* June 24, 2001, p. 42. Aaron McGruder's Web site can be found at http://www.boondocks.net. Jennifer A. Carbin, "Boondocks Speaks: An Interview with Aaron McGruder," *City Paper (Philadelphia),* November 5, 2001, http://www.alternet.org/story/11859. United Press Syndicate Web site, "Aaron McGruder," http://www.amuniversal.com/ups/features/boondocks/bio.htm. "Aaron McGruder: Cartoonist," Who2, Pearson Education, publishing as Infoplease (2000–2007), May 5, 2007, http://www.infoplease.com/biography/var/aaronmcgruder.html. Nancy Basile, "Aaron McGruder," About: Animated TV. May 5, 2007, http://animatedtv.about.com/od/theboondocks/p/aaronmcgruder.htm
2. The GEM study for 2007 reported that 44 percent of adults surveyed had thought about starting a business at some time. Only 5.9 percent had taken any actions toward starting one, and 5 percent of the population had actually started a business. Ivory Phinisee, I. Elaine Allen, Edward Rogoff, Joseph Onochie, and Monica Dean, *GEM United States 2006–2007 Executive Report* (Babson, MA: Babson College, 2008), Figure 25, http://www.gemconsortium.org/download.asp?fid=836.
3. Estimates peg new starts at around 4 percent of all businesses, which given 27.2 million firms, would place the estimate at 1,088,000. The SBA, counting only new firms with employees, reported 637,100 businesses opening in 2007. This number does not include partial-year businesses or sellers on the Internet based in the United States, so 1 million new businesses is a conservative estimate. Ivory Phinisee, I. Elaine Allen, Edward Rogoff, Joseph Onochie, and Monica Dean, *GEM United States 2006–2007 Executive Report* (Babson, MA: Babson College, 2008), Figure 25, http://www.gemconsortium.org/download.asp?fid=836. Office of Advocacy, U.S. Small Business Administration, "Frequently Asked Questions," September 2008. http://www.sba.gov/advo/stats/sbfaq.pdf.
4. This is the latest version of the idea called "fear of failure" by researchers in achievement motivation in the 1960s and 1970s. For fear of failure, see Ray Smilor, *Love and Fear: The Great Motivators of Entrepreneurial Achievement* EntreWorld, n.d., http://www.entreworld.com/content/topAdvise.com?ColumnID=192, July 9, 2005, or Emmeline G. de Pillis, "What's Achievement Got to Do With It? The Role of National Culture in the Relationship Between Entrepreneurship and Achievement Motivation," *Frontiers of Entrepreneurship Research* (Wellesley, MA: Babson College, 1998). http://www.babson.edu/entrep/fer/papers98/IV/IV_A/IV_A_text.htm. For the latest version, see Jeffrey Pfeffer and Robert I. Sutton, *The Knowing-Doing Gap: How Smart Companies Turn Knowledge into Action* (Cambridge, MA: Harvard Business School Press, 1999), or see Alan M. Webber, "Why Can't We Get Anything Done?" *Fast Company,* June 2000, http://www.fastcompany.com/magazine/35/pfeffer.html.
5. The 50 percent survival rate is the rate reported in SBA Office of Advocacy, *Small Business by the Numbers* (Washington, DC: Small Business Administration, 2004), http://www.sba.gov/advo/stats/sbfaq.pdf. This comes from original work done by the SBA and is reported in B. D. Phillips and B. A. Kirchoff, "Formation, Growth Survival: Small Firm Dynamics in the U.S. Economy," *Small Business Economics* 1 (1989), pp. 65–74 and B. D. Phillips, "Using Census Bureau Data by Firm Size, 1988–1996," in Jerome A. Katz (ed.), *Advances in Entrepreneurship, Firm Emergence and Growth Volume 4: Databases for the Study of Entrepreneurship* (Greenwich, CT: JAI Press, 2000). The survival figures can differ dramatically. For example, in 2009 the SBA's Frequently Asked Questions on Advocacy Small Business Statistics and research (http://web.sba.gov/faqs/faqIndexAll.cfm?areaid=24) used a figure of 44% of firms with employees surviving 4 years from a different study (Amy E. Knaup and Merissa C. Piazza, "Business Employment Dynamics Data: Survival and Longevity, II," by *Monthly Labor Review,* vol. 30, no. 9, Sept. 2007, pp. 3–10). However, this study follows firms during a period of boom and bust at the millennium, and while well done, really is best at telling us what survival rates are in bad times, not on average. The study also leaves open the survival figure for nonemployer firms. For comparison, a study done by the Census Bureau for the SBA and reported in SBA Office of Advocacy, ("Small Business Answer Card 1998, Table: Survival Rates of All Firms Existing in 1992 by 1996," 1998. http://www.sba.gov/advo/stats/answer.pdf) showed the four-year survival figure for all firms was 75.5 percent. For firms with no employees (owner-only firms) 72.4 percent survived. For firms with employees, the survival rate was 90.5 percent. For the text, we elected to report the conservative set of "average" figures.
6. James J. Chrisman, "The Influence of Outsider-Generated Knowledge Resources on Venture Creation," *Journal of Small Business Management* 37, no. 4 (October 1999), pp. 42–58. James J. Chrisman and W. Edward McMullan, "A Preliminary Assessment of Outsider Assistance as a Knowledge Resource: The Longer-Term Impact of New Venture Counseling," *Entrepreneurship: Theory & Practice* 24, no. 3 (Spring 2000), pp. 37–53. James J. Chrisman and W. Edward McMullan, "Outsider Assistance as a Knowledge Resource for New Venture Survival," *Journal of Small Business Management* 42, no. 3 (July 2004), pp. 229–244.
7. Devron A. Veasley, "Incubators Build Economies, Benefit Communities, in Depth: Small Business Resource Guide—Business Incubation," *Birmingham Business Journal*, 2003, http://birmingham.bizjournals.com/birmingham/stories/2003/08/11/focus6.html.
8. Alberta Charney and Gary Libecap, *Impact of Entrepreneurship Education* (Kansas City, MO: Kauffman Center for Entrepreneurial Leadership, 2000). Nancy B. Upton, Donald L. Sexton, and Carlos Moore, "Have We Made a Difference? An Examination of Career Activity of Entrepreneurship Majors since 1981" (abstract), *Frontiers of Entrepreneurship Research* (Wellesley, MA: Babson College, 1995), pp. 727–728. Zenas Block and Stephen A. Stumpf, "Entrepreneurship Education Research: Experience and Challenge." In Donald L. Sexton and John D. Kasarda (eds.), *The State of the Art of Entrepreneurship* (Boston, MA: PWS-Kent Publishing, 1992). Bryan W. Clark, Charles H. Davis, and Verne C. Harnish, "Do Courses in Entrepreneurship Aid in New Venture Creation?" *Journal of Small Business Management* Vol 22, no. 2 (April 1984), pp. 26–31. Calvin A. Kent, "Entrepreneurship Education at the Collegiate Level: A Synopsis and Evaluation," in Calvin A. Kent (ed.) *Entrepreneurship Education* (New York: Quorum Books, 1990), pp. 111–122. Lawrence A. Klatt, "A Study of Small Business/Entrepreneurial Education in Colleges and Universities," *The Journal of Private Enterprise* 4 (Fall 1988), pp. 103–108. Peter Robinson and Max Hayes, "Entrepreneurship Education in America's Major Universities," *Entrepreneurship: Theory & Practice* 15, no. 3 (Spring 1991), pp. 41–52. Donald L. Sexton and Nancy B. Upton, "Evaluation of an Innovative Approach to Teaching Entrepreneurship," *Journal of Small Business Management* 25, no. 1 (January, 1987) pp. 35–43. Van G. H. Clouse, "A Controlled Experiment Relating Entrepreneurial Education to Students' Start-up Decisions," *Journal of Small Business Management* 28, no. 2 (April 1990), pp. 45–53.
9. Ulla Hytti and Paula Kuopusjärvi, "Evaluating and Measuring Entrepreneurship and Enterprise Education," *Methods, Tools and Practices* (Turun Yliopisto, Finland: Turku School of Economics and Business Administration, 2004), http://webct.tukkk.fi/entreva/entredu/tiedostot/report_web.pdf. Lars Kolvereid and Øystein Moen, "Entrepreneurship among Business Graduates: Does a Major in Entrepreneurship Make a Difference?" *Journal of European Industrial Training* 21, no. 4 (1997), pp. 154–160. W. Edward McMullan and L. Murray Gillin, "Entrepreneurship Education: Developing Technological Start-up Entrepreneurs, A Case Study of a

Graduate Entrepreneurship Programme at Swinburne University," *Technovation* 18, no. 4 (April 1998), pp. 275–286. Teresa V. Menzies and J. C. Paradi, "Encouraging Technology-Based Ventures: Entrepreneurship Education and Engineering Graduates," *New England Journal of Entrepreneurship* 5, no. 2 (Fall 2002), pp. 57–64. Teresa V. Menzies and J. C. Paradi, "Entrepreneurship Education and Engineering Students: Career Path and Business Performance," *International Journal of Entrepreneurship and Innovation* 4, no. 2 (May 2003), pp. 85–96. Thomas N. Garavan and Barra O'Cinneide, "Entrepreneurship Education and Training Programmes," *Journal of European Industrial Training* 18, no. 8/9 (1994), pp. 3–13. Thomas N. Garavan and Barra O'Cinneide, "Entrepreneurship Education and Training Programmes," *Journal of European Industrial Training* 18, no. 11 (1994), pp. 13–22.

10. For the estimate of the number of firms, the source is U.S. Small Business Administration Office of Advocacy, *Frequently Asked Questions* (Washington DC: Small Business Administration, 2008), www.sba.gov/advo/research/sb_econ2006.pdf. For the estimate of the number of self-employeds three paragraphs later, the source is U.S. Small Business Administration, Office of Advocacy, *SBA Quarterly Indicators, 4th Quarter 2006* (Washington DC: Small Business Administration, 2007), www.sba.gov/advo/research/sbqei0604.pdf. If it seems strange that the number of firms is greater than the number of self-employeds, the reason is that many business owners organize their firms as corporations, and corporations with nonowner employees are counted separately. Unfortunately, "entrepreneur" or even "owner" is not a category the government uses when statistically profiling businesses.
11. For details on the SBA size standards, look at the Office of Size Standards Web site at the U.S. Small Business Administration—http://www.sba.gov/size/.
12. Even among small business owners, calling someone an entrepreneur can be problematic. About one owner in eight was offended by the term in a 2001 poll, although "small business owner" was almost universally accepted. *NFIB—National Small Business Poll—Success, Satisfaction and Growth* (Washington, DC: NFIB Research Foundation, 2001).
13. This fight among professors seems to have settled down to three competing camps—wealth creation, opportunity recognition, and firm creation. Wealth creation proponents usually define entrepreneurship as efforts to create wealth, especially through high-growth new ventures. Major centers for this approach are Harvard University and Babson College. The opportunity recognition approach is centered at University of Chicago and University of Virginia. This approach sees entrepreneurship occurring when an individual finds and exploits some technological, economic, or market mismatch. The firm creation approach says that starting a business is where entrepreneurship occurs, and it is the favored model at Clemson University and Saint Louis University.
14. M. Dell and C. Freedman, *Direct from Dell: Strategies That Revolutionized an Industry* (New York: Harper Business, 2000), http://www.amazon.com/exec/obidos/tg/detail//0756718775/102-2417352-1853726?v=glance&vi=excerpt.
15. Robert X. Cringley, *Accidental Empires: How the Boys of Silicon Valley Make Their Millions, Battle Foreign Competition, and Still Can't Get a Date* (New York: HarperInformation, 2000).
16. The Dynamic Capitalism Typology comes from the pioneering book by Bruce A. Kirchhoff, *Entrepreneurship and Dynamic Capitalism: The Economics of Business Firm Formation and Growth.* (Westport, CT: Praeger Publishers, 1994), http://www.questia.com/PM.qst?a=o&d=15462084. The model has been used in a variety of settings. The presentation here draws on William Bygrave, "Financing Entrepreneurs and Their Ventures," in Paul D. Reynolds, William D. Bygrave, Erkko Autio, and Others, *Global Entrepreneurship Monitor 2003 Executive Report* (Kansas City: Ewing Marion Kauffman Foundation, 2004); Bruce A. Kirchhoff, "Self-Employment and Dynamic Capitalism," *Journal of Labor Research,* 17(4), (1996), pp. 627–644; Gwen Richtermeyer and Cassy Venters, "Why Is Entrepreneurship an Important Economic Development Strategy?" National Association of Community Development Extension Professionals Convention (Las Vegas, NV, 2005), May 5, 2007, www.ncrcrd.iastate.edu/nacdep/researchroundtable/2-richtermeyer-venters-handout.pdf; and Sanders Wennekers and Roy Thurik, "Linking Entrepreneurship and Economic Growth," *Small Business Economics,* 13 (1), (1999), pp. 27–55.
17. William D. Bygrave with Mark Quill, *Global Entrepreneurship Monitor: 2006 Financing Report* (Babson, MA: Babson College, 2007), p. 13, www.gemconsortium.org/download.asp?fid=608. Ivory Phinisee, I. Elaine Allen, Edward Rogoff, Joseph Onochie, and Monica Dean, *GEM United States 2006–2007 Executive Report* (Babson, MA: Babson College, 2008), Figure 25, http://www.gemconsortium.org/download.asp?fid=836.
18. Jerome A. Katz, "A Psychosocial Cognitive Model of Employment Status Choice," *Entrepreneurship: Theory & Practice* 17, no. 1 (Fall 1992), pp. 29–37.
19. Marc Fleury, "Doing It Wrong, Getting It Right," Entrepreneur's Byline, *BusinessweekOnline.* September 3, 2003, http://www.businessweek.com/smallbiz/content/sep2003/sb2003093_8638.htm.
20. The "universally mentioned" rewards were those mentioned by 75 percent or more of potential or new small business owners—a much higher rate than working people in general mention. The "occasionally mentioned" rewards were those mentioned by less than 50 percent of potential or new small business owners, but were still mentioned more often than by working people. The "rarely mentioned" rewards were those in which entrepreneurs mention a reward significantly less often than working people do in general. The sample was 871 potential and new entrepreneurs, compared to a control group of 431 individuals. For details on the measures see Nancy M. Carter, William B. Gartner, and Kelly G. Shaver, "Career reasons." In William B. Gartner, Kelly G. Shaver, Nancy M. Carter, and Paul D. Reynolds (eds.), *Handbook of Entrepreneurial Dynamics: The Process of Business Creation* (Thousand Oaks, CA: Sage, 2004), pp. 142–152. The PSED analyses reported here were custom analyses performed by Dr. Jennifer Shaver.
21. Thomas J. Stanley, *The Millionaire Mind* (Kansas City, MO: Andrews McNeel, 2001). Thomas J. Stanley and William D. Danko, *The Millionaire Next Door* (New York: Pocket Books, 1996).
22. Devlin Smith, "Women of Substance—Experience: A Secret to Success," *Entrepreneur,* November 2003, http://www.entrepreneur.com/Magazines/Copy_of_MA_SegArticle/0,4453,311442— 2-,00.html.
23. See Endnote 2.
24. William D. Bygrave with Mark Quill, *Global Entrepreneurship Monitor: 2006 Financing Report* (Babson, MA: Babson College, 2007), p. 13, www.gemconsortium.org/download.asp?fid=608. Ivory Phinisee, I. Elaine Allen, Edward Rogoff, Joseph Onochie, and Monica Dean, *GEM United States 2006–2007 Executive Report* (Babson, MA: Babson College, 2008), Figure 25, http://www.gemconsortium.org/download.asp?fid=836. William J. Dennis, Jr., *National Small Business Poll: Economic Downturn* (Washington, DC: NFIB Research Foundation, 2008), http://www.411sbfacts.com/files/SBP_V8I1_EconDownturn.pdf.
25. Sarah Caron, "14 Big Businesses That Started in a Recession," insidecrm.com 24 May 2009, http://www.insidecrm.com/features/businesses-started-slump-111108/. Mandel, Michael, "Starting Successful New Companies in Recessions—BusinessWeek," Businessweek.com, May 3, 2009; May 24, 2009, http://www.businessweek.com/the_thread/economicsunbound/archives/2009/05/starting_succes.html. This list of airlines was based on Michael Masouras. "Companies founded after 2000—Freebase," Freebase.com. May 24, 2009, http://www.freebase.com/view/user/masouras/default_domain/views/companies_founded_after_2000, compared to operating airlines shown on "List of airlines—Planes," Plane.SpottingWorld.com, May 24, 2009, http://plane.spottingworld.com/List_of_airlines.
26. Anita Campbell, "What Are the Most Profitable Small Businesses in a Recession? Small Business Trends," *Small Business Trends,* January 27,

2009; May 24, 2009, http://smallbiztrends.com/2009/01/profitable-small-businesses-recession.html. Maureen Farrell, "The Most and Least Profitable Businesses to Start—Forbes.com," forbes.com, January 18, 2008; May 29, 2009, http://www.forbes.com/2008/01/18/citigroup-sageworks-nyu-ent-fin-cx_mf_0118mostprofitable.html. Mindy Woolen, "Industry Trends >> Blog Archive >> Most Profitable Industries of 2008," Sageworks.com January 28, 2009; May 24, 2009, http://www.sageworksinc.com/industrytrends/index.php/most-profitable-industries-of-2008/.

27. David Rottenberg, and Jeffrey Shuman, "Loser Chic—Entrepreneur.com," Entrepreneur.com, February 1999; May 24, 2009, http://www.entrepreneur.com/magazine/businessstartupsmagazine/1999/february/17228.html.
28. Mindy Carson, "Famous Mompreneurs and How They Made Their Fortunes—Associated Content," *Associated Content—Business & Finance,* April 21, 2009; May 29, 2009, http://www.associatedcontent.com/article/1662719/famous_mompreneurs_and_how_they_made.html. E.C., Hoffman III, "10 Famous Career Switchers," Businessweek.com June 28, 2007; May 29, 2009, http://images.businessweek.com/ss/07/06/0628_second_careers/index_01.htm.
29. "Young Millionares—Entrepreneur.com." Entrepreneur.com, May 25, 2009, http://www.entrepreneur.com/youngmillionaires.
30. Jerome Katz and William B. Gartner, "Properties of Emerging Organizations," *Academy of Management Review* 13, no. 3 (July 1988), pp. 429–441. Jerome A. Katz and Scott Safranski, "Standardization in the Midst of Innovation: Structural Implications of the Internet for SMEs," *Futures: The Journal of Policy, Planning and Future Studies* 35, no. 4 (May 2003), pp. 323–340. Sumit K. Kundu and Jerome A. Katz, "Born-International SMEs: Bi-Level Impacts of Resources and Intentions," *Small Business Economics* 20, no. 1 (February 2003), pp. 25–47. Jerome A. Katz and Susan Peters, "Understanding the Entrepreneur in the Growth Process of SMEs," *The International Journal of Entrepreneurship and Innovation Management* 1, no. 3/4 (2001), pp. 366–380. Nancy M. Carter, William B. Gartner, and Paul D. Reynolds, "Exploring Start-Up Sequences," *Journal of Business Venturing* 11, no. 3 (May 1996), pp. 151–166.
31. The theory was developed in the article: Jerome Katz and William B. Gartner, "Properties of Emerging Organizations," *Academy of Management Review* 13, no. 3 (July 1988), pp. 429–441. And extended in J. A. Katz and S. Peters, "Understanding the Entrepreneur in the Growth Process of SMEs," *The International Journal of Entrepreneurship and Innovation Management* 1, no. 3/4 (2001), pp. 366–380. Empirical work in the PSED study was reported in Nancy M. Carter, William B. Gartner, and Paul D. Reynolds, "Exploring Start-Up Sequences," *Journal of Business Venturing* 11, no. 3 (May 1996), pp. 151–166. An independent confirmation was reported in Sumit K. Kundu and Jerome A. Katz, "Born-International SMEs: Bi-Level Impacts of Resources and Intentions," *Small Business Economics* 20, no. 1 (February 2003), pp. 25–47. A shortened form of the scale they developed for the PSED remains in use in the Global Entrepreneurship Monitor.
32. Nancy M. Carter, William B. Gartner, and Paul D. Reynolds, "Exploring Start-Up Sequences," *Journal of Business Venturing* 11, no. 3 (May 1996), pp. 151–166.
33. Nancy M. Carter, William B. Gartner, and Paul D. Reynolds, "Exploring Start-Up Sequences," *Journal of Business Venturing* 11, no. 3 (May 1996), pp. 151–166 and Monica Diochon, Yvon Gasse, Teresa Menzies and Denis Garand, "From Conception to Inception: Initial Findings from the Canadian Study on Entrepreneurial Emergence (2001). ASAC 2001 Annual Meeting, www.sauder.ubc.ca/research/research_centres/era/arena5/papers/ASAC2001Revised%20Submission.pdf.
34. See Endnote 4.
35. The numbers are for 1999–2000, the latest year that data were available. SBA Office of Advocacy, *Small Business by the Numbers* (Washington DC: Small Business Administration, 2003), http://www.sba.gov/advo/stats/sbfaq.pdf.
36. SBA Office of Advocacy, *Small Business by the Numbers,* http://www.sba.gov/advo/stats/sbfaq.pdf and Z. J. Acs and C. Armington, "Endogenous Growth and Entrepreneurial Activity in Cities," Center for Economic Studies, U.S. Bureau of the Census, Working Paper #CES-WP-03-2, January 2003.
37. The last actual count was in 2000: small business—57.1 million, large business—56.9 million. SBA Office of Advocacy, *Small Business by the Numbers,* http://www.sba.gov/advo/stats/sbfaq.pdf.
38. Jerome A. Katz, "Modelling Entrepreneurial Career Progressions: Concepts and Considerations," *Entrepreneurship: Theory & Practice* 19, no. 2 (Winter 1994), pp. 23–40.
39. Jerome A. Katz, "A Psychosocial Cognitive Model of Employment Status Choice," *Entrepreneurship: Theory & Practice* 17, no. 1 (Fall 1992), pp. 29–37.
40. Joseph A. Schumpeter, *The Theory of Economic Development* (New York: Oxford, 1961) (1934).
41. Robert X. Cringley, *Accidental Empires: How the Boys of Silicon Valley Make Their Millions, Battle Foreign Competition, and Still Can't Get a Date,* (New York: HarperInformation, 1996).
42. Scott A. Shane, "Is the Independent Entrepreneur a Valuable Organizational Form?" *RISEbusiness,* http://www.riseb.org/shane.html.
43. SBA Office of Advocacy, *Small Business by the Numbers,* http://www.sba.gov/advo/stats/sbfaq.pdf.
44. History of Snowboarding Web site, http://www.sbhistory.de/.
45. "Behind the Earmuff," *Kids World,* http://www.kidzworld.com/site/p880.htm. Mary Bellis, "Chester Greenwood, Earmuffs," *Inventors,* About.com, http://inventors.about.com/library/inventors/blgreenwood.htm. "Fascinating Facts about the Invention of Earmuffs by Chester Greenwood in 1873," *The Great Idea Finder,* http://www.ideafinder.com/history/inventions/story091.htm.
46. Krisztina Holly, "Visual Voice(TM) Telephony Software," *Thinkquest,* http://library.thinkquest.org/26451/contents/inventors/krisztinaholly.htm?tqskip1=1; Mary Bellis, About.com, Inventors "Krisztina Holly," http://inventors.about.com/library/inventors/blholly.htm.
47. Don Debelak, "A Novel Dilemma: To Reach Potential Customers with an Avant-Garde Product, You'll Need to Have a Few Tricks Up Your Sleeve," *Entrepreneur,* June 2003, http://www.entrepreneur.com/Magazines/Copy_of_MA_SegArticle/0,4453,_308735—1-,00.html. And Drinksafe Technologies Web site, http://www.drinksafetech.com.
48. "Our Founders: Ed Lowe and Darlene Lowe," http://edwardlowe.org/index.peer?page=FDNfounders, July 9, 2005. Jenny Kee, "Author Mark Baven on Being Extreme: Do You Have What It Takes to Be an Extreme Entrepreneur? Let Mark Baven Show You the Ropes of Rule-Breaking, Risk-Taking Entrepreneurship," *Entrepreneur,* June 18, 2001, http://www.entrepreneur.com/article/0,4621,290325,00.html.
49. This table was inspired by a table on small business innovation in the 1994 edition of *The State of Small Business.* [U.S. Small Business Administration, *The State of Small Business: A Report of the President, 1994* (Washington, DC: U.S. Government Printing Office, 1995), p. 114.] I tracked down the inventors of several of the small business innovations listed in the report and added several new ones, as well as all the student started innovations. I found the video laryngoscope in Melnie Reid, "How a Shop Assistant Saw the Light and Saved Lives." *The Times,* July 17, 2008, http://www.timesonline.co.uk/tol/news/uk/scotland/article4354048.ece.
50. Small Business Administration, "The New American Revolution: The Role and Impact of Small Firms" (Washington, DC: U.S. Small Business Administration, Office of Economic Research, 1998).
51. Small Business Administration, *Rural and Urban Areas by Firm Size, 1990–1995* (Washington, DC: Office of Advocacy, 1999). http://www.sbaonline.sba.gov/advo/stats/urb_rur.pdf.
52. Economic development experts call these *central place theorems,* with the efforts to figure out how many stores a population can support called

demand-threshold studies. Examples tend to be fairly localized and include: Thomas R. Harris and J. Scott Shonkwiler, "Interdependence of Retail Businesses," *Growth and Change* 28 no. 4 (Fall 1997), pp. 520–533. J. Scott Shonkwiler and Thomas R. Harris, "Rural Retail Thresholds and Interdependencies," *Journal of Regional Studies* 36 (1996), pp. 617–630. H. Gale, Jr., "Retail Sales Pull Factors in U.S. Counties," *The Review of Regional Studies* 26 (1996), pp. 177–196. David Darling and Stephen Tubene, "Determining the Population Thresholds of Minor Trade Centers: A Benchmark Study of Non-Metropolitan Cities in Kansas," *Review of Agricultural Economics* 18 no. 1, (January 1996), pp. 95–102. G. Ebai and T. Harris, "Factors Influencing Trade Area Activity in the Great Basin Area," *The Review of Regional Studies* 27 (1997), pp. 251–276.

53. The idea that living spaces are important to creativity (such as the kind we find in entrepreneurial and high-growth ventures) comes from Richard Florida, *The Rise of the Creative Class: And How It's Transforming Work, Leisure, Community and Everyday Life* (New York: Basic Books, 2004).
54. Robert Berner, "P&G: New and Improved: How A.G. Lafley Is Revolutionizing a Bastion of Corporate Conservatism," *BusinessWeek*, July 7, 2003, http://www.businessweek.com/magazine/content/03_27/b3840001_mz001.htm. You can find information about Trillium Health Care Products at http://www.brockville.com/newsdetails.cfm?IDIn=172_01.htm or at their corporate Web site www.trilliumhealth care.com.
55. John E. Harmon, "On the Wings of a Buffalo or 'Mother Teressa's Wings'" *Atlas of Popular Culture in the Northeastern United States.* (Undated), http://www.geography.ccsu.edu/harmonj/atlas/buffwing.htm; Anchor Bar Web site, http://www.buffalowings.com/. Calvin Trillin, "An Attempt to Complile a Short History of the Buffalo Chicken Wing," *The New Yorker,* August 25, 1980, pp. 82–87 (Also reproduced in his book, *The Tummy Trilogy*) J. Ferrary, "Mother Teressa's Wings," *Travel-Holiday* 175, no. 5 (June 1992), p. 31.
56. Niels Bosma, Zoltan J. Acs, Erkko Autio, Alicia Coduras, and Jonathan Levie, *Global Entrepreneurship Monitor: 2008 Executive Report* (Babson, MA: Babson College, 2008), Figure 7, p. 21, http://www.gemconsortium.org/download.asp?fid=849.
57. Office of Trade and Industry Information, International Trade Administration, U.S. Department of Commerce, "Small & Medium-Sized Exporting Companies: A Statistical Overview, 2006," *Export.gov—Industry, Trade and the Economy: Data and Analysis,* February 7, 2008; May 31, 2009 http://ita.doc.gov/td/industry/otea/sme_2006/SME_index_2006.htm.
58. Sumit K. Kundu and Jerome A. Katz. "Born-International SMEs: BI-Level Impacts of Resources and Intentions." *Small Business Economics* 20.1 (2003): 25.
59. Jerome A. Katz, Scott R. Safranski, and Omar Khan, "Virtual Instant Global Entrepreneurship," *Journal of International Entrepreneurship* 1.1 (2003): 43.
60. eBay, "eBay Inc.—eBay Outlines Global Business Strategy at 2005 Analyst Conference," http://investor.ebay.com February 10, 2005; May 31, 2009, http://investor.ebay.com/releasedetail.cfm?ReleaseID=155513>.
61. The ideas for independent businesses come from Jerome A. Katz and William B. Gartner, "Properties of Emerging Organizations," *Academy of Management Review,* 13(3) (July 1988), pp. 429–441, and William B. Gartner, "A Conceptual Framework for Describing the Phenomenon of New Venture Creation," *Academy of Management Review* 10, no. 4 (October 1985), pp. 696–706. The social entrepreneurship ideas are built from a number of sources including L. Gregory Dees and Beth Battle Anderson, "For-Profit Social Ventures," *International Journal of Entrepreneurship Education, 2*(1), (2002), http://www.senatehall.com/journals.php?journal=1; Douglas Henton, John Melville, and Kimberly Walesh, "The age of the civic entrepreneur: Restoring civil society and building economic community," *National Civic Review, 6*(2), (1997), pp. 149–156; Janna Mair and Ignasti Marti, "Social entrepreneurship research: A source of explanation, prediction, and delight," *Journal of World Business,* 41, (2006), pp. 36–44; Julia Sass Rubin and Gregory M. Stankiewicz, "The Los Angeles Community Development Bank: The possible pitfalls of public-private partnerships," *Journal of Urban Affaris, 23*(2), (2001), pp. 133–153; and Sandra A. Waddock and James E. Post, "Social entrepreneurs and catalytic change," *Public Administration Review, 51,* (1991), pp. 393–401. The material on public entrepreneurship comes from Paula J. King and Nancy C. Roberts, "Policy entrepreneurs: Catalysts for policy innovation," *Journal of State Government, 60* (1987), pp. 172–178; Eugene Lewis, *Public Entrepreneurship: Toward a Theory of Bureaucratic Political Power* (Bloomington, IN: Indiana University Press, 1980); and Stefania Zerbinati and Vangelis Souitaris, "Entrepreneurship in the public sector: a framework of analysis in European local governments," *Entrepreneurship & Regional Development, 17*(1), (January 2005), pp. 43–64, while the material on corporate entrepreneurs comes from Peter Drucker, "What business can learn from nonprofits," *Harvard Business Review, 67*(4), (1989), pp. 88–93; Steven Klepper, "Employee start-ups in high-tech industries," *Industrial and Corporate Change, 10* (2001), pp. 639–674; and Donald F. Kuratko, R. Duane Ireland, Jeffrey G. Covin, Jeffrey S. Hornsby, "A Model of Middle-Level Managers' Entrepreneurial Behavior," *Entrepreneurship Theory and Practice* 29 (6), (2005), pp. 699–716.
62. The ideas behind the focuses of entrepreneurship come from an analysis of works such as Katz and Gartner, *op.cit.,* Gartner, *op.cit.,* King and Roberts, *op.cit.,* and Kuratko, Ireland, Covin, Hornsby, *op.cit.* as well as David Bornstein, "Changing the world on a shoestring," *The Atlantic Monthly,* 281(1) (1998), pp. 34–39; Gregory G. Dess, and G. T. Lumpkin, "The role of entrepreneurial orientation in stimulating effective, corporate entrepreneurship," *Academy of Management Executive, 19* (2005), pp. 147–156; Gillian Mort, Jay Weerawardena, and Kashonia Carnegie, "Social entrepreneurship: Towards conceptualization." *International Journal of Non-profit and Voluntary Sector Marketing, 8* (2003), pp. 76–88; Silvia Dorado, "Social Entrepreneurial Ventures: Different Values So Different Process of Creation, No?" *Journal of Developmental Entrepreneurship* (Dec 2006). FindArticles.com. 05 May. 2007. http://findarticles.com/p/articles/mi_qa3906/is_200612/ai_n17194471; Hans Westlund and Roger Bolton, "Local social capital and entrepreneurship," *Small Business Economics, 21*(2), (2003), pp. 77–113; and Fang Zhao, "Exploring the synergy between entrepreneurship and innovation," *International Journal of Entrepreneurial Behaviour & Research, 11*(1), (January 2005), pp. 25–41.
63. "Paul McCartney: Biography: Rolling Stone." rollingstone.com, May 25, 2009, http://www.rollingstone.com/artists/paulmccartney/biography; "Sir (James) Paul McCartney Biography—Biography.com." biography.com. May 25, 2009, http://www.biography.com/articles/Sir-(James)-Paul-McCartney-9390850. Steve. Shelokhonov. "Paul McCartney—Biography." *imdb—The Internet Movie Database,* May 25, 2009, http://www.imdb.com/name/nm0005200/bio.
64. John M. Mcguire, "Our Town 2000, They've Got the World on a Shelf," *St. Louis Post-Dispatch,* August 28, 2000, p. E1 (Everyday). Repps Hudson, "Small-Firm Owners Strive to Meet Their High Expectations," *St. Louis Post-Dispatch,* May 13, 2002, p. P. 22 (Business Plus). Janet Mcnichols, "Kirkwood City Council Honors Three Residents," *St. Louis Post-Dispatch,* January 1, 2001, p. P. 3 (West Post). John M. Mcguire, "Our Town 2000—Thai Dynamo Is a Reminder of How a Grocer Looks, Acts," *St. Louis Post-Dispatch,* August 28, 2000, p. E1 (Everyday). Dan Mihalopoulos, "Immigrant's Motto: "You Work Hard, You Can Make It," *St. Louis Post-Dispatch,* May 9, 1999, p. B 1 (Imagine St. Louis). Joan Little, "New Food Store Will Offer Exotic and Ethnic Variety: Opening of Global Food Market Set for March "99," *St. Louis Post-Dispatch,* November 26, 1998 p. P. 6 (West Post).

Chapter 2

1. Tim Hayden's story came from a 2003 classroom presentation in an Advanced Business Planning class Tim took with *ESB* co-author Jerome Katz at Saint Louis University.
2. The formal name for this overlap of entrepreneur and firm is called partial inclusion and was original to Daniel Katz and Robert L. Kahn, *The Social Psychology of Organizations,* 2nd ed. (New York: Wiley, 1978). A better-known approach for many comes from Karl E. Weick, *The Social Psychology of Organizing,* 2nd ed. (Reading, Mass: Addison-Wesley, 1979).
3. Definition is a paraphrase from Steve Robbins, *Essentials of Organizational Behavior,* 7th ed. (Upper Saddle River, New Jersey: Prentice-Hall, 2003), p. 231, and Edgar Schein, "The Role of the Founder in Creating Organizational Culture," *Organizational Dynamics,* Summer 1983, p. 14.
4. "Horizon-Chamber Collaboration Brings Wellness to Workplace." *The Business Monthly,* December 2007; May 25, 2009, http://209.116.252.254/12_2007/9.shtml. "Workplace Wellness Award," *The Horizon Foundation 2007,* May 25, 2009, http://www.thehorizonfoundation.org/ht/d/sp/i/1152/pid/1152. "Jolles Insurance," May 25, 2009, http://www.jollesinsurance.com/index.php. "WEPROMOTEHEALTH.COM," May 25, 2009, http://www.wepromotehealth.com/.
5. The profile is created from a series of interviews by *ESB* co-author Jerome Katz with Jim Allsup. The final version was approved by Mr. Allsup on May 30, 2009.
6. Kendra S. Albright, "Environmental Scanning: Radar for Success," Entrepreneur.com, (July 5, 2004), May 25, 2009, http://www.entrepreneur.com/tradejournals/article/117449440_2.html. Donald L. Lester and John A. Parnell, "Firm Size and Environmental Scanning Pursuits across Organizational Life Cycle Stages," *Journal of Small Business and Enterprise Development* 15.3 (2008): 540–554.
7. Patricia Carr, "Revisiting the Protestant Ethic and the Spirit of Capitalism: Understanding the Relationship between Ethics and Enterprise," *Journal of Business Ethics* 47, no. 1 (September 2003), pp. 7–16. Jeffrey R. Cornwall and Michael J. Naughton, "Who Is the Good Entrepreneur? An Exploration within the Catholic Social Tradition," *Journal of Business Ethics* 44, no. 1 (April 2003), pp. 61–75.
8. This is the concept of cognitive legitimacy as discussed in: John Freeman, Glenn R. Carroll, and Michael T. Hannan (1983). "The liability of newness: Age dependence in organizational death rates," *American Sociological Review, 48* (5), Oct, 692–710. Michael T. Hannan, and John Freeman (1984). "Structural inertia and organizational change," *American Sociological Review 49* (2), April, pp. 149–164. Howard E. Aldrich & C. Marlene Fiol (1994). "Fools rush in? The institutional context of industry creation," *Academy of Management Review, 19* (4), October, pp. 645–670.
9. Dean Shepherd and Andrew Zacharakis, "A New-Venture's Cognitive Legitimacy: An Assessment by Customers," *Journal of Small Business Management* 41, no. 2 (April 2003), pp. 148–167.
10. By the way, the fact that outsiders see entrepreneurs as a key source of legitimacy, while the entrepreneurs look outside themselves to their product as the legitimacy source, is a wonderful example of the classic psychological idea of causal attribution. People tend to see causes as being outside themselves, while outsiders are more likely to attribute cause to a person. For more on this in general, see Richard Nisbet, and Lee Ross, *Human Inference: Strategies and Shortcomings of Social Judgement* (Englewood Cliffs, NJ: Prentice Hall,1980). For an example in entrepreneurship, see Kelly G. Shaver, William B. Gartner, Elizabeth Crosby, Karolina Bakalarova, and Elizabeth J. Gatewood, "Attributions about Entrepreneurship: A Framework and Process for Analyzing Reasons for Starting a Business," *Entrepreneurship: Theory and Practice* 26, no. 2 (Winter 2001), pp. 5–32.
11. F. R. David, "An Empirical Study of Codes of Business Ethics: A Strategic Perspective," paper presented at the 48th Annual Academy of Management Conference, Anaheim, California, August 1988.
12. Kim T. Gordon, "Cross-Training: Join the Multichannel Marketing Revolution, and Get Ready to Pump Up Your Sales," *Entrepreneur,* July 2003. http://www.Entrepreneur.com/article/0,4621,309488,00.html.
13. Anat BarNir and Ken A. Smith, "Interfirm Alliances in the Small Business: The Role of Social Networks," *Journal of Small Business Management* 40, no. 3 (July 2002), pp. 219–232. T. A. Ostgaard and S. Birley "Personal Networks and Firm Competitive Strategy—A Strategic or Coincidental Match?" *Journal of Business Venturing* 9, no. 4 (July 1994), pp. 281–305. Herminia Ibarra, "Personal Networks of Women and Minorities in Management: A Conceptual Framework," *Academy of Management Review* 18, no. 1 (January 1993), pp. 56–87. Sue Birley,. "The Role of Networks in the Entrepreneurial Process," *Journal of Business Venturing* 1, no. 1 (Winter 1985), pp. 107–117.
14. Heidi M. Neck, G. Dale Meyer, Boyd Cohen, and Andrew C. Corbett, "An Entrepreneurial System View of New Venture Creation," *Journal of Small Business Management* 42, no. 2 (April 2004), pp. 190–209. Danny Mackinnon, Keith Chapman, and Andrew Cumbers, "Networking, Trust and Embeddedness amongst SMEs in the Aberdeen Oil Complex," *Entrepreneurship and Regional Development* 16, no. 2 (March 2004), pp. 87–106. Robert A. Baron and Gideon D. Markman, "Beyond Social Capital: The Role of Entrepreneurs' Social Competence in Their Financial Success," *Journal of Business Venturing* 18, no. 1 (January 2003), pp. 41–60. Sarah D. Dodd, "Social Network Membership and Activity Rates: Some Comparative Data," *International Small Business Journal* 15, no. 4 (July/September 1997), pp. 80–87. Eric L. Hansen, "Entrepreneurial Networks and New Organization Growth," *Entrepreneurship Theory and Practice* 19, no. 4 (Summer 1995), pp. 7–20. Tone A. Ostgaard and Sue Birley, "Personal Networks and Firm Competitive Strategy—A Strategic or Coincidental Match?" *Journal of Business Venturing* 9, no. 4 (July 1994), pp. 281–306. Howard E. Aldrich and Carlos Zimmer, "Entrepreneurship through Social Networks," in Donald L. Sexton and Ray W. Smilor (eds.), *The Art and Science of Entrepreneurship* (Cambridge, MA: Ballinger, 1986), pp. 3–24. Sue Birley, "The Role of Networks in the Entrepreneurial Process," *Journal of Business Venturing* 1, no. 1 (Winter 1985), pp. 107–117.
15. David A. Whetten and Alison Mackey, "A Social Actor Conception of Organizational Identity and Its Implications for the Study of Organizational Reputation," *Business & Society* 41, no. 4 (December 2002), pp. 393–414. Concept taken from p. 394.
16. Howard E. Aldrich and Nancy M. Carter (2004), "Social Networks," In William B. Gartner, Kelly G. Shaver, Nancy M. Carter, and Paul D. Reynolds (Eds.), *Handbook of Entrepreneurial Dynamics: The Process of Business Creation* (Thousand Oaks, CA: Sage, 2004).
17. Paula Caproni, *The Practical Coach: Management Skills for Everyday Life* (Upper Saddle River, NJ, Prentice Hall, 2000). Other articles that use similar approaches and show positive effects include: Jeff Gold, Dave Devins, and Alistair Johnson, "What Is the Value of Mentoring in a Small Business? Using Narrative Evaluation to Find Out," *British Journal of Guidance & Counselling* 31, no. 1 (February 2003), pp. 51–62. Tony Kent, Charles Dennis, and Sue Tanton, "An Evaluation of Mentoring for SME Retailers," *International Journal of Retail & Distribution Management* 31, no. 8/9 (2003), pp. 440–465. R. Sullivan, "Entrepreneurial Learning and Mentoring," *International Journal of Entrepreneurial Behaviour & Research* 6, no. 3 (2000), pp. 160–175.
18. Ivan Misner, "Start by Learning How to Tailor Your Networking Approach for Different Occasions," *Entrepreneur—Sales & Marketing,* March 22, 2004, http://www.entrepreneur.com/article/0,4621,314878,00.html. Kim T. Gordon, "Attracting Customers: Use Your Business's Assets to Bring in More Clients, *Entrepreneur,* August 07, 2000, http://www.entrepreneur.com/article/0,4621,278263,00.html. Dorothy P. Moore, *Careerpreneurs-Lessons from Leading Women Entrepreneurs on Building a Career Without Boundaries* (Palo Alto, CA: Davies-Black Publishing, 2001). Cynthia E. Griffin, "Gender Blender: Boys Don't Have Cooties, So Don't Be Afraid to

Mingle at Mixed-Gender Functions," *Entrepreneur* (October 2001), http://www.entrepreneur.com/article/04621,292826,00.html. Erin Chambers, "A Warm Reception for Female Execs," *BusinessWeek* online, December 9, 2004, http://www.businessweek.com/smallbiz/content/dec2004/sb2004129_3272_sb013.htm. Sherry Alpert, "Making a Network Connection," *BusinessWeek* online, September 18, 2003, http://www.businessweek.com/smallbiz/content/sep2003/sb20030918_4557.htm.

19. Amanda C. Kooser, "Crowd Control: Having Trouble Finding the Ideal System for Managing Your Customer Relationships? We've Got Advice to Get You Moving in the Right Direction," *Entrepreneur,* August 2003, http://www.Entrepreneur.com/article/0,4621309894,00.html. Kimberly L. McCall, "Contact Solution: Face It, Post-its and Spiral Notebooks Won't Cut It When It Comes to Contact Management. Go High-Tech and Save Yourself the Headache," *Entrepreneur,* June 2002, http://www.entrepreneur.com/mag/article/0,1539,299744,00.html. Kim T. Gordon. "Managing Your Contacts: Our Homebased Expert Tells You Why You Can't Live without a Good Contact Management Program," HomeOfficeMag.com, December 2000, http://www.Entrepreneur.com/article/0,4621,284147,00.html.

20. Tad Hogg and Lada Adamic. "Enhancing Reputation Mechanisms via Online Social Networks," *Proceedings of the 5th ACM conference on Electronic Commerce.* New York, NY, USA, 2004, http://protal.acm.org/citation.cfm?id=988772.988811. Catherine Holahan, "Social Networking Goes Niche: MySpace and Friendster's Runaway Popularity and Exposure Have Helped Spawn an Array of Targeted Networking Sites," *BusinessWeek* online, March 14, 2007, http://www.businessweek.com/print/technology/content/mar2007/tc20070314_884996.htm. Marko A. Rodriguez, Daniel J. Steinbock, Jennifer H. Watkins, Carlos Gershenson, Johan Bollen, Victor Grey, and Brad deGraf, "Smartocracy: Social Networks For Collective Decisionmaking," Hawaii International Conference On Systems Science (HICSS). IEEE Computer Society, 2007, www.cse.ucsc.edu/~okram/papers/smartocracy-hicss2007.pdf.

21. *BusinessWeek* online, Undated. "A Guide to Social Networking: Tip Sheet (CEO Guide To Technology: Tip Sheet)," http://www.businessweek.com/technology/ceo_tipsheet/2006_5.htm. Al Lautenslager, "It's Not Too Late to Get Your Business on MySpace," *Entrepreneur.* April 6, 2007, http://www.entrepreneur.com/marketing/marketingideas/guerrillamarketingcolumnistallautenslager/article176758.html. Pat Thomas and Susan Moisey, "Women Entrepreneurs: Informal Learning and the Internet," *Journal of Small Business & Entrepreneurship* 19, no. 2 (2006) pp. 183–201. Lena L. West, "Becoming More Social," Entrepreneur.com Online, April 9, 2007, http://www.entrepreneur.com/marketing/onlinemarketing/article176798.html.

22. Ian I. Mitroff and Murat C. Alpaslan, "Preparing for Evil," *Harvard Business Review,* 81, no. 4 (April 2003), p. 109. Ian I. Mitroff, *Crisis Leadership: Preparing for the Unthinkable* (New York: Wiley, 2003). D. Creelman, "Interview: Ian Mitroff on crisis leadership," 2004, HR.com, http://hradmin1.hr.com/HRcom/index.cfm/WeeklyMag/9A954EE7-B500-4-AC4-A13DF077B83214E2?ost=wmFeature.

23. Norman R. Augustine, "Managing the Crisis You Tried to Prevent," *Harvard Business Review,* 73, no. 6 (November/December 1995), pp. 147–158.

24. Dan Millar, "ICM Crisis Report: News Coverage of Business Crises during 2002" 12 no. 1 (May 2003). The Institute for Crisis Management http://www.crisisexperts.com/02creport.htm. Theresa Forsman, "Contemplating the Unthinkable: An Entrepreneur Who Lacks a Plan for Coping with Catastrophe Is a Victim in the Making, Says Crisis-Management Expert Debra Traverso," *BusinessWeek,* October 2, 2001, http://www.businessweek.com/smallbiz/content/oct2001/sb20011003_514.htm. Michael Seid and Kay Marie Ainsley, "Managing Your Reputation: Follow These Tips to Save Your Brand during a Crisis," *Entrepreneur,* October 22, 2001, http://www.entrepreneur.com/article/0,4621,294000,00.html. Christopher D. Lancette, "Critical Thinking: A Crisis Has Hit. Now What?" *Entrepreneur,* June 1999, http://www.entrepreneur.com/mag/article/0,1539,230335,00.html.

25. Daniel Tynan, "In Case of Emergency: A Smoke Alarm or a Life Preserver May Save Your Life, But They Won't Save Your Business. You Need a Real Disaster Plan Now. Your Business's Survival Depends on It," *Entrepreneur,* April 2003, http://www.Entrepreneur.com/article/0,4621,307161,00.html. Institute for Crisis Management, "Crisis Management and Crisis Communications" (Louisville, KY: The Institute for Crisis Management, 2000), http://www.crisisexperts.com/management.htm. Michael Seid and Kay Marie Ainsley, "Managing Your Reputation: Follow These Tips to Save Your Brand during a Crisis," *Entrepreneur,* October 22, 2001, http://www.entrepreneur.com/article/0,4621,294000,00.htm. Christopher D. Lancette, "Critical Thinking: A Crisis Has Hit. Now What?" *Entrepreneur* June 1999, http://www.entrepreneur.com/mag/article/0,1539,230335,00.html.

26. Scott J. Vitell, Erin B. Dickerson, and Troy A. Festervand, "Ethical Problems, Conflicts and Beliefs of Small Business Professionals," *Journal of Business Ethics* 28, no. 1 (November 2000), pp. 15–24. Ruth Clark and John Aram, "Universal Values, Behavioral Ethics and Entrepreneurship," *Journal of Business Ethics* 16, no. 5 (April 1997), pp. 561–572.

27. LaRue T. Hosmer, *The Ethics of Management,* 6th ed. (Boston: McGraw-Hill/Irwin, 2008.)

28. This example came from an interview conducted by Prof. Kathy Lund, Dean of Idaho State University-Pocatello, in May 2004. At the request of the entrepreneur, his name, his town, and his business's name are disguised.

29. Nichole L. Torres, "Ethically Speaking," *Entrepreneur,* December 2005. http://www.entrepreneur.com/magazine/entrepreneur/2005/december/81076.html.

30. Kimberly Blanton, "Dark Side of Subprime Loans—*The Boston Globe,*" boston.com, August 3, 2005; May 26, 2009, http://www.boston.com/business/personalfinance/articles/2005/08/03/dark_side_of_subprime_loans/. Steve Christ, "IMF Warns Toxic Debt May Exceed $4 Trillion," WealthDaily.com, April 9, 2009, May 26, 2009, http://www.wealthdaily.com/articles/imf-toxic-debt/1771. "Foreclosed: The Failure to Regulate Abusive Lending Practices: An Interview with Debbie Goldstein," *Multinational Monitor,* March 1, 2009, May 26, 2009, http://www.multinationalmonitor.org/mm2009/012009/interview-goldstein.html.

31. Lawrence M. Salinger, and Geis, Gilbert. "Caveat Emptor," *Encyclopedia of White-Collar & Corporate Crime.* (Thousand oaks CA. Sage, 2004). pp. 145–146; May 27, 2009 http://books.google.com/books?id=0f7yTNb_V3QC&pg=PA146&lpg=PA146&dq=%22caveat+emptor%22,+corporate&source=bl&ots=OeLuQT8JSV&sig=a6Wp4JC30KZrd77RDJQHdnopL6o&hl=en&ei=7JlcSqDHDoryMr_NsZIP&sa=X&oi=book_result&ct=result&resnum=6#PPA146,M1.

32. The negotiation approaches used here are adapted from Roger Fisher, William Ury, and Bruce Patton, *Getting to Yes: Negotiating Agreement without Giving in,* 2nd ed. (New York: Houghton Mifflin Harcourt, 1991).

33. Lisa Miller, "Ethics: It Isn't Just the Big Guys," *BusinessWeek* online, July 25, 2003, http://www.businessweek.com/smallbiz/content/10/2003/sb20030725_3531.htm.

34. M. H. Morris, M. Schindehutte, J. Walton, and J. Allen, "The Ethical Context of Entrepreneurship: Proposing and Testing a Developmental Framework," *Journal of Business Ethics* 40, no. 4 (November 2002), pp. 331–361. Hai Y. Teoh and Siang L. Foo, "Moderating Effects of Tolerance of Ambiguity and Risk Taking Propensity on the Role Conflict-Perceived Performance Relationship: Evidence from Singaporean Entrepreneurs," *Journal of Business Venturing* 12, no. I (January 1997), pp. 67–81.

35. For state government initiatives, see Amy Tsao, "A Primer on Drug 'Reimporting,'" *BusinessWeek* online, April 21, 2004. http://businessweek.com/bwdaily/dnflash/apr2004/nf20040421_1767_db_080.htm. For more about Rx Depot see Associated Press, "Judge Hears Testimony in Canada Drug Case." *St. Louis Post-Dispatch,* October 10, 2003, p C2. Also see Theresa Agovino, "Entrepreneur Fills an Order for Trouble," *St. Louis*

Post-Dispatch, October 8, 2003, p. E1. For information on online pharmacies and some of the issues lawmakers are wrestling with, see Amy Tsao, "An Iffy Prognosis for Online Pharmacies," *BusinessWeek* online, November 25, 2003. http://www.businessweek.com/technology/content/nov2003/ tc20031125_2272_tc136.htm.

36. Melissa S. Baucus and Caryn L. Beck-Dudley. "Designing Ethical Organizations: Avoiding the Long-Term Negative Effects of Rewards and Punishments." *Journal of Business Ethics* 56 (2005), pp. 355–370. BusinessWeek.com. SMALL BIZ—FEATURES, Online Extra: How to play with the Big Guys. September 10, 2001. http://www.businessweek.com/magazine/content/01_37/b3748628.htm; Brenda Joyner, E. Dinah Payne, and Cecily A. Raiborn, "Building values, business ethics and corporate social responsibility into the developing organization." *Journal of Developmental Enterpreneurship* 7, no. 1 (Apr. 2002), pp. 113–131. *Robert J. McGarvey,* "Lords Of Discipline: 'Gimme 10!' Is not the way to change your employees' behavior." *Entrepreneur,* January 2000. http//www.entrepreneur.com/magazine/entrepreneur/2000/January/18856.html.
37. Johnson, "The Gift," *Annual Advances 1990* (New York: McGraw-Hill, 1990), pp. 300–301.

Chapter 3

1. Information about Laura Tidwell can be found at "*Girl Geek of the Week,*" January 2001, http://www.girlgeeks.org/innergeek/gkwk/gkwk_tidwell.shtml (July 9, 2005). Kathleen Williams, "Enginehouse Media's CEO Honored by Business Community," *PRWeb,* December 15, 2000, http://www.prweb.com/releases/2000/12/prweb21075.htm (July 9, 2005). [no author], "Laura Tidwell: An Internet Entrepreneur's Tips for Success," Women of.com [no date], http://www.womenof.com/Articles/cb121800.asp (July 9, 2005). The Ad Firm Web site, www.theadfirm.com. "Laura Tidwell," WITI: Empowering Women Through Technology, 2000, http://www.witi.com/wire/witiwomen/ltidwell/ltidwell_complete.shtml (April 22, 2007).
2. There are some wonderful explorations on the history of the term *entrepreneur.* See R. F. Herbert and A. N. Link, *The Entrepreneur* (New York: Praeger, 1982). Here is the simple version. Trade, barter, and the family farm have existed since the earliest days of recorded history. Entrepreneurs—as people willing to take risks to pursue opportunities in order to gain wealth—have also been around a long time. Explorers like Marco Polo, ship captains, and the like were running businesses focused on the opportunity of attaining great wealth. The French economist Richard Cantillon was both an entrepreneur in his own right and the man who focused and popularized the term *entrepreneur* in its classic sense during the 1750s. Economists and early entrepreneurship researchers used the term in Cantillon's classic sense, with perhaps the last major study using the model being the Collins and Moore studies out of MSU in the early 1960s [Orvis F. Collins, David G. Moore, and Darab B. Umwalla, *The Enterprising Man* (East Lansing, MI: Michigan State University Bureau of Business and Economic Research, 1964); and Orvis F. Collins and David G. Moore, *The Organization Makers: A Behavioral Study of Independent Entrepreneurs* (New York: Appleton-Century-Crofts, 1970)], although organizational researchers of a psychoanalytic persuasion continued with such models even later. Abraham Zaleznik and Manfred F. R. Kets deVries, *Power and the Corporate Mind* (Boston: Houghton Mifflin, 1975); M. F. R. Kets de Vries, "The Entrepreneurial Personality: A Person at the Crossroads," *The Journal of Management Studies* 14, no. 1 (February 1977), pp. 34–75; Elliot Jaques, *A General Theory of Bureaucracy* (New York: Halsted, 1976); M. F. R. Kets de Vries and Danny Miller, *The Neurotic Organization* (San Francisco: Jossey-Bass Publishers, 1984); Danny Miller and Jean Marie Toulouse, "Chief Executive Personality and Corporate Strategy and Structure in Small Firms," *Management Science* 32, no. 11 (November 1986), pp. 1389–1409.
3. Small Business Administration, "SBA Quarterly Indicators: First Quarter 2009—the Economy and Small Business," (Washington DC: US Small Business Administration, Office of Advocacy, May 8, 2009), htttp//www.sba.gov/advo/research/sbqei0901.pdf.
4. The inclusion of new types of entrepreneurial personalities really started with Norman Smith's reanalysis of the Collins and Moore study. Norman R. Smith, *The Entrepreneur and His Firm* (E. Lansing, MI: Michigan State University Bureau of Business and Economic Research, 1967). Smith identified types he called the *opportunistic entrepreneur* (our modern classic entrepreneur), the *craftsman entrepreneur* (our small business owner), and a third possible group who consisted of technology-related entrepreneurs (what we call here the *idea generators*). Smith started a long productive collaboration with John Miner, and together over the next 40 years they and their colleagues published dozens of papers on the different entrepreneurial personality types, culminating in John B. Miner's *The Four Routes to Entrepreneurial Success* (San Francisco: Berrett-Koehler, 1996). Despite the title, Miner's book actually has six routes, with type combinations and what he calls a "sales or professional practice" which is the modern version of the small business owner or craftsman entrepreneur. But however researchers come to it, the idea of many personality types among the population of entrepreneurs remains the predominant model in consulting and research. See W. H. Stewart, Jr., Jo Ann C. Carland, and J. W. Carland, "Empirically Defining the Entrepreneur," *Journal of Business and Entrepreneurship* 8, no. 1 (1996), pp. 1–18. Smith's small business owner appeared in several other places. Sociologists had long studied small business owners, describing them as socially marginal individuals, but in general following the personality model given here. Charles M. Bonjean, "Mass, Class, and the Industrial Community: A Comparative Analysis of Managers, Businessmen, and Workers," *American Journal of Sociology,* 72, no. 2 (September 1966), pp. 149–162. Joel I. Nelson, "Participation and Integration: The Case of the Small Businessman," *American Sociological Review* 33, no. 3 (June 1968), pp. 427–438. Edna Bonacich and John Modell, *The Economic Basis of Ethnic Solidarity: Small Business in the Japanese-American Community* (Berkeley, CA: University of California Press, 1980). Psychologist Al Shapero popularized this model in an article in *Psychology Today.* Albert Shapero, "The Displaced, Uncomfortable Entrepreneur," *Psychology Today,* November 1975, pp. 83–88. Edgar Schein reported a group of MIT alums who were self-employed and carrying a career anchor he called *autonomy,* which was very similar. Edgar H. Schein, *Career Dynamics: Matching Individual and Organizational Needs* (Reading, MA: Addison-Wesley, 1978). Carland, Hoy, Boulton, and Carland established what has become the standard model for small business owners, and their differentiation from the contemporary classic entrepreneur. J. W. Carland, F. Hoy, W. Boulton, and J. A. C. Carland, "Differentiating Entrepreneurs from Small Business Owners: A Conceptualization," *Academy of Management Review* 9, no. 2 (April 1984), pp. 354–359. Today the small business owner profile is considered a distinct subgroup in the population of entrepreneurs and remains a lively topic of study. See for example T. M. Stearns and G. E. Hills, "Entrepreneurship and New Firm Development: A Definitional Introduction," *Journal of Business Research* 36, no. 1 (May 1996), pp. 1–4.
5. This model comes from Miner's "expert idea generator" as well as the entrepreneurial or creativity career anchor described by Edgar Schein, and the high-technology entrepreneur described by Ed Roberts of MIT. E. B. Roberts, *Entrepreneurs in High Technology* (New York: Oxford University Press, 1991).
6. This type is based on several sources also. Foremost is Miner's "Real Manager Entrepreneur," but even the psychoanalysts have mentioned this type, in Michael Maccoby, *The Gamesman* (New York: Simon & Schuster, 1976), as well as the power-oriented entrepreneurs in Wainer and Rubin's study of entrepreneurs. Herbert A. Wainer and Irving M. Rubin, "Motivation of Research and Development Entrepreneurs:

Determinants of Company Success," *Journal of Applied Psychology* 53, no. 3 (June 1969), pp. 178–184. Ed Roberts also talks about entrepreneurs who come in to manage high-technology companies and contribute managerial, as opposed to technological, skills.

7. Burt Helm, "Big Business Tactics for Small Outfits," *BusinessWeek* online, January 6, 2005, http://www.businessweek.com/smallbiz/content/jan2005/sb2005016_0877_sb013.htm.
8. Although Miner talks about the "supersalesperson" as an entrepreneurial type, it has been around by other names for a long time. Although Miner thinks in terms of growth-oriented firms, many part-time entrepreneurs are oriented toward the sales aspect of business, sometimes to the exclusion of good business sense. For example, the type had appeared earlier as the socially oriented entrepreneur in Wainer and Rubin's study of entrepreneurs, Herbert A. Wainer and Irving M. Rubin, "Motivation of Research and Development Entrepreneurs: Determinants of Company Success," *Journal of Applied Psychology* 53, no. 3 (June 1969), pp.178–184. Furthermore, in talking about entrepreneurial efforts in low-income groups, the socially driven entrepreneur type pops up, see S. Balkin, *Self-Employment for Low Income People* (New York: Praeger-Greenwood, 1989); and Eugene Gomolka, "Characteristics of Minority Entrepreneurs and Small Business Enterprises," *American Journal of Small Business* 2, no. 1 (July 1977), pp. 12–21. Among marketing based entrepreneurship researchers, the type has long been known. See Morgan P. Miles and D. R. Arnold, "The Relationship between Marketing Orientation and Entrepreneurial Orientation," *Entrepreneurship: Theory & Practice* 15, no. 4 (Summer 1991), pp. 49–65.
9. The modernization of the classic entrepreneur really began with the works of David McClelland in his books *The Achieving Society* (Princeton, NJ: Van Nostrand, 1961) and with David Winter, *Motivating Economic Achievement* (New York: Free Press, 1969). Central to this was the concept of moderate or managed risk taking, a concept proven in the early works of R. H. Brockhaus, "Risk-Taking Propensity of Entrepreneurs," *Academy of Management Journal* 23, no. 3 (September 1980), pp. 509–520. Economists revisited their definition of *entrepreneur,* adopting the modern version in the 1980s. See Mark Casson, *The Entrepreneur: An Economic Theory,* 2nd ed. (Cheltenham, UK: Edward Elgar Publishers, 2003). Today this modern version is called the *proactive entrepreneur* [see Jill Kickul and Lisa K. Gundry, "Prospecting for Strategic Advantage: The Proactive Entrepreneurial Personality and Small Firm Innovation," *Journal of Small Business Management* 40, no. 2 (April 2002), pp. 85–97] or the *high-growth entrepreneur* [see M. Y. Bhave, "A Process Model of Entrepreneurial Venture Creation," *Journal of Business Venturing* 9, no. 3 (May 1994), pp. 223–242].
10. H. Chang, "Atiba is the Success of a Self-Taught Man," *The Tennessean,* September 10, 2003; "Enterprise Executive Profile: J. J. Rosen, Chief Executive Officer," *Nashville Business Journal,* March 2, 2001, http://nashville.bizjournals.com/nashville/stories/2001/03/05/smallb1.html; M. Capps, "Bootstrapping Atiba Software Adds C-level Exec," *Venture Nashville,* February 13, 2009, http://www.venturenashville.com/news.php?viewstory=238.
11. There are two major models of entrepreneurial competency—Mitchell et al. and Chandler/Hanks models. The Mitchell *et al.* model has been validated cross culturally, with very strong results, while the Chandler/Hanks model has seen wider use in U.S. studies. Although each model labels the competencies differently, the content of the competencies is very similar. The model presented here builds from the Mitchell *et al.* and Chandler/Hanks models, mapping their specific competencies to the BRIE model of Katz and Gartner introduced in Chapter 1. The key article on competencies is Ronald K. Mitchell, J. Brock Smith, Eric A. Morse, Kristie W. Seawright, Ana Maria Peredo, and Brian McKenzie, "Are Entrepreneurial Cognitions Universal? Assessing Entrepreneurial Cognitions across Cultures," *Entrepreneurship: Theory & Practice* 26, no. 4 (Summer 2002), pp. 9–32. Note that what are called *competencies* in this text are called *scripts* in the Mitchell works. The scripts are observed through their related cognitions. Gaylen N. Chandler and Steven H. Hanks, "Founder Competence, the Environment, and Venture Performance," *Entrepreneurship: Theory & Practice* 18, no. 3 (Spring 1994), pp. 77–89.
12. This skill is called *business ability competency* by Mitchell et al. and *managerial competency* by Chandler and Hanks.
13. This is called *organizational resources and capabilities* by Chandler and Hanks, while in the Mitchell *et al.* model resources are a part of arrangement competencies. The social competencies that make these easier or harder for the entrepreneur come from R. A. Baron and G. D. Markman, "Beyond Social Capital: The Role of Entrepreneurs' Social Competence in Their Financial Success," *Journal of Business Venturing* 18, no. 1 (January 2003), pp. 41–60.
14. In the Mitchell et al. model these are called *willingness competencies,* while in the Chandler/Hanks approach they make up a part of the entrepreneurial competence factor.
15. In the Chandler/Hanks model, this is called the *quality of the opportunity,* while opportunity factors make up much of the arrangements competency cluster.
16. See R. Mitchell and S. Chesteen, "Enhancing Entrepreneurial Expertise: Experiential Pedagogy and the Entrepreneurial Expert Script," *Simulation & Gaming* 26, no. 3 (September 1995), pp. 288–306.
17. While this exact model is new to this text, three-part approaches to firms have been around more than 45 years. The two works that are the major contributors to the approach are Norman Smith's "Artisan, Technological and Opportunistic Firms" from his 1967 report, *The Entrepreneur and His Firm* (East Lansing, MI: Michigan State University Bureau of Business and Economic Research), Ron Mitchell and Susan Chesteen's 1995 article, "Enhancing Entrepreneurial Expertise: Experiential Pedagogy and the Entrepreneurial Expert Script," *Simulation & Gaming* 26, no. 3 September, pp. 288–306, which talked about novice, enhanced, and expert types in organizing a business.
18. You can learn more about ISO9000 certification from the International Organization for Standardization's web site at www.iso.org.
19. S. S. Smith, "Five Minutes with Author Jim Collins: What Does It Take to Be Great, Not Just Good? This Built to Last Author Reveals What It Takes to Reach the Top—and Stay There," *Entrepreneur,* October 1, 2001, http://www.Entrepreneur.com/article/0,4621,293352,00.html. For the Baldrige Award, see Malcolm Baldrige National Quality Award 1992 Winner—Granite Rock Company, http://www.quality.nist.gov/Granite_Rock_Co.htm.
20. In organizational theory, this favored business function is called a leading subsystem. D. Katz and R. L. Kahn, *The Social Psychology of Organizations,* 2nd ed. (New York: Wiley, 1978).
21. J. Plazonja and A. Zildjian, *Avedis Zildjian—The Father of Cymbals* (2003), http://www.zildjian.com/adaa/adaa_2003_legacy_6.asp (accessed July 9, 2005).
22. [No Author] Historical Timeline. Zildjian Company Web site, http://www.zildjian.com/EN-US/about/timeline.ad2 (July 10, 2005).
23. C. L. Shartle, *Occupational Information,* 3rd ed. (Englewood Cliffs, NJ: Prentice Hall, 1959), p. 23.
24. This approach builds on the career theory of Edgar Schein, from his work *Career Dynamics* (Reading, MA: Addison-Wesley, 1978). The original adaptation of Schein comes from Jerome A. Katz, "Modeling Entrepreneurial Career Progressions: Concepts and Considerations," *Entrepreneurship: Theory & Practice* 19, no. 2 (Winter 1994), pp. 23–40, with the entrepreneur's version presented here coming from Jerome A. Katz, "What Track Are You On?" *Inc,* October 1, 1995, http://www.inc.com/magazine/19951001/ 2430.html.
25. William Gartner [W. B. Gartner, "A Conceptual Framework for Describing the Phenomenon of New Venture Creation," *Academy of Management Review* 10, no. 4 (October 1985), pp. 696–706] defined the entrepreneurial event as the interaction of the entrepreneur, the business itself,

the process by which it is started, and the context or environment in which all this happens. Other works that have built on the Gartner idea include: L. Herron and H. J. Sapienza, "The Entrepreneur and the Initiation of New Venture Launch Activities," *Entrepreneurship: Theory & Practice* 17, no. 1 (Fall 1992), pp. 49–55; Douglas W. Naffziger, Jeffrey S. Hornsby, and Donald F. Kuratko, "A Proposed Research Model of Entrepreneurial Motivation," *Entrepreneurship: Theory & Practice* 18, no. 3 (Spring 1994), pp. 29–42; Carolyn Y. Woo, U. Daellenbach, and C. Nicholls-Nixon, "Theory Building in the Presence of 'Randomness': The Case of Venture Creation and Performance," *Journal of Management Studies* 31, no. 4 (July 1994), pp. 507–524; Richard C. Becherer and John G. Maurer, "The Proactive Personality Disposition and Entrepreneurial Behavior among Small Company Presidents," *Journal of Small Business Management* 37, no. 1 (January 1999), pp. 28–36. The term *entrepreneurial settings* follows the idea of environment in these studies. However, neither Gartner nor the subsequent researchers specified the exact nature of different types of settings. The settings described here are chosen because of their frequency.

26. Joseph Weber and Louis Lavelle, "Family, Inc." *BusinessWeek* online, November 10, 2003, http://www.businessweek.com:/print/magazine/content/03_45/b3857002.htm?mz.
27. R. Kurtz, "When Business Is in the Blood," *BusinessWeek* online, January 25, 2005, http://yahoo.businessweek.com/smallbiz/content/jan2005/sb20050125_3409.htm. D. Miller and I. Le Breton-Miller, *Managing for the Long Run: Lessons in Competitive Advantage from Great Family Businesses* (Boston: Harvard Business School Press, 2005).
28. Joseph Astrachan and Melissa C. Shanker, "Family Businesses' Contribution to the U.S. Economy: A Closer Look," *Family Business Review* 16, no. 3 (September 2003), pp. 211–219.
29. Joseph Weber and Louis Lavelle, "Family, Inc." *BusinessWeek* online, November 10, 2003, http://www.businessweek.com:/print/magazine/content/03_45/b3857002.htm?mz.
30. W. Gibb Dyer and Wendy Handler, "Entrepreneurship and Family Business: Exploring the Connections," *Entrepreneurship: Theory & Practice* 18, no. 1 (Fall 1994), pp. 71–83.
31. W. Gibb Dyer and Wendy Handler, "Entrepreneurship and Family Business: Exploring the Connections," *Entrepreneurship: Theory & Practice* 18, no. 1 (Fall 1994), pp. 71–83. Frank Hoy and Trudy Verser, "Emerging Business, Emerging Field: Entrepreneurship and the Family Firm," *Entrepreneurship: Theory & Practice* 18, no. 1 (Fall 1994), pp. 9–23.
32. David N. Laband and Bernard F. Lentz, "Like Father Like Son: Towards an Economic Theory of Occupational Following," *Southern Economic Journal* 50, no. 2 (October 1983), pp. 474–493. Bernard F. Lentz and David N. Laband, "Entrepreneurial Success and Occupational Inheritance among Proprietors," *Canadian Journal of Economics* 23, no. 3 (August 1990), pp. 563–579. Robert F. Scherer, James D. Bordzinski, and Frank A. Weibe, "Assessing Perception of Career Role-Model Performance: The Self-Employed Parent," *Perceptual and Motor Skills* 72, no. 2 (1991), pp. 555–560. Robert F. Scherer, James D. Brodzinski, and Frank A. Wiebe, "Entrepreneurship Career Selection And Gender: A Socialization Approach," *Journal of Small Business Management* 28, no. 2 (April 1990), pp. 37–44.
33. John L. Ward, *Perpetuating the Family Business: 50 Lessons Learned from Long Lasting, Successful Families in Business* (New York: Palgrave Macmillan, 2004).
34. A. P. Sherman, "Connect the Daughters: Sons Aren't the Only Offspring Taking Over Family Businesses," *Entrepreneur* 30, no. 2 (December 2002), p. 36.
35. Charles R. Stoner, Richard I. Hartman, and Raj Arora, "Work-Home Role Conflict in Female Owners of Small Business: An Exploration Study," *Journal of Small Business Management* 28, no. 1 (January 1990), pp. 30–38.
36. E. H. Updike, "How to Avoid a Dysfunctional Family Business," *BusinessWeek*, March 2, 1998, p. 3. K. E. Gersick, J. A. Davis, M. McCollom Hampton, and I. Lansberg, *Generation to Generation: Life Cycles of the Family Business* (Boston: Harvard Business School Press, 1997).
37. Nancy J. Miller, Mary Winter, Margaret A. Fitzgerald, and Jennifo Paul, "Family Microenterprises: Strategies for Coping with Overlapping Family and Business Demands," *Journal of Developmental Entrepreneurship* 5, no. 2 (August 2000), pp. 87–114. Frank Hoy and Trody Verser, "Emerging Business, Emerging Field: Entrepreneurship and the Family Firm," *Entrepreneurship: Theory & Practice* 18, no. 1 (Fall 1994), pp. 9–23. Eric G. Flamholtz, *How to Make the Transition from an Entrepreneurship to a Professionally Managed Firm* (San Francisco: Jossey-Bass, 1986).
38. Paul Edwards and Sarah Edwards, "How to Manage Your Home-based Time," Entrepreneur.com, May 13, 2003, http://www.entrepreneur.com/homebasedbiz/worklifebalance/advicefrompaulandsarahedwards/article61974.html (April 22, 2007). Lisa Kanarek, "Keeping Time," HomeOfficeMag.com, January 2001, http://www.entrepreneur.com/worklife/worklifebalanceadvice/timemanagementandorganization/article35806.html (April 22, 2007). Rosalind Resnick, "Secrets to Staying Focused in Your Home Office," *Entrepreneur.com*, May 17, 2004, http://www.entrepreneur.com/homebasedbiz/worklifebalance/timemanagement/ article70836.html (April 22, 2007). Sonja Treven and Vojko Potocan, "Training programmes for stress management in small businesses," *Education + Training, 47*, no. 8/9 (2005), pp. 640–652. Howard Van Auken and James Werbel, "Family Dynamic and Family Business Financial Performance: Spousal Commitment," *Family Business Review*, 19, no. 1 (2006), pp. 49–63.
39. Joseph Astrachan and Melissa C. Shanker, "Family Businesses' Contribution to the U.S. Economy: A Closer Look," *Family Business Review* 16, no. 3 (September 2003), pp. 211–219. Arthur Andersen Center for Family Business, *American Family Business Survey* (St. Charles, IL: Arthur Andersen Center for Family Business 1995). John Ward, *Keeping the Family Business Healthy: How to Plan for Continuing Growth, Profitability and Family Leadership* (San Francisco: Jossey-Bass, 1987). Ward suggested that around 88 percent of family firms fail by the third generation, with family infighting, rather than a lack of succession planning, taking a toll in later generations. Ward's sample was relatively small. A very large, multigenerational study of family firms in France suggested a much higher survival rate [see Dean Savage, *Founders, Heirs and Managers: French Industrial Leadership in Transition* (Beverly Hills: Sage, 1979)].
40. W. Gibb Dyer, Jr., *The Entrepreneurial Experience: Confronting Career Dilemmas of the Start-Up Executive* (San Francisco: Jossey-Bass, 1992), p. 184.
41. Ernesto J. Poza, *Family Business* (Mason, OH: South-Western, 2004), pp. 28–29, 33.
42. Ibid., p. 33.
43. John Ward, *Keeping the Family Business Healthy: How to Plan for Continuing Growth, Profitability and Family Leadership* (San Francisco: Jossey-Bass, 1987). Ward suggested that around 88 percent of family firms fail by the third generation, with family infighting, rather than a lack of succession planning, taking a toll in later generations. Ward's sample was relatively small. A very large, multigenerational study of family firms in France suggested a much higher survival rate [see Dean Savage, *Founders, Heirs and Managers: French Industrial Leadership in Transition* (Beverly Hills: Sage, 1979)].
44. William G. Shuster, "Family Business in Crisis: Letting Go," *Jewelers Circular Keystone*, (March 2003), p. 84.
45. David Whitford, "Century-Old Companies Built to Last," *Fortune Small Business* 12, no. 5 (2002), pp. 28–34.
46. Eric G. Flamholtz and Yvonne Randle, *Growing Pains: Transitioning from an Entrepreneurship to a Professionally Managed Firm* (San Francisco: Jossey-Bass, 2000), pp. 64–65.

47. W. Gibb Dyer, Jr., *The Entrepreneurial Experience: Confronting Career Dilemmas of the Start-Up Executive* (San Francisco: Jossey-Bass, 1992), p. 184.
48. Joseph Weber and Louis Lavelle, "Family, Inc." *BusinessWeek* online, November 10, 2003, http://www.businessweek.com:/print/magazine/content/03_45/b3857002.htm?mz.
49. W. Gibb Dyer, Jr., *The Entrepreneurial Experience: Confronting Career Dilemmas of the Start-Up Executive* (San Francisco: Jossey-Bass, 1992), p. 184.
50. Barnett Helzberg, Jr., "Sage Counsel for All Seasons," *BusinessWeek* online, August 13, 2003, http://www.businessweek.com:/print/smallbiz/content/aug2003/sb20030813_2077_htm?sb.
51. Ernesto J. Poza, *Family Business* (Mason, OH: South-Western, 2004), pp. 28–29, 33.
52. Ibid.
53. D. Bork, D. T. Jaffee, S. H. Lane, L. Dashew, and Q. G. Heisler, *Working with Family Businesses: A Guide for Professionals* (San Francisco: Jossey-Bass, 1996). N. C. Churchill and K. J. Hatten, "Non-Market Based Transfers of Wealth and Power: A Research Framework for Family Businesses," *American Journal of Small Business* 11, no. 3 (Spring 1987), p. 51. E. G. Flamholtz, *How to Make the Transition from an Entrepreneurship to a Professionally Managed Firm* (San Francisco: Jossey-Bass, 1986). R. Beckhard and W. G. Dyer, "Managing Continuity in the Family-Owned Business," *Organizational Dynamics* 12, no. 1 (Summer 1983), pp. 5–12.
54. S. Foley and G. N. Powell, "Reconceptualizing Work-Family Conflict for Business/Marriage Partners: A Theoretical Model", *Journal of Small Business Management* 35, no. 4 (October 1997), pp. 36–47.
55. Linda Moraski, "When a Partnership Turns Toxic," *BusinessWeek* online, December 17, 2003, http://www.businessweek.com:/print/smallbiz/content/dec2003/sb20031217_7845.htm?sb.
56. Robert D. Hisrich, *Small Business Solutions: How to Fix & Prevent the 13 Biggest Problems That Derail Business* (New York: McGraw-Hill, 2004), pp. 70–71. J. A. Cox, K. K. Moore, and P. M. Van Auken, "Working Couples in Small Business," *Journal of Small Business Management* 22, no. 4 (October 1984), pp. 24–30.
57. Howard E. Aldrich, Nancy M. Carter, and Martin Ruef, "Teams." In William B. Gartner, Kelly G. Shaver, Nancy M. Carter, and Paul D. Reynolds (eds.), *Handbook of Entrepreneurial Dynamics: the Process of Business Creation* (Thousand Oaks, CA: Sage, 2004), Table 27.1, page 307.
58. In Chapter 1, endnote 3, we explored the number of new firms annually. Applying the PSED findings from endnote 57 above, we have about 500,000 new firms started by teams.
59. The term *equity* comes from J. Stacy Adams motivational model called Equity Theory, which is often discussed in Introduction to Psychology courses. Two examples of applying it in partner situations include: Brian Tracy, "Is a Business Partnership Right for You?" *Entrepreneur,* February 21, 2005, http://www.Entrepreneur.com/article/0,4621,320162,00.html and John A. Gromala and David F. Gage, "Mediating Personality Differences Behind Internal Business Disputes," *The CPA Journal, 72,* no. 3 (March 2002), pp. 68–69.
60. Paige Arnof-Fenn, "The Partner Track: How To Decide if You Should Fly Solo Or Not: The Second In A Two-Part Series On Business Partnerships," *Entrepreneur,* July 14, 2005, http://www.Entrepreneur.com/article/0,4621,322335,00.html.
61. Robert D. Hisrich, *Small Business Solutions: How to Fix & -Prevent the 13 Biggest Problems That Derail Business* (New York: McGraw-Hill, 2004), pp. 70–71. Joe A. Cox, Kris K. Moore, and Philip M. Van Auken, "Working Couples In Small Business," *Journal of Small Business Management,* 22, no. 4 (October 1984), pp. 24–30.
62. Center for Women's Business Research, *Completing the Picture: Equally-Owned Firms in 2002* (Washington DC: Center for Women's Business Research, 2003), http://www.womensbusinessresearch.com/completingthepicture.htm (July 10, 2005).
63. Center for Women's Business Research, *Privately-Held, 50% or More Women-Owned Businesses in the United States, 2004: A Fact Sheet* (Washington, DC: Center for Women's Business Research, 2004), http://www.womensbusinessresearch.org/pressreleases/nationalstatetrends/total.htm.
64. Ibid.
65. Center for Women's Business Research, *Seizing the Opportunities: A Report on the Forces Propelling the Growth of Women-Owned Enterprises* (Washington, DC: Center for Women's Business Research, 2003), http://www.womensbusinessresearch.org/pressreleases/6-24-2003/6-24-2003.htm.
66. U.S. Small Business Administration Office of Advocacy *The Small Business Economy* (Washington DC: Government Printing Office, 2004), http://www.sba.gov/advo/stats/sb_econ2004.pdf. (July 10, 2005). U.S. Small Business Administration Office of Advocacy, Minorities in Business, 2001, Washington DC: US Small Business Administration Office of Advocacy, http://www.sba.gov/advo/stats/min01.pdf (July 10, 2005).
67. U.S. Small Business Administration Office of Advocacy, *The Small Business Economy* (Washington DC: Government Printing Office, 2004), http://www.sba.gov/advo/stats/sb_econ2004.pdf (July 10, 2005). U.S. Small Business Administration Office of Advocacy, Minorities in Business, 2001, http://www.sba.gov/advo/stats/min01. pdf.
68. U.S. Small Business Administration Office of Advocacy, *Minorities in Business,* 2001, http://www.sba.gov/advo/stats/min01.pdf.
69. Alicia M. Robb, "Entrepreneurial Performance by Women and Minorities: The Case of New Firms," *Journal of Developmental Entrepreneurship* 7, no. 4 (December 2002), pp. 383–397.
70. Karen E. Klein, "Women, the Loan Strangers," *BusinessWeek* online, May 28, 2004, http://www.businessweek.com/smallbiz/content/may2004/sb20040528_5382_sb010. htm. A. M. Robb, "Entrepreneurial Performance by Women and Minorities: The Case of New Firms," *Journal of Developmental Entrepreneurship* 7, no. 4 (December 2002), pp. 383–397.
71. Center for Women's Business Research, *Access to Markets: Perspectives from Large Corporations and Women's Business Enterprises* (Washington, DC: Center for Women's Business Research, 2003), http://www.womensbusinessresearch.org/pressreleases/ 2-4-2003/2-4-2003.htm.
72. K. S. Cavalluzzo and L. C. Cavalluzzo, "Market Structure and Discrimination: The Case of Small Business," *Journal of Money, Credit and Banking* 30, no. 4 (November 1998), pp. 771–792.
73. National Women's Business Council, *Federal Contracting with Women-Owned Businesses, FY1997 to FY2002* (Washington DC: National Women's Business Council, 2004), http://www.womenbiz.gov/IssuebriefFederal%20Contracts.pdf.
74. National Minority Supply and Diversity Council, MBE—Certification NMSDC Web site (2005), http://www.nmsdc.org/MBEs/tool_kit_certification.html. (July 10, 2005).
75. American Express Company, "Should You Consider Government Contracting?" Entrepreneur.com Web site (2002), http://www.entrepreneur.com/amex/article/0,5742,307414,00.html (July 10, 2005). J. B. Howroyd, "Minority Loan and Grant Programs: The Right Program Can Ease the Transition from Pre-Funding Planner to Full-Fledged Entrepreneur," *Entrepreneur Biz Startups,* May 20, 2002, http://www.entrepreneur.com/article/0,4621,299866,00.html.
76. Stephen Roper, "Entrepreneurial Characteristics, Strategic Choice and Small Business Performance," *Small Business Economics* 11, no. 1 (1998), pp. 11–24. Gangaram Singh and Alex DeNoble, "Early Retirees as the Next Generation of Entrepreneurs," *Entrepreneurship: Theory & Practice* 27, no. 3 (Spring 2003), pp. 207–226.
77. Joshua Kurlantzick, "About Face: The Face of Entrepreneurship Has Evolved Over the Years, and Today, It's Dramatically Different. But What Will the Entrepreneur of the Future Look Like?" *Entrepreneur,* January 2004, http://www.Entrepreneur.com/article/0,4621,312260,00.html.

David A. Baucus and Sherrie E. Human, "Second Career Entrepreneurs: A Multiple Case Study Analysis of Entrepreneurial Processes and Antecedent Variables," *Entrepreneurship: Theory & Practice* 18, no. 2 (Winter 1994), pp. 41–71. Wallace N. Davidson, Dan L. Worrell, and J. Fox, B. Jercary. "Early Retirement Programs and Firm Performance," *Academy of Management Journal* 39, no. 4 (August 1996), pp. 970–984.

78. Gangaram Singh and Anil Verma, "Is There Life after Career Employment? Labour Market Experience of Early Retires," in Victor W. Marshall, Walter R. Heinz, Helga Krueger, and Anil Verma (eds.), *Restructuring Work and the Life Course* (Toronto: University of Toronto Press, 2001).
79. Gangaram Singh and Alex DeNoble, "Early Retirees as the Next Generation of Entrepreneurs," *Entrepreneurship: Theory & Practice* 27, no. 3 (Spring 2003), pp. 207–226.
80. Andrea C. Poe, "Start a Business . . . Even After 50: Neither Shy nor Retiring, People over 50 Are Proving There's Life—and Profits—after Retirement as They Launch Second Careers as Entrepreneurs," *Entrepreneur* online—Entrepreneur Extra, August 19, 2003, http://www.Entrepreneur.com/article/0,4621,310607,00.html. G. Singh and A. DeNoble, "Early Retirees as the Next Generation of Entrepreneurs," *Entrepreneurship: Theory & Practice* 27, no. 3 (Spring 2003), pp. 207–226.
81. Andrea C. Poe, "Start a Business . . . Even After 50: Neither Shy nor Retiring, People over 50 Are Proving There's Life—and Profits—after Retirement as They Launch Second Careers as Entrepreneurs," *Entrepreneur* online—Entrepreneur Extra, August 19, 2003, http://www.Entrepreneur.com/article/0,4621,310607,00.html.
82. Nichole L. Torres, "Late Bloomer: If You're Just Now Realizing You're an Entrepreneur at Heart, Not to Worry. Here's Why Starting a Business after 40 Could Be the Best Thing that Ever Happened to You," *Entrepreneur's Be Your Own Boss,* October 2003, http://www.Entrepreneur.com/article/0,4621,311174,00.html.
83. "America's First Businessman: George Washington's Business Acumen," *The Businessweek Video Library,* May 18, 2009, http://feedroom.businessweek.com/. Associated Press, "A Taste of George Washington's Whiskey—U.S. and Canada—msnbc.com," msnbc.com, April 9, 2007; May 18, 2009, http://www.msnbc.msn.com/id/18025413/. Lisa Brown, "Washington's Whiskey Hits the Barrel after 200 Year Hiatus—USA-TODAY.com," USATODAY.com, April 15, 2009; May 18, 2009, http://www.usatoday.com/travel/destinations/2009-04-15-mount-vernon-whiskey_N.htm. John Fund, "Moonshine Patriot: George Washington, Whiskey Entrepreneur," *Leisure & Arts*—WSJ.com, February 21, 2007; May 18, 2009, http://www.opinionjournal.com/la/?id=110009692. George Washington's Distillers, "Making George Washington's Whiskey," *Making George Washington's Whiskey,* May 18, 2009, http://makinggeorgewashingtonswhiskey.blogspot.com/. Thane Peterson, "BW Online, June 17, 2003, Washington Sipped Here," Businessweek.com, June 17, 2003; May 18, 2009, http://www.businessweek.com/bwdaily/dnflash/jun2003/nf20030617_2197_db028.htm. Marta Roberts, "BW Online, May 22, 2001, George Washington Slept It Off Here," Businessweek.com, May 21, 2001; May 18, 2009; http://www.businessweek.com/bwdaily/dnflash/may2001/nf20010522_060.htm.

Chapter 4

1. This case is based on J. Samuelson, "Aaaaa-choo" *Forbes* 157 no. 5 (March 11, 1996), pp. 82–86; R. Lieber, *Upstart Start-Ups* (New York: Broadway Books, 1998); and information from the corporate Web site of Magnetic Poetry, www.magneticpoetry.com.
2. R. Lieber, *Upstart Start-ups* (New York: Broadway Books, 1998).
3. "Poetry Makes a Fashion Statement," press release, July 10, 2001, www.magneticpoetry.com.
4. C. M. Gaglio, "Opportunity Identification: Review, Critique and Suggested Research Directions," in J. A. Katz (ed.), *Advances in Entrepreneurship, Firm Emergence and Growth,* vol. 3 (Greenwich, CT: JAI Press, 1997), pp. 139–202. S. Venkataraman, "The Distinctive Domain of Entrepreneurship Research," in J. A. Katz (ed.), *Advances in Entrepreneurship, Firm Emergence and Growth,* vol. 3 (Greenwich, CT: JAI Press, 1997), pp. 119–138. I. Kirzner, *Perception, Opportunity, and Profit* (Chicago: University of Chicago Press, 1979). H. H. Stevenson and J. C. Jarillo, "A Paradigm of Entrepreneurship: Entrepreneurial Management," *Strategic Management Journal* 11, Summer 1990, pp. 17–27.
5. I. Kirzner, *Competition and Entrepreneurship* (Chicago: University of Chicago Press, 1973). I. Kirzner, *Perception, Opportunity, and Profit* (Chicago: University of Chicago Press, 1979). I. Kirzner, *Discovery and the Capitalist Process* (Chicago: University of Chicago Press, 1985).
6. C. M. Gaglio and J. A. Katz, "The Psychological Basis of Opportunity Identification: Entrepreneurial Alertness," *Small Business Economics* 16, no. 2, 2001, pp. 95–111.
7. G. E. Hills and R. P. Singh, "Opportunity Recognition." In *Handbook of Entrepreneurial Dynamics: The Process of Business Creation,* eds. W. B. Gartner, K. G. Shaver, N. M. Carter, and P. D. Reynolds. (Thousand Oaks, CA: Sage, 2004), Table 24.1, page 266.
8. Dame Anita Roddick, "Our history and values: a message from Dame Anita Roddick, The Body Shop founder" *The Body Shop* (corporate Web site), 2004, http://www.thebodyshop.com/bodyshop/company/index.jsp, accessed July 17, 2005.
9. Geoff Williams, "Innovative Model: Joey Reiman has thought up stuff you've only dreamed about—and now he's going to share his secrets of innovation with you," *Entrepreneur,* September 2002, http://entrepreneur.com/article/0,4621,302457-1,00.html, accessed July 17, 2005.
10. R. Lieber, *Upstart Start-ups* (New York: Broadway Books, 1998).
11. URL for this article http://www.entrepreneur.com/article/0,4621,307944,00.html.
12. Information comes from the corporate Web site of The Fat Hat Company, www.fathat.com.
13. G. E. Hills and R. P. Singh, "Opportunity Recognition," in *Handbook of Entrepreneurial Dynamics: the process of business creation,* ed. W. B. Gartner, K. G. Shaver, N. M. Carter, and P. D. Reynolds (Thousand Oaks, CA: Sage, 2004), Table 24.4, page 268.
14. M. Michalko, *Thinkertoys* (Berkeley, CA: Ten Speed Press, 1991).
15. G. Wallas, *The Art of Thought* (New York: Franklin Watts, 1926).
16. S. G. Isaksen, K. B. Dorval, and D. J. Treffinger, *Creative Approaches to Problem Solving* (New York: Kendall-Hunt Publishing Co., 2000).
17. L. K. Gundry and M. LaMantia, *Breakthrough Teams for Breakneck Times: Unlocking the Genius of Creative Collaboration* (New York: Dearborn Books, 2001).
18. Ibid.
19. C. W. Prather and L. K. Gundry, *Blueprints for Innovation* (New York: American Management Association, 1995).
20. Dean A. Shepherd and Mark Shanley, *New Venture Strategy* (Thousand Oaks, CA: Sage Publications, 1998).
21. Connie M. Gaglio and Jerome A. Katz, "The Psychological Basis of Opportunity Identification: Entrepreneurial Alertness," *Small Business Economics* 16 no. 2 (2001), pp. 95–111.
22. These results come from a custom analysis of the Panel Study of Entrepreneurial Dynamics (PSED) done by Dr. Jennifer L. D. Shaver. Additional information on the PSED can be found in *Handbook of Entrepreneurial Dynamics: The Process of Business Creation,* eds. W. B. Gartner, K. G. Shaver, N. M. Carter, and P. D. Reynolds (Thousand Oaks, CA: Sage, 2004).
23. This outline is adapted from, Ewing Marion Kauffman Foundation, *The Business Mentor CD-ROM,* Kansas City, MO: Ewing Marion Kauffman Foundation, 2001.
24. Michael V. Copeland and Om Malik, "How to Build a Bulletproof Startup," *Business 2.0 Magazine,* May 24, 2006 (June 2006 issue), http://i.cnn.net/money/magazines/business2/startups/bulletproof.pdf (accessed April 29, 2007). Janelle Elms, "Bring in eBay Customers with Your Site," *Entrepreneur,* August 2006, http://www.entrepreneur.com/ebusiness/

ebaycenter/boostingyoursales/article159936.html (accessed April 29, 2007). Mike Fitzgerald, "Lesson 5: Use Cheap Web Tools," *Inc. Magazine,* July 2006, http://www.inc.com/magazine/20060701/bootstrapping-15.html (accessed April 29, 2007). Gwen Moran, "If You Build It," Entrepreneur.com, April 01, 2007, http://www.entrepreneur.com/ebusiness/ebaycenter/boostingyoursales/article176310.html (accessed April 29, 2007). Jerome A. Katz, Scott R. Safranski, and Omar Khan, "Virtual Instant Global Entrepreneurship: Cybermediation for Born International Service Firms," *Journal of International Entrepreneurship* 1, no. 1, March 2003, pp. 43–57.

25. [No author], "Entrepreneur Profile: Paul Scheiter, Hedgehog Leatherworks, LLC" *EntrepreneurshipweekUSA.com,* http://www.entrepreneurshipweekusa.com/stories/profiles/sheiter.asp (accessed April 29, 2007). Rebecca Roussell, "Age Is Just a Number," *St. Louis Post-Dispatch,* Friday, December 15, 2006, p. D4. Additional information comes from discussion with Paul Scheiter and from his firm's Web site, www.hedgehogleatherworks.com.
26. [No author], "Entrepreneur Profile: Paul Scheiter, Hedgehog Leatherworks LLC," *EntrepreneurshipweekUSA.com,* http://www.entrepreneurshipweekusa.com/stories/profiles/sheiter.asp (accessed April 29, 2007).
27. A. Daniels, "Generating Great Ideas from Employees," *Entrepreneur* (September 18, 2000), http://www.entrepreneur.com/article/0,4621,279678,00.html.
28. The example of AltiTunes came from R. Lieber, *Upstart Start-ups* (New York: Broadway Books, 1998), and from the corporate Web site of AltiTunes, www.altitunes.com.

Chapter 4 Appendix

1. This feasibility study was developed by Laurel Ofstein, a student at DePaul University in May 2005, under the direction of Professor Lisa Gundry of DePaul University.
2. http://www.newmansownorganics.com/pet/home/index.php.
3. http://www.naturapet.com.
4. http://www.onlynaturalpet.com.
5. http://www.omhpet.com.
6. http://www.threedog.com.
7. http://www.flintriver.com.
8. http://www.howlinghound.com.
9. http://www.happydogtoys.com.
10. http://www.kongcompany.com.
11. http://www.fatcats.com.
12. http://www.woofonline.com.
13. http://www.dogztogz.com.
14. http://www.ruffruffandmeow.com.
15. http://www.sba.gov/starting/regulations.html.
16. http://www.illinoisbiz.biz/bus/step_by_step.html.
17. Mike Troy, "Knows No Bounds for Love of Fido," *DSN Retailing Today* 41, no. 23 (December 16, 2002), pp. 40–41.
18. Rebecca Gardyn, "Animal Magnetism," *American Demographics* 24, no. 5 (May 2002), pp. 30–37.
19. April Y. Pennington, "Hot Stuff: Want to Know What's Hot for 2004? We've Got the Businesses, Markets and Trends You Shouldn't Miss Out On," *Entrepreneur* (December 2003), http://www.entrepreneur.com/article/ 0,4621,311833,00.html. Steve Cooper, "Fever Pitch," *Entrepreneur* (December 2004), http://www.entrepreneur.com/article/ 0,4621,318038,00.html.
20. Alicia Suman, "Pet Owners," *Target Marketing* 26, no. 8 (August 2003), pp. 61–62.
21. Steve Cooper, "Fever Pitch."
22. "Organic Pet Food Gets Paws Up: Niche Grows Fast, Despite High Prices," *USA Today,* July 14, 2004, http://www.usatoday.com/ money/industries/food/2004-07-13-organicx.htm.
23. American Pet Products Manufacturers Association, Inc., "Fact Sheet: Industry Statistics & Trends." *American Pet Products Manufacturers Association, Inc.* (corporate Web site), http://site05.fuzweb2.fuzint.com/press_industrytrends. asp.
24. Alicia Suman, "Pet Owners" (citing Mediamark Research).
25. Alicia Suman, "Pet Owners" (citing U.S. Census Bureau).
26. Alicia Suman, "Pet Owners" (citing Mediamark Research and Third Wave Research Group analysis of BLS 1999 Consumer Expenditure Survey data).
27. http://site05.fuzweb2.fuzint.com/press_industrytrends.asp.
28. April Y. Pennington, "Hot Stuff."
29. June Campbell, "Mark Your Territory in the Pet Industry," *Entrepreneurnewz* (September 8, 2003), (http://www.entrepreneurnewz.com/entrepreneurnewz-19-20030908MarkYourTerritoryinthePetIndustry.html).
30. http://www.bccresearch.com/food.
31. Rebecca Gardyn, "Animal Magnetism" (citing pet industry analyst Julia Dvorko of Business Communications Co.).
32. http://site05.fuzweb2.fuzint.com/press_industrytrends.asp.
33. See endnote 32.
34. Joseph Tarnowski, "Pet Project: Giant Eagle Mixes Creative Merchandising, Special Events, and Just Plain Love to Create a Pet Program that Caters to Owners as Much as Animals," *Progressive Grocer* 83, no. 13 (September 15, 2004), p. 68.
35. http://egov.cityofchicago.org/webportal/COCWebPortal/COC_EDITORIAL/RetailChicago_2004_North_2.pdf.
36. http://www.petco.com.
37. http://www.petsmart.com.
38. http://www.omahasteaks.com.
39. http://www.oldnavy.com; http://www.harley davidson.com.
40. http://www.samandwillys.com.
41. http://egov.cityofchicago.org/webportal/COCWebPortal/COC_EDITORIAL/RetailChicago_2004_North_2.pdf.
42. http://factfinder.census.gov/servlet/QT_Table?_bm=y&-geo_id=86000US60657&-qr_name=DEC_2000_SF3_U_DP3&-ds_name=DEC_2000_SF3_U&-_lang=en&-redoLog=false&-_sse=on.
43. http://www.salary.com.

Chapter 5

1. Jerome Katz's interview with Kathryn Otoshi, Chicago, IL, March 2, 2007; Doug Chiang Studio, "Web Site Production Credits", 2006, http://www.dchiang.com/dchiang/webcredits.html#kathryn; Kathryn Otoshi, "KO Kid's Books-By Kathryn Otoshi" (Web site), 2007, www.kokidsbooks.com; LucasArts, "Lucas Company Greetings", December 08, 2003, http://www.starwars.com/community/news/holiday/news20031208.html.
2. PSED, question 331a asks people starting a business if they work for someone else more or less than 35 hours a week. 74.4 percent reported working for others full time, i.e., more than 35 hours a week.
3. Office of Advocacy, U.S. Small Business Administration, "Frequently Asked Questions," September, 2008, http://www.sba.gov/advo/stats/sbfaq.pdf.
4. Robert W. Fairlie, "Kauffman Index of Entrepreneurial Activity: 1996–2008," *SSRN eLibrary,* June 8, 2009, http://papers.ssrn.com/sol3/papers.cfm?abstract_id=1395945.
5. Telephone conversation with Brian Headd, U.S. SBA economist, May 28, 2009.
6. Sources include: Joseph J. Fucini and Suzy Fucini, *Entrepreneurs: The Men and Women behind Famous Brand Names and How They Made It* (Boston: G. K. Hall, 1985). Brendan Howard, "Making Time: Not Ready for the Burden of a Full-Time Business? How Do Your Evenings and Weekends Look?" *Entrepreneur,* June 2000, http://www.Entrepreneur.com/

article/0,4621,275163,00.html. Adam Cohen, *The Perfect Store: Inside eBay* (Boston: Back Bay Books, 2003), http://www.businessknowhow.com/manage/perfectstore2.htm.

7. David Gumpert in *Burn Your Business Plan* [Needham, MA: Lauson Publishing, 2002] suggests 100 hours, but the range is given as rules of thumb in government (http://bellzinc.sympatico.ca/en/content/503613?skin=sli) and commercial (e.g., http://www.capital-connection.com/bpconsulting.html) sites.
8. U.S. Census Bureau, "2007 Economic Census, Release Date: 3/17/2009, Sector 00: EC0700CADV1: All sectors: Core Business Statistics Series: Advance Summary Statistics for the United States (2007 NAICS Basis): 2007," *Detailed Statistics—American FactFinder,* March 17, 2009; June 4, 2009, http://factfinder.census.gov/servlet/IBQTable?_bm=y&-geo_id=&-ds_name=EC0700CADV1&-_lang=en.
9. Computed from numbers provided in Office of Advocacy, U.S. Small Business Administration, "Frequently Asked Questions," September 2008, http://www.sba.gov/advo/stats/sbfaq.pdf.
10. The material in this section is based on the following articles: Broderick Perkins, "Create the Ideal Space For Business at Home," 2001, http://www.startupjournal.com/howto/workhome/20011012-perkins.html; Meredith Gould, "Space Quest," *Entrepreneur,* 2000, http://www.Entrepreneur.com/article/0,4621,_280012,00.html; Broderick Perkins, "Realize the Dream of a Home-Based Business," 2001, http://www.startupjournal.com/howto/workhome/20011026-perkins.html; Cliff Ennico, "The Reality of Working from Home," *Entrepreneur,* 2002, http://entrepreneur.com/article/0,4621,301177,0.html; Paul Edwards and Sarah Edwards, "Handling Houseguests in Your Home Office," *Entrepreneur,* August 2003, http://entrepreneur.com/article/0,_4621,310492,00.html; Owen Thomas "You, Incorporated," *Business 2.0,* December 2002/January 2003.
11. An old listing can be found at http://www.cyburbia.org/directory/index.php?t=sub_pages&cat=217, but it is no longer being updated. A good listing of practical zoning help can be found at the Realtors' site at http://www.realtor.org/library/library/fg803.
12. Cliff Ennico, "Avoiding the Zoning Trap," Entrepreneur.com, August 15, 2005, http://www.entrepreneur.com/management/operations/location/article79464.html.
13. Paul and Sarah Edwards, "Dealing With Zoning Restrictions," HomeOfficeMag.com, December 2001, http://www.entrepreneur.com/magazine/homeofficemagcom/2001/december/46816.html; Paul and Sarah Edwards, "Bad Zoning Laws? Get 'Em Changed!" HomeOfficeMag.com, June 01, 2003, http://www.entrepreneur.com/homebasedbiz/worklifebalance/advicefrompaulandsarahedwards/article62418.html; Entrepreneur.com, 2007, "Zoning: Home Is Where the Business Is, And It's Also Where a Lot of Regulations Are," Entrepreneur.com (accessed May 26, 2007); http://www.entrepreneur.com/homebasedbiz/homebasedbasics/zoning/article38884.html; Karen E. Spaeder, "Is Your Home Zoned for Business?" Entrepreneur.com, January 26, 2004, http://www.entrepreneur.com/homebasedbiz/homebasedbasics/zoning/article68844.html.
14. Paul and Sarah Edwards, "Bad Zoning Laws? Get 'Em Changed!" HomeOfficeMag.com, June 01, 2003, http://www.entrepreneur.com/homebasedbiz/worklifebalance/advicefrompaulandsarahedwards/article62418.html; Karen E. Spaeder, "Is Your Home Zoned for Business?" Entrepreneur.com, January 26, 2004, http://www.entrepreneur.com/homebasedbiz/homebasedbasics/zoning/article68844.html.
15. Personal story, used with permission.
16. Meredith Gould, "Space Quest," *Entrepreneur,* October 2000, http://www.Entrepreneur.com/article/0,4621,280012,00.html. Reprinted with permission of Entrepreneur.com.
17. Azreila Jaffe, "When Is It Time to Move the Office Out of the Home?" http://www.jbsa.com/content/suites/hb_teleworking/time_to_move.shtml.
18. For more information regarding the impact of the Internet on small and medium businesses see Judith Jeffcote, Caroline Chappel, and Sylvia Feindt, "Best Practice in SME Adoption of e-Commerce," *Benchmarking,* 9, no. 2 (2002), pp. 122–132; S. McCue, "Small Firms and the Internet: Force or Farce?" *International Business Trade Forum,* 1999; B. Kleindl, "Competitive Dynamics and New Business Models for SMEs in the Virtual Marketplace," *Journal of Developmental Entrepreneurship* 5, no. 1 (2000), pp. 73–85; C. Chappel and S. Feindt, "Analysis of E-Commerce Practice in SMEs," 1999, http://kite/tsa/de, P. Haynes, R. Becherer, and M. L. Helms, "Small and Mid-Sized Businesses and Internet Use: Unrealized Potential?" *Internet Research: Electronic Networking Applications and Policy* 8, no. 3 (1990); Dick Anderson, "Marketplace: Creating and Nurturing a Premier E-business," *Journal of Interactive Marketing* 14, no. 3 (2000), pp. 67–78.
19. John, Horrigan, "The Internet and Consumer Choice," *Pew Internet & American Life Project,* May 18, 2008; June 7, 2009, http://www.pewinternet.org/Reports/2008/The-Internet-and-Consumer-Choice.aspx.
20. U.S. Census Bureau. "U.S. Census Bureau E-Stats: 2007 E-Commerce Multi-Sector Report," *E-Stats Main Page,* May 28, 2009; June 7, 2009, http://www.census.gov/eos/www/2007/2007reportfinal.pdf.
21. Conversation with David W. Peters, vice president of Letrah, used with permission, June 20, 2005.
22. Mary Kathleen Flynn, "No. 1 Tweeter about Twitter Is MKFlynn, says Klout (Dealscape—Technology)," TheDeal.com, May 19, 2009; June 9, 2009, http://www.thedeal.com/dealscape/2009/05/mkflynn_tweets_the_most_about.php. Mark Hefflinger, "StockTwits Gets $800K to Follow Investor Chatter on Twitter I Digital Media Wire," dmwmedia.com, May 19, 2009; June 9, 2009, http://www.dmwmedia.com/news/2009/05/19/stocktwits-gets-$800k-follow-investor-chatter-twitter. Peter, Kafka, "Twitter App Investors Still Writing Checks: StockTwits Raises a Round," *BetaWorks; MediaMemo,* May 18, 2009l: June 9, 2009, http://mediamemo.allthingsd.com/tag/betaworks/.
23. Don Debelak, "Working the Web," *Entrepreneur,* 1998, http://www.entrepreneur.com/article/0,4621,229049,00.html.
24. Gerry Grant, "Search Optimization Campaigns Build Brand," *Marketing News,* September 29, 2003; Yong Seck Sohn, Hangun Houn, and Dae Ryon Chang, "A Model of Consumer Information Search and Online Network Externality," *Journal of Interactive Marketing* 16, no. 4 (2002), pp. 2–14.
25. Nancy Einhart, "How to Get Them Buzzing to Your Site," *Business 2.0,* October 2003.
26. This pie chart was built from Nielsen ranking data. The actual counts were Google, 5,510,366, Yahoo, 1,406,416, Microsoft, 852,998, AOL, 321,205, Next 6 largest search engines, 517,503. The source was Nielsen MegaView Search, "Top 10 Search Providers for April 2009 (U.S.)," Nielsen Wire, May 15, 2009; June 7, 2009, http://blog.nielsen.com/nielsenwire/online_mobile/top-10-search-providers-for-april-2009-us/.
27. Philippa Gamse, "Are Search Engines Worth It Any More?" (2003), http://www.jbsba.com/cgi-bin/articlesbybtsub.cgi?art=441.
28. Figure 5.4 measures the number of SSL certificates issued to Web sites. SSL (secure socket layer) is a protocol for encrypting communications between a Web site and a user of the Web site. It is one of the key components of transaction security on the Internet, so the count of certificates gives a good approximatation of the number of e-commerce Web sites. Paul Mutton, "One Million SSL Sites on the Web—Netcraft," Netcraft.com, February 1, 2009; June 7, 2009, http://news.netcraft.com/archives/2009/02/01/one_million_ssl_sites_on_the_web.html.
29. U.S. Census Bureau, "U.S. Census Bureau E-Stats: 2007 E-Commerce Multi-Sector Report," *E-Stats Main Page,* May 28, 2009; June 7, 2009, http://www.census.gov/eos/www/2007/2007reportfinal.pdf.

30. The number of sellers on eBay is reported to be about 4 million, with roughly 500,000 who get their primary income from eBay or already have a full-time business and use eBay for a secondary sales outlet. These numbers come from Leslie Walker, "EBay Sellers Fell into Careers That Fill Their Lives," washingtonpost.com, June 20, 2005, http://www.washingtonpost.com/wp-dyn/content/article/2005/06/29/AR2005062902935_pf.html. The listing fees on eBay came from a search of eBay on June 7, 2009.
31. Miniwatts Marketing Group, "World Internet Usage and Population Statistics," *Internet World Stats: Usage and Population Statistics,* http://www.internetworldstats.com/stats.htm (accessed April 29, 2007).
32. Melissa Campanelli, "Anti-Fraud Measures for Your Site," *Entrepreneur,* September 2006, http://www.entrepreneur.com/ebusiness/operations/article166010.html (accessed April 29, 2007). Amanda C. Kooser, "Card Tricks," *Entrepreneur,* February 2002, http://www.entrepreneur.com/magazine/entrepreneur/2002/february/48322.html (accessed April 29, 2007). Tim Miller, "Chargebacks: A Huge Price to Pay," *Entrepreneur,* June 25, 2001, http://www.entrepreneur.com/money/paymentsandcollections/acceptingpayments/article41670.html (accessed April 29, 2007).
33. Sandy D. Jap, "An Exploratory Study of the Introduction of Online Reverse Auctions," *Journal of Marketing* 67 (July 2003) pp. 96–107.
34. Melissa Campanelli, "Help Wanted," *Entrepreneur,* 2003, http://www.entrepreneur.com/article/0,4621,310424,00.html.
35. Cliff Ennico, "Selling Your Specialty Merchandise Online," *Entrepreneur,* 2003, http://www.entrepreneur.com/article/0,4621, 311666,00.html.
36. Jacquelyn Lynn, "Let the Bidding Begin," *Entrepreneur,* 2003, http://www.entrepreneur.com/article/0,4621,310583,00.html.
37. Tim W. Knox, "The Secret to eBay Success," *Entrepreneur,* 2003, http://www.entrepreneur.com/article/0,4621,312476,00.html.
38. Compiled from information from Tim W. Knox, "The Secret to eBay Success," *Entrepreneur,* 2003, http://www.entrepreneur.com/article/0,4621,312476,00.html; Marsha Collier, "Ten (or So) Golden Rules for eBay Buyers and Sellers," *Entrepreneur,* 2002, http://www.entrepreneur.com/article/0,4621,305285,00.html.
39. Jacquelyn Lynn, Op. cit.
40. Michael Krauss, "EBay 'Bids' on Small-biz Firms to Sustain Growth," *Marketing News,* December 8, 2003.
41. Devlin Smith, "Parties Victorian: Build a Business around Tea Time . . . and Victorian Times," *HomeOfficeMag.com,* July 2001, http://www.entrepreneur.com/article/0,4621,290629,00.html.
42. Michael L. Sheffield, "Closing the Sale as a Network Marketer: How to Get a Commitment Out of Prospective Customers," *Entrepreneur* online, April 21, 2003, http://www.Entrepreneur.com/article/0,4621,308127,00.html.
43. Multilevel marketing resources are also available at *Entrepreneur magazine,* http://www.entrepreneur.com/search/dir/0,4733, 651,00.html.
44. Chris Penttila, "Retailiatory Strike: Don't Let the Big Boxes Win without a Fight. There's Plenty of Room for Start-ups to Make Their Mark in Retail," *Entrepreneur,* December 2002, http://www.Entrepreneur.com/article/0,4621,304515,00.html.
45. Jan Kingaard, "How to Select a Shopping Center Location: Your Plan for Retail Success Requires a Shopping Center or Mall Location," *Entrepreneur* online, Management Section. February 10, 2005, http://www.entrepreneur.com/article/0,4621,319969,00.html.
46. Jan Kingaard, "How to Select a Shopping Center Location: Your Plan for Retail Success Requires a Shopping Center or Mall Location," *Entrepreneur* online, Management Section. February 10, 2005, http://www.entrepreneur.com/article/0,4621,319969,00.html.
47. Paul Edwards and Sarah Edwards, "Treasure Hunt: Hit the Mark When You're Hunting for Products to Sell," *Entrepreneur,* December 2003, http://www.entrepreneur.com/article/0,4621, 312023,00.html.
48. Mike, Hogan, "Make Your Car an Office on Wheels—Entrepreneur.com," Entrepreneur.com, February 2006; June 8, 2009, http://www.entrepreneur.com/technology/newsandtrends/article82968.html.
49. Lisa, Druxman, "Mama Needs to Get out of the Home Office—Entrepreneur.com," Entrepreneur.com, August 21, 2008; June 8, 2009, http://www.entrepreneur.com/startingabusiness/mompreneur/mompreneurcolumnistlisadruxman/article196600.html.
50. J. A. Katz and W. B. Gartner. "Properties of emerging organizations." *Academy of Management Review* 13, no. 3 (July, 1988), pp. 429–441.
51. See endnote 2.
52. Mark Henricks, "Just To-Do It: Having Trouble Getting Organized?" *Entrepreneur,* August 2004, http://www.entrepreneur.com/article/0,4621,316414,00.html.
53. Nichole L. Torres, "Juggling Multiple Tasks: How to Find the Time to Do All You Need to Do—and Then Some," *Entrepreneur,* July 6, 2004, http://www.entrepreneur.com/article/0,4621,316299,00.html.
54. Another useful site is maintained by the U.S. Small Business Administration at http://www.sba.gov/hotlist/license.html.
55. American Express—The Open Network. "Learning to Delegate," *Entrepreneur,* December 09, 2002, http://www.Entrepreneur.com/article/0,4621,305082,00.html (accessed July 19, 2005), M. A. Johnston, "Delegation and Organizational Structure in Small Businesses: Influence of Managers Attachment Patterns," *Group & Organization Management* 25, no. 1 (March 1, 2000), pp. 4–22. Robert McGarvey, "To the Rescue: Always Stepping in to Save the Day?" *Entrepreneur,* March 2000, http://www.Entrepreneur.com/article/0,4621,229979,00.html. Alexander Ardichvili, Brian Harmon, Richard N. Cardozo, Paul D. Reynolds, and Mary L. Williams, "The New Venture Growth: Functional Differentiation and the Need for Human Resource Development Interventions," *Human Resource Development Quarterly* 9, no. 1 (Spring 1998), pp. 55–70. Robert McGarvey, "Ready, Set, Delegate! Handing Out Tasks Is the Key to Growing Your Business" *Entrepreneur,* July 1998, http://www.Entrepreneur.com/article/0,4621,228958,00.html. Glenn H. Matthews, "Run Your Business or Build an Organization?" *Harvard Business Review* 62, no. 2 (March/April 1984), pp. 34–39.
56. Dun & Bradstreet, D&B 21st Annual Small Business Survey Summary Report/Full Report, 2002, http://sbs.dnb.com/survey/2002survey.pdf. The sample was 543 firms with 1–25 employees, although only about half that number reported on the Web site and computer functions.
57. R. N. Lussier, "A Nonfinancial Business Success versus Failure Prediction Model for Young Firms," *Journal of Small Business Management* 33, no. 1 (January 1995), pp. 8–20. R. N. Lussier, and S. Pfeifer. "A Crossnational Prediction Model for Business Success," *Journal of Small Business Management* 39, no. 3 (July 2001), pp. 228–239.
58. Chris Penttila, "Close the Loop: If You're Outsourcing Projects Right and Left, Make Sure the Information You Need Is Rolling Back to You," *Entrepreneur,* October 2003, http://www.entrepreneur.com/Your_Business/YB_SegArticle/0,4621,311034,00.html. P. Jacobs, "So You Want to Be a Mountain Climber—Changing Careers One New Experience at a Time," *Global Career Coaching* (corporate Web site), http://www.gccoach.com/documents/SoYouWanttoBeAMountain_ClimberOct03_000.pdf. (accessed July 17, 2005); Additional information was also obtained from the Gourmet Gatherings corporate website. www.gourmetgatherings.com.
59. Teresa A. Sullivan, Elizabeth Warren, and Jay Westbrook, *Financial Difficulties of Small Businesses and Reasons for Their Failure* (Washington, DC: U.S. Small Business Administration, Office of Advocacy, 1998), http://www.sba.gov/advo/research/rs188tot.pdf.
60. Lynn Neeley, "Bootstrap Finance," Coleman Foundation White Paper, 2002, http://www.colemanchairs.org/files/documents/4/Neeley.pdf. Verne Harnish, "Finding Money You Didn't Know You Had," *Fortune Small Business* 12, no. 5 (June 2002), pp. 67–68. Mary Kay Sullivan, "Small Business Familiarity with Sources of Financing: Impact of Location and Size," U.S. Association for Small Business and Entrepreneurship,

annual meeting, 2000, www.usasbe.org/knowledge/proceedings/2000/sullivan.pdf. Bob Weinstein, "Walk This Way: Lessons in the Fine Art of Bootstrapping," *Entrepreneur,* October 1998, http://www.Entrepreneur.com/article/0,4621,229429,00.html. Howard E. Van Auken and Lynn Neeley, "Evidence of Bootstrap Financing among Small Start-Up Firms," *Journal of Entrepreneurial and Small Business Finance* 5, no. 3 (1996), pp. 235–249.

61. Stephanie Clifford, "How to Start a Business for (Almost) Nothing," *Inc.*, July 2006, www.inc.com/magazine/20060701/bootstrapping-intro.html (accessed April 29, 2007). Michael Fitzgerald, "CRM Made Simple," *Inc.* January 2007. www.inc.com/magazine/20070101/technology-tools.html (accessed April 29, 2007). Mike Fitzgerald, "Something for Nothing," *Inc.* November 2006, http://www.inc.com/magazine/20061101/handson-technology.html (accessed April 29, 2007). Derek Gehl, "12 Free Tools for Online Businesses," *Entrepreneur.com,* June 27, 2005, http://www.entrepreneur.com/ebusiness/ebusinesscolumnist/article78504.html (accessed April 29, 2007). *Inc.* Magazine Staff, "The Open-Source Advantage," *Inc.*, January 2007. http://www.inc.com/magazine/20070101/technology-software-adv.html. (accessed April 29, 2007). Gwen Moran, "If You Build It," Entrepreneur.com, April 01, 2007. http://www.entrepreneur.com/ebusiness/ebaycenter/boostingyoursales/article176310.html (accessed April 29, 2007).
62. Michael McMyne and Nicole Amare, *Student Entrepreneurs: 14 Undergraduate All-Stars Tell Their Stories* (St. Louis, MO: Premium Press America, 2003), pp. 42–50.
63. J. Finegan, "Bootstrapping: Great Companies Started with Less than a Thousand Dollars: CEOs from 11 different companies share tips and suggestions on how to fund a start-up with under $1,000," *Inc.*, August 1995, http://www.inc.com/magazine/19950801/2363.html (accessed July 17, 2005). Jerry Useem, "Should You Lie? Permissible or Not, Lying Has a Hallowed Place in the World of Business," *Fortune Small Business,* October 14, 1999, http://www.fortune.com/fortune/smallbusiness/managing/articles/0,15114,360720,00.html. MSGI Security Solutions Inc., "Board of Directors," MSGI Security Solutions, Inc. (corporate Web site), http://www.mediaservices.com/about/board.cfm (accessed July 17, 2005).
64. Carla Goodman, "The Big Time: You've Tested the Part-Time Waters; Now Take the Full-Time Plunge," *Business Start-Ups,* August 1998, http://www.entrepreneur.com/article/0,4621, 229016,00.html.
65. K. Petrova, "Part-Time Entrepreneurship and Wealth Effects: New Evidence from the Panel Study of Entrepreneurial Dynamics," Working Paper, Boston College Department of Economics, September 2004, http://www2.bc.edu/~petrovak/html/research/jmp.pdf (accessed July 17, 2005).

Chapter 6

1. This example comes from an interview by Professor Richard Green in April 2007.
2. Lyrics and tune by Paul Simon.
3. Ronald S. Burt and Holly Raider, "Creating careers: Women's paths to entrepreneurship." Unpublished manuscript (2002), University of Chicago, Chicago, IL, http://www.sfu.ca/~insna/SunbeltAbstracts/Abstracts/Burt_&_Riader.html (accessed 4-26-07). Arnold C. Cooper and William Dunkelberg, "Entrepreneurship and paths to business ownership," *Strategic Management Journal* (1986) 7, pp. 53–68. Calin Gurau, "Bio-Entrepreneurship in Different Economic Systems: A Comparative Analysis of Bio-Entrepreneurs' Profile in UK, France, and Germany," *International Journal of Biotechnology* (2006), 8, no. 3–4, pp. 169–186. Mary C. Mattis, "Women entrepreneurs: out from under the glass ceiling," *Women in Management Review* (April 2004), 19, no. 3, pp. 154–163.
4. B. Headd, "Redefining Business Success: Distinguishing between Closure and Failure," *Small Business Economics* 21, no. 1 (August 2003), pp. 51–61.
5. D. A. Veasley, "Incubators Build Economies, Benefit communities," *Birmingham Business Journal,* August 15, 2003; July 2005, http://birmingham.bizjournals.com/birmingham/stories/ 2003/08/11/focus6.html.
6. For example, see Oregon SBDC Network, *ASBDC Accreditation Self-Study* (Eugene, OR: Oregon, SBDC Network, November 2002). http://www.bizcenter.org/networkselfstudy/2002OregonSelf-Study.pdf; p. 25. J. J. Chrisman, "The Influence of Outsider-Generated Knowledge Resources on Venture Creation," *Journal of Small Business Management* 37, no. 4 (1999), pp. 42–58. J. J. Chrisman and W. E. McMullan, "A Preliminary Assessment of Outsider Assistance as a Knowledge Resource: The Longer-Term Impact of New Venture Counseling," *Entrepreneurship Theory and Practice* 24, no. 3 (2000), pp. 37–53. James J. Chrisman and W. Ed McMullan, "Outsider Assistance as a Knowledge Resource for New Venture Survival," *Journal of Small Business Management* 42, no. 3 (2004), pp. 229–244. A. Charney and G. Libecap, *Impact of Entrepreneurship Education* (Kansas City, MO: Kauffman Center for Entrepreneurial Leadership, 2000). L. Kolvereid and O. Moen, "Entrepreneurship among Business Graduates: Does a Major in Entrepreneurship Make a Difference?" *Journal of European Industrial Training* 21, no. 4 (1997), pp. 154–160. W. E. McMullan and L. M. Gillin, "Entrepreneurship Education: Developing Technological Start-Up Entrepreneurs. A Case Study of a Graduate Entrepreneurship Programme at Swinburne University," *Technovation* 18, no. 4, (1998), pp. 275–286. T. V. Menzies, and J. C. Paradi, "Encouraging Technology-Based Ventures: Entrepreneurship Education and Engineering Graduates," *New England Journal of Entrepreneurship* 5, no. 2 (2002), pp. 57–64. T. V. Menzies and J. C. Paradi, "Entrepreneurship Education and Engineering Students: Career Path and Business Performance," *International Journal of Entrepreneurship and Innovation* 6, no. 2 (2003), pp. 85–96. N. B. Upton, D. L. Sexton, and C. Moore, "Have We Made a Difference? An Examination of Career Activity of Entrepreneurship Majors since 1981" (abstract), *Frontiers of Entrepreneurship Research,* 1995 edition, pp. 727–728.
7. Brian Headd, "Redefining Business Success: Distinguishing between Closure and Failure," *Small Business Economics* 21, no. 1 (2003) pp. 51–61.
8. These statistics come from the Panel Study of Entrepreneurial Dynamics. William B. Gartner, Kelly G. Shaver, Nancy M. Carter, and Paul D. Reynolds (eds.), *Handbook of Entrepreneurial Dynamics: The Process of Business Creation* (Thousand Oaks, CA: Sage, 2004).
9. U.S. Small Business Administration, *The Small Business Economy* (Washington: DC: U.S. Small Business Administration, Office of Advocacy, 2004).
10. Jim Collins, *Good to Great* (New York: HarperCollins Publishing Company, 2001), p. 63.
11. R. Green, and J. J. Carroll, *Investigating Entrepreneurial Opportunities* (Thousand Oaks, CA: Sage 2000).
12. Professional Association of Innkeepers International (PAII), *Eighth Biennial Industry Study of Bed-and-Breakfast & Country Inns* (Santa Barbara, CA, 2003).
13. L. Marx and G. Shaler, "Bargaining Power in Sequential Contracting," Duke/UNC Micro-Theory Working Paper 3, 2002.
14. Financial Accounting Standards Board, "Statement of Financial Accounting Standards No. 142," *Goodwill and Other Intangible Assets* (2001).
15. McDonald's Corporation, *Annual Report,* 2002, p. 10.
16. Sarah E. Lockyer, "One Year Later: Ground Round Sizzles under Franchisee Co-op," *Nation's Restaurant News,* February 28, 2005. Carlye Adler, "The Ground Round Rebound: Stunned by a Sudden Bankruptcy, Stubborn Franchisees Step in to Buy Their Parent Company," *Fortune Small Business Magazine,* February 2005. Michael Peña, "Richmond's Job Center Gets Downsized," *East Bay Business Times,* April 2004.
17. Sandra King, "Organizational Performance and Conceptual Capability: The Relationship between Organizational Performance and Successors' Capability in a Family-Owned Firm," *Family Business Review* 16, no. 3

(September 2003), pp. 173–182. Patricia Schiff Estess, "Class Acts: Family Business Forums Are a One-Stop Education Resource," *Entrepreneur* December 1996, http://www.Entrepreneur.com/article/0,4621,226658,00.html. A. Ibrahim and W. Ellis, *Family Business Management: Concepts and Practices* (Dubuque, IA: Kendall/Hunt Publishing, 1994).

18. Rod P. Burkert, "A Good Deal Depends on Preparation," *Journal of Accountancy*, 196, no. 5 (November 2003), pp. 47–52.
19. Stephen Weinstein, "Add a New Owner to Your Firm," *Journal of Accountancy* 196, no. 2 (August 2003), pp. 43–48.
20. The ideas here are derived from Chris Kelleher, "Preventing Feuds in the Family Business: Handling Delicate Topics—Like Succession Planning—with Care Is Key to Keeping the Peace in Any Family Business," *Entrepreneur*, June 14, 2004, http://www.Entrepreneur.com/article/0,4621,315884,00.html. Nichole L. Torres, "Family Affair When Business and Family Mix, the Key to Success is Communication," *Entrepreneur's Be Your Own Boss*, September 2004, http://www.Entrepreneur.com/article/0,4621,316835,00.html. Patricia Schiff Estess, "Class Acts: Family Business Forums Are a One-Stop Education Resource," *Entrepreneur*, December 1996, http://www.Entrepreneur.com/article/0,4621,226658,00.html.
21. Dominique Besson and Slimane Haddadj, "Dysfunctions in Owner-Manager Succession Process in Family Firms and How a SEAM Intervener-Researcher Can Address Them," *Journal of Organizational Change Management* 16, no. 1 (2003), pp. 83–89.
22. Isabelle Le Breton-Miller, Danny Miller, and Lloyd P. Steier, "Toward an Integrative Model of Effective FOB Succession," *Entrepreneurship: Theory & Practice* 28, no. 4 (Summer 2004), pp. 305–328. William S. White, Timothy D. Krinke, and David L. Geller, "Family Business Succession Planning: Devising an Overall Strategy," *Journal of Financial Service Professionals* 58, no. 3 (May 2004), pp. 67–86.
23. Scott Bernard Nelson, "Leave It to Them: Make Sure Your Family Gets What It Needs by Including a Disclaimer Provision in Your Estate Plan," *Entrepreneur*, August 2004, http://www.Entrepreneur.com/article/0,4621,316380,00.html. Paul DeCeglie, "State of the Estate: What Is Estate Planning and Why Should You Be Doing It Now?" Entrepreneur's Start-Ups, January 2001, http://www.entrepreneur.com/article/0,4621,284549,00.html.

Chapter 7

1. This case is based on Nick Tostenrude, "Turning 25¢ into $1: The Unique Advantages and Disadvantages of Being Young Entrepreneurs," in Michael McMyne and Nicole Amare, *Student Entrepreneurs: 14 Undergraduate All-Stars Tell Their Stories* (Nashville: Premium Press, 2003).
2. G. E. Hills and R. P. Singh, "Opportunity Recognition," in *Handbook of Entrepreneurial Dynamics: The Process of Business Creation*, eds. W. B. Gartner, K. G. Shaver, N. M. Carter, and P. D. Reynolds (Thousands Oaks, CA: Sage, 2004), Table 24.1, p. 266.
3. Karl Vesper, *New Venture Strategy* (Prentice Hall, 1990).
4. Tax Resources, Inc., http://www.taxaudit.com.
5. "Initiative for a Competitive Inner City," Inner city 100 Winners 2003 SLR contracting, http://www.icic.org/vsh/oin/smRenderfs.php?phpsessid=b5238b7a7e0007c805caf97833ab6fda&cerror Fred O. Williams, Inner-City Success Story, *Buffalo News*, April 26, 2003, http://www. buffaloniagara.org/news.asp?ID=25&ARCHIVED=1.
6. The latest news can be found at the SBA's Regulatory Flexibility Act Enforcement Page, http://www.sba.gov/advo/laws/law_lib.html.
7. SIC codes are slowly being replaced by the North American Industry Classification System (NAICS). NAICS uses a six-digit code and offers original categories reflecting newer industries, such as those related to the Internet. For NAICS information, check out the NAICS page at the Census Bureau, http://www.census.gov/epcd/naics02/.
8. Thomas J. Stanley and William D. Danko, *The Millionaire Next Door* (New York: Pocket Books, 1996).
9. Anita Campbell, "Top 30 Most Profitable Small Businesses during 2008," *Small Business Trends* 2 (February 2009), June 11, 2009, http://smallbiztrends.com/2009/02/top-30-most-profitable-small-businesses-2008.html. Anita Campbell, "What Are the Most profitable Small Businesses in a Recession?" *Small Business Trends*, January 27, 2009; May 24, 2009, http://smallbiztrends.com/2009/01/profitable-small-businesses-recession.html. Maureen Farrell, "The Most and Least Profitable Businesses to Start—Forbes.com," forbes.com, January 18, 2008, May 29, 2009, http://www.forbes.com/2008/01/18/citigroup-sageworks-nyu-ent-fin=cx_mf_0118mostprofitable.html. Scott Shane, "Are There Recession-Proof Industries for Small Businesses?" *Small Business Trends*, December 1, 2008, June 11, 2009, http://smallbiztrends.com/2008/12/recession-proof-small-businesses.html. Mindy Woolen, "Industry Trends >> Blog Archive >> Most Profitable Industries of 2008," Sageworks.com, January 28, 2009; May 24, 2009, http://www.sageworksinc.com/industrytrends/index.php/most-profitable-industries-of-2008/.
10. Sarah Caron, "14 Big Businesses that Started in a Recession," insidecrm.com, May 24, 2009, http://www.insidecrm.com/features/businesses-started-slump-111108/. Michael Mandel, "Starting Successful New Companies in Recessions—BusinessWeek," Businessweek.com, May 3, 2009; May 24, 2009, http://www.businessweek.com/the_thread/economicsunbound/archives/2009/05/starting_succes.html. This list of airlines was based on Michael Masouras, "Companies Founded after 2000—Freebase," Freebase.com, May 24, 2009, http://www.freebase.com/view/user/masouras/default_domain/views/companies_founded_after_2000, compared to operating airlines shown on "List of Airlines—Planes," Plane Spotting World, May 24, 2009, http://plane.spottingworld.com/List_of_airlines.
11. Stanley and Danko, op. cit.
12. PSED Q327, "If someone asked you which kind of person you are, would you say that you preferred doing things better or doing things differently?" Of respondents, 63.3 percent said doing things better, while 32.4 percent said doing things differently.
13. The ideas in this section build on three works. Michael Porter talked about the topic in general in his 1980 masterpiece *Competitive Strategy* (Free Press). Karl Vesper really gave the first detailed workup of imitation-innovation strategies in his 1990 book *New Venture Strategy* (Prentice Hall). The most advanced thinking on the topic can be found in Dean Shepherd and Mark Shanley's 1998 book *New Venture Strategy* (Sage).
14. Sheila Himmel, "Feeling Welcome at Satay House," *The Mercury News*, May 3, 2002, http://www.bayarea.com/mld/mercurynews/entertainment/eye/3189323.htm.
15. [No author], "CONSUMER WEB SERVICES DVD Movie Rental Plot Pits Tiny Netflix Vs. Blockbuster," *Investor's Business Daily*, 1061–2890, March 21, 2001, p. A08. [No author], "DVD Renter Netflix Crafts New Plot Line; Molding Itself After HBO; The distribution company foresees its subscribers getting a host of content," *Investor's Business Daily*, 1061–2890, Nov 26, 2003, p. A04. [No author], "Blockbuster battles Netflix," *Variety*, 0042–2738, *v*395 i13 (August 16, 2004), p. 2. Tara Lemmey, "Push the Positive for Customers; Any Revenue Model That Takes Advantage of Human Frailty Is Vulnerable. Case in Point: Blockbuster. Opportunist: Netflix," *BusinessWeek* Online, Sept 13, 2005.
16. Michael V. Copeland, "Start Last, Finish First," *Business 2.0*, February 2, 2006, http://money.cnn.com/magazines/business2/business2_archive/2006/01/01/8368119/index.htm. Mauro F. Guillén, "Structural Inertia, Imitation, and Foreign Expansion: South Korean Firms and Business Groups in China, 1987–95," *Academy of Management Journal*, 45, (2002) pp. 509–525. Henrik Barth, "Fit among Competitive Strategy, Administrative Mechanisms, and Performance: A Comparative Study of

Small Firms in Mature and New Industries," *Journal of Small Business Management* 41, No. 2 (April 2003), pp. 133–147. David Newton, "To Spark Business Growth, Follow the Leader in Your Industry," *Entrepreneur,* October 2003, www.entrepreneur.com/magazine/entrepreneur/2003/october/64478.html.

17. Nichole L. Torres, "Designing Women—A 'by Women, for Women, about Women' Attitude Is Making this Greeting Card Company a Success," *Entrepreneur,* July 2001, http://www.entrepreneur.com/mag/article/0,1539,290274,00.html.
18. This is question Q291 in the PSED, "Within the first three to four years, what percentage of your customers do you expect to be . . . located within x miles?" Because the numbers are averages of percentages reported, they don't necessarily add up to 100 percent.
19. Adapted from discussion of the drivers of value and costs in Gordon Walker, *Modern Competitive Strategy* (Boston: McGraw-Hill, 2004) and in Michael Porter, *Competitive Strategy: Techniques for Analyzing Industries and Competitors* (New York: Free Press, 1980).
20. The model for life cycle comes from strategy texts like Gordon Walker, *Modern Competitive Strategy* (Boston: McGraw-Hill, 2004) and Gregory G. Dess and G. T. Lumpkin, *Strategic Management: Creating Competitive Advantage* (Boston: McGraw-Hill/Irwin, 2003). The discussion of the auto industry's growth comes from Renato Bertodo, "The Strategic Alliance: Automotive Paradigm of the 1990s." *International Journal of Technology Management,* 5, no. 4 (1990), pp. 375—388, Edward K. Miller, *Century on Wheels: The Story of the American Automotive Industry* (Houston, TX: Pioneer Publications, 1987), and H. Eugene Weiss, *Chrysler, Ford, Durant, and Sloan: Founding Giants of the American Automotive Industry* (Jefferson, NC: McFarland, 2003).
21. These generic strategies for business come from Michael E. Porter, *Competitive Strategy: Techniques for Analyzing Industries and Competitors* (New York: Free Press, 1980).
22. This list adapts and labels Shepherd and Shanley (p. 59) with two exceptions. One of their categories, "Products with special features appealing to specific niches" is treated here as a variant of customization. Second, the comprehensiveness supra-strategy (p. 61) is provided.
23. James Carpenter, "Little Guy Is No. 1 Volume Car Dealer," *The Salt Lake Tribune and Deseret Morning News,* http://www.utahbusinessandindustry.com/2003article/menlove2.asp.
24. Gary Nabham, "Food for Thought: Eating In—the Benefits of Locally Grown Food," *Sierra Magazine,* November/December 2002, http://www.sierraclub.org/sierra/200211/food.asp.
25. Michael Porter, *Competitive Strategy: Techniques for Analyzing Industries and Competitors* (New York: Free Press, 1980).
26. This section draws heavily on the original and interpreted works of Jay Barney. These include Jay Barney, *Gaining and Sustaining Competitive Advantage (2nd ed.).* (Upper Saddle River, NJ: Prentice Hall, 2002); Sharon Alvarez and Jay Barney, "Entrepreneurial Capabilities: A Resource-Based View," in G. Dale Meyer and Kurt A. Heppard, *Entrepreneurship as Strategy* (Thousand Oaks, CA: Sage, 2000); Gregory G. Dess and G. T. Lumpkin, *Strategic Management* (Boston: McGraw-Hill, 2003); and Gordon Walker, *Modern Competitive Strategy* (Boston: McGraw-Hill, 2004).
27. Adapted from "The Vermont Teddy Bear Company Story," http://store.yahoo.com/vtbear/ourstory.html; Elizabeth J. Goodgold, "Bear Market: How One Company Repositioned Itself for a Plush Success Story," *Entrepreneur,* September 2002, http://www.Entrepreneur. com/article/0,4621,302227,00.html. Joyce P. Vincelette, Ellie A. Fogarty, Thomas M. Patrick, and Thomas L. Wheelen, "The Vermont Teddy Bear Co., Inc.: Challenges Facing a New CEO," 1998, https://www. bus.iastate.edu/jdhunger/581AFall03/VermontTeddyBear.doc.
28. Elizabeth J. Goodgold, "Bear Market: How One Company Repositioned Itself for a Plush Success Story," *Entrepreneur,* September 2002, http://www.Entrepreneur.com/article/0,4621,302227,00.html.
29. Mark Henricks, "A Mixed Blessing: That Unexpected Windfall May Feel Like Winning the Lottery, but If You Aren't Careful, It Could Wreak Havoc on Your Business," *Entrepreneur,* July 2003, http://www.Entrepreneur.com/article/0,4621,309368,00.html.

Chapter 8

1. The ideas in this table come from David Gumpert, *How to Really Create a Successful Business Plan: Step-by-Step Guide* (4th ed.) (Needham, MA: Lauson Publishing, 2003), chap. 10. D. A. Shepherd and A. L. Zacharakis, "A New Venture's Cognitive Legitimacy: An Assessment by Customers," *Journal of Small Business Management* 41, no. 2 (April 2003), pp. 148–167. D. A. Shepherd and A. L. Zacharakis, "Venture Capitalists' Expertise: A Call for Research into Decision Aids and Cognitive Feedback," *Journal of Business Venturing* 17, no. 1 (January 2002), pp. 1–20. Dean Shepherd and Evan Douglas, *Attracting Equity Investors* (Thousand Oaks, CA: Sage, 1999). J. Hall and C. W. Hofer, "Venture Capitalists' Decision Criteria in New Venture Evaluation," *Journal of Business Venturing,* 8, no. 1 (January 1993), pp. 25–42. Robert Ronstadt, *Entrepreneurial Finance* (Gilmanton, NH, Lord Publishing, 1988), chap. 10.
2. Lisa K. Gundry and Aaron A. Buchko, *Field Casework: Methods for Consulting to Small and Startup Businesses* (Thousand Oaks, CA: Sage Publications, 1996). B. Honig, "Who Gets the Goodies? An Examination of Microenterprise Credit in Jamaica," *Entrepreneurship and Regional Development* 10 (1998), pp. 313–334.
3. John L. Nesheim, *High Tech Start-Up* (revised and updated ed.) (New York: Free Press, 2000).
4. Twenty-eight percent of owners wrote a formal plan while 26 percent had an informal or partial plan. Sarah Bartlett, "Seat of the Pants," *Inc.,* October 2002, http://www.inc.com/magazine/ 20021015/24772.html.
5. F. Delmar and S. Shane, "Does Business Planning Facilitate the Development of New Ventures?" *Strategic Management Journal* 24, no. 12 (December 2003), p. 1165. Nancy Upton, Elisabeth J. Teal, and Joe T. Felan, "Strategic and Business Planning Practices of Fast Growth Family Firms," *Journal of Small Business Management* 39, no. 1 (January 2001), pp. 60–72. Brian Gibson and Gavin Cassar, "Planning Behavior Variables in Small Firms," *Journal of Small Business Management* 40, no. 3 (July 2002), p. 171 (16 pgs).
6. F. Delmar and S. Shane, "Does Business Planning Facilitate the Development of New Ventures?" *Strategic Management Journal* 24, no. 12 (December 2003), p. 1165. B. Honig and T. Karlsson, "Institutional Forces and the Written Business Plan," *Journal of Management* 30, no. 1 (2004), pp. 29–48. B. J. Orser, S. Hogarth-Scott, and A. L. Riding, "Performance, Firm Size, and Management Problem Solving," *Journal of Small Business Management* 38, no. 4 (October 2000), pp. 42–58. Stephen C. Perry, "The Relationship between Written Business Plans and the Failure of Small Businesses in the U.S.," *Journal of Small Business Management* 39, no. 3 (July 2001), pp. 201–209.
7. B. Honig and T. Karlsson, "Institutional Forces and the Written Business Plan," *Journal of Management* 30, no. 1 (2004), pp. 29–48.
8. John L. Nesheim, *High Tech Start-Up* (rev. and updated ed.) (New York: Free Press, 2000).
9. Question 114 in the PSED: What is the current form of your business plan: unwritten or in your head, informally written, formally prepared, or something else?
10. Sources include: Cliff Ennico, "The 30-Second Business Plan: Want to Impress a Potential Investor Quickly? Here's Exactly What to Say," *Entrepreneur,* January 20, 2003, http://www.entrepreneur.com/ Your_Business/YB_SegArticle/0,4621,306110,00.html. Ben Casnocha, "Perfecting the Elevator Pitch: Learn to Rattle Off a Spiel Quickly about Your Company, and Soon You'll Have More Contacts Than You'll Know What to Do With," TeenStartUps.com, February 2003, http://www.entrepreneur.com/mag/article/0,1539, 306421,00.html. Stan Mandel, "The Elevator

Pitch: Engage People, Move to Action . . . in 2 Minutes," Wake Forest University, 2003.

11. A. L. Zacharakis, "Writing a Business Plan," in W. Bygrave and A. Zacharakis (eds.), *The Portable MBA in Entrepreneurship*, 3rd ed. (New York: Wiley, 2003).
12. Gregory G. Dess and G. T. Lumpkin, *Strategic Management: Creating Competitive Advantage* (Boston: McGraw-Hill/Irwin, 2003), pp. 27–29. Gordon Walker, *Modern Competitive Strategy* (Burr Ridge, IL: McGraw-Hill/Irwin, 2003), pp. 263–264. Guy Kawasaki, *The Art of the Start* (New York: Penguin Group, 2004).
13. Gregory G. Dess and G. T. Lumpkin, *Strategic Management: Creating Competitive Advantage* (Boston: McGraw-Hill/Irwin, 2003), p. 27.
14. Robert X. Cringley, *Accidental Empires* (New York: HarperBusiness, 1996).
15. Mark Henricks, "Words to Live By," *Entrepreneur*, September 1998, http://www.Entrepreneur.com/article/0,4621,229232,00.html.
16. Excalibur Seasoning, Mission Statement (Pekin, IL: Excalibur Seasoning), http://www.excaliburseasoning.com/About.htm.
17. Gregory G. Dess and G. T. Lumpkin, *Strategic Management: Creating Competitive Advantage* (Boston: McGraw-Hill/Irwin, 2003), pp. 28–29. Gordon Walker, *Modern Competitive Strategy* (Burr Ridge, IL: McGraw-Hill/Irwin, 2004) pp. 263–264.
18. Fantastic Gift Baskets, Inc., "Why We're Different." Raleigh, NC, http://www.fantasticbaskets.com/Different.html.
19. There is no standard time for elevator pitches. For example, the Wake Forest Elevator Pitch Competition allows two minutes for the pitch, but that is one of the longest times. For the MIT Enterprise Forums, the pitch is limited to one minute. Outside of these formal settings, communications experts tell us that listeners lose interest after 30 seconds. That in large part explains why 30 seconds is the length of the typical television commercial.
20. These come from AdSlogans.com, http://www.adslogans.com/samples/index.html.
21. Jim Horan, *The One Page Business Plan for the Creative Entrepreneur* (Berkeley, CA: One Page Business Plan Company, 2004).The version in this chapter is an adaptation of his approach and is included with his permission.
22. This outline for the full business plan was developed specifically for small businesses, but its roots are in a number of works on business planning. These include Jeffry Timmons and Stephen Spinelli, *New Venture Creation: Entrepreneurship for the 21st Century* (Boston: McGraw-Hill/Irwin, 2003); David Gumpert, *How to Really Create a Successful Business Plan: Step-By-Step Guide* (4th ed.) (Needham, MA: Lauson Publishing, 2003); Edward G. Rogoff, *Bankable Business Plans* (Thompson/Texere, 2004); Kauffman Foundation, *New Business Mentor* (Kansas City, MO: Kauffman Foundation, 2002); and J. D. Ryan and Gail Hyduke, *Small Business: An Entrepreneur's Plan* (Cincinnati, OH: Southwestern, 2003).
23. These numbers are fairly standard in a number of settings. For example, Linda Pinson and Jerry Jinnett gave these numbers in their SBA how-to guide, "How To Write A Business Plan" (Managing and Planning Series, MP-32, 1993), http://www.sba.gov/library/pubs/mp-32.txt or www.sba.gov/library/pubs/mp-32.pdf, and the same numbers are consistently used in the major business plan competitions.
24. Edward G. Rogoff, *Bankable Business Plans* (Mason OH: Thompson/Texere, 2004). David Gumpert, *How to Really Create a Successful Business Plan: Step-By-Step Guide*, 4th ed. (Needham, MA: Lauson Publishing, 2003). David Gumpert, *Burn Your Business Plan* (Needham, MA: Lauson Publishing, 2002).
25. Dean Shepherd and Mark Shanley, *New Venture Strategy* (Thousand Oaks, CA: Sage, 1998).
26. There is a tremendous range of models for different types of plans. Examples include: Edward G. Rogoff, *Bankable Business Plans* (Mason, OH: Thompson/Texere, 2004); A. L. Zacharakis, "Writing a Business Plan," in W. Bygrave and A. Zacharakis (eds.) *The Portable MBA in Entrepreneurship*, 3rd ed. (New York: Wiley, 2003); David Gumpert, *How to Really Create a Successful Business Plan: Step-By-Step Guide*, 4th ed. (Needham, MA: Lauson Publishing, 2003); Jill E. Kapron, *BizPlan Builder* (Mountain View, CA: JIAN/Southwestern, 1999); the ICVE model developed through R. K. Mitchell, J. B. Smith, K. W. Seawright, and E. A. Morse, "Cross-Cultural Cognitions and the Venture Creation Decision," *Academy of Management Journal*, 43 no. 5 (October 2000) pp. 974–993; and Dean Shepherd and Evan Douglas, *Attracting Equity Investors* (Thousand Oaks, CA: Sage, 1999).
27. Michael McMyne and Nicole Amare, *Student Entrepreneurs: 14 Undergraduate All Stars Tell Their Stories* (St. Louis: St. Louis University/Premium Press, 2003).
28. The approach here is inspired by three sources on the critical analysis of business plans: Robert C. Ronstadt, *Entrepreneurial Finance: Taking Control of Your Financial Decision Making* (Gilmanton NH: Lord Publishing, 1988); David Gumpert, *Burn Your Business Plan* (Needham, MA: Lauson Publishing, 2002); and most of all Dean Shepherd and Evan Douglas, *Attracting Equity Investors* (Thousand Oaks, CA: Sage, 1999).
29. R. K. Mitchell, J. B. Smith, K. W. Seawright, and E. A. Morse, "Cross-Cultural Cognitions and the Venture Creation Decision," *Academy of Management Journal* 43, no. 5 (October 2000), pp. 974–993. G. N. Chandler and S. H. Hanks, "Founder Competence, the Environment, and Venture Performance," *Entrepreneurship Theory and Practice* 19 (1999), pp. 77–89. G. N. Chandler, and E. Jansen, "The Founder's Self-Assessed Competence and Venture Performance," *Journal of Business Venturing* 7 (1992), pp. 223–236.
30. Margaret Fletcher and Simon Harris, "Seven Aspects of Strategy Formation," *International Small Business Journal* 20, no. 3 (August 2002), p. 297 (16 pgs).
31. C. L. Nicholls-Nixon, A. C. Cooper, and C. Y. Woo, "Strategic Experimentation: Understanding Change and Performance in New Ventures," *Journal of Business Venturing* 15, no. 5–6 (September–November 2000), pp. 493–521.
32. Adapted from "Michael Cain," in Michael McMyne, and Nicole Amare, *Student Entrepreneurs: 14 Undergraduate All Stars Tell Their Stories* (St. Louis: St. Louis University/Premium Press, 2003), pp. 59–67.
33. http://www.slu.edu/services/cc/jobsearch/chronologicalresume.pdf. Used with permission.

Chapter 9

1. http://www.beyondfleece.com/about_us/bio/
2. Susan Fournier, "Consumers and Their Brands: Developing Relationship Theory in Consumer Research," *Journal of Consumer Research*, March 1998, pp. 343–373.
3. Chiranjeev Kohli and Douglas W. LaBahn, "Creating Effective Brand Names: A Study of the Naming Process," *Journal of Advertising Research*, January/February 1997, pp. 67–75. See also Leonard L. Berry, Edwin F. Lefkowith and Terry Clark, "In Services, What's in a Name?" *Harvard Business Review*, September/October 1998, pp. 28–30.
4. Tomima Edmark, "On Your Mark . . . ," *Entrepreneur*, April 1999, http://www.entrepreneur.com/article/0,4621,230153,00.html.
5. Robert G. Cooper and Elko J. Kleinschmidt, "Benchmarking the Firm's Critical Success Factors in New Business Development," *The Journal of Product Innovation Management* 12 (1995), pp. 374–391.
6. Laura Tiffany, "Got a Lemon?" *Entrepreneur*, May 1999, http://www.entrepreneur.com/article/0,4621,230210,00.html. Tim W. Know, "Evaluating Your e-Business Idea," *Entrepreneur*, May 26, 2003, http://www.entrepreneur.com/article/0,4621,308896,00.html.
7. Albert H. Rubenstein, "At the Front End of the R&D/Innovation Process: Idea Development and Entrepreneurship," *International Journal of Technology* 9, nos. 5, 6, 7 (1994), pp. 652–678.

8. Don Debelak, "Inspired Minds Want to Know," *Entrepreneur,* January 1999, http://www.entrepreneur.com/article/0,4621, 229775,00.html.
9. Don Debelak, "Where's the Big Idea?" *Entrepreneur,* March 1998, http://www.entrepreneur.com/article/0,4621,228229,00.html.
10. Don Debelak, "Testing the Waters," *Entrepreneur,* February 1998, http://www.entrepreneur.com/article/0,4621,228009,00.html.
11. "McDonald's Tests Self-Service Kiosks," *Los Angeles Times,* July 6, 2004, p. C5.
12. Greg A. Stevens and James Burley, "Piloting the Rocket of Radical Innovation," *Research Technology Management* 46, no. 2 (Mar/Apr 2003), pp. 16–26. See also Greg A. Stevens and James Burley, "3000 Raw Ideas, 1 Commercial Success!" *Research Technology Management* 40, no. 3 (May/June 1997), pp. 16–27.
13. Phillip Kotler and Gary Armstrong, *Principles of Marketing,* 9th ed. (New York: Prentice Hall, 2000).
14. Don Debelak, "I Needed That," *Entrepreneur,* May 2002, http://www.entrepreneur.com/article/0,4621,299050,00.html.
15. Robert McMath and Thom Forbes, "Look Before You Leap," *Entrepreneur,* April 1998, http://www.entrepreneur.com/article/0,4621,228323,00.html.
16. Teresa McUsic, "Differentiate Those Differences to Stay Competitive," *St. Louis Post Dispatch,* April 17, 2000, p. BP17.
17. Kim T. Gordon, "Pros and Cons of Expanding Your Product Line," *Entrepreneur,* June 7, 2004, http://www.Entrepreneur.com/article/0,4621,315840,00.html.
18. www.kyptonitelock.com and http://www.kryptonitelock.com/inetisscripts/abtinetis.exe/templateform@psublic?tn=aboout_media.
19. Rosabeth Moss Kantor, "The 15-Minute Competitive Advantage" *Business 2.0,* February 2002, p. 87.
20. McMath and Forbes, op. cit.
21. Arundhati Parmar, "Where Are They Now?" *Marketing News,* April 14, 2003, pp. 1, 13, 14.
22. Adam Barak and Geoffrey Wilson, "Pricing Policies to Handle Patent Loss or Expiry," *International Journal of Medical Marketing* 3, no. 3, June 2003, p. 245.
23. Ibid.
24. Jay B. Lipe, "How to Set (and Get) the Right Prices," 2004, http://marketing.about.com/cs/advertising/a/pricingstrtgy_p.htm.
25. S.N. Lewis, "The Chateau Mouton Lockdown," *The Wall Street Journal Weekend Journal* (2007), pp. W1 and W8.
26. O.C. Ferrell and M.D. Hartline, *Marketing Strategy* (Mason, OH: Thompson–Southwestern, 2005), p.193.
27. Ibid., p. 194.
28. Kim T. Gordon, "How to Price Your Product," *Entrepreneur,* March 5, 2001, http://www.entrepreneur.com/article/0,4621,287402,00.html.
29. Roberta Maynard, "Take the Guesswork Out of Pricing," *Nation's Business,* December 1997, pp. 27–30.
30. Bob Weinstein, "What Price Success," *Entrepreneur,* March 1999, http://www.entrepreneur.com/article/0,4621,229999,00.html.
31. Jacquelyn Lynn, "The Middle of the Road," *Business Start-Ups,* December 1996, p. 33.
32. Julie Monahan, "Name Your Price," *Entrepreneur,* December 1999, http://www.entrepreneur.com/article/0,4621,231863,00.html.
33. Robert McGarvey and Babs S. Harrison, "Name Your Price," *Entrepreneur,* July 2000, http://www.entrepreneur.com/article/0,4621,276150,00.html. Beverly Williams, "The Price Is Right," *Entrepreneur,* October 3, 2000. http://www.entrepreneur.com/article/0,4621,280990,00.html. Ian Benoliel, "Pricing Your Product," *Entrepreneur,* July 22, 2002, http://www.entrepreneur.com/article/0,4621,301698,00.html. Rosalind Resnick, "Setting the Right Price," *Entrepreneur,* November 10, 2003, http://www.entrepreneur.com/article/0,4621,311820,00.html. Tim W. Knox, "Secrets to Setting Your Price," *Entrepreneur,* April 2, 2004, http://www.entrepreneur.com/article/0,4621,314970,00.html. Lipe, op. cit. Small Business Administration, "Pricing Your Product."
34. S. Seget, *Pharmaceutical Pricing Strategies* (London: Reuters Business Insight Healthcare, 2005).
35. European Telework Online, op. cit.
36. Darrell Zahorsky, "Super Charge Your Business with Profit Pricing Strategies," 2004, http://sbinformation.about.com/cs/marketresearch/a/pricing_p.htm.
37. "Inventing Success," *Business 2.0,* April 2003, p. 105.
38. Marty Nemko, "Perfecting Your Pricing Strategies," *Entrepreneur,* March 2000, http://www.entrepreneur.com/article/0,4621,267541,00.html. Michel A. Habib and Alexander P. Ljungqvist, "Underpricing and Entrepreneurial Wealth Losses in IPOs: Theory and Evidence," *The Review of Financial Studies* 14, no. 2 (Summer 2001), pp. 433–458.
39. Cliff Ennico, "Set the Right Price for Your Product or Service," *Entrepreneur,* June 1, 2003, http://www.entrepreneur.com/article/ 0,4621,309134,00.html.
40. J. R. Baum, E. A. Locke, and K. G. Smith, "A Multidimensional Model of Venture Growth," *Academy of Management Journal* 44, no. 2 (2001), pp. 292–303; see also, Elisabeth J. Teal, Nancy Upton, and Samuel L. Seaman, "A Comparative Analysis of Strategic Marketing Practices of High-Growth U.S. Family and Nonfamily Firms," *Journal of Developmental Entrepreneurship* 8, no. 2 (August 2003), p. 177.
41. Timothy Matanovich, Gary L. Lillien, and Arvind Rangaswamy, "Engineering the Price-Value Relationship," *Marketing Management,* Spring 1999, pp. 48–53.
42. J. Monahan, op. cit.
43. Ennico; and Knox, op. cit.
44. Gordon; Weinstein; and Monahan, op. cit.
45. Don Debelak, "Look What I Found!" *Entrepreneur,* July 2002, http://www.entrepreneur.com/article/ 0,4621,300831,00.html.
46. K. Carroll and D. Coates, "Teaching Price Discrimination: Some Clarifications," *Southern Economic Journal* 66 (1999), pp. 466–480.
47. Mark Hendricks, "The Art of (Price) War," *Entrepreneur,* April 2002, http://www.entrepreneur.com/article/0,4621,297992,00.html.
48. Small Business Administration, op. cit.
49. Eric Anderson and Duncan Simester, "Mind Your Pricing Cues," *Harvard Business Review* 81, no. 9 (September 2003), p. 96.
50. Joel Dean, "Pricing Policies for New Products," *Harvard Business Review* (November/December 1976), p. 141–153.
51. Jean-Noel Kapferer, "Managing Luxury Brands," *Journal of Brand Management,* July 1999, pp. 251–260.
52. Weinstein, op. cit.
53. Robert M. Schindler and Thomas Kilbarian, "Increased Consumer Sales Response through Use of 99-Ending Prices," *Journal of Retailing,* Summer 1996, pp. 187–199. See also Robert M. Schindler, "Patterns of Rightmost Digits Used in Advertising Prices: Implications for Nine-Ending Effects," *Journal of Consumer Research,* September 1997, pp. 192–201.
54. "When the Price is Right," *Entrepreneur,* http://www.entrepreneur. com/article/0,4621,302807,00.html.
55. http://www.makersmarkcollector.com/home.shtml.
56. Barbara Kiviat, "Sneaky Pricing," *Time Magazine,* September 19, 2003.
57. Priya Raghubir and Kim Corfman, "When Do Price Promotions Affect Pretrial Brand Evaluations?" *Journal of Marketing Research* 36 (1999), pp. 211–222.
58. Kiviat, op. cit.
59. Thea Singer, "Upstarts: Children's Hair Salons," *Inc.,* July 2001, http://pf.inc.com/magazine/20010701/22874.html.
60. Corliss L. Green, "Media Exposure's Impact on Perceived Availability and Redemption of Coupons by Ethnic Customers," *Journal of Advertising Research,* 25, no. 2 (March–April 1995), pp. 55–64.

61. Kapil Bawa and Srini S. Srinivasan, "Coupon Attractiveness and Coupon Proneness: A Framework for Modeling Coupon Redemption," *Journal of Marketing Research* 14, no. 4 (November 1997), pp. 517–525.
62. Peter Tat, William A. Cunningham III, and Emin Babakus, "Consumer Perceptions of Rebates," *Journal of Advertising Research* 28, no. 40 (August/September 1994), pp. 45–50.
63. John Burtzloff, "Keep Customers Coming Back for More," *Entrepreneur,* June 10, 2002, http://www.entrepreneur.com/article/0,4621,300846,00.html.
64. Ellen Rohr, "Keep Your Business from Closing," *Entrepreneur,* July 3, 2000, http://www.entrepreneur.com/article/ 0,4621,277102,00.html.
65. Gwen Moran, "Flash!" *Entrepreneur,* June 2000, http://www.entrepreneur.com/article/0,4621,274950,00.html.
66. Ennico, op. cit. also Tony Parinello, "Should You Offer Extra Services or Lower Prices?" *Entrepreneur,* July 1, 2002, http://www.entrepreneur.com/article/0,4621,301285,00.html.
67. See G. Bruce Friesen, "Dynamic Pricing: Teaching Your Clients to Dance," *Consulting to Management* 14, no. 1 (March 2003), pp. 33–38. Also Ellen Garbarino and Olivia F. Lee, "Dynamic Pricing in Internet Retail: Effects on Consumer Trust," *Psychology & Marketing* 20, no. 6 (June 2003), pp. 495–513.
68. Personal interviews with Dongzhou Gongbu and from a business plan for the Aba Sichuan Dairy Company written by Dr. Susan D. Peters, July 2002.

Chapter 10

1. This vignette was developed using material taken from an interview with Addie Swartz, conducted by Jill Kickul in April 2004, as well as excerpted from the Beacon Street Girls press release, "Introducing The Beacon Street Girls, Entrepreneur/Mother of Two Creates Fun, Values-oriented Books and Accessories for Girls Who Are 'Between Toys and Boys'," written by Ellen Miller and Alan Ryan.
2. Sherri Dorfman (March 1, 2006) "Value Proposition" *Marketing News,* 54; John Williams (February 6, 2006) "Building a Money-Making Brand," http://www.entrepreneur.com/marketing/branding/imageandbrandingcolumnistjohnwilliams/article83258.html, Dodo Zu Knyphausen-Aufsess, "Corporate Venture Capital: Who Adds Value?" *Venture Capital: An International Journal of Entrepreneurial Finance,* 7, no. 1 (January–March 2005), pp. 23–49.
3. R. Cooper, "Marketing From the Inside Out: Analyzing Your Market," *Entrepreneur,* May 28, 2002, http://www.entrepreneur.com/article/0,4621,300281,00.htm.
4. See for example, William O. Bearden, Thomas N. Ingram, and Raymond W. LaForge, *Marketing: Principles & Perspectives,* 4th ed., (Boston: McGraw-Hill, 2004), pp. 147–176.
5. Laura Clampitt Douglas (August 21, 2000), "Designing Your Promotion Materials," http://www.entrepreuner.com/homebasedbiz/homebasedbasics/marketing/article31668.html.
6. Lance E. Brouthers and George Nakos, "The Role of Systematic International Market Selection on Small Firms Export Performance," *Journal of Small Business Management* 43, no. 4 (2005), pp. 363–381. Laura Clampitt Douglas (August 21, 2000), "Designing Your Promotion Materials," http://www.entrepreneur.com/homebasedbiz/homebasedbasics/marketing/article31668.html.
7. Jean Brandau and Andrea Young, "Competitive Intelligence in Entrepreneurial and Start-Up Businesses," *Competitive Intelligence Review* 11, no. 1 (2000), pp. 74–84. Kathy J. Kobliski (2007), "Finding Ad Inspiration," http://www.entrepreneur.com/advertising/howtoguides/article44226.html.
8. Kim T. Gordon (November 2003), "Total Recall," www.entrepreneur.com/magazine/entrepreneur/2003/november/65130.html.
9. Ibid.
10. Jim Emerson, "Market Overview—Kid Power" (Special Report: Marketing to Children), *Direct Magazine* (Jul 26, 2005), http://directmag.com/exclusive/specialreports/2004_may_12_direct_listline_0/.
11. Lance E. Brouthers and George Nakos, "The Role of Systematic International Market Selection on Small Firms Export Performance," *Journal of Small Business Management* 43, no. 4 (2005), pp. 363–381. Roy Williams (April 11, 2005), "Target Your Market with Appropriate Ad Copy," http://www.entrepreneur.com/advertising/adcolumnistroyhwilliams/article76978.html.
12. Roy Williams (January 5, 2004), "Cheap and Effective Advertising Techniques," http://www.entrepreneur.com/advertising/adcolumnistroyhwilliams/article66236.html.
13. John Jantsch, *Creating an Effective Marketing Kit,* SBTV.com, http://www.sbtv.com/default.asp?segid=1173, February 14, 2007. Kathy J. Kobliski (2007), "Choosing the Best Ad Methods for Your Business," http://www.entrepreneur.com/advertising/howtoguides/article26188.html. James Stephenson with Courtney Thurman, *Entrepreneur Magazine's Ultimate Small Business Marketing Guide, 2nd ed.* (Irvine, CA: Entrepreneur Press, 2007).
14. Anonymous (December 6, 2006), "SCORE's Top Marketing and Public Relations Tips," http://www.entrepreneur.com/grow/score/index.html#market.
15. Michael Myser (June 2006), "Marketing Made Easy," *Business 2.0,* pp. 43–45.
16. Michael Warshaw, *Inc.,* November 2001.
17. Anonymous (December 6, 2006), "SCORE's Top Marketing and Public Relations Tips," http://www.entreperneur.com/article/0,4621,324728,00.html.
18. "301 Great Ideas for Selling Smarter," *Inc.,* January 1998.
19. Anonymous (December 6, 2006), "SCORE's Top Marketing and Public Relations Tips," http://www.entrepreneur.com/grow/score/index.html#market.
20. Michael C. Copeland and Om Malik (June 2006), "How to Build a Bulletproof Start-up," *Business 2.0,* pp. 76–92.
21. Kris Oser (January 23, 2006), "VH1, Bravo Get Content, Rating from Web Virals," *Advertising Age,* p. 10.
22. Gwen Moran (February 2007), "Get Your Biz Noticed Online—for Free," http://www.entrepreneur.com/magazine/entreperneursstartupsmagazine/2007/february/174106.html.
23. Jennifer Alsever (December 2006), "Flying off the Shelves," *Business 2.0,* p. 47. See also Michael V. Copeland and Andrew Tilin (June 2005), "The New Instant Companies," *Business 2.0,* pp. 82–94.
24. Copeland and Tilin, op.cit.
25. Todd Wasserman (December 2006), "Will Marketers' Filthy Lucre Corrupt the Blogosphere?" *Business 2.0,* p. 38.
26. Based on the following: Jack Ferrari (November 1, 2005), "Selling 101," http://www.entrepreneur.com/sales/aslestechniques/ article80782.html; Tom Duncan, *Principles of Advertising & IMC* (2nd ed.), (Boston, MA: McGraw-Hill, 2005), pp. 523–527. Barry Farber (January 2001), "On the Horizon" *Entrepreneur,* p. 119. Brian Caulfield (April 2004), "How to Land the Deal" *Business 2.0,* p. 85.
27. Alan J. Zell (undated; accessed 4/20/2003), "Business Etiquette—The Rule for Business Survival," http://sellingselling.com/articles/bizetq.html.
28. Cord Cooper, "The Art of Closing a Deal," *Investor's Business Daily,* March 2, 2003. Cord Cooper, "Deal with People Effectively—Stressing Value over Cost," *Investor's Business Daily,* January 27, 2005, p. A3. Cord Cooper, "Deal with People Effectively—Sidestep Sales Slip-Ups," *Investor's Business Daily,* February 24, 2005, p. A3. Cord Cooper, "Deal and Communicate Effectively—Hit Your Mark Each Time," *Investor's Business Daily,* July 14, 2005, p. A4. Cord Cooper, "Take Action—Art of a Successful Deal," *Investor's Business Daily,* November 23, 2005, p. A4. Cord Cooper, "Deal with People Effectively—How to Clinch the Deal,"

Investors Business Daily, September 7, 2006, p. A3. Cord Cooper, "Cut New Deals, and Win," *Investor's Business Daily*, March 27, 2007, p. A3.

29. For more information on the steps of personal selling, visit www.udel.edu/alex/chapt20.html and Sales & Marketing Top Secrets at www.entrepreneur.com.
30. William O. Bearden, Thomas N. Ingram, and Raymond W. LaForge, *Marketing,* 4th ed. (Boston, MA McGraw-Hill, 2004). Frederick F. Reichheld and W. Earl Sasser, Jr., 1990. "Zero Defections: Quality Comes to Services," *Harvard Business Review* 5, pp. 105–111. Rafi A. Mohammed, Robert J. Fisher, Bernard J. Jaworski, and Gordon J. Paddison, *Internet Marketing: Building Advantage in a Networked Economy,* 2nd ed. (Boston, MA: McGraw-Hill/Irwin-MarketSpaceU, 2004).
31. William O. Bearden, Thomas N. Ingram, and Raymond W. LaForge, *Marketing,* 4th ed. (Boston MA: McGraw-Hill, 2004). Robert L. Desatnick, *Managing to Keep the Customer: How to Achieve and Maintain Superior Customer Service Throughout the Organization* (San Francisco, CA: Jossey-Bass,1988). Rafi A. Mohammed, Robert J. Fisher, Bernard J. Jaworski, and Gordon J. Paddison, *Internet Marketing: Building Advantage in a Networked Economy,* 2nd ed. (Boston: McGraw-Hill/Irwin-MarketSpaceU, 2004).
32. Peter Alexander, "Tech Solutions That Help Keep Customers Satisfied," Entrepreneur.com, October 05, 2006, http://www.entrepreneur.com/technology/techtrendscolumnistpeteralexander/article168528.html. Ramon Ray, "Free Software You Should Consider," Entrepreneur.com, April 30, 2007, http://www.entrepreneur.com/technology/techbasicscolumnist/article177710.html.
33. Adapted from Rafi A. Mohammed, Robert J. Fisher, Bernard J. Jaworski, and Gordon J. Paddison, *Internet Marketing: Building Advantage in a Networked Economy,* 2nd ed., (Boston, MA: McGraw-Hill/Irwin-MarketSpaceU, 2004), p. 664.
34. Charles M. Futrell, *Fundamentals of Selling: Customers for Life through Service* (Boston, MA: McGraw-Hill/Irwin, 2006).
35. William O. Bearden, Thomas N. Ingram, and Raymond W. LaForge, *Marketing*, 4th ed., Boston: McGraw-Hill, 2004). Charles M. Futrell, *Fundamentals of Selling: Customers for Life through Service* (Boston: McGraw-Hill/Irwin, 2006). Vince Pesce, *A Complete Manual of Professional Selling* (New York: Prentice Hall, 1989).
36. Nichole L. Torres (June 2003), "Almost Famous," http://www.entrepreneur.com/magazine/entreperneursstartupsmagazine/2003/june/62194.html.
37. Anonymous (2007), "60-Second Guide to Generating Publicity for Your Business," http://www.entrepreneur.com/growyourbusiness/scoreresources/60secondguides/article81348.html.
38. Margie Fisher (April 6, 2006), "7 Ways to Milk Your Media Coverage," www.entrepreneur.com/marketing/publicrelations/article159500.html; Al Lautenslager (September 16, 2002), "Getting the Most from a Press Release," http://www.entrepreneur.com/marketing/publicrelations/gettingpress/article55540.html.
39. Based on information from the following: Al Lautenslager (2007), "A Press Release Primer," http://www.entrepreneur.com/marketing/publicrelations/gettingpress/article62050.html. Randall Hansen, "A Barebones Guide to Writing Successful Press Releases" (Deland FL: Stetson Marketing Department, 2005), http://www.stetson.edu/~rhansen/prhowto.html.
40. This is an actual title of a case study by Richard P. Green II and Susan D. Peters.
41. Catherine Seda (October 2006), "Make a Great First Impression," http://www.entrepreneur.com/ebusiness/gettingtraffic/ article167634.html.
42. Anonymous (undated; accessed 4/27/07), "Components of a Press Release," http://prntoolkit.prnewswire.com/entrepreneur/home1.shtml.
43. Excerpted from Randall Hansen, "A Barebones Guide to Writing Successful Press Releases" (Deland, FL: Stetson University Marketing Department, 2005), http://www.stetson.edu/~Rhansen/prhowto.html. Used with permission.
44. Al Lautenslager (2007), "The Ingredients of a Press Kit," http://www.entrepreneur.com/marketing/publicrelations/prbasics/article57260.html.
45. Charlotte Ryan, *Prime Time Activism* (Boston: South End Press, 1991), p. 35.
46. Based on information from the following: Al Lautenslager (March 15, 2004), "Implementing a PR Strategy in 7 Days," http://www.entrepreneur.com/marketing/publicrelations/prbasics/article69924.html; Margie Fisher (March 6, 2006), "The Making of a PR Story," http://www.entrepreneur.com/marketing/publicrelations/article83772.html. Al Lautenslager (April 19, 2004), "Who Should Receive Your Press Release?" http://www.entrepreneur.com/marketing/publicrelations/gettingpress/article70496.html. Mark Nowlan (July 10, 2006), "8 Ways to Get the Media Buzzing," http://www.entrepreneur.com/marketing/publicrelations/prcolumnist/article159508.html. Anonymous (December 6, 2006), "SCORE's Top Marketing and Public Relations Tips," http://www.entrepreneur.com/article/0,4621,324728,00.html.
47. Sean M. Lyden (July 22, 2002), "How to Generate Publicity," http://www.entrepreneur.com/marketing/publicrelations/publicspeaking/article53788.html.
48. Jane Applegate (2007), "How to Generate Publicity for Your Business," http://www.entrepreneur.com/marketing/publicrelations/article42738.html.
49. Al Lautenslager (July 15, 2002), "Using Publicity to Your Advantage," http://www.entrepreneur.com/marketing/publicrelations/prbasics/article53644.html.
50. For all her tips and more details, see: Margie Fisher (February 6, 2006), "10 Creative Ways to Get PR," http://www.entrepreneur.com/marketing/publicrelations/article83268.html.
51. Anonymous (December 6, 2006), "SCORE's Top Marketing and Public Relations Tips," http://www.entrepreneur.com/article/0,4621,324728,00.html.
52. Deborah L. Vence (October 27, 2003), "Cookie Dough," *Marketing News,* p. 10.
53. Excerpted from Kirk Hallahan, "A Publicity Primer," in Hallahan Course Resources (Web site), 1996, Fort Collins, CO: Colorado State University. http://lamar.colostate.edu/Hallahan/hpubty.htm. Used with permission.
54. Excerpt from "Fashion Statement," by Naomi Aoki, *Boston Globe,* May 13, 2004. Copyright © 2004 by Globe Newspaper Co. Reproduced with permission of Globe Newspaper Co. via copyright clearance center.

Chapter 11

1. Don Debelak, "Rookie Rules," *Entrepreneur,* September 1999, http://www.entrepreneur.com/article/0,4621,230661,00.html.
2. Gary L. Frazier, "Organizing and Managing Channels of Distribution," *Journal of the Academy of Marketing Science* 27, no. 2 (1999), pp. 226–240.
3. E. Rosen, *The Anatomy of Buzz: How to Create Word of Mouth Marketing* (New York: Doubleday, 2000).
4. David Stokes, "Entrepreneurial Marketing: A Conceptualisation from Qualitative Research," *Qualitative Market Research* 3, no. 1 (2000), pp. 47–54.
5. Lissan Levin and Jacob Zhavi, "The Economics of Selection of Mail Orders," *Journal of Interactive Marketing* 15, no. 3 (2001), pp. 53–71. Füsan F. Gonul and Byung-Do Kim, "Mailing Smarter to Catalog Customers," *Journal of Interactive Marketing* 14, no. 2 (2000), pp. 2–16.
6. Sean M. Lyden, "Make Newspaper Ads Work for You," *Entrepreneur,* May 27, 2002, http://www.Entrepreneur.com/article/0,4621, 300275,00.html. Reprinted with permission of Entrepreneur.com.
7. Kristin Zhivago "You and CAN-SPAM" January 23, 2004 http://www.marketing-technology.com/MT/canspam.cfm.
8. 2003 figures from the Outdoor Advertising Association of America, Inc. Web site (www.oaaa.org/outdoor/facts/cpmcomparison.asp).

9. Michael H. Morris, Minet Schindehutte, and Raymond W. LaForge, "Entrepreneurial Marketing: A Construct for Integrating Emerging Entrepreneurship and Marketing Perspectives," *Journal of Marketing Theory and Practice* 10, no. 4 (2002), pp. 1–19; K. J. Clancy and P. C. Krieg, *Counter-intuitive Marketing: Achieve Great Results Using Uncommon Sense* (New York: Free Press, 2000).
10. Don Debelak, "Lights, Camera, Action," *Entrepreneur,* April 2003, http://www.entrepreneur.com/article/0,4621,307359,00.html.
11. Michael McMyne, *Student Entrepreneurs* (St. Louis: Premium Press America, 2003).
12. Personal story, used with permission.
13. Kim T. Gordon, "Cross-Training," *Entrepreneur,* July 2003, http://www.entrepreneur.com/article/0,4621,309488,00.html.
14. Melissa Campanelli, "Fulfilling Orders," *Entrepreneur,* 2000, http://www.entrepreneur.com/article/0,4621,274296,00.html.
15. Art Avery, "Order Fulfillment for Your Small E-business: Should You Beg, Borrow or Buy?" (2000), http://wwwetailersdigest.com/resources/Specials/BegBorrow.htm.
16. George Matyjewicz, 'Doc' Don Avery, Kris Campbell, and Dave Campbell, "Online Logistics and Order Fulfillment Solutions for E-Tailers" (1999). http://wwwetailersdigest.com/resources/Specials/Logistics.htm.
17. Melissa Campanelli, "Delivering the Goods," *Entrepreneur,* 1999, http://www.entrepreneur.com/article/0,4621,229968,00.html.
18. Andy Gibbs, "How to Sell Your Product," *Entrepreneur,* 2000, http://www.entrepreneur.com/article/0,4621,279119,00.html.
19. Paul Edwards and Sarah Edwards, "It's in the Mail," *Entrepreneur,* 2003, http://www.entrepreneur.com/article/0,4621,307366,00.html.
20. For academic studies on e-tailers, see Heiko de B. Wijnolds and Michael W. Little, "Regulatory Issues for Global E-Tailers: Marketing Implications," *Academy of Marketing Science Review,* 2001, pp. 1–17; Gary J. Stockport, George Kunnarth, and Rashida Sedik, "Boo.com, the Path to Failure," *Journal of Interactive Marketing* 15, no. 4 (2001), pp. 56–70.
21. Don Debelak, "Who Needs 'Em?" *Entrepreneur,* 2000, http://www.entrepreneur.com/article/0,4621,276496,00.html.
22. Laura Tiffany, "Import/Export," *Entrepreneur,* 2001, http://www.entrepreneur.com/article/0,4621,290657,00.html.
23. Oystein Moen, "The Relationship between Firm Size, Competitive Advantages, and Export Performance Revisited," *International Small Business Journal* 18, no. 1 (1999), pp. 53–72.
24. Ibid.
25. Benjamin M. Oviatt and Patricia Phillips McDougall, "Towards a Theory of International New Ventures," *Journal of International Business Studies* 25, no.1 (1994), pp. 45–65. S. K. Kundu and J. A. Katz, "Born-International SMEs: Bi-level Impacts of Resources and Intentions," *Small Business Economics* 20, no. 1 (2003), pp. 25–47.
26. For more about SMEs and exporting, see Pierre-Andre Julien and Charles Ramagalahy, "Competitive Strategy and Performance of Exporting SMEs: An Empirical Investigation of the Impact of Their Export Information Search and Competency," *Entrepreneurship Theory and Practice* 27, no. 3 (2003), pp. 227–246; Neil A. Morgan, Anna Kaleka, and Constantine S. Katsikeas, "Antecedents of Export Venture Performance: A Theoretical Model and Empirical Assessment," *Journal of Marketing* 68 (January 2004), pp. 90–108.
27. Carla Goodman, "Going Global," *Entrepreneur,* 1996, http://www.entrepreneur.com/article/0,4621,226568,00.html.
28. Jerome A. Katz, Scott R. Safranski, and Omar Khan, "Virtual Instant Global Entrepreneurship: Cybermediation for Born International Service Firms," *Journal of International Entrepreneurship* 1 (2003), pp. 43–57.
29. S. K. Kundu and J. A. Katz, "Born-International SMEs: Bi-level Impacts of Resources and Intentions," *Small Business Economics* 20, no. 1 (2003), pp. 25–47.
30. "How to Take Your Country Global" *Entrepreneur,* 2003, http://www.entrepreneur.com/article/0,4621,312297,00.html.
31. George Matyjewicz, et al., op. cit.
32. Laura Tiffany, op. cit.
33. Carla Goodman, op. cit.
34. Beverley Williams, "Zoning Information and Resources," http://www.jbsja.com/content/suites/hb_teleworking/zoning.shtml.
35. Virginia Baldwin Gilbert, "Start-ups Are Poised to Fly Away from Incubator Nest," *St. Louis Post-Dispatch,* February 2, 2002, www.niduscenter.com/m_arts_html/post_02-25-02a.html.
36. Michael H. Seid and Kay Marie Ainsley, "What Makes a Location Great?" *Entrepreneur,* March 2001, http://www.entrepreneur.com/article/0,4621,287982,00.html.
37. Julie Bennett, "Location Is Everything to Franchise Hopefuls," http://startupjournal.com/columnist/franchiseinsight/20020814-bennett.html
38. Michael H. Seid and Kay Marie Ainsley, "Finding a Great Location," *Entrepreneur,* April 2001, http://www.entrepreneur.com/article/0,4621,288851,00.html.
39. Rieva Lesonsky, "Cart Blanche," *Entrepreneur,* 2003, http://www.entrepreneur.com/article/0,4621,265101,00.html.
40. Michael H. Seid and Kay Marie Ainsley, "Finding a Great Location," *Entrepreneur,* April 2001, http://www.entrepreneur.com/article/0,4621,288851,00.html.
41. Julie Bennett, op. cit.
42. Peter Carbonara and Maggie Overfelt, "The Dot-Com Factories," *Fortune,* 2000, http://www.fortune.com/fortune/print/0,15935,360353,00.html.
43. Michael H. Seid and Kay Marie Ainsley, "Finding a Great Location," *Entrepreneur,* April 2001, http://www.entrepreneur.com/article/0,4621,288851,00.html.
44. Michael H. Seid and Kay Marie Ainsley, "What Makes a Location Great?" *Entrepreneur,* March 2001, http://www.entrepreneur.com/article/0,4621,287982,00.html.
45. Cliff Ennico, "Franchise Business—Finding Space for Your Franchised Business," Entrepreneur.com, April 26, 2004, June 26, 2009, http://www.entrepreneur.com/management/operations/location/article70514.html.
46. The advice in the bullet points in this section come from Cliff Ennico, "Franchise Business—Finding Space for Your Franchised Business," Entrepreneur.com, April 26, 2004, June 26, 2009, http://www.entrepereneur.com/management/operations/location/article70514.html. Cliff Ennico, "Retail Business—Negotiating Your Shopping Center Lease," Entrepreneur.com, October 17, 2005, June 27, 2009, http://www.entrepreneur.com/management/operations/location/article80604.html. Rieva Lesonsky, "Commercial Leases," Entrepreneur.com, 1998, June 26, 2009, http://www.entrepreneur.com/management/operations/location/article21886.html. Jeffrey Steinberger, "How to Get out of a Commercial Lease," Entrepreneur.com, January 24, 2007, June 26, 2009, http://www.entrepreneur.com/management/legalcenter/legalissuescolumnistjeffreysteinberger/article173568.html. Nichole L. Torres, "Small Business—Lease Lessons," Entrepreneur.com, December 2004, June 26, 2009, http://www.entrepreneur.com/startingabusiness/startupbasics/location//article73744.html.
47. Rieva Lesonsky, "Commercial Leases." Entrepreneur.com, 1998, June 26, 2009, http://www.entrepreneur.com/management/operations/location/article21886.html.
48. Julie Baker, A. Parasuraman, Dhruv Grewal, and Glenn B. Voss, "The Influence of Multiple Store Environment Cues of Perceived Merchandise Value and Patronage Intentions," *Journal of Marketing* 66 (April 2002), pp. 120–140.
49. "Release Me?" *Entrepreneur,* 1998, http://www.entrepreneur.com/article/0,4621,266181,00.html.
50. Information from this case comes from Chris Taylor, "E-Commerce," *Fortune,* 2004, http://www.fortune.com/fortune/print/0,15935,575869,00.html; and Lisa Baertlein, "eBay Gets Boost as Middlemen Make Comeback" *Los Angeles Times,* (January 20, 2004).

Chapter 12

1. Personal and Internet interviews with Mingkit "Jerry" Lai conducted spring 2004 by Professor Susan Peters.
2. See Tim Mazzavol, "Do Formal Business Plans Really Matter?—A Survey of Small Business Owners in Australia," paper presented at the International Council for Small Business Conference, 2000. Available online at www.scbaer.acu.edu. See also R. Brooksbank, "The Basic Marketing Planning Process: A Practical Framework for the Smaller Business," *Marketing Intelligence and Planning,* 14, no. 1 (1996). G. Lancaster, and I. Waddelow, "An Empirical Investigation into the Process of Strategic Marketing Planning in SMEs: Its Attendant Problems and Proposals Towards a New Practical Paradigm," *Journal of Marketing Management* 14 (1998), pp. 853–878.
3. An Dugan, "The Value of Research," *Entrepreneur,* October 22, 2001, http://entrepreneur.com/article/0,4621,293951,00.html. Karen E. Spaeder, "Define Your Target Audience to Grow Sales," *Entrepreneur,* June 1, 2003, http://entrepreneur.com/article/0, 4621,309165,00.html.
4. Don Debelek, "Want Some of This?" *Entrepreneur,* June 2002, http://entrepreneur.com/article/0,4621,299768,00.html.
5. "Seems the Only Problem with New Products Is That They're New," *Brandweek,* August 22, 1994, pp. 36–40.
6. See, for example, G. Dean Kortge and Patrick A. Okonkwo, "Simultaneous New Product Development: Reducing the New Product Failure Rate," *Industrial Marketing Management,* 18, no. 4 (1989), pp. 301–306; Sharad Sarin and Gour M. Kapur, "Lessons From New Product Failure: Five Case Studies," *Industrial Marketing Management* 19, no. 4 (1990), pp. 301–314; Peter L. Link, "Keys to New Product Success and Failure," *Industrial Marketing Management* 16, no. 2 (1987), pp. 109–118. Gwen Moran, "3 Hours to a Great Marketing Plan," *Entrepreneur,* March 26, 2001, http://entrepreneur.com/article/0,4621,297622,00.html.
7. Laura Tiffany, "Researching Your Market," *Entrepreneur,* August 7, 2001, http://www.entrepreneur.com/article/0,4621,391713,00.html.
8. S. Hogarth-Scott, K. Watson, and N. Wilson, "Do Small Businesses Have to Practice Marketing to Survive and Grow?" *Marketing Intelligence and Planning* 14, no. 1 (1996).
9. Data for this table were extracted from www.Websurveyor.com.
10. See Gerald Zaltman, "Rethinking Market Research: Putting People Back In" *Journal of Marketing Research,* November 1997, pp. 424–437; Stephen Groves, and Raymond P. Fisk, "Observational Data Collection Methods for Services Marketing: An Overview," *Journal of the Academy of Marketing Science,* Summer 1992, pp. 216–224; Rebecca Piirto, "Socks, Ties, Videotapes," *American Demographics,* September 1991.
11. Stever Robbins, "Down and Dirty Market Research," *Entrepreneur,* August 12, 2002, http://entrepreneur.com/article/0, 4621,302407,00.html.
12. Judith Langer, "15 Myths of Qualitative Research: It's Conventional, But Is It Wisdom?" *Marketing News,* March 1, 1999, pp. 13–14.
13. See Janet Ilieva, Steve Baron, and Nigel M. Healey, "Online Surveys in Marketing Research: Pros and Cons," *International Journal of Marketing Research* 44, no. 3 (2002), pp. 361–376. Michael P. Cronin, "On-the-Cheap Market Research," *Inc.* June 1992, p. 108. Robert Hayes, "Internet-Based Surveys Provide Fast Results," *Marketing News,* April 13, 1998, p. 13; Phil Levine, Bill Ahlauser, Dale Kulp, and Rick Hunter, "Internet Interviewing," *Marketing Research,* Summer 1999, pp. 33–36.
14. Paul E. Green, Yoram Wind, Abba M. Krieger, and Paul Saatsoglou, "Applying Qualitative Data," *Marketing Research,* Spring 2000, pp. 17–25.
15. Don Debelek, "Want Some of This?" *Entrepreneur,* June 2002, http://entrepreneur.com/article/0,4621,299768,00.html.
16. Phaedra Hise, "Grandma Got Run Over by Bad Research," *Inc.,* January 1998, http://pf.inc.com/magazine/19980101/851.html.
17. See, for example, David M. Georgoff and Robert G. Murdock, "Manager's Guide to Forecasting," *Harvard Business Review,* January–February 1986, pp. 110–120. Angelo Guadagno, "Mastering the 'Magic' of Sales Forecasting," *American Salesman,* November 1, 1995; Carlo D. Smith, "An Integrated Model of Factors Affecting Sales Forecasting Management," *Academy of Marketing Science* 90, 1999; Donald McBane, "Benchmarking Sales Forecasting Performance Measures," *Journal of Personal Selling and Sales Management,* 2001.
18. Stever Robbins, "Down and Dirty Market Research," *Entrepreneur,* August 12, 2002, http://entrepreneur.com/article/0,4621, 302407,00.html.
19. Steven K. Baker, "Forecasting Your Sales Revenue," *Entrepreneur,* May 7, 2001, http://www.entrepreneur.com/article/0,4621, 389242,00.html.
20. David Carson and Audrey Gilmore, "Marketing at the Interface: Not 'What' But 'How,'" *Journal of Marketing Theory and Practice* 8, no. 2 (Spring 2000), pp. 1–8. Kenneth J. Cook, "Why You Are in Trouble if You Think Marketing Is Just Sales," *Small Business Forum* 14, no. 3 (Winter 1996–1997), pp. 43–49.
21. Rebecca Cooper, "Marketing from the Inside Out: A Coach's Perspective," *Entrepreneur,* May 20, 2002, http://entrepreneur.com/article/0,4621,299859,00.html.
22. G. David Doran, "Upper Crust," *Entrepreneur,* June 1999, http://www.entrepreneur.com/article/0,4621,230374,00.html; Ruth's Chris Steak House Web site www.ruthchris.com.
23. Ellen Rohr, "Price Wars," *Entrepreneur,* April 20, 2000, http://entrepreneur.com/article/0,4621,297622,00.html.
24. Personal and Internet interviews with Mingkit "Jerry" Lai conducted spring 2004 by Professor Susan Peters.
25. Laura Tiffany, "The Ingredients of a Marketing Plan," *Entrepreneur,* August 7, 2001, http://www.entrepreneur.com/article/0, 4621,291716,00.html.
26. Cook, op. cit.
27. Sumit K. Kundu and Jerome A. Katz, "Born-International SMEs: Bi-level Impacts of Resources and Intentions," *Small Business Economics,* 20, no. 1 (2003), pp. 25–47.
28. http://www.backbonemedia.net/clientBite.html.
29. Laura Clampitt Douglas, "Sizing Up Your Market," *Entrepreneur,* December 18, 2000, http://entrepreneur.com/article/0,4621, 284832,00.html. "Landing Customers," *Entrepreneur,* March 2, 2002, http://entrepreneur.com/article/0,4621,297622,00.html.
30. Karen E. Spaeder, "Who Is Your Market—and What Do They Want?" *Entrepreneur,* March 18, 2002, http://entrepreneur.com/article/0,4621,298041,00.html.
31. Cliff Ennico, "Expanding Your Target Market," *Entrepreneur,* October 28, 2002, http://www.entrepreneur.com/article/0,4621, 304103,00.html.
32. Based on www.entrepreneur.com/Home/HM Static/1,4472, formnet analysis,00.html.
33. Kathy Ellis, "Today's Marketing Plan," *The American Salesman* 49, no. 3 (March 2004), pp. 21–25.
34. Kim T. Gordon, "The Structure of a Marketing Plan," *Entrepreneur,* November 2000, http://www.entrepreneur.com/article/0,4621, 283011, 00.html.
35. Donald Lehmann and Russell Winer, *Analysis for Market Planning,* 6th ed., (Burr Ridge, IL: McGraw-Hill, 2005). Also see virtually any marketing textbook for similar layouts.
36. Laura Tiffany, "How to Create a Marketing Plan," *Entrepreneur,* August 7, 2001, http://www.entrepreneur.com/article/0,4621, 291706,00.html.
37. Larry Chiagouris and Brant Wansley "Start-Up Marketing," *Marketing Management* 12, no. 5 (September/October 2003), p. 39.
38. Lehman and Winer, op. cit.
39. Gwen Moran, op. cit.
40. Ibid.
41. Mark Henricks, "Change of Face," *Entrepreneur,* April 2000, http://www.entrepreneur.com/article/0,4621,269292.00.html.
42. This marketing plan was written by Shannon Shehee of California State Polytechnic University—Pomona, under the direction of Prof. Susan Peters.

Chapter 13

1. Interview by Richard Green with Tracy Butler, August 2, 2005. S. Dalin, "Brothers' IT Firm was Going Nowhere until Outside Analyst Set it Straight," *St. Louis Post-Dispatch,* http://www.stltoday.com/stltoday/business/stories.nsf/smallbusiness/story/E689F0D55F363DAD86257019008232887OpenDocument (June 07, 2005). M. Sorrell, "Butler's Acropolis a Rising Star in Computer Industry," *St. Louis Biz Journal,* July 18, 2003, http://stlouis.bizjournals.com/stlouis/stories/2003/07/21/focus18.html.
2. This is a loose interpretation of the bases for accounting. The definitive explanation is found in the FASB's Statements of Financial Accounting Concepts, numbers 1 through 7. Available in pdf format at http://www.fasb.org/st/#cons.
3. A complete description of the quality of financial accounting information is presented in Concepts Statement No. 2, "Qualitative Characteristics of Accounting Information." Available in pdf format at http://www.fasb.org/st/#cons.
4. It is common for these statements to be presented as only three separate documents by combining the statements of retained earnings and owners' equity into the equity section of the balance sheet. Regardless of whether they are combined or presented as separate statements, they contain the same information and follow the same general format.
5. An economist defines *income* as a change in wealth. This implies, for example, that if a business purchased a plot of land some time ago for $100,000, and today, because of the development of adjacent property, several potential buyers each offered to pay $200,000 to purchase the land, then the business has income equal to the $100,000 increase in the value of the real estate. Accounting does not, however, recognize as income the increase in wealth caused by the increase in value of the land. If, and only if, the land is sold to an outside party will the increase in value be recognized as income in the accounting statements. For accounting purposes, income, gains, expenses, and losses are recognized only when a transaction takes place between nonrelated entities.
6. An economist would say that it is converted without facing any discount from the true economic value of the asset.
7. C. Koornhof, "Accounting Information on Flexibility," Dissertation, University of Pretoria, 1997.
8. Technically, owners are insiders. However, absentee owners often have little, if any, access to the financial records of small businesses. Thus they are listed as outside investors for the purposes of using financial accounting statements for disclosure.
9. S. Holmes and D. Nicholls, "An Analysis of the Use of Accounting Information by Australian Small Business," *Journal of Small Business Management,* April 1988, pp. 57–68.
10. Airlines use "revenue passenger miles" as the measure of output. A revenue passenger mile is one paying passenger being flown one mile. Thus, a 100-seat commuter plane that flies 600 miles will produce 60,000 revenue passenger miles if full, but zero revenue passenger miles if empty.
11. R. C. Cressy, "Small Business Failure: Failure to Fund or Failure to Learn?" in Z. Acs, B. Karlsson, and C. Karlsson (eds.), *Entrepreneurship, Small and Medium Sized Enterprises and the Macro Economy* (Cambridge: Cambridge University Press, 1999), pp. 161–185.
12. C. Bianchi, "Commercial and Financial Policies in Family Firms: The Small Business Growth Management Flight Simulator," *Simulation & Gaming* 31, no. 2 (2000), pp. 197–230.
13. M. J. Peel and J. Bridge, "Planning Business Objectives and Capital Budgeting in Japanese, German and Domestic SMEs: Some Evidence from the UK Manufacturing Sector," *Journal of Small Business and Enterprise Development* 6, no. 4 (2000), pp. 350–365.
14. Dorothy A. Davis, "Internal Controls for the Small Owner-Operated Business," Small Business Institute Directors Association National Meeting, http://www.Sbaer.Uca.Edu/Research/Sbida/1991/Pdf/03.Pdf.
15. R. N. Lussier and S. Pfeifer, "A Cross-National Prediction Model for Business Success," *Journal of Small Business Management* 39, no. 3 (2001), pp. 228–239.
16. M. J. Peel, "Timeliness of Private Company Accounts and Predicting Corporate Failure," *The Investment Analyst: The Journal of the Society of Investment Analysts,* no. 83, pp. 23–27.
17. This definition is deliberately simple. The analysis as presented overstates both the price variance and the efficiency variance by ignoring the common variance. In practice this analysis is sufficient for all but the most sophisticated cost analysis systems.
18. H. A. Simon, "Rational Decision Making in Business Organizations," in L. Green and J. H. Kagel (eds.), *Advances in Behavioral Economics,* vol. 1 (Norwood, NJ: Ablex, 1987), pp. 18–47.
19. In practice, an outsourcing decision should not be made based solely on a financial analysis. Multiple factors, especially the effect upon the strategy of the business should be considered. See J. Bowles, "Outsourcing for Competitive Advantage," *Forbes,* June 7, 2004, p. 101.

Chapter 14

1. This follows some popular advice on managing cash flow using credit, see Doug Hood, "Can't Go With the Flow? Simple Solutions for Winning the Cash-Flow Battle," *Entrepreneur,* August 2001, http://www.entrepreneur.com/article/0,4621,291139,00.html.
2. Michael Selz, "Seasonal Business Struggles To Refinance Its Debt," *Wall Street Journal Startup Journal,* http://www.startupjournal.comfinancing/credit/200002290929-selz.html. Dwight B. Crane and Penny Joseph, "Be Our Guest, Inc." (Boston: Harvard Business School Publishing, 1999). Be Our Guest Web site http://www.beourguestpartyrental.com.
3. NFIB Educational Foundation, *National Small Business Poll: The Cash Flow Problem,* Washington, DC, 2001.
4. NFIB Education Foundation, "Business Starts and Stops" (Washington, DC: NFIB Education Foundation, 1999).
5. Evan Smith, "John Mackey," *Texas Monthly* 33, no. 3 (2005), pp. 122–132.
6. Federal Reserve Bank of Dallas, *Money, Banking and Monetary Policy,* 1995, p. 1.
7. In case the term is new to you, it comes from Joseph Heller's 1961 classic book (and 1970 movie) of the same name. It means that the situation is hopeless no matter what you do.
8. If you're interested, look at the 1998 Survey of Small Business Finance, which is conducted every five years. See "Financing Patterns of Small Firms: Findings from the 1998 Survey of Small Business Finance," done by the Federal Reserve and stored by the SBA at: http://www.sba.gov/advo/stats/ssbf_98.pdf. A particularly interesting look at financing (especially self-financing) comes from Charles Ou and George W. Haynes, "Uses of Equity Capital by Small Firms—Findings from the Surveys of Small Business Finances (for 1993 & 1998)," Paper presented at the Academy of Entrepreneurial Finance 14th International Conference, April 30–May 2, 2003, Chicago, Illinois.
9. http://www.startupjournal.com/financing/credit/20011005-clark.html; http://www.babyeinstein.com/B2C/about_founder_F32.shtml; http://www.usatoday.com/life/2002/2002-06-25-baby-genius.htm.
10. http://business.uschamber.com/P14/P14_1105.asp.
11. Paul Deceglie, "Fun with Funding: If You Left Your Creativity Somewhere with Your Coloring Books, You're Not Ready to Find Financing in the Post-Dot-com Era," *Entrepreneur,* BizOpp Zone, September 14, 2001, http://www.Entrepreneur.com/article/0,4621,292986,00.html. John F. Dalrymple, *International Business Profile Benchmarking for the SME Sector-Does it Work?* (RMIT University, Centre for Quality Management Research, 2001), http://www.cmqr.rmit.edu.au/publications/jdimprov.pdf. S. Mian and C. Smith, "Accounts Receivable Management Policy: Theory and Evidence," *Journal of Finance* 47 (1992), pp. 169–200.

12. Jonathan A. Scott and Morris G. Danielson, "Bank Loan Availability and Trade Credit Demand," *The Financial Review* 39 (2004), pp. 579–600, http://www.blackwell-synergy.com/links/doi/10.1111/j.07328516.2004.00089.x/pdf. A. N. Berger and G. F. Udell, "Small Business Credit Availability and Relationship Lending: The Importance of Bank Organizational Structure," *Economic Journal* 112 (2002), pp. 32–53.
13. Judy Gedge, "Does Your Collections System Need a Checkup?" *Entrepreneur,* March 29, 2004, http://www.Entrepreneur.com/article/0,4621,314904,00.html. Paul DeCeglie, "Gimme My Money: Steps You Can Take to Collect on Past Due Accounts Receivable," *Business Start-Ups,* August 2000, http://www.entrepreneur.com/mag/article/0,1539,277364,00.html. W. Lim and M. Rashid, "An Operational Theory Integrating Cash Discount and Product Pricing Policies," *Journal of American Academy of Business* 2(2002), pp. 282–288. W. Beranek, "Behavioral Relations, Operating Factors and the Optimal Cash Discount," the 7th International Symposium on Cash, Treasury and Working Capital Management, Chicago, October 1991.
14. See G. Udell, *Asset-Based Finance* (New York: The Commercial Finance Association, 2004); A. N. Berger and G. F. Udell, "Small Business and Debt Finance," in Zoltan J. Acs and David B. Audretsch (eds.), *Handbook of Entrepreneurship* (Norwell, MA: Kluwer Academic Publishing, 2003); M. R. Bakker, L. Klapper, and G. F. Udell, "The Role of Factoring in Commercial Finance: The Case of Eastern Europe," Working Paper, 2004.
15. See Mie-Yun Lee, "Factor Your Receivables for More Cash: Need a Quick Cash Infusion? A Factoring Service Can Help You Out," *Entrepreneur,* June 03, 2002, http://www.entrepreneur.com/article/0,4621,300447,00.html. Jan Norman, "How to Factor: Get Money to Grow!" *Business Start-Ups,* November 1998, http://www.entrepreneur.com/article/0,4621,229452,00.html.
16. One other approach is called *activity-based costing* (or ABC), which looks at which services, products, or internal operations add to your profits or add to your costs. It is used most often for companies with several different types of products, services, or markets and can help you pare down to those things that can truly make a positive difference in your bottom line. For an introduction, see Mark Henricks, "Beneath The Surface: Suspicious Not All Areas of Your Company Are Bringing in a Profit? Break It Down with Activity-Based Costing," *Entrepreneur,* October 1999, http://www.Entrepreneur.com/article/0,4621,230997,00.html.
17. For some other ideas, look at Jan Norman, "How to Manage Your Cash Flow: You're Making Sales, But Are You Making Money?" *Business Start-Ups,* June 1998, http://www.Entrepreneur.com/article/0,4621,228680,00.html.
18. Nancy R. Lockwood, "Work-Life Balance: Challenges and Solutions," Society for Human Resource Management, *2003 SHRM Research Quarterly,* 2003, http://www.ispi.org/pdf/suggestedReading/11_Lockwood_WorkLifeBalance.pdf. Aubrey C. Daniels, "Choosing an Employee Incentive Program: With So Many Choices Out There, How Do You Pick the Best One for Your Business?" *Entrepreneur,* September 02, 2002, http://www.entrepreneur.com/article/0,4621,302766,00.html. G. A. Marken, "Ten Low-Cost Steps to Keep Employees from Job Hunting," *Water Quality Products* 7, no. 4 (April 2002), http://www.wwdmag.com/wwd/index.cfm/powergrid/rfah=%7Ccfap=/CFID/2522697/CFTKEN/34858572/fuseaction/showArticle/articleID/3032. Marvin Collins, *The Human Use of Human Resources* (New York: McGraw Hill, 1981).
19. Mark Henricks, "Trading Up: No Cash? No Problem," *Entrepreneur's Be Your Own Boss,* February 2005, http://www.entrepreneur.com/article/0,4621,319918,00.html. Kirk Whisler and Nichole Torres, "Barter to the Cause: Does Cutting Costs Sound Like a Good Start-Up Idea?" *Entrepreneur,* October 2002, http://www.entrepreneur.com/article/0,4621,303206,00.html. Kurt J. Samson, "Better Business? Think Barter Business Why Trading for Products and Services Makes Great Financial Sense," *Home Office,* August 1999, http://www.entrepreneur.com/mag/article/0,1539, 270309,00.html.
20. See C. O'Gorman. "The Sustainability of Growth in Small- and Medium-Sized Enterprises," *International Journal of Entrepreneurial Behaviour and Research* 7, no. 2 (February 2001), pp. 60–75. Kevin Mole, "Business Advice to Fast Growth Small Firms" (Telford: University of Wolverhampton, 1999), http://mubs.mdx.ac.uk/research/Discussion_Papers/Business_and_Management/dpapmsno_4.pdf.

Chapter 15

1. Certainly, these investment vehicles are not truly risk-free. At the minimum, they have term risk. A full discussion of the elements of investment is far beyond the scope of this text.
2. The actual annual effective interest rate is 22.47 percent.

$$r = \left[\frac{fv}{c}\right]^{\frac{1}{n}} - 1 \quad r = (150{,}000/100{,}000)^{1/2} - 1 \quad r = 0.224745$$

3. Rendering is the process of converting dead animals into usable fats and protein.
4. J. A. Katz, "Modelling Entrepreneurial Career Progressions: Concepts and Considerations," *Entrepreneurship: Theory and Practice.* 19, no. 2 (Winter 1994), pp. 23–40. J. A. Katz, "A Psychosocial Cognitive Model of Employment Status Choice," *Entrepreneurship: Theory and Practice* 17, no. 1 (1992), pp. 29–37. J. A. Katz, "Secondary Analysis in Entrepreneurship: An Introduction to Data Bases and Data Management," *Journal of Small Business Management* 30, no. 20 (1992), pp. 74–86.
5. Crystal Detamore-Rodman, "The Search Is On: Entrepreneurs and Experts All Agree: If You're Willing to Hunt Around, You Can Score Financing to Get Your Homebased Business Off the Ground," *Entrepreneur's Be Your Own Boss,* June 2003, http://www.entrepreneur.com/article/0,4621,308997,00.html. Cliff Ennico, "Accepting Money from Friends & Family: 4 Ways to Get Your Cash without Wreaking Havoc on Your Personal Relationships," Entrepreneur.com—*Money & Finance,* May 06, 2002, http://www.entrepreneur.com/article/0,4621,299420,00.html. Stever Robbins, "Asking Friends and Family for Financing: Heed our Warnings before You Play This Dangerous Game," *Entrepreneur,* October 01, 2001, http://www.entrepreneur.com/article/0,4621,293174,00.html.
6. Actually, Freud most likely never made this statement; however, it has entered popular folklore and is usually attributed to him.
7. R. Cialdini, *Influence: The Psychology of Persuasion* (New York: William Morrow and Company, 1993).
8. A. Komter and W. Vollebergh, "Gift-Giving and the Emotional Significance of Family and Friends," *Journal of Marriage and the Family* 59, no. 3 (August 1997), pp. 747–757.
9. C. Ou and G. W. Haynes, "Uses of Equity Capital by Small Firms—Findings from the Surveys of Small Business Finances (for 1993 & 1998)," presented at the 14th Annual Conference on Entrepreneurial Finance and Business Ventures at the De Paul University Chicago, Illinois, on April 30–May 2, 2003, http://www.sba.gov/advo/stats/wkp03co.pdf.
10. R. Pettit and R. Singer, "Small Business Finance: A Research Agenda," *Financial Management,* Autumn 1985, pp. 47–60.
11. Ou and Haynes, op. cit.
12. Michael Stouder and Bruce Kirchhoff, "Funding the First Year of Business," in William B. Gartner, Kelly G. Shaver, Nancy M. Carter, and Paul D. Reynolds (eds.), *Handbook of Entrepreneurial Dynamics: The Process of Business Creation* (Thousand Oaks, CA: Sage, 2004).
13. U.S. Securities and Exchange Commission, "Accredited Investors," Securities and Exchange Commission Web Site, July 10, 2000, http://www.sec.gov/answers/accred.htm, accessed June 16, 2007.
14. Dirk De Clercq, Vance Fried, Oskari Lehtonen, and Harry J. Sapienza, "An Entrepreneur's Guide to the Venture Capital Galaxy," *The Academy of*

Management Perspectives, 20 (2006), pp. 90–112. Julian Lange, Benoit LeLeux, and Brenard Surlemont, "Angel Networks for the 21st Century: Best Practices in Europe and the US," D. Cetindamar (ed.), *The Growth of Venture Capital: A Cross-Cultural Comparison* (Greenwood Publishing Group, Quorum Press, 2002). Lloyd Steier and Royston Greenwood, "Newly Created Firms and Informal Angel Investors: A Four-Stage Model of Network Development," *Venture Capital—An International Journal of Entrepreneurial Finance* 1, no. 2 (April 1999), pp. 147–167.

15. James C. Brau and Jerome S. Osteryoung, "The Determinants of Successful Micro-IPOs: An Analysis of Issues Made Under the Small Corporate Offering Registration (SCOR) Procedure," *Journal of Small Business Management, 39*, 3, July 2001, pp. 209–227. "Direct Public Offering—DPO," Answers.com. Investopedia, Investopedia Inc. 2000. http://www.answers.com/topic/direct-public-offering-dpo, accessed June 16, 2007. North American Securities Administrators Association, *Directory of Securities Laws and Regulations*, NASAA, 2007, http://www.nasaa.org/Industry_Regulatory_Resources/Directory_of_Securities_Laws_Regulations/, accessed June 16, 2007. Regulation D Resources Enterprises, Inc. Web site, 2007, www.regdresources.com accessed June 16, 2007. U.S. Securities and Exchange Commission, "Q&A: Small Business and the SEC," Securities and Exchange Commission Web site, May 24, 2006, http://www.sec.gov/info/smallbus/qasbsec.htm, accessed June 16, 2007. U.S. Securities and Exchange Commission, "Microcap Stock: A Guide for Investors," Securities and Exchange Commission Web site, February 22, 2006, http://www.sec.gov/investor/pubs/microcapstock.htm, accessed June 16, 2007. David E. Vance, *Raising Capital* (New York, NY: Springer, 2005).

Chapter 16

1. B. Cummings, "They Even Stole a Backhoe in Broad Daylight," *The New York Times*, January 6, 2005.
2. C. D. Bader, "Construction Equipment Theft: A Billion-Dollar Problem," *Grading & Excavation Contractor*, November/December 2004.
3. Cummings, op. cit.
4. http://www.pprhealthcare.com/index.shtml.
5. REL's Annual Working Capital surveys, 2004, http://www.relconsult.com/website/website.nsf/Articles/.
6. Ellyn Spragins, "Get Paid First!" *Fortune Small Business* 15, no. 1 (February 2005), p. 85.
7. Rieva Lesonsky, "Inventory Control: When It Comes to Inventory, the Key Is Striking a Balance between Too Little and Too Much," *Entrepreneur*, 1998, http://www.entrepreneur.com/article/0,4621,265105,00.html.
8. Gwen Moran, "Cover Your Bases: If You Thought Database Marketing Was Just Wasting Your Time with Fliers and Mailing Lists, Take Another Look—at the Net," *Entrepreneur*, February 2000, http://www.Entrepreneur.com/article/0,4621,232630,00.html.
9. "Dell Does What Others Have Given Up," *Forbes World Media Digest*, 2005, http://Forbes.com/technology.
10. Mike Hogan, "The Outer Limits: With Larger PC-Makers Struggling, Why Is Alienware Doing So Well?" *Entrepreneur*, March 2005, http://www.Entrepreneur.com/article/0,4621,320044,00.html. "Cutting the Edge Hardware," interview with Alex Aguila, http://www.ownt.com/hardware/interviews/2003/alienware/alienware.shtm. Ed Duggan, "Alienware, a Miami Computer Maker, Could Top Sales of $50 million," *South Florida Business Journal*, August 16, 2002, http://www.bizjournals.com/southflorida/ stories/2002/08/19/smallb1.html?t5printable.
11. Jerome A. Katz, Scott R. Safranski, and Omar Khan, "Virtual Instant Global Entrepreneurship: Cybermediation for Born International Service Firms," *Journal of International Entrepreneurship* 1, no. 1 (March 2003), pp. 43–57.
12. Stephen Barlas, "Industrial Cleanser: The EPA Is Targeting Small Business for Pollution Cleanup," *Entrepreneur*, January 2000, http://www.Entrepreneur.com/article/0,4621,232505,00.html.
13. Amanda C. Kooser, "Who's Paying for Computer Recycling: The Newest Standard for Modems," *Entrepreneur*, August 2, 2002, http://www.Entrepreneur.com/article/0,4621,301626,00.html.
14. Because depreciation is a noncash expense, it causes net operating profit to be an amount less than net cash inflows, all other things being equal. (Refer to Chapter 13 "Accounting for Small Business" for a more complete discussion of depreciation.)
15. David A. Kirby and Stefan Kaiser, "Joint Ventures as an Internationalisation Strategy for SMEs," *Small Business Economics* 21, no. 3 (Spring 2003), pp. 229–242. Marc J. Dollinger, Peggy A. Golden, and Todd Saxton, "The Effect of Reputation on the Decision to Joint Venture," *Strategic Management Journal* 18, no. 2 (1997), pp. 127–140.
16. There is a caveat if you use Excel, however. The built-in net present value function of Excel does not provide for time period 0. Therefore, you must calculate the present value of the cash flows of periods 1, 2, 3, . . . , *n* and then add the initial negative investment cash flow to the number provided by the Excel function.
17. Stever Robbins, "How Much Is This Business Worth? If You're Interested in Purchasing an Existing Business, Here Are a Few Ways to Gauge Its Value," *Entrepreneur*, January 12, 2004, http://www.Entrepreneur.com/article/0,4621,312644,00.html.

Chapter 17

1. K. Kline, "No More Brush-Offs for This Crew," *BusinessWeek*, October 29, 2003.
2. Financial risk is discussed in detail in Chapter 15, "Small Business Finance."
3. Doris A. Christopher, "Small Business Pilfering: The "trusted" Employee(s)," *Business Ethics: A European Review* 12, no 3 (2003), pp. 284–297. Note that there is a lot of disagreement on how much theft there is. In an SBA-sponsored survey, only 2 percent of small businesses reported employee theft in the prior year, but it is better to be safe than sorry. The SBA study was Bonnie Fisher, "Small Businesses, Big Burdens: The Nature and Incidence of Crime within and against Small Business and Its Customers and Employees, Their Causes, Their Effects, and Their Prevention," Washington: U.S. Small Business Administration, Office of Advocacy Research Report no 176. March 1997, http://www.sba.gov/advo/ research/rs176.pdf.
4. Anita Dennis, "The Downside of Good Times," *Journal of Accountancy* 190, no. 5 (2002), pp. 53–55. Neil H. Snyder, O. Whitfield Broome, and Karen Zimmerman, "Using Internal Controls to Reduce Employee Theft in Small Businesses," *Journal of Small Business Management* 27, no. 3 (July 1989), pp. 48–55.
5. Thomas M. Sullivan, "Closing the Tax Gap and the Impact on Small Business," Testimony of the Chief Counsel for Advocacy to the U.S. House of Representatives, Committee on Small Business, April 27, 2005, http://www.sba.gov/advo/laws/test05_0427.html. W. M. Crain and T. D. Hopkins, "The Impact of Regulatory Costs on Small Firms," U.S. Small Business Administration, Office of Advocacy (SBAHQ-00-R-0027), October 2001, http://www.sba.gov/advo/research/rs207tot.pdf.
6. 42 USC Pub. L. 88-352, Title VII, Sec. 701 (b).
7. Except industries in SIC codes 55–69, 71–74, and 81–89.
8. M. Johnson, *Make Them Go Away: Clint Eastwood, Christopher Reeve and the Case against Disability Rights* (Louisville, KY: Advocado Press, 2003). K. Wexler, "Big Winners in Disabled Crusade? Lawyers," *St.Petersburg Times*, March 24, 2002. *Newsweek*, U.S. Edition: *Perspectives*, May 29, 2000. J. Vandehei, "Clint Eastwood Saddles Up for Disability-Act Showdown," *The Wall Street Journal*, May 9, 2000. B. Van Voris, "South Florida's ADA Industry," *National Law Journal*, July 9, 2000.
9. General Aviation Revitalization Act (GARA), 1994.
10. Gene Gable (ed.), "Heavy Metal Madness: Put on a Happy Face!" *Creativepro.com*, April 22, 2004, http://www.creativepro.com/story/

feature/21223.html. See also Yahoo's answer at http://ask.yahoo.com/ask/ 20011213.html, and the international angle on the "smiley face" story at http://www.goodbyemag.com/apr01/ball.html.

11. Separation of duties is discussed more fully in Chapter 16, "Assets: Inventory and Operations Management."
12. R. Hollinger, "National Retail Security Survey Final Report," University of Florida, 2001.
13. J. Wells, "2004 Report to the Nation on Occupational Fraud and Abuse," Association of Certified Fraud Examiners, Austin, TX, 2004, http://www.cfenet.com.
14. Thomas M. Sullivan, "Closing the Tax Gap and the Impact on Small Business," Testimony of the Chief Counsel for Advocacy to the U.S. House of Representatives, Committee on Small Business, April 27, 2005, http://www.sba.gov/advo/laws/test05_0427.html.
15. Leo Standora, "Heidi Has a Leg Up—$2m Insurance!" *New York Daily News*, September 7, 2004, p. 3.
16. Ibid.
17. Ibid.
18. U.S. Consumer Product Safety Commission, "Amusement Ride-Related Injuries and Deaths in the United States: 1987–2000," Bethesda, MD, 2001.
19. The Outdoor Amusement Association Web Site, November 27, 2004, http://www.oaba.org/facts2.htm/.
20. M. Holmer, "The Value of Social Security Disability Insurance," Public Policy Institute of AARP, Washington, DC, 2001.
21. T. Zayatz, "Social Security Disability Insurance Program Worker Experience: Actuarial Study No. 114," Social Security Administration, Washington, DC, 1999.

Chapter 18

1. This article is based on: Randall Roberts, "B-Money in the Bank: St. Louis Native B-Money Is Hanging with Rap's Heavy Hitters," *Riverfront Times*, December 6 2006 (St. Louis), http://www.riverfronttimes.com/2006-12-06/music/b-money-in-the-bank/. All quotes come from this article and are used with permission. Kevin C. Johnson, "St. Louisan Wins Grammy for Work with Beyonce," St. Louis *Post-Dispatch*, 02/22/2007, http://www.stltoday.com/stltoday/entertainment/columnists.nsf/kevinjohnson/story/6E9B89B710A94682862572880082B63D?OpenDocument. Randall Roberts, "STLOG: B-Money's Beat Kicks Off the New Jay-Z," Nov. 21, 2006 at 12:01:04 PM, http://blogs.riverfronttimes.com/stlog/2006/11/bmoneys_beat_kicks_off_the_new.php.
2. Robert A. Kagan, "On Surveying the Whole Legal Forest," *Law and Social Inquiry*, vol. 28, 2003, pp. 833–872, http://www.journals.uchicago.edu/cgi-bin/resolve?id=doi:10.1086/380082&erFrom=445040558813465220Guest. Christian Wollschlager, "Exploring the Global Landscapes of Litigation Rates," in Jürgen Brand and Dieter Stempel (eds.), Soziologie des Rechts: Fetschrift fur Erhard Blankenburg zum 60, Geburtstag. (Baden-Baden, Germany: Nomos Berlagsgesellschaft, 1998), pp. 587–88.
3. Pamela Rohland, "Follow Suit: What to Do when You Get Sued," *Entrepreneur—Business Start-Ups*, April 2000, http://www.Entrepreneur.com/ article/0,4621,269539,00.html.
4. Cliff Ennico, "How to Hire an Attorney: Hiring a Good Lawyer Is Crucial to Any Successful Business," *Entrepreneur*, January 20, 2003, http://www.Entrepreneur.com/article/0,4621,305623,00.html.
5. Karen E. Spaeder, "Is Your Home Zoned for Business? How to Research, Comply with and Change Local Zoning Laws in Your Home-Based Business's Favor," *Entrepreneur—Home Office*, January 26, 2004, http://www.Entrepreneur.com/article/0, 4621,313950,00.html.
6. Christopher L. Hansen, "Special Report: Home-Based Zoning: What Issues Are at Stake for Homebased Businesses Fighting Zoning Ordinances?" *Entrepreneur—Home Office*, January 1, 2001, http://www.entrepreneur.com/article/0,4621,285818,00.html. Laura Tiffany, "Zoning: Home Is Where the Business Is, and It's Also Where a Lot of Regulations Are," *Entrepreneur—Home Office*, March 21, 2001, http://www.Entrepreneur.com/ article/ 0,4621,287928,00.html.
7. "The Basics of Sole Proprietorships: Chances Are, You're Already Running a Sole Proprietorship," *Entrepreneur*, May 12, 2005, http://www.Entrepreneur.com/article/0,4621,321392,00.html.
8. These tips are adapted from Asheesh Advani, "Negotiation Tips for Start-Ups: Follow These Suggestions for Negotiating with Employees, Investors and Suppliers When Your Business Has No Revenue," *Entrepreneur*, April 4, 2005, http://www.Entrepreneur.com/article/0,4621,320642,00.html. Max H. Bazerman, "Creating Value, Weighing Values," *Negotiation*, April 2005, pp. 3–5. Tony Parinello, "Dealmaking Basics: Tips for Negotiating Your Way to a Smooth Sale," *Entrepreneur*, May 12, 2003, http:// www.Entrepreneur.com/article/0,4621,308526,00.html. Sean Silverthorne, "Five Questions for Max Bazerman," *HBS Working Knowledge*, September 4, 2001, http://hbswk.hbs.edu/item.jhtml?id=2472&t=negotiation&noseek=one. Max H. Bazerman and James J. Gillespie, "Betting on the Future: The Virtues of Contingent Contracts," *Harvard Business Review* 77, no. 5 (September/October 1999), pp. 155–160.
9. This is a variation of the idea of "tit for tat," where two parties immediately achieve balance.
10. Robert Axelrod, *The Evolution of Cooperation* (New York: Basic Books, 1984). See also the Evolution of Cooperation Web site at http://pscs.physics.lsa.umich.edu/Software/CC/ECHome.html. For a business-oriented approach, consider looking at John Stewart, *Evolution's Arrow: The Direction of Evolution and the Future of Humanity* (Steamboat Springs, CO: Chapman Press, 2000). The entire text is available for a free download at http://users.tpg.com.au/users/jes999/index.htm.
11. The key books on negotiating come from the Program on Negotiating at Harvard Law School (http://www.pon.harvard.edu/main/home/index.php3). They are R. Fisher, W. Ury, and B. Patton, *Getting to Yes: Negotiating without Giving In* (New York: Penguin Books, 1991): and W. Ury, *Getting Past No: Negotiating Your Way from Confrontation to Cooperation* (New York: Bantam Books, 1993). Another book you might find useful for working with very problematic types is R. M. Bramson, *Coping with Difficult People* (New York: Dell, 1981).
12. Internal Revenue Service, "Independent Contractor (Self-Employed) or Employee?" Internal Revenue Service, June 15, 2009, July 17, 2009, http://www.irs.gov/businesses/small/article/0,,id=99921,00.html.
13. Steven C. Bahls and Jane Easter Bahls, "RA-A-A-ID! Creepy Competitors Raiding Your Work Force? The Law Can Be the Perfect Bug Spray," *Entrepreneur*, September 2000, http://www.Entrepreneur.com/article/0,4621,278653,00.html.
14. Chris Kelleher, "5 Litigation Secrets: These Tips May Keep Your Business Out of Court—or Possibly Help You Win if You Get There," *Entrepreneur*, July 12, 2004, http://www.entrepreneur.com/article/0,4621, 316368,00.html.
15. David Rountree, "Head Over Heels: Former Auburn Gymnast and Husband Turn Her Talent into Success," *Birmingham Business Journal*, June 6, 2005, http://birmingham.bizjournals.com/birmingham/stories/2005/ 06/06/smallb1.html.
16. W. Michael Hoffman, Laura P. Hartman, and Mark Rowe, "You've Got Mail . . . and the Boss Knows: A Survey by the Center for Business Ethics of Companies' Email and Internet Monitoring," *Business and Society Review* 108, no. 3 (2003), pp. 285–307. American Marketing Association with the ePolicy Institute and Clearswift, *2003 E-Mail Rules, Policies and Practices Survey* (New York: American Marketing Association, 2003), http://www.amanet.org/research/pdfs/Email_Policies_Practices.pdf. Robert McGarvey, "Watch and Learn . . . or Watch and Feel Like a Slimy Interloper," *Entrepreneur*, December 2000, http://www.Entrepreneur.com/ article/0,4621,283614,00.html.

17. Chris Kelleher, "How to Protect Your Business's Trade Secrets: These Five Rules Will Help Safeguard Some of Your Company's Most Important Assets," *Entrepreneur,* May 1, 2005, http://www.entrepreneur.com/article/ 0,4621,321263,00.html.
18. Jane Easter Bahls, "The Name Game: You Can Shield Your Trade Name from Being Ripped Off by a Larger Company—If It's Distinctive Enough," *Entrepreneur,* January 2005, http://www.Entrepreneur.com/article/0,4621,318885,00.html. "The Source of the Nile(s):Trademark Law's Personal Name Rule Shows Flexibility," *Ideas on Intellectual Property Law* (Manchester, NH: McLane Intellectual Property Practice Group, October/November 2004), pp. 2–3. Eugene R. Quinn, Jr., *Beanie Babies Trademark Infringement?* (Albany NY: Hiscock & Barclay, LLP, 2004), http://www.hiscockbarclay.com/pdf/IPnewsletter_hb_0504.pdf.

Chapter 19

1. Talicia A. Flint, "Employees vs. Contractors Who Are the Best Players for Your Team?" HomeOfficeMag.com, May 2001, http://www.entrepreneur.com/mag/article/0,1539,289098,00.html.
2. U.S. Small Business Administration Office of Advocacy, "Private Firms, Establishments, Employment, Annual Payroll and Receipts by Firm Size, 1988–2004," Office of Advocacy–Firm Size Data: Statistics of U.S. Businesses and Nonemployer Statistics–U.S. Data—Classified By Employment Size of Firms—Totals, 1988–2004, n.d., http://www.sba.gov/advo/research/us88_04.pdf.
3. B. A. Kirchhoff, *Entrepreneurship and Dynamic Capitalism* (Westport, CT: Quorum Books, 1994). B. Phillips and B. A. Kirchhoff, "Formation, Growth and Survival Small Firm Dynamics in the U.S. Economy," *Small Business Economics* 1 (1989), pp. 65–74. D. Birch, *Job Creation in America* (New York: Free Press, 1987).
4. Joanna L. Krotz, "5 Tips for Hiring Your First Employee," Microsoft Small Business Center (2005). http://www.microsoft.com/smallbusiness/issues/management/recruiting_Staffing/5_tips_for_hiring_your_first_employee.mspx.
5. Ibid.
6. Gideon D. Markman and Robert A. Baron, "Individual Differences and the Pursuit of New Ventures: A Model of Person-Entrepreneurship Fit," in Jerome A. Katz and Theresa M. Welbourne (eds.), *Advances in Entrepreneurship, Firm Emergence and Growth,* vol. 5 (Oxford: JAI/Elsevier, 2002), pp. 23–54.
7. Allbusiness.com, "Is Employee Probation a Good Idea?" Allbusiness.com (2005), http://www.allbusiness.com/articles/EmploymentHR/749-33-1817.html. Wayne F. Cascio and Herman Aguinis, "Chapter 3: Staffing Twenty-First–Century Organizations," *Academy of Management Annals* 2, no. 1 (2008), pp. 133–165.
8. Krotz. "5 Tips for Hiring Your First Employee," op. cit.
9. Joanna L. Krotz, "Are You a Control Freak? 5 Ways to Stop," Microsoft Small Business Center (2005). http://www.microsoft.com/smallbusiness/issues/management/leadership_training/are_you_a_control_freak_5_ways_to_stop.mspx.
10. Ian O. Williamson, Daniel M. Cable, and Howard E. Aldrich, "Smaller but Not Necessarily Weaker: How Small Businesses Can Overcome Barriers to Recruitment. Managing People in Entrepreneurial Organizations," *Advances in the Study of Entrepreneurship Firm Emergence and Growth,* vol. 5 (Greenwich, CT: JAI Press, 2002), pp. 83–106.
11. Jeff Taylor, "A Monster Success," *The Economist* 307, no. 8368 (March 27, 2004), p. 66.
12. Chris Penttila, "How Embarrassing! Highly Publicized Dry Spells Are Poor Recruiting Tools," *Entrepreneur,* August 2002, p. 66.
13. Dale Duncan and Peter Hausdorf, "Firm Size and Internet Recruiting in Canada," *Journal of Small Business Management* 42, no. 3 (July 2004), p. 325.
14. Businesstown.com, "Hiring Top Performers," Businesstown.com (undated), http://www.businesstown.com/hiring/hiring-top.asp, adapted from Bob Adams and Peter Veruki, *Adams Streetwise Hiring Top Performers: 600 Ready-to-Ask Interview Questions and Everything Else You Need to Hire Right* (Cincinnati: Adams Media Corporation, 1997).
15. Joanna L. Krotz, "Tips for Outsourcing Your Small-Business Needs," Microsoft Small Business Center (2005). http://www.microsoft.com/smallbusiness/resources/management/recruiting_staffing/tips_for_outsourcing_your_small_business_needs.mspx.
16. Jerome A. Katz, Scott R. Safranski, and Omar Khan, "Virtual Instant Global Entrepreneurship: Cybermediation for Born International Service Firms," *Journal of International Entrepreneurship* 1 (2003), pp. 43–57. Robyn Greenspan, "Managing Virtual Employees," ecommerce-guide.com, February 28, 2002, //e-commerceguide.com/news/news/article.php/983281.
17. Gisda M. Pedroza, "Hiring Telecommuters, Before You Set Up Employees in Their Own Home Offices, Make Sure You Can Handle the Costs," *Entrepreneur,* January 2002, http://www.Entrepreneur.com/article/0,4621,295960,00.html.
18. Katz, Safranski, and Khan, op. cit. Greenspan, op. cit.
19. The ideas in the following section are from No-Cost Staffing Options on www.toolkit.cch.com.
20. Entrepreneur.com, "How to Write a Job Analysis and Description," *Entrepreneur.com,* October 23, 2002, http://www.entrepreneur.com/article/0,4621,304062,00.html.
21. Chris Kelleher, "Writing Great Job Descriptions," *Entrepreneur,* May 10, 2004, http://www.entrepreneur.com/article/0,4621, 315429,00.html.
22. Wayne F. Cascio and Herman Aguinis, "Chapter 3: Staffing Twenty-First–Century Organizations," *Academy of Management Annals* 2, no. 1 (2008), pp. 133–165. Cascio and Aguinis argue that most studies of selection device effectiveness using actual (vs. adjusted) statistics show results indicating a statistically significant but very small (low-power) improvement in predictive power. Meanwhile, using adjusted results has not been shown to work in real-world selection situations. They contend using *in situ* approaches such as internships and contingent work is the best way to sample. Cascio in earlier works (as well as Schmitt) have pointed out that behavioral interviewing is the next best approach.
23. Alison Doyle, "Behavioral Interview—Behavioral-Based Interviewing." About.com, July 20, 2009, http://jobsearch.about.com/cs/interviews/a/behavioral.htm. Susan M. Heathfield, "Behavioral Interviews: Use Behavioral Interviewing to Select the Best." About.com, July 20, 2009, http://humanresources.about.com/od/interviewing/a/behavior_interv_2.htm. Elaine D. Pulakos and Neal Schmitt, "Experience-Based and Situational Interview Questions: Studies of Validity," *Personnel Psychology* 48, no. 2 (1995), pp. 289–308. U.K. Work Ministry, "Work Ministry—The Interview," Work Ministry, 2004, July 20, 2009, http://www.workministry.com/resources/Interview3.shtml.
24. Adapted from the Mavens and Mogul Web site, http://www.mavensandmoguls.com/, and from Inc Magazine, "Entrepreneur of the Year: The Accidental Entrepreneur—Paige Arnof-Fenn," http://www.inc.com/entrepreneur/profile/index.php? arnof-fenn52.
25. The ideas here are excerpted and adapted from Gary Roberts, Gary Seldon and Carlotta Roberts, "Human Resources Management" Emerging Business Series, Monograph EB-4. (Washington DC: U.S. Small Business Administration, undated), http://www.sba.gov/library/pubs/eb-4.txt.
26. Adapted from "TechScribe Writing," *How to Write Instructions* (Sheffield, South Yorkshire, 2004), http://www.techscribe.co.uk/ta/ how_to_write_instructions.htm.
27. Excerpted from Gary Roberts, Gary Seldon and Carlotta Roberts, "Human Resources Management" Emerging Business Series, Monograph EB-4. (Washington DC: U.S. Small Business Administration, undated), http://www.sba.gov/library/pubs/eb-4.txt.
28. Allbusiness.com, "Secrets of Effective Employee Training." Allbusiness.com (2005). http://www.allbusiness.com/articles/EmploymentHR/1465-33-1817.html.

29. Jill Kickul, "Promises Made, Promises Broken: Employee Attraction and Retention in Small Businesses," *Journal of Small Business Management* 39, no. 4 (2001), pp. 320–335.
30. Adapted from Commerce Clearing House, "Building Employee Involvement," *Business Owners Toolkit* (Riverwoods, IL: Commerce Clearing House, 2005), http://www.toolkit.cch.com/text/P05_7200.asp.
31. Elcha Shain Buckman, "Motivating and Retaining Non-Family Employees in a Family-Owned Business." *The UMASS Family Business Center Online Newsletter* (Hadley, MA: The UMASS Family Business Center, 1998), http://www.umass.edu/fambiz/motivate_key_employees.htm.
32. This well-put concept was contributed by an anonymous user and reviewer of *Entrepreneurial Small Business.*
33. Buckman, op. cit.
34. Building Employees' Involvement, on www.toolkit.cch.com.
35. David Newton, "Of One Mind: Keep Employees by Getting on the Same Page from the Get-Go," *Entrepreneur,* August 2003, p. 23. http://www.entrepreneur.com/mag/article/0,1539,309926,00.html.
36. Alison Stein Wellner, "What Makes Employees Want to Stick Around?" *BusinessWeek,* March 2000, 3.20.00. http://www.businessweek.com/smallbiz/content/mar2000/sb000320a.htm.
37. Peter L. Allen, "Performance Appraisal Question and Answer Book," *Harvard Management Communication Letter* 6, no. 3 (March 2003), p. 3.
38. BizHelp23.com, "Employee Appraisal." *BizHelp23.com* (Sheffield, UK: BizHelp24.com, 2005), http://www.bizhelp24.com/personaldevelopment/employee_appraisal.shtml.
39. Gina Imperato, "How to Give Good Feedback," *Fast Company,* September 17, 1998, p. 144.
40. Allbusiness.com, "Making Performance Appraisals Work," Allbusiness.com (2005), http://www.allbusiness.com/articles/content/1383-33-1817.html.
41. David G. Javitch, "By Setting Clear Standards and Involving Employees in the Review Process, Your Entire Company Can Benefit from Formal Appraisals," Entrepreneur.com, April 05, 2004, http://www.entrepreneur.com/article/0,4621,314968,00.html.
42. This section is excerpted from an outstanding description of practical compensation management in small businesses which came from Allbusiness.com, "Key Compensation Components," Allbusiness.com, undated, http://www.allbusiness.com/articles/EmploymentHR/794-33-1773.html.
43. Staff of *Family Business,* "The Power of Base Pay," Inc., October 1999, http://www.inc.com/articles/1999/10/19037.html.
44. Allbusiness.com, "Key Compensation Components," op. cit.
45. Ibid.
46. Ibid.
47. Rich Mintzer. "20 Low-Cost Employee Perks," Entrepreneur.com, December 08, 2006, http://www.entrepreneur.com/humanresources/compensationandbenefits/article171630.html. Entrepreneur.com, "Low-Cost Benefits That'll Make Your Employees Happy," October 23, 2002, http://www.entrepreneur.com/humanresources/compensationandbenefits/article 56492. html. Aliza Pilar Sherman, "How Women Business Owners Reward Their Staff," Entrepreneur, September 2005, http://www.entrepreneur.com/humanresources/managingemployees/motivationandretention/article79320.html.
48. Catherine M. Daily and Marc J. Dollinger, *Alternative Methodologies for Identifying Family—versus Nonfamily-Managed Businesses* (Columbus, Ohio: Max M. Fisher College of Business, Ohio State University, 1994). John Ward and Christina Dolan, "Defining and Describing Family Business Ownership Configurations," *Family Business Review,* 11 (1998), pp. 305–310.
49. Eric Flamholtz and Yvonne Randle, *Growing Pains: How to Make the Transition from an Entrepreneurship to a Professionally Managed Firm* (San Francisco: Jossey-Bass, 2007).
50. Barbara Blouin, Katherine Gibson, and Margaret Kiersted, *The Legacy of Inherited Wealth: Interviews with Heirs* (Halifax, N.S.: Trio Press, 1995). Paul C. Rosenblatt, Leni de Mik, Roxanne arie Anderson, and Patricia A. Johnson, *The Family in Business* (San Francisco: Jossey-Bass Publishers, 1985).
51. Dennis T. Jaffe, *Working with the Ones You Love: Conflict Resolution & Problem Solving Strategies for a Successful Family Business* (Berkeley, CA: Conari Press, 1990). David Javitch, "David Javitch: Employee Management—How to Earn Employees' Respect," Entrepreneur.com, June 02, 2003, http://www.entrepreneur.com/humanresources/employ-eemanagementcolumnistdavidjavitch/article62284.html.
52. Flamholtz and Randle, 2007.
53. Rosenblatt et al., 1985.
54. David Bork, *Family Business, Risky Business: How to Make It Work* (New York, NY: AMACOM, American Management Association, 1986). Gideon Maas and Andre Diederichs, *Manage Family in Your Family Business* (Northcliff, South Africa: Frontrunner, 2007). U.S. Small Business Administration, *Challenges in Managing a Family Business,* Management and Planning Series, Monograph MP-3 (Washington DC: U.S. Small Business Administration, undated), http://www.sba.gov/library/pubs/mp-3.txt. Jeff Wuorio, "How to Fire a Family Member," Microsoft Small Business Center (2005), http://www.microsoft.com/smallbusiness/issues/management/employee_relations/how_to_fire_a_family_member.mspx.
55. Patricia Schiff Estess, "Strictly Business: Taking the Personal out of Personnel Isn't Easy When You're Talking about Family," *Entrepreneur,* January 2002, p. 118, http://www.entrepreneur.com/article/0.4621,232500,00.html.
56. Craig E. Aronoff and John L. Ward, *From Siblings to Cousins: Prospering in the Third Generation and Beyond,* Family Business Leadership *Series,* no. 22 (Marietta, GA: Family Enterprise Publishers, 2007). David Bork, *Family Business, Risky Business: How to Make It Work* (New York, NY: AMACOM, American Management Association, 1986). Eric Flamholtz and Yvonne Randle, *Growing Pains: How to Make the Transition from an Entrepreneurship to a Professionally Managed Firm* (San Francisco: Jossey-Bass, 2007). David G. Javitch, "By Setting Clear Standards and Involving Employees in the Review Process, Your Entire Company Can Benefit from Formal Appraisals," Entrepreneur.com, April 05, 2004, http://www.entrepreneur.com/article/0,4621,314968,00.html. Sandra W. King, George T. Solomon, and Lloyd W. Fernald Jr., "Issues in Growing a Family Business: A Strategic Human Resource Model," *Journal of Small Business Management* 39, no. 1 (January 2001), pp. 3–13. Paul C. Rosenblatt, Leni de Mik, Roxanne arie Anderson, and Patricia A. Johnson, *The Family in Business* (San Francisco: Jossey-Bass Publishers, 1985).
57. Patricia Schiff Estess, "Theory of Un-Relativity: How to Keep Nonfamily Managers Happy in Order to Grow Your Business," *Entrepreneur,* March 1999, www.entrepreneur.com/magazine/entrepreneur/1999/march/17328.html. Patricia Schiff Estess, "Attracting Non-Family Employees: As Appealing as the Cozy Atmosphere of a Family Business May Be, You Can't Beat Incentives for Hooking Good Managers," *Entrepreneur,* December 1999, http://www.entrepreneur.com/magazine/entrepreneur/1999/december/18656.html. Eric Flamholtz and Yvonne Randle, *Growing Pains: How to Make the Transition from an Entrepreneurship to a Professionally Managed Firm* (San Francisco: Jossey-Bass, 2007).
58. Craig E. Aronoff and John L. Ward, *From Siblings to Cousins: Prospering in the Third Generation and Beyond,* Family Business Leadership Series, no. 22 (Marietta, GA: Family Enterprise Publishers, 2007). Dennis T. Jaffe, *Working with the Ones You Love: Conflict Resolution & Problem Solving Strategies for a Successful Family Business* (Berkeley, CA: Conari Press, 1990). Nichole L. Torres, "Family Affair: When Business and Family Mix, the Key to Success Is Communication," *Entrepreneur's Start-Ups,* September 2004, http://www.entrepreneur.com/magazine/entrepreneursstartupsmagazine/2004/september/72314.html. Paul C. Rosenblatt, Leni de Mik, Roxanne arie Anderson, and Patricia A. Johnson, *The Family in Business* (San Francisco: Jossey-Bass Publishers, 1985).

Chapter 20

1. Look at Mark Hendricks, "Stage Right: Make Smarter Management Decisions by Knowing What Stage Your Company's In," *Entrepreneur,* April 1997, http://www.entrepreneur.com/mag/article/0,1539,227098—1-,00.html. The most famous model comes from Larry Greiner "Evolution and Revolution as Organizations Grow," *Harvard Business Review* 76, no. 3 (May 1998); pp. 55–68, a revisiting of Greiner's 1972 *HBR* article of the same name. Neil C. Churchill and Virginia L. Lewis adapted Greiner's model in "The Five Stages of Small Business Growth," *Harvard Business Review,* May–June 1983. A three-stage simplification follows the ideas expressed by Kelin E. Gersick, Ivan Lansberg, Michele Desjardins, and Barbara Dunn, "Stages and Transitions: Managing Change in the Family Business" *Family Business Review* XII no. 4 (1999), pp. 287–297, http://www.lgassoc.com/library/articles/112-Stages&Transitions.pdf; and in their book, Kelin Gersick, John Davis, Marion McCollum Hampton, and Ivan Lansberg, *Generation to Generation: Life Cycles of the Family Business* (Cambridge: Harvard University Press, 1997).
2. The model is derived from four major works on small business life stages: William J. Baumol, "Entrepreneurship in Economic Theory," *American Economic Review,* LVIII, no. 2 (May 1968), pp. 64–71; Gaylen Chandler & Steven H. Hanks, "Market Attractiveness, Resource-Based Capabilities; Venture Strategies and Venture Performance," *Journal of Business Venturing.* 9 no. 4 (1994), pp. 331–349; Neil C. Churchill and Virginia L. Lewis, "The five stages of small business growth," *Harvard Business Review* 61 (June 1983), pp. 30–40; and Jerome Katz and William B. Gartner "Properties of Emerging Organizations," *The Academy of Management Review* 13, no. 3 (July 1988), pp. 429–441.
3. The 7 percent rate comes from Heidi M. Neck, Andrew L. Zacharakis, William D. Bygrave, and Paul D. Reynolds, "Global Entrepreneurship Monitor: National Entrepreneurship Assessment—United States of America," 2002 Executive Report, http://www.gemconsortium.org/download/1061664039492/GEM%20US%202002.pdf. The drop off from those expressing an interest to those taking action comes from J. A. Katz, "Modeling Entrepreneurial Career Progressions: Concepts and Considerations," *Entrepreneurship: Theory & Practice* 19, no. 2 (Winter 1994), pp. 23–40. J. Katz, "Longitudinal Analysis of Entrepreneurial Follow-Through," *Journal of Entrepreneurship and Regional Development* 2, no. 1 (1990), pp. 15–25. Paul D. Reynolds, "Who Starts New Firms? Preliminary Explorations of Firms-in-Gestation," *Small Business Economics* 9 (1997), pp. 449–462.
4. Rieva Lesonsky, "It's Never Too Late," *Entrepreneur,* November 2003, http://www.Entrepreneur.com/article/0,4621,311458,00.html. Jacquelyn Lynn, "Don't Be Afraid: Are You a Big Scaredy-Cat? Here's How to Turn Terror into Super-Confidence," *Entrepreneur,* June 2000, http://www.Entrepreneur.com/article/0,4621,275016,00.html. Rieva Lesonsky, "What's the Big Idea? Start-Up Ideas Are All Around . . . Once You Know Where to Look," *Business Start-Ups,* November 1998, http://www.Entrepreneur.com/article/0,4621,229453,00.html. J. Katz, "Longitudinal Analysis of Entrepreneurial Follow-Through," *Journal of Entrepreneurship and Regional Development* 2, no. 1 (1990), pp. 15–25.
5. D. A. Shepherd and M. Shanley, *New Venture Strategy* (Newbury Park, CA: Sage, 1998). D. A. Shepherd, E. J. Douglas, and M. Shanley, "New Venture Survival: Ignorance, External Shocks, and Risk Reduction Strategies," *Journal of Business Venturing* 15 (2000), pp. 393–410. H. Robert Dodge, Sam Fullerton, and John E. Robbins, "Stage of the Organizational Life Cycle and Competition as Mediators of Problem Perception for Small Businesses," *Strategic Management Journal* 15, no. 2 (February 1994), pp. 121–135.
6. *Simpson's Contemporary Quotations,* compiled by James B. Simpson, 1988. Quoted by Thomas J. Peters and Robert H. Waterman, *In Search of Excellence* (New York: Harper & Row, 1982), http://www.bartleby.com/63/54/2254.html.
7. Mark Henricks, "Staying Power: Zero Defections Strategy Keeps Customers Coming Back," *Entrepreneur,* July 1997, http://www.Entrepreneur.com/article/0,4621,227415,00.html. Frederick F. Reichheld, *The Loyalty Effect, The Hidden Force Behind Growth, Profits, and Lasting Value* (Cambridge: Harvard Business School Press, 1996). Robert C. Blattberg, Gary Getz, and Jacquelyn S. Thomas, *Customer Equity: Building and Managing Relationships as Valuable Assets* (Boston: Harvard Business School Press, 2001). Roland T. Rust and R. L. Oliver, "Should We Delight the Customer," *Journal of The Academy of Marketing Sciences* 28, no.1 (2000), pp. 86–94. Sandy D. Jap, Control Mechanisms and the Relationship Life Cycle: Implications for Safeguarding Specific Investments and Developing Commitment," *Journal of Marketing Research* 37, no. 2 (May 2000), p. 227. F. F. Reichheld and W. E. Sasser, "Zero Defections: Quality Comes to Services," *Harvard Business Review,* 1990, pp. 105–111. R. T. Rust, A. J. Zahorik, and T. L. Keiningham, "Return on Quality (ROQ): Making Service Quality Financially Accountable," *Journal of Marketing* 59 (1995), pp. 58–70. Valarie A. Zeithaml, "Service Quality, Profitability, and The Economic Worth of Customers: What We Know and What We Need to Learn," *Academy of Marketing Science Journal* 28, no. 1 (2000), p. 67.
8. Zig Ziglar, *Zig Ziglar's Secrets of Closing the Sale* (Berkeley Pub Group, 1985). The ideas came from the long out-of-print Australian series, "10 Sales Cassettes by Dr. Joseph Braysich." Other good sources for this approach include: Kim T. Gordon, "Building Customer Relationships: Increase Your Sales through Better Relationships with Your Existing Customers," *Entrepreneur,* January 01, 2001, http://www.entrepreneur.com/article/0, 4621,285279,00.html. Nichole L. Torres, "Marketing Buzz 09/02: Sell Better by Understanding the Six Different Customer Types; How to Respond to Bad Press," *Entrepreneur,* September 2002, http://www.entrepreneur.com/mag/article/0,1539, 302387,00.html.
9. D. Guithues-Amrhein and J. A. Katz, "Assessing the Mortality Risk of a Business," *Journal of Enterprising Culture* 7, no. 3 (1999) or http://www.sbaer.uca.edu/Research/1998/ICSB/n004.htm. Joan Stableford, "Business Notes: It's Here: the Great Pumpkin," *Time* 136, no. 21 (November 12, 1990), p. 64. Joan Stableford, "For Sun Hill Industries, Success Last Year Was in the Bag," *Fairfield County Business Journal* 22, no 19 (May 27, 1991), p. 10. The pirate pursuit resulted in a legal battle, which was decided in Zinbarg's favor in 1999; see United States Court of Appeals for the Federal Circuit, 98-1498 (Serial No. 08/427,732), in Re Anita Dembiczak and Benson Zinbarg, http://www.law.emory.edu/fedcircuit/apr99/98-1498.wp.html.
10. mereChina, "Fun Chinese Lessons—9: Danger and Opportunity: The Chinese Expression for Crisis," http://www.merechina.com/language/chineselesson9.shtml.
11. Rod P. Burkert, "A Good Deal Depends on Preparation," *Journal of Accountancy* 196, no. 5 (November 2003), pp. 47–52.
12. Henry Gibbon, "Review of the Year—Global M&A Breaks 2000 Record: European M&A volume surpasses US$1.7trn following year of mega-mergers," *Acquisitions Monthly,* 2007, p. 6. Mrwavetheory, "Mr Wave Theory: 01/07—Silicon Valley Venture Capital and Tech News. Goldman Sachs Wins Again—M&A League Table 2006." 06/07/2007. Accessed 10 June 2007, http://mrwavetheory.blogspot.com/2007_01_07_archive.html.
13. The ESOP Association, "ESOP Facts and Figures," 2004, http://www.esopassociation.org/media/media_statistics.asp. C. Tawney and J. Levitsky, "Small Enterprise Development as a Strategy for Reducing the Social Cost of Restructuring and the Privatization Process: Public and Private Initiatives," Interdepartmental Action Programme on Privatization, Restructuring and Economic Democracy, Working Paper IPPRED-6, 2000, International Labour Organization (ILO), http://www.ilo.org/public/english/employment/ ent/papers/ippred6.htm. G. B. Hansen, "ESOPs in the USA", presentation to the ILO seminar "The Economies in Transition and the Employment Problem: The Role of Cooperatives and Associations," Kiev, Ukraine, 1993.

14. The ESOP Association, "ESOP Facts and Figures," 2004, http://www.esopassociation.org/media/media_statistics.asp.
15. The strategies come from the following overlapping sources: Kenneth J. Klassen and Richard C. Sansin, "A Model of Dynamic Tax Planning with an Application to Estate Freezes," *Journal of the American Taxation Association* 28, no. 1 (2006), pp. 1–24. Isabelle Le Breton-Miller, Danny Miller, and Lloyd P. Steier, "Toward an Integrative Model of Effective FOB Succession," *Entrepreneurship: Theory & Practice* 28, no. 4 (Summer 2004), pp. 305–328. C. J. Prince, "Death and Taxes—Entrepreneur.com." Entrepreneur.com, May 2006. July 21, 2009, http://www.entrepreneur.com/magazine/entrepreneur/2006/may/159926.html. William S. White, Timothy D. Krinke, and David L. Geller, "Family Business Succession Planning: Devising an Overall Strategy," *Journal of Financial Service Professionals* 58, no. 3 (May 2004), pp. 67–86. Remember that we strongly recommend finding a qualified estate planning attorney to make sure these strategies are done correctly.
16. Scott Bernard Nelson, "Leave It to Them: Make Sure Your Family Gets What It Needs by Including a Disclaimer Provision in Your Estate Plan," *Entrepreneur,* August 2004, http://www.Entrepreneur.com/article/0,4621,316380,00.html.
17. Paul DeCeglie, "State of the Estate: What Is Estate Planning and Why Should You Be Doing It Now?" *Entrepreneur Start-Ups,* January 2001, http://www.entrepreneur.com/article/0,4621,284549, 00.html.
18. N. Upton and B. Petty, "Funding Options for Transferring the Family-Held Firm: A Comparative Analysis," presented at the 18th annual meeting of the Babson Research Conference, Ghent, Belgium, April 1998. N. Upton and B. Petty, "Venture Capital Funding of Family Business Transition: An Exploratory Analysis," *Proceedings of the United States Association of Small Business and Entrepreneurship,* 1998, pp. 94–101. Neil C. Churchill and Kenneth J. Hatten, "Non-Market-Based Transfers of Wealth and Power: A Research Framework for Family Businesses," *American Journal of Small Business* 12, no. 2 (Fall 1987), pp. 53–66.
19. Brian Headd, "Redefining Business Success: Distinguishing between Closure and Failure," *Small Business Economics* 21, no. 1 (2003), pp. 51–61. Timothy Bates and Alfred Nucci, "An Analysis of Small Business Size and Rate of Discontinuance," *Journal of Small Business Management* 27, no. 4 (1989), pp. 1–8. Small Business Administration, U.S. "Small Business Economic Indicators for 2003" (Washington DC: Small Business Administration, August 2004).
20. This approach follows the practical concept pioneered by Dun & Bradstreet in its *Business Failure Reports.* What we call a walkaway was what D&B called a "business discontinuance" and referred to a business that closed having not left any creditors or legal actions pending. A "business failure" in D&B's language was a firm that closed with unpaid creditors or pending legal actions. These are called *failures* here. The source is Dun & Bradstreet, "Business Failure Record" (Murray Hill, NJ: Dun & Bradstreet, 1998), https://www.dnb.com/newsview/bfr96-97.pdf.
21. U.S. Courts Administrative Office, "Bankruptcy Filings Continue to Rise," *US Courts Newsroom,* June 8, 2009, http://www.uscourts.gov/Press Releases/2009/BankruptcyFilingsMar2009.cfm.
22. Brian Headd, "Redefining Business Success: Distinguishing between Closure and Failure," *Small Business Economics* 21, no. 1 (2003), pp. 51–61.
23. P. Jennings and G. Beaver, "The Performance and Competitive Advantage of Small Firms: A Management Perspective," *International Small Business Journal* 15 (1997), pp. 63–75. Brian Headd, "Redefining Business Success: Distinguishing between Closure and Failure," *Small Business Economics* 21, no. 1 (2003), pp. 51–61. J. Watson and J. Everett, "Do Small Businesses Have High Failure Rates?" *Journal of Small Business Management* 34, no. 4 (1996), pp. 45–62. J. Watson and J. Everett, "Defining Small Business Failure," *International Small Business Journal* 11, no. 3 (1993), pp. 35–48.
24. Stephen C. Perry, "A Comparison of Failed and Non-Failed Small Businesses in the United States: Do Men and Women Use Different Planning and Decision Making Strategies?" *Journal of Developmental Entrepreneurship* 7, no. 4 (December 2002), pp. 415–428. R. M. Hodgetts and D. F. Kuratko, *Effective Small Business Management* (New York: Wiley, 2002). L. Waghorne, "The Cold Hard Facts," *Chartered Accountants Journal of New Zealand* 79, no. 7 (2000).
25. Laura Tiffany, "Mail Order: Want to Go Retail but Don't Want to Deal with the Hassles of a Storefront? Follow the Paths Forged by Wards and Sears by Starting a Mail-Order Company," *Entrepreneur,* February 22, 2001, http://www.entrepreneur.com/ article/0,4621,287061-5,00.html.
26. Experts in management information systems have put in the most work applying CSF approaches to small businesses. For example, see Riyad Eid, Myfanwy Trueman, and Abdel Moneim Ahmed, "A Cross-Industry Review of B2B Critical Success Factors," *Internet Research: Electronic Networking Applications and Policy* 12, no. 2 (2002), pp. 110–123. T. Butler and B. Fitzgerald, "Unpacking the Systems Development Process: An Empirical Application of the CSF Concept in a Research Context," *The Journal of Strategic Information Systems* 8, no. 4 (1999), pp. 351–371. G. K. Kanji and A. M. Tambi, "Total Quality Management in UK Higher Education Institutions," *Total Quality Management* 10, no. 1 (1999), pp. 129–153.
27. Edward G. Rogoff, Myung-Soo Lee, and Dong-Churl Suh, "Who Done It?" Attributions by Entrepreneurs and Experts of the Factors That Cause and Impede Small Business Success. *Journal of Small Business Management* 42, no. 4 (October 2004), pp. 364–376. E. J. Gatewood, K. G. Shaver, J. B. Powers, and W. B. Gartner, "Entrepreneurial Expectancy, Task Effort, and Performance," *Entrepreneurship: Theory & Practice* 27, no. 2 (2002), pp. 187–206. K. G. Shaver, W. B. Gartner, E. Crosby, K. Bakalarova, and E. J. Gatewood, "Attributions about Entrepreneurship: A Framework and Process for Analyzing Reasons for Starting a Business," *Entrepreneurship: Theory & Practice* 26, no. 2 (2001), pp. 5–32.
28. J. J. Chrisman, "The Influence of Outsider-Generated Knowledge Resources on Venture Creation," *Journal of Small Business Management* 37, no. 4 (1999), pp. 42–58. James J. Chrisman and W. Ed McMullan, "A Preliminary Assessment of Outsider Assistance as a Knowledge Resource: The Longer-Term Impact of New Venture Counseling," *Entrepreneurship: Theory & Practice* 24, no. 3 (2000), pp. 37–53. James J. Chrisman and W. Ed McMullan, "Outsider Assistance as a Knowledge Resource for New Venture Survival," *Journal of Small Business Management* 42, no. 3 (2004), pp. 229–244.
29. Devron A. Veasley, "In Depth: Small Business Resource Guide—Business Incubation. Incubators Build Economies, Benefit Communities," *Birmingham Business Journal,* November 8, 2003, http://birmingham.bizjournals.com/birmingham/stories/2003/08/11/focus6.html.
30. A. Charney and G. Libecap, *Impact of Entrepreneurship Education* (Kansas City, MO: Kauffman Center for Entrepreneurial Leadership, 2000). L. Kolvereid, and O. Moen, "Entrepreneurship among Business Graduates: Does a Major in Entrepreneurship Make a Difference?" *Journal of European Industrial Training* 21, no. 4 (1997), pp. 154–160. W. E. McMullan, and L. M. Gillin, "Entrepreneurship Education: Developing Technological Start-Up Entrepreneurs. A Case Study of a Graduate Entrepreneurship Programme at Swinburne University," *Technovation* 18, no. 4 (1998), pp. 275–286. T.V. Menzies, and J. C. Paradi, "Encouraging Technology-Based Ventures: Entrepreneurship Education and Engineering Graduates," *New England Journal of Entrepreneurship* 5, no. 2 (2002), pp. 57–64. T. V. Menzies, and J. C. Paradi, "Entrepreneurship Education and Engineering Students: Career Path and Business Performance," *International Journal of Entrepreneurship and Innovation* 6, no. 2 (2003), pp. 85–96. N. B. Upton, D. L. Sexton, and C. Moore, "Have We Made a Difference? An Examination of Career Activity of Entrepreneurship Majors since 1981" (abstract), *Frontiers of Entrepreneurship Research* 1995 edition (Wellesley, MA: Babson College, 1995), pp. 727–728.
31. Brian Headd, "Redefining Business Success: Distinguishing between Closure and Failure," *Small Business Economics* 21, no. 1 (2003),

pp. 51–61. J. Katz, "A Psychosocial Cognitive Model of Employment Status Choice," *Entrepreneurship: Theory & Practice* 16, no. 1 (1992), pp. 29–37.

32. G. N. Chandler and S. H. Hanks, "Founder Competence, the Environment, and Venture Performance," *Entrepreneurship: Theory & Practice* 18, no. 3 (1994), pp. 77–89. R. K. Mitchell, B. Smith, K. W. Seawright, and E. A. Morse, "Cross-Cultural Cognitions and the Venture Creation Decision," *Academy of Management Journal* 43 (2000), pp. 974–993.
33. Robert A. Baron and Gideon D. Markman, "Beyond Social Capital: The Role of Entrepreneurs' Social Competence in Their Financial Success," *Journal of Business Venturing* 18, no. 1 (2003), pp. 41–60.
34. Gerard George, D. Robley Wood Jr., and Raihan Kahn, "Networking Strategy of Boards: Implications for Small and Medium-Sized Enterprises," *Entrepreneurship and Regional Development* 13, no. 3 (2001), pp. 269–285.
35. This is one of the oldest findings in small business research, starting with K. B. Mayer and S. Goldstein, "The First Two Years: Problems of Small Firm Growth and Survival," Washington: Small Business Administration; and continuing through Brian Headd, "Redefining Business Success: Distinguishing between Closure and Failure," *Small Business Economics* 21, no. 1 (2003), pp. 51–61.
36. Brian Headd, "Redefining Business Success: Distinguishing between Closure and Failure," *Small Business Economics* 21, no. 1 (2003), pp. 51–61.
37. Ibid.
38. D. A. Shepherd and M. Shanley, *New Venture Strategy* (Newbury Park, CA: Sage, 1998). D. A. Shepherd, E. J. Douglas, and M. Shanley, "New Venture Survival: Ignorance, External Shocks, and Risk Reduction Strategies," *Journal of Business Venturing* 15 (2000), pp. 393–410.
39. Susan A. Sherer and Bill Adams, "Collaborative Commerce: The Role of Intermediaries in e-Collaboration," *Journal of Electronic Commerce Research* 2, no. 2 (2001), pp. 66–77.
40. G. T. Lumpkin and G. G. Dess, "Clarifying the Entrepreneurial Orientation Construct and Linking It to Performance," *Academy of Management Review* 21, no. 1 (1996), pp. 135–172. G. T. Lumpkin and G. G. Dess, "Linking Two Dimensions of Entrepreneurial Orientation to Firm Performance: The Moderating Role of Environment and Industry Life Cycle," *Journal of Business Venturing* 16, no. 5 (2001), pp. 429–451. D. A. Shepherd and M. Shanley, *New Venture Strategy* (Newbury Park, CA: Sage, 1998).
41. D. A. Shepherd and M. Shanley, *New Venture Strategy* (Newbury Park, CA: Sage, 1998). D. A. Shepherd, E. J. Douglas, and M. Shanley, "New Venture Survival: Ignorance, External Shocks, and Risk Reduction Strategies," *Journal of Business Venturing* 15 (2000), pp. 393–410.
42. Dean A. Shepherd and Evan J. Douglas, *Attracting Equity Investors: Positioning, Preparing and Presenting the Business Plan* (Newbury Park, CA: Sage, 1999.)
43. W. Gibb Dyer, *The Entrepreneurial Experience: Confronting the Career Dilemmas of the Start-Up Executive* (San Francisco: Jossey-Bass, 1992) or Dorothy Perrin Moore, *Careerpreneurs: Lesson from Leading Women Entrepreneurs on Building a Career without Boundaries* (Palo Alto, CA: Davies Black, 2000).
44. This approach is called *open-systems theory* or *living systems theory* in the social sciences. Some of the most famous models for studying organizations are rooted in this approach such as Daniel Katz and Robert L. Kahn, *The Social Psychology of Organizations* (New York: Wiley, 1978), or William B. Gartner, "A Conceptual Framework for Describing the Phenomenon of New Venture Creation," *Academy of Management Review* 10 (1985), pp. 696–706.
45. The latest list comes from home-business gurus Paul Edwards and Sarah Edwards, "The Dark Side, Prepare Yourself for Being Home Based by Understanding the Downside," *Entrepreneur's Be Your Own Boss,* June 2003, http://www.entrepreneur.com/article/0,4621,308968,00.html.
46. Aliza Pilar Sherman, "Teaching by Example," *Entrepreneur,* December 2003, http://www.entrepreneur.com/mag/article/0,1539,311899,00.html.
47. Patricia Schiff Estess, "Gag Order," *Entrepreneur,* September 2000, http://www.entrepreneur.com/article/0,4621,278650,00.html. Quentin Fleming, *Keep the Family Baggage out of the Family Business* (New York: Fireside, 2000). Patricia Schiff Estess, "Close Encounters," *Entrepreneur,* July 1998, http://www.Entrepreneur.com/article/0,4621,228950,00.html.
48. Paul Edwards and Sarah Edwards, "The Dark Side: Prepare Yourself for Being Home Based by Understanding the Downside," *Entrepreneur's Be Your Own Boss,* June 2003, http://www.entrepreneur.com/article/0,4621,308968,00.html. Paul Edwards and Sara Edwards, *Working from Home* (Los Angeles: Tarcher, 1999).
49. Not surprisingly, there is a lot of disagreement on what exactly constitutes the triple bottom line. For example, for big businesses, the conventional thinking is economic, social, and environmental returns. See European Business Forum/PriceWaterhouseCoopers, "EBF on . . . Sustainable Development" (London: European Business Forum, 2003), http://www.pwc.com/pl/eng/inssol/publ/2003/corp_efb_rap.pdf, or Knowledge @ Wharton, "The Triple Bottom Line: Student Activists Demand More from B-Schools," Wharton School Public Policy and Management Web site, May 13, 2003. http://knowledge.wharton.upenn.edu/index.cfm?fa=viewfeature&id=773; or John Elkington, *Cannibals with Forks: The Triple Bottom Line of the 21st Century Business* (Gabriola Island, BC, Canada: New Society Publishers, 1998). In small businesses, the idea of firm, community, and personal returns is better established through works such as W. Gibb Dyer, *The Entrepreneurial Experience: Confronting the Career Dilemmas of the Start-Up Executive* (San Francisco: Jossey-Bass, 1992); or Dorothy Perrin Moore, *Careerpreneurs: Lesson from Leading Women Entrepreneurs on Building a Career without Boundaries* (Palo Alto, CA: Davies Black, 2000). A very good article on how the triple bottom line operates in family businesses can be found in Robyn Eversole, "Balancing Act: Business and Household in a Small Bolivian City," *Development in Practice* 12, no. 5 (2002), pp. 589–601.
50. Google, Inc., "Amendment No. 9 to Form S-1: Registration Statement, under the Securities Act of 1933" (Washington, DC: US Securities and Exchange Commission (2004) http://sec.gov/Archives/edgar/data/1288776/000119312504142742/ds1a.htm. Warren Bennis, "Warren Bennis: Google's Growth Engine," *CIO Insight,* June 1, 2004, http://www.cioinsight.com/article2/0,1397,1609425,00.asp. Mary Anne Ostrom and Matt Marshall, "Inside Google: Internet Search Engine's Founders Keep Ideas Rolling and Profits Pouring In," *Mercury News,* May 4, 2003, http://www.madville.com/link.php?id=39525&t=23.

PHOTO CREDITS

Chapter 1

p. 2 © 2005 Aaron McGruder. Dist. By UNIVERSAL PRESS SYNDICATE. Reprinted with permission. All rights reserved.
p. 7 Getty Images.
p. 10 Wells Fargo.
p. 11 Grill Bongarts/ Getty Images.
p. 17 Anchor Bar & Restaurant.
p. 20 (left) Robert Whitaker/ Getty Images.
p. 20 (middle) Michael Ochs Archives/Stringer/ Getty Images.
p. 20 (right) FilmMagic/Getty Images.

Chapter 2

p. 26 Courtesy Jerome Katz.
p. 31 David Perez Shadi/Getty Images.
p. 45 Courtesy Ronald Reagan Library.
p. 49 Carl Moore - AP Wide World Photo.

Chapter 3

p. 56 The Ad Firm.
p. 62 Courtesy Common Dog.
p. 65 © Stephane Cardinale/CORBIS SYGMA.
p. 70 © Getty Images.

Chapter 4

p. 78 Used with permission, Magnetic Poetry.
p. 82 Traction Experts, Inc.
p. 88 © Bonnie-Kamin/ PhotoEdit.

Chapter 5

p. 118 Courtesy Kathryn Otoshi.
p. 123 © Brand X/JupiterImages/ Getty Images.
p. 124 trbfoto/Brand X Pictures/ Jupiterimages.
p. 125 © BananaStock Ltd.
p. 131 The McGraw-Hill Companies, Inc./ John Flournoy, photographer.
p. 137 © Lars A Niki.
p. 138 Comstock/ PictureQuest.
p. 140 Courtesy Courtney Hennessey Hopson.

Chapter 6

p. 152 Courtesy Mike Tease.
p. 156 Courtesy Jerome Katz.
p. 158 Courtesy of NewProduct-Works www.newproductworks.com.
p. 161 Ryan McVay/ Getty Images/ MGH-DIL.
p. 170 © McGraw-Hill Companies, Inc./ Andrew Resek, photographer.

Chapter 7

p. 182 Courtesy EnableMart.
p. 190 Photo by Jon Perlmutter.
p. 193 Courtesy Jerome Katz.

Chapter 8

p. 212 © BananaStock/ PunchStock.
p. 217 Wake Forest University.
p. 236 Daniel J. Watkins Photography.
p. 266 MyLibros.com.

Chapter 9

p. 272 © 2006 - Brent Rubey - Beyond-Clothing.com.
p. 275 (top) Courtesy of zipcar.com.
p. 275 (bottom) PhotoLink/Getty Images.
p. 278 Photo reproduced by permission of Dyson Limited.
p. 282 Courtesy 3D Systems Corporation.
p. 284 Photo by Kryptonite, A registered trademark of Schlage Lock Company.
p. 285 © McGraw Hill Companies/Jill Braaten photographer.
p. 289 Screaming Eagle.
p. 290 Ildar Sagdejev.
p. 295 Courtesy Ultra-Pet.
p. 297 Courtesy of Makers Mark Distillery.
p. 298 Courtesy of United Parcel Service.

Chapter 10

p. 306 Courtesy B*tween Productions, Inc.
p. 310 Andrew Resek/ MGH-DIL.
p. 311 www.radiofiesta.net.
p. 313 (top, bottom) © Dave's Gourmet, Inc.
p. 316 © Corbis – All Rights Reserved.
p. 317 Digital Vision/ Getty Images/ MGH-DIL.
p. 319 Courtesy Legacy Ink/www.legacyinkdesign.com.
p. 320 Steve Cole/Getty Images.
p. 334 Vermont Teddy Bear Company www.VermontTeddy-Bear.com.

Chapter 11

p. 340 BaseballExpress.com.
p. 343 Photo Robert Hughes/1154 LILL STUDIO.
p. 348 Photo courtesy the michael alan group.
p. 358 © Kelly-Mooney Photography/ Corbis.
p. 360 www.census.gov.
p. 362 Dennis Light/ Light Photographic.

Chapter 12

p. 372 ZOU QING/AFP/ Getty Images.
p. 385 © Tom & Dee Ann McCarthy/ Corbis.
p. 386 (left, right) Bridgestone.

Chapter 13

p. 400 Mark Gilliland/ Acropolis.

Chapter 14

p. 440 Be Our Guest, Inc.
p. 444 AP/Wide World Photo.
p. 448 The Baby Einstein Company.

Chapter 15

p. 476 Courtesy INCELL Corporation, LLC.
p. 492 Corbis.

Chapter 16

p. 506 Jennifer Adleman, U.S. Geological Survey/DAL.
p. 509 Courtesy Dwight Cooper.
p. 513 Photo courtesy Alienware Corporation.
p. 515 http://barcodes.gs1us.org.
p. 517 © Dennis MacDonald/PhotoEdit.

Chapter 17

p. 538 © Hande/Zefa/Corbis.
p. 544 © Reuters/CORBIS.
p. 549 Photo provided courtesy of World Smile Corp. All rights reserved.
p. 553 AP Wide World Photo.
p. 560 © FRANCK PREVEL/Reuters/Corbis.

Chapter 18

p. 570 © Chuck Savage/Corbis.
p. 576 Business.gov.
p. 578 Corbis.
p. 580 (left, right) © St. Louis Bread Co./Panera Bread.
p. 589 Courtesy Litigation Fairness.gov.
p. 593 Robert Holmes/Corbis.

Chapter 19

p. 606 PerkettPR, Inc.
p. 612 © Royalty Free/Corbis.
p. 617 © Royalty Free/Corbis.
p. 623 www.salary.com.
p. 624 (top) www.salary.com.
p. 624 (bottom) www.salary.com.
p. 630 © Jon Feingersh/Corbis.

Chapter 20

p. 636 © Kayte M. Beioma/PhotoEdit.
p. 644 © Jack Hollingsworth/Corbis.

NAME AND ORGANIZATION INDEX

SUBJECT INDEX

A book about the businesses you might actually start...

This book focuses on the down and dirty of what you need to know about opening your design studio, buying a franchise, starting a retail store, opening a gym, starting your Web-based business, or expanding your family business. We know that most of you aren't going to go out and try to be the next Michael Dell. This book will give you the practical knowledge you'll need when starting your small business and information on where and how to get more information that you'll need along the way.

ESB focuses on issues like:

- Thinking creatively to turn your knowledge and skills into a business
- Funding the business with your own money
- How to write and "sell" a winning business plan
- How to tighten your belt in a cash crunch
- How to purchase a franchise
- Hiring and managing employees
- How to effectively price and market your product/service
- How to minimize risk by understanding legal issues
- Starting your business part time
- Personal selling skills
- How to assess competition

...and the skills you need to get there.

The book is full of Skill Modules that focus on basic skills that you'll need to develop as you start your small business. Here's a complete listing.